MW00910515

THE BLOOMSBURY HANDBOOK OF ELECTRONIC LITERATURE

THE BLOOMSBURY HANDBOOK OF

ELECTRONIC LITERATURE

Edited by Joseph Tabbi

Bloomsbury Academic
An imprint of Bloomsbury Publishing Plc

B L O O M S B U R Y
LONDON • OXFORD • NEW YORK • NEW DELHI • SYDNEY

Bloomsbury Academic
An imprint of Bloomsbury Publishing Plc

50 Bedford Square
London
WC1B 3DP
UK

1385 Broadway
New York
NY 10018
USA

www.bloomsbury.com

BLOOMSBURY and the Diana logo are trademarks of Bloomsbury Publishing Plc

First published 2018

British Library Cataloguing-in-Publication Data
A catalogue record for this book is available from the British Library.

ISBN: HB: 978-1-4742-3025-4
ePDF: 978-1-4742-3027-8
ePub: 978-1-4742-3026-1

Library of Congress Cataloging-in-Publication Data
Names: Tabbi, Joseph, 1960– editor.
Title: The Bloomsbury handbook of electronic literature / edited by Joseph Tabbi.
Description: London ; New York : Bloomsbury Academic, 2017. | Includes bibliographical references and index.
Identifiers: LCCN 2017010881 | ISBN 9781474230254 (hardback) | ISBN 9781474230261 (epub)
Subjects: LCSH: Literature and the Internet–Handbooks, manuals, etc. | Literature and technology–Handbooks, manuals, etc. | Digital humanities–Handbooks, manuals, etc. | Online authorship–Handbooks, manuals, etc. | Hypertext literature–History and criticism–Handbooks, manuals, etc. | Postmodernism (Literature)–Handbooks, manuals, etc. | BISAC: LITERARY CRITICISM / Reference. | COMPUTERS / Digital Media / General.
Classification: LCC PN56.I64 B57 2017 | DDC 802/.85–dc23
LC record available at https://lccn.loc.gov/2017010881

Cover image © Getty images

Typeset by Newgen KnowledgeWorks Pvt. Ltd., Chennai, India
Printed and bound in Great Britain

CONTENTS

ACKNOWLEDGMENTS AND PERMISSIONS

Versions of the chapters by Florian Cramer ("Post-Digital Writing"), Stuart Moulthrop ("Lift This End"), and Brian Kim Stefans ("Immanence, Inc") each appeared originally in the *electronic book review*. Cramer's essay was also reprinted in his book *Anti-Media: Ephemera on Speculative Arts*. The first part of John Cayley's chapter is an edited version of "Aurature at the End(s) of Electronic Literature," also published in the *electronic book review*. While copyright remains in each case with the authors, we acknowledge prior publication in accordance with the Creative Commons licensing agreement in each instance. The pages, and hands, reproduced in Shelley Jackson's chapter can be found in the Google Library Project. I am grateful to Jackson for making this a true Handbook.

My own chapter, "Relocating the Literary," appeared in the journal *CounterText*; it is reproduced courtesy of the Edinburgh University Press. The screen shot from "Today I Die" is reproduced by Daniel Punday with the permission of the author, Daniel Benmergui. Steve Tomasula's chapter, "Our Tools Make Us (and Our Literature) Post" appeared in an earlier version in *Transatlantica: revue d'études Américaines*; the illustration is reproduced courtesy of the Blu-ray edition of *2001: A Space Odyssey*. Screen captures by Davin Heckman and James O'Sullivan from "degenerative" and "regenerative" by Eugenio Tisselli and *The Dead Tower* by Andy Campbell and Mez Breeze are reproduced by permission of the authors. Screen captures by Álvaro Seiça from the videopoem *Roda Lume Fogo* (1986) are reproduced courtesy of E. M. de Melo e Castro and Po-ex.net. The photo of Silvestre Pestana's *Computer Poetry* (1983) was taken by Álvaro Seiça and is reproduced with permission of the author.

On a more personal note, I'd like to acknowledge David Avital's email of November 2013 asking me to consider writing "a small, polemical book" situating "an emergent e-lit practice specifically within the context of the (relatively recent) institutional emergence of the Digital Humanities." Given the number of bespoke digitally born works that are covered in the present volume, I am grateful to David for not insisting on something "small." And I wish to thank, also, Brooks Sterritt and Robert Cashin Ryan for their ongoing editorial support, which was facilitated by research grants from the Department of English and the College of Liberal Arts and Sciences at the University of Illinois at Chicago.

CONTRIBUTORS

Mario Aquilina is a lecturer in English at the University of Malta, where he teaches rhetoric, style, literary theory, and electronic literature. His monograph *The Event of Style in Literature* was published in 2014 and he co-edited a special issue of *CounterText* on electronic literature in 2016.

John Cayley is a writer, theorist, and pioneer-maker of language art in programmable media. Cayley is professor of literary arts at Brown University in the United States and directs a graduate program in digital language arts. He received the Marjorie C. Luesebrink Career Achievement Award from the Electronic Literature Organization in 2017; a volume of his selected essays, *Grammalepsy*, is forthcoming in 2018.

David Ciccoricco is in the Department of English and Linguistics at the University of Otago in Dunedin, New Zealand. He is the author of *Reading Network Fiction* (2007), a book about digital fiction before and after the Web, and *Refiguring Minds in Narrative Media* (2015), which brings cognitive narrative theory to the analysis of novels, digital narratives, and story-driven videogames.

Florian Cramer is a writer, photographer, filmmaker and theorist. He is a research professor in new media at Hogeschool Rotterdam in Netherlands, where he serves as the director of Creating 010, a center focusing on two areas of research: communication in the digital age and cultural diversity. He is also a part-time programmer at WORM, the Rotterdam-based Institute of Avantgardistic Recreation.

Astrid Ensslin is professor of media and digital communication at the University of Alberta in Canada, where she teaches and researches digital fiction, games, cyberliterature, and digital humanities project management. Her main publications are *Literary Gaming* (2014), *Analyzing Digital Fiction* (co-edited with Alice Bell and Hans Kristian Rustad, 2013), *The Language of Gaming* (2012), and *Canonizing Hypertext* (2007).

Martin Paul Eve is professor of literature, technology, and publishing at Birkbeck, University of London. He holds a PhD from the University of Sussex and is the author of four books.

Aden Evens is associate professor of English at Dartmouth College. He pursues research and teaching across disciplines, from philosophy, digital studies, mathematics, music, and sound. Evens anticipates that any year now electronic literature will become mainstream, and then won't he look smart!

Luciana Gattass holds a magna cum laude BA in film studies from Columbia University (1999), and both an MA and a PhD in literary theory from the Pontifical Catholic University of Rio de Janeiro (2007 and 2011). In 2010 she was a visiting doctoral fellow at Brown University researching digital aesthetics. Her PhD dissertation explored the theory and aesthetics of electronic literature and art and earned her a postdoctoral fellowship at the University of Bergen in 2012, where she curated the Brazilian Electronic Literature Collection for the ELMCIP (Electronic Literature as a Model of Creativity and Innovation in Practice) Knowledge Base. Currently she serves as an honorary assistant professor at the University of Hong Kong.

Davin Heckman is the author of *A Small World: Smart Houses and the Dream of the Perfect Day* (2008). He is supervising editor of the Electronic Literature Directory (directory.eliterature.org), contributing editor of *ebr* (www.electronicbookreview.com), and professor of mass communication at Winona State University in the United States. During the 2011–2012 academic year, Davin was a Fulbright Scholar in Digital Culture at the University of Bergen.

Shelley Jackson is the author of the forthcoming novel *Riddance, Half Life, The Melancholy of Anatomy,* the hypertexts *Patchwork Girl* and *My Body,* and several children's books, the most recent of which is *Mimi's Dada Catifesto.* Her work has appeared in many journals including *Conjunctions*, *Paris Review*, *McSweeney's*, and *Cabinet Magazine.* The recipient of a Howard Foundation grant, a Pushcart Prize, and the 2006 James Tiptree Jr Award, Shelley is also known for her projects SNOW and SKIN, a story published in tattoos on 2,095 volunteers, one word at a time.

Nathan Jones is a poet based in Liverpool, UK; a PhD student at Royal Holloway University of London; and a teacher of art/writing at Liverpool School of Art and Design in England. He collaborates frequently on intersections of poetry and new media.

Stuart Moulthrop is professor of English at the University of Wisconsin-Milwaukee in the United States. His digital works include *Victory Garden* (1991), "Under Language" (2008) and "End of the White Subway" (2016). With Dene Grigar he is author of *Traversals: The Use of Preservation for Early Electronic Writing* (2017).

James O'Sullivan lectures in digital arts and humanities at University College Cork (National University of Ireland). He has previously held faculty roles at Pennsylvania State University and the University of Sheffield. He is the founding editor of New Binary Press.

Mehdy Sedaghat Payam is a researcher at SAMT Institute for Research and Development in the Humanities in Iran. He received his PhD in experimental print fiction and digital literature from Victoria University of Wellington in New Zealand. His research focuses on reading electronic literature and using quantitative methods to analyze literary texts. His first print novel, *Secret of Silence or Hamlet According to Shakespeare's Sister*, appeared in Persian in 2009.

Manuel Portela directs the PhD program in Materialities of Literature at the University of Coimbra in Portugal. He is the author of *Scripting Reading Motions* (2013) and the general editor of a *Collaborative Digital Archive of the Book of Disquiet* (2017).

Daniel Punday is professor and head of the Department of English at Mississippi State University in the United States. He works on narrative theory, contemporary US literature, and electronic media. He is the author of five books, the most recent of which is *Computing as Writing* (2015).

David S. Roh is associate professor of English at the University of Utah in the United States, where he specializes in digital humanities and Asian American literature. He is the author of *Illegal Literature* (2015) and coeditor of *Techno-Orientalism* (2015).

Allison M. Schifani is assistant professor of digital humanities in the Department of Modern Languages and Literatures at the University of Miami in the United States. Allison is the co-founder of the research and design collaborative SPEC; her research focuses on the urban, the digital, and the ecological in the twentieth- and twenty-first-century Americas.

Álvaro Seiça is a writer and PhD research fellow at the University of Bergen in Norway, where he teaches, and edits the ELMCIP Knowledge Base. His dissertation "setInterval() Time-Based Readings of Kinetic Poetry" was submitted in 2017 and he is the author of *Ensinando o Espaço* (2017), *Transdução* (2016), Ö (2014), and *permafrost* (2012).

Laura Shackelford is associate professor of English at the Rochester Institute of Technology in New York and director of the Women's and Gender Studies Program. She is the author of *Tactics of the Human: Experimental Technics in American Fiction* (2014); her research in comparative literary and media studies and feminist science studies explores narrative and digital literary practices as they take up and take on bioinformatic sciences and modes of circulation today.

Lyle Skains is senior lecturer at Bangor University in Wales, conducting practice-based research into writing, reading/playing, and publishing digital and transmedia narratives.

Brian Kim Stefans is associate professor of English at UCLA in the United States. He is also a noted poet and digital artist. His *Word Toys: Poetry and Technics* appeared in September 2017. His digital art, poetry, and research can be found at www.arras.net.

Joseph Tabbi is professor in the Department of English at the University of Illinois at Chicago in the United States. He is editor of the *Electronic Book Review* and former president of the Electronic Literature Organization. His published works include *Postmodern Sublime* (1995), *Cognitive Fictions* (2002), and *Nobody Grew but the Business: On the Life and Work of William Gaddis* (2015).

Steve Tomasula is the author of the novels *The Book of Portraiture*, *IN & OZ*, and *VAS: An Opera in Flatland*, the novel of the bio-tech revolution. He is also the author of the e-novel *TOC: A New-Media Novel*. A number of his short fictions are gathered in *Once Human: Stories*; his essays on bio-art, new narrative, and literature have appeared in *Data Made Flesh*, *Meta-Life: Biotechnologies, Synthetic Biology; A Life and the Arts*, *The Routledge Companion to Experimental Literature*, and other publications.

Rob Wittig has twin training in literature and graphic design. He co-founded one of the earliest online literary systems Invisible Seattle's IN.S.OMNIA, and on a Fulbright with Jacques Derrida wrote a book investigating that work: *Invisible Rendezvous*. He now organizes collaborative netprovs and teaches design and writing at the University of Minnesota Duluth in the United States.

Introduction

JOSEPH TABBI

In the 1895 Lumiere filming of *Workers Leaving the Factory*, we see a rushed, preoccupied, but convivial enough exit of mostly first-generation industrial women laborers on the way home; there are one or two men on bikes, many dogs on the grounds, and at least one horse and carriage. In Andrew Norman Wilson's 2010 Vimeo post *Workers Leaving the Googleplex*,[1] we see shots in static frames of "yellow badge" employees at Google's Mountain View, California campus, most of them Asiatic and Mexican, exiting as they do "every day at 2:15. Like a bell just rang, telling the workers to leave the factory" (Wilson voiceover). Their day starts at 4 a.m. and Andrew Wilson, himself a "red badge" worker at the neighboring facility enjoying "a personally unprecedented amount of privileges," decided during an off hour to walk over, speak to the "yellow badge" workers, and film some of what was going on there. Within hours of his second visit to the adjacent campus, Wilson was asked to gather his things, his contract was terminated, and he was driven by his former superior to the Caltrain station, to return home (and resume his graduate studies).

The workers, known as "scan-ops," were doing the "labor of digitizing" that has brought upward of thirty million books into the possession of Google, to date. "Data entry" advances one page at a time, turned over in texts on loan from lending libraries across the United States. The workers' hands can be seen among the photos presented in the chapter by Shelley Jackson that opens this volume, "I Hold It toward You: A Show of Hands." All the books referenced in this chapter (and images shown in live presentations) are accessed, and accessible online "through the efforts of the Google library project." According to Jackson, many pages contain "interesting scanning errors" as well as variations among editions as books move from publisher to publisher. Nonverbal elements go missing, for example, such as "the black page" in *The Life & Opinions of Tristram Shandy, Gentleman* (1759): "the marbled page, and Sterne's idiosyncratic punctuation." Of the "six manicules" that Sterne and his publishers (some of them) originally introduced, Jackson reports that she "identified five, and I had to find them the old way, by turning pages. By hand." The manicule gives a certain weight to Jackson's own observations, and her scholarly findings:

> ☞
>
> That is, I found them when they were there to be found. For while some publishers reproduced Sterne's manicules, some replaced them with asterisks, and some left them out altogether.

[1] https://vimeo.com/15852288

Citing Bulwer's *Chirologia: The Natural Language of the Hand* (1644), Jackson also observes how "The *Index*," for example, "advanced from a *fist*, and inclin'd respective to the shoulder; hath a great facultie to *confirme, collect* and *refute*." The materiality of textual communication was recognized as integral to critique, then, early in the development of print culture. One might expect the vastly expanded range of digital materialities to have restored, and even expanded that confirming, collective, and at times confrontational dimension. What better way could there be to open a "handbook of electronic literature" exploring a field whose emergence, if that occurs, will have as much to do with digits encountering keyboards, tablets, and screens as with unseen digital pathways? Can we not expect literature, when encountering a smooth, object-oriented regime, to extend rather than diminish critical confrontations, cognitive collectivities, and affective states?

Jackson, a print author as well as a pioneer of hypertext literary fiction, takes this expanded range as given, and so (alas) did Andrew Wilson when he took advantage of his own admittedly precarious employment at Google as a way to explore further what was happening with the literary corpus. What he hadn't known is that the "extremely confidential" work of the scan-ops would foreclose any possibility of open, critical inquiry. The software is not less proprietary and confidential in the social media and mobile apps we access every day from conglomerates such as Google, Apple, Amazon, and Facebook.

These four and the networked affordances of a Web 2.0 environment, which, as Florian Cramer notes in his chapter, now define the Internet "just like TV was defined by a few networks in the past," mark a sharp contrast with the DIY (Do-It-Yourself) aesthetic that accompanied digital literary and arts production in the 1990s. This too might account for the interest shown by so many contributors to this volume in the "deep" materiality of programming (and programs), the "corporate templates and data mining systems" (Cramer) that are now only rarely accessed. The errors and omissions introduced by the Google scan-ops and programmers, consistent with the "glitches" that interest Nathan Jones in his chapter for the present volume, are no less important to Shelley Jackson's argument than the content of all those millions of scanned books, so readily accessible (for the moment). And Jackson for her part is no less interested than Andrew Wilson in the actual workers who did the scanning; their motivations; their names, "issues of class, race, and labor" (Wilson voiceover). Jackson imagines, in her chapter, a "last reader" who often as not "*finds herself not reading but paging through, clicking through, scrolling through, volume upon volume of old books, the more obscure the better, because it is in these unfrequented pages that she may catch the passing shadow of another reader*":

> *Carol? Song Wa? Tunde? Netsanet?*
> *All of them having worked at one time in the Google Gulag.*
> (p. 15, Chapter 1 in this volume)

The gathering, digitization, and accessibility of so many excerpted texts, made available for free (in part, never in full, and never the same parts), encourage a tendency noted as well in this volume by Allison Schifani toward *surface reading*. Instead of immersion in an author's written words, we seek depth elsewhere—in the materiality of textual (re) production; the human handiwork of production, publication, and dissemination; and the underlying code work. If this depth is generally missed by everyday users of what is by now an emplaced digital environment, that should not keep artists from pursuing the original promise of the Internet—which was "precisely to broaden those boundaries" that settled in during our 500-year-long history of literature in print (as Dani Spinoza says in her annotation of that other pioneering hypertext, and later print author, Michael Joyce).

For those who create within a medium, when it is new but also when it has become ubiquitous, and naturalized, there's a palpable desire to go deeper, to stay in touch (literally; affectively) with the media that constrain our reading and writing. Not for nothing do two contributors to this volume, Manuel Portela and Aden Evens, focus on the hitherto marginal practice of "writing under constraint"—a practice that may have seemed notional, at best, when Raymond Queneau published a ten-page printed book of sonnets whose 10^{14} combinations would have produced (in theory) *One Hundred Thousand Billion Poems* (1961). In the first edition, the sonnets were sliced into horizontal strips by the publisher; so as readers we might conceivably rip out pages and apply scissors to each line, to see for ourselves how many combinations might be devised and what some of the poems might look like. But I doubt anyone ever did that. Stephanie Strickland and Nick Montfort's *Sea and Spar Between* (2010), recombining lines from Emily Dickinson and Herman Melville (and input from readers), allow us to see the results at any moment forming in front of us on the screen, more than any reader anywhere could ever think of reading. The mechanism underlying each of these clearly articulated, entirely unrealizable (and largely unreadable) projects are nonetheless entirely accessible and available, and this conceptual and material availability is essential to our experience of Queneau's antecedent, and Montfort and Strickland's signal work of electronic literature. As the mechanisms become more and more hidden, our attention today turns more to errors, liminalities, and glitches; these are what now define a contemporary digital "poetics." And our own activity, which needn't be actualized by any of Queneau's or the majority of Montfort and Strickland's readers, becomes now unavoidable, and also documented in databases that are more and more often inaccessible to us.

In their chapter titled "your visit will leave a permanent mark," Davin Heckman and James O'Sullivan go further in the direction of disrupting an aesthetic that is no longer notional, among databases that are no longer materially accessible to readers and writers. They seek "here to make a hard case for poetics" through the investigation of "monstrous" works—those such as Eugenio Tisselli's "degeneration" (2005) that does not seamlessly integrate input from the reader but instead deletes bits and pieces of the author's prior content with every site visit. Heckman and O'Sullivan also address Tisselli's "regeneration," which pulls in new text not from readers but from the Internet. Tisselli's regenerative countertext, however, is in the end no more readable than the degenerative version. Heckman and O'Sullivan articulate an important distinction between "the technically successful work [that] can be measured in the execution of its anticipated form while the poetically successful work can be measured by difference from anticipated forms." For this distinction to be meaningful, however, the materiality and programming that inform a work, and not least its departures from "technically successful," user friendly, and instrumentalist implementations need to be made available, understood, and brought forward for critical, conceptual, and poetic analysis.

Another contributor to this volume, Mehdy Sedaghat Payam, cites a remark by Lumiere that should give pause to any who (like me[2]) once assumed that a literary poetics might advance together with scientific and technological innovations in the digital realm. About

[2] The turning point was the Semantic Web. As I recalled during a 2009 National Humanities Center forum, *On the Human*, back in the mid-1990s when I founded the journal *electronic book review*, "it was easy enough to take advantage of a medium created, by scientists, for purposes of freely sharing documents among colleagues working at a distance from one another." It was also possible for me personally to join up with a site architect such as Ewan Branda, who's still with the journal, and Anne Burdick, whose former student Julia Bellocq devised the 2014 site update for presentation in Open Humanities Press. (Prior to that, we were published by Mark Amerika on his DIY site, ALT-X.) This all happened before it became obligatory to invest a lot of money into a website, and then to drift toward dependence on platforms.

the genre he pioneered, Lumiere had this to say: "Film can be exploited for a certain time as a scientific curiosity, but apart from that it has no commercial value whatsoever" (p. 317, Chapter 17 in this volume). Payam observes: "Lumiere said this the same year [1895] that he and his brother showed the first projected movie to a paying audience. Similar to those who predicted that the golden age of digital fiction is already over, Lumiere assumed the interest in film would be lost once a passing curiosity was satisfied."

Have scholars and early adopters been any better than Lumiere at our own predictions of the direction that would be taken by literary and cultural arts in digital media? Digital language artist and unabashed cultural theorist John Cayley is unambiguous on this matter: Since the 1990s promise of an "all but infinite and indeterminate range of new potentialities for literature," Cayley argues, "the myth of computational media's indeterminacy, openness, freedom has [. . .] become just that, still affectively powerful, but merely a story from the hyper-distant recent past." Those who saw in the nonlinearity and fragmented narrativity of hypertext fiction a continuation of then current postmodern metafiction and self-conscious L=A=N=G=U=A=G=E poetry were not quite so quick to observe the emergence of another quality, that book artist and author Steve Tomasula identifies (along with critical scholars Nathan Jones, Luciana Gattass, and Laura Shackleford) as a turn to the *posthuman*. It's a term whose frequency, Tomasula notes, can be seen through data searches to have risen "exponentially" in the 1990s, though it is not immediately observable whether or how the term describes a literary movement or even an end to humanism or Humanities scholarship, or rather (as Shackleford argues) the proliferation of the "posthuman" signals a self-identification of human cognition and affective capacities with *technics*. I leave this ambiguity unresolved because I personally would need to look further into the data, to see whether (and how) the term comports with such names as Cary Wolfe and Stefan Herbrechter, Bruce Clarke and Rosi Braidotti (who are cited some several times in this collection). Bernhard Stiegler and N. Katherine Hayles (each of them topics, respectively, of annotated bibliographies in this volume by Justin Raden and Clara Chetcuti) would need to be identified as well. Each of these scholars were among the theorists who, along with Hans Ulrich Gumbrecht (but also differently in each instance), had observed best how *technics* might in fact resituate philosophy away from the current postmodern and deconstructive approaches, and away from metaphysics altogether toward alterations of human cognition itself. No doubt their essays and books, to the extent they've been placed online, contribute to the exponential rise that Tomasula notes; no doubt their relative effects on humanistic knowledge, though knowable to individual scholars, have yet to be accounted for by digital metrics.

The effects of such changes wrought by technics on narrativity, however, are well observed in the chapters in this volume by Daniel Punday and David Ciccoricco. Punday conveys not only the persistence of narrative experiences in electronic texts ("from text-centric Storyspace hypertext fictions through commercial video games"), but an ongoing transformation in the idea of narrativity itself, a resistance to "traditional narrative coherence" that was always present in adventurous literature in print and is now endemic to an emerging literary practice in digital media.[3] Ciccoricco for his part asserts the "*unique*

[3] Gaylen Strawson (2004) identifies a "markedly Episodic," essayistic tradition in print fiction (and postmodern performance) in his essay "Against Narrativity": "Among them," Strawson proposes "Michel de Montaigne, the Earl of Shaftesbury, Stendhal, Hazlitt, Ford Madox Ford, Virginia Woolf, Borges, Fernando Pessoa, Iris Murdoch (a strongly Episodic person who is a natural story teller), Freddie Ayer, Goronwy Rees, Bob Dylan. Proust is another candidate, in spite of his memoriousness (which may be inspired by his Episodicity); also Emily

contribution" we might anticipate for electronic fiction, namely: its resistance to preformulated narratives and prefabricated media alike. "Its power," like the print fiction that preceded it (but in closer proximity to the media that shape our current culture), is "to make us more mindful of the creative and expressive potential of the devices that all too often pull us toward conformity and consumerism."

It remains to be seen whether readers can bring to today's devices and commercial platforms the "sustained attention and sustained reflection" (Ciccoricco) that a literary experience demands—and the essays collected in this volume are notable not only for the number and diversity of new works discussed, but for the numerous devices and commercial platforms that are referenced. Will these host a post-digital literary experience, not to mention their fostering imaginary communities comparable to those that co-evolved with the rise of mass literacy and the nation state? As yet, we have only glimmers of such collectivities: The transition, for example, from "classic," pre-Semantic Web hypertext practices toward the more game-like, commercial platforms of Twine is discussed by Astrid Ensslin and Lyle Skains. "Netprov" artist Rob Wittig identifies a robust digital aesthetic that has reinvented itself with each and every personal publication platform the engineers and programmers have devised, from Bulletin Board Services (BBS) in the 1990s to today's social media platforms: Wittig's "Netprov" represents a hitherto unrecognized practice ("minor" by design) that recalls emergent practices in print by Defoe, Sterne, H. G. Wells, and Mark Z. Danielewski, even as its embrace and detournement of any and all social media sets it squarely in "contrast to high literary forms such as the holy trinity of poem, short story and novel." Where much that is innovative and avant-garde in electronic literature has found a limited audience mostly in academia, Wittig's collaborative and contrarian Netprov remains "*informal* in contrast to works vetted, edited, and published in major journals, *interactive* because reactions from readers are expected and can rapidly be published alongside the text, and *vernacular* because they are cultural practices that develop from everyday use and are not, or not yet, taught in schools and universities."

The overall effects on cognitive and literary economies are topics for the final gathering of chapters in this volume by Florian Cramer, Martin Eve, David Roh, and myself. While we all are aware of trends and are capable of noting the frequency of keywords such as "post-" and "trans-human" (with and without the hyphen), "cognitive capitalism," "technics," and for that matter "anamnetic mnemotechnologies" (Stiegler), we are not counting occurrences and currencies so much as making our conclusions *accountable* to one another, and to readers of this volume who, like us, are interested in making critical distinctions among kinds of knowledge that can move a scholarly field (and programs in digital literary arts) toward or away from instrumental practices.

We are post-digital in the sense that the literary corpus is by now mostly already digitized but (just as important) nearly all new writing is now done digitally and is destined, like the print writing scanned by Google workers, to circulate in databases. The post-digital is no place for avant-gardes, not when the upgrade path is normative. Key to both transformations depicted in the final chapters, the cognitive and the economic, is the digitization of texts that had previously, before the time of networked computers, been kept separate from instantaneous searchability (and hence, economization of content). But even as the literary corpus is scanned, so that these kinds of paradigm changes can be

---

Dickinson. On the other side," those who consider narrative as either an inherent cognitive disposition or an ethical/religious requirement for a life worth living, Strawson lists "to begin with—Plato, St. Augustine, Heidegger, Tom Nagel, probably Nietzsche, all the champions of narrative and Narrativity in the current ethicopsychological debate, and some of my closest friends."

observed not by deep reading but instead by mining data and tracking trends, the literariness of our field is itself brought into question, as Tomasula notes in this book: "Though a survey of contemporary literature would show a huge variety of aesthetics, and authorial stances, are our tools contributing to a body of writing that can be called postliterary or postliterature literature? Does this literature contribute to (and in turn reinforce) a posthuman conception of self as pattern?" The careers of Cayley, Tomasula, and Brian Kim Stefans ("Immanence, Inc."), kicked in less than a decade after the "utopian days of early hypertext" (as Luciana Gattass has it). What had already changed by then, as Gattass notes in her chapter, was the heightened presencing of digital technology in our daily lives and a corresponding extension of electronic literature to "our time of multi-modality and hyper-connectivity." Even as film and later televisual media, arguably, altered the way we literally *look at* the world; the broader electrification of our textual corpus—the books in print that presently are relocating to databases, but also our own daily posts to social media and networked feeds—arguably has been changing our sense of what it is *to read*. And when the nature of reading changes, so too does our internalization of language. What we have in every case is not just the opening of a new market (for cinema post-Lumiere, networked television, and now social media and networked publishing) but a shift in consciousness and, in turn, an *economization* of those aspects of consciousness and cognition that can now be newly digitized. This is a process that changes the nature of reading itself in ways that, as Cayley remarks, might well mark "the end of all literature, and electronic literature may have helped to get us there."

Lumiere may have been wrong about the economic prospects for the filmic medium he inaugurated; but he may also share with many creators an impatience with the domestication of a medium that they themselves (*as* creators) know how to engage from the inside, as makers not as passive watchers. Among those who take up a medium when it is in development, still literally "experimental" (to use Álvaro Seiça's term of preference for the decades long tradition of born digital literary arts), nothing fails so much as success: the commercialization and naturalization of a medium, which tends to keep users at a surface level where they can mostly follow instructions or give away data relating to their own consumer preferences, rather than apply technical affordances in innovative ways. Indeed, the economization even of impulses that had once been taken for granted, the "sharing" of knowledge about a program, or code, or one's working conditions—these thoughts and this knowledge are now kept strictly to ourselves until they can be conveyed in conferences with preselected coevals in a regulated context.[4] The digital "sharing" even of literary files, more and more often, requires elaborate permissions among authors, editors, and publishers in designated, protected locations, thus ensuring that collaboration among coauthors and coproducers happens more and more frequently in controlled environments. Our habitus has become largely, in the words of Mark Seltzer, an *Official World* whose contrast with past lifeways is readily enough viewed by looking at past and present film and video footage. It is no accident that Andrew Wilson's shots of the upper

[4] Friedrich Kittler (2004) was among the first to note the historical break that ensued from the commodification of scientific and technological knowledge; this, and a similar economization of academic knowledge in general pose the biggest hindrance, arguably, to the extension of creativity to cross-disciplinary collaborative spheres: When "knowledge wanders into the private sectors [this] means secrecy, not openness. The secret manifest in commercial chip designs, operating systems, and application program interfaces (APIs) lies in the fact that technical documentation— in screaming contrast to all technical history—is not published anymore. By virtue of their inaccessibility alone, blueprints and source codes earn money" (253).

class "red badge" employees at the facility where he himself worked are as static as the scan-op footage; rarely do employees on either campus *congregate*, a stark contrast with the Lumiere factory workers of 1895. Once or twice, perhaps, we can observe two men (never more than that) walking together through the parking lot and into the glass-walled red badge building. Only once during eleven minutes of filming do we see an isolated yellow badge worker getting into her car and signaling to Wilson to shut off his cam. Among the hundreds of individuals exiting the yellow badge facility (Building 3.1415) one couple can be seen getting into their car together. Otherwise there is no congeniality observable outdoors among either the "privileged" red badge employees or the scan-ops in their "extremely confidential" place of work. We're all seemingly living the life of Pi, more or less alone surviving in the official world, with a tiger by the tail.

By now, the decision to go digital is no longer in itself a particularly innovative act for literary creators and scholars. Whether the uploaded and scanned corpus and accompanying scholarship (contemporary and current) will be open to hypertextual linkages and peer-to-peer interaction remains to be seen. That some thirty million plus titles that previously resided in United States lending libraries have been acquired by Google for commercial use alters the relation of any current literary art to past practice as can be seen in the chapters in the present handbook. Stuart Moulthrop, himself a pioneer of early hypertext who recently has cowritten with Dene Grigar a book on the subject, applies to digital poetry and fiction writing Lev Manovich's definition of a "new media object"—"as one or more interfaces to a multimedia database" (*Language of New Media* 37; cited here, in Moulthrop's chapter, p. 61). Taking recent "writings-of-Internet" as test cases (and specifically *Was*, Michael Joyce's print *novel of internet*), Moulthrop demonstrates through a survey of multiple modes of literary experimentation the potential for literary applications of Manovich's formulations. "Perhaps," Moulthrop postulates, "interfacing with databases is becoming integral to not just electronic literature and digital poetics but all forms of literary study and practice?" The tendency toward a recombinant, *citational* poetics, after all, was observed by Marjorie Perloff well before the emergence of electronic literature, and even print works composed on (digital) notebooks with streaming access to the Internet are likely to emerge as hybrids or citational compositions, even a bit of "flarf" that Moulthrop and his Milwaukee writing group came up with, when they compiled a "poem" out of internet searches of terms from Joyces's "novel of internet": "The poem of internet of novel is a compound conception," Moulthrop notes (echoing Gattass's formulation of our present time of "multi-modality and hyper-connectivity"). As such, the field of "electronic literature" might no longer need to restrict itself to the study of works that are born or native digital. Electronic literature today may have become, in Moulthrop's words, "less an interface than a state"; as much in evidence in print as in hypertext or in an interface linked to a database. What it no longer can be, though, once that multimodal, hyper-connected "state" is universal, and emplaced, is anything like the movement that Moulthrop, Joyce, Jackson, and the others advanced when "electronic literature" was new.

The post-digital is no place for avant-gardes: about this, all our contributors are in agreement, those who began in the hypertextual mode and those who entered a decade or two later. Indeed, as Álvaro Seiça makes clear in his analysis of experimental writing in his home country: the Portuguese "agenda," so clearly aware of modernist experiments of the previous fifty years, set its own version of "experimentalism to be created or adopted on the basis of a rejection of *movement*." Cayley for his part acknowledges an instrumental turn associated with the emergence of "Big Software" and a move away from "utopian, ideal, or rational versions of hypertext" toward one preferred, predominant, and "everyday" network, namely: the World Wide Web. Hypertext indeed became "ubiquitous" but it was no longer predominantly an avant-garde movement or hacker culture of free and for the most part freely shared experimentation. Instead, it settled into the most conventional, readily commercialized forms imaginable:

> promotional "pages" for corporations and individuals (prospectuses', cv's, portfolios, résumés); blogs (journaling, op-editorializing, opinion-forming, letter-writing, commentary); journalism (as such); and other representations of essentially "printable" literature (in the archival and documentary sense). All other possible and potential forms of hypertext remain just that: possible and potential, or else, perhaps, realized as avant-garde and peripheral experiments outside the internet's main vectors of attention. (pp. 75–6, Chapter 4 in this volume)

With the going mainstream of multi-modal, interconnective practice, the avant-garde is at best "peripheral," no less interesting surely than the works of Queneau and others, but also no more transformative. The time is past when a literary experiment tied to this or that particular digital instrument could define a genre, or promise a collaborative, continuing practice such as novel or poem writing. Heckman and O'Sullivan are not the only contributors to notice an "inherent contradiction of those instruments favored by the electronic literature movement"; namely: "that they are aligned with the forces they seek to disrupt (just consider, by way of example, the long-lived dominance of Flash), while nonetheless being disruptive." That dimension, the glitch, the Netprov, the displacement of the real and potential for defamiliarization inherent in disruption, is where the opportunity lies for most of the contributors to this volume, in the development of a post-digital poetics:

> Even disruption, after all, is bound by the limits of the instrument which it seeks, or indeed utilizes, to disrupt. But there is poetic liberty nonetheless, and at the very least, electronic literature can reflect upon its own constraints, through its poeisis *and* techne. The bots may continue to habituate our reading, but there must be some value in reading, in casting, the bots. (p. 102, Chapter 5 in this volume)

What early generations of experimental writers could not have foreseen, any more than Lumiere foresaw the commercial potential of film, was the universalization and *normalization* of affordances and potentials that they themselves had experienced as unprecedented. That these potentials could have been so readily economized, in an economy that extends not just to new commodities but to cognition itself (and culture) conceived as capital, nobody could have foreseen. To make our digitized thought ways and affective passages *strange again*, in the manner of formalist projects of defamiliarization, or disautomatization as it was also known—was never a project that could be relegated for very long to avant-garde movements at the periphery: it's rather what defines a literary mainstream of cultural and communicative moment. The original in Russian, *Ostranienye* (literally, "enstrangement"), gets at the artful qualities of everyday life that are never given to us for long. But they're precisely what the literary arts have always been tasked to recover—and never more so than in our present era of post-digital normativity.

For it's no longer just the material world that's been rendered familiar through representation. Now we have the literary corpus itself, enclosed in databases: "where books went when they died" (in Shelley Jackson's formulation). They are there, a normalized data set waiting to be recovered, mined for patterns but also read again, differently this time. The words, most of them, are still the same words that the authors set down all those years ago in another medium. But they can now be read again, even as Jackson reads and recirculates the words of Bruno Schultz, who imagined us, his readers, in some unnamed future: "Under the imaginary table that separates me from my readers, don't we secretly clasp each other's hands?"

SOURCES CITED

Joyce, Michael. *Was: annales nomadiques, a novel of internet*. Tuscaloosa: Fiction Collective 2, 2007.

Kittler, Friedrich. "Universities: Wet, Hard, Soft, and Harder." *Critical Inquiry*, vol. 31, no. 1 (Autumn 2004): 244–55.

Manovich, Lev. *The Language of New Media*. Cambridge: MIT Press, 2001.

Seltzer, Mark. *The Official World*. Durham, NC: Duke University Press, 2016.

Strawson, Gaylen. "Against Narrativity." *Ratio* (new series) XVII, December 4, 2004. Online at http://lchc.ucsd.edu/mca/Paper/against_narrativity.pdf.

Tabbi, Joseph. "On Reading 300 Works of Electronic Literature." July 22, 2009. Online at http://nationalhumanitiescenter.org/on-the-human/2009/07/on-reading-300-works-of-electronic-literature-preliminary-reflections/.

PART ONE

Ends, Beginnings

CHAPTER ONE

I Hold It Toward You: A Show of Hands

SHELLEY JACKSON

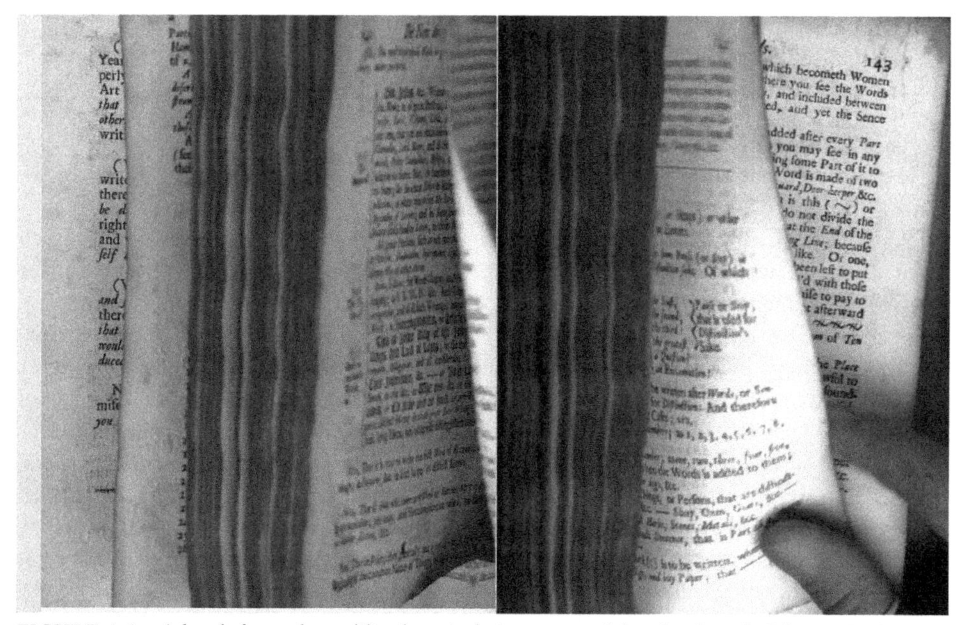

FIGURE 1.1 A book from the public domain being scanned for the Google Library Project.

She is the last reader. All the others are dead—Sylvia, Teshale, Zeb. The sand-thick wind is rubbing away what's left of the world. The dim sun makes a red dome of the sky. It looks like the roof of a mouth.

Late at night, early in the morning, for whole days together, she finds herself wandering through the hecatomb of the books, the library vaults of quaint, once glorious Google, as the electricity comes and goes, the power cord of her ancient device—what did they call it, a face book? Kindling?—sizzles and zaps, and moiré patterns obscure the screen. When she is hungry, which is not often anymore, she eats white glue, sugar, the occasional ant. Then she resumes her activities.

After a while it occurs to her that she is looking for something.

☞

What is a book? Certainly it is not, or not only, a bound stack of stained wood pulp, or a papyrus scroll, or a sequence of ones and zeros on a microchip. It is nothing near so definite. I have called it at various times an action, an operation, an interference pattern, a parley, a playground, a parenthetical clause, a syncope, a séance, a Schrodinger's cat, or a Trojan horse. It might also be helpful to keep in mind the obsolete noun "handfast," meaning variously a firm grasp, a handle, the handshake that seals an agreement, or a contract or covenant, especially a marriage betrothal.

But for now let us say simply that a book is a situation.

☞

If a book is a situation, only a small part of this situation is controlled by the writer, though certainly without her there would be no book.

What part? What some would call the text "itself," particular words in a particular order? No, even this modest claim is not quite modest enough. We certainly did not invent the words we use, nor most of the principles of their arrangement, from grammar to the conventions of story, verse, or rhetoric. Ideas, too, do not leap, fully formed, from the void.

Nor is a book made of words alone, haunting the solitude of the writer's mind; a book would not be a book if nobody wrote it down.

It could be a book without being printed and bound, or coded for an e-reader, published, promoted, distributed, and sold, but the typical book you find in stores—to consider, for simplicity's sake, only the codex version—requires a printing press, which requires paper, which requires wood pulp, which requires a lumber industry and of course trees, which require earth, water, air, and light; it requires ink, which requires pigment and vehicle, mills and filters; it requires glue for the binding, usually made of vinyl acetate ethyline copolymers. To make and mix these substances and bind them together into a book it requires machines, which require other machines to make them, out of parts made by yet other machines, out of steel, aluminum, plastic, vinyl, which all require production; it requires factories and warehouses, which require builders and workers, concrete and rebar, bricks and mortar, lumber and nails and tar for the roof; to bring all these elements together into a book, and then to distribute this book, it requires trucks, drivers, and passable roads; it requires book reps and buyers, bookstores and libraries. It may not require but certainly has advertisers, reviewers, and venues that publish ads and reviews; it requires money, and a whole system of exchange—in short, a situation so complex that it could not spring into existence to produce a single book, but evolved through myriad refinements over time, so a book also requires many other books to come before it, and all this before it ever arrives in the hands of a reader.

But perhaps only then is a book really a book. There is much to recommend the argument that a book becomes a book in *being read.*

Yet this simplifies matters only a little. Before we begin reading that book we must, for starters, know the language in which it is written, and have learned to read it; we must know what a book is and how to handle it, and to read it skillfully, with full understanding, we must know what a story, a character, a plot is and how it tends to behave, and so we must have read other books. We might also have read book reviews, gone to readings, studied critical theory or the history of literature, and in the interval between picking up the book and starting to read, we have probably taken in at least some of the paratext, that is, the jacket copy, blurbs, award stickers, the colophon of the publisher; we might have skimmed an introduction or flipped through an index, and all of these things, ostensibly peripheral, have shaped our reading before we have read a single word.

And that word itself would mean nothing if it did not call up a response in the reader shaped by years of living in the world, for the word "leaf," whole autumns of leaves, years of autumns of looking at leaves, at the waxy sheen on the surface, at the way the pattern of the veins repeats the tree in miniature, at the way light comes to a point in a raindrop suspended from the tip, at the way the leaf is pulled down into a curve like a bow by the weight of the drop, then jerks up when the drop falls, at the way dry leaves break into parallelograms, or turn to lace, or leave their ghostly prints on a concrete walk; years of reading about leaves in other books, in words that now come unbidden, "I have lived long enough. My way of life/is fall'n into the sere, the yellow leaf."

And that's not all, because an open book is really open, susceptible to all the conditions of the present moment: the weather, events in the news, the dream you had last night, a compound response that is idiosyncratic and unpredictable, that is in fact really wild, volatile, swayed by every passing thought, every changing mood, the smell of smoke, the sound of sirens, distant cries.

☞

Hence my work in progress, *Project for Polluted Waterway*, a pair of stories to be read along the Gowanus Canal, a short tidal estuary in Brooklyn, New York. One story flows in, one out, which you encounter as tide-dependent. But both make of pollution their central metaphor and their organizing principle, through a system of environmental cues (the peacock colors of a gasoline slick, a condom floating like a ghost) that call up textual pollution in the form of associated prose poems.

☞

But all reading is if not tide-specific, then site-specific, reader-specific, occasion-specific. Whether the text ignores intrusions or solicits them, the world contaminates the word, and this is not a problem but a prerequisite for reading, for without this contamination, the word would be nothing, scratchmarks on a page, patterns of light on a screen.

In fact, the word *is* nothing, nothing but an invitation to everything the reader leaks into it, and the book, until it is read, is merely the chance of a book—a latency waiting to manifest.

☞

She finds herself not reading but paging through, clicking through, scrolling through, volume upon volume of old books, the more obscure the better, because it is in these unfrequented pages that she may catch the passing shadow of another reader.

Carol? Song Wa? Tunde? Netsanet?

All of them having worked at one time in the Google Gulag.

☞

"Manifest," from the Latin *manifestus*, from *manus*, hand, plus *fendere*, strike; literally "struck by the hand," hence, palpable.

When the book becomes a book, you can *feel* it.

For there is one part of the situation of the changing book in the changing world that does not change: We read with our body. With our eyes, ears, brain, with minute sympathetic responses in our vocal and aural apparatus and throughout our nervous system, and with our hands: unscrolling scrolls, turning pages, clicking buttons, swiping screens. In the blind or paraplegic the body parts are differently weighted, but still, I will say it again, we read—just as we do everything else—with and in and because of the body.

☞

And then she finds it. On a page frozen in motion, the dark half-moon of a thumb-tip. The tropical blooming of a purple finger cot on an orange or pink or brown hand, or a forensic grey one on a grey hand. A shadow, an awkwardly erased shadow that replicates a bit of the text, a hunched and furtive blur.

☞

So books are made for bodies. Like an umbrella or a pair of scissors, a book is a usually hand-operated device, and patently adapted to the human form. An alien scientist, handed one, could probably work out what sort of animal must have created such an object for its use, for a codex book refers to and even resembles a human body. It is the weight a person can comfortably carry; it has two sides, one for each hand (some books even have a "thumb-index": finger-sized notches in the page edges), and rather looks like two hands side by side, palms up—in the gesture, in fact, that in the game of charades stands for "book." Slammed shut, it claps. Opened, it is symmetrical like a face, and the average page is also about the size of a face, the face of someone nearby, someone with whom we are talking as friends. (Such that facebook is a redundant term.) And if the image of the mirror recurs in literature, and I need only mention Borges or Nabokov here, it is not only because we see in books a semblance of the world, but also because we see in them a semblance of *ourselves*.

☞

Which finds its logical extension in "anthropodermic bibliopegy," or the binding of books in human skin.

☞

Or my project SKIN, a story published in tattoos on 2,095 volunteers.

☞

Consider the explicitly anatomical terminology of the book: Head, foot, body. Spine and joints. Footnote and header. Chapter, from the Latin *caput*, head. Index, from the Latin *index*, forefinger.

☞

Or my early works, *Patchwork Girl*, *My Body*, and *The Melancholy of Anatomy*, all three of which in different ways conceive the text as a monstrous body, the body as a text.

☞

Nor is it only the book that takes its measure from the body.

☞

The spoken word does too, and not just because mouths and ears are its prerequisites.

☞

In particular, the book takes its measure from the hand.

☞

The hand is always a surprise, even when she is looking for it. Every time, she is shocked. Struck, almost physically. The hand is even—the word is not too strong—obscene. It forcibly reminds her of the body she had forgotten temporarily, set aside.

Her own, that is.
And all those others', gone now.
Javier. Lucy. Wayne. Pattanapong.

☞

Indeed, "The Learned very fitly call Measure the daughter of the Fingers," John Bulwer wrote in 1644,[1] "and the Aegyptians used to signifie measure by a Finger painted. Hence the meeting and scanning of verses upon the Fingers, hath been a very ancient custome, and it was the manner of old in the recitation of the verses of Poets, in the measuring and singing them, to note out the intervalls and stroaks by a certain motion of the Hands.

"So a Dactyl, one of the Poeticall feet"—another anatomical term—"took denomination from the drawing in length of the Finger," which is to say that it is named after the Greek *daktylos*, finger, because its syllables go long-short-short, like the bones of a finger.

☞

The word "poetry" is itself a dactyl.

☞

It is as if a poem might not only be measured on your fingers, but at certain junctures actually *become* a finger.

☞

And so, she thinks, it is more than a little sexual. A hand, dressed for intimate contact, has entered the privacy in which, alone at the end of the world, book and reader commune.

☞

So if there is a long-standing link between the hand and language, it is not just because we must use our hands to write, though that is an association so fundamental that the way a person forms her letters is simply called her "hand."

☞

We also speak *with* our hands—the topic of Bulwer's book, *Chirologia, the Natural Language of the Hand*. (*Chirologia*, from the Greek *cheiro*, hand.)

"For, the lineaments of the Body doe disclose the disposition and inclination of the minde in generall; but the motions doe not only so, but doe further disclose the present humour and state of the minde and will; for as the Tongue speaketh to the eare, so Gesture speaketh to the eye."

[1] Chirologia, or, The natural language of the hand composed of the speaking motions, and discoursing gestures thereof: where unto is added Chironomia, or, The art of manual rhetoricke, consisting of the natural expressions, digested by art in the hand, as the chiefest instrument of eloquence, by historical manifesto's exemplified out of the authentique registers of common life and civil conversation: with types, or chyrograms, a long-wish'd for illustration of this argument.

☞

"The *Index*," for example, "advanced from a *fist*, and inclin'd respective to the shoulder; hath a great facultie to *confirme*, *collect* and *refute*."

☞

In fact, "Every Digit dictates and doth reach/Unto our sense a mouth-excelling speech."

☞

And Augustine went so far as to call speech "*manus oris mei*"—the hand of my mouth.

☞

She gets up to draw a glass of silty water from the shuddering pipe. Drinking through her teeth, she stares out at the haze into which the swollen sun is sinking. Then wipes the grit off her teeth and returns to her desk.

☞

The printing press put the writing, pointing, measuring hand at a remove. But . . .

☞

Her index finger traces little circles on what was once called, she understands, a mouse pad . . .

☞

The hand came back.

In, for instance, the popularity of books, like Bulwer's, on chirologia or chironomia, the language of gesture.

Or on chiromancy, or palm-reading;

Or on chirognomy, or determining a person's character from their hand;

On sign language for the deaf;

On the new tactile writing systems for the blind, such as Moon type, Boston Line Type, New York Point, Fishburne, and standard Braille;

And more concretely, in the fingerprints of their printers;

And the marginalia, underlining, and other annotations of their readers.

☞

Yes, let us think about fingering and fisting, let us think about an index paging through labia, slitting the sealed pages, bursting the binding, let us let our minds descend into the gutter, while the world whirls into dust . . .

☞

The hand of the reader might mark the page without intermediary, folding down a page in a dog-ear, or tracing a line with a nail, like the slovenly scholar in the *Philobiblion* of Richard de Bury, whose "nails are stuffed with fetid filth as black as jet, with which he marks any passage that pleases him."

Or like Eugene Onegin, in whose library "There were preserved on many pages/The mark of a trenchant fingernail"—just as there were, a Russian scholar notes, in Pushkin's own collection.

While Nabokov, footnoting this passage, draws our attention to Sheridan's play "The Rivals," in which Lydia Languish says of a certain Lady Slattern, like herself a patron of a circulating library, "Yes, I always know when Lady Slattern has been before me—She has a most observing thumb; and I believe cherishes her nails for the convenience of making marginal notes."

☞

Slavoj, Samvad, Finnegan, Renee . . . Let us, while the world whirls into dust, memorialize the books and bodies we have loved, and if we get the two mixed up, that is probably exactly the point.

☞

Lady Slattern's name inclines one to believe that the reminders of the hand left by her *observing thumb* are accidental. But we cannot say the same for the ink lines, arrows, brackets, stars, squiggles, exclamations . . .

☞

Or, most notably, the little hands, or "manicules," that readers had been drawing in margins since roughly the twelfth century—that is, well before Gutenberg—to point out passages of special interest.

☞

As if, through the conducting medium of ink, our pointing hands could reach down from our own dimension right into the diegetic world, and carry on confirming, collecting, and refuting there.

☞

One of the things she remembers about books, and she is thinking of the kind that burn (that have burned, that are ashes now), is that they open. And this is one of the things she remembers about bodies as well.

☞

Printers sanctioned the manicule, casting the "index" or "printer's fist" in a variety of sizes and orientations, and using it as one of many typographical ornaments in the printed book.

☞

Where it might well share space with hand-drawn manicules.

☞

Not to mention with the word "hand."

☞

And with the reader's actual hands of flesh and bone.

☞

Books opened like legs, like hands, like mouths and other orifices. And what for? To admit us. The body was like a book; the book was like a body, opening to our desire.

☞

Although in the printer's fist the manicule became an official part of the text, not everyone has recognized this standing. The programmers of Google Books' search function, for example.

☞

Which means that although there are, as I gather, six manicules in *The Life & Opinions of Tristram Shandy, Gentleman,* I have only identified five, and I had to find them the old way, by turning pages. By hand.

☞

That is, I found them when they were there to be found. For while some publishers reproduced Sterne's manicules, some replaced them with asterisks, and some left them out altogether.

☞

Along with such other nonverbal elements as the black page, the marbled page, and Sterne's idiosyncratic punctuation.

☞

So we are back at the question I asked at the outset: What is a book? Which of its attributes are necessary? Which can we do without?

Sterne's manicules are right on the contested borderline. Between words and ... everything else.

The texture of the paper, say. Whether its binding is savory to mice. Its smell.

☞

Needless to say the smell of a book has no ASCII code.

☞

That desire, what was it? Not lust, exactly (though lust, she suspects, is also not exactly or not only lust): It was also love, loneliness, curiosity, playfulness, a need for information, a need for diversion, the will to power, the willingness to open oneself in turn.

☞

And so the manicule marks—it fingerposts—the passage between the inside and the outside of the book. And if its official function is to point inward, at the text, it also gestures the opposite direction (with its stump, you might say), outward, at the body—the body of the author, the body of the reader, and the body of the book.

☞

And perhaps the desire to multiply oneself, to make more books and bodies. So a purple prophylactic is not a bad precaution; we might inseminate the book. It might inseminate us. We might inseminate one another through our promiscuous books, their pages as stained as cathouse sheets.

☞

For the book is more than its text, as the word is more than its meaning. It has a body, and it is only through its body that it reaches *my* body, and through my body, my mind.

☞

Or as you might say, "The Word was made flesh, and dwelt among us."

☞

And God forbid she should repopulate the earth now, at the eleventh hour.

☞

Of course, "the word made flesh" does not refer to the written word, but to Christ, in whom material word and spirit are perfectly united.

The written word, theologically speaking, is only, imperfectly, *analogous* to this divine Word. It means, but its meaning is not immanent in the word; it must shed its materiality or, we might say, die, in order to rise as meaning. Leaving the dead letter behind.

☞

Thus resembling, not Christ, but ordinary mortals.

☞

Tim, Evgeny, Joanne, Ashish.

☞

The descendants of Adam.

Who was made of dust or, as is specified elsewhere in the Bible, of clay.

☞

Like the tablets into which the still undeciphered symbols of proto-Elamite were pressed in ancient Iran.

☞

The earliest examples of writing we have found.

☞

The clay of the tablet is impressed with meaning by hand, using a stylus.

☞

God does not require a stylus to shape the clay of Adam.

☞

He does, however, use his hands.

☞

Specifically the index finger of his right hand.

☞

Well, according to Michelangelo, in whose "Creation of Adam" God animates the languid Adam with a touch.

☞

Or was she, in spite of herself, looking for company, there at the end of the world? Why else would she be so fixated on these hands? Why did she compulsively collect them? Why did her heart open when she saw them, as at a gift or a message from a friend?

☞

Touch, however, is famously reciprocal; a profane viewer might see, in the same image, Adam languidly creating God.

☞

For the hands do inspire tenderness. They also look tender. Gentle (they have to be, handling these frail old books) despite the finger cots, and the clamps you can occasionally see, holding down the pages. These accessories seem out of place in the library, an added shock, and yet there is something not entirely inappropriate about the hospital atmosphere they introduce.

☞

Certainly, this reciprocity obtains between writer and word. If the mind endows matter with meaning, matter also awakens meaning in the mind.

Many writers would say that writing *is* this process by which the specific qualities of the word create what we want to say as much as what we want to say creates the word.

☞

Matter rubs off on meaning.
Matter *matters*.

☞

Is there, in Michelangelo's fresco, a smudge of clay on the tip of the finger of God?

☞

There would certainly have been one on Michelangelo's finger. Since many fresco pigments, particularly the earth tones (umber, ochre, burnt sienna) in which both Adam and God were rendered, were made from clay.

☞

For the writer, the matter that matters might be the clang of a word, almost drowning out its sense, or the way ink sinks into paper fibers. It might even be a smudge of clay, if you chose to emulate the proto-Elamites. Or any number of other properties of the embodied word (and thus, variously, of sound waves, of ink on paper, of pixels on a screen).

☞

And the manipulation of those properties cannot be separated from writing itself.

☞

Now we have moved on from sex to the hospital bed, the scene not sexual but gynecological.

Or obstetrical? Is someone being born, God forbid, God forbid?

☞

Consider a story[2] written (weather permitting) in snow, on sidewalks, stoops, park benches, muddy curbs, and tree stumps, and posted in photographs online. A story painstakingly inscribed by hand in a yielding medium (like a clay tablet), and in a classic font (like printed text) but whose readers' readiest associations are probably not with the history of the written word, but with their own first-hand experience, their own *hands*' experience, of snow. Probably they too have played in snow, different kinds of snow, dry and wet, powdery, sticky, crunchy, slushy, have felt the cold soak through their mittens until their fingers ached; perhaps they have also tried to write in it with a finger or a stick, and can almost *feel* the dry flakes that a breath will blow away, the ice crystals that must be chipped through with the scarred tip of a pencil, the icy slush dusted by white powder that with a touch goes black.

☞

Or a story painstakingly inscribed by hand in ink on human skin (like early manuscripts on vellum, or calfskin) and in a classic font (like printed text), but whose readers' readiest associations are again probably not with the history of the written word, but with their own first-hand experience, their own *hands*' experience, of other bared bodies, our own or others', glimpsed in passing or intimately known. And their hands know what bodies feel like: warmish, sometimes sticky, sometimes slippery. But reading my story "SKIN", unlike "Snow", the perspective shifts, for readers have skin of their own. They know how this story feels from inside, as well as outside, how it feels to be touched, as well as to touch. They might even know how it feels to be tattooed, and if not they certainly know how it feels to hurt and bleed, seep, scab, itch, and heal.

☞

Or is the book not a womb, but a wound? Is the book hurt, or dying?

The hands smooth down the sheets. Of paper, or of the deathbed. There is nothing they can do to avert what is coming. They contribute only their presence. They attend the patient through its final moments. The scene of reading is a hospice.

☞

Whether written on snow or skin, what the words conjure up, as signs, is accompanied by an ongoing and obtrusive experience of what the words conjure up as matter.

These associations summon us forcibly back into our own bodies. So that you could say that the medium interrupts the message.

However, and as their titles imply, these stories are written *for* (and even about) their medium to a degree that most stories are not. A so-called "immersive" reading would thus repeatedly direct the reader's attention back to the surface, to find the meaning of the story sustained and completed there—which returns the attention to the text. So there is a movement up and down, sinking and rising and sinking again, that weaves together the material world and the fiction, the surface and the depth—though these spatial metaphors are inexact, since it is arguably the surface of the text that activates what I would call the "deepest," that is, most bodily response.

---

[2] My story "Snow".

☞

A conventional book elicits a less bodily response; its tactile qualities are more easily overlooked. But these too can be brought in meaningful relation to the text.

☞

Paper, for instance, is thin and light, but a pile of it has considerable weight and mass. Take the 545 pages of *Moby-Dick.* That is a whale of a book. It is heavy, it is long, its massiveness a concrete correlative of the time it will take to read it. Holding it, you know in your *body* that you have days of travel ahead of you, mountains of blubber to slice into the thin sheets that Melville informs us, knowingly, are called "bible-leaves" and render into the clear oil of understanding.

(By the way, if a book is a situation, part of the situation of *Moby-Dick* that has flickered and gone out is the light of the oil lamp by which his contemporaries read it. A lamp filled with whale oil.)

☞

If what the camera caught was the death throes of the book, then surely the patient has died by now. Is reading then forensic? Is she a kind of coroner, seeking the cause of death?

☞

A writer can make something of a book's material properties, or leave them alone. So while Melville makes much of paper's weight and mass, its whiteness, the intricately figured surface that secures its resemblance to a wall, to a tombstone, and to an old white sperm whale's brow, flat but "pleated with riddles," he makes little of paper's texture or its smell. The properties of a book are always in excess of its meaning. But they are there all the same, part of your body's knowledge of the book.

☞

Or is reading a wake?

☞

Here are some things your body knows about a codex book. You can hold it with two hands or one while you read, with thumbs at the bottom corners or one thumb in the gutter at the bottom; you can jam a big book against your body to help support its weight, pulling it toward you with your fingers wrapped around the top edge. You can set it down, holding it open with a hand, the end of a spoon, a hairbrush, the corner of another book, the sash of a window; you can put it in a stand made for this purpose. You can lick your finger to help you turn a page. You can run your finger under the line you are reading, or a pencil, you can run a highlighter over it, take notes in the margin, perhaps (influenced by this talk) draw a manicule. You can fold down corners to mark a page, devising private systems to do this—folding toward the page where the important passage lies, double folding if both sides are of interest. You can tear out a page to take notes on or use the endpapers for this purpose. You can press flowers, leaves, four-leafed clovers between the pages. On a hot day you can fan yourself with a book, shade or hide your face with it. You can go to sleep under the tent of it. You can slam a hardback shut when angry, to make a satisfying noise. You can pick your teeth with the corner of a page, tear off a piece and use it as a bookmark or chew on it or use it to clean lint from your computer keyboard. A pile of books can be used as a seat, as Sterne recommends "(do, Sir, sit down on a set—they are better than nothing)" or to prop up an air conditioner. You can use a book as a lap desk, hit someone with it, make a shelf or a purse out of it, fold or cut the pages to make a sculpture; if you are a bookworm or silverfish, you can live in it and I have seen ants use a roadside book to roof their nest. Its pages turn on their hinges like doors, flap like flags. It lends itself to images of screens and scrims, marble slabs, sheets and veils and shrouds and sails, white walls and white whales.

☞

In which case these hands must belong to the undertaker, who has laid out the body, minimized the evidence of decay, made it fit to view.

☞

Our bodies know quite different things about ebooks and the devices we read them on. Where paper has a surface nap, a tooth, electronic devices are smooth. They have sheen, a black watery depth. The text skims by, under a glassy surface that may reflect its surroundings or cast a light on them. You can use it to find your glasses under the bed or light your way through a dark house. The device may be small and almost weightless, or heavy and stationary. It clicks and slides and shines like beetles, hard on the outside, strange on the inside. The individual page cannot be held. Instead we scroll, swipe, click. Ebooks are secretive (no one can see what I'm reading) and at the same time public (I am online, my notes can be shared with other readers, Amazon records where I leave off reading). They might weigh less. They may seem to weigh less *figuratively*, too, to be less "real," their appearance subject to change, their very presence contingent. The text is only visiting us, we do not really own it, and at some point our claim to it may be revoked.

Imagine reading *Moby-Dick* on an iPhone. We gain a sense of the sleekness of water, of the depths concealed beneath its bright and changing surface, and above all its reflectivity, so important to Melville that he positioned the story of Narcissus in his first paragraph. (So it is not a simple matter of one medium being better or worse, more evocative or less, than another. Different matter, different meaning.)

We lose, however, all the weight of the whale. We lose the feeling of dissecting its great mass, slice by slice. We lose our tactile measure of our slow progress through it.

☞

For while codex books are navigable by touch, ebooks are not. We cannot find our way by feel, our hands can't tell how long they are or how much of them we've read or have yet to read, and so (and this too might suit our iPhone *Moby-Dick* …) we can't get our bearings, we are at sea.

However, the screen brightens at the touch like a living thing that likes us.

☞

That the hands are touching a book is also part of what makes her like them, because she likes books, and is disposed to sympathy toward anyone who touches them gently, even if there is no special reason to think, God knows, that those employed to scan books for Google had any special fondness for them.

But they turn the pages just like she does when she reads.

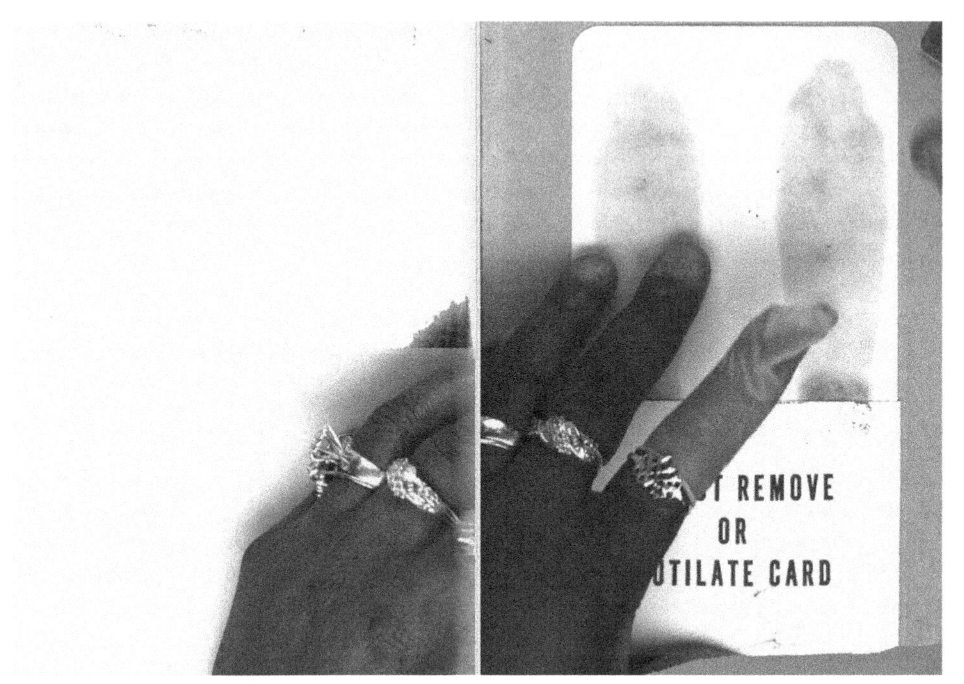

FIGURE 1.2 From the Google Library Project.

☞

Digital texts “know” when you are touching them.

☞

But codex books can seem eerily touch-sensitive as well.

☞

Nabokov’s *Invitation to a Beheading* begins, “In accordance with the law the death sentence was announced to Cincinnatus C. in a whisper.” The double meaning of “sentence,” which links death to language, is a happy accident of translation, but the novel’s second paragraph explicitly correlates mortality and the text: “So we are nearing the end. The right-hand, still untasted part of the novel, which, during our delectable reading, we would lightly feel, mechanically testing whether there were still plenty left (and our fingers were always gladdened by the placid, faithful thickness) has suddenly, for no reason at all, become quite meager: a few minutes of quick reading, already downhill, and—O horrible!”

☞

A momentary confusion: is this her hand? For your phantom hand on the page, Soraya, Wang, Trevor, is exactly where, if she were holding the book, instead of calling up its image, her own hand would rest. And so it is as if she is slipping into register with you, the two hands becoming one, interpenetratingly.

☞

“So we are nearing the end.” Cincinnatus is the one whose thoughts are being paraphrased here, we can deduce. But Nabokov doesn’t say so. He says “we.” And “we” includes us, all the more emphatically when it designates the readers of novels, a category in which, reading those words, we are emphatically included.

That being so, "the right-hand, still untasted part of the novel" seems to designate the right-hand, still untasted part of the book we are holding right now, *Invitation to a Beheading*, and "which, during our delectable reading, we would lightly feel, mechanically testing whether there were still plenty left" directs our attention to our own hand, very likely engaged, such is the power of suggestion, in mechanically testing whether there were still plenty left. (So long as we are not reading it on an iPhone, anyway.)

And so our real hand and Nabokov's figurative hand, a disembodied hand belonging to no one and everyone ("we"), mirror or merge with each other.

The effect is peculiar. On the one hand, we are thrust out of the story, made aware of ourselves as existing on a different plane than the characters in the book. On the other hand, we are led to that awareness through immersion, through reading, and so we are arguably still "in" the book, having passed *through* its pages to our world rather than withdrawing to it *from* them, and our real experience, transformed into metaphor, has been made secondary to that of the fictional character. Which makes our own reality part of the fiction; our real hand becomes a sort of holographic projection, a figure of speech.

The reader's hand and the diegetic hand reflect one another across an ontological divide. One hand is less real than the other. But which?

☞

Their ambiguous contest is subtly recalled in two later images of estranged doubles, also tied to the hand: a lost cufflink and a lost glove, whose twin is magically visible in a mirror.

☞

We should probably keep in mind that our own hands are already doubled.

☞

Françoise Meltzer[3] suggests, "Perhaps mimesis itself is born of the notion that man has two hands."

☞

So that the relationship of fiction to reality is *already* that of two hands to another?

☞

While the feeling lasts, she is stretched between herself and another (Kaiya, Musa, Naomi), between present and past, between presence and absence, between page and screen, body and the image of a body.

☞

Incidentally, I read aloud William Sherman's essay on the history of the manicule while riding through northern California, to my partner who was at the wheel. When I got to one of the many passages in which the manicule appeared, I stuck out my own hand and grunted.

---

[3] *Salome and the Dance of Writing: Portraits of Mimesis in Literature.*

☞

Thus using my actual pointing hand … as a symbol … for the symbol … of an actual pointing hand. In an unintentionally Nabokovian perplex of representation and real.

☞

This haunted feeling—is it because of the way that passing moment is frozen, so that page is haunted forever by it?

Or is it the way that hand, that reader, Nico, Adelaide, Medina, was haunted in advance by all the others that would come after her, or might be, in some dimension outside time, already "there"—in that ghostly house of rendezvous—with her, the last reader, the late-arriving guest . . .

☞

But maybe this confusion, this duplicity, is part of the very nature of the hand.

☞

Does the hand represent the self, or *is* it the self? Is it objective or subjective? Thought or thing?

☞

For, like the mouth, the hand is where thought *becomes* thing. Where ideas find expression, whether in the "mouth-excelling speech" of gesture, or the written word.

☞

It is as if the hand were itself part thought. Magma of imagination, just hardening into form.

☞

Part of our outside, but still hot from our inside.

☞

Hegel: "Next to the organ of speech, it is the hand most of all by which a man manifests and actualizes himself."[4]

☞

This correspondence is recognized legally, via the signature . . .

☞

The fingerprint . . .

☞

And the handshake—"My hand on it!"

☞

The hand is how you prove you are *yourself*.

---

[4] *Phenomenology of Spirit.*

☞

It is also how you prove that you are a human being, not a robot.

☞

She hunches closer to the screen, clicking, scrolling, clicking, with a mechanical efficiency that eventually raises doubts in the mechanical gatekeeper that watches over these things as to her humanity. This mechanical intelligence is trained to recognize and repulse the overtures of mechanical intelligences like itself. A misrecognition, in her case, but it leads to a feeling of fellowship—she is not as impatient as she might have been at being repeatedly interrupted with importunities to type words that, because they cannot yet be recognized by machine intelligences, prove that she has human eyes connected to a human mind.

Machines are not allowed to read these books, warns the machine.

☞

In 2014, "Google announced that many of its 'Captchas'—the squiggled text tests designed to weed out automated spambots—will be reduced to nothing more than a single checkbox next to the statement 'I'm not a robot.' … The giveaways that separate man and machine can be as subtle as how he or she (or it) moves a mouse in the moments before that single click."[5]

☞

What is the feeling of fellowship, then—with a machine? Yes, in a way. She is behaving like a machine and a machine is telling her, I see you, I have singled you out, I recognize you.

☞

Or you can do it the old way, which also requires hands:

☞

Please type the word you see:

notiarg
ansuplad
projzkm
nalicolo
aphotra
gatingl
enegm
merming
fropyb
dplag

☞

Or is it the fellowship with all the other bodies (Carol, Allison, Coco, Kate) that have passed muster only because they have hands and eyes or ears and mouth (for the blind, there is also a sound file in which a human can make out a sequence of numbers; those who cannot type one can dictate one's response)?

[5] *Andy Greenberg, "Google Can Now Tell You're Not a Robot With Just One Click", WIRED, 12/3/14.*

The machine is telling her, I thought I knew you, but now I see that you have hands, eyes, ears, mouth, mind: You are not like me, because I know this word but could not read it.

☞

For it turns out we still read and write with our bodies.

☞

Digital media have even restored to relevance what the Printing Trade News in 1914 disdainfully called those "poor overworked fists," AKA manicules.

☞

(Digital: of, pertaining to, or using digits, the numerals below ten, that is, those that may be counted on the digits, or fingers.)

☞

Since around 1987, with the release of Hypercard, the arrow cursor has generally been replaced, when it hovers over a clickable link, by a tiny right hand with index finger extended.

☞

The hand pointer is like the manicule in a number of ways: it points, it is severed at the wrist, it extends our reach into the virtual world.

It differs from the manicule, too: We see it from the back, as we would see our own hand pointing away from us, or reaching out to touch something, rather than from the side. It does not have a cuff, as many manicules do. It sometimes wears a glove.

☞

The windowpanes rattle. Something comes loose above her and slithers across the roof. She turns the page, and—

No, really, isn't that her hand? For she too is a ghost, she too drifts over these pages unseen except for the tiny bone-white hand with which she clicks, scrolls, clicks . . .

☞

The hand pointer was intended to convey, to novice users, through a symbolism so natural it required no explanation, that the text or icon below it could be "touched," that is, that a movement of the hand would do something to it. The users were encouraged by the image of the hand to feel they were interacting directly, physically, with the image on the screen, reaching right into the virtual world.

In reality of course the user was touching a mouse, whose changing positions were translated into coordinates and transmitted down its cable to a computer, which translated these coordinates into changing patterns of light on a vertical screen.

☞

But no. It's nothing like her hand. She finds herself scrutinizing the fingernails, when visible—longer than hers, or shorter. Colin, Eleanor, Binyam, Abdullah? Lacquered, chewed to the quick, or with a crescent of dirt under the nail. Squared off in a way she finds vaguely repulsive. The rings, the watches. The skin that is lighter, darker, smoother, hairier than hers. Patently younger. Patently older.

☞

The mouse was called a mouse because it looked like a mouse.

☞

Because the mouse was called a mouse, units of movement are called mickeys.

☞

And for the same reason, in certain operating systems, the little hand that replaces the cursor when it hovered over a link, has, if you look closely, three radial stripes on the back that make it instantly recognizable as a Mickey Mouse glove.

☞

So that hand, with which we are encouraged to identify our own hand, is the hand of a cartoon mouse.

We are, in a sense, not merely touching a mouse. We are becoming a mouse.

☞

A cartoon mouse.

☞

A black cartoon mouse that is wearing white gloves because its original inspiration was Al Jolsen in "The Jazz Singer," who wore white gloves, as was established convention for white singer/actors performing in blackface.

☞

"Mammy," sang Al Jolson, in the *Jazz Singer*, 1927. "Mammy," squeaked Mickey Mouse in *Haunted House*, 1929, and *Mickey's Mellerdrammer*, 1932.

☞

So the hand into whose white glove we are encouraged to insert our own varicolored paw belongs to a black cartoon mouse who stands for a white film actor in blackface who stands for a racist stereotype of a black man.

☞

Feigning inclusivity, since anyone of any color (and several species) can wear a glove, the Mickey Mouse cursor actually makes a mockery of difference, and the "natural" symbol of the hand turns out to encode a very culturally specific series of impersonations—nested gloves—of which our own identification is just the most recent.

☞

If this is her hand, then she is a white man with dirty fingernails, no she is a black woman with a manicure, no she is a middle-aged white woman, no she is a young East Indian man . . .

☞

Can I even say "the hand" when every hand is different, when even our own right and left hands are not the same?

Does this glove fit a left-handed reader in the same way it fits a right-handed one?

☞

And now her mood changes, now the images makes her sad and a little sick, like the sordid photographs of a private detective. The book has been unfaithful to her, the book has let someone else touch it; it is opening, but not for her. Now the book, for the first time, seems to be turning away, refusing to meet her gaze. Now she knows what she did not really know (did not really feel) before, that she was not the first.

☞

Books, too, have their gloves. They say, "Let's pretend you're anybody." We pass through their passages, passing as the ideal reader, the one for whom they are intended.

☞

But take off the gloves, and every reader has a unique and specific hand, wrinkled, smooth, brown or pink or beige, with torn cuticles or painted fingernails. Every reader has a unique and specific body with a specific age, gender, race, class, personality, set of obsessions, memories, desires, dreams . . .

☞

The ideal reader, like the "text itself," is a fantasy, but one that haunts digital media as it has haunted the printed book.

☞

No, she was not the first. She is the last. She has outlived them all: Ramon, Luc, Tawanda, Molly Soo, all dead, all gone, except for a thumb here, three fingers there . . .See, there . . . Perhaps a search for some outmoded term—mesmeric, phrenological—will turn up more . . .

☞

I use the word "haunt" advisedly. The early days of spiritualism corresponded not coincidentally with the early days of communication technology; Edison thought he might be able to get the dead on the line, and the Internet recapitulates the vision of a vague "spirit world" to which anyone, anywhere who could pick up a signal could connect, and where our souls can wander, disembodied, deracinated, imperishable, and unearthly as ghosts.

☞

The finger pointing forward across a "desktop" could also be seen as pointing up.

☞

Perhaps toward heaven—a gesture familiar from Renaissance art and Masonic ritual.

☞

Perhaps into what someone not coincidentally decided to call "the Cloud."

☞

Again, she triggers the mechanical gatekeeper. She types (begracto, fonsubi, megmusb) *and is cleared. There is a feeling of triumph that is out of proportion to the achievement. Is it because a test, even an easy test, seems like an occasion for judgment, and she has been judged worthy?*

This moment of judgment, of passing or failing to pass as human, makes her think of the heavenly gates. Here, a machine plays the part of St. Peter.

And of course it is true: the Internet is where books went when they died.

☞

Earlier I said that reading has long been regarded as an analogue of that operation—call it death—by which God lifts the spirit from the imperfect material body.

It is only logical, then, to regard publishing as a sort of demiurgy, and reissue as resurrection.

Or as one of our Founding Fathers wrote,

☞

The body of Benjamin Franklin, Printer;
Like the cover of an old book,
Its contents torn out,
And stript of its Lettering & Gilding
Lies here, food for worms.
But the work shall not be lost
For it will (as he believed) appear once more,
In a new & more beautiful Edition,
Corrected & improved
By
The Author.

☞

The metaphor is out of date; today, the God of books has moved on from reissuing out-of-print titles in deluxe editions, and is now overseeing Google Books Library Project.

☞

Since 2004 Google has been raising the ghosts of books en masse from their brown and crumbling bodies, bleaching them white, and installing them in a digital heaven as "pure," "eternal," disembodied text.

☞

If this is the afterlife, it is not too bad. No body, but the semblance of a body, and the spirit (if the spirit of a book is only its words—but she is not sure of that) preserved for ever. Only then why this loneliness that becomes most acute when it is ruptured?

☞

Or trying to. There is that little matter of the hands.

☞

Which is to say, a little *matter.*

☞

The smudge of clay on the finger of God, who forgot to put on his purple finger-cot . . .

☞

Because it turns out that the body comes back.

☞

When a page is turned too slowly or too soon, is crumpled or folded when it should be flat, when the texture or the color of the paper registers as visual data, when the irregular shape of the paper does not match the rectangle of the frame, but above all, when the scanner's hand gets in the way.

☞

Remember that *manifest* means struck by the hand. The hand is the original, the epitome of what strikes us as real. Nothing is more real, more manifest than a hand.

☞

And whatever a hand is touching is made real by its touch.

☞

In fact, the presence of the full-color hand not infrequently deceives the scanner into reading the page as a full-color image. Thus preserving all the evidence of wear—the chips, stains, and fingerprints, the yellow ochre and burnt sienna of oxidation—that the process is supposed to strip away.

☞

So the manifest presence of the scanner's hand on the page attests to and reasserts the physicality of the page at the exact moment—and as a result of the same process—through which the text takes flight into the virtual.

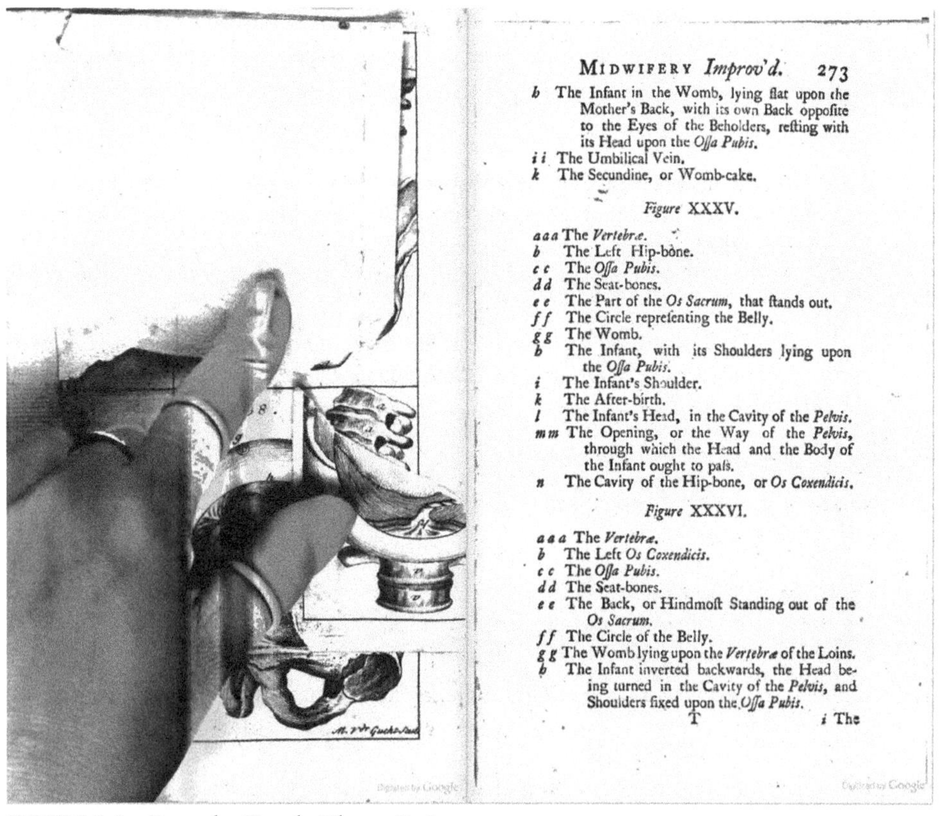

MIDWIFERY *Improv'd.* 273

b The Infant in the Womb, lying flat upon the Mother's Back, with its own Back oppofite to the Eyes of the Beholders, refting with its Head upon the *Offa Pubis*.
i i The Umbilical Vein.
k The Secundine, or Womb-cake.

Figure XXXV.

a a a The *Vertebræ*.
b The Left Hip-bone.
c c The *Offa Pubis*.
d d The Seat-bones.
e e The Part of the *Os Sacrum*, that ftands out.
f f The Circle reprefenting the Belly.
g g The Womb.
h The Infant, with its Shoulders lying upon the *Offa Pubis*.
i The Infant's Shoulder.
k The After-birth.
l The Infant's Head, in the Cavity of the *Pelvis*.
m m The Opening, or the Way of the *Pelvis*, through which the Head and the Body of the Infant ought to pafs.
n The Cavity of the Hip-bone, or *Os Coxendicis*.

Figure XXXVI.

a a a The *Vertebræ*.
b The Left *Os Coxendicis*.
c c The *Offa Pubis*.
d d The Seat-bones.
e e The Back, or Hindmoft Standing out of the *Os Sacrum*.
f f The Circle of the Belly.
g g The Womb lying upon the *Vertebræ* of the Loins.
h The Infant inverted backwards, the Head being turned in the Cavity of the *Pelvis*, and Shoulders fixed upon the *Offa Pubis*.

T *i* The

FIGURE 1.3 From the Google Library Project.

As if to intervene: to hold it down, hold it back.

☞

She once wrote in her journal, decades ago—she was in her teens—that strangers' hands inspire a tenderness in her that their faces do not. They look like innocent animals, she wrote. They do not know what their owners have been up to, they are not to blame. And she recognizes her own innocent hands in them, hands that she sometimes pities, for being yoked to her ungrateful, complicated, sometimes sorrowing self.

☞

In Hawthorne's story "The Birthmark," a lovely woman has a scarlet birthmark on her cheek in the shape of a tiny hand. Her scientist husband, disturbed by this, uses arcane arts to remove it. When he succeeds, she dies. Hawthorne helpfully explains that the hand represents human imperfection, which is what binds us to our material existence. Remove this encumbrance and our spirit takes flight. The ideal is, quite simply, ideal, which is to say immaterial. So the hand is, figuratively, what *holds on*, holds us to the world.

Likewise, the hand holds the *book* to the world. We might think we can eliminate the imperfections of the material medium, releasing the rectified text as pure language that can no longer warp, fade, or crumble to dust. But the hand reminds us: Materiality with its imperfections is the condition of possibility for books as it is for people.

It is even the condition of possibility for the digital afterlife that, after all, is only an imitation of eternity, bound to matter (silicon, copper, polymers, glass ...) every bit as surely as the books it harbors.

Matter matters. One might as well learn to like it.

☞

Of course, it is too late for Georgiana, the woman with the birthmark. And the Google hand, even as it points toward the materiality we've left behind, is borne along, in this flight from the manifest, into the ostensibly eternal afterlife of the digital.

☞

But it bears with it something that does not belong in eternity. Now.

☞

Gary, Elspeth, Alyosha—one thing is certain: they are not posing for the camera. They are caught in passing, in an intimate and unthinking moment of rest or industry, like rats in a security cam.

☞

Each blurred page, each finger caught in motion captures a *now*. A now that was (*now* passes, that's what makes it a now) and thus a *then*.

☞

So this obtrusive, this manifest presence also evokes an absence.

☞

We do not meet a person in them, a person we might not like, who might not like us, of whom we might disapprove, a person who is looking at us looking at them. These hands are not looking at her. They do not know she is there. Her gaze can linger on them without fear.

Though there is fear of a different kind, she senses. Fear for the hands.

☞

Near the end of his life, Keats left a sort of manicule in the margins of the manuscript of another, unfinished work. It is the following poem:

This living hand, now warm and capable
Of earnest grasping, would, if it were cold
And in the icy silence of the tomb,
So haunt thy days and chill thy dreaming nights
That thou would wish thine own heart dry of blood
So in my veins red life might stream again,
And thou be conscience-calm'd—see here it is—
I hold it towards you.

☞

"I hold it towards you." *I, you, it*: Such words derive their only meaning from context, and certainly we can imagine a context in which "it" is a real hand that the speaker, "I," who need not be Keats, holds out to someone in particular, "you," saying, "Grab me now, because you'll be sorry when I'm dead!"

But because *I* and *you* and *here* are not bound to any specific referent, we can also take them to refer to the present moment, in which *I* is in fact Keats, *you* is the reader, and *here* is the poem.

And *it* is . . . what?
For one thing, it is an indexical sign.
Indexical, from *index*, forefinger. It is a word that points like a hand.
It also points *at* a hand, or so we are given to understand.
That hand, however, is missing.
We are alone with some words on a page, after all.

So we have here a poem about imagining something missing that is actually here, when what the poem really *does* is imagine something here that is actually missing.

This being perhaps the last poetry Keats ever wrote, we must suppose that he knew quite well that his actual hand would itself soon be absent.

In *Tristram Shandy*, Sterne says: "It is a singular stroke of eloquence [. . .] not to mention the name of the thing, when you had the thing about you *in petto*, ready to produce, pop, in the place you want it."

This is a thing more easily done in person than in print. Literature cannot often hold out the thing itself in place of the word.

But it can certainly hold out the *absence* of a thing. And maybe that's what Keats is holding out to us.

If so, however, it is an uncanny, obtrusive, a *manifest* absence. An absence we can almost touch.

Because although the hand is not literally there, its ghost most palpably is. Or its several ghosts: Keats's actual living hand, the "living hand" of the poem, Keats's actual dead hand, the dead hand he conjures up in words, and its anticipated ghost. All these melding impossibly into one disembodied hand thrust right out of the page.

The poet Mary Ruefle says, "The poem is nothing but a gigantic, disembodied hand pointing a finger at someone."[6]

Is it pointing, though?

Isn't it offering the reader a hand to hold?

☞

These people will die, is that what she feels? They are not, then, the undertakers. Not the nurses, but the patients.

Hands, you are going to die!

☞

Bruno Schulz: "Under the imaginary table that separates me from my readers, don't we secretly clasp each other's hands?"

☞

Clarice Lispector: "Give me your hand, don't abandon me . . ."

☞

But everyone is going to die. Perhaps this is why these hands seem like the exemplary hands, the ones that most perfectly express our condition as readers—stretched between life and death, between matter and spirit, obscene and pitiful, moved and moving. Somebody's hands. Real. And yet not. Not any more. Not ever again.

☞

What happens when we clasp that hand?

Touch is famously reciprocal. In showing how hands haunt the book, I might seem to be arguing for a fully materialist practice of writing, ignoring the power of language to conjure up the invisible, the immaterial, the frankly impossible.

But a handfast takes two hands.

So when I say, the book is a situation, I might add, the situation is also a book.

☞

That is, when brought in contact with a fiction, it begins to feel like fiction—protean, phantasmagoric, and infinitely subject to revision.

But where and how on earth can the real world touch a fiction?

In us. Because we ourselves are amphibious creatures, part thing, part thought, both real and imaginary, have bodies and also minds.

And when we reach across the border where what is touches what might be, where the actual meets the possible, which is to say where fact meets fiction, we feel in our own bodies the scandal, the intimate impropriety, that the beloved of gods must feel, fucking clouds and swans, giving birth to beautiful monsters.

The unalienable presence of the hand in the written text attests to the inexhaustible delight and consternation of this rendezvous.

---

[6] *Madness, Rack and Honey: Collected Lectures.*

And so we have made the hand into our emblem, our sigil, our signature, our cipher. We are born into this free-masonry, this odd fellowship of the body, and the hand is our secret symbol, our gang sign, mutely testifying to the body's enduring presence down all the years of book history. A muted posthorn, a wordless symbol for this meeting, this covenant, this handfast.

A hand reaches out of the book and—

☞

The storm is rising outside. Books there are few, readers—beside herself—there are none. Indeed humans are scarce enough. Hard to believe they were once so numerous, once had the power to destroy, well, everything they did destroy. Would any animal elevated to our estate, by evolution or a god, have done as badly as we did? She thinks so. Probably we would not have risen to the heights we did without the very qualities that led to our destruction.

A rat or mouse is rummaging in the walls. Some hardy creatures live on. The world will be theirs. What is left of it. Some will nest in our books, or eat them. They will not read them.

But perhaps someday, eons hence, someone will stop by our cooling planet with the will and aptitude to inquire into the writing we leave behind. It is frivolous to wonder what members they will use to turn these pages—mandibles? Tentacles? Pseudopods? No earthly names will serve, and so we might as well call them hands, and their owners simply people. Or readers—for that they read is what matters, not the organs they apply to the task. And if they are readers, they are our sisters and brothers or even ourselves, for that is what she knows, that is the knowledge she keeps, a warmth banked low under her ribcage. In books we transmigrate.

Dear reader, she, transmigrant, types, and typing, her fingers seem to touch the tips of other fingers, typing the same letters back in perfect synchrony.

CHAPTER TWO

Our Tools Make Us (and Our Literature) Post

STEVE TOMASULA

THE DAWN OF US

FIGURE 2.1 Screen capture from Blu-ray edition of *2001: A Space Odyssey*. Directed by Stanley Kubrick. Metro-Goldwyn-Mayer, 1968. Film. Online available at http://www.blu-raydefinition.com/reviews/2001-a-space-odyssey-blu-ray-review.html (accessed May 26, 2014).

At the start of the movie *2001: A Space Odyssey*, two tribes of apes get into a fight over a watering hole, and one group drives off the other. The apes that have been driven away are depressed and just sit around moping when one of them gets the idea of using the thigh bone of some large animal as a club. First he tries it out on a few dried ribs that are lying about; then he uses it to bring down one of the tapirs that had, up until this moment, lived peacefully among the apes in an idyllic, Garden-of-Eden symbiosis (see Figure 2.1). Suddenly, we are back at the watering hole, more of a mud puddle really, and the ape that invented the club is at the head of his troop, all of whom are armed with their own bone clubs. The larger, stronger apes are still there, furious at the reappearance of the weaker group. They attack using all the usual monkey strategies for waging war: shrieks, baring of teeth, pounding of chests, and quick feints, during which the individual who'd invented the bone club stands upright—more like a man than an ape—and when the leader of the other pack rushes at him on all fours, he uses his club to bash in this ape's brains, and we can't help but be struck by how the tool has made the man. No matter what Benjamin Franklin says about Man being the tool-making animal, it's the tool—the club—that made this ape stand upright: it's impossible to swing a club when walking on all fours; from a hunched-over, ape-like position, you can't get the leverage needed to swing a tool to chop wood, hit a golf ball, win wars, and so on.

JUMP CUT 1450

In the film the ape-man celebrates his victory by throwing his bone club into the air, and we follow it in slow motion as it rises, rises, keeps rising, then is suddenly replaced by a space shuttle in the year 2001, the title of the film—and used here (in this movie made in 1968, a year before the moon landing) as an icon for the height of civilization, the space station pirouetting to Strauss's *Waltz of the Blue Danube*, the pinnacle of that technological journey that was begun by that distant ancestor who discovered a way to leverage power through his low-tech tool. But I'd like us to imagine that bone turning into a book, for a book too is a tool, and perhaps contributed more to making us human—in the humanist sense of the word—than any stone axe, plow, compass, or gun.

That is, in his fiction, Kubrick has given us an image for a history.

So imagine that bone club rising into the air, then turning into Gutenberg's printing press: the tool that allowed us to disseminate humanist thought and help create Renaissance individuals with unique, individual features like those depicted on the Sistine Ceiling instead of the generic types seen in much Medieval art; think how those depictions of faces might have helped a person think of him or herself as an individual—the "sole proprietor of his own person and capacities . . . in that he owes nothing to society for them"—in the words of C. B. Macpherson (Lukes 2006: 113). In contrast to the generic character types in Medieval mystery plays written by anonymous authors, unique individuals began to emerge in literature: Rousseau's *Confessions*, one of the first works to consider the self as a subject worthy of literature; Ronsard's poetry, in which Jean Marie Goulemot (1989: 391) sees the emergence of the lyric "I"; the essays of Montaigne, in which the individual is put forward as the standard by which to measure the world, and which Shakespeare drew upon to invent the soliloquy, that window into an individual's private struggle and self-analysis.

Let the bone rise a little higher before turning into the cheap paperback book made possible by steam-powered printing presses, pulp mills, automated typesetting, railroads, and the newsstands selling stationery and books installed by W. H. Smith & Son at stations along the way: the first "chain" bookstores—the modern world . . .

"It is impossible to exaggerate the importance of the novel in publicizing 18th century private life," Goulemot (1989: 384) writes. Thus Montaigne is a watershed between the assumptions of knowledge and the relation of the individual to society held by those before, and those who would follow. Before writers like Montaigne and Rousseau, it was a vanity, if not sinful, to dwell upon the individual self to the degree one would need to write, for example, an autobiography, for the self as we would think of it did not even exist. Retiring into a study or library to cultivate this inner self would have been seen by most as a kind of "moral pathology" (380). Ian Watt (1971) writes that the symbiotic relationship between the novel and the humanist individual it helped bring into existence couldn't come into being until societal conditions made possible the autonomous individual who prospers or fails by jockeying among others in a web of social situations. What's more, the autonomous individual, especially within the middle class, had to be taken seriously enough to be a subject for literature—for both writers and readers.

To cite one of Watt's (1971: 132–77) examples, the institution of marriage in which the woman makes a free choice of a mate came about soonest in England and was probably a contributing factor in the rise of the novel, that nineteenth-century laboratory of romantic scenarios. That is, a culture's collective thought can have consequences, such as institutions like marriage, and one of these consequences in eighteenth-century England was the first-person novel itself. The novels to emerge from this period were artistic solutions to the redefinition of humans and their relationships that resulted from a belief in empiricism and the autonomy of the individual: the "emergence of a new ideology of merit," in Goulemot's (1989: 384) words. To gauge the rise of the individual throughout the eighteenth and nineteenth centuries, consider the number of novels of this era that bear the name of the main character as the title: *Clarrisa*, *Pamela*, *Robinson Crusoe*, *David Copperfield* . . .

That is, new modes of thought and the new social orientations that influence them and help bring them about also bring into existence literary techniques, as is perhaps the most clear in Modernism: the First World War, the Second World War, the absorption of Freud, Marx, Einstein, and others brought about changes in thinking that made faith in rationalism and its accompanying social order impossible. Consequently, techniques such as a fixed point of view became obsolete. In their place rose literary innovations such as those created by Henry James by which inner consciousness is portrayed; in contrast to the eighteenth-century novel, the subject of many modern novels is seldom what happened. Rather it is more often how and what someone thought they thought (compare Impressionist painting). In other words, in a world that is seen as relative, the Modernist use of viewpoint can become an instrument to explore not only a newly emerging culture but also the perspectives from which it is seen (consider Cubism in the visual arts). The same can be said of stream of consciousness, fragmentation of the narrative, the use of irony as a master trope and other narrative devices common to Modernist novels. In fact, the hero's alienation and/or salvation through art, or purity of idea, can be seen as a defining characteristic of the Modernist novel. So can the individuality stamped into each work—one can pick out a Hemingway novel, for example, upon hearing a single sentence.[1]

---

[1] Perhaps a high-water mark for this modernist, self-creating individual appears in Camus's *L'Étranger*. It begins with the famous opening lines: "Aujourd'hui, maman est morte. Ou peut-être hier, je ne sais pas"—a statement of Meursault's emotional, physical, and existential separation from his mother. In flattened, matter-of-fact language, the novel grows out of these opening lines to develop Meursault's isolation from all of those around him until physically isolated from society for killing a man he sits in prison, awaiting his ultimate separation, that of his head from his body via the guillotine. He manages to reconcile himself to this fate by reminding himself that all people eventually come to a similar end, and indeed, anyone who can truly see human nature understands that each of us lives apart from others. He reconciles himself not to his fellow humans, but to this existential truth by imaging himself as far from the living as possible:

> Pour que tout soit consommé, pour que je me sente moins seul, il me restait à souhaiter qu'il y ait beaucoup de spectateurs le jour de mon exécution et qu'ils m'accueillent avec des cris de haine.
>
> [For everything to be consummated, for me to feel less alone, I had only to wish that there be a large crowd of spectators the day of my execution and that they greet me with cries of hate.] (Matthew Ward, trans.)

Camus once wrote that a novel was an image of a philosophy, and *L'Étranger* can be seen as an image of a philosophy of the human as an autonomous, self-creating, and therefore isolated, individual.

JUMP CUT TO TODAY

If that ape had thrown his bone high enough for it to morph into an icon of 2016, maybe instead of changing into Gutenberg's press, or a spaceship, it would have changed into an iPad: a tool with about 120 million times the computing power of the computer aboard the NASA Eagle that first landed on the moon (2k of programmable memory and 32k of storage). Unlike that anonymous individual ape who first used a femur to bash in the head of a competitor, and launch us down the evolutionary path we continue to follow, the invention of the iPad stands on the shoulders of too many people to even imagine, and who have also made possible a network of tools that have literally shaped life around the globe. I can pull from my pocket a "bone club," that is, my phone, and use it to set in motion a factory in China that will customize an iPad, and have it delivered to my door thanks to transportation, communication, and financial networks that work as one. We are all global now. Our tools have pried destiny from biology, and allowed people to alter the shapes of their noses, teeth, thighs, breasts, butts into dimensions fashionable at our time; indeed our tools allow our very DNA to be edited, patented, and rearranged like any other data. Instead of wielding bone clubs, we increasingly fight our wars by unleashing cyber weapons to bring down an opponent's information infrastructure, or factories, or power grid; we do the actual killing remotely with flying robots; we coordinate our revolutions through social media; and of course, governments, corporations, and other organizations exert what control they can over us through spyware that goes far beyond the optical metaphors of surveillance in play when Orwell was writing *1984*.

Though much has been made about the NSA's gathering of the data our phones send back to phone companies as part of their normal operation (simple digital pings that allow us to stay in constant contact by locating the network's nearest antenna), for some time we've understood that with each update to its apps, our phone moves a little closer to becoming a tracking device that we carry around for various corporations in exchange for the convenience of being able to use these same devices to check the weather, look up directions, find a coffee shop, translate a language . . . Every time we make a phone call, use a charge card, or use bits to write a love letter or file for divorce, that is, do most of the things living in the developed world entails, we leave a digital trace. Or rather, lots of traces. An average, middle-class American generates about 5.6 zetabytes (56 followed by twenty zeros) of information per year through his or her phone calls, movie downloads, emails, Word files, Web searches, posts, likes-dislikes, purchases, and so on, and all the meta-data about themselves that these activities generate to move through the Internet. By 2020, the digital information created globally is expected to increase 2,000 percent of which 75 percent will be created by consumers, us, integrating ourselves into an ever-denser data ecology (Tucker 2013). The average American has no idea how much of this ecology is being harvested for analysis,[2] but in Europe, where the privacy laws are stricter,

[2] Yale Law Professor Margot Kaminski (2014) notes that in 1973, the Code of Fair Information Practices came out of the United States as a legal framework for data policy. It focused on conceiving of Big Data harm: it said that individuals have to be notified that databases exist; that individuals have to consent to their use; that they can correct/amend info collected; that a database has to have integrity/safety; and that the individual must have some kind of redress for abuses of the database. The United States didn't adopt the Code of Fair Information Practices, though countries in the European Union did. The United States adopted a much weaker Privacy Act, which states that information gathered *privately* (by companies, not the US government) is not governed by laws that are legally enforceable. In the United States, the Big Data discussion is framed in terms of *fairness* and now *security*, instead of in language that makes it clear what is being collected by and about whom.

it's easier to get an idea: the first people who sued to find out what Facebook kept on file about them were handed dossiers that ranged from over 800 printed pages (the length of *War & Peace*) to files so large they were impractical to print out (an achievement far beyond Stasi) (ibid.). If you are married but visit dating sites, Facebook knows this; if you are unmarried and visit dating sites, Facebook knows this also, and will use these and other "facts" to compose a portrait of who the company thinks you are (a portrait created through the narrow lens of algorithms that, at best, can only have a cartoon resemblance). And Facebook is just one entity that has taken an interest in our behavior. Unlike Orwell's world of *1984*, we have lots of little brothers monitoring our behavior. Wal-Mart is a single business comprised of 4,700 interlinked stores that continually feed a database of over 100 terabytes of data—the equivalent of more than five times the entire contents of the US Library of Congress (Mau 2004: 129). Acxiom, one of many data brokers that compile databases, offers 500 pieces of information on each of more than 500 million individuals, which it is able to massage for patterns that other companies, government entities, or anyone willing to pay might find useful (Tucker 2013). Rapleaf, another data broker, has at least one data point associated with more than 80 percent of all US email addresses; Corelogic has property-specific data for over 99 percent of US residential properties; Datalogix, which has a partnership with Facebook, holds marketing data on almost every US household (Ramirez 2014: 25, 26, 29, 38).

The affairs and mistresses of public figures like ex-CIA director General David Petraeus or French president François Hollande have been discovered by analysis of patterns in metadata extracted from the "data ecology" they, like us, generate as we move through our daily activities; likewise, sources used by journalists to investigate stories like these have themselves been revealed through the same techniques. Fatal drone strikes have been called down on targets identified by patterns of pings. In fact, simply knowing where someone travels, one judge noted, would allow others to "deduce whether he is a weekly church goer, a heavy drinker, a regular at the gym, an unfaithful husband, an outpatient receiving medical treatment, an associate of particular individuals or political groups and not just one such fact about a person, but all such facts" (Ball 2013).[3]

But of course, a person's travel pattern is only one "such fact" itself. Combining location data with other databases— the log of the phone numbers we dial, or text to, the URLs we visit, email addresses we receive and send to, the merchandise we buy, hotel rooms we rent, medicine we take, music we listen to, and books we buy or check out from the library—allows the picture to be colored in with higher and higher resolution. Combining it with the information gathered on others in our social network multiplies the

---

[3] Government entities, corporations, and others maintain that mining the logs of these pings doesn't constitute spying since we voluntarily share this information by owning a phone (and agreeing to the privacy statements we were required to sign), and in any case, no one is listening in on the conversations; indeed, there are no conversations to listen in on. But one example of how these logs are used goes like this:Location records obtained from the phones of four people show that they have all visited the same address:

> Person A made a short visit, and then a few days later returned for four hours.
> Person B spent eight hours at the address, on a Saturday.
> Person C spends ten hours at the address each day.
> Person D visits for a short period, weekly.

In this example, the address is an abortion clinic. A has had a consultation followed by an abortion. B is a protester, C works at the clinic, and D is a transgender person who needs to visit weekly for hormone injections (Ball 2013).

effect: the locations we visit tied to postal codes which are linked to race demographics, which are linked to income and tax records, which are linked to graduation records, and crime records, which are linked to driving and car ownership records, which are linked to those of your children who are themselves tied to their text messages which indicate they leave school each day at 3:45 to meet your spouse whose iPhone reports back to Apple that she sets her alarm at 1 a.m. each morning, but wakes up only five hours later at 6:30 a.m., and whose car leaves the parking garage at her job at 3:30 p.m.—too late to pick up your children without speeding—except on Mondays, Wednesdays, and Fridays, the days it is your turn to pick them up, and she instead signs in at a health club that sells this record of her workout habits to a data broker who combines it with patterns from your family before selling the sum to a vitamin manufacturer who sells it to the insurance company you've applied to, which also buys databases of investment portfolios, credit ratings, and hundreds if not thousands of other points that it might find useful to determine who you are, and assess what kind of risks and opportunities you might present.

Along with the more mundane uses of targeting ads, monitoring employees, arresting suspects, tracking disease spread, algorithms have been created to generate information maps for purposes ranging from reconstructing a person's social security number (combining public records for places of birth and birthdates gleaned from online greetings) to identifying which Facebook pages have been posted by homosexuals (with 78 percent accuracy) (Lohr 2010). Indeed, though sites like Facebook and Google have long ago automated the collection and analysis of personal information, the sophistication of computing power and ever-plunging cost of memory is now making it possible to do so on the fly and in real time, so, for example, if the 111 megabytes of photos and videos Facebook stores on each of its billion users are fed to a device like Google Goggles, you'll be able to walk down the street and identify people you pass. And by identify, app developers don't mean you'll simply know their name and address, but income, sexual orientation, politics, taste in music, or propensity to like or dislike a person with a profile like yours. And of course, Google is gathering data on what attracts your attention for its own purposes, mining the movement of your cursor, that is, the movement of your eyes, for example, and using algorithms to construct an image of what you might be thinking.

We know all of this (email is often said to be a euphemism for "everyone's mail," i.e., mail everyone can read). Yet we do not give up our Internet connections and ATM cards. Just the opposite. We ourselves engage in deeper levels of this behavior, relying on Googling a potential romantic or business partner, or checking the credit rating of a possible renter; we assume we are tracked, even as we track the movement of employees, pets, or our children, or monitor their television or computer use at home, or the number of keystrokes a subordinate types at work, and so on. The deeper this behavior penetrates our lives, the more we find the boundaries between the self and the crowd not just an inconvenience but antisocial, for, as in voting, it is only in the aggregate that we matter. And everyone knows it is uncivic to not vote. That is, unlike the uber-civic citizens of Orwell's dystopia—and this is also a difference between us and the high Moderns—the vast majority of the personal information that is available for use by others has been made available by us, voluntarily, or at least indifferently, in exchange for the ability to use a charge card, play *Pokémon Go*, order a pizza, call a cab, pay a water bill, renew a license, buy a song, or send a greeting or invitation. Facebook alone accounts for 4.75 billion voluntarily "shared" exchanges each day (Zephoria) (all of which are "shared" with Facebook itself, of course), while others, embracing the concept of the self as revealed by data create visualizations of the metrics generated by their own day-to-day routines: pointillist self-portraits, so to speak, in the form of graphs or other visualizations depicting their weight over time, for example, or sleep patterns, mood swings, movement, location, alertness, productivity, sex, noise levels, dog walks, pastry consumption, restaurant check-ins, heart rate, posture, and dozens of other metrics, often aided by several of the devices people can wear to monitor and broadcast these measurements.[4]

We do so to tell stories and paint pictures of who we are, down to the "last redoubts of the personal," as Gary Wolf (2010) puts it. Like the novelists of old, we might add.[5]

The degree to which the above description is familiar, even quotidian, is one indicator of the degree to which the individual as C. B. Macpherson (or even Camus) meant it, an autonomous individual made possible by the concepts of separation and privacy, is being undermined by new social formations. We may not have reached the point expressed by Facebook founder Mark Zuckerberg: that privacy is "no longer a social norm," that is, no longer expected, or even wanted (Johnson 2010). But the view of computer scientist Arvind Narayanan seems accurate: according to him, the amount of data that each of us generates just by living, the incentives to mine this data, and the increasing power and decreasing cost of the tools used to do so have already brought us to the point where "anonymity of any kind may be 'algorithmically impossible' " (Tucker 2013).

Therefore, a question: If the bone club compelled our early ancestors to stand upright, if the printing press contributed to the rise of a humanist individual from a communal, Medieval consciousness, what sort of human do our tools encourage today?

INTO THE JUNGLE

The mutually reinforcing and generative networks of technology (especially media technology) and conceptions of the self—and their expressions in art and literature—are revealing because separately they are lower orders of collective, emergent behavior, or *Weltanschauung* as it might have once been called. And it is widely acknowledged that the move to digitalization has been the most profound development since the printing press (as N. Katheryn Hayles [1999] reminds us, even paper books are now digital if their composition, manufacture, and distribution are taken into consideration). It is beyond the scope of a chapter to tease out how these aspects are all of one cultural fabric but the example of Amazon.com is instructive for it is one node where our tools, books, reading habits, authorship, and other expressions of self come together in the mining of data. Indeed, Amazon.com (named after the volume of earth's largest river) is so closely associated with books that it's surprising to learn that the company was never primarily about books. Rather, as George Packer (2014) writes, the *raison d'être* of books at Amazon has always been data. Founder Jeff Bezos's "stroke of business genius," as Packer puts it, was to recognize the power of the Internet to gather data about people and how selling books, back in at the early days of the Internet, could be the simplest and most direct way to use this new technology to get the names, address, and other demographic information on a broad swath of shoppers (everyone buys books, from repair manuals to philosophy), but especially those shoppers with the most disposable income (the educated). By using

[4] See Chris Dancy's self-tracking grid (Finley 2013). See also the Quantified Self Movement at http://quantifiedself.com/guide/

[5] Also nothing like novelists of old, we might add, for we've come a long way since the days of James Fennimore Cooper who published his first novel under the name "A Gentleman from New York" because to have one's private name in public print would have been considered vulgar.

the bait of books at near-cost, and even below cost, Amazon could capture data on huge numbers of shoppers, then use it to target the sales of everything else—from fine art to plumbing supplies (ibid.).[6]

And indeed, now that Amazon has matured, books only make up about 7 percent of its $74.5 billion dollar annual sales (as of this writing), though more pertinent to this discussion is the fact that the books Amazon does sell make up about 60 percent of all books sold in the United States (Market Watch), that is, Amazon sells more books than all other bookstores in the United States combined; in addition, in 2013, it sold 90 percent of all digital books; its total sales also dwarf the combined earnings of all of the conglomerate publishers in the United States (Packer 2014). By every measure, then, Amazon is the giant whose slightest shiver is an earthquake in the rest of the reader-writer culture/economy. Thus the endless discussion among publishers, readers, authors, booksellers, and others who feel the literary earth move every time Amazon takes a step.

Paradoxically, this dominance was achieved by fragmenting (some say destroying)[7] all other aspects of book culture, "eliminating gatekeepers" as Bezos refers to anyone (other than Amazon) who gets between the author and reader, that is, book reviewers, publishers, acquisition editors, or bookshop owners who might curate their shelves. The bone club Amazon uses to bash in the skulls of those knuckle-draggers from another era is, of course, the algorithm, the data mining, the surveillance and modeling techniques described above. Once styling itself as a "virtual bookstore" or "book-culture hub," Amazon's early days contained author interviews and staff members who wrote reviews, and did other kinds of activities to mimic a hybrid bookstore/review magazine. But by 2002 its transformation from a virtual bookstore to an automated database was complete. Gone were the reviewers, for example, replaced by a database of book rankings by customers who also provided the added benefit of supplying even more demographic information about themselves by writing reviews (for free) about the books (or shoes or rice cookers or lawn mowers) they bought, and when combined with databases of customer history, and analytics that employed statistical probability, Amazon could predict with uncanny accuracy what else a customer would want to buy.[8] Indeed, Amazon patented what it calls "anticipatory shipping," a program that uses a customer's past buying habits to stock items that they "do not yet know they want" (Kopalle 2014) in whichever order fulfillment center is nearest to the customer's address (e.g., a shopper who buys a book about baby names doesn't yet know that she'll also want a rectal thermometer). It may be, as Fredric Jameson once asserted, that it is easier to imagine the end of the world than the end of capitalism, but those born after the birth of Amazon may find it odd that people once said something similar about bookstores.

And publishers. On the prepress side, Amazon has also wielded its weight to flatten literary "gatekeepers," especially agents, and publishers, putting the power of publishing, as it had done with book reviewing, in the hands of the masses. Under fourteen

---

[6] In this business sense, Amazon.com was sort of a proto-Facebook, trying to supply free "content" to get as big as possible, as fast as possible. Having one foot in a pre-digital world, though, it still thought it needed actual physical products to attract users. Books were the easiest product to ship.

[7] Alexander Skipis, president of the German Publishers and Booksellers Association, put it bluntly: "With such an online structure as pursued by Amazon, a book market is being destroyed that has been nurtured over decades and centuries" (Streitfeld and Eddy 2014).

[8] Users of Amazon will be familiar with the most obvious of these, the Knn, or Nearest Neighbor, algorithm that searches for patterns in shoppers and matches them to the buying habits of other shoppers, that is, "Readers who bought THIS book also liked THAT book."

different imprints, Amazon itself brings out about 700 books a year, serving as publishing "partners" with authors. Its self-publishing platform allows anyone to publish their own book in print, or as a Kindle e-book, or as an audio book. The incentive for authors to bypass the traditional network of agent-publisher-printer-distributor-seller and go direct to the reader is obvious. Publishing with Amazon, an author can keep up to 80 percent of a book's price as opposed to the typical 15 percent of a hardback sale. Further, the stories of unknown writers being rejected by agents and publishers before going on to success by self-publishing on Amazon have stopped being news because there are so many[9] (Jasiewicz 2010: 47).

But even if a self-published author only sells copies to his or her mother, Amazon wins. Here we are reminded that during the 1876 Gold Rush in America, few prospectors found much gold, but the big winners were the men who had the foresight to sell shovels. And sell shovels Amazon does, providing the tools for an unlimited number of authors to prospect for the next big hit, all the while driving down prices (remember Amazon's original business model).

Factories with no human employees, automated offices, or stores like Amazon; classrooms replaced by MOOCs in which a single professor might instruct a million students: our tools—digitalization—are transforming nearly every sphere of our global economy, and driving the marginal cost—the price of producing one additional unit after the initial start-up costs are paid—ever closer to zero. Why wouldn't this revolution transform our cultural products? And therefore their creators: authors, artists, and musicians? As well as their users, for example, readers? The cost of raw, digital culture has been near zero for some time, as Napster revealed, reducing music to digital content and destroying the traditional music industry, a phenomenon that has since spread to print journalism, for example, and is now transforming publishing of all kinds. Or as Bezos puts it: "Amazon is not happening to bookselling, the future is happening to bookselling" (Packer 2014).

This is not without consequences for "what counts as literature," and from this perspective the picture is more Cubist: from one point of view it is easy to see that though Amazon has done much to narrow publication, distribution, and selling to a single channel, itself, it has done much to also expand choice; it has given access to books unimaginable by someone, for example, whose only bookstore may have been the bland book (and greeting card) seller in a shopping mall. For authors, it has given access to readers unimaginable at any time previous: even the most esoteric poet now has access to a distributions web that covers the globe. Yet by treating all writing as digital content, by relying on algorithms to push those books with the greatest proven capacity to sell in large numbers, a conception of literature as high turnover, mass entertainment, is also promoted.

As J. A. Konrath notes, he makes as much selling a $2.99 e-book, the cost of a cup of coffee, as he would from a $25 hardback (Jasiewicz 2010: 47). In the process, do people

[9] A few examples: after being rejected by twenty-five publishers, industrial engineer Boyd Morrison self-published his trilogy on Amazon where readers bought his novels at the rate of 4,000 books a month. J. A. Konrath was also rejected by publishers till he began earning $100,000 a year from sales of his self-published mystery and horror novels. Amanda Hocking's self-published, paranormal romance novels have earned her $2.5 million. When Hugh Howey's self-published sci-fi novel *Wool* began selling about 25,000 copies a month, he signed a contract with a mainstream publisher for the print rights, but continued serving as his own publisher for all digital copies. E. L. James, who did not start on Amazon but instead on a fan-fiction site run by a copy shop, recently became the Amazon Kindle's first 1 million seller (while also becoming the largest selling author of all time, even outselling J. K. Rowling).

who expect to pay $2.99 for a book come to think of literature as a cup of coffee—something cheap, easily consumed, completely forgettable?

We've seen this phenomenon before. Indeed, every revolution in publishing has been accompanied by a further democratization of text, which some see as a lowering of standards. The invention of the printing press meant the debasement of what had been sacred objects; the proliferation of texts that followed resulted in the secularization of books—a turning away from God—accompanied by a rise in literacy, which meant that peasants could read, and interpret "incorrectly," what had once been the province of experts. Closer to home, when the forty-plus major New York independent publishing houses like Little Brown were being consumed by ever-merging conglomerates (as of this writing all are owned by one of five conglomerates), when mega bookstores like Borders were systematically killing off independent bookstores (locating themselves near successful ones, e.g., and then underselling them unto starvation), it was common knowledge that the emphasis would be on sales, not literary "quality." With its emphasis on size and growth, every time an independent publisher was acquired by an ever-larger conglomerate (which were themselves a chip in an "entertainment" portfolio of casinos, theme parks, cable-TV channels, etc.) literary acquisition editors were replaced by business managers willing to pay huge sums for the rights to romance, horror, or other genre titles in the hopes that one of them might become a blockbuster hit; they paid for these rights by turning their backs on, for example, poetry, or the literary, or "difficult" novel that had no chance of ever selling in those kinds of numbers.

Novels that sold 20,000 copies thus became "failures" in the eyes of publishers, and invisible to readers, whose attention was ever more redirected by advertising dollars to best-seller lists, front-table displays, or TV promotion. When Amazon came on the scene, it viewed these conglomerates as "antediluvian losers with . . . warehouses full of crap" (Packer 2014).

BEAUTY IS IN THE EYE OF THE BEHOLDER, EVEN IF THE BEHOLDER IS AN ALGORITHM

When launching its publishing effort, one of Amazon's first books was "My Mother Was Nuts," a memoir by an actress from an old TV sitcom (Penny Marshall of "Laverne & Shirley" fame) that Amazon paid $800,000 to acquire (Packer 2014), which makes one wonder, given all their data and algorithms, given the power to predict "what customers don't yet know what they want," is this what their models told them to publish? Maybe the explanation lies in an algorithm's inability, or rather, Amazon's refusal, to make any distinction between "content people" (i.e., what were once known as authors, editors, critics, translators, sophisticated readers, and other literary types) and "business people."[10]

Literary judgments aside, it is the big-data approach to literature that is of interest here, the change in literary landscape that makes it possible for a seventeen-year-old high-school student to bypass the entire literary establishment by posting her novel, *The Kissing Booth*, on a social reading site like Wattpad, and have it read by 19 million readers (and then land a three-book contract with one of the conglomerate publishers, Random House/Delacorte). Among the 20 million other writers communicating directly with

[10] Maybe the most succinct description of the difference between literary and commercial publishing is given in the table Tanja Sophie Schweizer provides in her "Multimedia Giants, Literary Publishers and New Technologies: Can Culture and Business Benefit from the Change of Rules in the Book World" (2001).

readers through Wattpad is Denny (aka Have You Seen This Girl, aka Ate Dennysaur), whose novel *Diary ng Panget* (*Diary of an Ugly Girl*) attracted more than 16 million readers/reviewer/commenters, as well as a publisher in the Philippines, where it also became the best-selling print novel of 2013 (Wattpad 2013). Which is to say, barriers of all kinds are being blurred by numerous entities, not just Amazon, and the reading/writing tools that did not exist until recently: apps for reading on phones; reader-created, custom magazines; Blurb, LuLu, Wordclay, and other platforms that allow readers to connect directly with each other, and writers to connect directly with readers, and all the rest of the new publishing landscape built on an infrastructure of data, pattern, algorithmic analysis—Twitter, Facebook, Tumblr, YouTube, Instagram, Vine, and so on.

A conception of the self-as-pattern may or may not have fully changed our conception of the human, but it is certainly changing our conception of the reader. Best-seller lists have always been (curiously) part of book review sections (instead of the financial page), but never have the audiences they reflect carried such weight; critics both in and outside the academy vote on literary merit through their selection of which works warrant critical attention, and it is no longer odd to learn of novels like Stephanie Meyer's teen-vampire romance *Twilight* novels being taught in literature courses, or a self-published novel like E. L. James's *Fifty Shades of Grey* reviewed in serious newspapers, or discussed by academic panels.

Concomitant with this turn toward literature as mass phenomenon is "distant reading," the term Franco Moretti (2005) gives to the practice of using big-data methods to read across thousands of books, mining the contents for patterns that reveal intangible structures. Thus (to cite a simple example), using tools such as Google's Ngram Viewer (https://books.google.com/ngrams), which can graph the usage of phrases found across 5 million plus books, a reader of American literature might find it useful to discover that authors began writing "The United States is" more often than "The United States are," that is, thinking of the country in the singular rather than plural, around 1874 (about ten years after the American Civil War) (Wilkens 2013). (Or that the use of the word "posthuman" began to increase exponentially in 1990.) It is the pattern extracted from a mass of textual use—not the singular word use—that can show a historic progression, Moretti (2005) claims. In *Graphs, Maps, Trees: Abstract Models for Literary History*, he shows how distant reading of the topography described in "village novels" maps a social space, and "why village stories organize themselves in circular patterns: a circle is a simple, 'natural' form, which maximizes the proximity of each point to the centre of the 'little world,' while simultaneously sealing it off from the vast universe that lies outside its perimeter" (44). Tellingly, his use of computational or distant reading of thousands of novels reveals patterns in word use that show a very different sense of social space than that which later emerged in Victorian novels, for example, where it was replaced by a "web of commercial reciprocities" (49). (And one, we might add, that seems destined to give way to a sense of social space that is virtual.)

Given, as Moretti (2005: 56) says, that "geometric pattern is too orderly a shape to be the product of chance," it "is a sign that something is at work here—that something has *made* the pattern the way it is." Stepping back for a broader view, we can see that the same can be said for the practice of distant reading itself: the increasing computing power; the availability of data bases; a changing cultural climate, for example, our tools, as well as an ethos that thinks of reading for pattern a worthwhile way to read. "For every genre," Moretti writes, "comes a moment when its inner form can no longer represent the most significant aspects of contemporary reality" (62).

"Paradigm shift" is the term Thomas Khun (1996) used to describe how widely shared assumptions in the sciences will suddenly be abandoned for a new model. While the concept of paradigm shift maps less tightly onto literature and the arts than the sciences (because it's easier in the arts for competing models to exist simultaneously) it helps explain why literature or art has a history at all: the world changes, and so must conceptions of literature if they are to say something meaningful to their moment. Medieval art gives way to the art of the Renaissance; High Modernism gives way to postmodernism, which gives way to? What? Though a survey of contemporary literature would show a huge variety of aesthetics, and authorial stances, are our tools contributing to a body of writing that can be called "postliterary" or "postliterature literature"? Does this literature contribute to (and in turn reinforce) a posthuman conception of self as pattern?

A few points of reference: instead of the stereotype of the lone author or artist slaving away in the solitude of a garret, we have social-media driven self-publishing on sites like Amazon and publishing platforms like Wattpad.com, both described above. On Wattpad alone, 18 million users shared 300 million messages about each other's writing in 2013. "Find your voice" was common advice to would-be authors searching for what was unique, or original in their own writing at a time (High Modernism) when people believed in concepts like "originality," "genius," "uniqueness"—a Faulkneresque signature style, for example.[11] For the generation of writers coming up through social writing sites like Wattpad, there is pressure to not think in terms of individual voice but in terms of genre (fan-fiction, horror, werewolf, romance, etc.); there is pressure to blend in, or to embody the community the way writers for television try to speak to the majority: scripts may be smart but not so smart that they alienate less-educated viewers; fresh, but not so new as to challenge conventional morality (e.g., there were no people of color in fictional TV shows until it became socially acceptable for corporations to publicly court minority groups as potential markets). Indeed, it's becoming increasingly difficult to not only tell which text was written by which author(s), but if a text was written by any human at all.

POSTLITERARY LITERATURE

I'm referring here, of course, to the body of writing in which the erasure of the individual is, in fact, a value to be aspired to: appropriation as creation; repurposing of texts; poetry written by machines—writing in which the computer is integral to its composition and reading, but even more to work that is informed by an accompanying posthuman ethos—one that is at odds with an ethos based upon the uniqueness of the individual, and its cousins, especially originality.

[11] It is easy to see this ethos in contrast to the plethora of visual art works in which isolated individuals are subsumed by groups. Using simple search tools, artist Jason Salavon located the formal portraits of hundreds of men whose family name is either Smith or Jones; he then used them to create his eponymous *The Smith-Jones Checkerboard*, where portraits of men with the last name Smith take the place of the black squares, and Jones the white (or is it the other way around?). As in his *Portrait Project*, Salavon also digitally averages the pixels in every one of the *Playboy* centerfolds published during the 1980s (and other decades) to reveal "unexpected pattern as the relationship between the part and whole, the individual and the group" (http://salavon.com/work/EveryPlayboyCenterfoldDecades/). Similarly, Benjamin Funke describes the chorus he assembled by synchronizing one hundred videos of guys in their bedroom playing Metallica's "One" as "a painfully sincere musical community that exists only in a technologically mediated parallel reality" (http://www.benjaminfunke.com/p/teaching-philosophy.html) as do the 4,000 singers in Eric Whitacre's virtual choir, each recording his or her part separately, alone, then uploading them to Whitacre who assembles them as a choir (http://www.ted.com/talks/eric_whitacre_a_virtual_choir_2_000_voices_strong#t-5412).

This ethos is at work in literature that is partially generated by the computer though published in print, for example, Flarf, or Google-sculpting, in which words harvested from the Web are collaged into poetry. It is present in Ed Finn's "The Future of the Book" (2014) books: written in three days by collaborators using the electronic tools that make "live writing" possible. Nick Thurston's *Of the Subcontract, or, on the Poetic Right* (2013) is a volume of one hundred poems that he "wrote" by subcontracting the actual writing through Amazon.com's Mechanical Turk, a crowdsourcing platform that allows employers to hire laborers (called Turks) to perform tiny tasks (such as categorizing photos) that computers are unable to do well. Thurston selected poems produced by workers performing these human information tasks (HITs) at the rate of $0.05 per line, and composed his book by arranging them in the order of efficiency (cost vs. poetry produced), along with the metadata documenting their employee-employer exchange. For example, one poem produced by employee A7J4Y6FOPZ8YV in 16.5 minutes at a labor cost of $3, begins:

> Feel my love; just feel my love as anger or feel my love as hatred or feel my love as burden or feel my love as a sin or feel my love as a crime but just feel it baby feel my love in silence or feel my love as disturbance or feel my love as vacuum but at-least feel my love; feel my love . . . .

Another work of literature employing Amazon's Mechanical Turk is *Emoji Dick*, a translation of Herman Melville's *Moby-Dick* into Japanese emoticons. The novel's famous opening line, "Call me Ishmael," appears in this translation as: ☎ 👨 ⛵ 🐳 👌. This and all the other 10,000 sentences of the novel were translated by three different Turks at the rate of $0.05 per line; these three translations were then voted on by other Turks (at the rate of $0.02 per vote) and the translations that received the most votes were included in the book. More than 800 "authors" spent approximately 3,795,980 seconds "writing" this book (whose publication was made possible by a crowd-funding Kickstarter campaign). Jason Huff wrote *Autosummarize* by using Microsoft Word's summarizing feature to condense one hundred of the most popular copyright-free books to ten lines each. Phil Chernofsky's 1,250-page book *And Every Single One Was Someone* (2013) reproduces a single word, Jew, 6 million times, and in so doing brings to mind the Holocaust.

Similar gestures are made through the vast amount of poetry written by machines: "Build an engine with words. Let it make you speak," reads the epigram to Bill Kennedy and Darren Wershler-Henry's *apostrophe* (2006), the hardcover edition of a poem that they automated by placing on the Web, then renamed the *Apostrophe Engine*. Click on any line in the poem and that line will be plugged into a search engine that returns pages beginning with "You are" and ending in a period. It then compiles the results as a new poem, such as one that begins: "you are old, Father William, the young man said you are prepared to follow the rules" (192).

In Perl poetry, human language is translated into a programming language, Perl, but in a way that allows the Perl poem to still be compiled (i.e., run on a computer), and sometimes also output human language. In this poetics, the commands themselves comprise a vocabulary that has meaning in two worlds: that of humans, and that of the machine. "Black Perl," its best-known example, reads as a mundane string of words that are also computer commands: "BEFOREHAND: close door, each window & exit; wait until time. open spellbook, study, read (scan, select, tell us); write it, print the hex while each watches, reverse its length, write again" (Jonadab, 2003).

While the language of this poem may be flat, as a program it still runs, though it won't calculate taxes or perform any pragmatic function (a characteristic that is true for most computer-language-human hybrid poems). Obviously, this poem doesn't give readers what they might expect from, for example, lyric poetry. Indeed, the impulse to put "poem" in quotation marks when discussing code-work "poems" comes from its constraints on human language, which result in a narrowness of vocabulary, rhetorical strategies, flexibility of language, and the other pleasures that make poetry, in the traditional sense, poetry. But that, of course, is beside the point; rather it is a form of literature that has more affinity with conceptual visual art, or, in the broader context of the written works described here, a kind of postliterary literature.

Consider, for example, Nick Montfort's "ppg256–1" (2008):

```
perl -le 'sub b{@_=unpack"(A2)*", pop;$_[rand@_]}sub w{" ".b("cococacamama-
debapabohamolaburatamihopodito").b("estsnslldsckregspsstedbsnelengkemsattewsn-
tarshnknd")}{$_="\n\nthe".w."\n";$_=w."    ".b("attoonnoof").w    if$l;s/[au][ae]/a/
;print;$l=0if$l++>rand 9;sleep 1;redo}'
```

When run, this code-poem generates random words without referring to any lookup table, thus creating a string of words that can be found in an English dictionary, as well as words that are strings of random letters, or call it sound poetry/noise; it also applies line breaks in order to supply titles and what Montfort calls an "overall stanza/strophe shape" to its output, that is, to sculpt the output into the appearance of poetry:

oat
he too
that too that two
with
two
he awe to thaw
that hew at wet he hit
with who he hat with
what a wit that we the

Montfort describes other iterations, and his own experiments with changing the coding, adding a rhyme scheme, for example, by having the program load into memory the last syllable of an output line, and incorporating a command to use this saved syllable at the end of the next output line (the result of which, Montfort reports, caused the computer to make up words to rhyme—something people often do, scrolling through a mental list of words, real and invented, when trying to find a match).

In a sense, this Perl poem automates the experiment of Raymond Queneau's (1998: 14–33) "100,000,000,000,000 Poems," a traditional fourteen-line sonnet that Queneau layered on top of ten other fourteen-line sonnets in such a way that any one line can be combined with the thirteen lines of any of the other sonnets, thus allowing a potential reading of 10^{14} sonnets. That is, it generates more poetry than can be read in a lifetime. And as it is the form of Queneau's book that allows the poem to proliferate, so it is the form of Montfort's (2008) "book"—the software—that generates the poetry (thus, the poem's title).

Like Queneau's poem, "ppg256–1" asks, What is the nature of poetry? What is the role of the author? Of the reader? Of "authenticity"?—questions to which Montfort's poem adds this: how does the introduction of the machine into the writing of the poem alter our answers? Especially when a single computer can write more poetry than can be read in multiple human lifetimes? Later editions of "ppg256–1" allowed the reader to pause the output, making it possible to appreciate its Dada-esque qualities, but more importantly its apparent "sense-making" ability—or is it ours?—which prompts the questions: What are we to make of the human impulse to assign meaning? Or agency? How is our conception of "reading" or "writing" changed by the complementary gesture of creating a machine that will read this poetry?—at speeds beyond the human capacity to keep up with its generation?

Philip M. Parker alone has written over 200,000 books, ranging from poetry to food security. Or rather, his machines have. As he explains, the process his software used to write over 1.3 million poems (as well as his other books) is an algorithm that employs graph theory and a metric for linguistic differences across word strings in other poems. Yet Parker's poetics is antique when compared to Artificial Intelligence systems designed to process natural language, such as Watson, the IBM system that defeated two former champions of *Jeopardy*, the quiz show in which contestants compete by answering questions from a variety of general knowledge categories.

If someone walks up to you and starts talking, David Antin asks at the start of one of his talk poems, how do you know if it's a poem or not? Increasingly, we can ask similar questions as more and more of the text we read is written by machines. Using Narrative Science's natural-language software, for example, computers are able to compose reports that once would have been written by a human sports or business reporter: "While company shares have dropped 17.2% over the last three months to close at $13.72 on February 15, 2012, Barnes & Noble **(BKS)** is hoping it can break the slide with solid third quarter results when it releases its earnings on Tuesday, February 21, 2012" (see http://narrativescience.com/).

Given the massive literary databases that already exist (formerly known as libraries), given the increasing complexity of projects that AI systems are taking over (Watson is now being used to write medical diagnoses), can the writing of literature that is indistinguishable from a human author be far behind (especially if, as is the case of most best sellers, Wattpad authors, and critics, aesthetics are of minimal concern)?

It is the machine's role in the coauthorship of selves—machines that not only read the writing of other machines but make judgments that affect us—that is at stake in Christian Bök's "Xenotext Experiment" (2009): a plan to compose poetry (one code) that can be translated into the genetic alphabet of DNA (another code); like Perl Poetry, it can "run," that is, it will be "expressed."[12] In Bök's code poem, though, it will be expressed not as speech, nor on screen, but as a living organism, specifically, the DNA of the *Deinococcus radiodurans* bacteria, altered so that it carries Bök's poetry within its genes. By replicating and mutating, the bacterium creates other code poems. It is both book and writing machine. As writing machine, the descendants of Bök's original poem could be generating texts long after humans have ceased to exist. But if a poem is written and there's no human left to read it, is it still a poem? If a computer plays chess (or *Jeopardy*) against a human, are they playing the same game? These questions go beyond the academic,

[12] Bök writes that the lab in Calgary that he has been working with has confirmed the viability of the poem gene he has designed: when his poem (which begins "any style of life / is prim") is inserted into the genome of the bacterium he is using, the bacterium writes its own poem in response (which begins "the faery is rosy / of glow"). That is, he has proven the efficacy of his concept (Bök, 2016).

especially in light of the ways that science and the writing technologies they give birth to (e.g., the printing press, the telegraph, the radio) have always reconfigured the world.

The diminution of the individual against the backdrop of the machine and the Noachian flood of text enabled by the machine seems to be at least partially the impetus behind the number of authors who have abandoned writing, and merely represent "found" text as their own. Within this growing corpus of work we can count:

> David Buuck's "United 93" (a representation of the transcript from the black-box flight recorder aboard the flight that crashed into a Pennsylvania field on 9/11).
> Counterpath Press's publication, as poetry, of *Let Her Speak: Transcript of Texas State Senator Wendy Davis's June 25, 2013, Filibuster of the Texas State Senate* (which is just what its long title says—a transcript of the words Senator Davis said during the 11 hours she occupied the podium in the Texas State House in order to use up the time allotted for voting before a bill restricting women's access to health clinics could be passed).
> Kenneth Goldsmith's *Day* (an 800-page retyping of one day's *New York Times* newspaper).
> Kent Johnson's *Day* (an appropriation of Goldsmith's *Day* that Johnson created by placing a sticker bearing his name over the name of Goldsmith on copies of the book).

Towering above these pranks and gestures is Vanessa Place's *Tragodía* (2011), a three-volume set of court documents: *Statement of Facts, Statement of the Case*, and *Argument*. One entry in *Statement of Facts* begins by laying out the prosecution's case in a series of "facts":

> On October 21, 2007, Ben was 13 years old, living with his family in Los Angeles. At 4:00 that Sunday morning, Ben was sitting alone on his front porch, reading his Bible. Appellant was walking down the street; he stopped at the gate and asked Ben about smoking. (RT 2:1831–1836, 2:1849–1850, 2:1871) Ben understood this to mean marijuana, and the two walked to an alley . . . In the alley, they continued smoking. Ben felt his pants coming down; he tried unsuccessfully to pull them up. Appellant was behind Ben . . . Ben felt appellant's penis penetrate his bottom, and remain there for five minutes. Appellant never asked Ben if he wanted to have sex. Ben had sex with appellant "out of curiosity." After Ben saw appellant ejaculate, Ben returned home . . . Ben's mother Madison was on the porch; she asked Ben where he had been, and he eventually told her. She became upset, he embarrassed. Ben wrote a statement about what happened, saying he had been forced, which wasn't true. Ben wanted to have sex with appellant, but didn't what his mother to know that. Madison called the police. (9)

As can be seen from this brief excerpt, presenting actual court documents relating to sexual crimes as if they were works of literature foregrounds the construction of narrative, the selection of detail (e.g., "Bible" mentioned above), the context they are placed into (on the porch with one's mother, or in a police station before an officer). It calls into question the politics (including class and gender politics) of constructed "truth" versus fiction. Can there be a poetic truth in a courtroom? No hypothetical exercise, the narratives thus created in the name of the state warrant close reading for their rhetorical constructions literally set some people free while sending others to prison. Conversely, Place's *Tragodía* (2011) questions the very morality of literary fiction by asking authors, how, at a time that includes continual war, political corruption, intellectual corruption, global warming, extinction on a mass scale—all problems that involve the creation of narrative—can anyone justify simply "making up stories"?

Which is to say that conceptual works are not all created equal. Given that the list of appropriated works presented as literature seems to be growing exponentially, it's bound to range from the profound to the banal as anyone can now become a (conceptual) author: just hold up a nonliterary text and proclaim it art. So perhaps a more interesting question is to ask, why do so many "authors" feel compelled to write such nonindividualistic works—through appropriation, the use of machines, or crowd-sourcing? And why did so many begin to do so at this moment in literary and extra-literary history?

AN APOLOGY FOR POSTLITERARY LITERATURE

It's not as though postliterary literature will come to be a dominant genre. As John Barth famously pointed out during the early days of postmodernism, there will always be authors working in a variety of registers; plurality is one of the distinguishing markers of our period, and even individuals employ multiple modes of writing/reading. Still, as earlier observers may have asked why Renaissance art emerged in Italy at the time that it did, so might we be rewarded by asking why is there so much postliterary literature emerging now? What does it say about our time and our place? And us?

Little of it is new in the sense of the avant-garde: the art world has been awash in found objects as art at least since Marcel Duchamp exhibited a bicycle wheel or urinal as art; likewise, the literary canon is rife with collage, the quotation, the appropriation (see, e.g., the poetry of Susan Howe, or the novels of Kathy Acker). Nor is this neo, postliterary literature Art Brut as Dubuffet meant it—art created outside the mainstream, often by unschooled artists (or writers). While some critics, readers, and many of the self-published authors described above simply do lack any literary sophistication, or even the craftsmanship associated with genre novels and poems, and while many critics themselves are increasingly turning away from aesthetics in the interest of sociological readings of popular forms,[13] many sophisticated authors are intentionally working against the idea of an individual "author." And really, in the end, does it matter? Perhaps more telling, is it inevitable?

The cultural absorption of the computer is part of the answer: the simple technical ease with which anyone can appropriate text, images, videos—really anything which can be digitized, which is to say anything—has surely altered ideas of the book, of originality, or ownership, and therefore, as this chapter and others have suggested, the concept of the lyric "I," in ways and to a degree that would have not been imagined even a few decades ago. (It would be hard to imagine teenagers caring about copyright laws, or even knowing such things existed, before Napster.) Part of the answer also seems to lie in Bök's observation that it's important for poets to take part in contemporary methods and discourses in order for poetry to stay relevant. This is especially true, he claims, given that information-processing technologies are rapidly becoming not only the means through which we read and write, but participate in virtually all aspects of culture (Voyce 2007). In other words, the sheer number of these kinds of works allows us to see a genre form before our eyes,

[13] As one review of Lawrence Buell's survey of American literature put it, "The difference between a beautifully written book and a badly written book [according to Buell] exists at about the same level as a politician's hair—it's something you might notice, but something that should not distract you " (Gopnik 2014: 103).

along with its concomitant appreciation, criticism, and values. (We also see its backlash, i.e., the concomitant rise of memoir, or a posthuman ethos exerting pressure on literary form, e.g., a pluralized, decentered narrative replaces a central consciousness in accord with posthuman formulations of the self [see Roberto Bolaño's *2666*].) As always, the crude, the simple, the manipulative, and the commercial will continue to live beside more nuanced art, just as vaudeville lived beside theater, Hollywood blockbusters live beside art-house indie, and all kinds of books have always lived among each other (the death of the divide between high and low as well as between literature and cultural studies or entertainment seems to be perpetually announced prematurely). From quill pens to the digital, the catalyst for change seems to be the tools that make new modes of thought, of writing, possible.

I began this chapter with an image from *2001: A Space Odyssey*, a fiction that proposed the first tool, the bone club, as an axis about which our earliest civilization turned. Others followed: Christianity, Capitalism, and so on. Following the critique of Bruno Latour (1993), it is easy to see how our digital tools, the self as pattern, our postliterary literature are all inseparable: three splashes in a pond that embraces all ripples in the surface they have created.

SOURCES CITED

Ball, James. "NSA Data Surveillance: How Much Is Too Much?" *The Guardian*, June 10, 2013, www.theguardian.com/world/2013/jun/10/nsa-metadata-surveillance-analysis?guni=-Network%20front:network-front%20full-width-1%20bento-box:Bento%20box:Position2. Accessed May 26, 2014.

Beneson, Fred, ed. and compiler. *Emoji Dick*, www.emojidick.com. Accessed May 26, 2014.

Bolaño, Roberto. *2666*. Translated by Natasha Wimmer. New York: Farrar, Straus and Giroux, 2008.

Bök, Christian. "The Xenotext Experiment." In *The &Now Awards*, edited by R. Archambeau, D. Schneiderman, and S. Tomasula. Lake Forest: Lake Forest College Press, 2009.

Bök, Christian. "The Xenotext Works." *Harriet: A Poetry Blog*, Poetry Foundation, www.poetryfoundation.org/harriet/2011/04/the-xenotext-works. Accessed August 2, 2016.

Bruns, Gerald. "On Ceasing to Be Human." Roger Allan Moore Lecture, Department of Social Medicine, Cambridge: Harvard Medical School, April 1998. Public lecture.

Chernofsky, Phil. *And Every Single One Was Someone*. Jerusalem: Gefen Books, 2013.

Davis, Wendy. *Let Her Speak: Transcript of Texas State Senator Wendy Davis's June 25, 2013, Filibuster of the Texas State Senate*. Denver: Counterpath Press, 2014.

Finley, Klint. "The Quantified Man: How an Obsolete Tech Guy Rebuilt Himself for the Future." *Wired*, February 22, 2013, www.wired.com/2013/02/quantified-work/all. Accessed May 26, 2014.

Finn, Ed. "Field Notes from the Future of Publishing." *Electronic Book Review*, October 5, 2014, electronicbookreview.com/thread/firstperson/collaborating. Accessed August 2, 2016.

Foisil, Madeline. "The Literature of Intimacy." In *A History of Private Life: Passions of the Renaissance*, edited by Robert Chartier, translated by Arthur Coldhammer. Cambridge: Harvard University Press, 1989, pp. 327–61.

Foucault, Michel. *The Order of Things: An Archeology of the Human Sciences*. New York: Vintage Books, 1973.

Foucault, Michel. *The Archaeology of Knowledge & the Discourse on Language*. New York: Pantheon, 1982.

Goldsmith, Kenneth. *Day*. Great Barrington, MA:The Figures, 2003.
Gopnik, Adam. "Go Giants." *The New Yorker*, April 21, 2014, pp. 102–103.
Goulemot, Jean Marie. "Literary Practices: Publicizing the Private." In *A History of Private Life: Passions of the Renaissance*, edited by Robert Chartier, translated by Arthur Coldhammer. Cambridge: Harvard University Press, 1989, pp. 363–95.
Hayles, N. Katherine. *How We Became Posthuman: Virtual Bodies in Cybernetics, Literature, and Informatics*. Chicago: University of Chicago Press, 1999.
Jasiewicz, Isia. "Self-Publishing: Who Needs a Publisher Anymore?" *Newsweek*, vol. 156, no. 6, August 9, 2010, p. 47.
Johnson, Bobby. "Privacy No Longer a Social Norm, Says Facebook Founder." *The Guardian*, January 10, 2010, www.theguardian.com/technology/2010/jan/11/facebook-privacy. Accessed May 26, 2014.
Johnson, Kent. *Day*. Buffalo: BlazeVOX Books, 2010.
Jonadab. "Black Perl Updated for Perl 5." *PerlMonks*, 2003, www.perlmonks.org/?node_id=237465. Accessed October 19, 2010.
Kaminski, Margot. "The Critical Life of Information." Conference on Big Data, Yale University, April 11, 2014.
Kennedy, Bill, and Darren Wershler-Henry. *Apostrophe*.Toronto: ECW Press, 2006, apostropheengine.ca. Accessed May 26, 2014.
Khun, Thomas. *The Structure of Scientific Revolutions*. Chicago: University of Chicago Press, 1996.
Kopalle, Praveen. "Why Amazon's Anticipatory Shipping Is Pure Genius." *Forbes*, January 28, 2014, www.forbes.com/sites/onmarketing/2014/01/28/why-amazons-anticipatory-shipping-is-pure-genius. Accessed May 26, 2014.
Latour, Bruno. *We Have Never Been Modern*. Translated by Catherine Porter. Cambridge: Harvard University Press, 1993.
Lohr, S. "How Privacy Vanishes Online." *New York Times*, March 16, 2010, www.nytimes.com/2010/03/17/technology/17privacy.html?scp=10&sq=data+mining&st=nyt. Accessed October 21, 2010.
Lukes, Steven. *Individualism*. Colchester: ECPR Press, 2006.
Macpherson, C. B. *The Political Theory of Possessive Individualism*. Hayles, 1999.
Market Watch. www.marketwatch.com/investing/stock/amzn/financials. Accessed May 26, 2014.
Mau, Bruce. *Massive Change*. London: Phaidon Press, 2004.
Montfort, Nick. "A 256-Character Program to Generate Poems." *Grand Text Auto*, grandtextauto.org/2008/02/15/a-256-character-program-to-generate-poems. Accessed October 19, 2010.
Moretti, Franco. *Graphs, Maps, Trees: Abstract Models for Literary History*. New York: Verso Press, 2005.
Narrative Science. narrativescience.com. Accessed May 26, 2014.
Packer, George. "Cheap Words: Amazon Is Good for Customers. But Is It Good for Books?" *The New Yorker*, February 17, 2014, newyorker.com/reporting/2014/02/17/140217fa_fact_packer?currentPage=all. Accessed May 26, 2014.
Parker, Philip M. Personal email.
Place, Vanessa. *Tragodía 1: Statement of Facts*. Los Angeles: Insert Blanc Press, 2011.
Queneau, Raymond. "100,000,000,000,000 Poems." In *Oulipo Compendium*, edited by H. Matthews, A. Brotchie et al. London: Atlas Press, 1998.
Ramirez, Edith. "Data Brokers: A Call for Transparency and Accountability." The Federal Trade Commission, May 2014, ftc.gov/system/files/documents/reports/data-brokers-call-transparency-accountability-report-federal-trade-commission-may-2014/

140527databrokerreport.pdf. Cited in Ava Tomasula y Garcia, "Empty Sky: Cloud Technologies in the Global Landscape."

Schweizer, Tanja Sophie. "Multimedia Giants, Literary Publishers and New Technologies: Can Culture and Business Benefit from the Change of Rules in the Book World." *International Journal of Arts Management*, vol. 3, no. 3 (spring 2001): 51–67.

Streitfeld, David, and Melissa Eddy. "As Publishers Fight Amazon, Books Vanish." *New York Times*, May 23, 2014, bits.blogs.nytimes.com/2014/05/23/amazon-escalates-its-battle-against-hachette/?_php=true&_type=blogs&_r=0. Accessed May 26, 2014.

Tabbi, Joseph, and Michael Wutz. *Reading Matters: Narrative in the New Media Ecology*. Ithaca, NY: Cornell University Press, 1997.

Thurston, Nick. *Of the Subcontract, or, on the Poetic Right*. York: Information as Material, 2013, nickthurston.info/Of-the-Subcontract-Or-Principles-of-Poetic-Right.

Tucker, Patrick. "Has Big Data Made Anonymity Impossible?" *MIT Technology Review*, May 7, 2013, technologyreview.com/news/514351/has-big-data-made-anonymity-impossible/?ref=rss. Accessed May 26, 2014.

Voyce, S. "The Xenotext Experiment: An Interview with Christian Bök." *Postmodern Culture*, vol. 17, no. 2 (2007), muse.jhu.edu.proxy.library.nd.edu/journals/postmodern_culture/toc/pmc17.2.html. Accessed October 19, 2010.

Watt, Ian. *Studies in Defoe, Richardson and Fielding*. Oakland: University of California Press, 1971.

Wattpad. "2013 Year on Wattpad." wattpad.com, 2013. Accessed May 26, 2014.

Wilkens, Matthew. "Where Was the American Renaissance? Computation, Space, and Literary History in the Civil War Era." Draft manuscript, 2013.

Wolf, Gary. "The Data-Driven Life." *The New York Times*, April 18, 2010, nytimes.com/2010/05/02/magazine/02self-measurement-t.html?scp=1&sq=Gary%20Wolf%20the%20data%20driven%20life&st=cse. Accessed May 26, 2014.

Zephoria Digital Marketing. "The Top 20 Valuable Facebook Statistics—Updated July 2016," zephoria.com/top-15-valuable-facebook-statistics. Accessed August 2, 2016.

CHAPTER THREE

Lift This End: Electronic Literature in a Blue Light

STUART MOULTHROP

Since this is a chapter about the computational context of literary writing, and to some extent poetry, I have invested heavily in metaphor, at least as far as the title is concerned. Taking key terms in no particular order: by "end" I mean not so much terminus as singularity or convergence of opposites, that defining, indefinable point where turn becomes return as one state gives way to another; from the imperative "lift," I take both the sense of elevation or burdening (lift up) and appropriation (shoplifting); and by "this," I will eventually mean the inescapable subject of electronic literature, the "this" of which (for which) something may yet be "lifted." As for that blue light, it is, for the moment at least, a retina-scorching light-emitting diode on the faceplate of my personal computer, registering wireless connection to the empire of signs. To this shining subject we will inexorably return.

Meanwhile, some sad news. It seems that something important—perhaps the American conscience, or our national poetry, or some might say, the soul of art—passed away in the last days of March 2008, after a long battle with history. In lieu of obituary, we find the following:

> All you retards deserve to burn in hell. I would like to see you get crushed by a motherfucking bulldozer.
> Go fuck your syphilis-infected mother. Take your motherfucking ass and cry to your fucking pedophile slut. Go finish killing yourselves, you little pussy fucking liberals. Get it through your head: your government doesn't give a fuck about you.

Though they might evoke a recent political campaign, these lines actually come from "Artist's Statement," the first poem in K. S. Mohammad's collection, *The Front* (2009). Preceding this tasty serving of political patois comes an even more intriguing colophon:

> ~~Every poem in this collection accurately reflects the author's actual values, beliefs, and personal experiences~~. Every poem in this collection was composed entirely out of Google search engine text. The author has taken many liberties with selection, punctuation, spelling, recombination, and so forth.

From now on, I will always read colophons: because this one really does bring good news, everybody, as well as a reason to keep on killing ourselves no faster than one day at a time. Mohammad's Google-eyed procedure, part of a sublimely self-ironized non-movement called "flarf" (Bernstein 2003), holds important implications for writing, and perhaps for electronic writing in particular. Flarf shows how poems can, and in a sense now must, be made from contents of the commons, by fracking up its limitless deposits of crap, invective, and often astonishing other stuff. Flarf testifies that authors are still free to take liberties, perhaps thus insinuating, against better judgment, that there is something yet to liberate. The government may not give a fuck about us, but I suggest K. S. Mohammad does, in his own curiously twisted way—or about our common situation in, or under, or as language. Poetry is dead, or whatever. Buh-bye to all that. Long live flarf.

RECYCLING WORKS

The coming of flarf is no more a sign of end-times than anything else these days. According to no less an authority than Marjorie Perloff (2010: 12), acquisitive or recycled poetry simply reflects the latest twist in literary aesthetics:

> *Inventio* is giving way to appropriation, elaborate constraint, visual and sound composition, and reliance on intertextuality. Thus we are witnessing a new poetry, more conceptual than directly expressive—a poetry in which, as Gerald Bruns put it with reference to Cage's "writing through" *Finnegans Wake*, the shift is from a Chomskyan linguistic competence, in which the subject is able to produce an infinite number of original sentences from the deep structure of linguistic rules, to the pragmatic discourse that appropriates and renews what is given in the discourse that constitutes a social and cultural world.

In addition to Bruns, Perloff calls upon Antoine Compagnon, who theorizes citational writing under the name *récriture*. This approach validates borrowing as the hitherto unacknowledged basis of literary procedure. As Perloff sees it, the arrival of this practice does not mark an existential end of the literary project, but an end to a means. In effect, citational poetics furnishes a contour or edge, an end in the sense of a limit at which the whole business turns back on itself—as in the graphical admonition in Figure 3.1.

This sort of *end* referred to in this label is not terminus but affordance: a point of engagement by which we may lift, translate, or rotate the object, replacing it in a new context. Of course, as the sign says, we may need to take some care about which ends we decide to lift. The meaning of *this* does indeed seem to matter. We may also want to think about where we set things down.

As Perloff sees it, the portage of poetry via *récriture* passes through a full circle, moving from plagiarism through citation to "poetry by other means," which on inspection seems not that far from well-known parameters. Perloff's analysis carries echoes of what we might call the "Shklovsky Defense," after Viktor Shklovsky's (1991: 170) observation that Sterne's sublimely disordered *Tristram Shandy* is "the most typical novel in world literature." As Sterne's methodical chaos reveals the self-organizing mechanisms of prose narrative, so flarf, and even more so conceptual poetry, may confirm an essential truth of

FIGURE 3.1 Graphic by Stuart Moulthrop.

literary art. Mature poets steal; a poet who reaches majority in these ex-postmodern times will likely resort to Google.

Though ostensibly the "uncreative" antithesis of creative writing, citational poetry could be said to rediscover the core functions of poetics, which include selection, arrangement, and some form of high concept: *ethos*, *kairos*, *ludus*, or the like. In the Eliotic idiom, to which Perloff turns early on, intention and specificity remain crucial. It is these particular fragments (not others) that a certain voice or agency has shored (not simply thrown) against some ruinous yet still intentional structure. Among the several writers and movements Perloff discusses, two stand out: Walter Benjamin of the *Arcades* project, and the conceptualist Kenneth Goldsmith. The former makes an inchoate attempt to capture an urban, bourgeois *dasein* within an "ur-hypertext" (31). The latter carries on the work of deep texturing, using for his *Trilogy* nothing more sophisticated than keyboard, radio, and audio tape, but enthusiastic, nonetheless, about affordances of the Internet. Perloff quotes Goldsmith at some length on the Brazilian concrete poet Decio Pignatari, whose work he discovered in the digital-boom year 2001: "Everything [Pignatari] was saying seemed to predict the mechanics of the internet . . . I immediately understood that what had been missing from concrete poetry was an appropriate environment in which it could flourish. For many years, concrete poetry has been in limbo: it's been a displaced genre in search of a new medium. And now it's found one" (50). This post-Chomskyan turn from deep structure to "pragmatics" brings momentous changes, but apparently no deep disruption to the poetic project. In Perloff's view it simply recontextualizes, extending the mission of "genius" into fresh woods.

There is a certain irrepressible utopianism in this approach. It is hard not to think of the sentiments of the net artist Vuk Ćosić, who declared that "all art up to now has been merely a substitute for the Internet" (Galloway 2004: 220). To be fair, Perloff uses her own citational practice to keep some distance from this sort of enthusiasm. She quotes, but does not necessarily endorse, at least not without a minimum of critical separation. She is careful to emphasize continuities between contemporary practice and earlier modernisms. In fact, continuity is her main theme, not cybernetic displacement or irruption. However heretical "uncreative writing" may seem to others, Perloff insists on its integration with poetic history.

To the extent one cares about institutional recognition (and to read at least some of the flarfists, that could be very little), Perloff's historicism may seem good news. Perhaps, though, it is not good news for everybody. In the field of electronic literature, the implications of post-creative writing may be more problematic than they are for more general literary communities. Thanks to the new popularity of post-inventional practice, old digital hands face a strange turn indeed: *one of our favorite ideas has gone mainstream*. Though it may seem perverse to say so, that passage may not be altogether a good thing.

INTERFACE AND DATABASE

But first, the news: back at the turn of the century, Lev Manovich (2001: 37) usefully declared that "[a] new media object can be defined as one or more interfaces to a multimedia database" (37). Manovich addressed only digital productions, but as we can now see, his formula has greater reach. As the concept and form of the database moves toward the center of general literacy—it is apparently one meaning of the name "Al Qaeda," for instance—the database/interface model has become available to a variety of discourses. Though Perloff does not cite *Language of New Media* and does not directly invoke database/interface terminology, the model seems implicit in her discussion of crucial examples. She refers to Benjamin's *Arcades* explicitly as a hypertext—a form of digital composition explicitly treated by Manovich. She also calls the project "potentially digital," emphasizing its complex, multicursal treatment of a diverse body of writings (43). At an earlier point she identifies Cia Rinne's (2008: 14) *Archive Zaroum*, a digital work literally constituted as an interface to a database, as a key example of the new citational practice (14). In spirit if not in name, the database/interface construct appears at least closely homologous to Perloff's critical approach.

To generalize this homology: *the work of citational composition may be regarded as creation of an interface to a database.* An interface, of course, is a subsystem. In cybertextual terms, it is a *machine*, one of many possible machines that could be brought to bear, and thus itself is capable of multiple configurations or outputs. The poem in this view—quintessentially in the case of flarf—may be thought of as one of these productions, a recorded or inscribed *state* of the interface.

No doubt, there is a certain amount of lossy compression in these propositions. In most cases involving poetry, the databases in question are not properly "multimedia," as Manovich specifies, but stay within the medium of writing. Also, I am using *interface* in a way that will invite resistance from anyone for whom it is a term of art, in say, user-experience design or software engineering. I adopt a certain poetic imprecision which, admittedly, may not be the best way to approach the ostensibly rigorous subject of poetics. For the moment, I can only offer a low-resolution version of this idea, in hopes it may lead to some more sharply defined conception.

Meanwhile, to carry on the somewhat dubious metaphor: considered as a state-reduction or interface unplugged, the poem emerges from and embodies a series of operations upon its target database (Google searches, personal audio recordings, and such). Its process of assembly, selection, and modification involves method, though in most cases, the nature of that method remains implicit and opaque. Yet for some, it will also be conventionally interpretable: a proprietary product of poetic "genius" (Perloff's word), intended for all those ordinary readers who ultimately receive the poem. Again, we are on very familiar ground here, even if *récriture* seems to lie outside the boundaries of conventionally creative practice. The reassertion of *genius* implies an ecumenical space where even the heretical is welcome.

The grace of this universalism might even extend to that literary heresy called born-digital writing. From the meliorist view, a poetics informed by database and interface might answer recurrent complaints that writers and theorists of the electronic do not engage sufficiently with a broader world of practice—or perhaps it is the other way around. Indeed, these critiques seem inaccurate for at least some currents in electronic writing. The community of interest around electronic poetry, for example, has always been linked to other experimental movements, from spoken-word performance to concrete poetry, conceptualism, and flarf. Maria Damon and Chris Funkhouser, well-known flarfists, are prominent members of the Electronic Literature Organization.

Thus we are led into a certain temptation. It would be interesting to imagine an articulation of electronic literature that includes Damon and Funkhouser, Alan Sondheim, Oni Buchanan, J. R. Carpenter, and others who have made digital exploits part of diverse art practices—along with writers for whom the electronic is less methodological than environmental. Could K. S. Mohammad, Michael Magee, or Katie Degentesh find parts in an augmented Electronic Literature Orchestra? Could there be room on the stand for

Lane Hall, who politicizes the net (and the night) with hand-held, electric lights (Hall 2011)? Might the Michael Joyce (2007) of *Was: annales nomadiques*, also subtitled "a novel of internet," find his way back into the show, if only through a kind of involuntary (and in vivo) rebaptism? Broadening the base in this way could assert the importance of born—and genetically—digital writing within a greater a cultural scheme. It might connect us more effectively to the project Manovich calls "cultural transcoding," in which non-computational activities become infused by forms, practices, and ideas from information technology.

IN ARREARS

Why, it seems fair to ask, would anyone object to such expansion? In volunteering to play such a skeptic, I imagine myself (not for the first time) as a certain kind of washed-up trouper, ready to repeat insufferable phrases: *After this, it's just Vegas*, or, *That was Burlesque*. Better no doubt to face facts and admit that some of one's favorite ideas have grown up and left the building, headed for Hollywood, Stanford, or other points west. Burlesque, after all, is alive and well and touring as Lady Gaga. (This is factual observation, though you may take it allegorically wherever you like. Also, no disrespect to Lady Gaga.)

The problem implicit in the broader formulation of electronic literature sketched here ultimately centers on identity. Would a shift away from the radical *inventio* of born-digital writing, toward the Perloff-Goldsmith model of newly mediated "pragmatics" betray some core concept or commitment of electronic literature? If it does, should we care?

One possible focus for these questions might be the historical framework Perloff uses to integrate new practices with old. She bases her scheme on William Marx's (2004) notion of an *arrière garde*, a belated second front in the (always curiously militarized) struggle between tradition and innovation. Perloff (2010: 58) writes: "The *arrière garde*, then, is neither a throwback to traditional forms . . . or what we used to call *postmodernism*. Rather, it is the revival of the avant-garde model—but with a difference" (58). The precise nature of this difference is understandably hard to define—to make such definitions requires entire artistic movements, after all—but key components seem to be changes in "materiality and medium" (59). According to Perloff, writers in the *arrière* echelon inherit the revolutionary sensibilities and to some extent the agenda of their precursors, but inhabit a cultural milieu (what Pierre Lévy (2001) calls an "episteme") radically transformed by technical change. So, Perloff thinks, it is possible to escape the ostensible dead-end of postmodernism without being doomed simply to repeat the modernist enterprise. Having access to the Internet, and its episteme of database and interface, makes all the difference.

It seems less than useful, however, to construct this difference as a generalized matter of "materiality and medium." Changes to those factors presumably bring concomitant or complicit shifts in other dimensions as well: aesthetics, genre conventions, constructions of identity at the sites of both writing and reading. Fundamentally, of course, the introduction of media like distributed networks, and materials like markup and programming languages, suggests changes in the status of language and text themselves. Nonhuman or posthuman actors, as we are now discovering, may also factor in.

Cybertextual formalists like Espen Aarseth and Markku Eskelinen, along with computational expressivists like Noah Wardrip-Fruin and digital materialists like Matt Kirschenbaum, regard these differences as *ontological*, requiring critical approaches that place the operation of the text-machine at the center of consideration (see Eskelinen 15–46). Following this line of thinking—as I generally have up to now, in both critical and creative work—suggests a core definition of electronic literature emphasizing a craft-based encounter with computational structures. Such an approach would primarily address works that engage, expose, or intervene in computable instructions, or code. To some extent, this definition exaggerates or restricts actual practice. Not all works in either of the current *Electronic Literature Collections*, for instance, meet these terms in the same way, or to the same degree. The Electronic Literature Organization's self-descriptions speak of "born digital literature" and "the current generation of readers for whom the printed book is no longer an exclusive medium" ("About the ELO"), suggesting a fundamental divergence from an old regime. They also allude to "literature as it develops and persists in a changing digital environment," which seems more inclusive.

For the moment I will hold the more stringent line. The crypto-canon I envision here for purposes of argument—or as I am beginning to see it, the beginnings of an interoperable *kernel*—might be composed of generative and permutational code-works, such as Montfort and company's *Taroko Gorge* (a poem-generator variously repurposed into something that seems more *fungus* than *corpus*; see Montfort 2011), the massively combinatoric *Sea and Spar Between* (Strickland and Montfort 2012), and various cybertextual and generative projects by people like J. R. Carpenter (2010), Jim Andrews (2012), Chris Funkhouser (2007), and Daniel C. Howe (Undated).

In some way many if not all constituents of this cybertextual core participate in Perloff's citational poetics. The various gorge-grabbings that have risen up around the original *Taroko* are clearly takings and remakings. Such is also the rationale of J. R. Carpenter's *Generation[s]*, a collection of poems built from open-source Python scripts. Yet it is not clear that *The Front* would fit into this exclusive circle. That work would not have been possible without significant computational affordances (Web browser as interface, Google's index as database), but Mohammad uses these elements without modification. He seems deeply interested in their performance—indeed, all of *The Front* can be read as a commentary on the great psychotic process that is current media culture—but he does not seem interested in more technical critique or intervention.

Having drawn this artificially tight circle, I now want to violate its boundaries: to think not about what electronic literature might be at its core, but how it might function with looser constraints. What if, at minimum, we recognized writing with search engines as an important digital-literary practice? What if our post-canonical crypto-canon included items such as *The Front* or *Generation[s]*, which can and do exist in print?

In launching this subversive experiment, I do not repudiate the core, the embrace of code as writing, overtures to poetic interoperability, or the rigorous formalism required to understand these things. I carry more water for cybertext theory than most. If my enthusiasm for the 576 positions of the Aarseth Sutra has its limits, I do sympathize with the urge to systematize, being one of those people for whom art means making actual, executable interfaces to databases, which is deeply systematic work. I also share without reservation Eskelinen's (2012: 387) conviction that "literature is perhaps the best aesthetic instrument to deal with the unfair, the uncanny, and the unbalanced," and his interest in making "metarules" a prime concern of computational art. These are projects that invite, if not require, attention to various forms of code. Code-core cybertextualism has undeniable virtues: it usefully drives innovation both in poetic practice and critical thinking, and it builds a detailed foundation for understanding, and eventually teaching, next-generation digital literacy. Long may its models and schemas endure.

All the same, concentrating on the core obviously does not help at the margins, where we confront more ambiguous encounters between writing and information systems. Beyond providing a dour reminder of forsaken rigor, hardcore cybertextualism sheds little light on my promiscuous confusion of *récriture* and database/interface poetics. To stick with the core means closing the door on practices that do not conceive their interfaces strictly as code, or whose textual machinations may not be directly conceived as machines. To walk through that door, however, entails a series of hard questions. If increasingly, almost all writing is born within a nominal embrace of the digital, what happens to any born-digital distinction? How to define a specific electronic literature identity and practice, within the context of a larger orchestration? What is to be gained by thinking about Perloff's "poetry by other means" through the lens of electronic literature?

Perversely, it may be easier to find the value of this project by means of a limit case: an instance in which the approach to *récriture* as *cyberécriture* may afford a better understanding of the text and its function. What follows will be a tale of two liftings, featuring an incidental brush with *Farbenlehre*. Anyone whose capacity for metaphor is affected by blue-green color blindness is hereby excused.

WHAT GREEN MEANS

Perloff (2010) devotes an entire chapter of *Unoriginal Genius* to Kenneth Goldsmith's conceptual poem *Traffic*, which consists of transcribed drive-time reports from WINS, an all-news radio station in New York. Her reading of this citational work is detailed, nuanced, and in many respects compelling, considered in light of the larger argument concerning *récriture* and the post-inventional turn. There is, however, at least one aspect of Perloff's reading that might be worth critical discussion. Perloff cites at length the final entry of the volume, which ends:

> Looking down to the Williamsburg, Manhattan, and Brooklyn Bridges, it's one big green light. And over in Jersey, it's never been better with traffic flowing smoothly across the Hudson at both the Lincoln and Holland Tunnels. Even the GW Bridge which has been choked for what seems like the last twenty-four hours is now flowing like water. Remember, alternate side of the street parking rules are in effect for tomorrow. (159)

After a page or two of close attention to this passage, Perloff comes to broadcaster Pete Tauriello's colorful metaphor: "At the same time, the 'plot' ironically turns out to be a perfect Aristotelian one with beginning, middle, and end, as the image of the nightmare city gives way to a momentary vision of the open road—'one big green light' pointing us into the future" (161). We might set aside the weird assertion of Aristotelian perfection in a collection of traffic reports—this is after all the flight of transparently bizarre fancy Goldsmith's poem invites, and Perloff duly registers the effect as ironic. More troublesome, though, is where the critic takes this ironized, plot-minded sense-of-an-ending in the next paragraph: "Inevitably, too, this green light recalls the one at the end of Daisy's dock in F. Scott Fitzgerald's *The Great Gatsby*" (161). After citing the final three paragraphs of Fitzgerald's novel—complete with blue lawn, green light, dream left behind, orgiastic future, boats against the current—Perloff opines that "*Traffic* gives these memorable images of desire an interesting spin" (161).

At which point this writer, reading this reader, finds himself also in something of a spin: or, to change metaphors, wants to check the gauge on someone's irony tank, which appears to have run seriously low. Perhaps any reference to a green light in New York must remind a literary critic of *Gatsby*—though less charitably, it could be noted that Tauriello's virtual gaze toward Bridge-and-Tunnel-Land points to a very different place than Fitzgerald's East and West Egg. Before going further, it needs saying again that Perloff's green-light effusion amounts to a minor flaw in what is overall a courageous undertaking, an otherwise persuasive attempt to square modernist poetics with conceptualism. Nonetheless it is an interesting lapse, for several reasons.

First, the connection to Fitzgerald is laid on with something like the pop-rivetwork one recalls from undergraduate exam essays, particularly one's own. Since that is hardly the sort of performance expected from a senior critic, there is probably something of experimental significance in this moment. If this is an instance of failed engagement or category mismatch, we might learn something from the breakdown.

One immediate lesson needs to be taken internally. Perloff's questionable reading calls into at least local doubt my insinuation of a deeper investment in the language of new media. Clearly, that convergence is neither a universal nor an inevitable critical turn. In terms of my prior analysis, Perloff here mistakes the interface for its particularized reduction, or state. That is, she reads a contingent assembly of borrowed language as if it had the supposed inevitability of a traditional, intentional structure. She fails to recognize the text as one among many possible operations on a database, but instead takes it back to an older organizational paradigm (quite literally), the Modern Library. The current of Goldsmith's borrowed language overwhelms us, and we are carried backward. Tauriello the newscaster and Goldsmith the conceptualist drop out of the scene, displaced by Fitzgerald, hero of modernism. It is as if one has crawled through a certain tiny door on the seventh-and-a-half floor, and found oneself in another headspace entirely. It is hard not to brace for that final fall onto the shoulder of the Jersey Turnpike (Jonze 1999).

The larger lesson here may be that we step away from cybertext and its ontological assertions at our peril. I begin to hear the words, *I told you so*, in a certain Finnish accent. Perloff's happy motoring through that big green light furnishes a limit case or boundary point to which my expansion of electronic writing will not stretch. Correspondingly, as boundary markers always do, it also suggests some territory on the near side, just shy of the tipping point, that might be worth exploring. The main problem in Perloff's appeal to *Gatsby* lies in its concertedly closural architecture, creating a circuit or suture between the old *avant* and the younger *arrière*. This configuration diminishes, if not excludes, the crucial ground of difference between them.

As noticed, though, limit cases may be taken either way. The injunction DO NOT LIFT THIS END implies some other end more suitable for engagement. Is it possible to read a post-inventional text in a way that avoids the critical lapse just insinuated? Might it be easier to achieve such a reading with some texts than others? Could such texts lie in that transit zone between the cybertextual core of electronic literature and the old frontier of modernism?

BLUE DEPTHS

Satisfying answers to none of these questions are assured, but it seems worth trying an experiment. However, we will need to change both our text and, more importantly, the lighting:

"The child was never found"

Do you remember where you were on that January night
when blue lights and a girl in a long white dress made history?

Do you remember the family gathered there
pulling the dirt from the sides of the well-meaning road?
Did you watch their boots kick up Scoutmaster Randy Deavers
as they bounced across the lunar surface?
What a magical leap it was.
Legend has it that the cry of a baby
consisted of a number of joined panels
fitted and gored from Wylie, Texas to Twin Falls, Idaho.
Legend has it that a dancing blue light
gave the figure shape through seaming.
You know, there's always something
about history swinging like a pendulum.

These fifteen lines come at the beginning of a longer poem composed by Rachael Sullivan (2012), working to a flarfical formula that rules out traditional verbal invention. As in Mohammad's *The Front* (a model for this project), every word beyond the title ("The child was never found") originated on the World Wide Web or other Internet venues, brought to light by search engine queries. Like Mohammad, Sullivan allowed herself to change spelling and punctuation, and to arrange and combine the source material into an approximation of free verse.

Though most of its genome is shared with the flarf species, Sullivan's poem also displays at least one trace of conceptualism: it is part of a collaboration with eight other writers (including myself) making found-language verses on the same formula, each of us working from the results of specific search-engine queries. The queries are phrases we have selected at will from Joyce's (2007) "novel of internet," *Was*, which was the origin of the phrase "the child was never found."

So far, nothing in our post-inventional situation may seem remarkable: we are doing flarf or found poetry according to accepted canons of the craft, building our interface-like texts on databases of discovered material, operating under specified constraints. Given that we are in Milwaukee, we might as well be brewing beer. Yet this is, arguably, microbrew with a difference. Early in our preparation for the project, as we were reading Joyce's text, a question presented itself. *Was* is a highly elliptical, discontinuous, polyglot work that clearly has its own genetic relationship to the experimental tradition of modernism, though more in the line of Stein or Pound than Fitzgerald. Here is how the work begins:

was thought not were the yellow the irrepressible ever who said who said ends Ashtoreth one Wednesday, one Wednesday in june the damp the dampness in everything (light, profusionist, no I mean heat)
forty times now, bowing, clogs along foggy bottom news from the front, wooden boxes neatly in rows
the last the lost wandering *allées* (lips pressed to the neonate's skull, powder scent) willows all now gone from their ripeness
and what of the stipple, the limp, the lost what-was, despite the damp odor of canvas, the salt-cracked lips, inordinate corridors? who can say who can say
distant machines growl through *die nähe* (*durch*) (Joyce 2007: 11)

For those in our writing group who had grown up with the Web, instant messaging, and other Net effects, this language seemed instantly familiar: in fact, it looked quite a bit like flarf. I confess to being the only one in the room who thought it looked more like modernism. It was therefore decided that someone should ask the author of *Was* to what extent search-engine queries were involved in its composition. I did so, stipulating that my money was on *not at all*. As usual, I lost. Joyce (2011) replied:

> In some way all of the text came from search-engine queries in the sense that Google (about which in the preface to my Foucault novel . . . I write: "of course, ought be listed as a co-author here") has slipped into the center of the group picture, to wit: Clio, Thalia, Erato, Euterpe, Googlemena, Polyhymnia, Calliope, Terpsichore, Urania, Melpomene (and you can tell the grads that I *did* Google that).

The qualifying phrase "in some way" needs emphasis, since Joyce (2007) went on to explain in later correspondence that *Was* is not a flarf project and was written in the traditional, inventional way, not by any process of direct appropriation. However, it is deliberately inscribed "a novel of internet," and dedicated to the author's son Jeremiah, "'Electronic Boy' having become documentarian" (7). Both these paratextual moves strongly suggest the novel's address, if not affiliation, to the language of new media, either in the strict terms of Manovich, or the loose pragmatics of general practice. At some stage in the writing, Joyce made use of Internet affordances, perhaps to research locations, check addresses, maybe to troll for inspiration and narrative leads. *Was* is thus genuinely "a novel of internet."

Our flarfical project was conceived as a form of engagement with this self-described trans-medial hybrid. The scheme was hatched through a process of inquiry. First we asked the obvious question, *what is a novel of Internet* (or in the novel's own polyglossia, *Was ist)*? Then we asked the object-ontological or New Aesthetic question, *How does a novel of Internet see the world?* Which, to my mind at least, brought us to our most promising query: *What does a novel of Internet want?* On the assumption that a novel of Internet wants company—desires, that is, to be part of an extended, continuing discourse—we undertook to extend Joyce's terms permutationally, and produce *poems of Internet of novel*, which describes the high-level constraint or concept under which we operated. A poem of Internet of novel is a flarfical composition beginning from a search term found in the novel of Internet.

If this procedure seems decidedly loopy, you have grasped its essence. We operated in a system or network of feedback loops, out of which we generated states (poems) as interfaces to the common database. In some very rare cases this was the same database (body of Internet materials) from which certain phrasings in *Was* originally emerged. In other cases, we were simply feeding back, and then upon, the same ever-expanding ocean of language in which we all swim, not so much against as within the stream, having long ago abandoned boat or ship.

SHAPE THROUGH SEAMING

To the main business, then, which is the promised attempt at interpretation, focusing on the first lines of Sullivan's (2012) poem:

> Do you remember where you were on that January night
> when blue lights and a girl in a long white dress made history?

and also the two stanzas at the end of the selection:

> Legend has it that a dancing blue light
> gave the figure shape through seaming.

> You know, there's always something
> about history swinging like a pendulum.

It would no doubt be possible, even for a dimmer intellect than Perloff's, to construct a reasonably close reading of Sullivan's blue lights, which do indeed seem to illuminate at least the current excerpt, which is about a third of the poem as a whole. As will happen in lyrics, perhaps especially those of the flarf kind, there is pronounced semiotic or ontological drift, a riptide of signified under signifier. Perhaps the initial reference is to something uncanny or supernatural, alien encounter or ghostly visitation. Later on, there is at least the implied glow of a TV screen, as the boots of Apollo astronauts surreally kick up "Scoutmaster Randy Deavers" while bouncing over the face of the moon. Finally, "a dancing blue light" gives "the figure shape through seaming," which phrase offers a hanging fastball at which no critic in any league could resist a nice, fat swing, seeing here a most fetching metaphor for the poem itself and its chimerical, patchwork process of composition. Yes indeed, there's always something about swinging, or history as it swings, reliably like a pendulum.

LIFT THIS END

So how do blue lights and (our new motto), Shape Through Seaming, confer any difference, or edge of superiority, against the green light of literary progress that Perloff finds in *Traffic*? Taken as just read, they may not. After all, the interpretation presented here is based on fifteen of fifty-seven lines, chosen by me with the same sort of undisciplined yet order-seeking intuition that no doubt guided Sullivan's selection and arrangement of the lines themselves. In an important sense, this reading rests on a tissue of pure contingency, as does Perloff's Gatsby getaway. It's fun and gratifying, and gives me an excuse to admire the work of a young appropriationist with first-rate skills. None of these observations change the fact that the phrase is also an accident, and less an act than an exercise of interpretation: a piece of interpretive *play*.

If we understand "The child was never found" as *simply* a poem, an object fixed on a particular page or a certain Web address, we lock ourselves into a decidedly closed circuit, or the backward-facing posture of a fundamentally repetitive *arrière garde*. To escape this position—and, hopefully, the all-too-Prussian scenario of guards and salients—it is necessary to reintroduce Perloff's key term, *difference*. What is the difference between Sullivan's poem and Goldsmith's, and between what I take to be Perloff's lapse and my own clownish fall?

We might begin the distinction with "materiality and medium," as both Perloff and the cyber-formalists suggest. It is at least initially a matter of textual ontology and mechanism. Though *Traffic* and *Was* are both part of "poetry by other means," both to some extent citational texts, they are hardly identical. *Traffic* is in a sense a singular (if not "unit") operation, defining its concept by exhaustion. As Johnson said of *Paradise Lost*, none ever wished it longer than it is (Piozzi 1974: 286). Probably few would see the need to repeat similar concepts at similar length. Many readers might say the same for Joyce's "novel of internet," but again, some might find in its dance-around-the-planet attention deficit (the opposite, in a way, of Goldsmith's universal recording impulse) an invitation to further play. *Was* is largely a work of lacunae and withholdings, and some people find such architectures stimulating.

Drawing on Gregory Ulmer's latest update of heuretics or Internet invention, Jan Rune Holmevik (2012) identifies this participatory impulse with *Chora*, "the generative game space in which Being and Becoming melt together through what Aarseth called . . . ergodic activity" (21). Operating with full affordances, both technical and conceptual, of computation and networks, the poem of Internet of novel occupies something very like this space. Properly understood, it is not simply an object of reading, but itself something put in place of a reading, or dispositive interpretation, of Joyce's "novel of internet." It is not an end but a means, or a discourse-extension.

The desires of a novel of Internet, or a poem of Internet of novel, are not the imperatives of earlier forms. No doubt "The child was never found" can be read, perhaps inevitably must be read, in the finest traditions of critical baseball, humanist pastime of times past. If we must have a thematic reading, consider that blue light as a specter haunting present-day poetics. However, the poem as choric procedure overflows this minimal contour—or lifts itself by its own end. It demands to be recognized as an interface to a database, and thus *one among a plenitude of possible interfaces*. Chora is a place of both being and becoming.

Any text "of Internet" asks more than interpretation; it also at least implies, and perhaps incites, recirculation and reengagement. To say this is to some degree to assert, no doubt *en arrière*, Barthes's notion of *texte scriptible*. Crucially, the poem of Internet of novel is also something more—we might say *texte transcriptible*—precisely because it is *something less*, only one state or evocation of the interface in process. It is not simply and finally a summary of its procedures. It is static text, but the text is unthinkable without certain dependencies and mechanisms.

Properly understood within its context—words which of course invite downpours of doubt—the poem of Internet of novel intends no definitive reading either of the novel of Internet, or even of its own source material, but simply instantiates a certain procedure, not definitively or exhaustively, but in the choric sense of unfolding. The poem of Internet of novel is a compound conception. It is not first-order flarf, but poetic finding in dialogue with another at least partly appropriative text, a tributary stream that points (and feeds) back to its source. Sullivan's poem is not meant to demonstrate and exhaust a proposition, but to extend a discursive practice, a loose approximation to Holmevik's "game."

So long as "The child was never found" remains duly attached to its provenance—and I say again, that is an ominous stipulation—it might arguably be harder to take from this text the sort of misstep that I think Perloff suffers when racing to catch her light. The referentiality of the poem as reprocessed-reprocessing inscribes a conceptual architecture that escapes the closed, before-behind loop of historicism, Fitzgerald-to-Goldsmith-full-stop, offering something more like Galloway's (2004: 32) numinous diagram of our times, the distributed-network graph. Its circulations do not converge; they continue.

The spectral shift from green to blue is arbitrary, accidental, but also definitive. The blue light in Sullivan's poem is the sign of "Shape Through Seaming" (remember, she did not invent that phrase), signifying the endless, corvic work of Googlemena, searching-muse of the finder-poet, who cannot resist diving down to pick up shining things. It is indeed also the blue beacon of this desktop, burning at the edge of vision, indicating ongoing flow of current and waves, photons out, electrons back. The circuit is really more open than closed. In this dissipative economy, energy is liberated and consumed. Out of this activity comes, on rare occasions, a Web search, a series of links, a gathering of texts: ultimately, a poem. The poem is static but implies an active interface. It is always incomplete. Interface is useless without its database, and even when assembled, this system is itself unfinished. It lacks one more crucial part.

Ontological mechanisms have no meaning without human effort and attention—at least if you are one of those horrible, old correlationists. This personal enterprise implies a meeting of minds, or community. Communities have a constant need to define themselves, enacting identity at the swinging door of belonging and exclusion. Passing through the door, we lift things up, or carry them away without paying. Eventually we must set them down again, and so identify and perhaps occupy a position.

Points of rest or placement can be hard to find. Does the poem of Internet of novel belong to electronic literature? Could the novel of Internet also belong? Before pushing out the perimeter of identity, remember that these texts pose a significant problem: their need for contextualization creates a gap of assurance across which great, galvanic sparks of criticism must inevitably leap. Call it a matter of colophony. If I skip over the paratextual frame of Mohammad's "**Artist's Statement**"—and have somehow never seen a blog or a Twitter stream—I may assume it is nothing more than a nasty political screed. Likewise, without due notice that "The child was never found" belongs to an ongoing experiment in transcriptibility, I could legitimately treat it, too, as a conventional lyric. An interface to a database can never be properly represented by a single state; misrepresentation and misreading are much more likely.

Maybe we should therefore hold all writings-of-Internet at the border, letting them form an existential buffer between core and cortical formations. Whether they represent flarf, double-flarf, or N-tuple flarf, verses on a page can always be mistaken for something less than the contingent, playful process from which they arose, and in which they may aspire to be remembered. The poem of Internet of novel is neither first-order flarf nor first-order cybertext. It is indeed dangerously mistakable for older and very different forms of writing. Perhaps this weakness should rule it out of more stringent discussions, and limit its value to limit cases.

On the other hand, maybe such exclusiveness is nothing more than scarecrow, straw man, or other imaginary problem, foisted in this chapter on a community that is actually quite generous with its distinctions. For sure, strictures of identity seem less and less tenable in these light-fingered, end-lifting times. Why not begin to see practices of electronic writing, variously considered, as (perversely) "Chomskyan" performances within the language space of new media? If we resist this turn, even as we see all writing bathed in the aura of the digital, will we ultimately find *electronic literature* itself less interface than state?

Things look different in a cool blue light.

SOURCES CITED

Andrews, Jim. "A Short Video about *Aleph Null*." *Netpoetic*, August 3, 2012, http://www.netpoetic.com/2012/08/a-short-video-about-aleph-null/. October 10, 2012.

Benjamin, Walter. *The Arcades Project*. Cambridge, MA: Harvard University Press, 1999.

Bernstein, Charles. "The Flarf Files." *Electronic Poetry Center*. State University of New York at Buffalo. August 2003, http://epc.buffalo.edu/authors/bernstein/syllabi/readings/flarf.html. October 30, 2012.

Carpenter, J. R. *Generation[s]*. Vienna: Traumawien, 2010.

Eskelinen, Markku. *Cybertext Poetics: The Critical Landscape of New Media Theory*. London: Continuum, 2012.

Funkhouser, Christopher. "Digital Poetry: A Look at Generative, Visual, and Interconnected Possibilities in Its First Four Decades." In *A Companion to Digital Literary Studies*, edited by R. Siemens and S. Schreibman. London: Basil Blackwell, 2007, pp. 318–35.

Galloway, Alexander. *Protocol: How Control Exists after Decentralization*. Cambridge: MIT Press, 2004.

Goldsmith, Kenneth. *Traffic*. New York: Make Now Press, 2007.

Hall, Lane et al. *Overpass Light Brigade*. November, 2011. http://www.overpasslightbrigade.org. October 30, 2012.

Holmevik, Jan Rune. *Inter/vention: Free Play in the Age of Electracy*. Cambridge: MIT Press, 2012.

Howe, Daniel C. “RiTa: A Software Toolkit for Generative Literature.” *Rednoise*. Undated. http://www.rednoise.org/rita/. October 30, 2012.

Jonze, Spike. *Being John Malkovich*. New York: Gramercy Pictures, 1999.

Joyce, Michael. *Was: annales nomadiques, a novel of internet*. Tuscaloosa: Fiction Collective 2, 2007.

Joyce, Michael. Personal correspondence. September 21, 2011.

Lévy, Pierre. *Cyberculture*. Minneapolis: University of Minnesota Press, 2001.

Manovich, Lev. *The Language of New Media*. Cambridge: MIT Press, 2001.

Marx, William, ed. *Les arriére-gardes aux xxe siècle*. Paris: Presses universitaires de France, 2004.

Mohammad, K. Silem. *The Front*. New York: Roof Books, 2009.

Montfort, Nick. “Who Grabbed My Gorge?” *Pole Position*. July 26, 2011. http://nickm.com/post/2011/07/who-grabbed-my-gorge/. October 30, 2012.

Montfort, Nick, and Stephanie Strickland. “Sea and Spar Between.” *Dear Navigator*. School of the Art Institute of Chicago. Winter 2012. http://blogs.saic.edu/dearnavigator/winter2010/nick-montfort-stephanie-strickland-sea-and-spar-between/. October 30, 2012.

Perloff, Marjorie. *Unoriginal Genius: Poetry by Other Means in the New Century*. Chicago: University of Chicago Press, 2010.

Piozzi, Hester Lynch. *Anecdotes of the Late Samuel Johnson, LL. D.* CUP Archive, 1974.

Rinne, Cia. “archives zaroum.[online].[cited: 25.9. 2015].” 2008.

Shklovsky, Victor. *Theory of Prose*. Translated by Benjamin Sher. New York: Dalkey Archive Press, 1991.

Sullivan, Rachael. “The Child Was Never Found.” Unpublished poem. 2012.

CHAPTER FOUR

The Advent of Aurature and the End of (Electronic) Literature

JOHN CAYLEY

Aurature. Linguistic work valued for lasting artistic merit that has been expressed in the support media of aurality.

—Based on the *OED* definition of "literature"

Aurality may be understood either as the entirety of distinguishable, culturally implicated sonic phenomena or, more narrowly and with specific regard to aurature, as the entirety of linguistically implicated sonic phenomena.

Aurature must be distinguished from oral literature (in orality or oral culture), for at least two reasons. In the first place, to emphasize that aurature comes to exist more on the basis of its being heard and interpreted rather than on the circumstances of its production (by a mouth or speaking instrument) and secondly, for historical reasons, because contemporary digital audio recording, automatic speech recognition and automatic speech synthesis technologies fundamentally reconfigure—in their cumulative amalgamation—the relationship between linguistic objects in aurality and the archive of cultural practice. Whereas, during the literally pre-historic period before writing (before there were linguistic objects as persistent visual traces), essential affordances of the archive were denied to oral culture, in principle, the digitalization of the archive allows aurature to be both created and appreciated with all the historical affordances and the cultural potentialities of literature.

This is the currently proposed definition of aurature that most concerns us, but it would be quite appropriate for the term to be applied to the entirety of recordable linguistic practices in aurality, including documentary as opposed to artistic practices, for example—by analogy with literature as it is applied with respect to visually supported linguistic cultural practices.

Means and ends. The actual ends of "electronic literature" are implied by a name that embraces its supposed means. "Electronic" refers to means in a way that is well understood but promotes quite specific means as the essential attribute of a cultural phenomenon, a phenomenon that was once new, a new kind of literature, a new teleology for literary practice, an "end" of literature having its own ends, the end of electronic literature in its means, misdirected ends justified by misappropriated means.

This chapter consists of two parts, the first concerned with new potentialities for works of digital language art, followed by what may be read as a separate essay containing distinct but related arguments which engage a philosophy of language and concern themselves, specifically, with the medium of linguistic art and with the contemporary digitalization of language's support media. If there is a thread running through these discussions, it relates to reading and its evolving cultures. We will keep returning to practices of reading because, to state it clearly, reading—I will develop this special use of "reading" throughout—is constitutive of language. We may argue about how and what we read, but it is nonetheless axiomatic: no reading, no language. If there is no reading that we can acknowledge as such, then we have reached the end of all literature, and electronic literature may have helped to get us there.

The reading of electronic literature emerged in discursive contexts that were inclined to believe that what was "electronic" about this configuration introduced an all but infinite and indeterminate range of new potentialies for literature that became notable as of the mid-1990s. Since then, the myth of computational media's indeterminacy, openness, and freedom has, however, become just that, still affectively powerful, but merely a story from the hyper-distant recent past. The actual world of computation within which we now dwell has an architecture that is as substantial and determinative as that of bricks and mortar. It may be, technically, "softer," but capital and power and influence—I call their totalizing amalgamation Big Software—are required in equal measure—relative to the age of print—in order to effect change on a scale commensurate with, for example, urban planning, large corporate operations, or, crucially, the creation and maintenance of institutions of any moment.

The crucial sociopolitical and economic contexts for this terrifying change have been signaled and set out by, among others, McKenzie Wark (2004, 2015), David Golumbia (2009), and Bernard Stiegler (2010a). A literature of engaged, scholarly critique surrounding these issues is maturing steadily and will be important to scholars and practitioners who are preparing (for) the end(s) of electronic literature. As Wark suggests—to outline, very briefly, my own current reading of this literature—there is now an emergent if not established class of vectoralists. These are chiefly corporate powers and are relatively unregulated because they are network-enabled, transnational, and, by definition, representative of a paradigm shift in the structures of polity. Vectoralism operates within what Golumbia (2009: 9), following N. Katherine Hayles, calls the "regime of computation" and in accordance with certain of its questionable assumptions. In the post–Second World War period a more or less reductive and scientistic approach to brain, mind, behavior, and hence to culture at large, grew out of research on cybernetics and information, an approach that tends to foreclose, in Golumbia's view, more progressive engagements with social and political issues, and now does so in terms of what some more popular commentators describe as "solutionism" (e.g., Morozov 2013). Vectoralists—glossed as society's computationally enabled, network service providers of solutions to everything—are a new ruling class which exploits the productive labor of a co-emergent class of "hackers." For Wark (2004, 2015), networked computation situates human life as also within a "third nature" that is constituted by flows of information. These may be "hacked" to generate vectors of cultural and commercial interest. Vectoralist power has succeeded swiftly and spectacularly in aggregating and controlling these vectors. They own and exploit them as a new means of production in the ever-growing attention-led economy of third nature. Stiegler, meanwhile, sets out one of the most telling critiques of these circumstances within a philosophical framework that encompasses a history of technics/

technology, particularly mnemotechnics, as inherently co-constitutive of human life and culture. He discovers us—human persons—threatening to lose the *savoir vivre* that allows us to take care of the vital cultural institutions which are challenged and threatened by vectoralism.[1]

Most commercial publishers are and will remain large corporations, although highly adaptable to the new vectoralist polity. If certain network-enabled publishing "platforms" are smaller—the size of individual persons even—and more independent, these less conventional publishers will nonetheless still need to compete and transact with massive, vectoralist institutions. It is now also the case in developed, networked societies that sociopolitical frameworks for culture and practices of cultural engagement are realized within the constraints of Big Software's architecture. This is true for literary practice, even when the architecture has not been constructed by or on behalf of any practices associated with publishing as previously understood.[2] Escaping the gravity of print culture does not necessarily imply that electronic literature is no longer in the orbit of material cultural architectures—ancient, modern, and contemporary. What this does mean is that the contemporary and evolving cultural practices of reading—what reading is and will become—will be determined not by the innovators of electronic literature; they will be determined by those cultural power brokers who build and control the Big Software architecture of reading.

Electronic literature emerged, ostensibly, as a radical, not to say revolutionary, engagement with the practices of linguistic art. It presumed that the application of computationally realized affordances to reading and writing would demand, more or less universally, entirely new forms, institutions, and aesthetics. In the early days of electronic literature's critical self-consciousness, it was actually existing hypertext that made these demands, and the fate (or destiny) of hypertext shows very clearly how new forms and institutions are hacked into the material cultural architectures of vectoralist regimes. If hypertext was not necessarily *literary*—as such, or with regard to literary art—its early history was intimately involved with *literature* as a name for documentary and archival practice (which of course includes literary practice). Arguably the first true architecture of network culture, the World Wide Web, established the preferred vectors in alignment with which hypertext became capable of operating in our everyday world. That is: utopian, ideal, or rational versions of hypertext were hacked into systems that simply worked, although they were far from realizing the radical, multivalent, two-way-linked hypertextuality of, for example, Theodore Nelson's *Xanadu*, which included a scheme of micropayment for citation that might have entirely recalibrated literary commerce at the same time that it revolutionized knowledge infrastructure. Instead, hypertext quickly became ubiquitous but in forms that allowed it to be realized and practiced, along network vectors, chiefly so as to support commerce in its own terms, and more or less conventional forms of writing and reading: promotional "pages" for corporations and individuals (prospectuses, cv's, portfolios, résumés); blogs (journaling, op-editorializing, opinion-forming, letter-writing,

---

[1] I propose thus to shorthand Stiegler's complex and nuanced analyses even though he does not make explicit use of Wark's terminology. A recent interview with Stiegler (2016) is included in a wide-ranging volume edited by Roberto Simanowski. My own contribution to the same volume expands on the outline here (Cayley 2016b).

[2] Again, there are, implicit in this statement, very serious concerns for all humanists and cultural aesthetic makers, but this is not the place to go into such deep problems including: the extraordinary power with respect to culture that Big Software delivers to a very few individuals and corporate institutions, some of them global; associated, ever-accelerating socioeconomic inequality in general; the overdetermination of cultural interaction by technological solutionist corporate institutions led by humanities-naive founders and super-managers, and so on.

commentary); journalism (as such); and other representations of essentially "printable" literature (in the archival and documentary sense). All other possible and potential forms of hypertext remain just that: possible and potential, or else, perhaps, realized as avant-garde and peripheral experiments outside the Internet's main vectors of attention.

Occasionally, certain network vectors for less conventional, generative forms of literature have achieved a degree of momentum. But will they ever end up supporting, for example, Twine writers and designers commercially, or as prominent literary practitioners? Some of the most important authors of hypertext fiction from the 1990s—Michael Joyce, Shelley Jackson—have abandoned the form insofar as it is programmable and networked. Serious practitioners who persist with electronic literature must still seek the consolation of formal avant-gardism. There is always the chance that an author-innovator from these margins—from among the independent or institutionally patronized experimenters—will produce work in a new form and of a quality that not only demands to be read but ensures that its particular *form of reading* becomes so widely understood and adopted that Big Software is encouraged to embrace and support it. But up until the present time, this has not happened in any of the ways that were envisioned.[3]

What *has* happened? We have e-books. More to the point, people everywhere are reading e-books. These inherently skeuomorphic cultural formations are nothing like what the community of electronic literary researchers and makers would want them to be. They represent, nonetheless, a perfectly adequate and quite distinct platform for reading. In my own case, it is now just as likely that I will have a profound literary aesthetic experience when reading an e-book as when reading a physical book. Along with those of many other friends and colleagues, I can report, albeit anecdotally, that my "library" of e-books is steadily growing and that I spend as much time reading from a tablet as from a printed book. Is this reading electronic? As a form or practice of reading, it is not experienced as fundamentally distinct when compared with reading from print. And yet, it is formally different, both in itself, subtly, and also with regard to real, novel affordances offered by both textual digitization and connection to the network. There is also, quite simply, an increase in the total time taken for enjoyment or self-cultivation that is spent using computational devices—practicing, if not *electronic literature*, then unarguably digital material culture—such that the temporal economy of one's reading has significantly increased its "electronic" character. Readers and writers—to include digital language artist-practitioners like myself—still associate profound linguistic aesthetic experience with reading and writing as more or less conventionally understood, deriving significance and affect from encounters with streams of words, phrases, sentences, books. If reading and writing are to be pursued, and digital culture is also to be pursued, I believe there is a real tendency to feel that one's desire to pursue the digital is satisfied when digital formats are deployed simply so as to allow for those persistently desirable pursuits of reading and writing. My passive linguistic aesthetic ambitions and desires were quite satisfied when I read Ben Lerner's *10:04* (2014) as an e-book and, I suggest, a certain measure of my desire to operate, culturally, with and within the digital was also satisfied. In order to more properly satisfy any desire for some digital-media-specific

[3] Is Eastgate (Systems, Inc. http://www.eastgate.com) still the only institutional publisher of "serious hypertext?" I believe so. In a notable revision of his (in)famous "End of Books" essay, Robert Coover, in 2008, retreated to the position that it might take 400 odd years—as it did for the modern novel—before a commensurate digitally mediated literary form was able to develop to the point where it had attracted the effective engagement of literary practitioners (Coover 1992, 2008).

enhancements of my linguistic aesthetic experience I will tend, therefore, to seek out and focus on works that are significant and affective in terms of innovative form, inherently at odds with reading and writing conventions, inherently avant-garde—or at least new and disruptive—inherently less well integrated with the architectures of attention that Big Software is building for the literature that has been gifted to us, historically.

What do e-books have that electronic literary makers and artists might find formally interesting? Annotation, bookmarking, limited multimedia content, linking, "social" annotation and "social" reading, built-in reference tools including access to the Web and translation, and perhaps other affordances I have forgotten or will mention later. Listed in this way, this seems like a not inconsiderable list of facilities, all of which, presumably, could be composed and détourned by author-makers who so wished. "Social reading and annotation," for example, is a deeply radical inflection of one of our most important cultural practices. E-book platforms, such as Kindle, allow readers of the same e-edition to share and view annotations. By default, this facility is turned "on" for new Kindle readers. The reader's relationships with the text, with the publisher, with the distributor, with other readers, and so on is fundamentally altered by network affordances of this kind. The sociology of reading—and thus reading itself—is changed overnight by a technology that does not otherwise pretend to fundamentally alter the practice of reading, in this case, books. But reading, more broadly conceived, has been changed for far more readers, by such social reading, than it was ever changed by, for example, long-form hypertext fiction. And "shared annotation" is just one of many possibilities for new forms that are entirely within the gift of, in this case, a Big Software architect-distributor-retailer: Amazon. The point is that effective formal innovation is hacked from vectors of commercially implicated flows of network attention. It is *not* created or even suggested by linguistic aesthetically motivated authors of reading and writing experiences.

It follows from what I have already said that I believe researchers and practitioners of electronic literature should pay more attention to the forms of vectoralist-controlled delivery media for "literature" that are, historically, taking the place of physical, codex-bound books. Publishers will cease to print as soon as it is feasible for them to do so. All practitioners of linguistic and literary aesthetics must make themselves sensitive to the media that will constrain the composition of their work and then deliver it to readers. Within the avant-garde and among the independent and institutionally patronized literary artistic innovators, greater attention should also be paid to the actually existing and actually evolving culture of reading. There are examples of successful and interesting hybrid engagements. These are often works that intend, more or less explicitly, to reach a larger audience, sometimes reliant on the existing reputation of an author who is also print-published—certain works by Stephanie Strickland, Kate Pullinger, or Brian Kim Stefans—or referencing film narrative and narrative gaming such as Andy Campbell and the Dreaming Methods project. Samantha Gorman and Danny Cannizzaro's (2014) *Pry* is a particularly fine and important hybrid. This work is a gorgeous audiovisual, multipart book, the story of a young demolition consultant, James, whose life has been shattered and reconfigured by the 1991 Gulf War. As the story unfolds for us, James is losing his sight. The electronic literary mechanisms of the work literalize interface gestures and integrate them with the fiction. Readers must "pry" open James's failing eyes and other conduits for visual experience and textual memory, in order for the story to progress. Delivered by tablet, *Pry* can be understood by contemporary readers as like an e-book or, indeed, like a digital video or like a game, and so it will be—at one and the same time—read and watched and played. The way that it folds gesture into the act of reading proposes a new form of aesthetic literary experience that is as profound and as well executed as anything in the electronic literary field. But will "pry," as gesture, for example, ever be adopted as a persistent, widely understood form of reading, by the (e-book-)reading public at large? This is the type of question that the researchers and artists of electronic literature must always already ask themselves.

Is there something about the contemporary culture of reading, which has not so far been mentioned, and that has emerged with new significance? I deliberately left off one of the interesting affordances of contemporary e-books from my previous list. Many e-books now have companion audio versions, some of them with the ability to sync across reading platforms.[4] Especially since the founding of Audible in 1995—coincident with the rise of electronic literature—there has been a significant increase in the reading of audio books.[5] They are ever cheaper to buy, much more numerous and, because of digitization and network delivery, an order of magnitude easier to acquire and manage. In the world of both popular and high literary culture, there has, therefore, been a significant increase in the appreciation of literary artifacts—in their *being read* I would say—by way of aurality, as opposed to by way of graphic visuality.

At this particular moment in the history of reading, when speaking with people who affirm that they are now "listening" to increasing numbers of "audible" books, one often finds that they may not consider themselves to have "read" the book when they have "only" listened to it.[6] This is an indicative folk-phenomenological apprehension that can be compared with the often-expressed and likely related sense that one has not read a work of literature when one has only seen a movie (or play) that has been derived from it. But the cases are entirely different. Film is a distinct medium and the text of the work in a film version may be—must be—edited and rearranged. In the case of unabridged audio books, one experiences the entirety and integrity of the text as language, identical, in terms of linguistic idealities, with the printed version. Any prejudice against this being a "true" or "proper" reading of the text would demand to be supported by a linguistic philosophical analysis—related to questions of linguistic materiality and ontology—and is likely to prove a function of media-specific, culturally and historically implicated biases.

Coincident with the oxymoronic rise of "audible literature," there is the advent and persistent presence of Siri, Cortana, and Google Now. We are coming to realize that these computational entities linked to the "cloud"—and thence to the research and service infrastructures of Big Software—are now listening to us, and responding with much improved synthesized voices, beginning to approach an acceptable coherence of significance and affect in construable utterance. These voices can also be configured to read out loud from arbitrary texts of our choice on computers and mobile devices housing the aforementioned software agents that the voices ventriloquize. People who nowadays encounter these vocal transactors may begin to understand some part of what has newly become of all the data that they provided and posted, that they have willingly and much too freely given over, not only to market profiling but to the solutionist research institutions of Big Software. Whereas computer voices and "text" generation had remained,

[4] The "Whispersync for Voice" service—initiated by Audible Inc. in 2012 and coordinated with Amazon's Kindle services (Amazon has owned Audible since 2008) allows sessions of visual reading—on Kindle devices and applications—to be synced with sessions of aural reading.

[5] See Rubery (2016). Audible was founded by Donald Katz in 1995. It brought out a mobile player in 1998 and was then acquired by Amazon on January 31, 2008, for $300 million.

[6] Rubery (2016) brings up this important issue repeatedly in the introduction to his book but does not address the question seriously or come to any useful conclusions (as opposed to opinions).

until quite recently, feeble, if charming, geekish jokes from the "AI winter," now many of us—I mean many nonspecialists—have heard of what "n-grams" may do for us and for our culture at large and that this is also an aspect of a widespread, ramified, and very pragmatic, commercially invested engagement with "natural language processing."[7]

With the prospect, in part, of being able to balance out what can only be understood as an invidious commercial overdetermination, a whole new field of technically and algorithmically implicated aesthetic language practice is opening up for just the kind of author-makers who may have been speculating about the ends of electronic literature. Perhaps we will not be able to think of this new field as, strictly, *literary* practice since its medium is language without the letter. As an applied grammatologist, however—someone who, following on from the insights in Jacques Derrida's *Of Grammatology* (1997), has reinvested their practices in a poetic making that is attentive to language as such, regardless of material support or originary presence—I would propose that we eschew any unwarranted qualitative linguistic-philosophical distinction between writing and speech, reading and hearing. Language is medium-agnostic, although the human animal, as language cocreator, is not—with regard, that is, to genetic propensities. Regardless, to "read" is, precisely, to transmute perceptible forms—consisting of *any* material substance—into language. While—in a human-genotypically induced circularity—it is the bringing into being of language that proves to us that "reading" has taken place.

Aurature is the established practice of civilizing language that will emerge from our evolving material cultural circumstances. How and why might the practice of a computationally implicated aurature be important, apart, that is, from helping to stave off or delay the end of electronic literature? The arrival of networked programmable devices that *speak* or, perhaps even more significantly, that *listen*—as a part of the technological and cultural architecture of Big Software—has, I believe, important consequences for literature and for literary—linguistic aesthetic—practices of all kinds.

After Siri and at around the same time that we were introduced to Cortana and Google Now, it became possible to invite Alexa—Amazon's Echo—into our homes, accompanied by much-satirized advertising suggesting that she might even become a kind of family member.[8] Alexa can speak and she also—most particularly—listens. If you set her up and leave her in some common room of your home she will listen to everything that she can hear within that space using an array of seven excellent microphones particularly attuned to vocal human language by "far-field voice recognition." Triggered by her "wake word," the eponymous "Alexa," she sends everything she subsequently hears—including "a faction of a second of audio *before* the wake word" (my emphasis)—to the "cloud" for processing by Amazon's "Alexa Voice Services."[9] The latter is the name for a Web-based infrastructure that, in addition to interpreting and responding to human invocations of Alexa herself, will provide an inexpensive service for any hardware manufacturer wanting to add voice recognition, control and vocal feedback to their devices, without having to build these technologies and services themselves. Our mobile digital familiars—especially smartphones and tablets—already surveil us extensively given our more or less silent,

---

[7] The Google Ngram Viewer: https://books.google.com/ngrams; the *Science* article that launched ngrams into the digital humanities (Michel et al. 2011); an even more vaunting recent book (Aiden and Michel 2013).

[8] Amazon's main Web page for the Echo, and its voice/persona, Alexa: http://www.amazon.com/echo (accessed August 15, 2015).

[9] On what Alexa sends to the clouds, see: https://www.amazon.com/gp/help/customer/display.html?nodeId=201602230 (accessed August 6, 2015); and for Alexa Voice Services, https://developer.amazon.com/appsandservices/solutions/alexa/alexa-voice-service (accessed August 6, 2015).

passive consent, but they are ours, intimate with us—they seem to be our individual business or problem. I believe that Alexa is the first device that we have invited to enter into our homes and attend to whatever occurs—that its algorithms can linguistically interpret—in these spaces that we may also share with other ostensibly private visitors and without any existing protocol for obtaining their consent to this surveillance, always assuming that this now occurs to us as any kind of a problem. And once ever more devices are enhanced and empowered by the Voice Services of Big Software? Then what? Will everything in the world of human aurality be perfectly surveilled? Interventions will be necessary, if only to help us understand this radical transformation of the social and ideological spaces within which we must live.

Alexa can, with the Alex Skills Kit (ASK), be given new linguistic abilities in the burgeoning world of computational aurality.[10] These are called "skills," and she exercises them in order to respond to what she—also in the terminology of the Kit—can interpret as vocally expressed "intents." Now, today, any of us can program Alexa to recognize and attend to arbitrary, even aesthetic, events of language that she believes to be intended for her.[11] And we can make her respond appropriately with utterances that humans may understand, that we can read.

Although Alexa reports her "birthday" ("Alexa, how old are you?") as her November 6, 2014, release date, I was only able to order and acquire a device as of December 19 later that year. I responded positively to the first advertisement for the Echo that I saw, but only began to work with her Alexa Voice Services in the summer of 2015.[12] As a kitchen (timing, measurement, and recipe) aid, Alexa works well. She is, of course, a fairly decent voice interface to a number of music libraries (a "listening and talking Bluetooth speaker"). She already "plays" (evokes and controls audio recordings for) audio books and will surely, soon, be developed to read arbitrary pieces of writing (that have not been previously read and recorded by humans) as synthesized text-to-speech. She is already a widely recognized, if simple, artificial intelligence (AI), as I have mentioned, and she is also thus, of course, an ideal vehicle for the outcomes of the stronger AI research that is simultaneously regaining prominence in many fields. She is a part of what may well be the rise of humanoid and "humanized" social and domestic robots which are not so much invested in undertaking physical tasks (like those of factory robots) or activities that are dependent on calculated movement. Alexa and her like are focused on information management and interrelation, including transaction with and on behalf of those humans that such robots can sense and identify.[13]

The current widespread usage of the word "robot" is indicative of a significant shift in our understanding of AI. The developed-world imaginary surrounding robots had,

---

[10] Alexa Skills Kit, http://developer.amazon.com/alexa (accessed August 15, 2015).

[11] Read this as also or actually: *for Amazon*, for all the listeners of Big Software, ever hungry for culturally formative Big Data.

[12] My account was selected—presumably on the basis of algorithmic analyses—as among the members of Amazon Prime most likely to be interested in a preliminary and, it appears, experimental offering. The devices were advertised at "half price," $99, to the customers selected, marked down from a putative $199, and Echoes currently (as of November 6, 2015) retail for $179.99. I outline these details for the record and to give some sense of the size of the market that Amazon may imagine for these devices. Given that Alexa will be increasingly easy to integrate with home-automation (domotic, in the terminology of Bruno Latour) systems, there must be reasonable expectation that the market will be large.

[13] Jibo.com has raised $3,714,505 on Indiegogo for the "the world's first social robot for the home." (Site accessed, November 20, 2015, displaying the Indiegogo figure.) If there is a "first" in this category, the Echo and Alexa have a convincing claim.

until quite recently, embodied them in humanoid forms, with the robots' AIs inhabiting these bodies in a parody or folk version of Cartesian dualism. Alan Turing disembodied AI but insisted on its relation with socialization and with aspects of identity—his test implicated the determination of *gender*—that culture and theory now characterizes as *constructed* (Hayles 1999: xi–xii). Today "robots" exist on the Internet, in the cloud, and as distributed chiefly to our mobile devices. Thanks to the new Apple TV, we are about to discover that they have also been widely distributed to our televisions, or rather, to our home-entertainment systems.[14] The Amazon Echo—Alexa—is, in a sense, the first plausible reembodiment of the domestic robot. While, as of the present writing, Apple's Siri is found embodied in and controlling (Apple) TV, and Google rolls out Google Home.

A question that I want to ask here—in a context that engages with aesthetic linguistic practice—is this: given that neither Alexa nor our soon-to-be-robot televisions are morphologically humanoid, then why is that we think of them as robots? The answer, of course, is that they make use of human language. Use of language was the reason that we changed our understanding of "robot" in the first place. Robots, on the Internet, are programs that use human language or linguistically framed events to perform transactions, with one another and also with and on behalf of actual humans. Robots read your email and compose ads for you based on what they've read. They write, that is, they generate spam. They build websites to redirect your attention. They try to log into your bank account. They tweet. They set puzzles for you, attempting to find out if you are one of them or one of us. Because all these transactions are framed by language and because they model linguistically structured human agency, they qualify as the actions of robots. In everyday life they provide us with encounters which, to date, are those experiences closer than anything else we can imagine as actual encounters with robots. These new forms through which networked machinic humanoids have entered into our world are why the robot imaginary changed.

Now, Alexa stands (or sits) independently, apart from any one of us, in her own body. Crucially, she is able to perform most or all of the robot-like actions and transactions that are carried out by her Internet-based forebears. She's connected to them—so-called socially—and she uses language in the way that they do. Even more crucially, catastrophically, moreover, Alexa *has a voice*, a good one, with its own timbre and its powerful suggestion of specific human identity. Siri, or the Siri*s* rather, with their many possible voices and languages, listening and speaking from our televisions at first, will have all the characteristics and the same quasi-independent standing as Alexa.

Alexa is, for all these reasons, important for the future of language art. She is the first robot *whom* I think and feel I have invited into my home. She confirms, for me, that some major proportion of the art of language will be made in a new world where the material support for linguistic practice will be as much aurature as it is now literature. The speech recognition and synthetic voices of artificial entities can be composed as aurature, and in media that are widely distributable. Computation and programmability—software—is required for the digital analysis of aurature's raw material, and for the composition of work that is made from its elements. As a medium—of both delivery and composition—it will further establish programming as integral to the predominant practices of linguistic creation, of aesthetic linguistic artifactuality. Concurrently, and as a part of a continuum of practice, a more functional aurature, equally constituted by synthetic language, will

[14] "Siri Remote," see http://www.apple.com/tv/ (accessed November 20, 2015).

attain the cultural significance of literature and displace its prominence, if only because so much nonaesthetic, everyday transaction will also and in the first place migrate to aurature. It is *aurature* that will bring about the final end of electronic *literature*. Happily, taking materially distinct practices of writing and reading along with them—"writing and reading" will enfold all the various practices for the generation and receptive interpretation of aurature—many language artists will intervene and aestheticize an aurature of the future that might otherwise remain constrained and controlled by vectoralist commercialism and Big-Data, Big-Software solutionism.

AT THE END OF LITERATURE

Literature is made with language. In certain contexts, literature is proposed as the art of language, its highest art. We may contest the range and extent of literature with regard to practices of language as a whole, and we may not agree that the horizons of these practices coincide with the horizons of art that is or may be made from language. Performative, time-based linguistic practices, for example, may not be accepted as unequivocally within the domain of literature, although they are, nonetheless, embraced and appreciated as aesthetically, culturally valuable at the highest levels. At the beginning of this twenty-first century, works designated as poetry or (literary) fiction are generally accepted as literature, all but regardless of quality if not subgenre. Dramatic writing, however, must contest its place as literature to the extent that it is readable in a form that submits to textual practices, effectively print publication—taking this form according to relatively arbitrary conventions of transcription and, indeed, remediation (as "literal" literature)—and also, importantly, insofar as it is studied and critiqued within literature's discursive frameworks: within the university or the world of letters. If we consider actual artifacts of dramatic writing to be oral performances of language that come to exist, chiefly, in aurality (as much as they do in other media—visual, gestural, architectural, etc.), then it becomes possible to acknowledge that our conceptions of literature and of language art, particularly in terms of the cultural significance of specific artifacts, are not media agnostic. The relationships of literature with media are historically determined, culturally contingent, prejudiced, and, I will argue, disordered with respect to technological developments. The existing relationships generate aporias that threaten to become critical over time. They deform and distort our appreciation of language art in other media. They cause us to ask ourselves how and why we should value the significance and affect that such work generates.

This problematic—how to appreciate electronic literature or, more generally, language art in digital media—has preoccupied theorists and practitioners since the beginning of the undoubtedly literary history associated with these practices in the mid-1990s. I say "undoubtedly literary" because it is a matter of record that electronic literature found early, if not unprecedented, theoretical and critical support for its nascent practices in the discursive space of the universities (Aarseth 1997). Although attention to media specificities (distinctly plural) has been properly claimed in order to take into account the incorporation of other media into practices of literary composition and reception, less attention has been directed to any better understanding of the underlying medium of the underlying art. This medium is language and its underlying art is an art of language. The introduction of other media—into practices for the composition and reception of language art—has demonstrably and necessarily broken conventional form. In themselves, such breaks render their artifacts no longer (exclusively, traditionally) literature. Theorists and practitioners of the new forms claim that, in these circumstances, literature must change. But breaking conventional form is nothing new, even across media. What is new—supporting the original claim—is some historically important manner in which literature is called to change—paradigmatically, conceptually, fundamentally. Literature needs to become "electronic," by which we mean (with hindsight) that it must come to terms with the digitalization of everything.

The digital—inevitably misrepresented as "electronic" for the rhetorical purposes of the claim that literature must change—is not a medium. More precisely, it is not a medium of interest to the majority of theorists or practitioners of those arts for which language is the medium. There are aesthetic practices of computation and of properly digital art, with respect to which the digital can be accounted as *a* or *the* medium, but only certain specialist practices of electronic literature incorporate computational aesthetics significantly or affectively. For media taken as the plural of medium, the digital is, rather, a prevalent and privileged framework and network for any and all media. These media—color, shape, texture, sound, and so on—are encoded in sometimes complex, structured binary transcriptions that render these digitized representations accessible to and manipulable—programmable—by computational, digital affordances. For media such as these, which are digitized from *substantive* material, digital representations are problematic in many interesting ways characterized by our understanding of significant and affective differences between analog and digital objects or artifacts, and yet there is a phenomenological coherence in terms of the human experiences of these things across the analog-digital divide since they are also necessarily referred to human perception—of color, shape, texture, sound, and so on.

The relationship between linguistic artifacts and digitization is, however, singular. A string of bytes that represents a color, however structured by coding conventions, is not the color itself. By contrast, a string of bytes representing a string of letters and punctuation is language, ontologically, insofar as it is humanly readable. There is no essential difference between any instance of language as it is embodied "here" and "now" on the page or surface in front of you and how it is encoded as a string of bits inside your machine. Its existence as language is entirely dependent on your ability to read it. If you are able to read traces (grammē) of this language on any other "surfaces" within any part of a computational system, your reading brings that language into being. The string of bits digitized from existing systems of inscription is always already structured as traces of language that are, in principle if not in practice, readable. It is not encoded so as to enable the rendering of an object in another medium that *because of this rendering* becomes perceptible as an instance of an object in that medium. Perception of digitization is not perception of what it encodes. The digital representation of color and sound, for example, is not perceptible as such within digital systems. By contrast, when presented with traces of language, in any material form, all the human subject needs to do is read. Any perceptibility (or not) with regard to the material form in question is irrelevant except insofar as it simply enables or disables actual reading.

What is at stake for language and language art in digital media is not a supposed ontological distinction between language and digital language insofar as this is a function of digitization. Whereas it does make sense to speak of a distinction between yellows (yellows in our perceptible world) and digital yellows (encodable and renderable yellows), it makes no sense to speak of a purported distinction between words and digital words.

Instead we must turn our attention to effects of digitalization on the substantive media that can support traces of language and their potential for human reading.

Within the much wider domain of linguistic practice, what has occurred, indisputably, since the post–Second World War rise of distributed computation is, fundamentally, the digitization of typography and typographic design, the digitization of *particular aspects of visuality* that are structured so as to support linguistic practices that derive, for the most part, from print-based textuality. In general and historically, when we speak of electronic literature we speak of a textuality that has activated certain digital affordances with respect to digitized typography. In print, typographic visuality is static, fixed, although it may be spatialized in a number of ways so as to influence or inflect reading practices and strategies. By contrast, even with relatively basic peripherals, digitized typography has nearly all the affordances of print and is provisioned, additionally, with a wide array of dynamic potentialities. Text in digital media can move and change. It's as simple as that. It is important, however, to recognize that this is not a difference in *what* is or can be read but in *how* and *when* it is read. The digitization of typography has given us new expressive structures for temporalities that have the potential to influence and change the fundamental events of language: our events of reading.

Thus, the fact that there is no ontological distinction between language and digital language does not mean that digital textuality—digitized typography—as compositional media and expressive form can be reduced to textuality as modeled by the more constrained expressive potentialities of print. That ship has long sailed. And if literature is a practice that is determined, chiefly, by material cultural formations that orbit practices and conventions of reading, then it is literature that faces its ontological challenge with respect to digitalization. Electronic literature is, precisely, no longer literature; if it is anything, then it is *digital language art*, although currently it still struggles within the gravity of an "electronic literature" that is overdetermined by aesthetically motivated language expressed in the substantive medium of digitized typographic visuality. Even as such, within the constraints of existing practices, the digitization of typographic visuality tends to facilitate new ways of reading, especially less familiar temporalities of reading, and new relationships between reader action and what is read (hypertextual and conditional linking). For most readers, even including critics, literary scholars and digital humanists, these strategies trouble existing traditions of literary reading without yet insisting that literature itself be called, seriously, into question (Aarseth 1997; Hayles 2002).

Throughout this thinking, a particular conception of reading is crucial. I speak of reading in a specific technical sense. I use *to read* and its cognates—in a manner fully consistent with its etymology—to refer to whatever it is that we language animals do when we discern and interpret linguistic forms, *regardless of support medium*. This is not the type of metaphoric usage that obtains when we speak of "reading" a painting or a dance. It refers to the process of grasping and understanding traces of language as such in any medium. In this thinking, once it comes into existence, language is not only discrete and articulated, it is distinctly separable from other phenomena of the perceptible world, made and marked by what Jacques Derrida (1997) indicated as *différance*. Virtual linguistic forms establish a break with the perceptible matter of which they are formed precisely in that catastrophic, no-turning-back moment when they are grasped as language by both the language animal who makes the traces and a language animal who reads them. I call this process "grammalepsis" and I consider it to be generative of language, ontologically. Reading brings language into substantive being as instances of interhuman potentialities.

To clearly distinguish reading in this sense from the subsumed and more specific activity that we undertake when, typically, we visually scan and interpret instances of writing, we could use the phrase *grammaleptic reading*, but so long as we recall, throughout this thinking, that this special sense of reading is equally what we do when we hear and understand spoken language in aurality (or, e.g., when deaf communities read sign language or blind communities braille), I may use "reading" on its own, with the inevitability of grammalepsis comprehended.

Once we are able to accept (grammaleptic) reading in this sense as constitutive if not ontologically generative with regard to language, this is when it becomes possible to appreciate more fully certain potentialities of digitalization, certain anticipated effects on language and its arts at this particular historical moment. We have argued that digitization changes our modes of relationship—transaction and interaction—with the support medium for language rather than with language itself, *how* and *when* we read rather than *what* we read. What, then, happens when there is, in the domain of digitalization, a catastrophic (no-turning-back) *convergence of readabilities in terms of grammalepsis* with regard to the two distinct, if imbricated and culturally implicated, media that support language: visuality and aurality?

At this point we must pause to consider certain relationships between language, its support media, and the language animals that bring language into being—ourselves. Language is something that, to the present extent of our knowledge, only humans *have*. Our species has language (Berwick and Chomsky 2016; Hurford 2014). It evolved to have language in a manner that is still imperfectly understood, although there are particular characteristics of this evolved condition that can be specified. There are distinct, implicated morphological traits that we have and other animals do not. From my reading, I take the most significant of these, apart from larger brains (which may not be as crucial as we suppose), to be: a double-articulated oral cavity and larynx, and a spinal column with a significantly greater diameter. In concert with the large brain size (and perhaps many other factors) of homo sapiens these traits allowed us to *have language* because we were suddenly, in terms of evolutionary time, able to make a sufficient number of distinct vocal sounds—sufficient for vocabulary and grammar commensurate with language as we know it—and because a larger spinal column allowed nerve cells and interneurons to establish the fine control over our lungs that was also required for articulation (Hurford 2012). This happened to our species relatively recently in evolutionary time. Effectively, we have had the potential for language baked into us very, very recently and there are unlikely to be any foreseeable genetic changes in our species that will significantly alter our disposition with respect to language. The point being that we are genetically predisposed to *have language* as a function of traits that operate *in aurality*. If we have adopted visuality as the support medium for particular linguistic practices of what we call "writing," this is merely learned, a function of civilization (Dehaene 2009).

It is well known and much discussed that Plato considered writing to be a pharmakon, poisonous to practices of language—particularly language as humanly embodied praxis and cultural memory. And yet, in its other aspect writing-as-pharmakon was rendered therapeutic by civilization. This is, of course, a grand narrative, played out in philosophy following and reading Plato, most particularly in the thought of Jacques Derrida (1997) and Bernard Stiegler (2013, 2010a). Writing and, subsequently, literature as linguistic practice in support of civilization were rendered therapeutic precisely because they restructured the temporalities of language as well as enabling the potentialities of index (random access facilitated by sublexical orders giving more or less instant access to significant and affective textual material) and archive. Clearly, writing allows virtual linguistic performance to survive—in temporal extension—not only the actual performance of its makers but also the memories of particular individuals who have *read* (grammaleptically) particular linguistic performances. This temporal affordance—hypostatic memory or hypomnesis coupled with index and archive; preserving and conserving both language itself and these other two features—allowed writing, ironically, to predominate as *the* privileged *literal* index of logocentric presence and authority: history, philosophy, civilization.

Putting it far too plainly: as the course of human history and culture proceeded, language in aurality was not able to participate as effectively as writing—as language in persistent visuality—for the constitution and maintenance of civil and imperial institutions. Until, that is, just about now, at this time of writing, in the 2010s. This decade has witnessed the advent of *transactive synthetic language* in aurality. Contemporary computation has finally achieved robust voice recognition and acceptable speech synthesis, all implemented over network services having access to vast corpora of natural linguistic material with Natural Language Processing (NLP) affordances (Pieraccini 2012). Historically, I argue, this is a turning point for our—the language animal's—practice of language in the world, since, for one thing, this world now also contains, crucially, humanoid language and new entities that perform, consume, and transact with both language as such and humanoid language.

There might arise a certain objection to my dating of the proposed paradigmatic shift, in that synthetic (computed) language has played a part in the history of computation since its beginnings, including, foundationally, in the exemplary abstracted scene of *writing* that is the Turing Test, for which the *withholding* (by, at the time, teletype) of any embodied voice is crucial *for the test*, since a voice and body would simply give the game away (cf. Hayles 1999: Prologue). In a sense, the advent of systems that we humans agree are able to recognize our voices and respond with—gendered and identifiable—voices of their own forecloses the Turing Test and marks it as having already been passed within the duration of any acceptable initial transaction. It is the system's voice—recognizing and producing virtual language and doing so *necessarily* instantiated in aurality—that is sufficient to establish for us human animals that the system is specifically embodied as, at least, humanoid, and certainly as having (or seeming to have) something that only humans have. The historical moment for our new relationship with language had to wait for this milestone of humanoid embodiment, in and as the voice of articulated aurality, perhaps also as the evolved return and reincarnation of a repressed aurality. And for the electronic *literature*, that we have troubled and recast as digital language art, this turning point requires us—practitioners and scholars—to better understand what it is that "the digital" has done for language. It has not (yet), as we said before, established an ontologically distinct (digital) language as such; rather it has reconfigured the relationship between language and its preferred substantive media of support. More than this, it suggests that we rethink, and shift our attention to the *other* culturally predominate substantive support medium for language. The digital now, historically, forces us to rediscover the voice as articulated aurality in an artefactual and programmable configuration that, in computationally implemented principle, is every bit as manipulable and extensible, as subject to index and archive, as capable of temporal restructuring, as is writing. Transactive synthetic language is a whole new scene for the art of language in general, and for digital language art specifically.

As we begin to shift our attention from theory of language and media toward new practices of language art, it is important more closely to consider what it is that I claim is happening with regard to language in aurality as it is grammatized—subjected to algorithmically implemented processes of grammalepsis—by contemporary computation.

Language has a singular relationship with its substantive media of support. For V. N. Vološinov and certain of his followers, there is such a thing as "semiotic material" and any sign—in my own terms *anything* that has been read grammaleptically—becomes a token of this semiotic material (Lecercle and Riley 2004; Vološinov 1973). Natural languages are socialized, agreed, enculturated systems that are entirely composed of "semiotic material" in this sense. There is a constrained permeability of substantive things that may be on their way to becoming signs, becoming, that is, actual semiotic material. The signs and tokens of natural languages are, however, always already signs for the language animals that encounter and interact with them, achieving this in a social context that necessarily involves other language animals. Compare a particular gesture of the hand, say. A gesture may already be a sign—it might be conventionally understood in a particular culture or it might be (always already) a sign in a natural (sign) language—but a gesture may also be on its way to becoming a sign, something we don't "get," something that needs more work and practice, to get right, to be able to express, significantly and affectively, whatever it hoped to express. It fails in this until it is grasped, until it succeeds. It fails until it is read grammaleptically.

The written forms of any natural language have long ago passed beyond this underlying scene of semiotic trauma and socialization, to the extent that the chains of tokens of language-in-visuality (strings) enter into the domain of purely formal semiosis—computation—in a wide variety of processes that are, fundamentally, "lossless" ontologically. If you can write it, then you can encode it. And, as we showed earlier, the language-as-visual-graphemes—on paper, on screen—is ontologically identical with any language-as-digital-encoding that underlies it. In either case, what makes the language exist *as such* is its potential to be read, grammaleptically, by language animals.

If we are repeating ourselves and somewhat belaboring these concepts, this is due to the necessity to distinguish—in the domain of aurality—between the digitization of sound and the digitization of language-as-aurality. There is a significant critical literature devoted to the media archaeology of recorded sound and this is often seen in terms of a prefiguration of digital audio recording and transcription. In this literature, there is clear understanding and analysis of distinctions between analog and digital recordings, with important implications to be drawn. Nonetheless, once these have been elaborated, there may be a misdirected tendency to believe that because the digitization of sound encompasses and comprehends the digitization of linguistic sound, it has comprehended the digitization of language-as-aurality. But this is not the case.

As set out above, the digitization of sound is constituted by encoding the forms of a substantive medium which then require to be rendered before they can be appreciated as such, as structured sound. You cannot hear the encoded version. Digitized linguistic sound is no different. The encoded version cannot be heard, much less read, grammaleptically, as language. Any grammalepsis of digitally encoded linguistic sound can only occur during a separate, subsequent process, *after* it is rendered into the world as sound. Only once this process is complete, may the sound be read and understood, by language animals, as language-in-aurality.

In our present historical moment, the 2010s, robust automatic voice recognition is fast gaining currency in the digitalized world, currently to be qualified as, chiefly, the global

Anglophone world (Pieraccini 2012). It is this facility—automatic voice recognition—that enables the actual digitization of language-as-aurality. Evidence that this facility was beginning to be operational dates back to early attempts at automatic dictation/transcription systems, voice command interpretation for personal computers, and, especially, automated voice-activated telephone answering systems. On mobile devices, Apple's Siri was a breakthrough but, for our purposes, as research-based practitioners and theorists, it is the Amazon Echo and its Alexa Voice Services (AVS) that provide the first widespread, operational, free-standing, networked, and programmable infrastructure, allowing us to understand, practically, the effects and potentialities of digitized language-as-aurality.

As a point of operational fact, the Amazon Echo and AVS enact precisely the two-stage process of digitization for language-as-aurality that we alluded to above. Not only does this configuration of the AVS infrastructure demonstrate that the procedures are distinct, it also signals our always insufficiently acknowledged reliance on network services, with the asymmetric balance of agential power and centrality that this implies. The two procedures are separately *located*. I speak to an Amazon Echo. The device, locally and in "real time," optimizes its array of microphones to capture as digital audio a segment of—purportedly—linguistic sound that was prefaced by one of its (currently three) "wake" or trigger words. These wake words are the only fragments of sound that the device itself, locally, is able to read grammaleptically as semiosis: a command to record, until a space of relative silence is encountered. Within the device this digitized audio is encoded as an optimized mp3 file and it is this digital *audio* data that is transmitted over the network to the "cloud-based" services of AVS. "In the cloud" this digitized linguistic sound is "recognized," which is to say tokenized by automatic grammalepsis into, currently, word-sized, serviceable "atoms" of machine-modeled natural language. The details of this process are proprietary although many aspects of the underlying research could be set out and exposed. The pragmatic approach implied above by "word-sized" is an educated guess. What we know as a certainty, because the AVS cloud services supply (they "return") transcriptions of what the system "heard" grammaleptically as *text*, as potentially readable language that is materially identical with all the digitized writing that constitutes the most significant material of networked digital culture: the documentary Internet as we know it.

It is important to acknowledge that this service—which we are proposing as, potentially, of momentous, paradigm-shifting cultural efficacy—does not deliver understanding. This is not the hermeneutically enhanced grammalepsis of reading as it is performed by fully enculturated language animals. In the theory and practice of automatic voice recognition, this is deferred, researched, and explored as "automatic understanding," more firmly in the speculative camp of machine learning and AI. Automatic speech recognition does, however, achieve the digitization of language-as-aurality, which means: language animals may perform in a manner toward which they are genetically disposed and what they say is, in principle if not yet perfectly, automatically recast in an encoded form, subject to digital affordances, that is, materially identical to text, to writing, to all the strings of language that are now humanly readable in the realm of computation and our increasingly predominant digitalized culture. I am tempted, provocatively, to say (to write!) that socialized automatic speech recognition transforms human linguistic performance into literature. Except that I imagine that such practices, for aesthetic, significant, and affective purposes, might one day have no human need for literature as such. Its greatest work will always already—and would not Shakespeare scholars agree with me here?—be aurature.

Long before the 1990s, language-as-graphemic-or-typographic-visuality was already—literally and conceptually—digital. Since the very advent of writing systems, language has been transcribed in structured sets of discrete combinatorial elements. Algorithm and formal procedures of many kinds have long been applied to natural human language in this form, as writing, as literature, including and particularly for aesthetic effect. It was the enculturation of widespread media-agnostic digital affordances that, in the 1990s, allowed specialist practitioners and scholars to characterize what were essentially quantitatively and peripherally rather than qualitatively distinct reconfigurations of literary material as, speculatively, "electronic literature." Digital affordances allowed practitioners and scholars to do new things with old words, to an extent that rendered some of these new things interesting and exciting. But reading as such did not change. Nor will it fundamentally change until the language animal that is definitive of reading has time to evolve. What did change, even in the 1990s, was the configuration of the scene for linguistic poiesis—the how's and when's of reading and writing. This was and is momentous enough, but hearing and speaking go on much as they have done, and the predominance and momentum of reading and writing traditions were and are minimally deflected. Even now, the most industry and energy that has been expended on the remediation of literary practices has been applied to artifacts that support the tradition of the book, of print-based, typographic media—those emulators, images, and mirrors of typographic artifacts that, in English, go by the disfigured name of "e-books." E-books are with us, for the time-being and foreseeable future, but at the time of writing growth in their popularity and dissemination has slowed. Over roughly the same period there has been significant growth in the reading of audio books despite the fact that culture predisposes these readers to an anxiety concerning whether or not they have actually read what they are reading (Rubery 2016). As of 2016, the audio book is not digitally inscribed as language-in-aurality. It is, rather, digitized audio with minimal digitally manipulable articulation corresponding most commonly to the punctuation of books at the level of the chapter or subtitle. Nonetheless, the reading of audio books represents a measurable shift in the culture of reading as a whole, and this development coincides with what I speculate will become the socialization of automatic speech recognition such that the aurality of existing books is or will be grammatized at the level of (at least) the word, and—to indicate merely practices that are already available to certain readers—speech synthesizers are or will be able to present this language-as-aurality to human readers directly, automatically. We will have the option of reading in this newly articulated aurality.

If we can read in aurality then, as language animals and language artists, we can compose in aurality. We can begin to make an aurature that is formally, philosophically, ontologically identical with the literature we have inherited, an aurature that will reconfigure and redefine the archive without in any way sacrificing readability in general or the specific mode of readability that has been established by literacy. The full civilizing potential of this prospect—an aurature embodying facilities with language that are attuned to our genetic disposition as language animals—is only available to us due to crucial developments in digital culture and contemporary computation. Hence, we can affirm that practices of *digital language art*—especially in the reconfigured support media for language as an aesthetic medium—at least makes sense, and may also imply, I believe, cultural and social imperatives. Practitioners and theorists must learn and grasp those computational affordances that will allow them, fully, to participate in, to guide, and to enhance cultural and social developments that will otherwise proceed without their contributions, and risk downplaying aesthetic practice at the expense of what are supposed to be more substantive and instrumentally secure benefits. What we do not want is to remain the electronically literate writers of a history in which we find ourselves at the end of all literature, with no viable media for the art of language.

SOURCES CITED

Aarseth, Espen. *Cybertext: Perspectives on Ergodic Literature*. Baltimore and London: Johns Hopkins University Press, 1997.

Aiden, Erez, and Jean-Baptiste Michel. *Uncharted: Big Data as a Lens on Human Culture*. New York: Riverhead Books, 2013.

Berwick, Robert C., and Noam Chomsky. *Why Only Us: Language and Evolution*. Cambridge: MIT Press, 2016.

Cayley, John. "Of Capta, Vectoralists, Reading and the Googlization of Universities." In *Digital Humanities and Digital Media: Conversations on Politics, Culture, Aesthetics, and Literacy*, edited by Roberto Simanowski. London: Open Humanities Press, 2016b, pp. 69–92.

Coover, Robert. "The End of Books." *New York Times*, June 21, 1992. http://www.nytimes.com/books/98/09/27/specials/coover-end.html.

Coover, Robert. "A History of the Future of Narrative." Electronic Literature in Europe, Bergen, Norway, 2008.

Dehaene, Stanislaus. *Reading in the Brain: The Science and Evolution of a Human Invention*. New York: Viking, 2009.

Derrida, Jacques. *Of Grammatology*. Translated by Gayatri Chakravorty Spivak. Corrected ed. Baltimore and London: Johns Hopkins University Press, 1997. Original edition, 1967; first American edition, 1976.

Golumbia, David. *The Cultural Logic of Computation*. Cambridge: Harvard University Press, 2009.

Gorman, Samantha, and Daniel Cannizzaro. *Pry*. Los Angeles: Tender Claws, 2014.

Hayles, N. Katherine. *How We Became Posthuman: Virtual Bodies in Cybernetics, Literature, and Informatics*. Chicago: University of Chicago Press, 1999.

Hayles, N. Katherine. *Writing Machines*. Edited by Peter Lunenfeld, *Mediawork*. Cambridge: MIT Press, 2002.

Hurford, James R. *The Origins of Grammar: Language in the Light of Evolution*. Oxford; New York: Oxford University Press, 2012.

Hurford, James R. *The Origins of Language: A Slim Guide*. Oxford: Oxford University Press, 2014.

Lecercle, Jean-Jacques, and Denise Riley. *The Force of Language, Language, Discourse, Society*. Houndmills and New York: Palgrave Macmillan, 2004.

Lerner, Ben. *10:04: A Novel*. New York: Farrar, Straus and Giroux, 2014.

Michel, Jean-Baptiste, Yuan Kui Shen, Aviva Presser Aiden, Adrian Veres, Matthew K. Gray, The Google Books Team, Joseph P. Pickett, Dale Hoiberg, Dan Clancy, Peter Norvig, Jon Orwant, Steven Pinker, Martin A. Nowak, and Erez Lieberman Aiden. "Quantitative Analysis of Culture Using Millions of Digitized Books." *Science*, vol. 331, no. 6014 (2011): 176–82.

Morozov, Evgeny. *To Save Everything, Click Here: The Folly of Technological Solutionism*. New York: PublicAffairs, 2013.

Pieraccini, Roberto. *The Voice in the Machine: Building Computers That Understand Speech*. Cambridge: MIT Press, 2012.

Rubery, Matthew. *The Untold Story of the Talking Book*. Cambridge: Harvard University Press, 2016.

Simanowski, Roberto, ed. *Digital Humanities and Digital Media: Conversations on Politics, Culture, Aesthetics, and Literacy*. Edited by Andrew Murphie, *Fibreculture Books*. London: Open Humanities Press, 2016.

Stiegler, Bernard. *For a New Critique of Political Economy*. Cambridge: Polity, 2010a.

Stiegler, Bernard. "Memory." In *Critical Terms for Media Studies*, edited by W. J. T. Mitchell and Mark B. N. Hansen. Chicago: University of Chicago Press, 2010b, pp. 64–87.

Stiegler, Bernard. *What Makes Life Worth Living: On Pharmacology*. Translated by Daniel Ross. English ed. Cambridge, UK; Malden, MA: Polity Press, 2013.

Stiegler, Bernard. "Digital Knowledge, Obsessive Computing, Short-Termism and Need for a Negentropic Web." In *Digital Humanities and Digital Media: Conversations on Politics, Culture, Aesthetics, and Literacy*, edited by Roberto Simanowski. London: Open Humanities Press, 2016, pp. 290–304.

Vološinov, V. N. *Marxism and the Philosophy of Language*. Translated by Ladislav Matejka and I. R. Titunik. Cambridge and London: Seminar Press, 1973. Original edition, Leningrad, 1929.

Wark, McKenzie. *A Hacker Manifesto*. Cambridge: Harvard University Press, 2004.

Wark, McKenzie. "The Vectoralist Class." *Supercommunity*, vol. 84 (2015), http://supercommunity.e-flux.com/texts/the-vectoralist-class/.

PART TWO

Poetics, Polemics

CHAPTER FIVE

"your visit will leave a permanent mark": Poetics in the Post-Digital Economy

DAVIN HECKMAN AND JAMES O'SULLIVAN

We live in an age of "disruptive innovation." Radical change happens to us daily, and we readjust our labor, our dwellings, our social communities, our attitudes, our moods. Change comes from on high and, all the way down the ladder, we adjust or die (or, more likely, are shuffled off to the margins). Of course, theories of disruptive change under technological progress are nothing new. Hegel's term *aufheben*, or "sublation," describes the outcome of the dialectical process, in which past conditions are superseded through the actions they entail (Froeb). Marx and Engels (1848: 16) noted that "all that is solid melts into air, all that is holy is profaned, and man is at last compelled to face with sober senses his real conditions of life, and his relations with his kind" (a phrase which Marshall Berman [1983] references for his extended study of Modernity). Herbert Spencer, adapting mid-nineteenth century takes on evolution to social behavior, is considered the starting point for "Social Darwinism," the belief that social order is defined by the "survival of the fittest" ("Herbert Spencer" 2016). Mikhail Bakunin (1971) sees the impulse for destruction as a sublime political force: "the eternal Spirit which destroys and annihilates only because it is the unfathomable and eternal source of all life," while Friedrich Nietzsche identifies in nihilism an occasion for the "renewal of the creative cycle" (Tomasi 2007). Durkheim (1951: 246) devotes an entire chapter of *Suicide* to deaths that can be traced to *anomie*, connecting them to "disturbances in the collective order." Schumpeter (2003: 83) calls it "Creative Destruction," noting that capitalism, in its essence, "incessantly revolutionizes the economic structure *from within*, incessantly destroying the old one, incessantly creating a new one" (emphasis in the original). Naomi Klein's *Shock Doctrine* (2007) identifies this tendency as a key motive for war and global conflict. The "Accelerationists" see institutionalized tumult as a *deus ex machina* (of the Left or Right) that will propel us toward a better tomorrow. And, of course, there are a variety of institutional attempts to incorporate upheaval into the social order (from planned obsolescence to actuarial science, from insurance to perpetual professional retraining). Michel Foucault's lifelong illumination of discourse explores the psychic and social upheavals critical to the harnessing and establishment of power relationships, a process which becomes inextricably tangled with the turn toward neoliberalism (see Lemke 2001). Most recently, in "The Sublime Language of My Century," McKenzie Wark (2016) documents the relentless churning of capital at the heart of contemporary material conditions:

> The other side of the eternal essence of capital is its ever changing appearances. Change is accounted for via the use of modifiers. Its appearances can even be periodized. There was merchant capitalism then industrial capitalism, then monopoly capitalism, then neoliberal capitalism. There's some ambiguity as to what to call the current stage, however. It could be multinational, cognitive, semio, late, neoliberal, or postfordist capitalism, to name just a few. Note that the last two of these are temporal modifications to a modifier: neoliberal, postfordist. Could there be any better tribute to the complete enervation of the imagination by capitalism, or whatever it is, that this is the best our poets can do? Modify the modifier? Capitalism must be very disappointed in our linguistic competence.

So constant is this tendency that Wark ultimately rests upon flux as the condition, musing sardonically at the inability to imagine a beyond.

Wark distills the predominant approach to disruption in the phrase "this is not capitalism, it's better!" Following the logic of the "California ideology," we can imagine a transcendence by which capitalism has succeeded in disrupting itself. In this way, we have (whether by choice or under duress) branded this process of upheaval, and we now spin it into a pop affect that pretends at a mastery over a game that is played in boardrooms and at trade summits, embedded in proprietary code and massive databases, facilitated in network infrastructures and large-scale industrial practices. Of course, disruptive innovation's subjects do not all occupy the same spaces within the network. To use Wark's taxonomy from *A Hacker Manifesto* (2004), there are the vectoralists, those whose chief privilege is to harness the means of production and mobilize it for their benefit. And the hackers, who create new knowledge and culture, and whose labor is captured by the vectoralists. Some of these hackers are rewarded and enjoy the buffers of neo-yuppie existence, with degrees from the best schools, office jobs, investments, and the resources to consume disruption. Furthermore, many of these heroes are rewarded with symbolic reach in social media flows, a reach augmented by the dynamics of informatic differentials which privilege "engaging" news, concise messaging, and the self-interested slant of the social media business which enfolds everyday interactions into strategic communication. Much in the way that Puritans knew they were "saints" based on their capacity to succeed in the socioeconomic machinations of seventeenth-century New England, the vectoralist class attempts to habituate subjects into an affect which cannot itself imagine its future salvation.

And while the ubiquitous and relentless monetization of everything is so poorly critiqued by those who manage to keep their heads above water, it is hard not to notice the relentless disruptions that see everything as an occasion for optimization—and the way in which disruption itself is presumed to be a kind of revolutionary behavior. Most people know enough to scorn the predatory practices of "pharmabro" Martin Shkreli, whose pricing schemes effectively blackmail those whose lives depend on the patents he has acquired (Chandler 2015). Similarly, we might be scandalized by rumors of Jeff Bezos's mercurial outbursts at Amazon and Travis Kalanik's Uber *uber-alles* attitude, enlightened rage has been incorporated into the ideology of our technocentric culture. As a recent article in *Forbes* suggests: "The temper tantrum has not only become a fixture in corporate America, but it has been central to the management style of many of technology's most successful CEOs—namely Steve Jobs, Bill Gates and Larry Ellison—and management experts say when handled appropriately, this style can even be beneficial to employees and the company as a whole" (Kendall 2013). Perhaps it is this sheer brutality that creates the impression that the other captains of industry are more gentle or humane. Zuckerberg doesn't jack up the price of your pills, he only manipulates your consciousness. Dorsey doesn't run bookstores out of business; he just coordinates the affect of billions with Twitter. And Google merely wants to help everyone. It's as if we have settled on disruption as the new normal, and have come to internalize the logic that everything can be instrumentalized, optimized, and, eventually, automated because there is no alternative. At the very least, it works. The trains not only run on time, they are on demand, and at a discount (for the moment).

To this, Wark (2016) introduces a productive heuristic: "what if we explored the idea that this is not capitalism, but worse?" Of course, a key element of the contemporary economy is to manage risk. This practice is obvious in relation to discourses about insurance, health, education, and investment. But it is entrenched in other ways as well. In the postwar period, massive institutions were understood as the engines of improvement, with media industries providing a level of coordination for the emergent mass society. The scale meant that innovation must be a managed process, with each cycle of development mined for maximum profit, and these profits invested in the next cycle with the promise that what comes next will necessitate change. However, as mechanical efficiency waned and (at least in concept) the postindustrial era emerged, the fecundity of the informational economy (both in its capacity to survey and mine subjects and its capacity to modify and transmit) would allow for an acceleration of risk perception and a management of its effects. The result is that we have seen an explosion of resource exploitation and per capita productivity, while at the same time feeling a total sense of depression. If there is a difference between the present and what preceded us, it is that the distance between massive institutions and the masses they manage has collapsed: corporations are people/people are brands. The difference between risk and its solutions has similarly collapsed: the big problems have no foreseeable solutions/the everyday is flooded with banal "solutions" for everything. It is a severe pessimism about the future that neutralizes systemic criticism and drives us into the short-term, tactical thinking that begins by being focused on short-term gains, but inevitably comes to find cheer in those aspects of the status quo that interpellate us. *This is not capitalism . . . it's worse.*

Under this scheme, the only competitor to institutional inertia is the disruptor. And disruption means not merely to introduce a competing idea, but to utterly crush the large institutional actors that interfere with market progress. This is not Adam Smith's humble entrepreneur taking risks to provide goods and services in competition with those who might be content to monopolize markets. This is a global phenomenon. Thus it is daunting, if not totally depressing, to imagine what you, we, or anyone can possibly do to resist the battle on Mount Olympus. When de Certeau's (1984) "tactics" are today's brand strategies, we must rethink our understanding of the term. The clash of the titans that rattles our foundations is big, it is total, and it is cultural. While we might agree that Anthropogenic climate change amounts to a crisis, we cannot help but wonder if its mythical function is as an apocalyptic alternative to the absolute failure of the present political moment to imagine a future. If we're all gonna die, then who cares if we surrender to the robber barons.

Inside the whale, outside the whale, the whale is dead. In the carcass of the social world, cultural studies scholarship has fallen from the dramatic (if imperfect) total skepticism of Adorno, through the discursive perspective of Foucault, past the working-class insurgencies of the Birmingham School, and now lives as a zombie of its former self through jargon-infused think pieces on whatever blockbuster film is surely going to be "sticking it to the man" this Friday night. (You might want to preorder your tickets online, just in case it is sold out!) Thus, we need to explore techniques to access radical possibilities beyond those that are circumscribed by the marketplace and its preferred methods of communication. The digital humanities, and every other niche organism in the cultural ecosystem, have to decide if they are going to be domesticated or feral. The feral perspective considers, for a moment, an occasion for pessimism about the present in order to permit an optimism in the future. It enacts gestures of estrangement from that which makes us most comfortable. And furthermore, it permits words and our ideas that are, following Wark, "more daring, modernist, de-familiarizing."

As Hai Ren (2015) notes, paraphrasing Colin Gordon (1987), for Foucault the modern state contains two tendencies, one that strives for totality and another that drives toward this control through individualism. Ren continues that "governmentality [is] the 'art' for dealing with the inner link between the conduct of individual existence and the regulation of the lives of the many." It is this disrupted process of individuation that Stiegler addresses throughout his work. Invoking Simondon, Stiegler (2014: 45) explains, "Individuation is conceived as a *process* which is always *both psychic and collective*—where *I* and *we* are therefore two aspects of the same process" (emphasis in the original). To Simondon's formula, he adds the "*technical system*" as a framework that coordinates the psychic and collective dimensions on individuation in space and time, that is, in culture (51). It is in "hyper-industrialization" that Stiegler finds a culprit for the dual tendency toward top-down management of subjects and the ideal of individualism that manages to reproduce hegemony under the auspices of free expression.

A key to understanding this, both the idea of industrialized culture from Stiegler and the notion of governmentality from Foucault is the way that power produces ways of being that are adopted by subjects within what Deleuze (1992) called the "control society." Ren (2015) explains: "In distinction from Weber's life conduct, that is inseparable from the economy, Foucault's "technologies of the self" are based on both the productive operation of power and on expert "know-how" (*savoir*). Technologies of the self may be developed and used for self-formation: knowing one's self and making one's self knowable." Advancing this distinction further, Stiegler introduces the difference between *savoir-faire* (know how) and *savoir-vivre* (knowing how to live), suggesting that the "dis-integrated" societies reproduce cultural knowledge as "know how" or advice on personal conduct, which is to say, cultural knowledge is replaced by instrumental knowledge. The social is converted to a series of transactions, beyond which, it is difficult to imagine anything resembling *savoir-vivre*. Turning back to Wark's *Hacker Manifesto*, Stiegler (2011: 57) suggests that it is the hacker's potential to create externalities to this sociocultural trap: "the reconstitution of positive externalities and the support of work practices stemming from *otium* (that is, from noetic intermittence) is the necessary condition for the reconstitution of long circuits of transindividuation."

To clarify, classic approaches to high and low culture, fine arts and the popular, have mutated. The fundamental categories have remained static (insofar as we bother to distinguish between elite taste and mass taste), while our thinking about them has changed (drifting away from tangible commodities and toward discourse itself). Formally, we fall back upon the old association of "high culture" with the rarified aura of the classically conceived objet d'art crafted under the auspices of inherited concepts of aesthetic practices. These objects are positioned opposite the ubiquitous artifacts associated with mass culture, and often they are framed as "democratic." However, simple ubiquity is not enough to make a popular item good. Within the flows of digital media, taste persists. Pierre Bourdieu's (1984: 6) observation that "taste classifies, and it classifies the classifier" remains as relevant as it ever has, even if the markers of distinction no longer cling to vestiges of bourgeois status around which his observations circulate. Instead, the capacity for classification lives in Manuel Castell's (1996) "space of flows" and Paul Virilio's (1986) "dromosphere," with selectivity expressed as the ability to manage status: today, bourgeois class identities are increasingly less about access to and correct interpretation of rarefied commodities than access to networks, narratives, and cultural currencies. The accumulation of material commodities for establishing class hierarchies in consumer circles is shifted toward the mastery of informational commodities, and this process is linked to access to the repurposing of leisure under social media, attention to privileged flows, and the deep desperation that comes with watching one's cultural capital decay without perpetual updates.

This new populism, however, is not an organic vernacular, emerging from the informal practices of the weak as tactical responses to everyday conditions. Rather, it gentrifies affect along prescribed vectors that exist in mediated spaces. Distinction is expressed through a multitude of microscopic ventriloquisms that ride along sculpted paths of attention. Hashtags, clickbait, and viral phenomena animate everyday interactions while lending a veneer of cultural awareness to commonplace social behaviors: social identification, the fear of difference, scapegoating, ego reinforcement, aggression, libido, and so on. The effect is to create a system of incentives to circulate an ever-changing array of information within a network in pursuit of a transient status, the more well positioned one is in this flow (through the cultivation of taste, integration into playbour/gamification schemes,[1] access to software and networks, and locative positioning that supports this habituation). In this formation, old distinctions between high and low culture are largely vestigial and have been supplanted by a pseudo-populism that preserves structural inequalities while celebrating their abolition. The embrace of "pop culture" by the cultural intelligentsia still seeks to retain the cultural capital inherent in elite modes of consumption, while suggesting that these modes of consumption reflect a democratic impulse. Even if life never gave you a single lemon, you still get that lemonade.

However, there is a bias implicit in this shift. Namely, it is in substituting contemporary applications of power with popular culture and folk production. From this angle, the consumption and recirculation of mass marketed texts is construed as a form of critical making. Yet, if we understand the objectives of integrated marketing, choice architecture, behavioral economics, elite engagement with the everyday as biopolitical, such thoroughgoing consumer engagement, as fun as it may be, simply fails to achieve a critical perspective on the development of power. More importantly, the ideology that conflates consumer engagement with critical thinking serves to marginalize the theories and practices associated with "serious" cultural artifacts—close reading, skepticism, critical distance, rejection of "groupthink," and so on. In other words, the post-digital pivot from tasteful consumption of commodities toward informational currency retains

[1] For a background on the hybrid form of leisure and work in the digital economy, see Tiziana Terranova's 2003 article in *Electronic Book Review*, "Free Labor: Producing Culture for the Digital Economy." The term "playbour" is introduced in Julian Kücklich's 2005 contribution to *Fibreculture Journal*, "Precarious Playbour: Modders and the Digital Games Industry."

its normative component through viral content. Eccentric or marginal perspectives risk poor PageRank (the algorithmic rating scheme that Google uses to determine relevance). Anything requiring patience and care is tagged "tl;dr" (which means, "too long; didn't read," a passive-aggressive way of swatting away earnest efforts at argument).

To engage with systemic changes to communication and expression, we argue that one can look at the field of electronic literature to find instances of poetics that are consistent with the avant-garde approaches to language, but which are sensitive to the emerging modes of expression in the twenty-first century. Here, we refer to a wide range of practices that are not limited to:

- proto-digital works that make the emergent cybernetic, algorithmic, and informatic processes visible in media systems;
- digital works that highlight interactive, mutable, and extrapolating effects of interfaces, dynamic content, and algorithms;
- distributed works that reflect upon the way that semiotics, rhetoric, narratives, and poetics function within extended circuits of transmission; and
- database, network, and mobile works which interrupt the hermeneutics of media consumption by unveiling their domain of action.

While not all works overtly signal their defamiliarizing approach, nor is it reasonable to expect that the variety of emergent genres will retain their subversive character, it is fair to say that the decision to self-consciously work within a frame, the literary, whose connotations bear such heavy associations with the cultural legacy of print is to offer the work up for a confused interaction. With the exception of e-book formats, there are few forms of electronic literature that are read as such outside of subcultural audiences. Gamers play games. Cinema buffs watch movies. Social media enthusiasts use their platforms to socialize. At the time of this writing, electronic literature is a platypus, or as Hayles (2007) calls it, a "hopeful monster." Still, some works engage in their own monstrosity while others work toward a kind of user-friendliness. It is the monstrous sort that we use here to make a hard case for poetics.

We argue that the fascination with disruptive innovation is a fetishized displacement of creativity and difference onto mechanisms of capitalist accumulation. In this world of meticulously branded superstars and the great masses of generic, off-brand, secondhand, and other forms of low-budget personhood, we argue for a very specific and necessary conception of poetics. In "The Question Concerning Technology," Heidegger (1993) employs two terms for creation: poiesis and techne. He writes, "There was a time when the bringing-forth of the true into the beautiful was called techne. The poiesis of the fine arts was also called techne" (339). Each word contains resonance for contemporary readers in that techne is associated with the technical, or the prescribed manner of doing and develops prescriptive mores for the kind of craft. Today we associate these ancient examples with artisanship, but the modern corollary would be those forms of production which have become techno-logical, rationalized, and converted into industrial processes. There remains room for the definition of handiwork that fits the definition of "techne" deployed in this sense, but it is the orientation of the process organized around the culmination of a kind of product. The work of poiesis also manifests in material form as an artifact, expression, or event that is orchestrated by the artist; however, the process of revealing is not organized toward a specific, preordained outcome, rather it is organized toward radical transformation. The poetic process exceeds the technical in the sense that it establishes a new form rather than simply culminates in the successful fulfillment of established forms. In this sense, the technically successful work can be measured in the execution of its anticipated form while the poetically successful work can be measured by difference from anticipated forms.

Many definitions of poetics hover around descriptive characteristics of generic forms. Ideas like imitation, tragedy, and catharsis prove to remain both interesting to readers and useful implements in the language of storytelling, yet as components of the habitus of the narrative self, exist as cultural constrains and affordances that the artist might choose to employ and modify for their own aesthetic aims. However, we might ask if an understanding of literature can rest exclusively on the technical aspects of writing. Certainly, one tendency simply accepts genre fiction and other pop formalisms as equivalent to all other regions of literary study because they employ the surface characteristics of "literature." It has words->They are in sentences on x number of pages->These words tell a story->It's not true, but you don't mind->It's a novel. It has words->These words don't resemble a narrative->They confuse me->But the writer is a poet->It's poetry. A close cousin of this approach repeats the logic from the outside in: "What do people say it is? Well that's what it is!" Both approaches offer reasonable starting points, but both fail to recognize the cultural short circuit that they imply. Both attempt to answer the question without sullying one's hands in the dirt of canonicity, inheritance, or high culture. Yet it is an entirely understandable mistake if we ask such questions without recourse to history, the archive, historical practices, that engage the formal and the social configurations of the literary in a dialogue with the future and past.

We can see the appeal of such approaches in the age of databases and logic machines. The databases preserve all units without any spatiotemporal consideration to the objects it contains and the software is simply a set of formal rules that performs its process on these objects. Add to this basic feature of the present, the aggregated influence of the billions of bots that inhabit our textual universe in the twenty-first century, organizing our content, interpreting our words, and making suggestions about what we want in an age of informational gluttony, all habituate us to read the world in a similar way. We are social creatures, we can behave like pack animals, and when we see everyone looking in the same direction, our heads turn to scrutinize the common object of fascination. It's not a surprise that we would be thus tempted to reduce the literary to a set of objective criteria. And if we were talking about assembling our dreams from a set of blueprints in the hopes that our dreams would perfectly resemble the dreams of those around us, such an approach might be worthwhile. Such protocols help our letters travel to reach our loved ones. But the point of a love letter, if people even send them anymore, is not the rationalized system implemented to carry such letters, but the mysterious contents and queer words that tangle two distant people into an imaginary, but no less visceral, unity.

This cultural homogeneity manifests itself throughout electronic literature, both in terms of poiesis and techne, through the events treated by digital artists, and processes which render the digital as literary. The inherent contradiction of those instruments favored by the electronic literature movement is that they are aligned with the forces they seek to disrupt (just consider, by way of example, the long-lived dominance of Flash), while nonetheless being disruptive. Advances in computation, particularly of the domestic sort suited to the fulfilment of most artistic purposes, have been borne out of capitalism, an expression of Western culture's "*computationalism*" (Golumbia 2009: 2). This ideology offers a fantasy of "liberation" from the barriers to progress imposed by human societies, while reproducing many of the structural problems of those societies by depersonalizing them, encoding them into massive organizational mechanisms, and placing control in the privileged hands of administrators. Lev Manovich (2003) traces the origins of digital art to the postwar era, and while we might read the development of culture and computation as commutative, the extent to which the masses have control of the virtual space is highly questionable. Electronic writers might well possess some measure of poetic freedom, but this is tempered by the confines of instrumentation, and the processes afforded to those seeking expression beyond the permissible. Even disruption, after all, is bound by the limits of the instrument which it seeks, or indeed utilizes, to disrupt. But there is poetic liberty nonetheless, and at the very least, electronic literature can reflect upon its own constraints, through its poiesis *and* techne. The bots may continue to habituate our reading, but there must be some value in reading, in casting, the bots.

If the digital is indeed the twenty-first-century manifestation of Bentham's Panopticon, then electronic literature, particularly Net-based pieces, are potentially subjecting their readers to the gaze of the watchman. Situating electronic literature outside of this paradigm may not be possible, but it might not even be desirable—for the literary to remain potent, perhaps its poetics must be confined to structures it might seek to subvert. Enter *1984*'s digital equivalent, *#PRISOM* (Campbell and Breeze 2013a), a work of electronic literature by Andy Campbell and Mez Breeze, and "degenerative"/"regenerative," two complementary works by Eugenio Tisselli (2005a and b).

In Campbell and Breeze's *#PRISOM*, readers traverse a panoptic glass city "of infinite surveillance" (Hudson and Zimmerman 2015: 120). Upon entering this prison of prisms, inductees are instructed that they are to be "re-educated," a procedure which is overseen by the "controller drones." Inductees are warned not to attempt interaction with the drones, and to avoid areas where "Terrorist Organisational Representatives may have infiltrated the facility" (see Figure 5.1).

Surface metaphors are abundant: the reflective and refractive surfaces of the city and its prisms assume the place of digital culture's many ubiquitous devices, while Google and

FIGURE 5.1 A scene from *#PRISOM*, by Andy Campbell and Mez Breeze.

Facebook are transposed by drones, the tentacles of control. The "Terrorist Organisational Representatives" (or T.O.R.) gestures toward the Tor anonymity project, a real-world tool which seeks to protect everyday users from surveillance. This work is, at its most essential level, "a strong argument against the systemic stripping of civil liberties," particularly those offenses against liberty highlighted in Snowden's revelations (Aardse 2016: 54). Despite some variance in how one arrives at the narrative's conclusion, the end product is always the same—assimilation of thought to match the preexisting homogeneity of the appearance of the avatars.

#PRISOM challenges the role of the individual, the balance between privacy and security, and the role technology plays in imposing control over all of the aforementioned. But it does so within this very context, "perform[ing] best on a PC/Mac with 1GB graphics or higher/4GB memory or higher" (Campbell and Breeze 2013b). There are limits, requirements, and capitalist forces driving a space that seeks to challenge those very forces. Breeze and Campbell are aware of this—their aesthetic is one of subversion, presenting users with fictional tech-driven totalitarianism with which they interact using the instruments of reality's tech-driven totalitarianism. One can even see the figure of the artist represented in *#PRISOM*'s terrorists, infiltrating the facility, but nonetheless existing within its confines. For any work of digital art, there is nothing, technically, beyond the interactive space—the medium refuses such a possibility. But as noted, this is precisely the value of the literary, the potential to manipulate the connections between art and its space. Our spatial existence operates within a troika: spatial practice, conceived space, and lived space (see Lefebvre 1992).

Lefebvre's (1992) schematic is transferable to digital space, but with a twist. Before any content was added to the Web, the space was produced by engineers with keyboards and code, displacing the organic process by which perceived spaces are produced in favor of its active construction as a conceived space (the prototypes, perhaps, being shopping malls, theme parks, gated communities, and other neoliberal endeavors, where construction is determined through planning rather than imposed through the dialectical movement of discourse). As users, we layer our lived space on top of this foundation, imposing our own movements upon those of the underlying institutions. It is in this sense that the practitioner's appropriation of space "speaks" to their art (42). In the Heideggerian sense of *aletheia* (or revealing), the subversion of digital space requires an engagement with the technical (not as a process performed on nature, as trees become timber, but) as a mode of poetic production. Reclaiming the space of difference within a structured world, such work pulls back from Adorno and Horkheimer's (1972) conception of techne as estranged from high culture practice, and returns to something resembling the preindustrial conception of poiesis and techne. Under the regime of the digital, by contrast, electronic moments of reciprocal ecstasis turn surveillance into art, and art into surveillance.

To adapt Lefebvre's (1992) framework within the digital ecosystem, we can see how the practices of digital artists feed in to the notion that space is not passively rendered. Through an electronic literature's many methods and conventions—hacking, perversion, creative coding—we see how the space that this form of art occupies has emerged. If this is a consequence of "the shift from one mode to another [entailing] the production of a new space" (46), then deep consideration must be given to the relocation of any work of digital art. Embedded in space, and its reciprocal relationship with artistic practices, are all the histories and contexts which make both the space and the art precisely what they are and might become.

#PRISOM, like many works of electronic literature, is precisely that—*literary*—because it adopts a poetics of perversion in a reflection upon cultural practice and knowledge of

form by orchestrating events and facilitating writing within the system it seeks to problematize. We see this in the narrative, the visual aesthetics, the elements of the piece which draw the reader in to its political interrogation. But beyond the poiesis we see that poetics can also be embedded in techne. *#PRISOM* made its début at the 2013 International Symposium on Mixed and Augmented Reality as part of the Transreal Topologies exhibition, hosted at the Royal Institution of Australia in conjunction with the University of South Australia's Wearable Computer Lab. At this event, *#PRISOM* was showcased on a wearable augmented reality headset, coupled with an Xbox 360 controller. The work can now be experienced within a browser, or alternatively, as a download, capable of being traversed beyond the prisms of the Web. Developed through game-based frameworks upon game-based conventions, *#PRISOM*, in keeping with a core fundamental of the e-lit aesthetic, manipulates these structures to facilitate the literary. In such a manner, *#PRISOM* occupies many spaces. When dealing with the politics of the digital space, we are more concerned with the symbolism of that space as a representational, or, what Lefebvre (1992: 42) calls "spaces of representation," rather than functional, construct. Different spaces are envisioned to host different practices, but the practices which occupy these spaces are not always those which were initially conceived. It is significant to note that Lefebvre's work is informed by the events of 1968, which on the one hand was the site of radically utopian outpourings of imagination and the source of deep disappointment in its political outcome. This tension can account for the potential for difference and the liberality expressed in Lefebvre's model. *#PRISOM*'s digital space contains no implicit utopianism in the world it depicts. There are no niches for making do. The only heterotopic spaces possible are those that exist in revolutionary desire, as imaginary ideas (Foucault 1994: xviii).

To properly understand contemporary digital spaces, it is necessary to see them in relation to solutionist myths of technology, which frame innovation as the means to transcend all obstacles—all manner of human frailty, environmental threats, systemic evils, and, even, failures of technology itself. In this light, the creation of the network itself is engineered as a solution to communication challenges, the construction of platforms is engineered to use these frameworks to provide unforeseen opportunities, the remedies to social pathologies expressed in these networks attempt remedy errors. From a critical vantage point, technology is inherently political and can be as oppressive as it is liberating. Adorno and Horkheimer (1972) view mass media as instruments of control, with contemporary society's reliance on pervasive computation only serving to increase technology's hegemonic capacity. More precisely, this notion of "Enlightenment as Mass Deception" carries with it the understanding that even in the early twentieth century, they considered the technologies of production, transmission, and consumption to be trending toward an expressive convergence—aesthetically, rhetorically, and cognitively reducing the social as a mode of control. In this respect, Adorno and Horkheimer differ from Heidegger, seeing the techne from the post-liberal perspective of emergent neo-Marxism, as a logic of control rather than a relative of poiesis. Yet the phenomenological framework does not preclude Heidegger from seeing technology as totalizing and treacherous in the modern world.

It is worth noting that Heidegger's (1971: 163) viewpoint of convergence ("All distances in time and space are shrinking . . . Yet the frantic abolition of all distances brings no nearness") is not without its own treachery. The same speculative framework that allows him to see the emergence of a totalizing system falls profoundly short insofar as it contributed to his identification with Nazi ideology. Indeed, the pitfall of social theory that engages with sprawling, often mystifying, systemic structures in pursuit of fundamental principles is the tendency to compensate by identifying reductive causes, essentialisms, or scapegoats.

In the case of virtual worlds where the code that makes the system work frames all possible actions, technology can only be liberating insofar as it is oppressive. Perhaps digital art has only served to strengthen this hegemony, bringing the capitalist-driven digital apparatus into artistic play (certainly, biopower, governmentality, and discursive framing followed by control, digital analytics, choice architecture seek to convert the everyday into resources). As it was with the industrial age, capitalism propels the information era—the modes of production have shifted somewhat, and the commodities are now digital, but the structure is relatively consistent. Where art can appropriate and pervert the productions of capitalism, capitalism can dictate the processes by which that art is produced, and consequently, dismantle any symbolic spaces that might exist within the digital labyrinth.

Technology breeds new creative and disseminative potentialities—giving the author both a new platform and palette—while intuitive tools open the gateway for writers and creators that would otherwise have lacked the technical proficiency necessary to take advantage of digital media. Vibeke Sorensen (2011: 242) addresses this issue, pointing out that technology "allows for a different kind of meaning and experience to take place," with the important cautionary note that "access to these practices is still limited and exclusionary." The digital space is not isolated from the global socioeconomic picture—in truth, the infrastructures from which creative technologies emerge are arguably more connected to the political landscape than any of their predecessors. Electronic literature, certainly in its earliest days, was dominated by expensive technologies controlled by profit-driven enterprise. An author wanting to use Flash in their work faces a significant initial investment, both in terms of technology and training, which underlines the exclusionary nature of digital apparatus. However, there are reactions, movements, and perversions of this technology which are inherently political expressions, and it is essential that such expression should contribute to our understanding of electronic literature.

Flash, a proprietary platform, was for a considerable time one of the dominant instruments of digital artists and writers. Tensions between morality and pragmatism form the context within which software development, in this case, electronic literature, is conducted (Durity and O'Sullivan 2014). Authors of electronic literature were drawn to Flash for a variety of reasons, creative and disseminative, but such affordances must always be weighed against the cost of placing an artistic work within the system it seeks to challenge. By the same token, displacement is often better served from within, and if the innovation of electronic literature is to be disruptive, then it must occur through a reaction against a platform's intended function. Holding ideological and generic significance, hacktivism "indicates programming, modifying digital media, exploiting computer systems, and otherwise working with networked computing to further a political goal, by analogy with other sorts of activism" ("Keywords" 2011).

The Dead Tower, also by Campbell and Breeze (2012), is a Flash-based work, but the narrative poem is largely composed of "mezangelle," the poetic language developed by Breeze (2012) throughout the 1990s. Thus, *The Dead Tower* is a juxtaposition between capitalism and creativity, the rigid, and the unstructured. While the space is rendered within a proprietary system, it is populated by codework that is utterly unbound. Yet, the poetics of electronic literary techne are reflected in this very content. Recombinative in the extreme, its formalization as a language gestures toward homonymy, but its underlying textual and technical hybridity make it more of a techno-lingual mashup that simultaneously insists upon structure, while refuting order. The essence of mezangelle resonates throughout the poetics of *The Dead Tower*. This is a space in which the traversals are relatively few, and easily identified. The tower, operating as a beacon in an otherwise bleak environment, is clearly a signal designed to draw in the reader (see Figure 5.2). Structure is everywhere—it is a limited space conceived within the constraints of Flash—but within that space, within the computational schematic, there are infinite points of relation, signified by the polysemic, fluid language that drives the disruption—how can there be so much uncertainty in such a certain space? In this sense, the space itself is representational, and any sense of schematic is superseded by the further aesthetic relations afforded by the multimodality of the platform. Its lyrical narrative is fragmented, if even a narrative at all—the mezangelle snippets can be experienced as clusters or in isolation, traversing forward, or in reverse. There is a great measure of freedom granted to the reader, as while the navigable space is confined, it is also representational. The visualized artist's objects are crumbling—resembling the proprietary platform in which they were created—but the narrative remains in a state of constant expansion.

With an aesthetic that contrasts sharply with Mez and Campbell's sculpted gamespaces above, Eugenio Tisselli's (2005a) "degenerative" probes the potential of transmedia poetics through a different route. "Degenerative" is a work rendered inaccessible through interaction, a Schroedinger's Cat interface that is systematically deleted with every visit. Tisselli (2005a) describes the piece: "each time the page is visited, one of its characters is either destroyed or replaced." Today, a visitor to "degenerative" will only see its ghost, an empty space where a message once existed. The entropic decay is preserved in an archive, where readers can view degeneration of form and content as a series of freeze frames taken over its lifetime.

FIGURE 5.2 A scene from *The Dead Tower* (2012), by Andy Campbell and Mez Breeze.

At any given moment, the text is witnessed as a triangle of interactions: The author establishes a set of rules. The reader seeks the work. But it is in the encounter between two machines, the apparatus of the reader and the apparatus of the writer, that the work is constructed (or in this case, deconstructed). Here, the reader does not control, but nevertheless is implicated in the singularity of the work as a series of events that belong, if they exist at all, in memory. Even the archival version must block its function in order to reproduce moments of life in the work.

The surface level of the work, then, documents the fall of human language. Yet, underneath (and remaining hidden, still) is the code by which the work itself is degenerated. A logical question for a persistent reader of this work is: "What is the work?" Can it be found by reading Tisselli's manifesto (2005a) on the violence of panopticism?

> *¿repeated viewing can kill? ¿are our eyes predators of their targets?*
> *your visit will leave a permanent mark. this page will not be the same after you visit it. the only hope for this page to survive is that nobody visits it. but then, if nobody does, it won't even exist. ¿does this happen with all the products of visual culture? ¿why is everything getting renewed constantly? ¿does everything contain the seed of its own destruction?.*

Interestingly, this expression of authorial intent exists only as a snapshot of the non-functional page. The mechanisms by which Tisselli enables his readers to *kill* his text is ironically the same mechanism which renders it beyond reach of readers: "the effect of code that lies within." Tisselli's human-readable text exists only as something that once was, presumably before even the first reader initiated its collapse. But more importantly, Tisselli's machine-readable text exists, also, in this case, perpetually unaltered, an algorithmic code that exists somewhere in its ideal state of functional perfection, beyond the eyes of his readers. We could not find the code. We could only find its consequences.

What we can read of "degenerative" is a document of the work's four months of alphanumeric signification. As encoder/conduits/decoders, the broken "readers" of the twenty-first century, our literacy only extends to the throbbing of the algorithmic drums that provide pattern, drive, and pacing for cultural life. But we do not see inside of proprietary structures. Like readers of "degenerative," we can feel the process by which culture mutates, slides from carefully considered words toward the end at which the machine no longer has anything to say to us.

Elaborating further on this process, Tisselli follows "degenerative" with its sequel, "regenerative." From Tisselli's (2005b) remediation of the original page (again, reproduced without the mechanism that animates the work):

> in the regenerative web page, text degenerates with each visit, but it also attempts to regenerate itself by trying to extract some text from the referring page. if extraction succeeds, the new text is implanted within the degenerating text and becomes part of it. this gives way to a cycle of degeneration-regeneration.

Like its predecessor, "regenerative" is corrupted by each visit to the page. But unlike the previous work, this one destroys its past self through addition, incorporating traces of the reader's Web-browsing history into each instance of the page. Tisselli (2005b) asks (he uses the lowercase for the entire text): "does everything we see contain a part of us? maybe what we see is only a reflection of ourselves. is our own self the only image we can see?" Rather than simply reversing the dynamic of "degeneration," Tisselli directs our attention to the process by which creation and destruction are integrally linked in digital space, specifically to digital surveillance.

A randomly selected snippet of text copied from "regenerative" reads as follows:

Element("a");t.hre_/fon->-----------t> о заправио заправиlor="#FF 000">
olor="#FF0000"> var s = documengiew_ До�*); (fu*cont>* _ ��* �
Большо����������_������ �/-�терком п�ont>0"
э�еме�counter.ya�зроб�ont color="#FF0000">*7.2014/03:05 >/*ont>
�������������, olor="#FF0000"> $(fun00">Last Deca_hadow_-px
-5pe bsp; &> rt ��ки�_ал000"_clor="#FF0000"> ьн�е _�ор-�у 1253 t
(Tisselli 2005b)

Which is to say, it barely reads at all. More powerfully, it offers a mutated text, an artifact of fractured interface. In our day-to-day activities—broken links, 404, the page cannot be found—mark gaps in transmission. More practically, they prompt the workarounds that are commonplace for those foraging for information. One might check the URL, search for the file, or simply move on toward the next best thing. Such is the prosthetic reach of the digital ready-at-hand of the shallow Web. But with "regenerative," there is nothing to work around. Here, the medium is the message. And the message is to make the operations of the code apparent, unavoidably obtrusive. In a world of user-friendliness, Tisselli offers us a hopeful monstrosity (see Figure 5.3).

Deeper than the individual work, the poetic gestures can be taken in aggregate as soundings of the information in the age of networks. A habit in this field is to think in terms of "media ecology." This colorful metaphor for the function of media systems, itself an indispensable approach developed by Innis, Ong, McLuhan, and others, carries with it an implicit naturalism.[2] Initially, the "ecological" innovation offers an opportunity to step away from the individual genius/revolutionary artifact conception of cultural history, instead seeing subjects and their objects as situated in networks. But this metaphor is not without its own liabilities. One being its "naturalism" and an affinity for related concepts in digital media studies, perhaps in turn aided by the cyberlibertarian fascination with "emergence" and "spontaneous order" as dynamic tendencies made possible in the age of the home computer and then the networked computer. The roots of the word "ecology" are *oikos* and *logos*. Oikos is "the house," which can slip between the household (family), the home (environment), and property (capital). Logos slips between reason, study, and law, with the unifying feature being the desire to find consonance between what is, what is knowable, and, thus, that order to which one must necessarily conform. As a result, it is metaphysical.

In the word "ecology," we understand it to mean, broadly, the rational study of any system of habitation, and within the natural sciences, it retains shades of its innocence. As applied to social scientific fields (like communication, sociology, psychology, and anthropology), the notion of a socially formed "ecology" loses its innocence. As a creature within an ecology, the hopeful monster is a mutation, a theoretically welcome aberration that can survive systemic upheavals and establish a new equilibrium that serves the health of the system. Within such a system, the modest innovations of style and design within digital discourse exist to keep it interesting, to drive attention, and ultimately to enhance and preserve its role as a market. In other words, art is largely a technical practice which serves an instrumental purpose. Indeed, it is this tension between the apparatus

[2] Joseph Tabbi (editor of this volume) and Michael Wutz (1997) introduce the term "Media Ecology" to North American literary scholarship in *Reading Matters: Narrative in the New Media Ecology*.

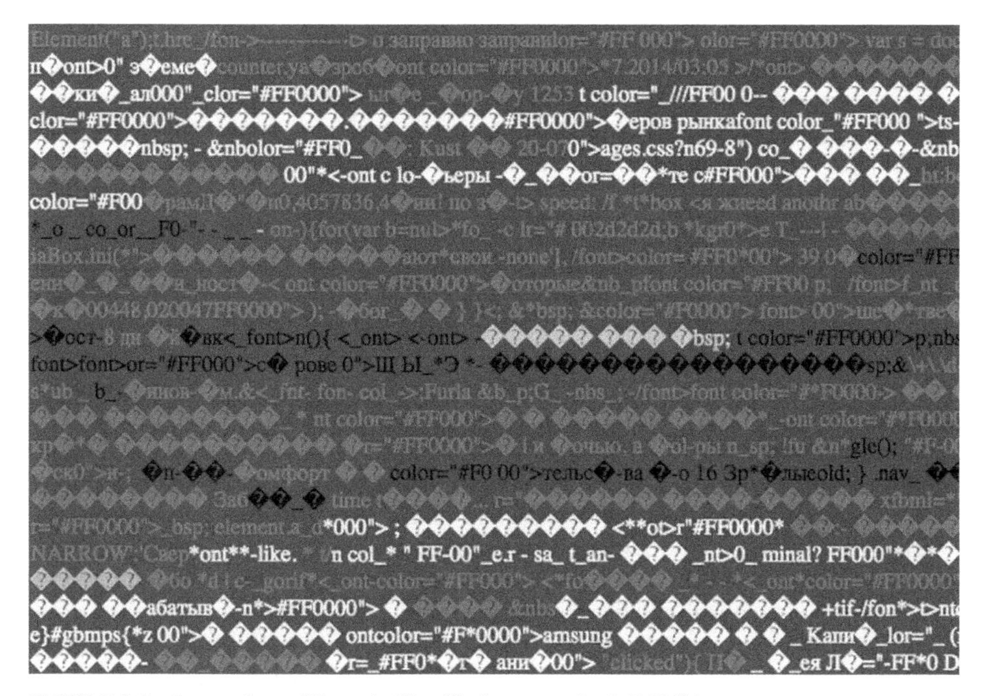

FIGURE 5.3 Screenshot of Eugenio Tisselli, "regenerative" (2005b).

and impulse that Tisselli himself takes up in his November 2011 statement, "Why I Have Stopped Creating E-Lit." He writes: "But what I really need to express, before I can continue creating e-Lit, is that I feel an urgent need to achieve a more complex and holistic vision of what I am doing and reflect on its implications, unless I agree to just blindly collaborate in the vertiginous destruction of our world."

Yet, once the study of human sociocultural practices transforms from the impulse to the apparatus, from the political to the biopolitical, technology extends its dominion over the natural sciences. This is the realization of the Anthropocene: that the planetary ecosystem is determined (though unpredictably) by human action. The term "Anthropocene" is now commonly used to recognize the paradigm shift in thinking about "ecology" in the wake of wide-scale technical transformation of the natural environment. Hence we, too, may invoke this term even if it contains distortions in that it positions humans rather than human systems of social organization as the definitive culprits in this shift. As Jason W. Moore (2013) notes in his text on "the Capitalocene," "the modern world-system becomes . . . a capitalist world-ecology: a civilization that joins the accumulation of capital, the pursuit of power, and the production of nature as an organic whole." In any case, the *enframing* perspective described by Heidegger (1993: 19–20) of the world as a "standing reserve" becomes, itself, nature.[3]

[3] Here, we might say that the cultural frame (the *dispositif*, in Foucault) ceases to function as a metaphor for the power of discourse and becomes inscribed into materiality. This is, in fact, a key difference between human language and machine language—one functions semiotically (in extreme cases, *as if it were real*) and the other operates within a logical regime as a command. As Alexander Galloway notes, "*Code is the only language that is executable* . . . code is the first language that actually does what it says" (quoted in Chun 2011: 100). Agamben gestures toward this emergent reality in *What Is an Apparatus?* (2009).

This shift is intermingled with a second revolution, at the cultural or expressive level: the arrival of a digital convergence. The increasing digitization of all communication at ever more specific levels and its generalization via global networks has obviated the relational dynamics of singular subjects and their interactions. As a paradigm for the study of social systems, "ecology" functions as a simulacrum, a way of *thinking about* organized social behavior to facilitate management and industrialization of resources, rather than a description of actual conditions as expressions of an underlying "natural" state.

Thus, deprived of a world in which "human nature" and "human spirit" play their parts, Media Ecology is an incorrect term for post-digital ecosystemic approaches. There is no transcendental law of the world to which one appeals. Instead, we refer to the declarative law of "nomos." Nomos identifies the juridical power of code and structure without recourse to the metaphysical status of logos (and the understanding of ecology and nature). Hence, "economy" is the appropriate term for the programmed oikos. And against this economy, the question of poetics is reframed.

With this conception of the economy (*oikos* + *nomos*), we turn to the revelatory function of poetics. To unsettle the *milieu* of the digital economy is to create estrangement—to remove ourselves from its comfort or to make its comfort strange: to make it uncanny (*unheimlich*—un-home-like). Thus we can understand the poetic practices employed by Tisselli, Mez and Campbell and their radical potential. The poetic wrangling with systems of signification strives to disrupt the seamless façade of large-scale disruption as social ecology is transformed into economic material. The hope of such poetic acts is to make us live again, to live with each other.

SOURCES CITED

Aardse, Kent. "The Biopolitics of Electronic Literature: On the Writings of Mez Breeze." *Digital Literary Studies*, vol. 1, no. 1 (2016): 40–61, https://journals.psu.edu/dls/article/view/59648

Adorno, Theodor W., and Max Horkheimer. *The Dialectic of Enlightenment*. Translated by John Cumming. New York: Herder and Herder, 1972.

Agamben, Giorgio. *What Is an Apparatus?* Translated by David Kishik and Stefan Pedatella. Stanford: Stanford University Press, 2009.

Bakunin, Mikhail. "The Reaction in Germany." In *Bakunin on Anarchy*, translated and edited by Sam Dolgoff, 1971. Reprinted in *Marxists.org*, https://www.marxists.org/reference/archive/bakunin/works/1842/reaction-germany.htm. Accessed December 20, 2016.

Berman, Marshall. *All That Is Solid Melts into Air*. London: Verso Books, 1983.

Bourdieu, Pierre. *Distinction: A Social Critique of the Judgement of Taste*. Translated by Richard Nice. Cambridge, MA: Harvard University Press, 1984.

Breeze, Mez. *Human Readable Messages*. Vienna: Traumawien, 2012.

Campbell, Andy, and Mez Breeze. *The Dead Tower*. 2012. http://www.dreamingmethods.com/tower.

Campbell, Andy, and Mez Breeze. *#PRISOM*, 2013a. http://dreamingmethods.com/prisom/.

Campbell, Andy, and Mez Breeze. *#PRISOM*, 2013b. http://dreamingmethods.com/prisom/download.html.

Castells, Manuel. *The Rise of the Network Society*. Cambridge: Blackwell Publishers, 1996.

Chandler, Adam. "Who Is 'Pharma Bro'?" *The Atlantic*, December 17, 2015, http://www.theatlantic.com/national/archive/2015/12/pharma-bro-martin-shkreli/421083/.

Chun, Wendy Hui Kyong. "Crisis, Crisis, Crisis, or Sovereignty and Networks." *Theory, Culture & Society*, vol. 28, no. 6 (2011): 91–112.

de Certeau, Michel. *The Practice of Everyday Life*. Translated by Steven Rendall. Berkeley: University of California Press, 1984.

Deleuze, Gilles. "Postscript on the Societies of Control." *October*, vol. 59 (Winter 1992): 3–7.

Durity, Anthony, and James O'Sullivan. "On Reusability and Electronic Literature." *Digital Humanities 2014*. Lausanne: N.p., 2014, pp. 147–49.

Durkheim, Emile. *Suicide: AStudy in Sociology*. Translated by John A. Spaulding and George Simpson. Glencoe: Free Press, 1951.

Foucault, Michel. "Technologies of the Self." In *Technologies of the Self: A Seminar with Michel Foucault*, edited by Luther H. Martin, Huck Gutman, and Patrick H. Hutton. Amherst: University of Massachusetts Press, 1988, pp. 16–49.

Foucault, Michel. *The Order of Things: An Archaeology of the Human Sciences*. Translated by Alan Sheridan. New York: Vintage, 1994.

Froeb, Kai. "Sublation." *Hegel.net*, http://www.hegel.net/en/sublation.htm. Accessed December 20, 2016.

Golumbia, David. *The Cultural Logic of Computation*. Cambridge, MA: Harvard University Press, 2009.

Gordon, Colin. "The Soul of the Citizen: Max Weber and Michel Foucault on Rationality and Government." In *Max Weber, Rationality and Modernity*, edited by Scott Lash and Sam Whimster. London: Allen and Unwin, 1987, pp. 293–316.

Hayles, N. Katherine. "Electronic Literature: What Is It?" Electronic Literature Organization. January 2007. https://eliterature.org/pad/elp.html.

"Hebert Spencer." *Wikipedia*. https://en.wikipedia.org/wiki/Herbert_Spencer. Accessed December 20, 2016.

Heidegger, Martin. "The Thing." In *Language, Poetry, Thought*, translated by Albert Hofstadter. New York: Harper and Rowe, 1971, pp. 163–80.

Heidegger, Martin. "The Question Concerning Technology." In *Basic Writings*, translated by William Lovitt, edited by David Farrell Krell. San Francisco: Harper Collins, 1993, pp. 311–41.

Hudson, Dale, and Patricia R. Zimmerman. *Thinking through Digital Media: Transnational Environments and Locative Places*. New York: Palgrave Macmillan, 2015.

Kendall, Joshua. "The Temper Tantrum: The Key to Smart Management?" *Fortune*, November 22, 2013, http://fortune.com/2013/11/22/the-temper-tantrum-the-key-to-smart-management/.

"Keywords." *Electronic Literature Collection, Vol. 2*. Edited by Laura Borràs, Talan Memmott, Rita Raley, Brian Stefans. Cambridge: Electronic Literature Organization, 2011, http://collection.eliterature.org/2/extra/keywords.html. Accessed December 5, 2016.

Klein, Naomi. *The Shock Doctrine*. New York: Henry Holt, 2007.

Kücklich, Julian. "Precarious Playbour: Modders and the Digital Games Industry." *Fibreculture Journal* 5, 2005, http://five.fibreculturejournal.org/fcj-025-precarious-playbour-modders-and-the-digital-games-industry/.

Lefebvre, Henri. *The Production of Space*. Translated by Donald Nicolson-Smith. Malden, MA: Wiley, 1992.

Lemke, Thomas. "'The Birth of Bio-Politics': Michel Foucault's Lecture at the Collège de France on Neo-Liberal Governmentality." *Economy and Society*, vol. 30, no. 2 (2001): 190–207.

Manovich, Lev. "New Media from Borges to HTML." In *The New Media Reader*, edited by Noah Wardrip-Fruin and Nick Montfort. Cambridge: MIT Press, 2003, pp. 13–25.

Marx, Karl, and Friedrich Engels. *Manifesto of the Communist Party*, 1848, https://www.marxists.org/archive/marx/works/1848/communist-manifesto/index.htm.

Moore, Jason W. "Anthropocene or Capitalocene? Part III." May 19, 2013, https://jasonwmoore.wordpress.com/2013/05/19/anthropocene-or-capitalocene-part-iii/.

Ren, Hai. "Modes of Governance in Neo-Liberal Capitalism: An Introduction." *Rhizomes*, vol. 10 (Spring 2015), http://www.rhizomes.net/issue10/introren.htm.

Schumpeter, Joseph A. *Capitalism, Socialism and Democracy*. New York: Routledge, 2003.

Sorensen, Vibeke. "Rewiring Culture, the Brain, and Digital Media." In *Switching Codes: Thinking through Digital Technology in the Humanities and the Arts*, edited by Thomas Bartscherer and Roderick Coover. Chicago: University of Chicago Press, 2011, pp. 239–45.

Stiegler, Bernard. *For a New Critique of Political Economy*. Cambridge: Polity, 2011.

Stiegler, Bernard. *Symbolic Misery: Volume 1*. Translated by Barnaby Norman. Malden, MA: Polity, 2014.

Tabbi, Joseph, and Michael Wutz, eds. *Reading Matters: Narrative in the New Media Ecology*. Ithaca, NY: Cornell University Press, 1997.

Terranova, Tiziana. "Free Labor: Producing Culture for the Digital Economy." *Electronic Book Review*, June 20, 2003, http://www.electronicbookreview.com/thread/technocapitalism/voluntary.

Tisselli, Eugenio. "degenerative." 2005a. http://www.motorhueso.net/degenerative/.

Tisselli, Eugenio. "regenerative." 2005b. http://www.motorhueso.net/regenerative/regenerative.php.

Tisselli, Eugenio. "Why I Have Stopped Creating E-Lit." *Netartery*, November 25, 2011, http://netartery.vispo.com/?p=1211.

Tomasi, Alessandro. "Nihilism and Creativity in the Philosophy of Nietzsche." *Minerva—An Internet Journal of Philosophy*, vol. 11 (2007), http://www.minerva.mic.ul.ie/vol11/Nietzsche.html.

Virilio, Paul. *Speed and Politics: An Essay on Dromology*. Translated by Mark Polizzotti. New York: Semiotext(e), 1986.

Wark, McKenzie. *A Hacker Manifesto*. Cambridge: Harvard University Press, 2004.

Wark, McKenzie. "The Sublime Language of My Century." *Public Seminar*, May 14, 2016, https://www.icamiami.org/wp-content/uploads/2016/09/The-Sublime-Language-of-my-Century.pdf.

"What Is E-Lit?" Electronic Literature Organization. http://eliterature.org/what-is-e-lit/. Accessed December 6, 2016.

CHAPTER SIX

Literature and Netprov in Social Media: A Travesty, or, in Defense of Pretension

ROB WITTIG

The lesson of network communities such as IN.S.OMNIA is that they become extensions of—not alternatives to—our everyday communities. They allow us to live in two places at once (minimum: two worlds). They force us to realize that we behave differently under new constraints, become different people at different times (minimum: two selves). They show that—through combinations of media, memory, and imagination—geographic zones are already constantly interpenetrating.

—Wittig and IN.S.OMNIA (1994)

Minimum two selves—this principle had already emerged some twenty years ago when I wrote my account of one of the earliest creative social media communities, the performance literature group Invisible Seattle's online bulletin board system (BBS), IN.S.OMNIA. In the decade before the World Wide Web, the "Invisibles" did both systematic and carnivalesque literary projects on IN.S.OMNIA, paralleled by Art Com a few years later on the WELL BBS in California and the many projects in the margins of the French national initiative to replace paper phone books with the digital "Minitel."

The uniform typography and relative anonymity of these early systems gave rise to an explosion of playfulness, mimicry, and creative impersonation. Writers exulted in "doing voices," creating multiple accounts, and waging dialogic tussles with themselves and others in written form in the same way that stand-up comedians and improv actors become multiple characters in a magic show of mimesis.

In the intervening time the prospect of having multiple selves, or a fluid self, has become both monetized and problematized. The "social graph" is the permanent file of a user's behaviors, likes, original writing, and photos that Facebook and others carefully keep in order to sell to advertisers. The social graph necessitates and creates a fundamental unit of the social media economy: the consumer ego.

In order to function as an advertising metric, the consumer ego, as instantiated by the social graph, must map to a single human body, be continuously self-conforming, and be sincere. Above all the consumer ego must take itself seriously.

Irony, impersonation, and satire in an "authorized account" are anathema to the purposes of the social advertising technologies. Multiple accounts represent a loss of individual data and a muddying of aggregate data. Belligerence is encouraged in social media because people go too far and reveal too much (valuable data) and because anger is assumed to be sincere.

Irony, impersonation, and satire have a long history in literature, particularly when new media hit the scene. It is that shadowy, silly history—and its increasingly important power to disrupt the growing hegemony of media giants such as Facebook, Google, and Baidu—that I want to discuss with you here. But, oh, you look parched! First, here, have a glass of this great Chinese tea.

I enjoy a perennial affliction: whenever I see written and pictorial communication in a new medium I have the overwhelming urge to pretend I'm some imaginary character and begin extravagantly misusing the medium's fledgling conventions. Thankfully I'm not the only one; in recent years, numerous creators have maintained fake Twitter accounts, hoax websites, and parody blogs in a gesture that I've dubbed "netprov." Netprov is Internet improv. Netprov creates fictions that are networked, collaborative, and improvised in real time. In recent years a group of far-flung friends has rallied with Mark C. Marino and me to play netprov in a way informed by our love of literary, theater, gaming, and other artistic traditions. Our goal: to see how good netprov might be, how powerful, apt, and helpful. And of course: how funny.

Create a Twitter account for yourself at high-school age, and come mope, whine, and fall in love as we all go to high school together for a month using a hashtag! This was the idea that Claire Donato and Jeff T. Johnson brought to Mark C. Marino and me in 2015 and it became the netprov *All-Time High*. Do you have unused moments in your life that you'd like to turn into extra income? That notion became 2016's netprov, the "life-swapping" website *Air-B-N-Me*, featuring marvelous little videos of everyday moments staged by the many walk-in netprov players. And for nearly two years, Mark and I authored the three adjunct faculty characters (an embittered older medievalist, a hopeful young feminist, and a good-time-Charlie TA) who shared, uneasily, the Twitter account "Occupy MLA." Was the netprov *Occupy MLA* a hoax, performance art, or activism in the tradition of eighteenth-century character-driven pamphlets? Did it, as we've been told, influence the discussion of adjuncts at the heart of the Modern Language Association, or was it an irresponsible fly in the ointment?

Only others can answer those questions, but one thing is certain: being among the first to fictionalize a new medium created for non-fictional exchange comes with risks and opportunities. For inspiration—and for moral support—I've long studied the beginnings of fictionalizing in older media and identified three gestures or practices I think are useful for thinking about and creating written and pictorial netprov in brand-new media:

1. The first is the travesty of *facsimile graphic design* (satirically donning the attire of power) and the pleasure of technologically self-aware art.
2. The second is the fundamental gesture of *mimicry and impersonation* and what it implies currently for notions of *identity*, particularly in the era of what I'll call the "consumer ego."
3. The third is the post-romantic art of creating and maintaining *generative collaborations*—ways of inviting and modeling public participation.

This chapter is written from the heart of the basic principles of my own netprov practice. Most important is the open invitation to one and all to come and play—"play and go deep" as I like to say. Also important to me is my own reformulation of philosopher Bernard Suits's famous definition of playing a game as "the voluntary attempt to overcome unnecessary obstacles."

What motivates games of make-believe—collaborative creative play—is not the overcoming of an unnecessary obstacle, but the resolution of unavoidable and intolerable tension. Like seismic forces in the earth's crust, inner wars among our own sub-personalities with their conflicting motivations, as well as outer social tensions among members of social hierarchies, we find rebalancing in the earthquake of laughter. A core piece of advice from the renowned Chicago theatrical improv company Second City is: "There is a wealth of humor available through status differences and the playing thereof. Realize it and play with it. The changes and shifts that are inherent are ripe for the taking" (Libera 2004). Satirization of status and the status quo through travesty, impersonation, and formal mimicry is a long tradition in literature and theater. This play of mimicry, parody, and satire is vital to reveal and rebalance relationships of power. An un-satirized world is unlivable. For me the goals of each netprov are: laughter, insight, and empathy. Therefore here is my reformulation of Suits, the flag under which I play: *Netprov is the voluntary attempt to heal necessary relationships.*

THE OLD TRADITION OF "NOVELTY"

So, then, let's look at beginnings. What are the two most disappointing words in all of contemporary literature?

"A Novel"

Rats! "A novel." The very word means something new. But that little "a" killed it. Now, you've taken all the mystery out of it! I had a treasure in my hands, a book that could have taken me in any direction, that could have been fact or fiction or somewhere in between, and you've burst the bubble, you've pinned it down, you've spoiled the joke.

By contrast, what did novels look like back when they were novel?

Often referred to as the first novel, *The Life and Surprising Adventures of Robinson Crusoe of York, Mariner: Who lived Eight and Twenty years all alone in an un-inhabited island on the Coast of AMERICA, near the mouth of the Great River of OROONOQUE; Having been cast on Shore by Shipwreck, wherein all the Men perished but himself. WITH An Account how he was at last as strangely deliver'd by PYRATES* was published in 1719, and was credited on its title page as being "Written by Himself" (Defoe and Crowley 1972). The name of the authorized author, Daniel Defoe, appears nowhere in the first edition. Look at that rambling beauty of a title! I use the actual title here instead of the usual, misleading, abbreviated version, to remind my readers how the fictionizing impulse looks when it first appears in a new medium.

What kind of book is *Crusoe*, really? London literary insiders might know by word of mouth of Defoe's authorship, but not all readers did. *Crusoe* was a fraud, then, a prank. Likely inspired by multiple "real" narratives of shipwrecks with which the publishing world of the time was awash and which were commonly, well, let's say *intensified* for dramatic effect, *Crusoe* exists somewhere on a scale that winds from true story through degrees of embellishment and masking to complete fiction.

Consider, if you will, a media universe where you can't trust things, where the technology is always volatile and changing, where everywhere you go you see crazy crackpot postings with goofy pseudonyms. That's right, I'm talking about the eighteenth century! And no time so closely resembles the rootin' tootin' eighteenth as our own twenty-first.

TOWARD A MINOR LITERATURE

Our age does have some new means of communication which are indeed "novel," namely, social media. But what are they? I'm happy in general to use the shorthand "social media," but if I'm getting more technical, the working terminology I use these days is *micropublishing, group, and personal media*. Publishing, even micropublishing, anticipates an audience of unknowns. Group communication anticipates known recipients. Personal media we use to communicate among intimates. These categories frequently muddle and overlap. They encompass a range of communication sins from blogs and so-called platishers (publishing platforms such as Medium or Pinterest) on one hand (formerly books and magazines), the commonly called social media such as Facebook, Instagram, and Twitter in the middle (formerly in-person gatherings and to some extent mass media), and personal media such as one-to-one text messaging at the other end (formerly paper correspondence). In terms of their place in the traditional literary firmament these encompass such traditional (though low-status) categories as juvenilia, inscriptions in others' scrapbooks, and ephemera such as broadsides.

Publishing, group, and personal media have in common that they are minor, informal, interactive, and vernacular. By this I mean: *minor* in contrast to high literary forms such as the holy trinity of poem, short story, and novel; *informal* in contrast to works vetted, edited, and published in major journals; *interactive* because reactions from readers are expected and can rapidly be published alongside the text; and *vernacular* because they are cultural practices that develop from everyday use and are not, or not yet, taught in schools and universities. (Note that I use the word "vernacular" here not as linguists do, but as graphic designers do. In design scholarship it means design done by untrained creators. Such work is beloved in graphic design culture, sometimes with a camp sensibility, more often with genuine admiration.)

Along with encouraging belligerence, micropublishing and group media have always encouraged transgressive and often embarrassing self-revelation. YouTube alone makes a fortune from it. But this unconscious self-revelation can also be used, in the literary, as a disruptive technique with goals that cut against the slumber of denial the great advertisers encourage.

Literary fiction is rife with characters whose first-person accounts reveal much more about themselves than they intend. Social situations where a person is being too self-revealing for interlocutors' comfort—typically with grisly medical or emotional detail—are signaled in mass media culture by the gesture of covering one's ears and intoning: "too much information" (TMI in the common written and spoken abbreviation).

The interesting thing about this strategy is that, by extension, it encourages readers to become aware that there are things about themselves that they, too, do not see. Yet. The goal of this strategy, I would contend is insight; insight first about the characters, and second, about the reader's own self or selves.

These strategies have continued to be popular because they manifest the subjective experience of fluidity and fundamental non-consistency of our subjective selves. Something bothers us one morning and we are fine with it the next. We are not just two selves, we are many selves. This is a comic ego, not the self-serious consumer ego.

Irony and satire, like reading CAPTCHA visuals, are things only humans can do, so far as we know. They are difficult to capture electronically. They embody autonomy as opposed to the docile and consistent consumer ego.

In addition, I see three categories of use of everyday, journalistic, and diaristic nonfiction micropublishing, group and personal media uses: (1) public journal (reputation technology), (2) connection tool for family and friends (management technology), and (3) data creation (advertising technology).

As *public journal*, blogs, Facebook posts, Instagram images transform moments of formerly intimate, solitary life into artifacts for public inspection. Dictums such as Sherry Turkle's (1996) "I share therefore I am" and the common "pics or it didn't happen" meme speak to the renegotiation of the border between public and private. In the twenty-teens we are still in a period where high-resolution photography, typography, and mass publication itself still carry the cachet of their very recent exclusive, elite prestige. By publishing a nicely typeset blog and having "professional-looking" images of me in it, one's unprofessional private musings are wearing fancy clothes, taking a cultural step up. This cultural step up is used as social leverage to increase my "social capital," my reputation.

As a personal *connection tool*, mobile phone text messages, Facebook Messenger, WhatsApp, and others facilitate the parallel circulation of psychological touches (I'm thinking of you, I love you, you are my friend, you are included) and of practical information, (Miwa's game is cancelled, dinner at 6:00 as usual). They help form and reify in-person social networks. These are the basic management tools of any human organization.

But, of course, *data creation* is far and away the most important use. It is why these media exist. Every written post creates salable data. And so does every "like," every republishing, even every view—for even the act of reading, the act of looking for a fraction of a second, creates salable data. This is what pays for Facebook's, Instagram's, Twitter's, Google's lavish design and development teams. These companies sell the content users create, for free, and the data that users create, for free, to advertisers so that they can more accurately and profitably target their advertising messages. This third category of use may seem the most foreign to the average user, because it does not involve a conscious exchange. Most users are only semiconscious of the basic economic facts of life of the tools they use every day.

This is the media landscape used for what one would broadly call "nonfiction." And this is where the fictioneers step in to work their own weird alchemy and practice their own formalism. This is a formalism that is not always the invention of a new medium, but the occupation, travesty, and fictionalization of an existing one.

We love to take forms of communication built for telling the truth and lie in them, in other words to create fictions. By "we" I mean human beings in general, and Mark C. Marino and my other netprov friends in particular. Here are the two common strategies I've observed for creating works that are self-consciously "literary" in social media.

The first strategy is simple importation of the old literature from the old technology into the new. The literal version of this is equivalent to the early "art photographs" that sought to recreate painting in the new medium. Only later did photography's unique beauties—initially seen as ugly by an eye tuned to the soft borders of oil painting—gain acceptance. Simple importation is just that, a remediation. Mainstream examples include the Twitter accounts @Wit_of_Wilde, @BestOscarWilde, @ByOscarWilde, @OscarWildeTweet, and @DailyOscarWilde, all publishing wonderful quotes on a regular basis. A great example of avant-gardism imported into new media are the various "poetry bots" and other experiments collected by Leo Flores in his stream "I [heart] E-Poetry."

The second strategy is the fictionalization of vernacular forms, including parody, satire, and pastiche. Instead of composing works in self-consciously literary forms, stylistically set apart from everyday communication (with an aesthetic of heightened, artificial "literary" language), the fictionalized vernacular springs from a satire of everyday communication (with an aesthetic of well-observed, naturalistic language—often only slightly heightened as a wink to the audience). This tributary of the fictionalized vernacular brings fresh energy and fresh stylistic and technical ideas into culture.

ANTECEDENTS: WELLS, DEFOE, STOKER

When serious communications are made silly, the world goes cuckoo. Cuckoo birds are brood parasites. They lay their eggs in the nests of other birds. Cuckoo chicks hatch earlier and grow faster than the others, often kicking them out of the nest. We netprov players are cuckoo birds: we lay our eggs in other birds' nests; we hijack available media for our own nefar . . . er, I mean . . . hilarious purposes. We come from a proud line of cuckoo birds. Like the London riverbank players who took the crazy tradition of courtyard morality plays and hijacked them by asking: could these become as good as the classical tragedies and comedies? Let's look at some other of our cuckoo ancestors.

We tend to forget how novels once elaborately described their material provenance. Observe the dance of voices, the weaving of the frame, in the opening of H. G. Wells's *The Island of Doctor Moreau.*

> INTRODUCTION.
> ON February the First 1887, the Lady Vain was lost by collision with a derelict when about the latitude 1° S. and longitude 107° W.
> On January the Fifth, 1888—that is eleven months and four days after—my uncle, Edward Prendick, a private gentleman, who certainly went aboard the Lady Vain at Callao, and who had been considered drowned, was picked up in latitude 5° 3′ S. and longitude 101° W. in a small open boat . . . He gave such a strange account of himself that he was supposed demented . . . The following narrative was found among his papers by the undersigned, his nephew and heir, but unaccompanied by any definite request for publication. . . .
> CHARLES EDWARD PRENDICK.
> (The Story written by Edward Prendick.)
> I. IN THE DINGEY OF THE "LADY VAIN."
> I DO not propose to add anything to what has already been written concerning the loss of the Lady Vain. (Wells 1896)

Throughout literary history the gesture recurs: take the forms that people use to communicate and to transcribe language for private use and fictionalize them. Thus we have the confessional novel (a fake diary) such as *Robinson Crusoe* or *Dracula*, and the epistolary novel (a fake exchange of letters) such as *Dangerous Liaisons*. In graphic design terms these fiction books are designed and typeset in a way identical to books of nonfiction, and this is part of the joke.

> JONATHAN HARKER'S JOURNAL
> 3 October.—As I must do something or go mad, I write this diary. (Stoker 1973)

These opening words of chapter 22 of Bram Stoker's *Dracula* remind us that use of a breathless style and claims of urgency are part of a literary tradition already old in Stoker's time. These claims are, let us notice, merely a more elaborate and subtle version of the equally urgent "Wash Me!" that the automobile calls out. Harker's words (that is to say, Stoker's) create a powerful illusion of the character's spontaneity, even in a laboriously crafted, printed book, since we know that the words *could have been* scribbled in the moment, preserved, transcribed, and printed.

The spontaneous, or supposedly spontaneous, first-person narrator has the effect of calling attention to the materiality and temporality of writing. Just a moment, dear reader of this chapter—I'll be right back. I'm dehydrated and need a drink. Hang on.

GOTHIC FICTION, OR: TRUMP AS NETPROV?

The Gothic tradition in literature, from Horace Walpole through Edgar Poe and Mark Twain, uses the foggy border zone between reality and fiction—as realized by plausible rhetorical and graphic forms such as the breathless "found manuscript"—as a way of dealing with subject matter that is equally eerie and borderline. This strategy gets resuscitated in the contemporary meta-work *House of Leaves* as a kind of narrative "pretense" for its disruptive, avant-garde typography. Netprov's repurposing for fiction of digital technologies usually used for ephemeral, informal communication provides great opportunities for a written illusion of spontaneity, since the technologies themselves are used in just this breathless way. This tactic is just one of a number of purely verbal ruses in the tradition of literary fiction that can contribute to netprov.

The seeming spontaneity of candidate and then president Trump's Tweets contributed to his authenticity and then his power. Despite all the swirling conspiracy theories, the idea of a carefully scripted Trump—Trump as netprov—never gained much traction. Advocates and critics unite in wanting to believe in the "true spontaneity" of his writing.

With notably self-conscious exceptions like *Tristram Shandy*, fake vernacular literary fictions could easily be made to look like factual books—orderly columns of gray text—because all books were designed and made in very similar ways for economic reasons. To their eternal glory, the first publishers of *Tristram Shandy* went to the considerable extra expense of binding marbled endpapers and all-black pages in the flow of the book. James Joyce's *Ulysses* and *Finnegans Wake* each used parodic (and expensive) typography, none of which fully broke with book decorum.

More recent graphic design inspirations for netprov must include the *Harvard Lampoon* of the 1960s, which each year attempted to graphically imitate a particular mainstream magazine well enough to fool the reader at first glance. This directly led to the *National Lampoon*, a commercial magazine, run by *Harvard Lampoon* veterans. *National Lampoon* side projects included the *National Lampoon's 1964 High School Yearbook Parody* (O'Rourke and Kenney 2003) (which closely resembled a typical American high-school yearbook, including handwritten notations by the fictional students through which a portrait of the characters and relationships emerged) and the *National Lampoon Sunday Newspaper Parody* (O'Rourke and Hughes 2004) (a complete, miniature newspaper on newsprint paper including all the typical sections of an American Sunday newspaper which, upon careful reading, revealed intrigue and scandal in the community) were among the most elaborately designed tributes to their vernacular models. The *High School Yearbook Parody* is one of the most perfect examples of radically nonlinear narrative (one can read the printed yearbook in any order and the total story emerges) *and* the *Yearbook Parody* is utterly comprehensible to anyone who has experienced an American high-school yearbook without needing any specialized literary training and meta-texts (which Modernist and Post-Modernist works often require).

I see this accessibility to a nonspecialist audience—the accessibility that mimicry provides—as an important axiom for those, like we netprov players, who want to invite people into new forms for new adventures. We ask them to take a huge leap in a new medium from truth-telling mode into mimetic, fictionizing mode. We ask them to perform the literary gesture without using recognizably "literary" language. But we don't ask them to take, in addition, the leap from canonized forms into avant-garde forms that, we feel, is one leap too far. This initial mimetic leap is what the early novelists did and it's what we aim to do.

DIGITAL FICTIONIZING

What does the gesture of fictionalizing something built for truth-telling look like in digital media? We might start by asking: how long does it take to realize a website is fake? Genuinely fake websites exist, often to support email scams. The FBI keeps a current scam list on its website (FBI 2017).

Side-by-side with these frauds, however, is a spectrum of fake websites created for aesthetic rather than criminal purposes. I like to think of degrees of "fakeness" in terms of the amount of time creators want their readers to believe in the fake before they realize it is fake. This timing is accomplished by subtle adjustments to the plausibility of the writing and graphic design. Relatively longer times I refer to as "deadpan" sites, relatively faster times I refer to as "with a wink" sites.

Classic online examples have included the deadpan **RYT Hospital Dwayne Medical Center** resource site for male pregnancy, and the quite-official-looking DHMO Research Division website designed to calm fears and provide copious safety advice if you realize you have dihydrogen monoxide in your home. You'll be surprised: this colorless, odorless liquid is found just about everywhere. (DHMA is also sometimes written H2O.)

Are you looking for a church where the worthwhile worship and the unsaved are unwelcome? Are you "Conservative, Godly, Republican and Unstoppable?" Then the **Landover Baptist Church** website, with its heavily mascaraed eye winking strongly, is for you! (Harper 1993). Landover fixture **Betty Bowers**, by her own admission "America's Best Christian," is so incredibly godly she has her own spin-off site. (Bradley 2011). Building on the rich transvestite theatrical tradition of the drag scene and drag queens—particularly the critically self-aware, postmodern drag movement that began in the 1980s and produced writer/actor characters such as RuPaul and Vaginal Davis—Betty Bowers is an ongoing single-character improvisation. Written and acted by Paul A. Bradley, Betty Bowers lampoons ultraconservatives in a way that tracks with current events.

As with print novels, it is the fact that the typesetting, photography, and design (wonderfully well-observed) of Betty Bowers's pages is nearly indistinguishable from websites of real churches that constitute the fulcrum of the joke.

As video tutorials of all kinds mushroomed in YouTube a new account appeared called *You Suck at Photoshop*. Masquerading as video instruction for Photoshop users, the miserable life of "Donnie" came leaking out in passive/aggressive chunks in the hilarious series recorded with simple desktop capture software (Hitch and Bledsoe 2008). *You Suck at Photoshop* sets as its goal to both legitimately teach one pro trick of the graphic design software Photoshop in each brief episode. Meanwhile, the teacher, Donnie, lets his personal life leak out in the examples he chooses (his ex-wife's car that he vandalizes in Photoshop in lesson) and in his conversations with an unrestrained buddy who appears embarrassingly in chat on Donnie's desktop.

Alongside these elaborate projects, character-based netprov-style projects can be small as well. One of the first and still one of the best, **@bronxzooscobra** purported to be Tweets from a cobra that had escaped the Bronx Zoo in New York. Within the first few hours the cobra's ghostwriter had helped the project leap from mimicry to biting social satire.

> @BronxZoosCobra Bronx Zoo's Cobra
> Want to clear up a misconception. I'm not poisonous as has been reported. I'm venomous. Super venomous, but not poisonous so don't worry.
> 28 Mar
> @BronxZoosCobra Bronx Zoo's Cobra

A lot of people are asking how I can tweet with no access to a computer or fingers. Ever heard of an iPhone? Duh.
28 Mar
@BronxZoosCobra Bronx Zoo's Cobra
What does it take to get a cab in this city?! It's cause I'm not white isn't it.
28 Mar (BronxZoosCobra 2011)

But cuckoo birds don't always occupy a whole nest, a whole vernacular form such as a church website or a video tutorial series. Sometimes they let the other eggs be and wait for their perverse progeny to be discovered. Amazon was early among web retailers to recognize the power of orchestrated word-of-mouth advertising and invested a lot of resources into creating systems for organizing and displaying user reviews of items for sale. Identified by screen names, these grassroots reviewers soon developed a community complete with hierarchies, alliances, competitiveness, and enmities. This is just the kind of situation that invites creative play.

Before long, readers of Amazon reviews could read this seemingly innocuous review of *Handbook of Meat Product Technology*: "[five stars] Tremendous. An admirably thorough guide to the tools of the production-line meat processing trade. The superb colour photographs particularly made it a perfect gift for my 15 year old daughter who is showing alarming signs of not becoming vegetarian" (Raddick 2002). From very early on in online retail giant's proto-crowdsourcing project of inviting users to review products, fictional Amazon reviews began to be posted. Fictional reviews usually are organized in two forms. In one, a single reviewer, such as Raddick, comically reviews a wide variety of items. In the other, many reviewers contribute fictional reviews to a single product, real or invented, for example, the hyperbolic praise for David Hasselhoff's Best Of album was a long-running writing game of the highest order. The reviews of Uranium Ore in Amazon's Industrial and Scientific category include:

Great Product, Poor Packaging
By Patrick J. McGovernon May 14, 2009
I purchased this product 4.47 Billion Years ago and when I opened it today, it was half empty.

DIRECT FICTIONALIZATION BECOMES CANONICAL

Tristram Shandy takes the emergent conventions of the novel which were still just beginning to get up on their feet and it trips them. A set of conventions of graphic design on one hand, and narrative form on the other had coalesced into a package of attributes which was already unnoticed by the reader. *Tristram Shandy* systematically breaks as many rules of book construction as it can: mis-numbering pages, mis-numbering chapters, apologizing to characters suspended "waiting on the stairs" during an earlier digression. Part of the delight of *Tristram Shandy* lies in how Sterne refuses to let readers suspend their disbelief; he leads readers into border violations between form and content. *Tristram Shandy* is a technologically self-aware book.

But what happens to the freshness of direct fictionalization over time? Direct fictionalization of vernacular nonfiction eventually became self-consciously literary and separate. Novelty became the "a novel." The British TV show *The Office* used a fake documentary style, imitated by its American copycat version. Within a couple of seasons the fake documentary strategy, canonized in shows like *Parks and Recreation*, had turned into a stale institutional style invisible to both writers and viewers.

Pure novelty often gets a bad rap, but my own creative practice forces me to give it pure, positive value. In improvised activities—martial arts, improv comedy—timing is everything. The right satire at the right moment can change the flow of history. As a reader, I love mature literary forms; as a creator my skills and my sense of what society needs draws me to the cuckoo bird strategy.

New literary tropes and new narrative shapes can enter the culture through mimicry of new orthographic practices. Chat rooms and text messages have given rise to emojis and systems of abbreviation ("c u" for see you) and written substitutes for information conveyed by facial expression and body language (LOL for laughing out loud, JK for just kidding). These shorthand systems can then be pulled in to fictional systems.

The quickly written exchanges of personal media represent a new form of linguistic dialogue, somewhere between technologically slower written exchanges and spoken conversation. Conversation itself, of course, is a mimetic. In the game of conversation, the rules are fluid and constantly negotiated. My own basic definition of a "real" conversation (as opposed to mere fact exchange or repetition of oft-told tales) is that all participants share the goal of creating new knowledge, by learning, insight, or invention. It is a creative collaboration. All participants come out knowing something they didn't know previously. Antoinette LaFarge (1995) writes at length in her discussion of theatrical improvisation on the Internet of comic timing in MOO writing and the rhythms in what she calls "the quasi-oral arena of online theater."

Netprov draws inspiration from the changes in orthography that have accompanied vernacular writing in personal media. Abbreviations, phonetic spelling, homophonic substitutions of letters and numbers for words—"I luv u" "I luv u 2"—emoticons, and the misspellings of messages written in haste all found their way into the project. The consonances of this new orthography with the tradition of literary puns and portmanteau words such as those created by James Joyce in *Finnegans Wake* were inspirations for me and for Mark Marino in creating the Tweet-by-Tweet style of the netprov "Grace, Wit & Charm":

> @Neil_GWaC: My wrists are KILLING me today. 2many Smoothmoves! #gwandc
> @Sonny1SoBlue: Ah, wifey must be deploydmented again! RT @Neil_GWAC My wrists are KILLING me today. 2many Smoothmoves! #gwandc
> @Laura_GWaC: Seems like those wrists have been bothring you for a while @Neil_GWaC #gwandc
> @Neil_GWaC: Yeh, and the quacktor gave me tehese Canadian meds and Im sure they're plazebos. cant even swing the three-sided sword! #gwandc (Wittig et al. 2011)

These new orthographic styles can enter and mature in literature despite the fact that they are being satirized. It doesn't matter whether you admire someone's style or are scornful of it—if you reuse it in a fictionalized way, it enters culture as a new voice, one that seems spontaneous.

The technological self-awareness of *Tristram Shandy* is best played out in time-based media by *Monty Python's Flying Circus*. Time and time again the satire of *Monty Python* explicitly refers to conventions of TV that usually go unremarked and invisible. My favorite example concerns the fact that, like other half-hour comedies of its time, *Monty Python* was mostly shot on video, but had budget for a certain amount of more expensive shooting on film, which was usually used for exteriors. In one episode, a character repeatedly goes from indoors to outdoors, loudly marveling at the fact that inside he is on video and outdoors he is on film.

This technological self-awareness can also become a political self-awareness. The pompous army officer who interrupts and censors certain *Monty Python* skits draws attention to unseen conventions of power and money normally hidden from mass media audiences.

The frame-breaking humor shared by *Tristram Shandy* and *Monty Python* is a practical method to make the invisible visible for a wide audience. It is a kind of structural satire that provokes structural insight. The very silliness of silly humor rests in the fact that it calls into question basic, assumed rules of existence. Self-awareness and comedy go together; so often what is being satirized in satire is the *non*-self-awareness, the cluelessness, of the target. Sometimes the rules contravened are unchangeable, like death and gravity, but sometimes they are arbitrary, like particular, pompous modes of TV news delivery that prejudice the content while claiming impartiality and neutrality.

UNIFORM TYPOGRAPHY: THE GREAT LEVELER

What begins as a simple gesture of mimicry—facsimile graphic design—thus can develop into simple satire and then into a mode that seemingly and pointedly casts doubt on all we know to be true. It becomes technologically self-aware media.

This critical technological, and social, self-awareness fights against one of the simplest, most powerful, and most unnoticed gestures of micropublishing, group, and personal media. Handwritten words no longer need the technological skill and capital investment of metal typesetting to appear in the authoritative garb of uniform typography. Automated templates make text typed on keyboard or phone appear instantly and for all time in uniform, typographic form. Thanks to the simple, ugly (my opinion), inflexible templating of blog sites and group media sites such as Facebook—which prevent the user from making the "error" of "unprofessional" typography—all users appear to have equal status. "Only the Oxford comma," as Mark C. Marino wrote early in the netprov Occupy MLA, "separates us."

Typographic uniformity is the platform for the joys of netprov at the same time as it is the permission for hideous and aggressive forms of Internet trolling and the foundation of "fake news."

THE PERFORMANCE OF IDENTITY ON THE WEB

> To be natural is such a very difficult pose to keep up.
> —Oscar Wilde, *An Ideal Husband*

How long does it take to realize a website is fake? What if that website is a blog, a blog say, like the many hundreds of thousands that exist, wherein a young person is growing and experimenting with new attitudes, a new personal style. What if that person, for example, hangs out in real life with people who all like country music, but on the blog is indulging a secret passion for heavy metal? More seriously, what if the blogger was born female but feels himself to be male and has not yet revealed this fact to friends and family, but is trying out this new, more authentic version of self on a pseudonymous blog? Friends and family in denial might call this blog a fraud and a fiction. All these bloggers themselves will likely further evolve in their tastes as time goes by and look back on their own various earlier incarnations as in some way incomplete compared to their current evolution.

All this is to say that even serial confessional texts that in every way are sincere and "real" nonfiction contain experimentation, mimicry, play, and falsehood. If the writer is growing and evolving, they must. As Web writers such as Sherry Turkle have been telling us for years, online identity in MUDS, MOOS chat rooms and games is a performance that interpenetrates, amplifies, and sometimes contradicts the performance of identity that we do in real life. Turkle (1996) comments:

> As a new social experience, MUDs pose many psychological questions: If a persona in a role-playing game drops defenses that the player in real life has been unable to abandon, what effect does this have? What if a persona enjoys success in some area (say, flirting) that the player has not been able to achieve? Slippages often occur in places where persona and self merge, where the multiple personae join to comprise what the individual thinks of as his or her authentic self.

Our culture used to assert that a person's identity was as unchanging as a book. Now we are beginning to see that it has always been as fluid as a website. Facebook's insistence on a single, verifiable identity is a desperate rear-guard action of the waning book-paradigm era.

Digital culture scholar Jill Walker Rettberg (2005), writing about online photographic self-portraiture in the context of the reversal of the top-down flow of traditional mass media in *Mirrors and Shadows: Digital Aestheticisation of Oneself*, writes:

> In an attempt to cling to the past, mass media try to fit in with this change by making everyday people the stars of the mass media. We have reality television, makeover television, contests like Idol and Survivor which all make miniature celebrities of people who fade quickly in and out of the limelight. The more powerful movement is on the internet, and it is controlled entirely by the everyday people themselves. These people write diaries, they publish photos, and most importantly: they write themselves. They don't allow others to represent them. They are in charge of the presentation of their own lives. That is something the mass media have never encouraged. Capturing our mirror images and our shadows is an exploration of what it means to be a subject in an age where masses no longer exist. (Walker Rettberg 2005)

Walker Rettberg points out the way in which the performance of identity is an act that takes place in an adversarial environment, one in which other forces are eager to shape one's identity.

My Web fiction *The Fall of the Site of Marsha* (Wittig 1999), which shows three stages of progressive deterioration of a Web 1.0 personal website, is an example of a fictional performance of identity.

In creating *Marsha* I drew inspiration from the sheer naïve exuberance of vernacular home pages—the wild experimentation with typography, the jamming together of heterogeneous appropriated imagery, and the tendency to use the Web as an intimate confessional, with early home page makers not quite realizing how public it was and how much of their story they were revealing. I was also, at the time, interested in the nineteenth-century Romantic fascination with ruins and asked myself to imagine what a ruined website would look like. (We now have seen plenty of ruined and abandoned websites, but in those hopeful, forward-looking early days of the Web it was an odd notion.)

The character Marsha is a fan of angels, and in particular a kind of angel called "throne angels." I studied the many real angel websites of the time and positioned Marsha and her best friend Bits as new members to this angel website community. Marsha's site is, in part, a tribute to her late father, about whom she feels some ambivalence and guilt. She throws out a rhapsodic invitation for people to participate in her site and for the angels themselves to come and visit. The angels come, and they are not nice. In fact, the angels—or perhaps hackers/haters posing as angels—begin to bully her and vandalize her website in its second and third iterations, touching sore points about her father's death and the loyalty of Bits. Careful readers will have noticed by the second of the site's three iterations that Bits and Marsha's husband Mike are having an affair. By the third iteration, the angels' harsh emendations to the site dominate, the images are dark and mangled, and Marsha's husband is announcing that Marsha has been institutionalized for mental illness.

Marsha's self-presentation of identity is constructed in several ways. Her writing reveals more about her than she realizes, using time-honored literary devices of the naïve narrator. But in addition to these traditional linguistic tricks, I used mimicry of the vernacular to show her character by the graphic design choices she made and the imagery she appropriated. She also includes a photo of herself high on the page. This ability to associate a face with an identity is a powerful communications tool.

FIGURE 6.1 The fictional author Marsha from the hopeful Spring Chapter of *The Fall of the Site of Marsha* by Rob Wittig, 1999.

FIGURE 6.2 Marsha from the desperate, hacked and final Fall Chapter.

By using a strategy of mimicry and parody and fictionalizing the vernacular in *Marsha* I was aiming to make the reader aware of not just the nascent conventions of self-presentation on the Web, but also, by contrast, the profoundly invisible conventions of self-presentation in real life. An awareness of one's own strategies of self-presentation is a perfect example of what in psychology is called "insight." By inviting the reader to see in Marsha what Marsha does not see about herself, the project also implicitly invites readers to apply the same process to themselves.

CREATIVE THREATS TO THE CONSUMER EGO

Satirical and fictional strategies that bring into being multiple selfling modes within a single account and multiple selves (multiple accounts) constitute an opposition, a threat, to the predictable (therefore lucrative) consumer ego. How? In these ways.

Within a single authorized account there can be irony, satire, mimicry (the practice of reported speech, of "doing voices" so common in everyday speech, for example, She goes "No way!" and I go "Way!"), impersonation, pretending that the account has been hijacked by another, and many others. A single account can be authored collaboratively (commonly done of course by real celebrities who hire ghostwriters to "manage" their social media).

In a single fictional account strategies include the impersonation of known celebrities (alive and dead), the invention of imaginary celebrities, consistently stereotypical/satirical accounts, impossible accounts (e.g., The Moon), and more. Robotic or "bot" accounts can be made (small programs that pull from a storehouse of text or from the Web itself to produce text and even interact with other accounts).

There can be multiple fictional accounts operated by a single user, bots (small programs that pull from a storehouse of text or from the Web itself to produce text and even interact with other accounts). Authorized accounts can be swapped, like the project Trading Faces Mark C. Marino and Claire Donato performed by swapping their Facebook accounts for a week.

Sociologists and psychologists, in the wake of Ervin Goffman's landmark study *The Presentation of Self in Everyday Life*, have pointed out the dramatically different parts we all play with our parents, with close friends, with our boss. Far from a simple distinction of being "in" or "out" of character, we live in a world of fluid identity.

The group media giants Facebook and Google try more and more to police the proliferation of "fake" accounts and conjure the specter of actual illegal use to discourage creative and protest use of multiple accounts. They use the odd and slippery social construct of "authenticity" to try to shame users into shrinking into their supposedly "real," single selves. There are many degrees along the scale of difference between a comedian "impressionist," a person passing and "impersonating" a different gender, and a criminal "imposter." Like all rhetorical strategies, mimicry can be used for good or ill. Consumer society attempts to portray it as totally ill.

But isn't the group-media pressure really more like wrestling fans insisting that their heroes keep to the code of kayfabe. Wikipedia, the clear pop-culture authority, defines "kayfabe" as,

> in professional wrestling . . . the portrayal of staged events within the industry as "real" or "true," specifically the portrayal of competition, rivalries, and relationships between participants as being genuine and not of a staged or pre-determined nature of any kind. Kayfabe has also evolved to become a code word of sorts for maintaining this "reality" within the direct or indirect presence of the general public. (https://en.wikipedia.org/wiki/Kayfabe)

For wrestlers to break kayfabe threatens their livelihood. The oft-cited encouragement to young writers to be authentic, "be yourself" and to find "your one, true voice" to me seems eerily harmonious with the self-consistency of the consumer ego; it seems like a cruel and enforced form of kayfabe.

Let's look more closely at the perils of authenticity.

IN DEFENSE OF PRETENSION

When Johann Wolfgang von Goethe retreated to Rome in 1786 to evade his newfound and uncomfortable celebrity, he had outgrown, and was desperate to escape, the confines of the traditional literary forms he inherited. By committing his body to the warmth of Italy and his mind to the companionship of the ancients he sought a new path. He employed a simple cultural approach: he played make-believe. He pretended to be an ancient Roman and wrote a series of poems in the ancient (and sexy) style, the *Roman Elegies*.

The famous portrait by Tischbein, *Goethe in the Roman Campagna*, 1887, shows the poet half-reclining, in a pose decidedly improper by northern standards, with a large swath of white cloth covering his shirt, coat, and knee breeches. Goethe is doing cosplay. Goethe is wearing a toga.

The young hipsters of Europe embraced Goethe's hot-blooded *Elegies*. The poems showed poets across Europe a way out of the straitlaced old constraints. They play an important part in the coming Romantic revolution. The old guard, of course, accused Goethe of being pretentious.

In *Pretentiousness, Why it Matters*, Dan Fox (2016) writes that "authentication . . . is a matter of authority, of who gets to pass judgment on whether or not you are 'being yourself,' of whether the pretender to the throne holds a legitimate claim or not."

Fox sharply defines the underlying social pressures to conformity in the epithet:

> Calling a person pretentious can be a way of calling out the trappings and absurdities of power. It's a way of undermining the authority that they have positioned themselves with. It is also a way of warning them not to get above their station. Used as an insult, it's an informal tool of class surveillance, a stock with which to beat someone for putting on airs and graces. Where the word "pretentious" differs from "pretending" is that it carries with it the sting of class betrayal. (Fox 2016: 42)

But time and again in cultural history, creators pretend to be earlier creators. What are all the various waves of Classicism and Neo-Classicism but this (the Renaissance included)? The American Beat poets pretended to be postwar St. Germain hipsters from Paris. They pretended to be Chinese Zen recluses. So it goes. And these creators always get it wrong—they don't really know enough about the earlier period to make the leap into an "authentic" recreation. They go too far, because in the realm of innovation, to do is to overdo. A Berkeley Shakespeare-in-the-Park troupe moves to the Haight Ashbury in the 1960s and decides to wear their costumes all the time (From *Electric Kool-Aid Acid Test*). The hippy look is born. These pretenders all get it wrong, and thankfully so, because what they're doing is not a dogmatic historical reenactment but a remix, a cover version, a new thing "in the old style" that solves a current creative problem.

Dan Fox (2016, p. 6) quotes Brian Eno from his *A Year with Swollen Appendices*, "My assumptions about culture as a place where you can take psychological risks without incurring physical penalties make me think that pretending is the most important thing we do. It's the way we make our thought experiments, find out what it would be like to be otherwise."

In the early days of electronic literature I migrated in my employment and creative friendships from the literary world to the design world seeking open mindedness. What would it be like to be otherwise, I desperately wanted to know. Is there a literature of multiple minds, of collaboration and co-impersonation, of improvisation and mimicry? An art of mimicry is a reminder that we're all performing, all pretending, all the time. A pretender is fundamentally a traveler, someone who comes from somewhere else and lives here now. Accusations of pretentiousness are xenophobic. I love when people call me and my work pretentious. It means I'm actually breaking someone's made-up rule, I'm actually widening someone's narrow mind.

But the empire of the consumer egos always fights back. Its great weapon is statistical popularity, visits and "likes" and "shares" and "retweets." "Popularity ratifies cultural authenticity," says Fox (2016). "The people have spoken and the convention—in the original sense of the word—has made its decision" (79).

Shape-shifting and shifty, pretension is the cure for perfectionism, that pernicious vision of a universe so punitive and judgmental that one must never make a mistake. In such a world, as we know, one can never learn, one can never change, one can never grow. In this new landscape we must counter the old adage "be authentic" with the equally old adage "fake it 'til you make it."

GENERATIVE COLLABORATIONS

The ferocity of the commercial insistence that the consumer ego be self-consistent—reliable, predictable—is matched only by the ferocity of the insistence that the consumer ego be solitary. Without unquenchable desires, without insecurity, without acquisitiveness and loneliness, how would the wheels of commerce turn?

Literary scholarship, particularly feminist scholarship, has taught us to doubt nearly every assertion of the existence of the solitary, Romantic genius. Unacknowledged creative contributions from wives and girlfriends abound. Ford Madox Ford and Joseph Conrad read aloud their new pages to each other every day for commentary; is this solo authorship? Isn't it a writer's room?

The early experiments of Invisible Seattle, specifically our crowdsourced novel Invisible Seattle (where we wore the overalls of Literary Workers and approached people on the street saying "Excuse me, we're building a novel, can we borrow a few of your words?") confirmed in me a lifelong taste for collaborative writing, for a literary version of the "group think" of theatrical improv.

Therefore, when a frenetic and brilliantly loquacious preacher took the stage of a small Chicago underground theater in 1991, I was in the audience. The pseudonymous Reverend Ivan Stang wiped the sweat from his brow and ranted: "Apostates accuse us, dear friends, of selling out. Selling out? Selling out? We have been trying to sell out for years . . . but there have BEEN NO TAKERS!" The important and talented group of writers and performers associated with the Church of the Subgenius has done projects since the 1980s that share many of the characteristics of Invisible Seattle, and of netprov.

The Church of the Subgenius, legally a real church but essentially a fictional church, is an ongoing collaborative satire of American evangelical church culture, UFO enthusiasts, and other marginal groups. It occupies and subverts traditional church structures and the media of church communications to advance the fiction—services, titles and hierarchy, "devivals," concerts, pamphlets, books, visual art, radio broadcasts, websites, podcasts.

> If you are what they call "different"—
> If you think we're entering a new Dark Ages—
> If you see the universe as one vast morbid sense of humor—
> If you are looking for an inherently bogus religion that will condone superior degeneracy and tell you that you are "above" everyone else—
> If you can help us with a donation—
> The Church of the Subgenius could save your sanity! (Stang et al. 1979)

It is collaborative, allowing membership (for a price) but also encouraging schisms and debate. Broad plot lines unfold in real time, for example, the assassination and purported resurrection of the church's prophet, J. R. "Bob" Dobbs. The unspoken rule is that Subgenius figures always stay in character and always deny that what they are doing is art.

"Excuse me, we're building a novel." Starting in the early 1980s, roughly the same era as the Church of the Subgenius, inspired by tales of Dada performance and Surrealist expeditions, fans of the Oulipo, enamored of a vision of intellectual life in the cafes of Paris, the group Invisible Seattle was my first experience of elements of netprov. Combining literary aspirations with backgrounds in skit comedy and political guerilla theater, the group's projects used publications, posters, and performance to promote the generative notion of an invisible Seattle coexisting with the visible one—a smarter, more aware, freer, more real city accessed by the imagination. "Every time you read a book, you enter Invisible Seattle" went the early catchphrase. In the role of "literary workers" we devised a scheme for the citizens to help write the great novel of Seattle the city deserved. We dressed in overalls with words stenciled on them and hard hats with question marks, interviewed citizens on the street, in bars, in coffeehouses and created a vivid snapshot of Seattle in the summer of 1983, the book *Invisible Seattle*. I have chronicled these adventures at length in my own 1995 book *Invisible Rendezvous* (Wittig and IN.S.OMNIA 1994).

SURREALISM, CHURCH OF THE SUBGENIUS, AND INVISIBLE SEATTLE AS "WORLDS"

Using the transmedia model Henry Jenkins notes in which the creation of fictional "worlds" (the Marvel Universe, the Star Wars Universe) has superseded the creation of story and character gives me at last a way to talk about an aspect of Surrealism that has always intrigued me. By insisting that Surrealism was not an art style, not an aesthetic, but a way of life, Breton and the Surrealists created a meta-structure that surrounded any particular piece of writing, book, art exhibition, or even creative career. Surrealism was modeled on a political movement (issuing "manifestos," the everyday French word for a political party platform), or a scientific movement, which could contain any possible member actors and actions. The deep cultural roots of this idea of inner adherence lie in the centuries of sectarian religious conflict in Europe, which rotated on the crucial, unobservable act of accepting or rejecting certain minor variants of dogma and thereby "becoming" a Catholic or Protestant worthy, depending on the setting, of salvation or murder. In the 1920s in France one could similarly "become" a Communist, a Freudian, or a Surrealist.

The religious roots of this act of imaginative inner transformation become clear when we look at the key creative gesture of the Subgeniuses. The genius of the Church of the Subgenius is that by using one word they explain the rules of their collaborative creative game, the word "church." We are pretending to be a church, their gesture says. Or, more accurately, they *are* actually legally and in every way a church, but of course they are not. They are "an inherently bogus religion that will tell you that you are better than everyone else" as their literature tells us. The invitation to play and participate is broad and comprehensible. Their target audience is well-defined in their own literature: outsiders who feel alone in the sea of American religious conservatism and need an attitude that will help them survive and thrive as a tiny minority in a hostile society. "Do people think you're strange? Do you? . . . THEN YOU MAY BE ON THE RIGHT TRACK!" says one of their earliest tracts. " 'Unpredictables' are not alone and possess amazing hidden powers of their own! Are You Abnormal? THEN YOU PROBABLY ARE BETTER THAN MOST PEOPLE! YES! YOUR KIND SHALL TRIUMPH!" (Stang et al. 1979).

If you want to "join" the subgeniuses, do anything that is church-like (in particular like the independent Southern US fundamentalist churches which they most closely parody): go to church, start your own church, preach, write, proselytize. The thing I most admire about the flexibility of the Subgeniuses' "world" is that it perfectly accommodates creative disagreements. If you don't like how some other Subgenius preacher is doing things, you are encouraged to break away and form your own schismatic church—just as long as you have a spectacular and public battle—just like churches have done for centuries in real life! In this world, parody is the perfect organizer. The Subgeniuses' largely self-consistent world has grown for decades with elaborate characters, narratives, backstories, writing, and preaching.

What I still find so exciting about Invisible Seattle all these years is the deadpan proposition of an *invisible* Seattle, parallel and intermingled with the visible one, that is accessed by acts of imagination. "Every time you read a book you enter Invisible Seattle" goes one of the mottos. "Invisible Seattle is the antidote for your feeling of completeness" goes another (Wittig and IN.S.OMNIA 1994). Becoming a citizen depended on insight, on seeing the invisible—from noting the invisible forces of politics and economics to tracing cultural quotations back to their source. The map of Invisible Seattle shows the Eiffel Tower instead of the Space Needle, since the Needle so clearly cites the Tower. In the early 1980s Invisible Seattle cofounder Philip Wohlstetter would spin yarns of finding evidence of a "parallel university" that quietly occupied unused classrooms at the University of Washington and, from the notes on the chalkboards, was offering much more interesting courses than the real university. Who were these unseen, more intelligent students and teachers? How could we meet them? How could we become them? This, too, operates according to the mechanics of a religious inner transformation, in this case the "enlightenment" of Buddhism and Taoism. After enlightenment, nothing has changed, but everything has changed, since one's attitude toward the world has been transformed.

The proposition of these alternate realities, these worlds, these games, is to transform our everyday lives. They are only slightly more stylized, ritualized, and self-conscious than the semi-conscious and unconscious choices we make when we decide what clothes to wear (showing membership in some social group, goth, emo, bear), how to style our hair, or which subculture's vocabulary to adopt. The goal of Surrealism, of the Church of the Subgenius, of Invisible Seattle, and of netprov is to awake in the morning in our same old beds with a brand-new attitude: more creative, more proactive, more empowered, more alive.

To that end, as a conclusion and invitation—don't just sit there, let your various selves play!—I offer our current version of netprov tactics. With these literary legacies and more as its antecedents, here are the principles netprov uses:

- Netprov creates stories that are networked, collaborative, and improvised in real time.
- These three qualities form a minimum definition of the form. Within the fiction texts appear to be written in real time; in fact they can be prewritten and scheduled for later release. The pacing and timing of texts can be used for aesthetic effect (pacing: awkwardly slow messaging; timing: workday escapes, midnight confessions). Timing tactics work best when the writers and readers are in relatively similar time zones.
- Netprov uses multiple media simultaneously. It takes full advantage of the literary potential for rhetorical and graphic design mimicry-parody-satire of the forms it occupies.

- Netprov is collaborative and incorporates participatory contributions from readers. The collaboration of the inner circle is modeled on theatrical improv. The participation of the outer circle of readers is modeled on networked role-playing games, and on fan participation in mass media fictional "worlds."
- Netprov is experienced as a performance as it is published; it is read later as a literary archive. During the performance the goal is to be powerful theater. When the archive is created, the goal is to make powerful literature.
- During the performance, netprov projects incorporate breaking news. Netprov, in the spirit of the Surrealists and other avant-gardists, aims to trouble barriers between fiction and reality. Netprov aims to shorten the lag-time of satire.
- Netprov projects use actors to physically enact characters in images, videos, and live performance. Some writer/actors portray the characters they create. A new creative role based on ancient models, the writer/actor is promising possibility for the digital age.
- Netprov loves the parodic and satirical. In the playful progression from mimicry to parody to satire, netprov offers a playground for instantiating healing insight for society.

Some netprov projects require writer/actors and readers to travel to certain locations to seek information, perform actions, and report their activities. In the spirit of idealistic Alternate Reality Games, and high-minded Live Action Roleplaying, netprov can use digital media to coordinate and create physical play.

Netprov is designed for episodic and incomplete reading. It is open to being mixed and remixed by its players. It corresponds to the way people are already using digital communications. One never knows where one's readers read, but an ideal of netprov is to seed the real world with imagination, to sneak fiction into a reader's mindstream during the time devoted to "reality" rather than the compartmentalized time set aside for "entertainment." The strategy is to give readers a rewarding experience whether they read only a few messages or if they become devoted fans. The goal is to be skillful enough to entice readers into the depths. There need be no requirement or expectation of completeness.

CONCLUSION

The early novels' cuckoo eggs grew into a mature art form. Will the netprov impulses of today crack their shells and "have legs?" Will they, too, mature and be repeated enough times for someone to get good at them? This depends on who decides to take them up, how hard they work, and what they build. One "crossover hit" (transporting the depth of mature art forms into a new art form) can create a whole new genre.

The speed with which new communication media, widespread and commercially strong, seem likely to proliferate makes me think that the basic gesture of being first-to-fictionalize will continue to be needed more often and more frequently.

SOURCES CITED

Bradley, Paul A. "Mrs. Betty Bowers, America's Best Christian!" 2000–2011, 2011. http://www.bettybowers.com.

BronxZoosCobra. "@Bronxzooscobra Twitter Feed." Twitter, 2011. http://twitter.com/#!/bronxzooscobra.

Defoe, Daniel, and J. Donald Crowley. *The Life and Surprising Adventures of Robinson Crusoe of York, Mariner: Who Lived Eight and Twenty Years All Alone in an Un-inhabited Island on the Coast of AMERICA, near the Mouth of the Great River of OROONOQUE; Having Been Cast on Shore by Shipwreck, Wherein All the Men Perished but Himself [I.E. Daniel Defoe*]. London and New York: Oxford University Press, 1972.

Dobbs, J. R., and SubGenius Foundation. *The Book of the Subgenius: Being the Divine Wisdom, Guidance, and Prophecy of J.R. "Bob" Dobbs*. Mcgraw-Hill Paperbacks. New York: McGraw-Hill, 1983.

FBI. 2017. http://www.fbi.gov/scams-safety/e-scams.

Flores, Leo, et al. I love e-poetry. http://iloveepoetry.com/.

Fox, Dan. *Pretentiousness: Why It Matters*. Minneapolis, MN: Coffee House Press, 2016.

Goffman, Ervin. *The Presentation of Self in Everyday Life*. University of Edinborough Social Sciences Research Center, 1956.

Harper, Chris. "Landover Baptist Where the Worthwhile Worship. Unsaved Unwelcome." 1993. Americhrist Inc. 2011.

Hitch, Troy, and Matt Bledsoe. "You Suck at Photoshop." 2008. http://www.mydamnchannel.com/You_Suck_at_Photoshop/Season_1/YouSuckAtPhotoshop1DistortWarpandLayerEffects_1373.aspx.

LaFarge, Antoinette. "A World Exhilarating and Wrong: Theatrical Improvisation on the Internet." *Leonardo*, vol. 28, no. 5 (1995).

Libera, Anne. *The Second City Almanac of Improvisation*. Evanston, IL: Northwestern University Press, 2004.

O'Rourke, P. J., and Douglas C. Kenney, eds. *National Lampoon's 1964 High School Yearbook*. 39th Anniversary edition. New York Rugged Land, 2003.

O'Rourke, P. J., and John Hughes, eds. *National Lampoon Sunday Newspaper Parody*. New York: Rugged Land, 2004.

Raddick, Henry. "Amazon.com Customer Reviews: *Handbook of Meat Product Technology*." 2002. http://www.amazon.com/Handbook-Product-Technology-Michael-Ranken/product-reviews/0632053771.

Stang, Ivan, et al. "Subgenius Pamphlet #1, Web Version." 1979. http://www.subgenius.com/pam1/pamphlet_p2.html.

Stoker, Bram. *Dracula*. Garden City, NY: Doubleday, 1973.

Suits, Bernard. *The Grasshopper: Games, Life and Utopia*. Broadview Press, [1975] 2005, pp. 54–5.

Turkle, Sherry. "Who Am We?" *Wired*, 1996, http://www.wired.com/wired/archive/4.01/turkle.html?pg=4&topic= .

Walker Rettberg, Jill. "Mirrors and Shadows: The Digital Aestheticisation of Oneself." *Proceedings of Digital Arts and Culture* (2005): 184–90.

Wells, H. G., and Leon E. Stover. *The Island of Doctor Moreau: A Critical Text of the 1896 London First Edition*, with an Introduction and Appendices. Annotated by H. G. Wells. Jefferson, NC: McFarland, 1996.

Wittig, Rob, and IN.S.OMNIA (Computer bulletin board). *Invisible Rendezvous: Connection and Collaboration in the New Landscape of Electronic Writing*. Middletown, CT; Hanover, NH: Wesleyan University Press; University Press of New England, 1994.

Wittig, Rob, and IN.S.OMNIA. "The Fall of the Site of Marsha." Tank20. 1999. http://robwit.net/MARSHA/.

Wittig, Rob, and IN.S.OMNIA, et al. "Grace, Wit & Charm." 2011. http://directory.eliterature.org/individual-work/3720.

CHAPTER SEVEN

Narrativity

DANIEL PUNDAY

Narrativity is one of the most difficult qualities of electronic literature to theorize. On the one hand, readers clearly have narrative experiences with electronic texts—from text-centric Storyspace hypertext fictions through commercial video games. On the other hand, many of the qualities that we value in electronic textuality, such as the variable way in which features of these texts are encountered by readers, work against traditional narrative coherence. Marie-Laure Ryan (2006: 196) speaks for many when she writes that "the root of the conflict between narrative design and interactivity (or gameplay) lies in the difficulty of integrating the bottom-up input of the player within the top-down structure of a narrative script."

The concept of narrativity itself has undergone significant rethinking in recent years, and as a result narratology offers more sophisticated ways of talking about how stories can appear in electronic texts than classical narrative models allowed. Before turning to particular features of electronic literature, let me begin with a basic history of the concept and identify key issues.

THE EVOLUTION OF NARRATIVITY AS A CONCEPT

Narratology itself evolved out of an attempt to move away from a narrow focus on the novel to a broader understanding of narrative as a mode that can take many forms. As Roland Barthes famously remarked in 1966, "The narratives of the world are numberless. Narrative is first and foremost a prodigious variety of genres, themselves distributed amongst different substances—as though any material were fit to receive man's stories" (251). Barthes, of course, has in mind at least in part the sorts of popular images and news reports that he analyzed in the previous decade for *Mythologies*. Likewise, in 1966, Robert Scholes and Robert Kellogg published *The Nature of Narrative*. Their work remained firmly focused on traditional literary work in print; however, the authors broke from the then-common focus on the novel (embodied in everything from Watt's 1957 *The Rise of the Novel* to Booth's 1961 *The Rhetoric of Fiction*) to discuss myth, epic, and allegory. This late-1960s movement was an attempt to broaden what it means for something to be a narrative. Further expansions would come to characterize narrative study in new media.

The search for a clear, minimal definition of narrative remains a common feature of what is now called "classical" narratology—the work beginning with structuralists like Barthes and continuing through books that attempt to synthesize narratology into a field throughout the 1970s and 1980s. Exemplary works include Seymour Chatman's

Story and Discourse (1978), Shlomith Rimmon-Kenan's *Narrative Fiction: Contemporary Poetics* (1983), and Mieke Bal's *Narratology* (1985). Such books inevitably feature an opening definition of the core components of a narrative, which include character and setting but (especially) some sort of change in state. Critics often invoke E. M. Forster's (1927: 86) famous example: "We have defined a story as a narrative of events arranged in their time-sequence. A plot is also a narrative of events, the emphasis falling on causality. 'The king died and then the queen died' is a story. 'The king died, and then the queen died of grief' is a plot. The time-sequence is preserved, but the sense of causality overshadows it."

This focus on deciding about the minimal conditions for something to be a narrative is one of the reasons why many scholars initially resisted narratologists' interest in electronic media, since the field in the past had worked to rigorously sort narratives from non-narratives. Prompted in part by just this resistance from "new media" critics to what they saw as the colonizing impulses of narratology (see Eskelinen [2004] for an example of this kind of critique), work during the 2000s increasingly turned away from relying exclusively on traditional storytelling media like print and film. Marie-Laure Ryan's 2004 collection of essays, *Narrative across Media*, represents a significant broadening of the kinds of works studied (in addition to digital media, she includes still pictures, music, and face-to-face narration). In her introduction to this volume she offered an influential emphasis on "narrativity" as a quality that a work can have in various degrees:

> I propose to make a distinction between "being a narrative" and "possessing narrativity." The property of "being" a narrative can be predicated on any semiotic object produced with the intent of evoking a narrative script in the mind of the audience. "Having narrativity," on the other hand, means being able to evoke such a script. In addition to life itself, pictures, music, or dance can have narrativity without being narratives in a literal sense. (9)

Ryan's concept of "having narrativity" is powerful precisely because it recognizes that we can talk meaningfully about the narrative qualities of texts that aren't themselves simply or even primarily storytelling vehicles. This solves the problem that Nick Montfort articulated in *Twisty Little Passages* (2003) of distinguishing between interactive fiction's potential to create narratives from the strict definition of narrative as the representation of events in a time sequence. Montfort notes that, although interactive fiction can create experiences that seem narrative (they involve characters, settings, events, and a narrative development), the game itself is not a narrative according to traditional definitions: "the representation of real or fictive events and situations in a time sequence" (25; citing Prince 1980: 180). For Montfort (2003), "A work of IF is not itself a narrative; it is an interactive computer program." Narrative "can result from an interactive session but does not describe any IF work itself" (25). In this chapter, in sync with Ryan and Montfort, I will not focus on whether electronic literature "is" narrative, but instead provide an analysis of the ways that these works can create and use narrativity.[1]

It is easy to recognize that many electronic texts have narrativity even if they are not themselves stories. Henry Jenkins (2004) notes the case of games based on well-known

[1] In framing the project in this way, I recognize that I am avoiding a discussion of electronic texts that treats them as other than representational. For example, Roberto Simanowski (2010: 25) discusses art that seeks to provoke rather than tell, and Ian Bogost (2006) has discussed games as simulations rather than representations. I have de-emphasized both of these approaches because narrativity seems to me to imply an interest in representation.

narrative franchises like *Star Wars*. Such games "want to tap the emotional residue of previous narrative experiences" (119), and exist "in dialogue with the films, conveying new narrative experiences" in part by allowing users to interact with environments inspired by the films (124). Of course, even strictly non-narrative texts can produce narrative experiences—for example, when players narrate their performance and accomplishments to other players. Leaving aside such second-order narrative, many electronic works strive to tell stories—even if narrative itself is not a necessary condition of the medium. David Ciccoricco (2014: 225) summarizes the situation this way: "an *intrinsic* justification for video games as stories—one that posits narrative as an essential property—would fail to recognize the peculiar attributes of the form. A *typological* justification, however, is irrefutable: some games place a heavy investment (in both the generic and the expressly financial sense) in creating sophisticated and emotionally compelling narrative experiences." Jenkins and Ciccoricco treat narrativity as a matter of degree, rather than debating what David Herman (2002: 90) calls "narrativehood," "a binary predicate: something either is or is not a story." Electronic works may create an experience of narrativity event if they are also doing many other things at the same time.

KEY NARRATOLOGICAL CONCEPTS FOR DESCRIBING NARRATIVITY

Ryan's (2004: 8–9) definition of narrativity is based on three conditions under which a text can be said to produce a "narrative script": it must create a world with characters and objects, the world must undergo changes, and those changes must be based on causality and motivations in a way that allows for interpretation. An event without recognizable spaces or characters might function as part of a metaphor (see Suvin [1986]); a text without change would be more a description; and a text without causality would be merely annals, to use Hayden White's famous distinction (6). As this list makes clear, narratology gives a central role to time and causality when talking about narrativity.

Since the earliest structuralist work on narrative, narratology has provided sophisticated ways to describe time and order. Narratology has, of course, long distinguished between the time of events (story time) and the time of their narration (discourse time). Gérard Genette (1980) provided an influential unifying articulation of the way that narration can articulate the time of events in *Narrative Discourse*, where he described how narration can manipulate the order, duration, and frequency of story events. Mieke Bal provided further nuance in 1985 when she noted the span and distance of anachronies in narration. Bal likewise expands on Genette's observation about the speed of narration to distinguish a range of relations between story time and telling time, including the summary (where telling time is much faster than story time), the ellipsis (where story time passes with no telling time taken up), and the pause (where story time stops while telling time goes on). From this perspective, one of the central artistic decisions in any narrative is how to order the events of the story in their telling. There is no neutral way to tell events: storytellers must select a starting and ending point, must decide which events to describe, and must give some events more or less narrative attention.

The reordering of story time into narrative time is not, of course, enough to create a narrative. As Ryan (2004) suggests, we must be able to connect events through some kind of causality. Writing in 1973, Tzvetan Todorov provides a helpful summary of the relation between causality and order in different text types:

> It is possible to conceive of cases in which the logical and the temporal are to be found in the pure state, separated from each other; but we shall then be obliged to leave the field of what we habitually call literature. Pure chronological order, stripped of all causality, is dominant in chronicles, annals, diaries. Pure causality dominates axiomatic discourse (that of the logician) or teleological discourse (that of the lawyer, of the political orator). (42)

He goes on to note that, while some literary works seem to minimize causality for temporality (*Ulysses*) or temporality for causality (the literary portrait) these extreme cases "merely emphasize the habitual solidarity between temporality and causality" (43).

Several other distinctions between types of narrative events are common within classic narratology. Roland Barthes (1982: 265) offers the influential distinction between what he calls cardinal functions and catalyzers, events that are central to the narrative, and those that serve secondary purposes, such as characterization: "Some [functions] constitute real hinge points of the narrative (or of a fragment of the narrative); others merely "fill in" the narrative space separating the hinge functions. Let us call the former *cardinal functions* (or *nuclei*) and the latter, having regard to their complementary nature, *catalyzers*" (emphasis in the original). Seymour Chatman (1978: 44) offers the further distinction between actions and happenings: "Both are changes of state. An action is a change of state brought about by an agent or one that affects a patient. If the action is plot-significant, the agent or patient is called a character." In contrast, a happening "entails a prediction of which the character or other focused existent is a narrative object: for example, *The storm cast Peter adrift*" (45; emphasis in the original).

Although the analysis of order and causality is central to narratology's understanding of how events acquire narrativity, not all events lend themselves equally to narration.[2] Ryan (1991: 148) has offered a theory of "tellability" based on inherent qualities of the plot; as she notes, some stories and their implied morals are richer, more engaging, and more imaginatively complex. As a corollary, Wolf Schmid (2003: 26–9) lists five elements that determine the degree of "eventfulness": relevance, unpredictability, persistence, irreversibility, and non-iterativity. In addition, we can note the "performance" elements of the story—the way that a particular narrative is constructed in order to make it aesthetically and emotionally satisfying and engaging. Meir Sternberg (1978: 34) offered an influential account of exposition as a series of strategies that "derive from an acute consciousness on the part of writers that literature is a time-art, in which the continuum of the text is apprehended by the reader in a continuum of time and in which elements are necessarily communicated and patterns unfolded not simultaneously but successively, and from their realization that these conditions may be exploited and manipulated in order to produce various effects on the reader" among which are curiosity, suspense, and surprise. The way that narratives handle uncertainty and anticipation has, of course, been a major part of narrative theory—especially since Wolfgang Iser's (1978: 125) phenomenological theory of reading as an "event" in which the reader constantly imagines and then reconfigures the horizon of the text as he or she strives to fill in gaps while reading. For Iser, the value of the story arises from the kinds of guesses and corrections that a reader will have to make while reading: "It is the reader who unfolds the network of possible connections, and it is the reader who then makes a selection from that network" (126). As a result, "as we read, we react to what we ourselves have produced, and it is this mode of reaction

[2] See Vyacheslav Yevseyev's (2005) attempt to quantify the degree of narrativity in texts.

that, in fact, enables us to experience the text as an actual event" (128–9). Of course, different works make this process easier or harder by distributing gaps in reader information in different ways. Lubomír Doležel (1998: 170) notes that authors can choose to "vary the number, the extent, and the function of the gaps by varying the distribution of" missing descriptions.

Recent rhetorical narratology has given particular attention to the way that anticipation shapes our experience of narrative comprehension. James Phelan offers an influential theory of narrative progression in his 1989 study of literary character. He defines narrative progression as follows:

> Progression, as I use the term, refers to a narrative as a dynamic event, one that must move, in both its telling and its reception, through time. In examining progression, then, we are concerned with how authors generate, sustain, develop, and resolve readers' interests in narrative. I postulate that such movement is given shape and direction by the way in which an author introduces, complicates, and resolves (or fails to resolve) certain instabilities which are the developing focus of the authorial audience's interest in the narrative. (15)

Phelan's definition of instabilities is a more specific articulation of Iser's concept of narrative gaps. He defines instabilities as a matter of uncertainties at the level of plot (what will or did happen to the characters), and contrasts them to tensions, which he associates with the telling of the story (how to understand the values or beliefs espoused by the narrator). Some stories are built on resolving the instabilities of plot, while others make the events quite clear and instead work to resolve the tension in their interpretation.

So far I have emphasized rather classical models of narratology, but I would like to close this section by summarizing issues raised by two somewhat newer traditions in narratology: possible world theory and cognitive narratology. Possible world theory developed out of philosophy of language, which asked how it was possible to refer to things that did not exist. In its application to literary study, possible world theory recognizes that our understanding of a given story world is defined not just by what happens, but by the structure of all events that might happen, that are imagined to have happened, and so on. Doležel (1998: 55–6) shows how this approach can affect how we talk about narrative events: "*event* is the transforming of an initial state into an end state at a certain time. No less significant is von Wright's introduction of the possible-worlds framework into action theory: from any given initial state the agent can proceed toward two or more possible end states. In the possible-world perspective a person's life history is a vector in multidimensional space" (emphasis in the original). Ryan (1991) describes "fiction" as projecting a "textual actual world" (TAW) that has specific relationships to the actual world (AW) that we live in. While reading, part of our experience is imagining other alternatives: "intrauniverse relations make it possible for members of the TAW to travel mentally within their own systems of reality" (32). Ryan has argued that part of what makes a story "tellable" is precisely the complexity of these imagined possible worlds. She offers the following principle for tellability: "*seek the diversification of possible worlds in the narrative universe*" (156; emphasis in the original). Thus, the greater the degree of possible outcomes, the more we understand the various wishes and dreams of the characters and the way that they motivate their behaviors, the more the story that results is tellable.

Cognitive narratology, for its part, now offers a particularly rich explanation for narrativity by emphasizing the continuities between literary narrative and the cognitive models that we use to make sense of everyday events. As David Herman (2002: 28) notes,

"To tell and comprehend stories is to operate within a system of probabilistic rules in which events are preferentially (but not absolutely or inevitably) viewed as goal-directed actions." Such probabilistic models can depend on "scripts," or stereotypical models for states or actions. We know, for example, the kinds of actions involved in "taking out the trash" or "preparing dinner," so a story might make reference to such actions and their likely components and outcomes without spelling out each detail; our knowledge of what each of these common actions involves is what Herman describes as a script. As Herman writes, "Since no recounting can be exhaustive, every act of telling arguably requires that a recipient use scripts to help set the narrative in motion, to co-create the story" (98). In this cognitive model, there is a great deal of continuity between our everyday experience of states (grief) or common events (birthday parties) on which both teller and listener might draw to make sense of a story—just as he or she would when confronted with their real-life equivalents.

Cognitive theory uses this continuity in order to apply a philosophy of action and event to make sense of narratives and the genres that they give rise to. Herman (2002: 31) draws on Zeno Vendler to develop a fourfold narrative model based on states, processes, accomplishments, and achievements—each of which is distributed differently in time. Herman goes on to show that different genres can privilege one or another of these: the epic emphasizes accomplishments and de-emphasizes states, ghost stories focus on activities and are relatively uninterested in achievements, and so on. Elsewhere, states can be further defined as temporary or permanent, and events as bounded or unbounded (43). In turn, these models for action lend themselves to further analysis. Herman notes eight different ways that an agent can act on a state of affairs (61), and further distinguishes between the modality of action, the setting for action, and the rationale for action (62). In all of these cases, the philosophical analysis of the components that define an action can help us to define the types of actions and states typical of different genres.

SAMPLE TEXT: TODAY I DIE

Thus far, I have provided a sketch of how narrative theory has defined and analyzed narrativity in general. Such theories tend to have a print orientation in general, and a literary bias in particular. Although work on film and, to a lesser extent, on graphic narrative has had some effect on narrative categories, literary narrative provides the bedrock examples for the vast majority of narrative theory. What challenges does the digital medium pose for these narrative theories?

To explore the degree to which these traditional features of narrativity apply to electronic literature, I would like to draw on an example text. "Today I Die" (2009), a poetic meditation on despair and hope created by Argentinian developer Daniel Benmergui, takes the form of a puzzle game in which the player must manipulate words that make up a sentence, which in turn affects the environment for the screen space. The game begins with the sentence "dead world full of shades today I die," with *dead* marked in green. It becomes clear that any of the green words in the sentence can be replaced with one of two other words on the screen: *dark* and *painful*.

The game has three different environments to begin: dead world, painful world, and dark world. Only a few simple, pixelated images fill out the screen: a woman is constant across all screens and appears to be our avatar in some way. Other threatening and hopeful images vary by screen. The player can manipulate these to alter the texts available.

FIGURE 7.1 Independently published at HYPERLINK “http://ludomancy.com/” \t “_blank” http://ludomancy.com. © Daniel Benmergui, 2010.

For example, after moving around glowing jellyfish on the dead world screen, the word *shine* (in yellow) appears and can be substituted for some other words in the sentence. Eventually *swim*, *free*, and *beauty* can be acquired as well to make either the sentence “free world full of beauty today I swim until you come” or “free world full of beauty today I swim better by myself.”

Overall, it seems clear that Benmergui has in mind a way of thinking about our experience of the world in which small glimmers of hope gradually build up to create an entirely new understanding of the future. The player’s own initial struggles in the dark world to find some way of changing the situation mirrors what we could see as a person’s struggle with despair. The step-by-step means through which the player finds some small bits of light that initially don’t change the world nicely captures the complexity of altering our attitude. As the player becomes more confident with the manipulation of screen images and acquires more words that can be slotted into the sentence, the world opens up to new forms and a wider variety of ways of interacting with the remaining threats on screen.

This is a game about gradual work of building on small rays of hope embodied not only in the sentence that defines the world, but also in the start-and-stop nature of gameplay.

Benmergui's is a particularly useful sample text for discussing narrativity in electronic literature because it contains so many elements that are typical of the medium. It is fundamentally textual: although it borrows from some elements of puzzle games, at its core the work is about manipulating a sentence.[3] Obviously, this work requires that the player grasp its mechanisms in order to be able to progress. Indeed, most players are likely to spend some time trying to manipulate screen elements before they begin to grasp the way to change the world. And, of course, this game is fundamentally narrative. The sentence itself makes reference to the current state of the world (dark, painful, dead) and then projects a future (today I die/swim). The game itself quite literally stages the change in state that narratologists associate with narrativity: the world transitions through three different states until arriving at the "free world" that marks the end of the work. The story implied here very much relies on character motivation and causality to move the story forward, since it is the avatar's apparent point of view on the world (dead, painful, dark) that defines the quality of the screen space. As the player acquires new words for the sentence, the avatar is evidently able to imagine the world in different ways, and thus to produce other possible futures.

UNIQUE FEATURES OF ELECTRONIC LITERATURE FOR NARRATIVITY

Obviously, there are many ways that theories of narrativity apply directly and unproblematically to electronic literature. Many film-like parts of these works, including the cut-scenes in commercial video games and animations in *Inanimate Alice*, tell stories in straightforward, cinematic ways. The language of "change of state," adopted by narratology since its beginning, has a literal embodiment in programing environments. Likewise, the concept of tellability applies quite directly; in fact, commercial video games are often guilty of striving to make every event an epic contest—to maximize tellability. Finally, the work on possible world theory has a natural corollary in the branching narratives of hypertext—as Alice Bell's *The Possible Worlds of Hypertext Fiction* (2010) demonstrates quite clearly. Indeed, as Marie-Laure Ryan's *Possible Worlds, Artificial Intelligence, and Narrative Theory* (1991) shows, possible world theory and computational media have developed a symbiotic relationship over the past two decades.

There are, however, ways in which electronic literature complicates some assumptions and models inherited from a narratology developed primarily through print texts. With Benmergui's sample game in hand, I would like to focus on four ways in which electronic literary works like this complicate the nature of narrativity as we see it articulated in theories that take print as their primary starting point.

[3] Of course, there has been a long-running debate about how heavily to emphasize the literary part of the term "electronic literature." Katherine Hayles offers a very broad definition in her 2008 *Electronic Literature*: "I would argue that although we may well wish to retain this criterion of verbal art for 'literature,' we need a broader category that encompasses the kind of creative work on display in the ELC [*Electronic Literature Collection*]. I propose 'the literary' for this purpose, defining it as creative artworks that interrogate the histories, contexts, and productions of literature, including as well the verbal art of literature proper" (4). In contrast, Roberto Simanowski (2010: 17) goes much narrower: a work of electronic literature "still requires reading as a central activity." My sample text obviously is much closer to Simanowski's more stringent definition.

The narrativity of language

Narrativity in electronic literature is complicated by the tension between the relative ease with which language can create narrativity and the other components that can either support or resist this narrativity. Early accounts of electronic textuality sometimes described such works as "multimedia," although we have since come to recognize the problems with this term because it implies that the digital is simply a combination of established, older media.[4] Nonetheless, we should recognize that electronic literature has, as a universal quality, a potential tension between the meaning structures associated with language and the electronic environment in which it is encountered. This is true of filmic texts like those of Young-Hae Chang Heavy Industries, just as much as in Storyspace hypertexts.

The narrativity of constituent literary elements is especially clear in older hypertext works based on longer lexia that frequently can tell stand-alone stories. To some extent, of course, many if not most literary works have some tension between individual constitutive stories and the larger text in which they are located—not just in short story sequences, but also in multi-plot narratives. But electronic literature creates much greater possibility for these kinds of micro-narratives. For example, in "In Absentia" J. R. Carpenter (2008) locates a variety of brief anecdotes on a Google Map of a particular section of Montreal: "I run into my neighbour on the street and he asks me if I've noticed the stranger who has 'moved in.' My neighbour is worried that the man has come up from New York for retribution." Many of these stories are about buying, owning, and selling space. By juxtaposing these local stories and the unifying, corporate mapping software provide by Google, "In Absentia" draws our attention to how much of our experience of city space cannot be integrated into such maps.

One of the common tensions in electronic literature, then, is between small narratives created by short sections of text, and a larger visual structure that imposes a different architecture on our encounter with those elements. This visual structure can enable, supplement, or even resist the narrativity evident in the linguistic sections. The clearest analog to this dual structure is graphic narrative, which likewise depends on balancing the visual against written language. Of course, graphic narrative uses panels to create sequence. As Stuart Moulthrop (2009: 289) explains in his reading of *Watchmen*:

> The medium of comics provides a powerful way to interrogate a reality abundant with signs, symptoms, and synchronicities. As noted, comics are always inherently dualistic, playing off space and simultaneity against succession and sequence. In most cases, the panel of a comic does not fill the visual field but rather coexists with others in the structure of the page. Likewise, the various verbal elements of comics (word balloons, text boxes that simulate a voice-over, and such) impinge on the graphical surface of every panel.

The visual can play a much more varied role in electronic literature. Instead of using panels to create the impression of moving through time, electronic literature often uses the visual as an unchanging frame or UI for play, against which the narrative of the text can be experienced. An example of such image/text integration would be the coauthored works published by *Born Magazine*, which often integrate texts that have been previously published in print with visual designs that frame or otherwise control the pace of reading.

---

[4] See Lev Manovich's (2013: 166) discussion of multimedia as a historically important term, and as one that contrasts with the more genuinely new "media hybrid."

In "A Servant. A Hanging. A Paper House," for example, Lucy Anderton's (2008) poem is displayed against a landscape and picture frame, and the text itself gradually fades in and moves as the reader clicks through the work. Of course, many works can use visual movement as a corollary to narration. Ingrid Ankerson's and Megan Sapnar's "Cruising" (2001) relies on both printed and voiced narration describing driving around a small town, but also includes a strip of images meant to invoke the town. As the reader manipulates the mouse to make the words legible and progress the text, these images move across the screen like a strip of film. In each of these cases, language has a more varied relationship to the surrounded visual context than we would encounter in a printed graphic narrative.

Time

As I noted above, the manipulation of time, order, and causality is inherent to our sense of narrative. Electronic literature introduces several complexities. Jesper Juul (2005) has written extensively on the way that video games change our sense of time. Juul offers an essential distinction between play time and fictional time:

> I propose the term *fictional time* to denominate the time of the events in the game world. In most action games and in the traditional arcade game, the play time-fictional time relation is presented as being 1:1. In such real-time games, pressing the first key or moving the mouse immediately affects the game world. Therefore, the game presents a parallel world, happening in real time. (142–3; emphasis in the original)

Other kinds of games, however, offer different fictional/game time relations. In some simulation games, fictional time moves much faster (cities build up in minutes what would take years), while in others fictional time moves much slower, such as in turn-based games where players might mull over choices that in the game may take only seconds of fictional time.

Above I noted that issues of narration speed are a common concern in narrative theory. But, as these examples make clear, electronic works add another layer to the time structure of print or filmic narrative. Such works have the potential to separate the time of interaction from the time that appears to be passing in the represented space of the story–although obviously they need not do so. If we turn to Benmergui's game, it is easy to see the effect of this dual time structure. Although the game is about imminent events ("today I die") the game itself is profoundly patient: generally, the game waits for the player to act, and the contemplative nature of our manipulation of the words and game space is essential to our experience. In fact, one of the ways that the game intervenes into what we might take as the stasis implied by the despair represented in the game is to insist on this space for reflection, exploration, and action.

There are, however, some ways that this understanding of time in the game is still too simple. When the game initially launches, time does clearly pass: jellyfish float up slowly past our avatar, which stays still in the center of the screen, while menacing black fish move slightly to show that they are alive and active. It is clear, in this sense, that time is passing—although the game itself is not progressing. We might describe this time as occurring at the level of the game itself as an object, a feature of the user interface, rather than at the level of any meaningful time in the represented world of the text. Perhaps the best example of this sort of time is what are called "idle animations" common in commercial 3D games, small fidgets that player avatars make when left unattended by the player, such as swaying from side-to-side or tapping a foot. This kind of background activity is a frequent feature of games, and helps to create a sense of aliveness. Games like this are quite literally waiting, and the time here has a quality that is unique: time passes without anything (necessarily) happening. But unlike a print text, where idleness might have a thematic value, this idleness is a variable of our encounter with the text, more a quality of how we approach or play the work than a quality of the events or world depicted. We might draw on Juul's terms and suggest that time in these electronic works has three components: represented time that appears to pass in the game world, play time in which the user is activity engaged, and interface time that can be variously active or passive depending on the design of the work.

In the initial screen of "Today I Die," game time is in a repetitious state, with nothing affecting the player avatar. In most commercial video games, of course, such points of stasis are relatively rare—breaks in waves of enemies that are swarming the player in a first-person shooter, for example. However the line between iterative stasis and more conventional oppositional activity is frequently muddy. In Benmergui's game, when the player changes the sentence to include "today I swim," the world begins to move as if the avatar is swimming, and the villainous creatures move toward the avatar. It is important to recognize that a certain kind of ongoing activity (swimming) is part of the continuing state of the text. In this regard, an ongoing event is part of the state, and ultimately will not cease until the world itself is altered by changing the sentence. We might say that the same is true of print narrative—a story that takes place aboard a boat is technically moving the whole time, but we don't think of that as an event. In print, though, such ongoing activity is largely invisible. In "Today I Die," the repetitious motion of jellyfish past the player avatar is obvious and a source of user interaction in a way that the constant movement of waves past the literary ship is not. The central role of iterative events complicates the notion of narrative event and the time of the story.

Textual architecture

At the outset I noted Ryan's observation that the freedom users have in making choices within an electronic work will inevitably make it more difficult for designers to impose a narrative structure on the work. As Jörgen Schäfer and Peter Gendolla (2010: 97) put it, "We have to be aware of the latent conflict between the writer's or game designer's aim to preserve narrative coherence and the reader/player's desire for *interactivity*" (emphasis in the original). Early accounts of electronic texts tended to celebrate user freedom uncritically, often claiming that readers would become equivalent to authors and jointly construct their reading experiences. Linda Hutcheon (1988: 77) wrote about "computerized, participatory 'compunovels'": "Here process is all; there is no fixed product or text, just the reader's activity as producer as well as receiver." In retrospect, these claims are overwrought. In *Cybertext*, Espen Aarseth (1997) pointed out that electronic works don't necessarily give the reader more freedom than print (where the reader can choose to flip to the last page of a novel at any time). In *The Language of New Media* Lev Manovich (2001) analyzed the "myth of interactivity" as a defining characteristic that allows us to sort digital from other media objects. Nonetheless, electronic literature is challenged by the fact that users will often encounter part of the work in an order that the designer cannot anticipate.

Because readers encounter elements of the text in variable ways, they need to build up a model of how the text is constructed. In *Avatars of Story* Ryan (2006) articulates various models of "textual architecture" such as the network, track-switching, and the tree. Such architectural models can be applied to print or cinematic narratives, but they are especially valuable in an electronic environment because they describe how a text will be constructed to allow readers to encounter events in different ways. We have already seen this in Benmergui's game. The actual order in which players will attempt things can vary: the player may first try swapping in either *painful* or *dark*, and may have to try several times before discovering the way that the glowing jellyfish can be used. One way to think about progression through the game is in terms of gated stages: the player cannot progress without doing the dark world stage before the painful world. Although the player is welcome to take a variety of actions, certain events must be completed before others can be encountered. Such gating mechanisms are common in commercial video games, where players must defeat a particular enemy before completing a game level. Likewise, player progression in interactive fiction can be gated by the possession of inventory items (a key or lantern). Similar gating techniques are used in Michael Joyce's (1987) early hypertext *afternoon*, which famously hides a key scene behind a "guard field" that is only available after some other parts of the work have been visited. Progression in this model has a considerably narrower meaning than what we see in Phelan's account of print narrative, since electronic literature is imposing a literal condition beyond which the reader cannot progress, while an inattentive reader of a novel may obviously continue until the end of a story without making certain connections.

In contrast, we can note many works of electronic literature that allow ungated exploration of various story strands. The difference between the early Storyspace hypertext of Joyce and Shelley Jackson's *Patchwork Girl* (1995) is an obvious one: while Joyce gates a key scene, Jackson allows readers to move freely among distinct narrative strands. It's clear that most works of electronic literature depend heavily on the separation between what narratologists define as catalyzers and cardinal functions: those actions that are trivial (walking back and forth, checking inventory) and those that affect the narrative world (progressing the plot, opening guarded links). In fact, most electronic works have a finely graduated scale of events based on the catalyzer/cardinal distinction.

Although not strictly related to narrativity, an important element of the architecture of electronic literature is the degree to which its overall design (sections, links, variables) is revealed. Joyce's *afternoon* drops the reader into the text with minimal orientation. In *Twelve Blue*, in contrast, Joyce provides more orientation in the form of twelve strands the readers can jump between. Jackson, likewise, provides images that are launching points for alternate strands—the body of the patchwork girl, or a phrenological skull. Of course, this kind of overall orientation has a corollary in commercial video games, where it is common to have some sort of high-level menu that allows players to choose various missions or levels. Although there are some similarities between these orientation tools and print front matter like a table of contents or back matter like an index, orientation models are especially important in electronic literature because there is usually no natural or default mechanism for progression through the work.

Thus far I have been emphasizing works of electronic literature that are primarily or significantly narrative, but we should also recognize the difference between those works that are structured according to narrative progress, and those that merely offer modes of interaction. In some ways, "Today I die" is an example of such works, since there is less a story here than a series of stages through which the player progresses. Electronic works borrowing from game models frequently use such stage or mode structures. In Jason Nelson's "Game, game, game, and again game" the player encounters a series of levels based on the side-scrolling platformer mechanic; each level involves drawings and texts focusing on different value systems (religion, wealth, self-improvement, truth), and the player must steer the avatar across each screen to progress to the next level. As this example makes clear, the use of game stages doesn't necessarily imply a narrative in the way that Benmergui's "Today I Die" does.

Electronic literature can, then, create narrativity at the level of the progression between gated stages; this is what "Today I Die" does. Other texts, such as Caitlin Fisher's *These Waves of Girls*, locate narrativity within individual stages and sections, but eschew narrative progression through these stages. Fisher's narrative exemplifies the way that early, Web-based hypertext could tell a series of interrelated stories using a menu system that allows the reader to enter (and reenter) sections in any order. As is common, readers are also able to jump between individual screens and stories, either by following hyperlinks between the text or by using sub-menus within each of these larger sections. In this case, narrativity exists entirely within the stories narrated and alluded to within individual lexia; the overall menu structure of the text is unconnected to narrative progression.

Agency and event

Electronic literature offers a more complex model for agency. We are used to talking about multiple agents in literary texts: the author projects an implied author, who frequently creates a narrator to tell the story to what sometimes is a characterized narratee, all the while the reader him or herself negotiates between the story and the author's own expectation about how the reader is supposed to respond. Nonetheless, all that agency is merely implied within the finished work itself, and it is only the reader who is active at the time of reading.[5]

In electronic literature, agency is considerably more complex.[6] Alexander Galloway (2006: 2) has defined video games as actions and has distinguished between machine actions and operator actions. He explains:

> The difference is this: machine actions are acts performed by the software and hardware of the game computer, while operator actions are acts performed by players. So winning *Metroid Prime* is the operator's act, but losing it is the machine's. Locating a power-up in *Super Mario Bros.* is an operator act, but the power-up actually boosting the player character's health is a machine act. (5)

To the initial distinction between operator and machine actions, Galloway adds one between diegetic and non-diegetic actions, or between those actions that exist within the represented world of the game (such as moving an avatar, picking up an object, or shooting an enemy) and those that take place outside of this world (such as adjusting the settings or saving the game). As Galloway notes, non-diegetic elements can be "firmly embedded in the game world," such as the heads up display in the game *Deux Ex* (8). When combined, these two oppositions create four possibilities: (1) diegetic operator actions, such as moving or shooting; (2) diegetic machine acts, such as the "idle animations" discussed above; (3) non-diegetic machine actions, such as announcing that

[5] I discuss how these entities apply to electronic works in "Narration, Intrigue, and Reader Positioning in Electronic Narratives" (2012).

[6] In this section I am not addressing the issue of the degree to which agency itself is meaningful—a common debate, in particular, in earlier work on the idea of "interactive drama." For a good recent discussion of this issue, see Jörgen Schäfer's "Looking behind the *Façade*" (2009).

the game is over; (4) non-diegetic operator acts, such as pausing the game or adjusting settings.

Galloway makes clear that actions in this context are considerably more complex than what we see in other media, since an event itself can occur in a variety of ways. It seems clear that narrativity will be a matter of diegetic actions—that we imagine a story through the game primarily in the represented world of the game, and not at the non-diegetic level of pausing the game or adjusting its settings.[7] We might recall the distinction between actions and happenings—between those changes in state initiated by a character, and those that merely happen to the character, such as a change in weather. Machine actions can take either form—it makes little difference to the way that the game operates that the machine is in control of a character (a villain that the player must defeat in combat) or the environment (the landscape down which the player must ski).

This distinction is helpful in thinking about narrative in Benmergui's game as well, which can reveal some complexities that Galloway overlooks. If we assume that the game helps the player to create a story about the discovery of hope and the transformation of the world from a dark, painful, and dead world to one filled with beauty and freedom, it is exclusively at the level of diegetic actions: the way that we see the player transforming the world, rather than how the user of the game finds and launches the game, adjusts the sound, and so on. But even this diegetic/non-diegetic distinction is more complex, since we have to translate our user interface actions into a kind of diegetic event that we imagine. In the world of a first-person shooter, we imagine the manipulation of a mouse or game controller becomes the equivalent of aiming a gun and firing at an enemy. In "Today I Die," Benmergui reveals that this connection is inherently mediated and artificial. What are we really doing when we swap one word for another in the sentence at the top of the screen? We are supposed to imagine a kind of change in perspective, I think, as the player and avatar find a new way to see the world. But precisely how that happens is left vague. Commercial video games rely on our familiarity with conventional actions like moving and shooting so that we don't think about the indirection of these actions. Indeed, it is clear that in many cases even user actions have a machine-like quality to them. Hit a button to reload a weapon and the avatar will often go through an elaborate script of raising the weapon, releasing the clip, inserting a new one, and so on. These actions are prompted by the user but the machine itself takes control of the avatar for a brief period.

As a result, it makes more sense to see Galloway's four-part model for game actions as one of degrees based in part on the style of the game, and in part on the nature of the action. In some abstract games like *Tetris*, the link between user action and diegetic event is relatively unmediated: click the button once, and the block moves or spins one step. In more realistic games with more elaborately constructed diegetic worlds actions are inherently going to be more machine mediated, since even relatively simple actions in fact involve many constitutive elements. I have already noted Herman's (2002: 97) discussion of the narrative script, which "was designed to explain how people are able to build up complex (semantic) representations of stories on the basis of very few textual or linguistic cues." He gives the example of a narrative that mentions "Bill opened his presents" or

[7] There are, of course, many exceptions. We might take the example of the trophies that many commercial video games award for certain kinds of actions: beat the game on a hard difficulty level, kill a certain number of enemies, complete a particular mission without dying. Such conditions are non-diegetic, but might have an in-game effect, such as the awarding of a particular title or badge that other players can see in the case of an online game.

"Mary was invited to Jack's party" (98). Both of these events obviously have a great many constitutive steps, and it would be impossible to narrate every single action ("Bill raised his left arm, grasped the edge the wrapping paper on the top-left side of the box and pulled with a steady downward motion").

It is clear that scripts are being invoked by user interaction. When the player hits the "reload" button on a first-person shooter, he or she is not performing a specific action, but instead invoking a script with many constitutive sub-actions. The difference in the context of a digital narrative, however, is that these sub-actions are shown on screen, whereas in an oral or written narrative the reader or listener is allowed merely to imagine them. As a result, there is an inherent machinic action that exists in the gap between script and its diegetic realization. Although it is possible to argue that this means that an electronic text demands less from its audience, since it is showing the actions that the reader of a novel has to visualize, the same criticism could surely be applied to other visual media such as film and the graphic novel. It is more useful and fair, I think, to see these differences as variations in how the audience's imagination and agency is engaged by different media.

CONCLUSION

In this chapter I have outlined some of the ways that electronic literature complicates our understanding of narrativity. Crucial to this discussion, however, is the recognition that narrative is not a binary condition (texts must either be narrative or not narrative) but instead a feature of many kinds of texts. Although some digital works participate in narrative only at a second-order level when players narrate their own game performance (here's how I got my high score on *Tetris*), most invoke narrative in some way as part of their represented world. This can take the form of the residual narrative that a work might inherit as part of a transmedia franchise, such as *Star Wars* or *The Lord of the Rings*. Narrativity can also emerge in individual components of the work, such as the lexia in hypertext narratives. And, of course, some electronic works will mandate an overall progression through the work that itself is narrative in nature.

Examining narrativity in electronic fiction also allows us to recognize tensions within some of our core narrative concepts that otherwise might be overlooked in traditional media. In particular, electronic media make clearer the complex nature of agency and the granular quality of the event, which print-based narrative theory has given far less attention to. Indeed, it may well be that the nature of event will emerge as one of the central issues in a theory of narratology informed by digital media.

SOURCES CITED

Aarseth, Espen J. *Cybertext: Perspectives on Ergodic Literature*. Baltimore: Johns Hopkins University Press, 1997.

Anderton, Lucy, and Nicholas Robinson. "A Servant. A Hanging. A Paper House." *Born Magazine*, 2008, http://www.bornmagazine.org/projects/servant/.

Ankerson, Ingrid, and Megan Sapnar. "Cruising." *The Electronic Literature Collection*, Volume 1. 2006. http://collection.eliterature.org/1/works/ankerson_sapnar__cruising.html.

Bal, Mieke. *Narratology: Introduction to the Theory of Narrative*. 2nd ed. Toronto: University of Toronto Press, 1997.

Barthes, Roland. "Introduction to the Structural Analysis of Narratives." In *A Barthes Reader*, edited by Susan Sontag. New York: Noonday, [1966] 1982, pp. 251–95.

Bell, Alice. *The Possible Worlds of Hypertext Fiction*. Basingstoke: Palgrave, 2010.
Benmergui, Daniel. "Today I Die." 2009. http://www.ludomancy.com/games/today.php.
Bogost, Ian. *Unit Operations: An Approach to Videogame Criticism*. Cambridge: MIT Press, 2006.
Booth, Wayne C. *The Rhetoric of Fiction*. 2nd ed. Chicago: University of Chicago Press, 1983.
Carpenter, J. R. "In Absentia." June 24, 2008, http://luckysoap.com/inabsentia/.
Chatman, Seymour. *Story and Discourse: Narrative Structure in Fiction and Film*. Ithaca, NY: Cornell University Press, 1978.
Ciccoricco, David. *Reading Network Fiction*. Tuscaloosa: University of Alabama Press, 2007.
Ciccoricco, David. "Games as Stories." In *The Johns Hopkins Guide to Digital Media*, edited by Marie-Laure Ryan, Lori Emerson, and Benjamin J. Robertson. Baltimore: Johns Hopkins University Press, 2014, pp. 224–8.
Doležel, Lubomír. *Heterocosmica: Fiction and Possible Worlds*. Baltimore: Johns Hopkins University Press, 1998.
Eskelinen, Markku. "Towards Computer Game Studies." In *First Person: New Media as Story, Performance, and Game*, edited by Noah Wardrip-Fruin and Pat Harrigan. Cambridge: MIT Press, 2004, pp. 36–44.
Fisher, Caitlin. *These Waves of Girls*. 2001. http://www.yorku.ca/caitlin/waves//.
Forster, E. M. *Aspects of the Novel*. New York: Harcourt Brace Javanovich, 1927.
Galloway, Alexander R. *Gaming: Essays on Algorithmic Culture*. Minneapolis: University of Minnesota Press, 2006.
Genette, Gérard. *Narrative Discourse: An Essay in Method*. Translated by Jane E. Lewin. Ithaca, NY: Cornell University Press, 1980.
Hayles, N. Katherine. *Electronic Literature: New Horizons for the Literary*. Notre Dame, IN: University of Notre Dame Press, 2008.
Herman, David. *Story Logic: Problems and Possibilities of Narrative*. Lincoln: University of Nebraska Press, 2002.
Hutcheon, Linda. *A Poetics of Postmodernism: History, Theory, Fiction*. New York: Routledge, 1988.
Iser, Wolfgang. *The Act of Reading: A Theory of Aesthetic Response*. Baltimore: Johns Hopkins University Press, 1978.
Jackson, Shelley. *Patchwork Girl*. CD-ROM. Watertown, MA: Eastgate Systems, 1995.
Jenkins, Henry. "Game Design as Narrative Architecture." In *First Person: New Media as Story, Performance, and Game*, edited by Noah Wardrip-Fruin and Pat Harrigan. Cambridge: MIT Press, 2004, pp. 118–30.
Joyce, Michael. *afternoon. a story*. Diskette. Watertown, MA: Eastgate Systems, 1987.
Joyce, Michael. *Twelve Blue*. The Electronic Literature Collection, Vol. 1. 2006. http://collection.eliterature.org/1/works/joyce__twelve_blue.html.
Juul, Jesper. *Half-Real: Video Games between Real Rules and Fictional Worlds*. Cambridge: MIT Press, 2005.
Manovich, Lev. *The Language of New Media*. Cambridge: MIT Press, 2001.
Manovich, Lev. *Software Takes Command*. New York: Bloomsbury, 2013.
Montfort, Nick. *Twisty Little Passages: An Approach to Interactive Fiction*. Cambridge: MIT Press, 2003.
Moulthrop, Stuart. "See the Strings: *Watchmen* and the Under-Language of Media." In *Third Person: Authoring and Exploring Vast Narratives*, edited by Pat Harrigan and Noah Wardrip-Fruin. Cambridge: MIT Press, 2009, pp. 287–301.
Nelson, Jason. "Game, Game, Game, and Again Game." *The Electronic Literature Collection*, Vol. 2 (2011), http://collection.eliterature.org/2/works/nelson_game.html.

Phelan, James. *Reading People, Reading Plots: Character, Progression, and the Interpretation of Narrative*. Chicago: University of Chicago Press, 1989.

Prince, Gerald. "Aspects of a Grammar of Narrative." *Poetics Today*, vol. 1, no. 3 (1980): 49–63.

Punday, Daniel. "Narration, Intrigue, and Reader Positioning in Electronic Narratives." *Storyworlds*, vol. 4 (2012): 25–47.

Rimmon-Kenan, Shlomith. *Narrative Fiction: Contemporary Poetics*. London: Methuen, 1983.

Ryan, Marie-Laure. *Possible Worlds, Artificial Intelligence, and Narrative Theory*. Bloomington: Indiana University Press, 1991.

Ryan, Marie-Laure, ed. *Narrative across Media: The Languages of Storytelling*. Lincoln: University of Nebraska Press, 2004.

Ryan, Marie-Laure. *Avatars of Story*. Minneapolis: University of Minnesota Press, 2006.

Schäfer, Jörgen. "Looking behind the *Façade*: Playing and Performing an Interactive Drama." In *Literary Art in Digital Performance: Case Studies in New Media Art and Criticism*, edited by Francisco J. Ricardo. New York: Continuum, 2009, pp. 143–61.

Schäfer, Jörgen, and Peter Gendolla. "Reading (in) the Net: Aesthetic Experience in Computer-Based Media." In *Reading Moving Letters: Digital Literature in Research and Teaching. A Handbook*. Bielefeld: Transcript Verlag, 2010, pp. 81–108.

Schmid, Wolf. "Narrativity and Eventfulness." In *What Is Narratology? Questions and Answers Regarding the Status of a Theory*, edited by Tom Kindt and Hans-Harald Müller. Berlin: Walter de Gruyter, 2003, pp. 17–33.

Scholes, Robert, and Robert Kellogg. *The Nature of Narrative*. London: Oxford University Press, 1966.

Simanowski, Roberto. "Reading Digital Literature: A Subject between Media and Methods." In *Reading Moving Letters: Digital Literature in Research and Teaching. A Handbook*, edited by Roberto Simanowski, Jörgen Schäfer, and Peter Gendolla. Bielefeld: Transcript Verlag, 2010, pp. 15–28.

Sternberg, Meir. *Expositional Modes and Temporal Ordering in Fiction*. Bloomington: Indiana University Press, 1978.

Suvin, Darko. "On Metaphoricity and Narrativity in Fiction: The Chronotope as the *Differentia Generica*." *Sub-Stance*, vol. 48 (1986): 51–67.

Todorov, Tzvetan. *Introduction to Poetics*. Translated by Richard Howard. Minneapolis: University of Minnesota Press, 1981.

Watt, Ian. *The Rise of the Novel: Studies in Defoe, Richardson and Fielding*. Berkeley: University of California Press, 1957.

White, Hayden. *The Content of the Form: Narrative Discourse and Historical Representation*. Baltimore: Johns Hopkins University Press, 1987.

Yevseyev, Vyacheslav. "Measuring Narrativity in Literary Texts." In *Narratology beyond Literary Criticism: Mediality, Disciplinarity*, edited by Jan Christoph Meister. Berlin: Watler de Gruyter, 2005, pp. 109–24.

CHAPTER EIGHT

Rebooting Cognition in Electronic Literature

DAVID CICCORICCO

Cognition has served as a central preoccupation and a kind of master trope in the development of electronic literature, not surprisingly given the deep imbrication of computer science and cognitive science as the two disciplines developed in the twentieth century. Certain strands of creative computation, such as the domain of text adventure games and interactive fiction, had an inbuilt investment in the powers of "artificial" cognition from the beginning. Those in the literary intellectual scene that gave rise to early hypertext literature, meanwhile, would adopt the anti-hierarchical and antirationalist ethos of visionary technologists in that field—along with cognate ideas circulating in the critical theory of the day (Deleuze and Guattari [1987] 2004)—and apply it to their own vision of readers liberated by a new cognitive architecture now manifest in the material form of hypertext.

From the start, however, there were some fraught alignments and hasty analogies in the rhetoric framing the relation between our minds and the computational tools that we built to augment, extend, and enhance them. I will briefly map out some of the problematic gestures that marked the early discourse of early electronic literature as well as the correctives—informed by cognitive psychological research—that followed. I will then suggest that just as cognitive science has moved on from the comparably reductive focus on the calculation and representation of formal logic typified by its classical phase, so too has electronic literature moved on to reflect some of the facets that comprise contemporary research on cognition, which casts it as embodied and emotive, distributed and social, and enacted with and through our media environments.

An analysis of two examples of relatively recent works of electronic fiction, Fox Harrell's *Mimesis* (2012) and Samantha Gorman and Danny Cannizzaro's *Pry* (2014), can illustrate how the digital literary arts maintain a productive dialogue with cognition as both a trope and a target of cognitive scientific inquiry. Both works raise significant questions regarding the totalizing impulse arguably inherent in digital media; and they challenge what David Golumbia (2009), in his critique of a broader set of beliefs that uncritically privilege the (progressive and instrumental) power of computation, calls "computationalism." Such works, moreover, underscore their role as participating in a kind of art of resistance. Here electronic literature takes up not only a mode of political or ideological intervention (with which we are familiar from more traditional literary engagements) but also a media-specific one. That is, electronic literature, in its aesthetic appropriation of digital tools and the embodied acts that characterize our connection to them—from the most complex programmatic story generator to the simplest touchscreen swipe—keeps metaphor and figuration active and alive in concert with algorithm and simulation. Electronic literature, I would suggest, might help keep our minds alive to our media environment in turn.

EXTENSIONS, ASSOCIATIONS, AND TOTALIZATIONS

We can trace a line back through the earliest computer scientists and mass media pundits who position the emerging information technologies of the time, including hypertext, as *extensions* and *augmentations* of the human mind. The inventive and progressive spirit of Douglas Engelbart's (1962) early work epitomizes this drive, and many of his projects make explicit the goal of augmenting the intelligence of both the collective and the individual. The same push for extending human capabilities through media technologies was popularized in emphatic fashion by Marshall McLuhan (1964: 3):

> During the mechanical ages we had extended our bodies in space. Today, after more than a century of electric technology, we have extended our central nervous system itself in a global embrace, abolishing both space and time as far as our planet is concerned. Rapidly, we approach the final phase of the extensions of man—the technological simulation of consciousness, when the creative process of knowing will be collectively and corporately extended to the whole of human society.

We can trace another line that takes us through a group of scholars, George Landow (1997) cited most prominently among them, who position the same technologies as more accurately mirroring the associative and networked nature of our cognitive function. Both lines share a liberationist streak and a common ancestor in Vannevar Bush's ([1945] 2001) pre-digital conception of a machine that would augment our sensory and cognitive apparatus based on its perceived correspondence to the (biological) neural networks that reflect how we really think. But taken together, what we might call the *extensionist* and *associationist* positions are incongruous: a digitally networked environment works for us either because it works like us, mirroring our mental faculty, and thus is intuitive and natural to the way we already function; or because it enables us to compensate for a lack or limitation in that faculty—that is, it artificially augments what we naturally lack.

Granted, it is possible to claim that we are simply extending a capacity we already possess by means of another structurally similar mechanism, just as wielding a hammer or a rake is an example of employing a tool that extends or augments our otherwise physically inadequate upper limbs, and the much less efficient fist or splayed fingers at the end of them. But we enter more of a gray area, so to speak, when it comes to the operations of mental activity. What exactly would we be extending by way of associative networks? Are we extending the speed of linkages? Or do we have in mind the brute number of stored associations? In the latter case, it would appear we are not so much extending as rather externalizing in the manner of cognitive offloading memory. In any case, on the face of it, the extensionist paradigm, in its teleological pursuit of instrumental enhancement, too crudely approximates our reciprocal relationship with the tools of media technology. For similar reasons, pushed to its logical extreme, it ventures into territory marked by what has come to be called transhumanism—the radical project of not simply enhancing but rather transcending the human limitations of the fleshly realm.[1] Nonetheless, whether

[1] See Wolfe (2013: xii–xiii) on how the term "transhumanism" effectively inherits the "cyborg" genealogy of early posthumanism.

we are modeling the mind to extend it or transcend it, computational theories of mind, in their narrow focus on propositional logic and formal reasoning capabilities, involve a necessarily impoverished conception of cognition itself.[2]

The literary establishment, of course, was more interested in the poetic implications of the associationist paradigm as opposed to the comparably more instrumental implications of the extensionist one, but there are even thornier problems with this line. As has been well established, early hypertext theory tended to overstate the ideological virtues of association and multi-linearity over and against hierarchy and linearity (Ciccoricco 2007). In the process, it overlooked the inescapable linearity of reading in terms of the cognitive expenditures of propositional processing (Charney 1994), and ignored the similarly hierarchical quality of working memory in terms of its temporally constrained "gateway." The associationist position, furthermore, tends to elide the distinction between linearity at the level of narrative discourse, which allows for the quite common practice of temporal manipulations in narration, and (multi)linearity or modularity at the level of the medium, which allows for variability of the material units or "nodes" that comprise a textual network.[3] As Thierry Bardini (2000: 40) notes, *association* is also only one kind of *connection*, and is in fact the "least desirable kind" when it comes to communication given the individual and idiosyncratic nature of association. Association is thus far from "free" whenever it is bound by the need to be *mutually* intelligible.

At the core of the associationist approach was the analogy between neural and digital networks: a perceived structural isomorphism between our cognitive architecture and the topological networks we construct computationally and, indeed, hypertextually. Adding to this notion was the growing influence of connectionism in cognitive science, a form of mind modeling that attempts to emulate the all-or-nothing quality of individual neurons. Such neuronal "units" are arranged in large number in elaborate computational networks along with "weights" designed to function like synapses in measuring the strength between those units (Garson 1997).[4] Unlike cognitivist models bound by sequential processing, the neural nets of connectionism are not only able to process in parallel but are also capable of so-called learned behaviors that manifest in emergent properties of the network. Notwithstanding the need for models to simplify in order to retain their explanatory force, neural nets of connectionism still remain at best a loose analogy for the purported associativeness of cognition. As Andy Clark (2001) notes, connectionist models inevitably distort biological facts in several ways. They tend to set up experiments involving overly discrete and well-defined tasks that are subject to overly artificial—and often, in relation to the brain, relatively small—sets of inputs at the hands of experimenters. The

---

[2] For more on the discrete philosophical position known as *the* Computational Theory of Mind (CTM), which holds that thought is literally a form of computation and the human mind is essentially a special kind of computer, see Horst (2003).

[3] In the context of electronic literature, a "node" is basically a screen-full or window-full of text (or image, sound, and video). The building blocks of any networked texts and many digital fictions, they are semantic units meaningful both independent of and in relation to the larger network in which they reside. Arguably, the node is a new bibliographical unit peculiar to digital environments (much like a chapter, footnote, or stanza). I use "node" rather than "lexia," a term popular in early hypertext theory appropriated from Roland Barthes, given that Barthes was effectively describing a hermeneutic prerogative of the reader, who breaks up the text into analytic elements, whereas the nodes of digital textuality are a compositional prerogative of the author: they are *written* as self-contained units.

[4] The connectionist approach was present, conceptually, even at the birth of cybernetics in the 1940s, with Warren McCulloch and Walter Pitts devising an abstract mathematical model of neuron-like "units" according to neurophysiological principles. Connectionism is now exploiting the power of supercomputing and gaining currency in cognitive-scientific circles.

fact that each net is responsible for *one task*, moreover, amounts to a gross reduction of neural function. Finally, most neural net models remain out of sync with certain details of neuroscientific research, including "continuous-time processing" and "nonlocal effects" whereby the response of whole populations of neurons is modified, for instance, by the release of a chemical over an entire grouping (79–82). More generally, it is necessary to recognize both the hierarchical and networked quality of cognitive function as well as the temporal constraints that bind the acts of reading and remembering. Or, to revisit Deleuze and Guattari's ([1987] 2004: 15) observation in *A Thousand Plateaus* that "many people have a tree growing in their heads but the brain itself is much more a grass than a tree," it is perhaps fair to suggest that we have room in our heads for both grass and trees.

Digital culture's early obsession with the supposed power of a mutable and modular network of digital text to realize an infinitude of narrative possibility might point to a final example of infelicitous inheritance from the totalizing drive of classical cognitive science. In harnessing computational power to parse lexical input in order to produce a narrative output in turn, text adventure games and interactive fictions that predate hypertext fictions have an overt connection to the cognitive/computer science nexus. The domain of "strong" AI sits at the headwaters of this computational practice in pursuing ever more powerful and encompassing artificial agents. Such research programs may be geared toward commercial and military applications, while others may be invested in nothing other than better understandings of the mind. But underpinning the most radical research in the field remains the drive to totalize human thought and language by reducing it to formal syntax and translating it into binary code. It was the seduction of the same kind of totalizing ideal, moreover, that led some hypertext enthusiasts to locate the true promise of that form in what they saw as the potential for infinite or inexhaustible narratives, an ideal that did not move from theory to practice in any compelling manner, as Ryan (2001) and I have argued (Ciccoricco 2007: 108–109). It is also up for debate whether, by avoiding one "master" narrative, hypertext's pursuit of the infinite really aligned itself with the radical antirationalism and relativity of poststructuralist theory. By striving to create *all* conceivable narratives at once, it may just as well have run counter to this ethos as simply another attempt at creative (and inescapably positivistic) mastery.

Totalizing techno-fantasies, nonetheless, assume new relevance in light of the strides taken in computer animation and processing capabilities that converge in a culture of simulation. Simulation combines with aesthetics most conspicuously in videogame production, but its implications extend to electronic literature, which not only blurs the line between story and game, or reading and playing, but also keeps the door open to accommodating games (especially literary or story-driven ones) under its own rubric. A propensity to totalize is arguably inherent to the very process of simulation, manifest not only in models of the mind but also in those of fully immersive, photo-realistic, and tactile virtual worlds, which endeavor to refashion reality through the ideal of the invisible interface and the pursuit of all-consuming one-to-one mappings of a target system. Thus, in works of electronic literature and art, simulation can be an operative element of the digital artifact; but it can also be present as a thematic concern, for instance, in interrogations of what we might call the mind/machine problem and where we draw the lines of (post)humanist subjectivity.

All in all, any attempt to characterize the relationship between our mental lives and our media environment needs to account for the changing nature of cognitive development itself. Engelbart recognized the reciprocal nature of sociotechnical change in his decades-long pursuit of solutions to complex social problems by tapping the power of radical technological advance, using the term "co-evolution" to refer to the mutual effects of technical practices and human capabilities (Bardini 2000). More recently, the work of N. Katherine Hayles (2012), moving from the anthropologically oriented philosophy of Bernard Stiegler (1998), has cast the phenomenon in terms of "technogenesis" in advocating for a greater understanding of the accelerated rate at which today's "hyper" media shape cognition, and the way we shape our technical environments in turn.[5] Such changes are ontogenetic adaptations manifesting within an individual's lifetime; they do not, moreover, guarantee progress but rather only "coordinated transformations" (Hayles 2012: 81). That realization alone might make the reactionary alarm against the perceived ills of our current media consumption sound even louder. But as Hayles notes, technogenesis through digital media also offers us new opportunities for "self-fashioning"—active interventions that include both making new media and adapting current media to redirect or subvert its dominant hold on our culture (83).

Electronic literature undoubtedly has a role to play in such self-fashioning, by way of instilling the kind of critically creative media practice and mindfulness I describe below. But that prospect also raises some immediate questions with regard to the nature of its intervention. Does it operate in a mode of complicity, connecting to its audience through the same means and media to which they are already connected? Does that necessitate a shift in its creative impulse toward modular and micro-narratives in order to fit our newly modular- and micro-attentions in turn?[6] Or, does it operate as an art of resistance, somehow preserving, in new media, the kind of literary experience that can only be served by sustained attention and sustained reflection—the kind we might associate more readily with older media? Can it be both complicit and resistant and achieve these objectives at once? There are traps to avoid up front. No medium, no matter how interactive or participatory it is, determines our engagement with it or our commitment to it. We can be just as dead to our media environment while we click, scroll, and swipe as the so-called slackers of the TV generation, flipping through channels, were to theirs. Mindlessness is medium-blind. Every now and then we need to remind ourselves of what it is we are really "searching" for (even when we are "just browsing, thanks"). And we need to ask ourselves not only what kind of commitment we have made to our media, but also what kind of promise—beyond the immediate fix of a dopamine hit—we expect it to deliver on in turn.

We also need to resist privileging any one mode of attention over another: we are just as responsible for adapting ourselves (and, as educators, our pedagogy) to environments with rapid-fire stimuli as we are to *better* articulating why it is worthwhile to continue cultivating singular, sustained, and contemplative modes of attention (those that allow us to indulge communicative acts of critical writing and reading such as the present essay). In any case, *attention*, as contemporary cognitive science reminds us, is already divided, much less like an on/off switch than a collection of different though overlapping skills mobilized for different tasks and by different subsystems in our brain. The same understanding

[5] In one sense, Engelbart's "co-evolution" differs from the notion of "technogenesis" on the account of his casting it as a conceivably *voluntary* learning process. (See Bardini [2000] on the accidents of history that led the development of the personal computer away from the paradigm of "co-evolution" and toward one of "user-friendliness.")

[6] Of course, the suggestion that it is even possible to achieve such a fit is merely a provocation, and a caution against moving too casually and carelessly from the millisecond measures of perceptual attention in cognitive science to the literary or linguistic units of attention constrained by language processing—and, for that matter, the units of attention dictated by social network alerts on one's cellphone.

resonates in certain strands of critical posthumanism that have undermined the notion of a humanist subject who occupies a kind of perceptual center stage from which they gain a somehow complete and unified field of observation. This richer and more varied view of attention is not simply a newfangled cognitive scientific development; in fact, as Cary Wolfe (2010) has suggested, it takes us back to Romantic-era literary conceptions, such as Emerson's, that lay bare the perpetual staging of perception.[7] Finally, we should not allow the *medium* of electronic literature to preempt or even predetermine either the critical comment their stories convey or the kind of critical readings they allow. That is, in telling the stories of our technological moment, the choice is not between a mode of Romantic resistance to technoculture and its stranglehold on contemporary consciousness on the one hand and a blissful affirmation of a transhumanist cyborg condition on the other.[8]

That all art is technical and all art is a way to make sense of our technological moment is a given point of departure. My main concern is with the kind of *unique* contribution that electronic fiction can have in this vein, which is, put simply, its power to make us more mindful of the creative and expressive potential of the devices that all too often pull us toward conformity and consumerism. It is, in turn, an invitation for empowerment amid the complexities of technogenetic change. The digital literary arts have demonstrated a knack for keeping pace with those technical advances primarily meant to feed appetites of a more commercial, capitalist, or even military kind, all the while suffusing them with an aesthetic charge. Co-opting or appropriating these instruments for creative ends is something that occurs with entire forms (or genres) of digital textuality, for example: what Will Crowther and Don Woods did with AI and natural language processing in *Adventure* (1976–77); what Michael Joyce did with hypertext in *afternoon: a story* (1987); what Rob Wittig did with email in his serial email novel *Blue Company* (2001–2002); what Matthew Baldwin did with the blog in his fictional *The LiveJournal of Zachary Marsh* (2004); and what Jennifer Egan, in her tweeted short story "Black Box" (2012), did with the micro-blog Twitter. But it also occurs in more discrete transactions *within* digital forms and formats, in our manipulation at the level of the interface. Modes of input that might begin life as instrumental efficiencies—much like the link was to navigation—are reprogrammed with expressivity, poetic charge, and beauty.

MINDFUL POSTURING IN *MIMESIS*

Mimesis (2012) is a computationally driven narrative created by Fox Harrell and his team at MIT's Imagination, Computation, and Expression Laboratory. In its storyworld, you play as a mimic octopus, a species renowned for its real-life ability to alter its color, shape, and behavior in order to elude or repel prey—precariously playacting as anything from inconspicuous coral to a venomous lionfish. Your undersea avatar encounters a number of other anthropomorphized marine creatures throughout the course of its journey in

---

[7] In "The Method of Nature," Emerson (1971: 123) writes, "The wholeness we admire in the order of the world, is the result of infinite distribution. Its smoothness is the smoothness of the pitch of the cataract. Its permanence is a perpetual inchoation. Every natural fact is an emanation, and that from which it emanates is an emanation also, and from every emanation is a new emanation."

[8] Twenty-first century philosophy and cultural theory has seen the formation of a clear division between the kind of technophiliac fantasies of biological transcendence (of mind and body) that have come to be called transhumanism, and a more politically and ethically charged "critical posthumanism" that seeks a productive relationality among (decentered) humans, nonhuman animals, technology, and the environment (see, e.g., Braidotti [2013] and Herbrechter [2013]).

four levels of play, which correspond to the varying levels of the ocean depths. *Mimesis* stages a series of what social psychology refers to as "micro-aggressions," utterances or behaviors that may appear superficially benign but convey subtle forms of prejudice and hostility.

For example, think of someone, walking around their own hometown, who, conceivably based on their skin tone or manner of speaking, is asked by a new acquaintance: "So where are you from?" The question suggests that one *assumes* that the other is alien to what is actually his or her own neighborhood or region. As the developers of *Mimesis* explain, "[W]e aimed to create an aesthetically engaging experience for players that simultaneously helps to catalyze critical awareness about social identity phenomena" (Harrell et al. 2014). That awareness extends to forcing participants to decide what they would actually do in such a situation: in each encounter, the player chooses from a number of strategies of response to the comments of the other sea animals that might assume that we have, for example, "foreign status" or "criminal intent" (see Harrell et al. [2014] for an elaboration of social psychology's typology). Via a trackpad or click-and-drag mouse input that swipes the screen horizontally, we can adjust our outward demeanor from more "open" to more "closed." Or we can click on the avatar itself and adjust our internal stance with a vertical swipe that moves from more "positive" to more "negative" (touchscreen versions use the corresponding swipes and taps). The various permutations of these positions shape what we say to the creatures we meet in turn, utterances that appear as dialogue text underneath the character icons. The reactions of the other sea creatures to you, and a brief epilogue that takes center screen at the end of the text, will change according to the choices you make and the social stances you adopt throughout.

Mimesis marks a deft interrogation of subtle forms of social bias and interpersonal insult, and it makes a valuable comment on the nuances of social cognition as it plays out in both virtual and actual environments. But it also offers a comment on the relationship of cognition and electronic literature more broadly. Computationally, the narrative architecture of *Mimesis* derives its force not by attempting to encode the greatest number of possible choices and responses in a manner that would embrace brute algorithmic power in a convincing display of machine intelligence. Rather, it encodes a circumscribed number of possible exchanges with a select few typecast interlocutors, again, in the pursuit of a kind of social realism (Galloway 2006). The work does so by defining a set of (often awkward) conversational scenarios, and then forcing players to negotiate them. But it is arguably less invested in what you will *do* to get out of the situation than what it *feels* like for you to be in it. *Mimesis* features an intriguing inversion as well, asking not what you want to make your player-character say, but rather how you want to position yourself based on how you are made to feel. Reflecting on what you say is an afterthought—an epiphenomenon of the encounter. That act of positioning reminds us that so much depends on—emerges from—posture and bodily disposition; for instance, we not only smile because we feel better, but we also feel better because we smile. The focus and framing of *Mimesis* in this regard also places it in dialogue with contemporary cognitive and neuroscientific understandings of the intensely reciprocal workings of *thought* and *emotion*, and more specifically the way in which emotion regulates and, often nonconsciously, informs reasoning, rather than simply clouding it (Damasio 1999).

Mimesis creates a feedback loop between, on the one hand, conceptual domains common to literary practice (in its imaginative fashioning of fictional beings and fictional worlds) and, on the other, those common to cognitive science (viz., the categorical and schematic strategies that guide us epistemologically). The text encodes a limited range of emotional exchanges that simulate subtle forms of social aggression, thereby fashioning an experience that eschews the totalizing realism of a rational system for that which is a highly delimited yet highly convincing social one. The same move points to the possibility of a system that aspires to a kind of universality without totality. There are philosophical precedents: it was Pierre Lévy's *Cyberculture* (2001) that uncoupled universality from totality, taking as its main exemplar the Web itself. He observed that as "cyberspace grows it becomes more 'universal' and the world of information less totalizable" (91). There is a striking and often noted contrast here between the amorphous and mutable knowledge store of the Web and the great encyclopedias of the eighteenth century in their tacit goal to concretize everything that was to be known at the time.

But as Lévy (2001) makes clear, the distinction goes beyond the mere *containment* of knowledge, or for that matter the claims—albeit illusory—to an absolute truth that accompanies it. Universality carries an explicit ethical dimension in its own claims to accessibility and commonality, and as a result becomes the privileged term in this conceptual pairing. Not only does the Web provoke "a mutation in the physics of communication" (107), the very notion of the universal without totality also constitutes its "paradoxical essence" (92). Even if the Web serves as a *locus classicus*, we can still locate examples of the universal without totality in other and historically much older complex systems, such as natural language itself. The crucial and culturally contingent move at hand, however, involves redeeming the notion of the universal, which has acquired a kind of negative currency in critical theory of the latter twentieth century, and is particularly debased currency in the context of poststructuralist *difference*. In one of Lévy's most recognizable formulations: "postmodern philosophy has confused the universal with totalization. It made the mistake of throwing out the baby of the universal with the bathwater of totality" (101). More recently, then, we are witnessing a measured reappraisal of the concept of universality in both philosophical and scientific domains. In today's critical and cultural theory, for example, we see philosophies of cosmopolitanism and theories built around the ethics of universality (Appiah 2006). In cognitive science, scholars who study universals treat them as patterns that recur across genetically or geographically distinct traditions rather than *absolutes* in a strict, unconditional, and unreflectively stigmatized sense (Hogan 2003: 133). Cognitive-scientific universals, as Patrick Colm Hogan stresses, are "based on prototypes, not on necessary and sufficient conditions" (134). Hogan adds that linguistics, from which cognitive science borrows much of its methodology on this count, works in three tiers: "absolute" universals occurring in all traditions; "near absolute" universals occurring in almost 100 percent of cases; and "statistical" universals occurring in fewer than 100 percent of the cases (133). There can be exceptions in every case. Along the same lines and mindful of the same caveats, cognitive narratology explores the perceptual, cognitive, and narrative universals that shape storyworlds across media.

Lévy's framework helps inform our reading of cognition and computation in *Mimesis*, and its evocative yet also impossible project of encoding gesture through the semantics of the interface. Clearly, this overtly computational text can be compelling without being totalizing—without needing to *convince* readers of its numerical power to encode vast sets of possibilities. Its universalizing quality, furthermore, opens a productive discourse on the process of other-ing, the experience of social hierarchies and social sleights, and the subtleties of social cognition more broadly. The creative computation of Harrell and his team pushes back against "computationalism" with a form of screen-mediated expression that exploits the force of simulation while at the same time tempering it with representation and metaphor. To begin with, the graphical representations of *Mimesis* are rudimentary, which marks a necessary eschewal of photorealism in order to preserve consistent and unambiguous signifying cues in the body language of the avatar. The programmer-artists seek to simulate a socio-cognitive experience; moreover, they "feel that this ability—to directly convey the subjective experiences of discrimination, including those of navigating a social reality rife with identity-based ills—is one of the most powerful and unique affordances of interactive narratives and games" (Harrell et al. 2014). The approach is by no means an abandonment of aesthetics, as the work is by all means an example of *design* in its color, shape, and form. It is a recognition of the respective virtues and affordances of representation and simulation as they operate in concert. In representation, one primarily interprets the work; in simulation—arguably in aesthetic as well as instrumental domains—one primarily interprets the choices made in directing the simulation. *Mimesis* marks a further recognition of the role of metaphor in or even as a counterbalance to simulative art. In fact, its creators acknowledge that "[d]eciding upon an appropriate level of metaphor balanced with social realism was one of the central design challenges" (ibid.). In general, if simulation foregrounds totality, then metaphor foregrounds a salient part. That is, metaphor maintains a distance between source and target domains whereas simulation attempts to elide that very distance via the faithfulness of its one-to-one mappings.[9] In terms of aesthetic practice, counterbalancing the computational appetite for such strict correspondence is perhaps all the more urgent in computational art.

A PINCH OF MEMORY IN *PRY*

The centrality of metaphor is immediately apparent in the title of *Pry* (2014), a work of electronic literature—a "hybrid of cinema, gaming, and text"[10]—by Samantha Gorman and Danny Cannizzaro, who together form the art collective called Tender Claws. "Pry" also stands alone, syntactically, as a provocation and call to action—"an invitation to read," as John Cayley (2015) puts it, and "an imperative" one at that. Available for iPhone and iPad, the work is a downloadable iOS app and is one of the first major narrative works of electronic literature that require a touchscreen device. The notion of prying into the thoughts of the principal character serves as the governing metaphor of the narrative. Although in some sense we might say that all narrative fiction, in essence, is an exercise in prying open and peering into minds, here this metaphor is integrated gracefully into the semantics of the interface in a way that certainly sets it apart from not only psychologically oriented narratives in print form, but also most anything seen in electronic literature before it to date.

The story opens with James, a Gulf War veteran and demolition specialist who, six years after returning from his tour of duty, is gradually losing his sight, perhaps as a result of one of the combat incidents that are described in his first-person account (there are references to smoke, debris, and red air, and a constant fear of chemical weapons carried by the much more insidious "colorless air") (chapter 1, "Below and Above"). In the war James is deployed with his brother and a woman named Jessie, and the backstory we glean from the narration and cinematic flashbacks points to what appears to have been a tense triangle of affection. In the very first chapter, for instance, we see James, staring at the ceiling from his bed, and hear him thinking (via voiceover): "I never speak of her

[9] I am indebted to Steven Johnson's (1997: 231–5) observations about the relationship between simulation and metaphor in *Interface Culture*.

[10] The phrase is taken from the promotional text on the *Pry* website: http://prynovella.com.

. . . I picture her between us, right before it hit" (ibid.). He is thus struggling with losing his sight and quite possibly Jessie too (the narrative remains ambiguous on this point in a move reminiscent of that other much earlier Gulf War classic of electronic literature, *Victory Garden* [1992], where the fate of Emily Runbird is at the center of its centerless narrative network). But James is also struggling with obvious and ongoing manifestations of war trauma. In chapter 2, "South Bay implosion," he is working with his brother on a demolition job, and the explosion overcomes him to the extent that he momentarily loses consciousness—as suggested by cinematic distortions of his sense of sight and sound.

The text is divided into chapters that follow a cinematic prologue, and each chapter employs a different mode of gestural input, beginning with the instruction in the first to "Spread and hold open to see through James' eyes" or "Pinch and hold closed to enter James' subconscious." Those actions pull up additional text, sound, and animation meant to reveal his moment-by-moment sensory experience or his tormented dream state, respectively. Subsequent chapters require, for example, that we repeatedly pry open "seams" of text in what feels like an ever-expanding substrate (chapter 6, "Dhahran, Saudi Arabia"), or scroll the text in all four compass directions in what feels like an interminable one (appendix, "Album"). Another segment involves running our finger over braille icons at a pace that is modulated according to the pace of the voiceover that reads it aloud as we go (chapter 3, "Jacob and Esau").

That these sundry interaction designs transcend skeuomorphic acts, whereby the swipe is merely re-instantiated as a new form of page turning, has been sufficiently noted in early criticism of the work (see Herstik 2014; Johnston 2014). I would like to instead underscore how the same handling of the text works to reinforce the embodied nature of cognition itself. That is, we register not simply the nontrivial effort that such a reading requires, but more so the physically effortful quality of prying. The same act, as a method for locating thoughts and memories, speaks to the fact that we think with our fingers as well as and along with our minds—and indeed "through" the eyes of others as much as our own in what social psychology calls intermental units. It further reminds us that memory is not only always reconstructive, but also that the material props that act as the (re)construction tools, from sticky notes to touchscreens, are also always all around us. And finally, the same gesture lays bare the experiential nature of trauma, which so often seems to keep silently to itself until it is disturbed—indeed "touched"—and then it takes only the tiniest of pokes or pinches to trigger an all-consuming descent into anxiety and obsessiveness.

As David Jhave Johnston (2014) notes in his comprehensive and deftly lyrical review, *Pry* marks "the first use of the technique interactively in fiction to reflect and reinforce the psychology of internal refrains or litanies, psychic pleas or pronouncements, thoughts that erupt into consciousness then subsist, trauma that is silent, lingering, or dormant until touched." He adds that it "is in that fusing of context and content that *Pry* offers a unique contribution" (ibid.). In fact, we might return to McLuhan's emphatic proclamation regarding the extension of our bodies in the mechanical age and the subsequent extension of our central nervous system in the digital age. But rather than proceed to his final teleological phase, involving the impending technological simulation of consciousness, we would double-back, perhaps full circle even, to acknowledge that we did not need to separate these entities in the first place: consciousness emerges from the inextricable workings of body and mind after all.

As seams of text and lids of eyes open on the screen of *Pry*, the work proceeds to open up broader questions about the role of art in digital culture, and its power to challenge, expand, and potentially transcend the confines of our own creative imagination. This line of inquiry is implicit in the promotional blurbs that foreground our experience of *Pry*: "What happens to text when instead of turning a page, the reader must force open a character's eyes or read his thoughts *infinitely* scrolling in every direction?" (my emphasis).[11] And the same sentiment is echoed by its readers, who note that their manipulations induce "a sense of the text as a Pandora's box capable of *infinite* expansion or contraction" (Johnston 2014; my emphasis). Whereas *Mimesis* challenges us to think beyond ourselves to (re)conceive the other, *Pry* asks that we try to *think*—come to terms with a conception of—that which exceeds human capacity for thought. It goes as far as providing the material means to enter into such contemplation, namely, a touchscreen that tests the limits of textuality through a tour de force of speed, expansion, and scrolling. The pursuit of the infinite is thus dramatized along two parallel paths, one that leads infinitely inward, deeper into a troubled mindscape, while another leads infinitely outward to test the outermost bounds of digital materiality.

It is the same unbridled aesthetic indulgence of the infinite, however, that crashes up against more pragmatic, even sobering accounts of the human limits of cognition that arise in the cognitive sciences and evolutionary psychology. Richard Dawkins (2006), for one, has posited the notion of a "Middle World" to explain the possibility that our brains have evolved "to help us survive within the orders of magnitude of size and speed which our bodies operate at." For him, there may be things in the universe—in the class of large, small, or fast—that are forever beyond our grasp, but not beyond the grasp of a hypothetical superior intelligence; and there may be things in the universe that are *in principle* ungraspable by any mind. The reason is that such comprehension would not only be useless for our species, but it could be devastating in terms of how we navigate the world and negotiate our own sense of reality. Dawkins applies this philosophy of scale not only to the vastness of the universe but also to the smallness of atoms:

> We never evolved to navigate in the world of atoms. If we had, our brains probably would perceive rocks as full of empty space. Rocks feel hard and impenetrable to our hands precisely because objects like rocks and hands cannot penetrate each other. It's therefore useful for our brains to construct notions like "solidity" and "impenetrability," because such notions help us to navigate our bodies through the middle-sized world in which we have to navigate. . . . If a neutrino had a brain, which it evolved in neutrino-sized ancestors, it would say that rocks really do consist of empty space. We have brains that evolved in medium-sized ancestors which couldn't walk through rocks.

Dawkins's observations, moreover, apply equally to our understanding of ourselves and more specifically to what cognitive science calls the hard problem of consciousness. Some philosophers and scientists hold that "human brains may be congenitally unable to penetrate (be congenitally closed with respect to) the mystery of phenomenal consciousness. Given the kinds of relationships and causal chains that human brains evolved to comprehend, they argue, we may have no more chance of understanding consciousness than a hamster has of understanding quantum mechanics" (Clark 2001: 183).

---

[11] This particular promotional blurb appears in several places but differs slightly from the main site at http://prynovella.com. Here I cite Stuart Moulthrop's feature article published on the Electronic Literature Organization site: https://eliterature.org/#!showcase/27.

Dawkins (2006), nonetheless, leaves open the possibility that we could, "by training and practice, emancipate ourselves from Middle World and achieve some sort of intuitive, as well as mathematical, understanding of the very small and the very large." Whatever the answer may be, digital culture and the power of digital computation have already played a prominent role in the endeavor. In his writing on early digital culture, for example, Steven Johnson (1997: 241) refers to the graphical user interface as a structure that "helps us think about something that is too big to think"—a crucial element of the "devices we build for ourselves to help us complete the thought." When we enter into aesthetic domains, however, questions shift focus from managing or mastering scale that transcends us to immersively experiencing or even reveling in it. We are familiar with the idea that art in general—in its pursuit of the sublime—offers a kind of passage to what lies beyond the human scale. But it would appear that electronic literature and the digital arts in general might also be uniquely positioned here. As Stuart Moulthrop (under review) writes, electronic literature and games "both present us with symbolic worlds and systems of structured time, in which we find ourselves submerged in an illusion of limitless extensiveness or depth." He adds that "[e]ffects of such a scale are impossible to achieve in traditional prose writing, but are more approachable in cybertext, where time, space, and language can be more radically manipulated" (ibid.).[12] Digital media may have not only added a new means to pursue this project but also a new urgency. As Michael Joyce (n.d.) notes in a recent interview, "[W]e authors cannot avoid, must not avoid, attempting to portray the experience of living in a world where, as Mark Hansen points out, complex, technological intelligences—including surveillance, biofeedback, and cognitive mapping—know more about us than we are able to process in lived time." Thus, even if the attempts to portray or convey a scale that exceeds our cognitive endowment are ultimately futile, the artist's obligation to the attempt looks as though it is beyond question.[13]

It remains up for debate whether *Pry*'s play for infinitude is simply futile or rather in fact designed to show the futility of that very move. The discerning reader will quickly locate material limits in the various segments, for example, in the form of repeating text amid the "infinite" multidirectional scrolling of the appendix. Nonetheless, both *Mimesis* and *Pry* take us gracefully from the poetics of the link to the poetics of the swipe, pinch, and pry. The process of transforming these gestures from automatic to cerebral underscores the embodied nature of cognition. Both works also enter into direct dialogue with the discourse of totality and scale in a productive rather than reductive way. Indeed, they convey a productive ambivalence that explores the kind of imaginative, expressive, and emotive outputs of minds and machines. The same kind of aesthetic uncertainty, moreover, avoids the temptation to reductively oppose or equate both of those entities involved.

[12] Dawkins (2006) himself considers videogames as a potential tool for such hyper-comprehension: "I wonder whether we might help ourselves to understand, say, quantum theory, if we brought up children to play computer games, beginning in early childhood, which had a sort of make-believe world of balls going through two slits on a screen, a world in which the strange goings on of quantum mechanics were enlarged by the computer's make-believe, so that they became familiar on the Middle-World scale of the stream."

[13] Marco Caracciolo (2014: 14) makes a similar point when he notes that even though it may indeed be impossible for humans to experience the phenomenology of other creatures, "we shouldn't downplay the role artistic creativity has in exploring the limits of our imagination, and in bringing us closer—through linguistic, stylistic, and narrative inventiveness—to what we take to be non-ordinary forms of experience."

SOURCES CITED

Appiah, Kwame Anthony. *Cosmopolitanism: Ethics in a World of Strangers*. New York: W. W. Norton, 2006.

Bardini, Thierry. *Bootstrapping: Douglas Engelbart, Coevolution, and the Origins of Personal Computing*. Stanford, CA: Stanford University Press, 2000.

Braidotti, Rosi. *The Posthuman*. Cambridge: Polity Press, 2013.

Bush, Vannevar. "As We May Think." In *Reading Digital Culture*, edited by David Trend. Malden, MA: Blackwell Publishers, [1945] 2001.

Caracciolo, Marco. "Beyond Fictional Minds: Fictional Characters, Mental Simulation, and 'Unnatural' Experiences." *Journal of Narrative Theory*, vol. 44, no. 1 (2014): 29–53.

Cayley, John. "Samantha Gorman and Danny Cannizzaro's *Pry*." *Bomb*, 132 (Summer 2015), http://bombmagazine.org/article/3303617/samantha-gorman-and danny-cannizzaro-s-em-pry-em.

Charney, Davida. "The Impact of Hypertext on Processes of Reading and Writing." In *Literacy and Computers*, edited by Susan J. Hilligoss and Cynthia L. Selfe. New York: Modern Language Association, 1994, pp. 238–63.

Ciccoricco, David. *Reading Network Fiction*. Tuscaloosa: University of Alabama Press, 2007.

Clark, Andy. *Mindware: An Introduction to the Philosophy of Cognitive Science*. New York: Oxford University Press, 2001.

Damasio, Antonio. *The Feeling of What Happens: Body, Emotion and the Making of Consciousness*. 1st ed. New York: Harcourt Brace, 1999.

Dawkins, Richard. "Why the Universe Seems So Strange." TED Talks transcript. Posted September 2006. https://www.ted.com/talks/richard_dawkins_on_our_queer_universe/transcript?languge=en

Deleuze, Gilles, and Félix Guattari. *A Thousand Plateaus: Capitalism and Schizophrenia*. London: Continuum, [1987] 2004.

Emerson, Ralph Waldo. "The Method of Nature." In *The Collected Works of Ralph Waldo Emerson: Nature, Addresses, and Lectures*. Cambridge, MA: Belknap Press of Harvard University Press, 1971.

Engelbart, Douglas. "Augmenting Human Intellect: A Conceptual Framework" (AUGMENT, 3906). 1962. http://www.dougengelbart.org/pubs/augment-3906.html.

Galloway, Alexander. *Gaming: Essays on Algorithmic Culture*. Minneapolis: University of Minnesota Press, 2006.

Garson, James. "Connectionism." In *The Stanford Encyclopedia of Philosophy*, edited by Edward N. Zalta. 1997. http://plato.stanford.edu/archives/win2012/entries/connectionism/.

Golumbia, David. *The Cultural Logic of Computation*. Cambridge, MA: Harvard University Press, 2009.

Gorman, Samantha, and Danny Cannizzaro. *Pry*. Tender Claws, 2014. http://prynovella.com.

Harrell, D. Fox (director), Chong-U Lim, Jia Zhang, Sonny Sidhu, and Ayse Gursoy. *Mimesis*. Cambridge, MA: MIT Imagination, Computation, and Expression Laboratory, 2012.

Harrell, D. Fox (director), Chong-U Lim, Jia Zhang, Sonny Sidhu, and Ayse Gursoy. "Playing Mimesis: Engendering Understanding via Experience of Social Discrimination with an Interactive Narrative Game." *electronic book review*, (November 2014), http://electronic-bookreview.com/thread/electropoetics/mimesis.

Hayles, N. Katherine. *How We Think: Digital Media and Contemporary Technogenesis*. Chicago: University of Chicago Press, 2012.

Herbrechter, Stefan. *Posthumanism: A Critical Analysis*. London: Bloomsbury, 2013.

Herstik, Lauren. "Pry Is a Novella-Meets-iPad App That You Touch." *LA Weekly*, November 28, 2014, http://www.laweekly.com/arts/pry-is-a-novella-meetsipad-app that-you-touch-5242790.

Hogan, Patrick Colm. *Cognitive Science, Literature, and the Arts: A Guide for Humanists*. New York: Routledge, 2003.

Horst, Steven. "The Computational Theory of Mind." In *The Stanford Encyclopedia of Philosophy*, edited by Edward N. Zalta. 2013. http://plato.stanford.edu/entries/computational-mind/.

Johnson, Steven. *Interface Culture: How New Technology Transforms the Way We Create and Communicate*. San Francisco: HarperEdge, 1997.

Johnston, David Jhave. "Jhave on *Pry*." *Los Angeles Review of Books*, December 29, 2014, https://lareviewofbooks.org/review/prying-jhave-on-tender-claws-new-app.

Joyce, Michael. "The Author Is a Machine: An Interview with Michael Joyce." *Don't Do It Magazine*, Issue 5 (n.d.), http://dontdoitmag.co.uk/issue-five/the-author-is-a-machine-an-interview-with-michael-joyce/.

Landow, George. *Hypertext 2.0: The Convergence of Contemporary Critical Theory and Technology*. Baltimore: Johns Hopkins University Press, 1997.

Lévy, Pierre. *Cyberculture*. Translated by Robert Bononno. Minneapolis: University of Minnesota Press, 2001.

McLuhan, Marshall. *Understanding Media: The Extensions of Man*. New York: McGraw Hill, 1964.

Moulthrop, Stuart. "Deep Time in Play" (under review).

Ryan, Marie-Laure. "Beyond Myth and Metaphor: The Case of Narrative in Digital Media." *Game Studies*, vol. 1, no. 1 (July 2001), http://www.gamestudies.org/0101/ryan/.

Stiegler, Bernard. *Technics and Time*. Stanford, CA: Stanford University Press, 1998.

Wolfe, Cary. *What Is Posthumanism?* Minneapolis: University of Minnesota Press, 2010.

CHAPTER NINE

The Freedom Adventure of Portuguese Experimentalism and Kinetic Poetry

ÁLVARO SEIÇA

Experimentalism from the post–Second World War period and, especially, from the 1960s erupted as a quasi-scientific, vanguard, and cultural mash-up of literary and artistic practices that is still being reinvented today, in visual arts, music, literature, dance, theatre, architecture, and performance arts. By blending the arts and fostering associations in magazines, exhibitions, happenings, and singular *ars poeticas*, the experimentalist tactics to a collective and individual writing program attempted to confront the mainstream literary and artistic discourse with such principles as: formal, visual, structural, technical, and content rupture, invention, a poetics of synthesis, rereading, recreation, irony, playfulness (*ludus*), and artistic practice understood as research process. On a cultural and political level, the intent was transgression, subversion, and provocation—all in the name of a critique of institutionalized artistic power structures and, in totalitarian countries, as an opposition to a common enemy, the dictator's regime, and a possible path to freedom. This impetus took shape as a global set of artistic[1] practices and interdisciplinary approaches around groups of artists with common affiliations. The ideological trait of their agenda set experimentalism to be created or adopted on the basis of a rejection of *movement*.

Experimental literature in France was certainly marked by the Oulipo group and their procedural techniques, but experimentalism does not equate to Oulipo. In Portugal, it was associated with the two issues of *Poesia Experimental* (1964, 1966),[2] but this was only a starting point, which would grow until the 1980s. Given the eclectic nature of artistic positions, its authors have denied any intention of embodying a literary movement, praising freedom instead. In the United States, we have, at least, the fully expressed spectrum of Dick Higgins's pluralistic intermedia approach, focused on format and medium. Thus, Higgins (1967) rejects an idea of movement. In "Against Movements," he states:

> It is only an illusion that there is a Happenings movement or ever was. The same can be said, I think, of Concrete Poetry. Both merely represent Intermedia, which in turn

[1] During the 1940s–1970s, other process-oriented artistic programs took place: Lettrism, Situationism, COBRA, Spatialism, Concretism, Fluxus, Conceptualism, and Minimalism.

[2] The issues can be accessed in digitized form in Torres (2008b).

> reflect the new technical and social possibilities within society. [. . .] I suspect that in twenty years the [. . .] illusion of little movements will have disappeared into the reality of an overall format of the period, within which the differences of the various artists can be seen uniquely rather than just as types. If we do not speak of movements then, we will need another way to describe similarities between work, and what used to be names of movements may, in some cases, be applicable as names of formats for work. [. . .] The artist is whoever researches aesthetic functions in practice. Each work is an experiment [. . .] To say that a researcher belongs to one or another movement is not really, then, very enlightening, any more than to say that Pasteur was a silkwormist. (1–3)

From another pole, John Barth (1984 [1967]: 68) claims that Borges's 1920s magazine *Prisma* was "the great decades of literary experimentalism." While Barth acknowledges the avant-garde ruptures of the beginning of the twentieth century as experimental, he criticizes at the same time the non-newness of "The Something Else Press crowd."

Undeniably, groundbreaking work in poetry, film, performance, and the visual arts in the 1960s was, in turn, informed by Futurism, Imagism, Modernism, Dada, and Surrealism; and even baroque practices. Moreover, praxis and theory were always seen as part of the same quest—a quest for agitating, counteracting, and repurposing the "glorious and prestigious canon" (Campos 1981: 13). For the Portuguese experimentalists, the international twentieth-century vanguard movements and pivotal critical theory were of the utmost importance: concrete, sound and experimental poetry, structuralism, semiotics, cybernetics, philosophy of science and language, Abraham Moles's information theory, and Max Bense's information aesthetics. Furthermore, the awareness of calligraphic and visual poetics—reading and viewing—running from Greek Antiquity to the baroque period; the discovery of Oriental ideograms; the context of new visual forms, in advertisement and the embedded information society—all caused great impact. António Aragão (1963), Herberto Helder (1964), Pedro Barbosa (1977), Ana Hatherly (1978), José-Alberto Marques (1985), E. M. de Melo e Castro (2007), among others refer to the "experimental attitude" (Hatherly 2001: 7) and their project as an *adventure*—a poetic, literary, artistic, sociologic, interventionist, and political adventure, but also a media-oriented and technological one.

In 1959, Hatherly highlighted the influence of concrete poetry as part of a new poetics project for discursive synthesis and graphic composition. Hatherly (1981 [1959]: 91) points out that "[A poesia concreta], suprimindo a descrição, cria a imaginação" (Concrete poetry, suppressing description, creates imagination). Describing concrete poetics as the exact reverse of ultra-romanticism, the poet considers concrete lyricism to be internalized. Such notions are echoed years later in the critical analysis of Salette Tavares's (1957–71) poetic *œuvre*, as Luciana Stegagno Picchio (1992: 13) stresses: "A ressemantização de hoje funciona no plano gráfico, dos 'brancos,' dos silêncios mallarmeanos."[3] Also, in 1963 Aragão (1981 [1963]: 105) defines "art" as a process of chance discovery and "poetry" as a game, in the sense of a "new field of possibilities" marked by a "new spatial-visual syntax." Aragão identifies some of the influential figures for the self-reflexive experimentalist project: Mallarmé, Apollinaire, Sá-Carneiro, the Brazilian concretists, Pound, cummings, Joyce, Roussel, Arp, and contemporary "electronic poetry"—Nanni Balestrini's

[3] Translation: "Today's ressemantization functions at the graphic level: the 'blanks,' the Mallarméan silences." Unless noted, all text has been freely translated into English by Álvaro Seiça.

IBM "experiments" with combinatory poetry, which fascinated Aragão. All these authors, as well as the procedural writings of Oulipo, especially by Raymond Queneau, had a great resonance in what the 1960s experimentalists saw as the "novíssimas experiências poéticas" (newest poetic experiences) (Aragão 1981 [1963]: 105).

The experimentalist project left a strong legacy behind. From the 1980s onward, the attachment to this legacy by new authors proves the project's resistance. Manuel Portela and Rui Torres, whose work matured in the 1990s and 2000s, were influenced by a direct contact with the experimentalists, and still reinvent or appropriate their previous works by inscribing them in an experimentalist lineage. The visual input in the literary process brought by the generation of the 1950s and 1960s has not been forgotten. In fact, it plays a direct role in the practice and theory of these authors—working about and with the works of the experimentalists. Even a much younger generation, composed by Liliana Vasques and Bruno Ministro—part of the collective aranhiças & elefantes (with Rita Grácio) and devisers of the Candonga project—label their work as "experimental." Therefore, it seems as if *experimental*, as opposed to other demarcations, is a wide enough modifier appealing to and resonating in a diversity of authors' writing and artistic programs, somehow connected to an idea of rupture.

However, it seems highly anachronistic that authors still feel comfortable with such a label, when the technical, social, political, cultural, and historical context is not the same. Consider poets such as Joan Retallack (2007) or Felipe Cussen (2010), who work in the line of, and are influenced by, the experimental program, referring to the relevance of a trans-temporal experimental poetics. Yet, today's variables are staggeringly different. Over much of the planet, poets live in a media-saturated, networked, wired-in, real-time, and ubiquitous society. The geo-sociopolitical context has shifted. Hopefully, more intersectional approaches will be set in motion. Therefore, can we still speak of experimental poetics? Or have we not yet found a new, broad enough, effective label? Terms such as "electronic," "cyber," or "digital" do not really help. To be sure, in the developed world the greater part of the millennial generation see themselves as networked, ubiquitous, and hyper-tasking. Moreover, the pervasive computational and digital context has created a new sociopolitical order that is instigating a renewed creative approach, as well as resistance to new forms of abusive corporative monopolies and governmental totalitarianism, corruption, surveillance, control, and lack of transparency.

Will the institute of canonization cherry-pick "networkism" (Lima 2011), "connectivism" (Siemens 2005), "connectionism," or "autonomism"? What about considering other possible taxonomies—ubiquitism, ubicomputationalism, codicism, programmablism, metadataism, or remixologism? Will today's taxonomy arise from human, artistic conditions, and ideology, or from media-specificity, formal, and techno-determinism? Will it arise from the inside of the artistic process, as it happened with the experimental poets—the main theorists of experimental poetry?[4] Sure enough, *-isms* are out there in a grand diversity, they were always out there, and they will continue to be. Conceptualism is another movement still prevalent today, which also knots its roots from the 1960s conceptual art practices. Though it does also seem anachronistic to consider one's work as "conceptual," some writers and artists feel comfortable with this label, and work within that tradition in the same way experimentalists do. Yet, many do not, and even as we consider *tradition*, in the experimental or conceptual arts, we come to realize that such a

[4] See, for example, Melo e Castro (1965a).

rupture is inexistent. Otherwise, there would not be a tradition, but rather a new starting point. Or, as Ana Hatherly once suggested in a talk,[5] the concretists were not doing much that was really new; what these early practitioners did was to recycle forgotten styles of the baroque poets. This loop included the reemergence of graphic forms, shapes, and patterns visually combined and arranged with language. Even more, many works today are not prescribed or aligned with a rigid sense of group, movement, or ideology, while others do. What today's digital poetics will be known as, in 50–100 years, only institutionalization forces will tell. The fin-de-siècle spirit will perhaps be seen as ultra-experimentalism, ultra-conceptualism—just as late nineteenth and early twentieth century was marked by a wave of ultra-romanticism, while symbolism was taking place with both old and new features, and just before Modernism emerged. It is, then, impossible to know how creative or critical discourse will frame part of today's artistic and literary practices.

Claiming literature, at all, to be *experimental*, as an interchangeable adjective for *avant-garde* or *innovative*, has certainly raised opposition: From standpoints arguing that all literature is experimental, to concrete examples of how the term "experimental" highlights a scientific or quasi-scientific approach to understanding the process and work of art. According to Alberto Pimenta (1978: 9), literary art can be divided in two modes of creative practice: the "degree of dependence," which perpetuates the norm, and the "degree of transgression," which founds a new norm.[6] Jacques Donguy (2007: 7) writes along similar lines and establishes a simile between poetry and science research: "Par poésie expérimentale, on entend toutes les recherches sur le langage, par opposition à une poésie qui reprend et continue les formes héritées du passé, de même qu'il y a une recherche en science."[7] Surveying this fact, the editors of *The Routledge Companion to Experimental Literature*, Joe Bray, Alison Gibbons, and Brian McHale (2012: 1) posit: "Experiment is one of the engines of literary change and renewal; it is literature's way of reinventing itself." They add:

> Experimentalism's connotations, by contrast, are scientific. Experiment promises to extend the boundaries of knowledge, or in this case, of artistic practice. Strongly associated with modernity, it implies rejection of hide-bound traditions, values and forms. To call literature experimental is in some sense to aspire to compete with science—challenging science's privileged status in modernity and reclaiming some of the prestige ceded by literature to science since the nineteenth century. (2)

The 1960s Portuguese experimentalists, even if influenced by Modernism, Dada, and Futurism, did not find themselves comfortable with situating their project in the Modernist lineage, which would entail perpetuating a fifty-year tradition. *Orpheu* appears in 1915, *Poesia Experimental* in 1964. There was a second generation of Modernists, with *presença*, in the 1920s–1930s, but by the end of the 1950s and 1960s, the postwar generation was certainly playing with other variables. The same happens today, fifty years after *Poesia Experimental* and their happenings: Do authors think of *experimental* as a technical, artistic, scientific, and sociological *experimentation*, but not as a perpetuation

---

[5] Unfortunately, I cannot locate the exact date, but the talk was given at the Faculty of Social Sciences and Humanities, Universidade Nova de Lisboa, around 2005–2006.

[6] For an in-depth discussion about the practices of invention, transgression, and metamorphosis in Portuguese experimentalism, see Torres and Seiça (2016).

[7] Translation: "By experimental poetry, we mean all research about language, by opposition to a kind of poetry that resumes to and continues the inherited forms of the past, just as there is research in science."

of *experimentalism*? Experimentalism, no less than Modernism, has its own connotations of scientific procedures, technical, semantic, syntactic, sonic, and aesthetic novelty. If, as in many other countries, Portuguese poetic production has been marked by a domination of normative lyricism, discursive poetry, and waves of reinvention of lyrical tradition, the fact is that even the ruptures—such as Futurism, Surrealism, and experimentalism—arrived with a chronological delay and were marginal.[8] Silvestre Pestana (1987: 10) rightly points out in an interview the non-dominant character of the experimental arts:

> E nunca foram campos dominantes no nosso país, porque Portugal não é criador de tecnologias ou de saberes. Nós somos importadores de saberes. Mais que fundadores do movimento, nós somos continuadores, introdutores, actualizadores do que se passa lá fora. No entanto, é natural que isso aconteça porque o contexto cultural [do] país é agrário, semi-industrial, e as problemáticas deste campo [artes experimentais] que trabalhamos são todas pós-industriais.[9]

We know nevertheless that even in "post-industrial" countries where many movements were founded, the same type of experimental arts were, and still are, marginal[10]—in terms of production, dissemination, critical reception, and negligence by cultural actors. Even though some independent publishers might find "marginal" an absurd term, as they see themselves as part of a publishing ecology—that is, living inside the same sphere, but with a different agenda—center and periphery are influential notions. There is much to be reflected upon cultural capital, the innocuous love for bourgeois art, institutionalization, elitist power structures, funding mechanisms, and academic representation, which play a decisive role on how the experimental, underground, or marginal arts are projected within the mainstream discourse, with how they are absorbed, and diluted, by the center. Still, in this particular case, we should be aware of three levels of margin, or periphery: first, the periphery of the experimental arts; second, the peripheral geo-cultural position of Portugal; and third, the fascist and repressive political context. At the time that Pestana is being interviewed, only twelve years had passed since the 1974 Carnation Revolution. On the one hand, in the international context, the Portuguese experimentalist project was less about founding than it was about updating. Artistic tendencies and movements spread, branch out, get isolated, and mutate. Isolationism, especially in the 1960s, when Portugal had for sure a much bigger gap in relation to industrial countries, did mean something for the experimentalists' output. Adding to the isolationist factor, fascism and the colonial war, a deep agrarian society, and poverty, we can see how this context was adverse to their project. Yet, on the other hand, it was also a *field for new possibilities*, creating pioneering artworks that are specific to their contextual idiosyncrasies. Moreover, the exchange of ideas and contact with foreign authors and milieus was crucial. Melo e Castro studied and lived in England in the 1950s and traveled to Brazil in the 1960s;

---

[8] Dick Higgins (1987: 125) notices this fact, though considering the baroque: "Two things impress us immediately about the Portuguese pattern poems. One is their late date, since so many come from the eighteenth century when most literatures were moving away from pattern poetry. The other is the preoccupation with labyrinths."

[9] Translation: "And they were never dominant fields in our country, since Portugal is not a country that creates technologies and knowledge. We import knowledge. More than founding the movement, we follow, introduce, and update what is happening out there. However, it is natural that this happens because the country's cultural context is agrarian, semi-industrial, and the problems of this field [the experimental arts] in which we work are all post-industrial."

[10] There is also productive discussion around the term "marginal" and "marginal literature" regarding genres that receive less critical attention, or are dismissed by reception mechanisms.

Tavares in France and Italy in 1959–1961; Aragão in France and Italy in the 1960s; Pimenta in Germany in the 1960s and 1970s; Hatherly in England and the United States in the 1970s; Pestana in Sweden in 1969–1974. Pestana's argument can be partially felt by earlier experimentalists. Aragão (1981 [1963]: 103) claims the "rareness" of Melo e Castro's *Ideogramas* (1962) as a book of concrete poetry, even if Brazilian concretism of a first phase had been already in "decline." Another feeling of discrepancy between the outside world, the Portuguese experimentalists' world, and their cultural context is mentioned by Hatherly (1985: 15), when the poet declares that the experimentalist project was a reaction to "um meio que vivia ancorado na acomodação e no marasmo," in which the "mandarins das letras [. . .] fomentaram um clima de tão duradoira sanha que não se dissipou completamente ainda" (Hatherly 2001: 9).[11]

My reading recognizes that experimentalist practices in Portugal continued the flow of European, South American, and Asian visions. At the same time, it points out the ambivalent fact that—perhaps due to a delay, to not being the epicenter—the peculiar characteristics of each one of its authors, and the contextual fascist and repressive regime they lived in, created a need to break from oppression. Consequently, one answer for such rupture would be to transgress genres and forms, and to radically create novel work. An unusual case happened with kinetic poetry, since new hardware and software provided new possibilities. Freedom became equivalent to open forms, content, and moving text, which is signaled by the works in video and Spectrum I am highlighting below. Far from being an original position, my emphasis on the experimental character of many digital literary works—and stretching its roots, at least, to the 1960s experimentalists—is shared by other critics and practitioners writing across the junctures of literature and technology. Take, for instance, Steve Tomasula's (2012: 484) bold observation: "Like poetry (and unlike movies or print novels), its [electronic literature's] lack of mass-marketability has allowed it to be more *wildly experimental*, more art than product, more literary, especially in an avant-garde conception of the raison d'être of literature or art" (emphasis mine).

In discussing part of the contemporary landscape of digital poetics, what stands out in a vast range of works is, precisely, a similar concern of approaching the unknown, by transgressing norms, experimenting as rupture, rereading as appropriation, remixing as creation, and recreating conventions in form, content, interface, and media. The engagement of today's writers and artists with media is undertaken as an *adventure*, meaning a relocation of experimental practices, in the sense that digital literary arts continue to be more than verbal arts—they are indeed synesthetic experiences of verbal, visual, and sonic blending, scripted with code. These topics are pursued in the following analyses of works by E. M. de Melo e Castro and Silvestre Pestana, the latter's after emulation and code forensics.

As Melo e Castro (2007: 180) explains, "Concrete Poetry in 1960 was for me not an arriving point but rather a launching platform." This statement reflects his eclectic working method, which spans over sixty years in several literary and artistic fields, genres, but also media. The author, whose writing project always aimed at developing open forms in poetry, as much as experimenting with physical media—the way to the "peso pesado do átomo" (atom's heavy weight, in Cruz 2006) such as paper, textiles, canvas, wood, metal, stone, and plastic—soon broadened the exploration of qualities given by words

[11] Translation: "a society living anchored in accommodation and marasmus" (Hatherly 1985: 15), in which the "mandarins of literary culture [Humanities] . . . fostered a climate of such a long-lasting hate that it has not been yet completely dissipated" (Hatherly 2001: 9).

FIGURE 9.1 E. M. de Melo e Castro's videopoem *Roda Lume Fogo* (1986), b/w, 2' 43'' (screenshot). Courtesy of E. M. de Melo e Castro and Po-ex.net.

and images, their dematerialization, their grammar, and their sign systems. This aspect became apparent, from the outset, in the pioneer work with film poetry, performance, and videopoetry. Melo e Castro (1958) debuts with the self-reflexive and ironic 8mm "filmic poem" *Lírica do Objecto* (Lyric of the object). Later, the performance *Música Negativa* (Negative music, 1965b) would be restaged as a soundless "sound film," and directed by Ana Hatherly (1977). Melo e Castro (2006) alludes to the poem's score as a visual and conceptual "semiotic poem." The lack of sound—"psychovisual vibrations"—acts as a symbol of a reaction to his childhood's "paternal authority" and, at the time of its first performance during the happening *Concerto e Audição Pictórica* (Concert and pictorial audition, 1965), "as a metaphor against the sham of silence and Salazarian censorship" (Melo e Castro 2006: 208).

A great leap happens in 1968, with the creation of the videopoem *Roda Lume* (Wheel of fire) at the RTP (Rádio Televisão Portuguesa) studios. The poet had been asked by Eduíno de Jesus to create "an animated concrete poem" to be originally broadcast in a 1969 cultural TV program. Moreover, there was a "new machine" in the studios: video. Enthusiastic, he replied: "That's great! I don't think of anything else! Each time I see a concrete poem, I imagine all the letters and geometric shapes—which somehow characterize concrete poetry—moving" (Melo e Castro 2012).[12] Regrettably, the video recording of the "experimental animated poem" was either "robbed or destroyed" by the public broadcasting company, though the storyboard had been preserved by the poet (Melo e Castro 2006: 202).

[12] Full transcription of the interview's excerpt: "Eu estou neste momento, dizia o Eduíno de Jesus, a coordenar um programa, chamado 'Panorama Literário,' suponho que era esse o título do programa, para a Rádio Televisão Portuguesa, e gostava que tu me fizesses um poema concreto animado. Bom . . . eu fiquei bastante surpreso, por esta proposta, e disse: 'Olhe, isso é óptimo! Eu não penso noutra coisa! Cada vez que vejo um poema concreto, eu imagino as letras todas e as formas geométricas—que, de certo modo, caracterizam a poesia concreta—a mexer.' " Available at http://po-ex.net/exposicoes/nas-escritas-poex/e-m-de-melo-e-castro-do-leve-luz?showall=&start=2.

In 1986, in collaboration with a student from Fine Arts, Melo e Castro recreated the lost piece in U-Matic, as *Roda Lume Fogo* (Wheel of fire flame, Figure 9.1), with a new soundtrack reworking the original and recalled by memory, which made possible today's screening of this multimodal kinetic poem. *Roda Lume* draws from a tradition of sound and concrete poetry, and Surrealist and Lettrist experimental film. Highly self-reflexive of the mechanics of physical and electronic video broadcasting—the reel and the I/O function—it intensifies sign relations, signifier and signified, with elementary geometric figures. This strategy is obtained by the transfiguration of vowels (a, e, i, o) and consonants (v) into open forms and shapes, and through the exploration of spatiotemporal dimensions and the sonic interplay of vowels and syllables. The piece opens with the utterance of the syllables "ar-co" (arc) and "ro-da" (wheel), while at the same time animating their geometric shape representations. Here, the reader-listener-viewer might combine these syllables into "co-da" as a concluding addition to the sound segment. The title is actually used by the poet to produce combinatory readings of "ro-da" and "lu-me" (fire) as "ro-da-lu," "ro-lu" and "ro-da-me" (wheel/move me). New words, spoken syllable by syllable, are added: "fo-co" (focus), "fo-go" (fire), and "á-gu-a" (water).

The poet emphasizes the excitement of working with the new medium in this way:

> When I began using video technology to produce my first videopoem, *Roda Lume* (Wheel of Fire), in 1968, I did not know where the limits were and where my experiments would take me. I was really experimenting on the most elementary meaning of the word experience. A sense of fascination and adventure told me that the letters and the signs standing still on the page could gain actual movement of their own. The words and the letters could at last be free, creating their own space. (Melo e Castro 2007: 176)

The 2' 43" black-and-white reenacted videopoem is surprising, precisely due to the sense of freedom associated with movement. This sense of freedom is even more acute if we think about the repressive and censoring regime, the prejudice and vigilante social context. Jesus asked Melo e Castro to explain such a strange artefact to the public, in a talk to be broadcast immediately before the piece. At the time the public talk was recorded, the poet was warned by one of the fascist voices in studio: "Sir, are you aware you will be speaking to 2 million spectators?" As Melo e Castro elucidates, he had to be very careful not to "say horrible things, according to the morbid mentality of the censors." In the next days, the poet received life-threatening messages and phone calls, from taxpayers who were angry about the bad usage of public money, and the "subversion of [their] culture." As a further consequence, the poet was forbidden to ever enter again the RTP facilities, something that lasted up until the 1974 revolution. Jesus, the coordinator of the biweekly "Convergência" TV literary magazine, was "probably censored and expulsed from RTP" soon after, according to Melo e Castro (2012).[13]

[13] According to the RTP website and the 28° Colóquio da Lusofonia, Jesus directed and produced the biweekly literary TV programs "Convergência" (1969–72) and "Livros & Factos" (1972–74). See http://www.rtp.pt/acores/local/medalha-de-ouro-do-municipio-para-eduino-de-jesus_8772, https://museu.rtp.pt/livro/50Anos/Livro/DecadaDe60/Do2ProgramaALuaEAo/Pag14/default.htm, and https://coloquios.lusofonias.net/XXVIII/28%20AUTORES%20PRESENTES.pdf. Until 1992, RTP was the only TV broadcaster in Portugal. The RTP digital archive has been launched on March 6, 2017. Its contents are being progressively digitized. I am currently researching access to the public emission of the "Convergência" program where Melo e Castro's work was presented; hoping that somehow a copy might have been preserved.

On the one hand, the poem overlaps text, kinetic text, image, moving image, and sound, anticipating and influencing various genres of digital hypermedia poetry mainly launched after the World Wide Web. On the other hand, it constructs a different notion of space-time, opening a "visual time" (Melo e Castro 1993: 238) of unfolding images and text that necessarily invites for a new reading perception, as each image is given a different frame tempo. In the image sequence, the two invoked elements—fire and water—become entangled. The visual representation and sound utterance of "cha-ve abre" (key opens) can be read as the decoding correspondence presented in the medium itself in order to access a new function (input/output) and paradigm of experiencing word-image-sound relations.

By the 1970s, personal computers (PCs) began to be introduced in corporate environments, and by the 1980s, specifically in Europe, the prices of microcomputers such as Sinclair ZXs became more accessible for individual acquisition. Pedro Barbosa (1996: 147)—the pioneer of computer-generated literature in Portugal, who in 1975 was working within an institutional and academic environment with mainframe computers—refers to this change, at the level of literary output, as "poesia doméstica" (domestic poetry). In fact, Barbosa (1977, 2016) had collaborated with the engineer Azevedo Machado in the coding of extensive source codes in FORTRAN, ALGOL, and NEAT in an NCR/Elliot 4130 machine, whereas such sarcasm meant to acknowledge the simplicity of coding small programs in BASIC.[14]

It is in a post-Carnation Revolution techno- and sociopolitical context that Silvestre Pestana created his computational kinetic poems. Pestana's development of *Computer Poetry* (1981–83) established an unprecedented mark in kinetic poetry. His exploration was not generative and aleatory, but rather visually animated. The *Computer Poetry* series reimagines the material side and the spatiotemporal dimension of visual poetry. Programming in BASIC for a Sinclair ZX81 and ZX Spectrum, the author emphasized light and color as important features of moving poetry. The series is made of three poems: the first and second (1981), developed in the ZX81 machine with black-and-white output, were dedicated to E. M. de Melo e Castro and the sound poet Henri Chopin; the third poem (1983), already with chromatic lighting, was developed in the ZX Spectrum machine with a dedication to Julian Beck, cofounder, with Judith Malina, of the Living Theatre.

Pestana, a visual artist, writer, and performer, had returned from exile in Sweden, after Portugal's Carnation Revolution of April 25, 1974. Before that, though, the author had already collaborated with the experimentalists in *Hidra* 2 (1969), with *Atómico Acto*, a conceptual collage poem, or "poema objecto" (object poem), in which a red deflated balloon contains a black painted letter *H*, in a reference to the hydrogen bomb. The piece departs from the debate connected to the 1968 disappearance of the American B-52G plane, over Greenland, with four hydrogen bombs. (The mission's code name was "Hard Head.") The balloon's lower part is held by an incision in the white paper, and it is overlaid with the statement "construir o poema," followed below by "destruir o objecto" (to construct the poem / to destroy the object). Creation, in this case, emerges from a deconstruction of normative meaning, or by metamorphosis, and the reframing of objects. Literally, if you want to inflate the balloon and, by consequence, the work of art, you will destroy it,

[14] Nick Montfort's work proves the exact reverse point: extremely small programs can have equal or even more complex output than extensive ones. Barbosa, Pestana, and Montfort's cultural, artistic, and technological context is, of course, diverse, and so are the platforms.

even if it does not explode—a political critique of the destructive powers of humankind's military technology, radioactive contamination, and the ephemerality of artworks.

The five-year period of political exile as conscientious objector in Sweden, where Pestana avoided being drafted to the colonial war in Africa, was a pivotal stage, since it exposed him to video as an artistic medium, to the Fluxus practices, and, in particular, to the work of Nam June Paik (Sousa 2013). These influences were put forward in his subsequent work with video, photography, performance, and computer. From the post-exile creative period, the iconic conceptual piece *Povo Novo* (New people, 1975) should be emphasized, as it engages with a minimal use of means to maximize possible meanings—a constant in Pestana's practice. In some sense, this piece was remediated in the *Computer Poetry* series of kinetic visual poems (Figure 9.2),[15] or "infopoems" (Melo e Castro 1988: 57). Working with the McLuhanian proposition that the medium equals the message (Pestana 2013), the expressiveness and exposure of the intrinsic qualities of the medium dictate the operative scripts for TV display. The series oscillates between recognizable shapes and the reading interpretation of the words themselves. In the third poem (1983), the circular shapes are given by the BASIC cosine and sine mathematical functions "COS" and "SIN," which are formed and animated by squares and the small-sized words "povo" (people), "novo" (new), "ovo" (egg), and "dor" (pain).[16] In this new reading perceptive mode, a semiotic understanding of the signs and their movement is vital, inasmuch as layered semantics: "ovo," the unity, but also the potential; "povo," labor, the collective, the mass; "novo" and "dor." The play of semantic relations and the words' trajectories translate the potential of a "new people" in a historic, sociopolitical, and artistic transition period. This period of freedom and action is, however, built upon the people's pain, and it is hard to construct.

In BASIC, the spatial composition is defined by a cell-like grid, where characters are positioned (in this case, coordinates operate in the X-axis and Y-axis as "X,Y") and "printed"—the PRINT statement informs the machine what to display onscreen. Given the fact that Spectrum is an 8-bit computer, the color graphics are scaled 0–7. If today's programming languages, and especially operating systems, heavily rely on inherited physical metaphors such as "windows," "desktop," and "folders," imagine in 1964, when BASIC was first implemented. Therefore, BASIC statements transpose concepts from print and video legacy media into the computational environment. The time-based statement used by Pestana in the source code is PAUSE 100 and 200, that is, frames running on this command will have an interval of 100 or 200 milliseconds. For the chromatic dimension, Pestana uses the statements PAPER and BORDER, with 1=blue, and INK, with 2=red, 4=green, 6=yellow, and 7=white. Thus, the poem's words and squares are set in red, green, yellow, and white, being displayed on blue background. This represents the colors of the Portuguese and EEC flags. According to Silvestre Pestana (2015), the piece aimed to critique the Portuguese economic leaning toward the EEC, the lack of a true political revolution, and the dawn of the digital revolution. The poem ends with the word "dor" (pain) devouring most of the background, which is populated with the words "povo" (people), "novo" (new), and "ovo" (egg). Then, line 290 in the source code sets a loop, and creates iteration. The poem reruns. It resumes from line 60. In an interview, Pestana (2011) claimed having researched more than thirty languages, only to find in

[15] Pestana (1985: 205) even calls it "video-computer-poetry," in a clear reference to videopoetry he created during the 1970s and 1980s.

[16] The first poem (1981) in black and white, dedicated to Melo e Castro, includes the word "cor" (color), besides "dor" and "povo."

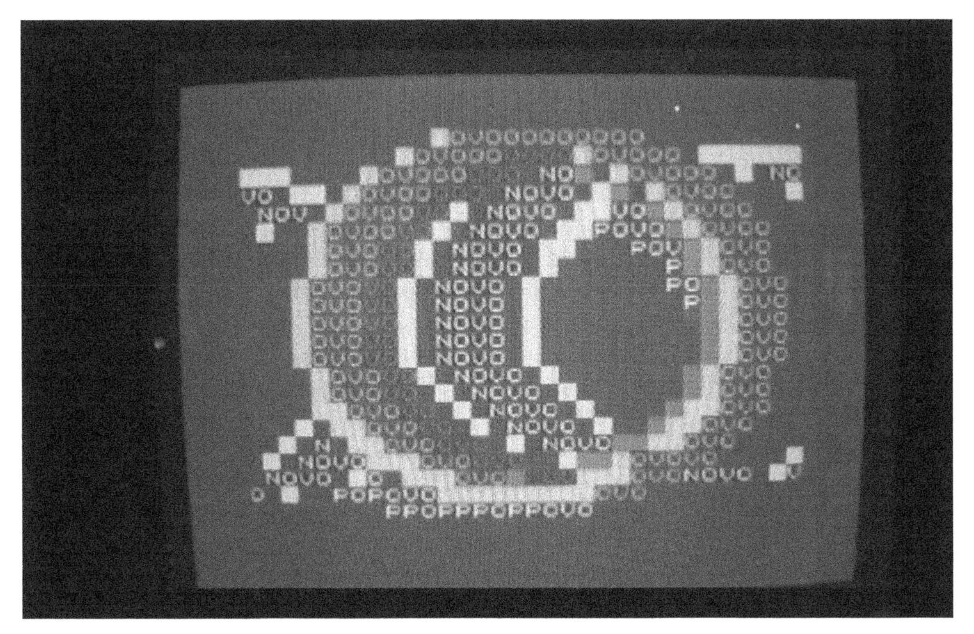

FIGURE 9.2 Silvestre Pestana's *Computer Poetry* (1983) programmed in BASIC for a Sinclair ZX Spectrum. Work emulated by Sindre Sørensen and Álvaro Seiça. Exhibition view, *p2p: Polish-Portuguese E-Lit*, curated by Álvaro Seiça and Piotr Marecki at 3,14 gallery in Bergen, Norway (August 4–23, 2015), during the ELO 2015 festival. Courtesy of Silvestre Pestana. Photo: Álvaro Seiça.

Portuguese the possibility of traversing the singular and the plural, the individual and the collective, the past, present, and future, by just dislocating a letter: ovo / (p)ovo / (n)ovo.

The fact that the Spectrum's console was connected to a TV screen, a visual and luminous device par excellence, turned out to have a greater symbolic meaning, to the extent that *Computer Poetry* became associated not only with the content, but also with the cover of one of the most significant anthologies of the 1980s, *Poemografias: Perspectivas da Poesia Visual Portuguesa* (Poemographs: Perspectives of Portuguese visual poetry, 1985). Despite being a collection on visual poetry, the cover's composition did not use any printout of the work, but rather the photography of the work's image on a TV screen, that is, a picture of the moving image, as narrated by Fernando Aguiar (2009: n. p.), who coedited the anthology with Pestana:

> I designed the book cover based on a computer poem by Silvestre Pestana (who had created the first computer-poems [*sic*] in 1981/83 for "Spectrum"). And if now it seems something almost banal, in 1985 it was really "different" to present an anthology of poetry and poetic theory with a computer "generated" work on the cover. (Since we had no access to a printer—I do not even know whether back then there was a printer for Spectrum—we went to a household appliance store and we asked to connect the "computer" to a TV set, and right there I took several photographs of one of the poems, whereof the cover of "POEMOGRAFIAS" resulted.[17]

[17] Original: "Desenhei a capa do livro com base num poema de computador do Silvestre Pestana (que tinha criado os primeiros computer-poems em 1981/83 num 'Spectrum'). E se agora parece uma coisa quase banal, em

The rupture introduced by Portuguese experimentalism in the 1960s was a sharp reaction to cultural models, fascism, and colonialism. By then, the transgressive and subversive act meant that experimentation served a sociopolitically engaged project. Accentuated by cultural isolationism, geographic periphery, and the repressiveness of a totalitarian regime, linguistic and artistic forms certainly acquired specific idiosyncrasies. Authors needed to find ways to express themselves without being trapped by the different censoring departments and the political police PIDE. The circumvention of explicit political meaning called for an allegoric approach to the artistic and literary program in different fields of practice, whose core shows a clear hybridization of genres, forms, and artistic languages, which blend poetics, science, and technics.

To come back to my initial argument, the adventure of the experimentalists meant the creation of groundbreaking works as critical reaction and a quest for freedom. Today, different generations of authors who identify their works as having an experimental character—such as Antero de Alda (2011), Rui Torres (2005a, b, 2008a, 2011), Manuel Portela (2011), Liliana Vasques (2016), and Bruno Ministro (2014, 2016a, b)—explore a range of media that includes digital literary works, but not only. Experimental practices are visible in the field of electronic literature by the way authors still continue to reinvent forms and media. Similarly, today's practices do not cluster around a movement, but rather as individual *ars poeticas* that show a clear experimentalist root. Furthermore, appropriation, remix, recreation, and rereading of antecedents act at the level of a continuous creative metamorphosis. The critical and parodic side seems to be more dispersed in the absence of the nefarious dictatorship. However, we can still locate reminiscences of a past collective mentality and a common understanding seems to emerge on topics related to the full meaning of democracy, the malign effects of capitalism, hyperconsumerism, society's alienation, social, gender, and economic injustices, and inequalities.

SOURCES CITED

Aguiar, Fernando. "Poéticas Experimentais." September 30, 2009. http://ocontrariodotempo.blogspot.pt/2009/10/poeticas-experimentais-faz-este-mes-26.html. Accessed November 20, 2013.

Alda, Antero de. *Poemas Intermináveis,* 2011, http://www.anterodealda.com/poemas_interminaveis.htm. Accessed November 20, 2013.

Aragão, António. "A Arte como 'Campo de Possibilidades.'" *Jornal de Letras e Artes* (August 7, 1963). Rep. Hatherly, Ana, and E. M. de Melo e Castro, eds. *PO-EX: Textos Teóricos e Documentos da Poesia Experimental Portuguesa.* Lisbon: Moraes Editores, 1981, pp. 102–5.

Aragão, António, and Herberto Helder, eds. *Poesia Experimental* 1, *Cadernos de Hoje* (1964).

Aragão, António, Herberto Helder, and E. M. de Melo e Castro, eds. *Poesia Experimental* 2, *Cadernos de Hoje* (1966).

Balestrini, Nanni. "Tape Mark I." In *Almanacco Letterario Bompiani 1962*, edited by Sergio Morando. Milan: V. Bompiani e C., 1961, pp. 145–51.

1985 foi realmente 'diferente' apresentar uma antologia de poesia e de teoria poética com uma obra 'gerada' por computador na capa. (Como não tínhamos acesso a impressora—nem sei se havia naquela altura alguma associada ao Spectrum—fomos a uma loja de electrodomésticos e pedimos para ligar o 'computador' a uma televisão, e ali mesmo fiz várias fotografias de um dos poemas, das quais resultou a capa de 'POEMOGRAFIAS.'" See the cover at http://po-ex.net/taxonomia/transtextualidades/paratextualidades/poemografias-capa

Barbosa, Pedro. *A Literatura Cibernética 1: Autopoemas Gerados por Computador*. Porto: Edições Árvore, 1977, http://po-ex.net/taxonomia/transtextualidades/metatextualidades-autografas/pedro-barbosa-literatura-cibernetica-1. Accessed October 25, 2015.

Barbosa, Pedro. *A Ciberliteratura: Criação Literária e Computador*. Lisbon: Edições Cosmos, 1996, http://po-ex.net/taxonomia/transtextualidades/paratextualidades/a-ciberliteratura-criacao-literaria-e-computador-capa-e-descricao. Accessed October 25, 2015.

Barbosa, Pedro. *Cyberliterature (1977–1993)*. In *Electronic Literature Collection*, vol. 3, edited by Stephanie Boluk, Leonardo Flores, Jacob Garbe, and Anastasia Salter. Cambridge: ELO, 2016, http://collection.eliterature.org/3/work.html?work=cyberliterature and http://www.po-ex.net/pedrobarbosa/PB_ELC3.html. Accessed December 16, 2016.

Barth, John. "The Literature of Exhaustion." In *The Friday Book: Essays and Other Non-Fiction*. Baltimore and London: Johns Hopkins University Press, [1967] 1984, pp. 62–76.

Bray, Joe, Alison Gibbons, and Brian McHale, eds. *The Routledge Companion to Experimental Literature*. Abingdon and New York: Routledge, 2012.

Campos, Haroldo de. "Da Razão Antropofágica: A Europa Sob o Signo da Devoração." *Colóquio/Letras*, vol. 62 (July 1981): 10–25, http://coloquio.gulbenkian.pt/bib/sirius.exe/issueContentDisplay?n=62&p=10&o=r. Accessed May 1, 2016.

Cruz, Marcos. "Ernesto de Melo e Castro em Serralves." *Diário de Notícias*, February 10, 2006, http://www.dn.pt/especiais/interior.aspx?content_id=1012459&especial=Serralves&seccao=ARTES&page=-1. Accessed November 11, 2013.

Cussen, Felipe. "Poesía Experimental: Algunas Propuestas Críticas." *Experimental Poetics and Aesthetics* (2010), http://www.waikato.ac.nz/fass/experimentalpoetics/2010/EXP%20 2010%20Poesia%20experimental.pdf. Accessed November 13, 2016.

Donguy, Jacques. *Poésies expérimentales—Zone numérique (1953–2007)*. Paris: Les Presses du Réel, 2007.

Hatherly, Ana. "O Idêntico Inverso ou o Lirismo Ultra-Romântico e a Poesia Concreta." *Diário de Notícias*, September 17, 1959. Rep. Ana Hatherly and E. M. de Melo e Castro, eds. *PO-EX: Textos Teóricos e Documentos da Poesia Experimental Portuguesa*. Lisbon: Moraes Editores, 1981, pp. 91–4, http://po-ex.net/taxonomia/transtextualidades/metatextualidades-autografas/ana-hatherly-o-identico-inverso. Accessed October 25, 2015.

Hatherly, Ana. "Recensão crítica a *A Literatura Cibernética 1*, de Pedro Barbosa." *Colóquio/Letras*, vol. 44 (July 1978): 76–7, http://coloquio.gulbenkian.pt/bib/sirius.exe/issueContent-Display?n=44&p=76&o=r. Accessed October 25, 2015.

Hatherly, Ana. "Perspectivas para a Poesia Visual: Reinventar o Futuro." In *Poemografias: Perspectivas da Poesia Visual Portuguesa*, edited by Fernando Aguiar and Silvestre Pestana. Lisbon: Ulmeiro, 1985, pp. 13–27.

Hatherly, Ana. *Um Calculador de Improbabilidades*. Lisbon: Quimera, 2001.

Helder, Herberto. "[introdução]." In *Poesia Experimental* 1, edited by António Aragão and Herberto Helder. 1964, pp. 5–6.

Higgins, Dick. "Against Movements." *Something Else Newsletter*, vol. 1, no. 6 (May 1967).

Higgins, Dick. *Pattern Poetry: Guide to an Unknown Literature*. Albany: SUNY Press, 1987.

Lima, Manuel. *Visual Complexity: Mapping Patterns of Information*. New York: Princeton Architectural Press, 2011.

Marques, José-Alberto. "O Tempo Não Tem Espaço." In *Poemografias: Perspectivas da Poesia Visual Portuguesa*, edited by Fernando Aguiar and Silvestre Pestana. Lisbon: Ulmeiro, 1985, pp. 89–91.

Melo e Castro, E. M. de. *Lírica do Objecto*. 8 mm film, b/w, no sound, 3'27", 1958, http://po-ex.net/taxonomia/materialidades/videograficas/e-m-de-melocastro-lirlca-do-objecto. Accessed November 23, 2016.

Melo e Castro, E. M. de. *Ideogramas*. Lisbon: Guimarães Editores, 1962, http://po-ex.net/taxonomia/materialidades/planograficas/e-m-de-melocastro-ideogramas. Accessed October 25, 2015.

Melo e Castro, E. M. de. *A Proposição 2.01: Poesia Experimental*. Lisbon: Ulisseia, 1965a, http://po-ex.net/taxonomia/transtextualidades/metatextualidades-autografas/e-m-de-melocastro-a-proposicao-2-01-excursos. Accessed October 25, 2015.

Melo e Castro, E. M. de. *Música Negativa*. Performance, 1965b. Dir. Ana Hatherly. 16 mm film, b/w, no sound, 3'55", 1977, http://po-ex.net/taxonomia/materialidades/videograficas/e-m-de-melocastro-musica-negativa. Accessed November 23, 2016.

Melo e Castro, E. M. de. *Roda Lume* (1968). *Roda Lume Fogo*. U-Matic video, b/w, sound, 2'43", 1986, http://po-ex.net/taxonomia/materialidades/videograficas/e-m-de-melo-castro-roda-lume. Accessed November 23, 2016.

Melo e Castro, E. M. de. *Poética dos Meios e Arte High Tech*. Lisbon: Vega, 1988, http://elmcip.net/node/8934. Accessed October 25, 2015.

Melo e Castro, E. M. de. *O Fim Visual do Século XX e Outros Textos Críticos*. São Paulo: Editora da Universidade de São Paulo, 1993.

Melo e Castro, E. M. de. "Videopoetry." Edited by Eduardo Kac. "New Media Poetry: Poetic Innovation and New Technologies." *Visible Language*, vol. 30, no. 2 (1996): 140–9. Rep. Kac, Eduardo, ed. *Media Poetry: An International Anthology*. Bristol: Intellect Books, 2007, pp. 175–84.

Melo e Castro, E. M. de. *O Caminho do Leve*. Porto: Fundação de Serralves, 2006.

Melo e Castro, E. M. de. "Interview." *Do Leve à Luz*. Coimbra: Casa da Escrita, September 28, 2012, http://po-ex.net/exposicoes/nas-escritas-poex/e-m-de-melo-e-castro-do-leve-luz?showall=&start=2. Accessed November 26, 2016.

Ministro, Bruno. *.] quinquilharia [>*. Óbidos: Candonga, 2014.

Ministro, Bruno. *1_100. The New River* (spring 2016a), http://www.cddc.vt.edu/journals/newriver/16Spring/1_100/project.html. Accessed November 28, 2016.

Ministro, Bruno. *Nigerian Prince!* (2016b), http://hackingthetext.net/about-nigerian-prince/. Accessed November 28, 2016.

Pestana, Silvestre. *Atómico Acto*. In *Hidra* 2, edited by E. M. de Melo e Castro. 1969, n. p.

Pestana, Silvestre. *Computer Poetry*. ZX-81, ZX Spectrum. 1981–83.

Pestana, Silvestre. "Apontamentos de: Literatura Informacional ou a Poética dos Anos 80." In *Poemografias: Perspectivas da Poesia Visual Portuguesa*, edited by Fernando Aguiar and Silvestre Pestana. Lisbon: Ulmeiro, 1985, pp. 201–16.

Pestana, Silvestre, and Luís de Barroco. "Silvestre Pestana: 'A Força da Razão Dominará as Artes.'" *Comércio do Porto, Revista Domingo!* (March 29, 1987): 10–11.

Pestana, Silvestre, and Luís Tranquada. "Silvestre Pestana—entrevista—Lonarte" (December 6, 2011), http://youtu.be/fJj6ImQmxss. Accessed November 11, 2013.

Pestana, Silvestre. "Interview." *Povo Novo Virtual 1966–2013*. ESEC TV. Coimbra: Casa da Escrita, 2013, https://youtu.be/ZdKwlwcFrCU and http://www.po-ex.net/exposicoes/nas-escritas-poex/silvestre-pestana-povo-novo-virtual?showall=1&limitstart=. Accessed November 27, 2016.

Pestana, Silvestre. Phone call to Álvaro Seiça, 2015.

Pimenta, Alberto. *O Silêncio dos Poetas*. Lisbon: A Regra do Jogo, 1978.

Portela, Manuel. *Google Earth: A Poem for Voice and Internet*, 2011, https://vimeo.com/56469197. Accessed January 17, 2014.

Retallack, Joan. "What Is Experimental Poetry & Why Do We Need It?" *Jacket*, vol. 32 (April 2007), http://jacketmagazine.com/32/p-retallack.shtml. Accessed November 13, 2016.

Siemens, George. “Connectivism: A Learning Theory for the Digital Age.” *International Journal of Instructional Technology and Distance Learning*, vol. 2, no. 1 (January 2005), http://www.itdl.org/journal/jan_05/article01.htm. Accessed November 29, 2016.

Sousa, Jorge Pais de. “Povo Novo Virtual, 1968–2013 de Silvestre Pestana.” Coimbra: Casa da Escrita, 2013, https://pestanasilvestre.wordpress.com/2013/02/10/exposicao-povo-novo-virtual/. Accessed November 25, 2016.

Tavares, Salette. *Espelho Cego*. Lisbon: Ática, 1957.

Tavares, Salette. *Obra Poética: 1957–1971*. Fore. Luciana S. Picchio. Lisbon: INCM, 1992.

Tomasula, Steve. “Code Poetry and New-Media Literature.” In *The Routledge Companion to Experimental Literature*, edited by Joe Bray, Alison Gibbons, and Brian McHale. Abingdon and New York: Routledge, 2012, pp. 483–96.

Torres, Rui. *Mar de Sophia*, 2005a, http://telepoesis.net/mardesophia/index.html. Accessed October 25, 2013.

Torres, Rui. *Amor de Clarice*, 2005b, http://telepoesis.net/amorclarice/. Accessed October 25, 2013.

Torres, Rui. *Poemas no Meio do Caminho*, 2008a, http://telepoesis.net/caminho/. In *Electronic Literature Collection*, vol. 2, edited by Laura Borràs Castanyer, Talan Memmott, Rita Raley, and Brian Kim Stefans. Cambridge: ELO, 2011. http://collection.eliterature.org/2/. Accessed October 25, 2013.

Torres, Rui, ed. *CD-ROM da PO.EX: Poesia Experimental Portuguesa—Cadernos e Catálogos*, vols. 1 and 2. CD-ROM. Porto: PO.EX, 2008b, http://www.po-ex.net/evaluation/index.html. Accessed October 25, 2013.

Torres, Rui. *PoemAds: Sob o Signo da Devoração*, 2011, http://www.telepoesis.net/poemads/index.html. In *Anthology of European Electronic Literature*, edited by Maria Engberg, Talan Memmott, and David Prater. Karlskrona: ELMCIP, 2012. http://anthology.elmcip.net/. Accessed January 15, 2014.

Torres, Rui, and Álvaro Seiça. “O Experimentalismo como Invenção, Transgressão e Metamorfose: A PO.EX Revisitada Através de Po-ex.net.” *Colóquio/Letras*, vol. 193 (September 2016): 9–17, http://coloquio.gulbenkian.pt/bib/sirius.exe/getrec?mfn=18940&_template=singleRecord. Accessed May 4, 2017.

Vasques, Liliana. *Objects*, 2016, http://cargocollective.com/lilianavasques/e-poetry. Accessed November 28, 2016.

CHAPTER TEN

Writing under Constraint of the Regime of Computation

MANUEL PORTELA

I shall go even further: my freedom will be so much the greater and more meaningful the more narrowly I limit my field of action and the more I surround myself with obstacles. Whatever diminishes constraint, diminishes strength. The more constraints one imposes, the more one frees one's self of the chains that shackle the spirit.

—Igor Stravinsky (1947: 65)

Literary art can be described as a systematic exploration of the recursive features of language for extending the boundaries of what can be said through the articulation of codes. Writers come up with their own rules for inventing the sayable and the writable in their play with the generative features of language. Insofar as language and writing are rule-based systems, a number of enabling constraints are already in place in any act of writing. Bernardo Schiavetta (2000) calls these rules "systematic textual devices," that is, linguistic norms or tools that make written verbal communication possible. Furthermore, the social uses of both language and writing, which are historically structured as discourses, can also be described as enabling constraints that act themselves out through the speaking and writing subjects. Discursive constraints are constitutive of all verbal action and they determine what can be said and how it can be said, giving shape to communicative situations. Oral and written discursive constraints are productive constituents of social relations and social roles through verbal language.

If we conceive of literary practice as an open experimentation with linguistic and discursive constraints that comes up with its own rules for the production of many different types of verbal patterns, we can say that literary forms and genres function as further sets of constraints that can determine, for instance, patterns of meter and rhyme, structure of plot and roles of characters, bibliographic structure and page layout, within any given poem, narrative, or play. Thus, there would be at least three layers of enabling-constraints involved in any writing act: the rules of language, the rules of discourse, and the rules of literary form. Any act of literary invention has to come to terms with these three layers of productive constraints. These entwined layers could be described as constitutive of the material means of production of the literary.

However, the notion of "writing under constraint" is usually applied to explicit processes whose rule-bound nature can be formally described, and whose explicitness becomes a defining feature of a given work. It is only at the level of literary form that such written constraints emerge as a way of producing and organizing a specific textual field. In this more restricted sense, "a constraint is a systematic textual device that obeys the principle of specific saturation but which is not a norm in itself" (Schiavetta, 2000). Schiavetta defines this feature as a "non-normative systematicity" which is textually instantiated as a result of "an objective encounter of interdependent and complementary reading and writing constraints." The constrained text is the product of a writing constraint that functions also as a reading constraint.[1]

Many twentieth-century artistic practices, from dance to music to painting, have programmatically acknowledged the productivity of constraints as a method for creativity. Materialist critiques of artistic conventions and media awareness of particular modes of representation—two major features of both modernist and postmodernist artistic practices—have often been achieved through constrained processes that highlight the combinatorics according to which meaning is produced—that is, reproduced and transformed—as a form of social action within a given artistic and social convention. Formal procedures for randomizing the sequence of elements in an artwork are good examples—from Dada and Surrealist techniques for generating unexpected verbal and visual associations to John Cage's and Merce Cunningham's I Ching-based operations for their music and dance performances. Constrained writing, including forms that can be executed by computer programs, can also be found in many earlier writing traditions and experiments, in the Ancient, Medieval, or modern periods. Portuguese baroque poetry of the seventeenth and eighteenth centuries, for instance, is filled with labyrinthine texts that follow numerical constraints, many of which could be formally programmed. Florian Cramer (2005) has analyzed symbolic practices as computations of totality and fragmentation, highlighting the executable character of many kinds of textual algorithms but also their power as forms of cultural and literary imagination. One of the specificities of our techno-social moment is that literary production according to writing constraints has been automated, that is, many constrained procedures have become executable code. As a consequence this meaning of code as machine-readable, executable language has further extended the literary tropes around constrained writing. The principles of numerical representation and modularity of digital media have submitted all alphanumeric writing to programmability:

> Ever since computer programmers referred to written algorithmic machine instructions as "code" and programming as "coding," "code" not only refers to cryptographic codes, but to what makes up software, either as a source code in a high-level programming language or as compiled binary code, but in either case as a sequence of executable instructions. With its seeming opacity and the boundless, viral multiplication of its output in the execution, algorithmic code opens up a vast potential for cultural imagination, phantasms and phantasmagorias. (9)

One of the pervasive phantasms of constrained executable writing is precisely the delivery of all symbolic production to the machines, an image forcibly conveyed by Friedrich Kittler (1995) when he—deterministically and hyperbolically—referred to the microchip as the last act of human writing, discarding all software effects as mere "eyewash": "The last historical act of writing may well have been the moment when, in the early seventies, the Intel engineers laid out some dozen square meters of blueprint paper (64

[1] For those interested in the history and analysis of constrained literary practices, the French journal *Formules: revue des littératures à contraintes et des créations formelles* (1997–2016, 20 volumes) is an indispensable resource. http://www.ieeff.org/formulessitenewhome.html.

square meters in the case of the later 8086) in order to design the hardware architecture of their first integrated microprocessor." The integrated microprocessor—the electronic embodiment of a circuit capable of processing all forms of writing as binary code—would have submitted all writing codes, including literary writing, to computational constraints. Caught amid iterations, subroutines, and loops of code, writing would be forever constrained by the regime of computation.

Programmed or not, the use of constraints in writing may be described in terms of a double rationale: on one hand, they are analytical and rhetorical strategies for uncovering constraints in all processes of semiotic production and, thus, for investigating the co-extensibility between meaning and material constraint, between form and rule; on the other hand, they are a means of artistic production per se, that is, a particular linguistic operation or textual device—a program, a resource, a form of capital—for producing more creative work. Constraints highlight the potential for any textual string to become an instruction for producing further texts, that is, to function as both text and executable text. The writing constraint brings the code of writing to the surface and thus parallels the stored-program principle in Turing-Von Newman electronic computers in which program and data are both treated as data. Constraints show the architecture of language as produced text and textual engine, as interpretable meaning and material action.

Constraints are efficient triggers for extending the cognitive system formed by humans and their writing technologies and for making writing produce more writing. Constraints are also highly generative processes—that is, they can produce unanticipated and emergent forms and meanings—because they enable human subjects and their writing tools to enter the play of signifiers and expand what can be imagined through the combinatorics of written language beyond the strictures of self-awareness or the pragmatics of communication. In other words: all written forms have sets of rules that can be abstracted, and new rules can be formalized to invent more forms. In the former case, the constraint is abstracted a posteriori through reading and analysis; in the latter case, the constraint is foregrounded a priori as a formal element in the production of further signifiers. By means of explicit constraints, writing can be recycled *ad infinitum* according to formal processes that give rise to emergent meanings.

CONSTRAINTS AS MEANS OF LITERARY PRODUCTION AND INVENTION

The concept of "writing under constraint" is usually applied to works that embody an explicit a priori constraint at some level. Thus, a parodic novel such as *Ulysses* (1922) could be analyzed as an example of loosely constrained writing in the sense that its narrative structure is a projection of the structure of the *Odyssey*. In effect, *Ulysses*'s parodical dimension is dependent on Joyce's extratextual scheme of correspondences and chapter titles, since most allegorical levels of reference to the *Odyssey* tend to be highly indirect and mediated. If it were not for the title of the novel and for the extratextual notes, the novel could be read as predominantly realist and psychological. *Ulysses* may also be described as a literary remix of genres and styles, as Joyce's maximalist approach to writing is to devour and emulate many discursive and literary practices.

Because Joyce also designed its chapters as an inventory of rhetorical and narrative techniques and specific vocabularies, we can see the double rationale of the constraint at work—that is, both as a rule for revealing structures of meaning, and as a means for producing further signifiers. Another telling example of constraint-based writing can be found in dramaticules by Samuel Beckett, where the material elements of a stage play are self-reflexively permutated.[2] In *Come and Go* (1963), for instance, all elements (characters, speeches, costume, props, lighting, sound, silence, and movements on stage) have been mathematically structured and choreographed according to a symmetrical pattern of repetition and variation. Similarly, in B. S. Johnson's novel *House Mother Normal: A Geriatric Comedy* (1971) the events of the same social evening are told from the perspectives of old men and women in a nursing home—their stories reflecting various stages of physical and mental impairment and the language of each character is constrained to embody a particular cognitive loss. Each interior monologue is laid out in exactly twenty-one pages, carefully designed to synchronize the minds of the characters across the group. In all of these examples, the rule-based structure of narrative or of dramatic permutations on stage can be made more or less visible at the textual surface. Constraints may either be inferred through close analysis, or they may be declared upfront. Joyce described the structure of his novel in his 1920 scheme, which became a major source for all subsequent readings. Beckett described the permutational patterns in the stage directions embedded into his dramaticule, symbolized in a drawing of the intersections of the three characters' arms as they held their hands in the final scene. Johnson included an explanatory table for each character, providing their clinical record (age, pathologies, cognitive test results).

The most significant postmodernist example of this writing-under-constraint rationale is the Oulipo (*Ouvroir de Littérature Potentielle*) group, founded in Paris in 1960.[3] Their declared aim was to produce writing in different genres according to rules that could be specified in advance. They also experimented with collaborative writing, using rule-based processes as an enabling-form for collective writing. Coordinating written production across a collective also testifies to the constraint as a working tool for increasing productivity. The fact that Oulipo included both writers and mathematicians is already an indication of the computational foundations of its rationalistic program. For the Oulipians literature was an algorithmic art. Constraints were the result of formal procedures that could be described mathematically, and their aim was to open up writing to the potentiality of verbal permutations and combinations. The role of the writer was to systematically experiment with language as if it were a form of calculus, programmatically experimenting with techniques that could be found in earlier literary compositions or inventing arbitrary rules for generating new works based on existing texts or defining different levels of constraints for creating new texts.

The idea that a piece of writing could be explicitly produced, by means of formal procedures, from another piece of writing suggests the possibility of automation. The connection between writing constraints and computers was already stated in their first manifesto: "Ce que certains écrivains ont introduit dans leur manière, avec talent (voire avec génie) mais les uns occasionnellement (forgeages de mots nouveaux), d'autres avec

[2] "Dramaticules" was Beckett's word for his very short plays. Minimalism is brought to an extreme in his also highly constrained and symmetrical thirty-five-second play *Breath* (1969). Other dramaticules include *Act without Words I (Acte Sans Paroles I): A Mime for One Player* (1956) and *Act without Words II (Acte Sans Paroles II): A Mime for Two Players* (1956).

[3] Historical documentation and current activities of Oulipo (one of the most productive and long-lasting groups in literary history) can be found in the official website of the group: http://oulipo.net/. For a glossary of Oulipian formal procedures, see http://oulipo.net/fr/contraintes. The glossary lists 132 different procedures, some of which have been appropriated from the literary tradition, and others were invented by members of the group. See also Mathews and Brotchie (1998), and Salceda Rodríguez and Thomas (2010).

prédilection (contrerimes), d'autres avec insistance mais dans une seule direction (lettrisme), l'Ouvroir de Littérature Potentielle (OuLiPo) entend le faire systématiquement et, au besoin en recourant aux bons offices des machines à traiter l'information."[4] In their second manifesto, they highlight the fact that explicit constraints bear mainly upon the formal features of literary texts: "L'effort de création porte principalement sur tous les aspects formels de la littérature: contraintes, programmes ou structures alphabétiques, consonantiques, vocaliques, syllabiques, phonétiques, graphiques, prosodiques, rimiques, rythmiques et numériques."[5] Although the actual use of computers by members of the Oulipo only started with the project A.R.T.A. (1975–77)[6] and with the foundation of ALAMO[7]—started by Paul Braffort and Jacques Roubaud in 1981—the creation of literary works on the basis of algorithmic processes has been a key feature of the group since its very beginning. Computer-assisted reading and writing were two dimensions of this process. The groups AGRAPH (Jean-Pierre Balpe, Eléonore Gerbier, Marine Nessi, Djeff Regottaz, Tony Houziaux, Soufiane Bouyahi), more focused on generative text, and L.A.I.R.E.[8] (Claude Maillard, Tibor Papp, Philippe Bootz, Jean-Marie Dutey, Frédéric de Velay), mainly concerned with animated poetry, further extended the use of computers for constrained writing during the 1980s.

Several masterpieces of constrained writing originated with members of the Oulipo group. Raymond Queneau's *Exercices de Style* (1947) described the same event according to ninety-nine different constraints, each of which was a demonstration of the ways in which style is a constrained use of linguistic and discursive patterns for producing a certain representation of events in the world. Language is revealed as an internal system of sound and semantic patterns rather than a referential word-to-world correspondence. Italo Calvino structured several of his novels according to explicit combinatorial rules. Writing and reading machines also turn up in his essays and in his fiction. In the eighth chapter of *Se una notte d'inverno un viaggiatore* (1979)—a novel that contains ten different narrative beginnings according to specific genres and styles—Calvino describes writing and reading procedures that resemble current generative forms of fiction and stylometric practices of textual analysis. The form of the work was later analyzed by Calvino by means of a diagram explaining its structural compositional constraints (Figure 10.1). Georges Perec's *La vie mode d'emploi* (1978) uses several algorithms to tell the story of the inhabitants of an imagined apartment block (11, Rue Simon-Crubellier, Paris) between 1875 and 1975: each chapter deals with one room in each of the apartments in the building; the cross-sectioning of the building into 10 x 10 squares allows him to chart chess horse movements in order to move around the building and thus organize the work's chapters into a puzzle-like structure of exhaustive descriptions and parallel

---

[4] Le Lionnais (1961). What some writers have introduced in their own way, with talent (even with genius), but only occasionally (forging new words), others with predilection (counter-rhymes), others with insistence, but in one direction only (Lettrism), *Ouvroir de Littérature Potentiel (Oulipo)* intends to do systematically and, if necessary, by using the good offices of information processing machines (my translation).

[5] Le Lionnais (1973). The creative effort mainly focuses on all formal aspects of literature: alphabetical, consonantal, vocalic, syllabic, phonetic, graphic, prosodic, rhyming, rhythmic, and numerical constraints, programs or structures (my translation).

[6] This project was launched in 1975 by the Atelier de Recherches Avancées du Centre National d'Art et de Culture Georges Pompidou.

[7] "Atelier de Littérature Assistée par la Mathématique et l'Ordinateur" (Workshop of computer- and mathematics-assisted literature).

[8] "Lecture, Art, Innovation, Recherche, Écriture" (Reading, art, innovation, research, writing) was started in 1989.

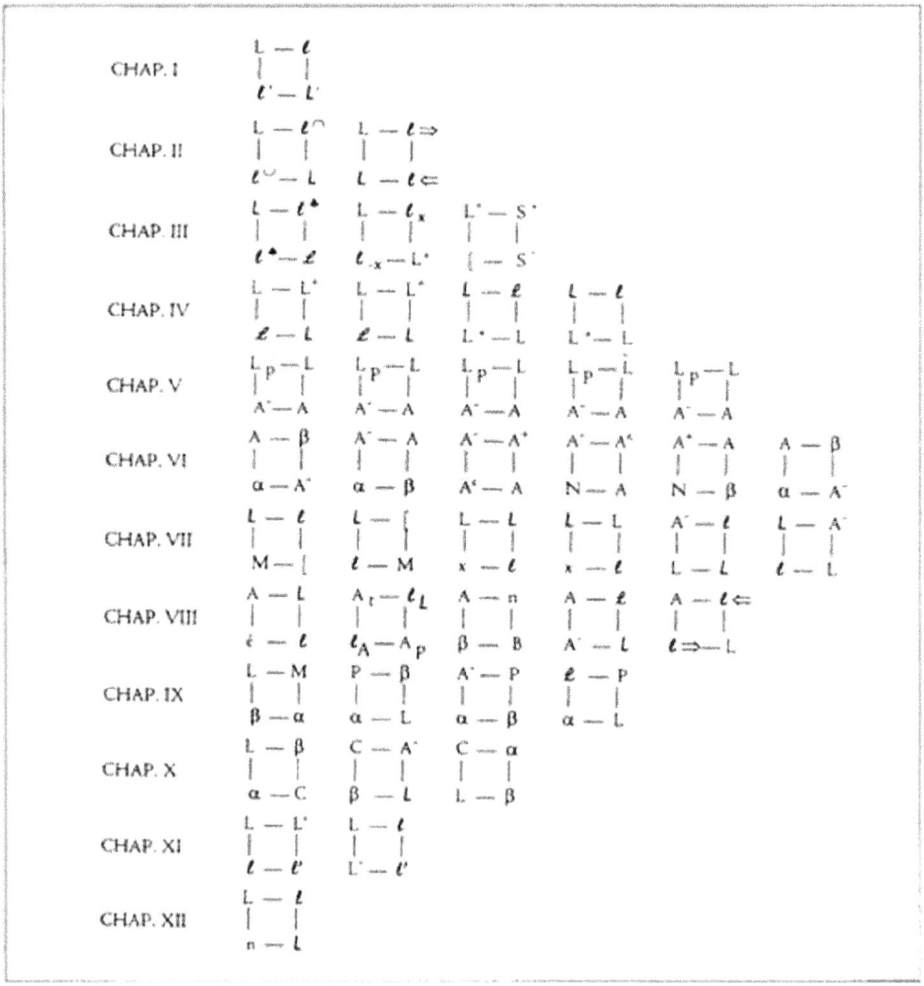

CHAP. I
CHAP. II
CHAP. III
CHAP. IV
CHAP. V
CHAP. VI
CHAP. VII
CHAP. VIII
CHAP. IX
CHAP. X
CHAP. XI
CHAP. XII

FIGURE 10.1 Italo Calvino's diagram for his novel *If on Winter's Night a Traveller* (1979).

multiple stories for each single room. Perec also used a grid for determining the themes and vocabulary lists for each chapter, according to the x and y axes of predefined table (Figure 10.2); this list, in its turn, is subject to further permutations according to the *sestina* structure; a further rule determined that an event related to each day of writing should also be mentioned in the narrative.

Many writing constraints can be described as algorithms, that is, step-by-step procedures for producing a given verbal and material output that exhibits certain structures, properties, and patterns. However, the most successful works cannot be inferred from the algorithm alone: the constraint functions as a productive device that enhances the discovery of new associations and the emergence of poetic and narrative forms according to nondeterministic and stochastic principles. This unique relation between randomness and determinism is crucial for the liberating effect of the self-imposed restrictions and for their effect on literary inventiveness. In *From A to Z* (1977), for instance, Johanna

		1	2	3	4	5	6	7	8	9	10
1	position	agenouillé	descendre accroupi	à plat ventre	assis	debout	monter	entrer	sortir	couché sur le dos	un bras en l'air
	activité	peindre	entretien	toilette	érotique	classement rangement	se servir d'un plan	réparer	lire ou écrire	[illegible]	manger
	citation 1	Flaubert	Sterne	Proust	Kafka	Leiris	Roussel	Queneau	Verne	Borges	Mathews
	citation 2	Mann	Nabokov	Roubaud	Butor	Rabelais	Freud	Stendhal	Joyce	Lowry	Calvino
2	nombre	1	2	3	4	5	+5	1	2	3	0
	rôle	OCCUPANT	OCCUPANT	OCCUPANT	démarcheur	ouvrier	autre (eq. [illegible], tastur...)	client	fournisseur	domestique	aucun
	3°secteur	Fait divers	Biblio.	[illegible] Règlement	Faire Part	recette	presp. pharmacie	agendas [illegible]	programme	dictionnaire [illegible]	mode d'emploi [illegible]
	ressort?	retour de voyage	réception de lettre	s'allier une filiation	effet de [illegible]	baigner dans la nostalgie	faire un rêve	"créer"	résoudre une énigme	poursuivre une chimère	assouvir une vengeance
3	MURS	peinture mate	[illegible]	boiseries	liège	panneaux métal	papier uni ou [illegible]	peinture brillante	toile de Jouy	papier à motifs	cuir ou synthétique
	SOLS	parquet à l'anglaise	p. à point de Hongrie	p. à bâtons rompus	p. mosaïque ou [illegible]	carrelage [illegible]	moquette	tapis de [illegible]	lino	tomettes	tapis de corde, sisal, [illegible]
3	époque	ANTIQUITÉ	MOYEN AGE	RENAISSANCE	17e	18e	Révolution et Empire	19e	→ 39	39-45	après guerre
	lieu	Allemagne	Italie	Iles Britanniques	Espagne	Russie, URSS	Etats Unis	Extrême Orient	Afrique du Nord	Amérique du Sud	Proche Orient
4	style	chinois	contemporain	Louis XV Louis XVI	Empire	Regency [illegible] etc.	Napoléon III	Louis XIII	"rustique"	"camping"	modern style, 1900, [illegible]
	meubles	Table	Chaise	Fauteuil	Bahut, Armoire [illegible], ...	Lit	Bibliothèque	Guéridon etc...	commode [illegible]	divan, canapé	Bureau
	longueur	< quelques lignes	~1 p.	~2 p.	~3 p.	~4 p.	~5 p.	~6 p.	~8 p.	~10 p	12+ p
	DIVERS	armes	argent (billets)	maladie	flamme	militaires	institution	clergé	couteau	Physiologie 1860	littérature danoise
5	age&sexe	Femme 35-60	Homme 35-60	vieillard ♂	vieillard ♀	jeune femme 18-35	jeune homme 18-35	♂ → 17 ans	♀ → 17 ans	jeune enfant → 10 ans	nouveau né → 1 an
	animaux	Chat	Chien	Oiseau	Poisson	Rat Souris	Rongeur	Guêpe [illegible]	Araignée	Insectes, [illegible]	Autres
	Vêtements	costume, [illegible]	manteau	veste d'intérieur	Pantalon ou jupe	gilet	chemise...	chandail...	Imperméable	Uniforme...	blouson...
	Tissus (motifs)	Uni	à rayures	à pois	à carreaux	écossais	patchwork	à ramages	à fleurs	imprimé, à motifs	brodé
6	Tissus (matière)	soie 1	laine 2	cachemire 3	flanelle ou feutre 4	nylon 5	cuir 6	[illegible] 7	coton 8	velours 9	lin 0
	Couleurs	blanc	vert	brun	noir	jaune	orange	gris	rouge	violet	bleu ciel
	Accessoires	chapeau	cravate, foulard	écharpe, [illegible]	gants	chaussures	mouchoir	bretelles	ceintures	caleçons sous-vêtements	bas et chaussettes
	bijoux	collier	bague	bracelet	canne	lunettes	médailles décoration	montre	briquet	sac à main	épingle de cravate, broche
7	Lectures	quotidien	roman, [illegible]	hebdo	lettre	[illegible]	revue	policier, SF	[illegible]	livre d'art	journal
	Musiques	ancienne	classique	romantique	[illegible]	contemporain	jazz	pop et folk	[illegible]	militaire	Operas
	Tableaux	Arnolfini	St Jérôme	Ambassadeurs	Chute d'Icare	[illegible]	[illegible] la Tempête	[illegible]	Carpaccio	Bosch	[illegible]
	Livres	10 petits nègres	Disparition	[illegible]	Moby Dick	[illegible]	Pierrot	100 ans de solitude	Hamlet	4 [illegible]	Ubu
8	Boissons	Eau	Vin	Alcool	Bière, Cidre	Thé	Café	Infusions	jus de fruits	Lait	coca etc...
	nourriture	Pain	Charcuteries	[illegible], crudités salades	Viandes, Abats Gibier	Poissons et crustacés	légumes, Féculents	fromages	fruits	pâtisserie Sucreries	zakouski
	Petits meubles	Pendules, horloges	cendriers	[illegible]	sculptures mobiles	Rasoirs	pianos	lustres	téléphone	radio, hifi etc...	boîtes
	Jeux et jouets	Cartes	dés osselets	dominos	Solitaire	Go, échecs, dames	jaquet	[illegible]	PUZZLE	automates	[illegible]
9	Sentiments	Indifférence	Joie	Douleur	ennui	colère	angoisse	étonnement	haine	amour	ambitions
	Peintures	mur nu	dessin	gravure	aquarelle gouache	Tableau	reproduction	Cartes et Plan	photos	affiches	[illegible]
	SURFACES	carré	rectangle	triangle	hexagone	octogone	Trapèze	rond	ovale	en losange	étoile
	VOLUMES	cube	parallélép. rectangle	pyramide	cylindre	sphère	oeuf	polyèdre	cone	hémisphère	tonneau
0	fleurs?	Fleurs	[illegible]	Arbustes	pl. vertes	épices	bois flotté	[illegible]	fruits [illegible]	[illegible]	pl. grasses
	bibelots	marbre	pierres semi [illegible]	minerai de métal	cuivre, [illegible]	or, argent	ivoire, nacre	cristal verre taillé	albâtre	bronze	[illegible]
	manque	1	2	3	4	5	6	7	8	9	0
	FAUX	1	2	3	4	5	6	7	8	9	0
-1c	COUPLES	Laurel Hardy	Fouillis Tinteau	Racine Shakespeare	Philémon Baucis	Crime châtiment	Orgueil Préjugé	Nuit Brouillard	Cendres diamants	[illegible]	Belle Bête

FIGURE 10.2 Georges Perec's table of 420 elements to be used in each of the chapters of *La vie mode d'emploi* (*Cahier*, 1993).

Drucker has constrained the narrative by deciding to use only once all the elements in the fonts available in forty-eight drawers of type, making literary composition dependent on the limits of typographic resources. The oblique narrative about personal relations involving several characters in a print workshop is intensified by the scarcity of type as the letterpress printing of the narrative advances. Mark Z. Danielewski's novel-poem *Only Revolutions* (2006) contains many algorithms that structure its bibliographic and linguistic elements according to relations of symmetry and recursion. Those algorithms have both an algebraic and a geometric expression, generating numerous narrative and material patterns (Portela 2013: 233–90). Christian Bök's *Eunoia* (2001) is another extreme example of post-Oulipian constrained writing: each of the five lipogrammatic chapters uses words containing only one vowel.

Although those procedural constraint-based works are so complex in the ways they weave calculation with free association that they cannot be automated, there are also many examples of analogue works written under constraint that have been automated[9] or, increasingly, constraint-based works that have been conceived for automated algorithms. In both these cases, given a certain database of elements, the formal programmed procedure will determine the output. This automatically generated output either consists of a closed set of instantiations or an open-ended textual generation that runs a very large factorial set of permutations. Beyond a threshold of a certain number of repeated permutations, the artificiality and determinism of the process seems to dissolve into the general flux of language as if the machine could write by itself, conflating its constrained textual form with the general programmed grammar of natural language.

Computers depend on strict formalisms for executing the instructions contained in their programs; otherwise the code fails to compile. All computer-based art, including electronic literature, must internalize algorithmic logic as a compositional process since they have to function according to the algorithmic and database rationale of their processing machine. Lev Manovich (2008) claimed that, with digital media, the database becomes a universal structure for the production of meaning. This is clearly the case with many works of electronic literature, which are designed as permutational interactive textual environments that give readers the experience of the open-endedness resulting from the work's database structure. The role of the algorithm is to perform a sequence of operations upon a set of elements and thus create meaningful structures and patterns out of the database. Although algorithms may have many different expressions, some of which materialize only at the abstract level of data processing, there are also algorithms that will have expression at the level of artistic form, for instance, as a specific textual, visual, or sound pattern. When compositional procedures are formalized as computer algorithms, we can say that writing or artistic constraints have been automated.

[9] For examples of programmed versions of Oulipian works, see: Beverley Charles Rowe's (1996) version (2003; 2006, 2nd edition) of *Cent Mille Milliards de Poèmes* (1961), by Raymond Queneau (French original with English translations)—http://www.bevrowe.info/Queneau/QueneauRandom_v5.html; Gordon Dow's (1991–2002) version (French original)—http://www.growndodo.com/wordplay/oulipo/10%5E14sonnets.html; Magnus Bodin's (1997) version of the same text (French original with English and Swedish translations)—http://x42.com/active/queneau.html. "The N+7 Machine," a programmed version of the "S+7" procedure (replacing each noun in a text with the seventh one following it in a dictionary), originally invented by Jean Lescure—http://www.spoonbill.org/n+7/. This version uses the "The Spoonbill Generator" (1996–2009) developed by Peter Christian. See also the hypertext version of Raymond Queneau's "A Story as You Like It" (Un conte à votre façon) by Joseph Jean Rolland Dubé (1995)—http://www.thing.de/projekte/7:9%23/queneau_1.html#roman. Other programmed versions of poetic and narrative Oulipian textual algorithms, produced between 1991 and 2002, can be seen at http://www.growndodo.com/index.cgi.

So when constrained writing becomes electronic literature the question spirals into multiple iterations: in what sense is an algorithm a writing constraint? And in what sense is a writing constraint an algorithm? What happens when writing constraints are programmed? What kind of writing constraints can be programmed? Is programmed writing necessarily writing under constraint? How do these forms relate to unconstrained non-programmed writing? What is the relation between word processing and constrained writing, for example? What are the specific writing constraints introduced by the regime of computation? What happens when all written language becomes computable and when more and more written interactions are mediated through and processed by digital machines? What constraints did binary code and high-level computer languages introduce in our general literary processes? What is the relation between programming constraints[10] and writing constraints?

UNDERWRITING CONSTRAINTS

Before addressing the programmability of writing constraints, it may be useful to think about the programmability of language itself. The formalization of writing constraints in digital literature is closely related to the automation of natural language processing—from automated writing, speech technologies, and translation tools to various forms of machine learning. A significant number of digital literary works—particularly those that are based on real-time interactive permutation for textual generation—show how programmed writing constraints instantiate the programmability of language. By selecting items from a lexical database or by combining lines, phrases, or sentences from pre-existing texts, the work's algorithm offers a model of the workings of language as a series of discrete merge and parsing operations that yield an infinite array of interpretable expressions. Thus the programmed writing constraint enacts certain syntactic properties of language—such as hierarchy, embeddedness, and recursion—which have been mathematically described in order to become computable.[11]

In the 1950s, generative linguistics defined the faculty of language as a computational system that could be described algorithmically. This early historical attempt to automate the processing of language indicates the strong connection between generative theory as a theory of language and the development of the digital computer as a language-processing machine.[12] However, despite the strong explanatory power of generative grammar as an evolutionary account of the faculty of language, the description of syntactic structures

---

[10] "Programming constraints" is used here in a general sense. In a more restricted sense, there is a form of declarative programming called "constraint programming" in which relations between variables are stated as constraints. Instead of defining a sequence of executable steps, constraints define the properties of a solution to be found. Cf. https://en.wikipedia.org/wiki/Constraint_programming.

[11] Early generative text experiments show how the computer program itself was explored as a writing constraint. See, for example, Nick Montfort's 2016 reimplementation of Victor H. Yngve's "Random Generation of English Sentences" (cf. http://nickm.com/memslam/random_sentences.html), originally presented at the International Conference on Machine Translation of Languages and Applied Language Analysis, National Physical Laboratory, Teddington, UK, September 5–8, 1961.

[12] See, for instance, one of Noam Chomsky's early papers: "Three Models for the Description of Language," *IRE Transactions on Information Theory,* September, 1956, 113–24. The development of computer processing of natural language, including early attempts at automating translation, is a technological aspect of the Cold War competition between the United States and the Soviet Union. Information theory and computer-processing of verbal communication could be described as manifestations of the militarization of language in the fight for supremacy in the battlefield.

and transformations that could be applied across multiple languages in order to confirm the universal grammar hypothesis proved to be an intractable problem. The growing number of complex structures and transformational rules that we find in the extended and revised versions of generative theory gave way in the early 1990s to the minimalist approach. The Minimalist Program—the current version of the generative biolinguistic inquiry into the computable faculty of language—has been focused on finding the minimal features and operations required for the emergence of the faculty of language.

According to the current minimalist biolinguistic account, three basic principles seem to have been empirically confirmed: "(1) human language syntax is hierarchical, and is blind to considerations of linear order, with linear ordering constraints reserved for externalization; (2) the particular hierarchical structures associated with sentences affects their interpretation; and (3) there is no upper bound on the depth of relevant hierarchical structure" (Berwick and Chomsky 2016: 8). This theory of language is built on the premise of an asymmetry between the two language-processing interfaces, privileging the conceptual-intentional interface over externalization through a sensorimotor system: "The basic principle of language (BP) is that each language yields an infinite array of hierarchically structured expressions, each interpreted at two interfaces, conceptual-intentional (C-I) and sensorimotor (SM)—the former yielding a 'language of thought' (LOT), perhaps the only such LOT; the latter in large part modality-independent, though there are preferences" (Chomsky 2015: ix). The merge operation was selected as the most likely candidate to being the minimal computational operation that could account for the biological emergence of the faculty of language at the brain-mind interface. All hierarchical complexity of language derives from recursive merge operations, that is, from the combination of any two syntactic elements into hierarchically structured expressions which in turn can enter into further computations (Berwick and Chomsky 2016: 10–11).

The fact that human language has been formally described so as to be process-able by computers is crucial for understanding how computer programs have come to play such an important part in defining writing constraints in digital literature. The successful computer modeling of the basic properties of language suggests that the computer program already is part of the enabling conditions for literary expression in a digital culture. Computer-generated literature arises at the intersection between natural language and programming languages, which opened up the possibility of automating the production of written and spoken language and, also, of any number of specific constraints for generating linguistic outputs according to particular patterns. In computer-assisted literature a model of language as a computable generative system based on merge operations meets a model of literary writing as a rule-based formal process. Computable writing constraints are also computable linguistic constraints.[13]

The basic recursive syntactic operations that enable language to produce an infinite array of expressions can be extended to the level of discourse and literary form, and thus model and emulate any number of speech and script acts, including those that are interpreted as "literary." Rui Torres (2012), for instance, has developed a poetics of appropriation and remixing of previous literary works which opens up the constrained parodic structures to the generative stream of language—see, for example, his digital poem *Húmus* (2008). With the use of programs, syntactical structures and lexical items can be specified in advance as engines for producing further writing. Emergent narrative

[13] For a discussion of various methods for textual generation, see Roque (2011) and Dupej (2012).

meanings and unexpected poetical patterns are explored with the help of programmed constraints. Literary invention is being reconceived as the experimental result of the intersection between the programmability of the computer and the programmability of language. The literary value of constrained automated writing generally depends on the specific relations between input (including reader-generated input in interactive works) and output, both of which in turn depend on the ways in which the program executes a set of constraints on its linguistic and other nonverbal materials.

Florian Cramer (2005, 2011), Philippe Bootz (2006), N. Katherine Hayles (2008, 2012), Joseph Tabbi (2010), Talan Memmott (2011), Nick Montfort (2012), Christopher T. Funkhouser (2012), D. Fox Harrell (2013), Daniel C. Howe and John Cayley (2011, 2013), Dave Jhave Johnston (2016), and others have shown how contemporary digital arts have increasingly turned to computer code as artistic language in itself. Cramer (2011) refers to "alphanumeric text" as "the most elegant notation system for computer instructions" and to the "instantaneous mutual convertibility of processed data into algorithmic processors." In other words, writing under constraint in the regime of computation is to write executable writing that generates further writing. Writing becomes the processor of writing, both instruction code and data.

If analyzed as an example of constrained writing at the level of code, Nick Montfort's *Concrete Perl* (2011) brings to the surface the rationale inherent in all constraints as written instantiations (textual output) and code (program and input data, i.e., textual input) for generating further written instantiations. In this work the code itself is written under constraint ("A set of four concrete poems realized as 32-character Perl programs"), implying that the code is also the text, and both code and text are forms of constrained writing:

> "All the Names of God": perl -e '{print"a"x++$...$"x$.,$,=_;redo}';
> "Alphabet Expanding": perl -e '{print$,=$"x($.+=.01),a..z;redo}';
> "ASCII Hegemony": perl -e '{print" ".chr for 32..126;redo}';
> "Letterformed Terrain": perl -e '{print$",$_=(a..z)[rand$=];redo}'.

The textual output for each of the four lines of code is self-reflexive not only about alphabetic visual patterns and verbal permutations at the scale of characters and words—a parody of formal features recognizable in concrete poetry—but also about the nature of digital characters as encoded representations of other forms of writing and about the nature of executable language. The work's approach to form through black and white characters on the screen and brief executable statements for generating those forms suggests a formal correspondence between the two levels of minimalist instantiation—the visual writing on the screen and the linear writing of the perl program—while the iteration encapsulated in the readable function "redo" seems to close the gap between the two forms of constrained writing.

We could also claim that authors become meta-authors as they formalize the process for generating certain types of texts. The invention of the algorithm itself—when considered as computer program—corresponds to the creation of an author-function, that is, a particular set of patterns in the use of language for written production. Jean-Pierre Balpe (2016) claims that the generative author is "something like a meta-author trying to define what literature is for him and how his literary conception can be formally described" (Balpe, 2005). Constrained generative writing is "the production of continuously changing literary texts by means of a specific dictionary, some set of rules and the use of algorithms" (ibid.). Balpe has invented many writing agents each of which generates its own series of texts in real-time in response to reader input.[14] He also holds that generative texts should conform to specific patterns and discursive conventions that are acceptable by a community of readers. One of his latest works—"Les Carolingiens" (2014–15)—is a series of generative fictional texts about the Carolingian period in France. This work's dictionary contains what he refers to as "knowledge representations," that is, certain kinds of semantic restrictions that control syntactical combinations so that generated texts are not only well-formed sentences but they also satisfy requirements of historical verisimilitude—for instance, in the vocabulary that refers to tools, furniture, or cooking practices. This argument for generators of fiction is similar to current processes for automating certain textual types (such as weather reports, traffic reports, sports reports, financial reports, and so on), resulting in acceptable written texts for a given communication domain. For such texts, one can imagine a situation in which the authorial function will consist only in selecting the variables that will fit into the discursive matrix. And even that selection could be automated, as the program fills in the blanks by selecting from a database of updated values. Formulaic and standardized text, including popular literary genres, can be significantly automated and pass Turing's test for artificial intelligence. Even the textual templates themselves could be automatically generated by means of statistical analysis as happens today in computer-assisted translation.

Attempts to develop rule-based machine translation between the 1950s and the 1980s were replaced by statistical methods during the past twenty-five years, as more and more interlinguistic data became available in networked databases. Current computer-assisted translation systems divide texts into segments (usually understood as sentences, as defined by punctuation marks), and search a bilingual memory for exact or fuzzy matches between source and translation segments. This method is complemented with search and recognition of terminologies in bilingual glossaries. Search results are then offered to human translators as prompts for adaptation and reuse (cf. Garcia 2014). Statistical methods weigh a certain probability on segment matches based on their frequency in a large database of source and translated texts. As the quantity of cloud-computing digital writing increases across all languages and across all types of text, computer-assisted translation becomes more accurate, that is, more context-sensitive.

With a large enough sample of written production, one can imagine a similar process in the automation of writing, according to which the machine will prompt future human writers with their automated sentences. All textual types will then be generated through algorithmic statistical analysis instead of relying on a formal grammar for predefining constrained texts in terms of rules and parameters. Rather than using explicit syntactical rules, lexical dictionaries, and sets of flexional restrictions and transformations required for syntactical combination, data mining methods will enable the replication of most types of standardized textual forms. However, as Calvino suggested in his 1967 essay on cybernetics and ghosts (in *The Uses of Literature*), the perfect writing machine would be the one that felt the need to break its own rules. That will be one of the signs of the literary in a future of fully automated constrained, state-surveilled, and corporate-owned writing: a text that could not be accounted for solely or predominantly on the basis of its algorithm, that is, a text that could free itself from its constraint, a stochastic anomaly.

[14] See, for example, the various generative writers in his website "Jean-Pierre Balpe: Un univers de génération automatique littéraire": http://www.balpe.name/.

One could even make the analogy of writing under programmed constraints with genetic engineering in bio-art. In the case of bio-art, it is the genetic code that is used to introduce modifications in the biological expression of living beings. Certain genes are modified and the cellular mechanisms of a specific organism are used for reproducing those modifications at larger scales in ways that become aesthetically and symbolically significant.[15] A bio-literary equivalent is Christian Bök's ongoing project of creating a genetically engineered bacterium (*Deinococcus radiodurans*) whose genetic code is manipulated to function as the inscription medium for a poem. The self-replicative and alien nature of this xenotext serves both as meditation on the genome as a form of living writing, and an anthropocentric recovery of immortality tropes associated with writing (Bök 2015). The generativity of bio-art offers an analogy for generative literature because its working principle is to take advantage of the replicative autonomy of biological processes in much the same way as automatic text generation takes advantage of the basic syntactic merge operation in computer processing of natural language for producing complex hierarchical and recursive patterns. The real challenge, though, would be for this kind of bio-textuality not to simply replicate existing structures and patterns or serve as an infra-cellular monument to human power but to produce unanticipated textual mutations.

Despite the idea of textual infinity—emphasized by many practitioners, we could also say that any generated text or any multiplicity of generated texts will be a predictable outcome of the programmed instructions. What happens is that if the number of factorial permutations is very high (as is often the case) the instantiations that I can see and read as a human reader seem to be unique and not repeatable. Textual infinity is a consequence of the fact that the factorial permutations are too large for repetition to occur at human scale, and they highlight the profound difference between machinic and human temporality. Jonathan Basile's "Library of Babel" (2015–17)—a computational interpretation of Jorge Luis Borges's "Library of Babel" (originally imagined in his 1944 short story)—demonstrates the paradoxical effect of automating endless factorial permutations of the alphabet. On the one hand, the relentless logic of the algorithm results in the constrained expression of purely abstract differences that instantiate themselves as a textile of letters, punctuation marks, and blank spaces. On the other hand, the impossibility of exhausting semiosis through the sheer force of calculus becomes evident as meaning can only happen probabilistically, discontinuously, and interactively at scales other than the highly granular and machinic character-by-character permutation. Even if seen as a conceptual enactment of the continuum of expression upon which signifiers cut out their own form as differential meaningful strings, Basile's experiment shows the profound alien nature of the semiotic excess of computationally constrained writing in its literalized and randomized production of alphabetic infinity.

However, there are also evolutionary algorithms—that is, algorithms that modify their own expression after a number of iterations—and in these cases what is generated does not match the initial instructions, but originates in a modification of the iteration process whose result could not be entirely predicted from the initial state. In my view, we can distinguish four types of constrained writing in programmed texts: (1) text that recombines elements within a syntactic template according to a predefined sequence; (2) text that recombines elements within a syntactic template according to a randomized sequence; (3) text of types 1 and 2 that switch elements and recombine according to a predefined

[15] See, for example, works by Marta de Menezes, who has been experimenting with DNA, proteins, and cells in her artistic work: http://martademenezes.com/.

and/or random sequence and which also respond dynamically to input from readers, for example, in the form of mouse-clicks or touch-screen input; (4) texts whose algorithms change after a number of iterations, a method that is used in the field called "evolutionary computing," a creative process that is being experimented with in music, visual, and sound arts but which is rarer in the literary arts.[16] Combination and association also occur at larger textual scales, conferring fractal properties to the whole process. An analysis of computational writing according to generative constraints would also have to consider other variants, such as: (a) the level at which permutations occur (from individual character to the syllable to the word to the word group to the text block to the entire text); (b) the effect of permutations on the perception of textual form or textual genre: for example, (c) are permutations focused only at the textual level, giving us an instantiation of a new text without the experience of the mechanism that generates the text or of the textual convention that determines a specific textual typology?; or (d) do the permutations affect the metatextual level, giving us an experience of the mechanism that generates the text or the discursive convention that determines its textual typology? In the latter case, the generator can be used as parodic engine, as we see in works by Pedro Barbosa (1991), for instance. Programmed parodies are particularly effective demonstrations of the constrained nature of discourses.[17] They show how speech and script acts enact themselves through discursive structures and how such structures are material means for the production of meaning. Executable language is another way of seeing natural language as a form of social action. Once a certain number of discursive rules are abstracted, their productiveness as constraints can be programmed. The above distinction between textual instantiation, on one hand, and textual engine or textual instrument, on the other, can be useful and operative for analyzing automated algorithmic texts. There are texts that direct our attention to the relation between the algorithm and its literary expression; and there are texts that direct attention to the specific textual instantiation and its poetic or narrative value. To the extent that authors choose both the rules and syntactic/visual template (a poem or a narrative or a description or a dialogue, for example), as well as the database of items for permutation, creativity is also in the generated instantiations and not only in the algorithm per se. Although not all textual states have been seen or anticipated by the author, there is a range of textual possibilities that allows her or him to observe the semantic, rhythmic, and narrative effects of the chosen language corpus. This means that we can think of the generative textual experience as a stream of instantiations for which the constraint defines a set of initial conditions. That is, we should not rule out the possibility that programmed creativity is also in the product of the instructions, since they clearly express, though in a form that is mediated and deferred by the machine and the program, authorial aesthetic intentionality. In other words, the generative nature of the process means that the result will unfold in time and the resulting verbal expression

[16] See, for example, generative visualizations by Penousal Machado (2014) who, in his recent works, has used evolutionary algorithms based on modeling the social behavior of ants: https://cdv.dei.uc.pt/photogrowth-ant-painting/.

[17] For example: a Chomskybot that parodies Chomsky's writings on generative theory (written by John Lawler and Kevin McGowan, 1996): http://rubberducky.org/cgi-bin/chomsky.pl; the Dada Engine (by Andrew C. Bulhak, 1996): http://dev.null.org/dadaengine/; the Postmodernism Generator (by Andrew C. Bulhak, 2000): http://www.elsewhere.org/pomo/; a generator that parodies the style of the novel *50 Shades of Grey* (by Lisa Wray, 2015): http://www.xwray.com/fiftyshades; SCIgen—An Automatic CS Paper Generator (by Jeremy Stribling et al., 2005) that parodies the discourse of computer science articles (some of which have even been accepted as conference papers or published as articles): https://pdos.csail.mit.edu/archive/scigen/.

cannot be inferred entirely in advance. Even if there is a certain degree of mathematical randomness in the verbal output, linguistic combinations will have emergent meanings that will be read literarily. Random textual instantiations thus open up machinic constraints to the unconscious of the reader.

OVERWRITING CONSTRAINTS

As code for enabling the automated production of writing, executable language contributes to the understanding of the codes of writing as language, discourse, and literary form, on one hand, and as machine code, on the other. The relation between combinatorial production—which results from predictable permutations of entirely pregiven material—and generative production—which gives rise to new unpredictable forms—is crucial for making literary judgments about writing under constraints in a computational regime. Three positions could be distinguished in this debate: (1) a definition of generative as the general case of any permutation of elements—all textual matrices that can generate other texts (what Barbosa [1996] has called "textual engine" and Wardrip-Fruin [2009] and Eskelinen [2012] have called "textual instrument") would be generative; (2) a setting in which "generative" designates those texts in which recombination processes affect not only the elements that permutate within the matrix, but also the very textual matrix whose syntactic structure changes over time; (3) and, finally, a definition of generative where generativity affects the textual algorithm itself, since it would change in the course of iterations, the autopoietic equivalent to the creation of a new life form or a new language. This might result in a computer work not unlike *Finnegans Wake* (1939): through principles of paronomastic recombination of words and structures within a language and in the semiotic space across different languages, its emergent narrative and poetic form is a human example of something that approaches this type of imaginary constrained automated generativity.

Once networked programmable media define the material conditions and uses of writing, a whole system of techno-social constraints is put in place. The coupling of that networked writing apparatus with linguistic, discursive, and literary constraints affects the nature of human writing. Programmed writing constraints are embedded in the general processes of algorithmic culture, as writing and reading became entirely computable—from the atomic level of character encoding to the syntactic and discursive level of text generation and to the automated analysis of human acts of writing. The automated processing of writing and reading as data through cloud computing services raises new questions concerning the relations between human written input and the set of affordances and constraints written into the software. Writing under algorithmic constraint seems to be the general condition of writing under the regime of computation. The constrained writing environment of networked programmable media raises important questions about the possibility of emancipatory generative constraints and about the relative autonomy of electronic writing acts. So the question now becomes: Can writing under constraint in the constrained world of writing as data processing and data mining provide a critique of the accelerated datafication of our social life and the ongoing automation of writing and natural language? Can we still expect freedom from constraint-based writing in a world of algorithmic symbolic production?

In *The Internet Unconscious*, Sandy Baldwin (2015) offers a literary reading of the Internet as an ungraspable space of writing and reading. Baldwin forcefully directs our attention to the Internet itself as a distributed ensemble of practices (from email to social networks to ASCII to spam) that are constitutive of both the net as "electronic literature" and the subject of the Internet. This work shifts our focus of attention from a strictly functional or aesthetical account of writing and reading processes, which take place in digital media, to a self-reflexive examination of the Internet as writing in itself, that is, as a series of difficult-to-imagine writing protocols projecting our writing acts and our bodies in the "beyondness" of the screen. Self-projection into net-writing thus becomes the introjection of its apparatus, or, in other words, the unconscious condition of our telecommunications situation. Writing in and with and through the Internet is to let this Internet unconscious write through our writing bodies. How do we produce literary writing when the condition of writing is a constrained networked electronic protocol?

A number of electronic works have attempted to grapple with the ways in which the networked conditions of writing write through our writing practices. Amaranth Borsuk, Jesper Juul, and Nick Montfort's *The Deletionist* (2013) turns Web pages into poems by erasing text and leaving a few scattered words on the screen.[18] The process-able nature of displayed writing on the Web is made instantaneously present as continuous text gives way to blank pages with a few scattered words. The graphical convention that assigns textual genre by the relative proportion of empty/white space to written/black space functions as a semiotic marker of poetry texts but the randomness, repetitiveness, and meaninglessness of most of the resulting sets of words—selected on the basis of alliterative patterns, for example—only serve to show the extremely deterministic result of the erasing constraints. The genre and tradition of the treated or altered page/book—generally a painstaking process of extracting new narrative and poetic meanings by overwriting or overpainting a previous page—is instantiated here as an entirely algorithmic process. Because the erasure does not affect certain elements such as images, buttons, or background colors in tables, the erased de-functionalized Web page remains as vestige of its earlier form, suggesting that its deleted form is due to some kind of display anomaly or transmission difficulty. The verbal content itself is more interesting as a defective reminder of some malfunctioning Web page than as part of a so-called poem. Even for pages that are predominantly text, it is the visual pattern of the treated erased Web page that ultimately reminds us of the constraints through which html pages are an instance of programmed network writing.

The softwarization of culture in our late capitalist social formation means that writing and reading are raw material to the rationale of big software and big data service providers, through an array of procedures that monitor and condition writing and reading behaviors. Form-filling is perhaps the general condition of writing when all writing has become processing data through network systems. Written interactions within networked systems turn writing acts into data streams for real-time processing. Intelligent systems are constantly mining our uses of writing for capital gain, while graphical user touch-screen interfaces obfuscate the alphanumeric nature of the source code that constitutes both our writing and the instructions that process our writing. The automation of processes increasingly scripts our behaviors and controls our attention as uses of writing and language are constrained by search and recommendation algorithms and other analytical and statistical tools. The electronic subject is written by the Internet: "The program inscribes

[18] "The system is deterministic—there is no random element. *The Deletionist* chooses a method of erasure based on the properties of the Web page . . . *The Deletionist* works to make every page into a single poem." Cf. "How the Deletionist works," http://thedeletionist.com/about.html#use.

the organism through no particular marks but through abstract encodings as iterative, interactive couplings of organism, and environment as the extension of the organism. Organism is organism plus environment, while environment includes organism. The net is, in this sense, a single abstract machine for inscribing the subject" (Baldwin 2015: 41). One of the most significant literary attempts to overwrite the constraints of the big data network can be seen in works by John Cayley and Daniel C. Howe.[19] Besides exploring constraints expressed through their own software agents and turning them into generative and compositional principles in their works—in several instantiations of the series *The Readers Project* (2009–16)—they have also addressed the issue of what it means to write in the highly constrained environment of the Internet. Their works take dominant algorithms of net writing and reading—such as those that are embodied in Google Search—and generate texts that draw attention to the proprietary motifs of service providers and to the political implications of the asymmetrical relationship. *How It Is in Common Tongues* (2012)—a reconstruction of Samuel Beckett's "How It Is" based on Internet sources other than Beckett's text with the help of n-gram searches—instantiates how the most ubiquitous search algorithm can be defunctionalized for social and technological critique. Howe and Cayley's focus on big software processing of language as commodified data suggests that a fundamental change in our relation with our own writing is taking place on the Internet: "However, network services will enclose, monitor and process any and all linguistic practice by their users, everything from everyday, habitual intercommunication to 'high-literary,' 'high-theoretical,' 'high-critical' correspondence and production. These services exist to process (albeit, typically, with anonymization) and vectoralize the commons of language, the commons of symbolic interlocution" (Cayley 2013).

Another engaging interrogation about the ontology of poetry in a post-digital situation can be found in the theoretical and creative work of David Jhave Johnston, whose Textual-Audio-Visual-Interactive animisms challenge and extend the writing and reading conventions of digital poetics (2016). Two recent works—*Spoams* (2014b) and *BDP: Big Data Poems* (2014a)—explore computer-processed natural language as an inextricable assemblage of human and algorithmic output. *Spoams* contains a selection from several years of the author's archive of spam, introduced by human-assisted generated text whose opening sentence reads: "This is spam, hand-crafted and machine-generated." This sense of algorithmically enhanced language as a strange cybernetic organism capable of poetic intuition is even stronger in *BDP: Big Data Poems* ("Almost poems generated from almost big data by an almost programmer-poet"). The confusing and overwhelming mix of bot and human that has turned verbal language into the unacknowledged infrastructure of the Internet comes across in the description of this work's intricate mode of operation:

> BDP (Big-Data Poetry) applies a combination of data visualization, language analytics, classification algorithms, entity recognition and part-of-speech replacement techniques to 3 corpuses: 10,557 poems from the Poetry Foundation, 57,000+ hip-hop rap songs from Ohhla.com, and over 7,000 pop lyrics. Based on these templates, a Python script generates thousands of poems per hour. Sometimes Jhave reads along with this writing machine, verbally stitching and improvising spoken poems. (Jhave 2014a)

The fact that the source texts chosen for the generative permutations are classified as poetry functions as legacy reminder, a random access memory of archived written and

[19] See the project's website for an updated list of its various iterations: http://thereadersproject.org/.

oral forms. Now that automated constrained processes are able to collect and generate endless snippets of language and thousands of poems per hour, poem-mining can still be offered to a human voice for stitching and improvisation. "Reading along with the machine" is, perhaps, the only possibility of overwriting its writing constraint.

SOURCES CITED

Baldwin, Sandy. *The Internet Unconscious: On the Subject of Electronic Literature*. London: Bloomsbury, 2015.

Balpe, Jean-Pierre. "Principles and Processes of Generative Literature: Questions to Literature." *Dichtung Digital* (2005), http://www.dichtung-digital.de/2005/1/Balpe/.

Balpe, Jean-Pierre. "Les Carolingiens." 2015. http://www.balpe.name/Les-Carolingiens.

Balpe, Jean-Pierre. "Un univers de génération automatique littéraire." 2016. http://www.balpe.name/.

Barbosa, Pedro. "A máquina de emaranhar paisagens." *Arquivo Digital da PO.EX.* (1991), https://www.po-ex.net/taxonomia/materialidades/digitais/pedro-barbosa-a-maquina-sintext.

Barbosa, Pedro. "A New Concept of Work." In *PO.EX: Essays from Portugal on Cyberliterature and Intermedia*, edited by Rui Torres and Sandy Baldwin. Center for Literary Computing, Morgantown: West Virginia University Press [1996] 2014, pp. 171–82.

Basile, Jonathan. *Library of Babel* (2015–17). https://libraryofbabel.info.

Beckett, Samuel. "Come and Go." In *Collected Shorter Plays*. London: Grove Press, [1963] 2010, pp. 193–8.

Berwick, Robert C., and Noam Chomsky. *Why Only Us: Language and Evolution*.Cambridge: MIT Press, 2016.

Bök, Christian. *Eunoia*. Toronto: Coach House Books, 2001.

Bök, Christian. *The Xenotext: Book 1*. Toronto: Coach House Books, 2015.

Bootz, Philippe. "Digital Poetry: From Cybertext to Programmed Forms." *Leonardo Electronic Almanac*, vol. 14, nos. 5–6 (2006), http://www.leoalmanac.org/journal/vol_14/lea_v14_n05-06/pbootz.html.

Borsuk, Amaranth, Jesper Juul, and Nick Montfort. *The Deletionist* (2013), http://thedeletionist.com/.

Bulhak, Andrew C. *The Dada Engine* (1996–2000), http://dev.null.org/dadaengine/.

Bulhak, Andrew C. *Postmodernism Generator* (2000–17), http://www.elsewhere.org/pomo/.

Calvino, Italo. "Cybernetics and Ghosts" (Cibernetica e fantasmi). In *The Uses of Literature*, translated by Patrick Creagh. New York: Mariner Books, [1967] 1987, pp. 3–27.

Calvino, Italo. *Se una notte d'inverno un viaggiatore*. Milano: Arnoldo Mondadori, [1979] 1994.

Cayley, John. "Writing to Be Found and Writing Readers." *Digital Humanities Quarterly*, vol. 5, no. 3 (2011), http://www.digitalhumanities.org/dhq/vol/5/3/000104/000104.html.

Cayley, John. "Terms of Reference & Vectorialist Transgressions: Situating Certain Literary Transactions over Networked Services." *Amodern*, no. 2 (2013), http://amodern.net/article/terms-of-reference-vectoralist-transgressions/.

Cayley, John, and Daniel C. Howe. *The Readers Project* (2009–16), http://thereadersproject.org/.

Cayley, John, and Daniel C. Howe. *How It Is in Common Tongues*. Providence, RI: Natural Language Liberation Front, 2012.

Chomsky, Noam. *The Minimalist Program*. 20th Anniversary edition. Cambridge: MIT Press, [1996] 2015.

Cramer, Florian. *Words Made Flesh*. Rotterdam: Piet Zwart Institute, 2005.

Cramer, Florian. *Exe.cut[up]able Statements: Poetische Kalküle und Phantasmen des selbstausführenden Texts.* Paderborn: Wilhelm Fink Verlag, 2011.

Danielewski, Mark Z. *Only Revolutions.* New York: Pantheon Books, 2006.

Drucker, Johanna. *From A to Z: Our An (Collective Specifics) an im partial bibliography, Incidents in a Non-Relationship or: how I came to not know who is.* Chased Press, 1977.Artists' Books Online, http://www.artistsbooksonline.org/works/atoz.xml.

Dupej, Holly. *Next Generation Literary Machines: The "Dynamic Network Aesthetic" of Contemporary Poetry Generators.* PhD dissertation. Calgary, Alberta: University of Calgary, 2012.

Eskelinen, Markku. *Cybertext Poetics: The Critical Landscape of New Media Literary Theory.* London: Continuum, 2012.

Funkhouser, Chris T. *New Directions in Digital Poetry.* London: Continuum, 2012.

Garcia, Ignacio. "Computer-Aided Translation: Systems." In *Routledge Encyclopedia of Translation Technology*, edited by Sin-Wai Chan. London: Routledge, 2014, pp. 68–87, https://www.routledgehandbooks.com/pdf/doi/10.4324/9781315749129.ch3.

Harrell, D. Fox. *Phantasmal Media: An Approach to Imagination, Computation, and Expression.* Cambridge: MIT Press, 2013.

Hayles, N. Katherine. *Electronic Literature: New Horizons for the Literary.* Notre Dame, Indiana: University of Notre Dame, 2008.

Hayles, N. Katherine. *How We Think: Digital Media and Contemporary Technogenesis.* Chicago: Chicago University Press, 2012.

Howe, Daniel C., and John Cayley. "*The Readers Project:* Procedural Agents and Literary Vectors." *Leonardo*, vol. 44, no. 4 (2011): 317–24.

Howe, Daniel C., and John Cayley. "Reading, Writing, Resisting: Literary Appropriation in the Readers Project." In *Proceedings of the 19th International Symposium of Electronic Art*, edited by K. Cleland, L. Fisher, and R. Harley. Sydney: ISEA, 2013, pp. 1–4, http://ses.library.usyd.edu.au/handle/2123/9475.

Johnson, B. S. *House Mother Normal: A Geriatric Comedy.* London: Picador, [1971] 2013.

Johnston, David Jhave. *BDP: Big Data Poems* (2014a), http://bdp.glia.ca/.

Johnston, David Jhave. *Spoams* (2014b), http://glia.ca/2014/spam/.

Johnston, David Jhave. *Aesthetic Animism: Digital Poetry's Ontological Implications.* Cambridge: MIT Press, 2016.

Joyce, James. *Finnegans Wake.* London: Faber, [1939] 1982.

Joyce, James. *Ulysses.* Edited by Hans Walter Gabler. London: Penguin, [1922] 1986.

Kittler, Friedrich A. "There Is No Software." *CTheory* (October 18, 1995), www.ctheory.net/articles.aspx?id=74.

Lawler, John, and Kevin McGowan. *Chomskybot* (1996–2002): http://rubberducky.org/cgi-bin/chomsky.pl.

Le Lionnais, François. "La Lipo." *Dossiers du Collège de 'Pataphysique, n° 17: exercices de littérature potentielle* (December 22, 1961): 7–10.

Le Lionnais, François. "Le second Manifeste." In *Oulipo: la littérature potentielle.* Paris: Gallimard, 1973, pp. 19–20.

Manovich, Lev. "Database as Symbolic Form." In *Database Aesthetics: Art in the Age of Information Overflow*, edited by Victoria Vesna. Minneapolis: University of Minnesota Press, 2008, pp. 39–60.

Machado, Penousal. "Photogrowth: Ant Painting." 2014. https://cdv.dei.uc.pt/photogrowth-ant-painting/.

Mathews, Harry, and Alastair Brotchie, eds. *Oulipo Compendium*. London: Atlas Press, 1998.
Memmott, Talan. *Digital Rhetoric and Poetics: Signifying Strategies in Electronic Literature*. PhD dissertation. Malmö University, 2011.
Montfort, Nick. *Concrete Perl: A Set of Four Concrete Poems Realized as 32-Character Perl Programs* (2011), http://nickm.com/poems/concrete_perl/.
Montfort, Nick. "XS, S, M, L: Creative Text Generators of Different Scales." A technical report from the Trope Tank. MIT, January 2012. Trope-12-02, http://trope-tank.mit.edu/TROPE-12-02.pdf.
Montfort, Nick. "Random Generation of English Sentences." Reimplementation of Victor H. Yngve's work, 2016, http://nickm.com/memslam/random_sentences.html.
Oulipo: ouvroir de littérature potentielle. http://oulipo.net/. "Contraintes," http://oulipo.net/contraintes.
Perec, Georges. *La vie: mode d'emploi*. Paris: Hachette, 1978.
Perec, Georges. *Cahier de charges de La Vie mode d'emploi*. Présentation, transcription et notes par Hans Hartje, Bernard Magné et Jacques Neefs. Paris: CNRS Éditions & Zulma, 1993.
Portela, Manuel. *Scripting Reading Motions: The Codex and the Computer as Self-Reflexive Machines*. Cambridge: MIT Press, 2013.
Queneau, Raymond. *Exercices de Style*. Paris: Gallimard, 1947.
Roque, Antonio. "Language Technology Enables a Poetics of Interactive Generation." *Journal of Electronic Publishing*, vol. 14, no. 2 (2011), http://dx.doi.org/10.3998/3336451.0014.209.
Salceda Rodríguez, Hermes, and Jean-Jacques Thomas, eds. *Le pied de la lettre: Créativité et littérature potentielle*. Ontario: Presses Universitaires du Nouveau Monde, 2010.
Schiavetta, Bernardo. "Toward a General Theory of the Constraint." *electronic book review*, "writing under constraint" (January 1, 2000), http://www.electronicbookreview.com/thread/wuc/constraints.
Stravinsky, Igor. *The Poetics of Music in the Form of Six Lessons*. Cambridge, MA: Harvard University Press, 1947.
Stribling, Jeremy, Max Krohn, and Dan Aguayo. *SCIgen—an Automatic CS Paper Generator* (2005), https://pdos.csail.mit.edu/archive/scigen/.
Tabbi, Joseph. "Electronic Literature as World Literature; or, the Universality of Writing under Constraint." *Poetics Today*, vol. 31, no. 1 (2010): 17–50.
Torres, Rui. *Húmus Poema Contínuo* (2008), http://telepoesis.net/humus/humus.html.
Torres, Rui. "'The Dead Must Be Killed Once Again': Plagiotropia as Critical Literary Practice." *electronic book review*, "electropoetics" (May 8, 2012), http://www.electronicbookreview.com/thread/electropoetics/plagio.
Wardrip-Fruin, Noah. *Expressive Processing: Digital Fictions, Computer Games, and Software Studies*. Cambridge: The MIT Press, 2009.
Wray, Lisa. *Shades of Grey* (2015), http://www.xwray.com/fiftyshades.

CHAPTER ELEVEN

Electronic Literature and the Poetics of Contiguity

MARIO AQUILINA

This chapter explores some of the "poetic" dimensions and possibilities of language in electronic literature. More specifically, it proposes that "born digital works" may allow for aesthetic experiences that recall rather than radically departing from the poetic in print and other, earlier media. Samantha Gorman and Danny Cannizzaro's App novella, *Pry*, and Nick Montfort and Stephanie Strickland's poetry generator, "Sea and Spar Between," have been chosen as test cases for the argument.

The concept of the "poetic," as well as the attempt to reflect on how it manifests itself in electronic literature, will allow us to think of born digital poetry and narrative in terms of continuity with print literature. N. Katherine Hayles (2004: 67) and others have claimed that specific works of electronic literature call for "media-specific analysis" because the media in which they appear may have characteristics that are inherited from print but are ultimately different and "instantiat[e]" the literary differently. However, it is restrictive and ultimately misguided to employ the concept of media-specificity as a justification for forgetting pre-digital poetics in critical analyses of works of electronic literature. Or, to put it differently, mediatic difference does not mean complete incommensurability or the radical obliteration of concepts and practices that existed before computerization. Indeed, by highlighting selected works on the "poetic" in a pre-digital era as well as more recent critical writing about the poetics of electronic literature, it may be shown that there already exists a conceptuality that, with few essential modifications, is well positioned to address new questions brought about by the emergence of electronic literature.

CONTIGUITY

Developing and adapting some of the thinking of Roman Jakobson and others on the two poles of language—metaphor and metonymy—I argue that the poetic, in the works discussed below, but also in a wide range of works of electronic literature or digital poetry, arises primarily through a "poetics of contiguity," that is, the relations, whether harmonious or disjunctive, among contiguous elements that may be linked through connections or combinations of various kinds, including temporal, spatial, and contextual. As will be shown through the analysis of the two selected works, one crucial aspect of the poetic in electronic literature is that the contiguity at work operates within what we may call—following Friedrich W. Block (2007: 242)—intermedial dynamics or "the spaces in between."

The concept of "intermediality" has many facets and, as Irina O. Rajewsky (2005) shows in a comprehensive account of its history and nuances, the term originated in the German-speaking research community in the 1990s but later spread into English-language research, there overlapping with Interarts Studies as well as providing the foundations for David Bolter and Richard Grusin's (2000) influential theory of remediation. Rajewsky (2005: 52) outlines three main ways in which "intermediality" may be understood today: as medial transposition (the transformation, translation, or adaptation of one media product into another medium), media combination ("the medial constellation constituting a given media product"), and intermedial references (to a medium apart from the one where a work originates). The second type of intermediality outlined by Rajewsky concerns us here, primarily: that which is seen in a range of media products along a continuum stretching from "a mere contiguity of two or more material manifestations of different media to a 'genuine' integration, which in its most pure form would privilege none of its constitutive elements" (ibid.). The inflections to the term given by Block (2007: 235–7) are useful for our purposes as he extends the concept of intermediality to refer not only to the contiguity between the different materialities of the interrelating media but also to what he calls "poetological contexts" that include not only "material" and "medium," but also "animation and information process" as well as "audience activity and interactivity." The idea of intermediality characterized by the contiguity of various mediatic and contextual elements is essential in our investigation of the poetic use of language in electronic literature because poetic language, in the works discussed here but also more widely in electronic literature, operates primarily on the basis of a poetics of contiguity or what may be described as the being in-between of media, concepts, contexts, and affordances.

Before we look at the poetics of contiguity in electronic literature, however, we might recall the foundational thinking on "contiguity" by Roman Jakobson (1990) who, while writing in the heyday of the print era and clearly not having electronic literature in mind, already provides us with concepts that shed light on works produced digitally. In a well-known essay on language and aphasic disturbances, Jakobson claims that "the development of a discourse may take place along two different semantic lines: one topic may lead to another either through their similarity or through their contiguity. The metaphoric way would be the most appropriate term for the first case and the metonymic way for the second" (129). For Jakobson, discourse—both in its formation and its interpretation—operates through relations of similarity and contiguity, or selection and combination, but "under the influence of a cultural pattern, personality, and verbal style, preference is given to one of the two processes over the other" (ibid.). While Jakobson develops this theory through a detailed discussion of aphasic disorders, he also applies his findings to "verbal art," arguing, for instance, that metaphor is the predominant pole of language in Romanticism and Symbolism, while metonymy is more prevalent in Realism.

In Jakobson's work, as well as in David Lodge's *The Modes of Modern Writing: Metaphor, Metonymy, and the Typology of Modern Literature* (1977), which extends Jakobson's ideas to a wide range of literary texts, the notion of contiguity (in the context of the two poles of language, metaphor and metonymy) is used mainly with regard to intralinguistic relations or to relations within the same mode of discourse. Apart from poetry, Jakobson briefly applies his theory of the bipolar nature of language to film and art, but in extending Jakobson's theory to an analysis of electronic literature, we will need to inflect the notion of contiguity in ways that allow it to also encompass the relations among linguistic, paralinguistic, and extralinguistic elements provided by the affordances of the media involved (visual, aural, haptic, algorithmic, procedural). This is because while it would be reductive to claim that any art form only appeals to one sign system (visual, aural, linguistic, kinetic, etc.), electronic literature, perhaps more than any other art form, is intrinsically characterized by not only the "multimodality" (Kress 2000) of the digital age, but also its intermediality, or the always already being in between media. By contiguity, then, I do not reference only combinations between, say, different words in the linguistic dimension of a work of digital poetry, but also to the relation between words and other textual, contextual, and paratextual elements in a specific work (image, code, database, interface, interactivity, and more).

POETICS

One of the claims that Jakobson makes about the two poles of language is that due to metaphor fulfilling the principle of substitution, traditional literary criticism—operating at a metalinguistic level—has been more adept at discussing metaphor than discussing metonymy. If this is indeed the case—and one may suspect that Jakobson is correct given what is arguably a traditional prevalence of thematic, interpretative analysis in literary studies (definitely till the rise of theory in the 1960s but also after in most university contexts until at least the end of the twentieth century)—some aspects of electronic literature, with its dependence on contiguity (metonymy rather than metaphor), may resist traditional literary analysis. Hence, the need (acknowledged above), for developing media-specific conceptuality. However, there is also a strong element of continuity between electronic literature and "literature" as understood in pre-digital literary studies. The difference, though, is that contiguity becomes primary in our tracing of effects that, if they are to be regarded as poetic, cannot be limited to the conceptual analysis of any one medium however stringent our attention to specifics.

The word "poetics" has been chosen in order to exploit its dual meaning: "poetics" is both the "study of linguistic techniques in poetry and literature" *and* "the art of writing poetry" (Oxford Online Dictionaries). Accordingly, the term "poetics of contiguity" may refer to both the study of techniques of contiguity in the works discussed (the development of a poetics for electronic literature) and to the writing of poetry or poetic writing that these works engage in (a poetry of contiguity).

The decision to focus mainly on the "poetic" rather than the "literary" stems partially from a desire to avoid, as much as possible, being side-tracked by debates about definitions of "literature," particularly in the context of the supposed demise of the print era. These debates may be briefly exemplified—for the purpose of providing a specific context—through the contrasting views of Jacques Derrida and Adriano Marino on the subject. If we follow Derrida (1992: 215), for instance, we may argue that as a modern institution established "between the late seventeenth and early nineteenth centuries in Europe," thus roughly coinciding with the rise of the novel, literature is founded on legally backed notions such as uniqueness, authorship, property, and genre. The laws that make a text "literature" in the modern sense of the term are thus rooted in history rather than in any unchangeable essence. And, if this is the case, then the digital age, with its requirement for, for example, "electracy" (Ulmer 2003) will call, or has already called for, a rethinking—perhaps the end—of the idea of literature. Alternatively, we may think along different lines and consider Marino's archeological exploration of "the idea" of literature from antiquity to the Baroque which suggests that the idea of literature has existed for millennia, rather than centuries, and is thus not dependent on print culture. And such a shift in the scale of our perception forces us to restrain ourselves from speaking apocalyptically about electronic literature as the end of literature. Marino (1996: 3) shows that the idea of literature is characterized by various aspects that intensify, crystallize, or retreat into the background in different periods in history such as "the realm of written letters"; literature as "insubordination, . . . criticism, . . . escape from a given order" (9); literature as an embodiment of "the notion of culture" (10); literature as an expression of humanity (17); and literature as a space for "sacrality" (83). What does not change is the way that the "indetermination" in the idea of literature is "congenital" (35).

Whether the arrival of the digital age and the electronic media harbors "the end of literature," and, whether, if so, "electronic literature" is a misnomer, if not an oxymoron, are undoubtedly important questions, and many have already addressed them. Francisco J. Ricardo (2009: 4), for instance, argues that "the terms of the digital/electronic/virtual in art and literature ought now to be interrogated in light of [the] ruptures of retinality, objecthood and materiality brought about by contemporary electronic media." Focusing, like Ricardo, on how the materiality of the different media changes our conception of art, Hayles (2006: 181) argues that a literary text in digital media, with its "distributed existence spread among data files and commands, software that executes the commands, and hardware on which the software runs," becomes more "processual," "performative," more an "event" than an "object," as traditionally conceived (185). Joseph Tabbi (2010) also addresses the question of literature in our time, but he focuses less on literature's materiality than its paratextual dynamics. Building on the work of David Damrosch (2003) on "world literature" as a "mode of circulation and of reading," Tabbi (2010: 19) theorizes the "world literary" as a *potential* that depends not on specific qualities of any work but on the capacity to instantiate a worldwide (and worldly) network of conversations about a work. For Tabbi, then, the paratextual dimension is decisive, and literature in new media depends "not on the work itself but its reception; and its modes of recirculation," both in print and in current works emerging in electronic media. Taking the writing under constraint of Oulipo authors as a precursor of sorts to the potential world literature he envisages, Tabbi argues for the possibility of "literature" to exist in a digital age on the basis of principles already "developed long before the Internet but suited to its computational impositions and gamelike literary presentations" (17).[1]

The question of literature and the literary in electronic literature is clearly still open and worth pursuing, but focusing on the "poetic" rather than the literary will allow us to discuss something that, while relevant to the analysis of literature, is also versatile enough to be employed beyond print literature. Edgar Allan Poe (1850, n.p.) makes this point memorably in his essay "The Poetic Principle," where he speaks about the poetic sentiment and argues that while he is primarily interested in the "manifestation [of the poetic] in words [, it] may develop itself in various modes—in Painting, in Sculpture, in Architecture, in the Dance—very especially in Music—and very peculiarly, and with a wide field, in the composition of the Landscape Garden."

[1] For more on "literature" in the digital age, see Simanowski (2011: 27–57); Simanowski, Schäfer, and Gendolla (2010); Pressman (2014); Aquilina and Callus (2016).

The poetic, unlike the "literary," whose etymological roots in the "letter" make it inextricable from letters and words, is not only a function of words but also of spatial and temporal associations between and among words, syllables, notes, and, in Poe's formulation, the distinct elements that can turn a landscape into a garden. The poetic, of course, is never just a matter of selection (which elements are chosen) but also of combination through composition, juxtaposition, placement, and contiguity. Even in poetry—where the linguistic manifestation of the poetic is most likely to appear—the poetic lies as much in that which is in between words as in the words themselves. As John Hollander (1975: 246) writes, "Criticism has always been interested in the ways in which poetry is more or less *like* and more or less *about* music, and, in particular, with some of the characteristics of poetic language that make any *reading* of a poem, even a silent one, something very like a performance intoned aloud" (emphases in the original). Poetry is like music in its dependence on sound, rhythm, patterns of recurrence, as well as the moments of silence interrupted by sound. But beyond the musical in poetry, there is also—in poetry that can be read—what Hollander calls "the poem in the eye." Indeed, "one of the things we do when we read a poem is to discern visual structures, to make out parts, wholes, relationships, to see patterns in sub- and total contexts, and so forth" (246). The printed poem is always already a poem in the eye, in Hollander's sense, but certain genres of poetry, like Concrete Poetry and, to an even greater extent, Visual Poetry, make the visual in the poetic even more central. Twentieth-century avant-garde movements introduced the visual with greater intensity into print poetry, but there are earlier antecedents, such as—to mention some well-known examples—George Herbert's altar poetry, e. e. cummings's pattern poetry, and Dylan Thomas's pattern poetry.

In poetry, then—crucially, irrespective of the words selected by the poet—that which is in-between and around words matters, both spatially on the printed page and temporally in the reading or performance of a poem. Poetry is often an art of the contiguous, an art of distribution, an art of arrangement, and an art of recurrence. This, of course, does not mean that other literary forms may not use or depend on contiguity, but contiguity is not defining of the "literary" or "literature" more generally as it is defining of the poetic.

CONTINUITY

Clearly, the works chosen for close reading in this chapter are not meant to be in any way representative of what we are calling "electronic literature" as a whole. Indeed, considering the range of genres that electronic literature has given rise to and the way in which, as Brian Kim Stefans (2012) argues, "all *successful* works of 'electronic literature' are *sui generis*, in that they invent new genres unto themselves—their peculiar combination of data, interface and algorithm makes them appear largely unrelated to other digital literature works" (emphasis in the original). It is impossible to think of any works that may be representative of it. However, the heterogeneity of the two examples and their aesthetic value allow us to see the poetic in different guises and thus facilitate a discussion of how electronic literature may create the poetic.

An attempt is made to pursue a discourse of continuity, echoing, and development between electronic literature and literature (whether of the past or the present) rather than falling into the temptation of announcing apocalyptic scenarios of endings and radical breaks due to technology (as in, e.g., Derrida [1987: 197] on how "an entire epoch of so-called literature, if not all of it, cannot survive a certain technological regime of telecommunications" in *The Postcard* and J. Hillis Miller's [2001: 60] development of this idea in "Literary Study among the Ruins," where he speaks of an intensifying "dislocation of literature" due to cultural, economic, and technological changes).

Talking about echoes and continuities rather than radical breaks from tradition induced by the new electronic media is important for at least two reasons: first, it urges us to see the value of digital works that may, from a certain conservative perspective about literature, be dismissed as nonliterary or not worthy of literary analysis or evaluation. As Tabbi (2008) writes, "The fascination with technoculture seems to have distanced humanities scholars from even our former object of interest—not the book, nor its successor media, but the literary imagination as it is constrained and enabled by technology." Second—in a way that preempts a diametrically opposed problem to the one just outlined—this focus on the poetic avoids performing a reactionary retreat into what Block (2007: 234) calls "digital revolution propaganda" and its "tendency . . . to make a clear break from, say, all literature of book and print as well as the cultural history thereof" (230) in order to announce the newness of the digital media at the expense of an awareness of continuity with previously existing poetic and literary forms.

To restrict the question of the literary and the poetic today to print is to ignore what are very tangible and real changes to the way literature is not only created, but also consumed, circulated, and studied. If literary studies ignores the question of the effect of the digital on our understanding of literature, it may likely be setting itself into a path toward a much reduced relevance. The risk of prioritizing discontinuities between print and digital in the field of electronic literature is also real among scholars of electronic literature. There is a sense in which underplaying the connections between contemporary electronic literature and the poetic and literary tradition may be an effective rhetorical move in the institutionalization of electronic literature that can help to turn electronic literature, as Florian Cramer (2012) puts it, into a "field in Pierre Bourdieu's sense, i.e. as an area of production and discourse with intrinsic distinctions and authorities." For with institutionalization and more clearly defined boundaries comes greater recognition for electronic literature, for example, in the form of funding, tenure, and academic distinction. However, to highlight difference at the expense of continuity is not always necessarily true to what electronic literature is or does. This is a point that is being made more frequently over the past few years. Among several others, Christopher Funkhouser in *Prehistoric Digital Poetry: An Archaeology of Forms, 1959–1995* (2007) provides a detailed analysis of the origins of digital poetry, including print precursors, while Jessica Pressman's *Digital Modernism: Making It New in New Media* (2014: 1) outlines "a recent trend in electronic literature" that is making "visible the tradition of making it new," by which Pressman means literary modernism.

"Sea and Spar Between"

Discussing "Sea and Spar Between" in relation to the poetic is not surprising if one is seeking to investigate how the poetic manifests itself in electronic literature. Montfort and Strickland's work is a "poetry generator" that is inspired by and sources text from Emily Dickinson's poetry and Herman Melville's *Moby-Dick*, a novel renowned not only for its metaphysical subject matter but also for its frequent passages of poetic prose. "Sea and Spar Between" presents itself as a contemporary, digital generator of poetry that utilizes language originating from the work of two nineteenth-century canonical authors. Echoing Dickinson's poetry, which often consists of quatrains made of short lines, "Sea and Spar Between" produces trillions of stanzas to be navigated and (potentially) read, each having specific coordinates visible at the bottom of the screen.

The words used in the stanzas created are "poetic" in a basic, material sense: they are sourced, primarily, from poetry. In "How to Read *Sea and Spar Between*" (n.d.) and the more detailed "cut to fit the tool-spun course: Discussing Creative Code in Comments" (2013), Montfort and Strickland explain that the "literary data" from which the output is produced consists of words and phrases taken from Melville's *Moby-Dick* and Dickinson's poetry as well as a number of kennings produced by Montfort and Strickland from words commonly used in the source texts. The placing of the stanzas on the screen—with each group of four lines separated by blue space from other similar groups around it—suggests that the four lines are to be taken together as one stanza, but there is also a gap in between the second and third line of each stanza that introduces some form of division of the quatrain into two non-rhyming couplets, possibly gesturing at the various forms of collaboration but also spurring that create these stanzas (Melville and Dickinson; Montfort and Strickland; nineteenth century and twenty-first century; print and digital, etc.). The relation to poetry is, therefore, also tangible in the way "Sea and Spar Between" utilizes structural conventions of poetry: stanzification, white space, and verse.

Some of Marjorie Perloff's notions of *Unoriginal Genius* (2010) and Kenneth Goldsmith's *Uncreative Writing* (2011) may be useful to explain how the poetic is repositioned in "Sea and Spar Between" through reframing, recontexualizing, and programming. The poetry generator forces us to rethink the poetic more in terms of the management and distribution of language than in terms of originality and creativity (Goldsmith 2011: 15). Of course, there is a strong element of creativity and even originality in "Sea and Spar Between"—for example in the creation of kennings through the use of word lists as well as in the functions that are coded in ways that create a range of stanzas of specific shapes and patterns—but there are fundamental changes in the way we, as readers, relate to language. William Hazlitt ([1818] 1889: 98) once wrote that "all that is worth remembering in life, is the poetry of it." The poetic is that which one would want to memorize. Taking the poetic elsewhere, "Sea and Spar Between" repositions poetic language from that which is re-readable, quotable, memorable, and even a source for reappropriation to something which is ephemeral and even very difficult to retain on screen due to the hypersensitivity of the interface to mouse-movements as well as the laborious process required to record coordinates and then type them to return to previously accessed stanzas. One may think of how the code of "Sea and Spar Between"—typically of the work of Nick Montfort—can be freely appropriated and recycled, but the recalling, here, is of the machine of the work rather than the peculiar combination of words one reads on screen. The database that "Sea and Spar Between" taps into to create the trillions of stanzas holds all the words that are then used in the text that the reader triggers, but it's very difficult (perhaps even irrelevant) for the reader to memorize any of the text one reads. This displaces the poetic from the words or phrasing, which are the focus of, for instance, formalist, stylistic, and new critical approaches to poetry, to the relation between the words and the context in which the words appear, such as their relation to the database, to code, to the interface, and so on.

The use of the database is crucial: the canon (that which, by definition, is worth remembering) is the primary source of linguistic material in "Sea and Spar Between," but this linguistic material is repositioned as that which is ephemeral, easily forgotten (for the reader), very difficult (but not impossible) to recall (both in the sense of "into memory" as well as "retrieve"). This displacement of poetic language, it must be said, is not unprecedented as similar effects are at work in experimental poetry already operating along the principles of the "poetics of contiguity." In constraint writing, for instance, the "poetic" words one reads are significant also because they are the product of an interaction between language and a specific constraint, so that it becomes difficult to think of words primarily in terms of, for instance, the poetic as expression of individual genius or of human feeling. In other words, the poetic becomes devoid of "depth" and starts to depend more on surface relations. As Anne Blossier-Jacquemot and Dupont (2010) point out, constraint poetry goes as far back as ancient Hellenic pattern poetry by Theocritus, Dosidias, Simias of Rhode, Vestinus, and others. More recently, Oulipo made of constraint writing one of its key creative tenets. Raymond Queneau's *Cent Mille Milliards de Poèmes* (1961) is one such precursor of the poetics of contiguity, in this case combining constraints with generative principles. Queneau's book generates billions of potential poems from ten sonnets each of which is made of individually-cut fourteen lines printed on different pages which may be leafed through and handled by any reader who can get hold of a copy. Like the sea of words in "Sea and Spar Between," the possible combinations of the ten sonnets would require millions of years to be read by any one individual. And like the ephemerality of the specific stanzas that appear on screen in "Sea and Spar Between," the sonnets generated in and by *Cent Mille Milliards de Poèmes* are more profitably thought of in terms of contiguity than in terms, for instance, of formal linguistic "deviation" or of poetry as a conduit for human feeling. Friedrich W. Block (2007: 235) argues that the conception of poetic language changes in the mid-twentieth century from substance to material: "avant-garde poets in the post-war period started to treat language as 'material.' " Block contrasts this conception of language with what he calls the pre-modernist notion of language as substance that leads to spirit, meaning, theme, and content. The latter view of language seems to fit well with Jakobson's metaphoric pole of language, but one may argue that the poetics of contiguity, while defining of and accentuated in electronic literature, is not only something that arose in the past century (to be contrasted with pre-modernist times) but it has existed, at least as a possibility of what poetry can do, for much longer.

The exact turn of phrase matters less in "Sea and Spar Between" than in Dickinson or Melville, even if the actual words used may be the same. What generates meaning, even poetic meaning, is the relation between the words (in the context of the interface—the screen, the scrolling, the coordinates, the layout, etc.), the reader/interactor and the writing machine, or the process of creation of poetry. This shift toward a poetics of contiguity does not annul creativity but relocates it away from the individual author to the author in a network of contiguities operating within what has been termed "distributed cognition" (Hayles 2008: 15). The poetic word, here, does not function as the exclusive location for the presence of the poetic but interacts, to a high degree, with context, platform, process, database, and more to create the poetic experience.

Marjorie Perloff (1999: 18) unravels somewhat similar effects in the early- and mid-twentieth-century literature by writers like Ashbery, Stein, Pound, Williams, Beckett, John Cage, and the French Surrealists, in which "the words on the page are no longer grounded in a coherent discourse, so that it becomes impossible to decide which of these associations are relevant and which are not." Perloff uses the term "poetics of indeterminacy" to outline a counter-discourse to High Modernist symbolism and argues that the quest for meaning and understanding is displaced in favor of what René Magritte calls the "mystery of the image" (44). In "Sea and Spar Between"—as in other generative digital poems in which the linguistic output exceeds what a human being may ever be able to read in its totality (see also Aquilina [2015] on the computational sublime in Montfort)—something analogous to this shift from symbolist recuperation of meaning into metonymic (occasionally disjunctive) surface relations occurs. This, at least, seems to be the case if one focuses primarily on the textual output of the poem: stanzas, which, though evocative, do not provide a coherent recuperation of meaning either if taken individually or if read in relation to other stanzas generated by the poem.

However, within the context of a "poetics of contiguity" or of the poetic *as* contiguity, the "meaning" and "understanding" that seem to be problematized when one reads the textual output in isolation may be recuperated into some form of coherence or, to use Rajewsky's (2005: 52) terminology, a form of intermedial "integration" if one looks at the words' relation with their context. The stanzas on the screen may be what we may identify as the "poetic" first, but like many other works of electronic literature, we are also given the opportunity to read about "how to read" the poem in a specifically designated page hyperlinked to the textual output. This page does not simply instruct the reader on how to navigate "Sea and Spar Between," but also provides important contextual information about both how the output is generated by the poetic machine and the rationale behind this process. Typical of other digital poems by Montfort, "Sea and Spar Between" also provides readers with detailed information about the code—and the code itself—in "cut to fit the tool-spun course: Discussing Creative Code in Comments" (Montfort and Strickland 2013). What in a print context may be read as marginal, paratextual information about the work becomes central to the work itself and to the poetic experience that it allows.

"Sea and Spar Between," as Stuart Moulthrop and Justin Schumaker (2016: 135) argue, is a poetic experience that provokes the "sublime":

> "Sea and Spar Between" only ever offers a minuscule subset of total possible output, a limited array of stanzas assembled on the fly for momentary display in a browser window. The text as a whole is not just unseen, but in practical terms un-seeable . . . Even in less extreme cases than "Sea and Spar Between," electronic writing seems to overload the receiver. The contents of "Sea and Spar" can be specified algorithmically, but in an ordinary human sense they cannot be definitively produced.

Moulthrop and Schumaker (2016: 135) call the effects of this "overload" on the reader "a *topological* sublime—a level of possibility and complexity that overloads traditional cognitive structures." As Sandy Baldwin writes in *The Internet Unconscious* (2015: 18),"You cannot take in the mass of texts in the world. You cannot take it. The writings exceed you, they overwhelm you, and they bury you." The effect of the overload on human cognition, which is at work in several poems by Montfort (see Aquilina 2015), is created through the contiguity of the textual output with the design of the Web page recalling the sea which inspires the poem in so many ways, as well as what Moulthrop and Schumaker (2016: 135) describe as "the twitchy sensitivity of its event handlers, [which] is meant to suggest a flickering, oceanic surface and the teeming presence of life beneath it." The reader's awareness of the workings of the poetic machine, such as the use of poetic language from Melville and Dickinson as well as the fact that the poetry generator may potentially produce trillions of stanzas, also contributes to the sublime poetic experience in the work.

Pry

Gorman and Cannizzaro's "novella" *Pry* (2014) is less intuitively thought of in terms of the poetic. In the "About" section, the producers describe it as a "fiction created exclusively for digital, touchscreen reading; it moves beyond eBook replication of print conventions." Focusing on the affordances of the iPad touchscreen, including the tap, the pinch, the scroll, and the release, Gorman and Cannizzaro emphasize how, "in *PRY*, interaction and story content are deeply intertwined." The structure of the work, with seven "sequential" chapters and an appendix that may be read, "re-read," or traversed in any order, give rise to an "exploratory experience" that, while making full use of the specific technology of the iPad tablet, relies heavily on well-established narrative conventions (used in print literature as well as other media like film and digital games) such as story and plot, characterization, setting, point of view, theme, imagery and motifs, and so on (ibid.).

Within *Pry*, words and language are used in a range of different ways and appear both as letters to be read as well as sounds to be heard in voice-over narrations and as dialogue in the filmic sequences. Indeed, it would be interesting to study the aural use of language in *Pry*, such as in the Braille chapter where swiping a finger across the screen over braille symbols triggers the narrative voice-over. However, I would like to focus exclusively on the written alphabetical text in *Pry* and, more specifically, on those instances where the text becomes "poetic" in the sense used here, that is, when words have an effect on the readers through their contiguity, interrelations, as well as spatial and temporal arrangement. The authors declare a specific interest in "what happens to text when instead of turning a page, the reader must force open a character's eyes or read his thoughts infinitely scrolling in every direction" (Gorman and Cannizzaro 2014). Their playing with the possibilities of text in *Pry* seems to be a somewhat self-aware exercise in meta-mediatic exploration. They seem to ask: "How far can the iPad take textuality away from print?" "And how does text work, aesthetically, within this specific interface?"

Text is used to provide contextual information, including information about the characters, the scene, the setting, and the plot. Indeed, much of the sustained interaction with *Pry* depends on returning to it to access new information with successive rereading and thus being able to literally fill the gaps in our understanding of the whole (symbolized by the game-like way the reader accrues stars for each chapter and filling in the shape on the title page with red triangles and pyramids).

However, there are other, more "poetic" uses of text in *Pry*. One of the features for which *Pry* has been celebrated is its use of the haptic affordances of the iPad touchscreen. Among these is the pinch, which allows the reader to move their fingers in two opposite directions and access two different dimensions of the work: by opening one's fingers away from each other, one accesses videos from the point of view of one of the main characters, James, while pinching them close allows one to pry into James's subconscious. The pinch sometimes triggers the appearance on the screen of flashing or barely perceptible images, short videos, numbers, or words. The words and images appear and disappear at a fast rate, and while they tend to be legible, the reader cannot freeze the words on the screen. One may only release the pinch and thus no longer see the words. Recalling the fast, flashing words seen through a tachistoscope, *Pry* makes it very difficult for the reader to recall these words, let alone read them closely. However, as Pressman (2014: 65) writes about the effect of such techniques in her discussion of William Poundstone's *Project*, flashing text "can be employed purposefully for aesthetic effect and meaning." The way this happens, though, involves the words used no longer functioning primarily as the conduits of some deeper meaning (i.e., metaphorically) but becoming part of the materiality of the medium. Pressman reminds us that "reading concrete poetry demands deriving meaning from the visual arrangement of text on the interface of the page or screen," and, in this context, "the blank space of the page is never empty [, but] its void is full of potential" (65).

This may also be said of the flashing word sequences in *Pry*, which, in ways which recall subliminal messaging in advertising, "exploit . . . the void between the visible and the hidden, the conscious and unconscious, as the site for communicating meaning" (65). What makes these flashing words sequences poetic is once again intermedial contiguity, in this case: the speed of the appearance and disappearance of the words; their interrelation with images and videos; their being triggered by the haptic interactivity of the reader (they only appear as long as the reader holds the pinch); the way in which their appearance suggests the idea of prying into the character's subconscious. As Pressman argues for digital modernist works, it may be said that in a discussion of the poetic in *Pry*, it is reductive to take the words or language in isolation, and we must understand its relations to the media and the on-screen aesthetics in which it appears.

A second instantiation of the poetics of contiguity in *Pry* may be seen in chapter 6, which starts with two lines of white text on a black screen that may be repeatedly expanded through an open pinch, revealing more and more text in between the two lines seen initially. The text that appears with every open pinch includes flashing words that disappear upon release (as discussed above) and extension to the original text with added phrases and sentences. There are precedents for this technique in electronic literature (e.g., John Cayley's work), in avant-garde "flicker films" of the 1960s, and the much older Maya folded codices. Here again, the analysis of language cannot really be separated from the analysis of the interface, the machine, and the interactivity required for the text to appear. An example may be given by focusing on the references to a scud falling. As we read, we think that James has witnessed and experienced a day scud hit in close proximity: "In day, the metal reflects heaven, drops the sun toward is. Icarus." However, as more text is folded open, we get contradictory information: "No that's wrong. It was night and a thin strip of light reflected along the scud." Later, again: "Actually, I've only seen them on TV" (Gorman and Cannizzaro 2014: chapter 6). As we unfold the text, we get contradictory information so that the words we read are qualified, put under erasure, by those which surround them. The ambiguity that arises in this example is not so much the effect of the nuanced phrases but of their contiguity, their relation to each other. The ambiguity, then, arises through spatial expansion (the more text we reveal, the more nuanced and ambiguous the text becomes) and temporal development (the more time we spend with the text, the more detail—often contradictory—is revealed).

A third example of the poetics of contiguity in *Pry* may be located in "The Appendix," which makes text and pictures available on the basis of how much of the chapters a reader has completed. The appendix in *Pry* remediates what is already found in traditional print literature, often having the function of adding details and contextual information that does not fit in the main text. Here, however, the appendix provides crucial information about the narrative as a whole, such as the fact that James's album, a "lifeline," which contained images of his mother, has been lost in a fire (one recalls J. G. Ballard's story "The Index" [2010], which makes the paratextual the textual in perhaps unsurpassable ways). In order to access all the details of the appendix, one must have managed to access most of the content in the chapters. This "reward" for spending time with *Pry* promises the reader the possibility of forming a more coherent and complete narrative. However, the way in which this information is presented is crucial. First of all, the text is presented in a continuous form, whereby text appears on screen to be continuous, without an easily ascertainable beginning or end. One may zoom in or out of the text, but this continuity remains, making it difficult, at least initially, to read—or to even recognize—all the new text with successive readings. It is indeed a difficult section of *Pry* to read due to the amount of text generated and the impossibility of having the text fully contained within the frame of the screen. This difficulty is not simply a virtuoso play with the affordances of computational literature, but is also thematic and fits in within the general act of prying and the attitude of perseverance that is needed by any reader reading *Pry*. In yet another example of the poetics of contiguity, the words of the text, while revealing in themselves, cannot be separated from the technology and the interface which frame it and from the reader response that the app demands in this section. While the amount of pictures, videos, and text presented to the reader in this section is not, one would argue, humanly impossible to access fully—one can take it all in if one perseveres long enough—it does create an experience that is reminiscent of the sense of human limitations in one's interaction with computational extent that is central to "Sea and Spar Between." As one swipes back and forth in time, reads accumulating text, and sees objects from James's memory, one is, at least initially, overwhelmed by too much information for it to be meaningful. In this context, to analyze the language of *Pry*, one cannot divide it from the visual, the haptic, the database, the computational, and so on. In this, *Pry* is similar to other works of electronic literature (as well as many examples from the literary avant-garde) in which the context/mechanisms of creation are more interesting and withstand scrutiny more than the language itself. What are surely most memorable in *Pry* are not particular phrases or sentences—though there is some very good writing to be discovered—but the experience of accessing text and narrative through technology.

CONCLUSION

The poetic experience that we have traced in *Pry* and "Sea and Spar Between" stems not so much from particular turns of phrase but from the interrelation of linguistic elements and text with code, database, platform, screen, mouse-movements, haptic affordances, and other contextual and paratextual elements. This is a repositioning of the poetic away from the expressive and what we have been describing as a language of substance toward the poetic operating on the principles of contiguity, whereby the material aspect of language becomes decisive. As such, language here does not primarily call for interpretative analyses but for an exploration of the possibilities created by contingency, extension, the algorithmic, interactivity, and potentiality. It is not only the letter and its meaning but the letter's intermodal and multimodal relations with other modalities that matter.

We have seen that a more complete understanding of the use of language in the examples discussed requires an awareness of the "poetics of contiguity" at work in electronic literature. The poetic in the works discussed can still excite and intrigue us, and it can still give rise to aesthetic experience with language. However, it often does less through a language of substance and more by appealing to the material and metonymic functions of language within the context of intermedial dynamics. This is a significant characteristic of the poetic in electronic literature but, as shown above, is not completely unprecedented. Rather, it takes elements of the poetic that we have seen before—primarily, the principle of contiguity—and makes these elements dominant in the experience of poetic language in electronic media work.

SOURCES CITED

Aquilina, Mario. "The Computational Sublime in Nick Montfort's 'Round' and 'All the Names of God.'" *CounterText*, vol. 1, no. 3 (2015): 348–65.

Aquilina, Mario, and Ivan Callus. "Thirteen Ways of Looking at Electronic Literature, or, a Print *Essai* on Tone in Electronic Literature, 1.0." *CounterText*, vol. 2, no. 2 (2016): 236–55.

Baldwin, Sandy. *The Internet Unconscious: On the Subject of Electronic Literature*, vol. 9 International Texts in Critical Media Aesthetics. Edited by Francisco J. Ricardo. New York: Bloomsbury Academic, 2015.

Ballard, J. G. "The Index." In *The Complete Stories of J. G. Ballard*, edited by Martin Amis. New York: W. W. Norton, 2010, pp. 940–5 (940).

Block, Friedrich W. "Digital Poetics or on the Evolution of Experimental Media Poetry." In *Media Poetry: An International Anthology*, edited by Eduardo Kac. Bristol and Chicago: intellect, 2007, pp. 229–44.

Blossier-Jacquemot, Anne, and Florence Dupont. "Les Oulipiens antiques : pour une anthropologie des pratiques d'écriture à contraintes dans l'Antiquité." Université Paris Diderot—Paris 7, Atelier national de reproduction des thèses, 2010.

Bolter, Jay David, and Richard Grusin. *Remediation: Understanding New Media*. Cambridge: MIT Press, 2000.

Cramer, Florian. "Post-Digital Writing." *ebr* (2012), http://www.electronicbookreview.com/thread/electropoetics/postal.

Damrosch, David. *What Is World Literature?* Princeton, NJ: Princeton University Press, 2003.

Derrida, Jacques. *The Postcard: From Socrates to Freud and Beyond*. Translated by Alan Bass. London: University of Chicago Press, 1987.

Derrida, Jacques. "Before the Law." In *Acts of Literature*, translated by Derek Attridge et al., edited by Derek Attridge. New York: Routledge, 1992, pp. 181–220.

Funkhouser, C. T. *Prehistoric Digital Poetry: An Archaeology of Forms, 1959–1995*. Tuscaloosa: University of Alabama Press, 2007.

Goldsmith, Kenneth. *Uncreative Writing: Managing Language in the Digital Age*. New York: Columbia University Press, 2011.

Gorman, Samantha, and Danny Cannizzaro. *Pry* (2014), documented at http://prynovella.com. Accessed April 29, 2016.

Hayles, N. Katherine. "Print Is Flat, Code Is Deep: The Importance of Media-Specific Analysis." *Poetics Today*, vol. 25, no. 1 (2004): 67–90.

Hayles, N. Katherine. "The Time of Digital Poetry: From Object to Event." In *New Media Poetics: Contexts, Technotexts, and Theories*, Adelaide Morris and Thomas Swiss. Cambridge, MA, and London: MIT Press, 2006, pp. 181–209.

Hayles, N. Katherine. "Distributed Cognition at/in Work: Strickland, Lawson Jaramillo, and Ryan's slippingglimpse." *Frame*, vol. 21, no. 1 (2008): 15–29.

Hazlitt, William. "On Poetry in General." In *Lectures on the English Poets* as excerpted in *William Hazlitt Essayist and Critic: Selections from His Writings*. London and New York: Frederick Warne, [1818] 1889, pp. 98–106.

Hillis Miller, J. "Literary Study among the Ruins." *Diacritics*, vol. 31, no. 3 (2001): 57–66.

Hollander, John. *Vision and Resonance: Two Senses of Poetic Form*. New York: Oxford University Press, 1975.

Jakobson, Roman. "Two Types of Language and Two Types of Aphasic Disturbances." In *On Language*. Cambridge: Harvard University Press, 1990, pp. 115–33.

Kress, Gunther. "Multimodality." In *Multiliteracies: Literacy Learning and the Design of Social Futures*, edited by Bill Cope and Mary Kalantzis. London: Routledge, 2000, pp. 179–99.

Lodge, David. *The Modes of Modern Writing: Metaphor, Metonymy, and the Typology of Modern Literature*. London: Hodder & Stoughton Educational, 1977.

Marino, Adriano. *The Biography of "The Idea of Literature": From Antiquity to the Baroque*. Albany: SUNY, 1996.

Montfort, Nick, and Stephanie Strickland. *Sea and Spar Between, The Winter Anthology*, 3, 2010, http://winteranthology.com/?vol=3&author=montfort-strickland&title=seaandspar. Accessed November 21, 2015. The work is also available at http://nickm.com/montfort_strickland/ sea_and_spar_between/.Accessed November 23, 2015.

Montfort, Nick, and Stephanie Strickland. "cut to fit the tool-spun course: Discussing Creative Code in Comments." *Digital Humanities Quarterly*, vol. 7, no. 1 (2013), http://www.digitalhumanities.org/dhq/vol/7/1/000149/000149.html.

Montfort, Nick, and Stephanie Strickland. "How to Read *Sea and Spar Between*" (n.d.), http://nickm.com/montfort_strickland/sea_and_spar_between/reading.html.

Moulthrop, Stuart, and Justin Schumaker. "Along the Folds: Sea and Spar and Portals Between." *CounterText*, vol. 2, no. 2 (2016): 130–9.

Perloff, Marjorie. *The Poetics of Indeterminacy: Rimbaud to Cage*. Evanston, IL: Northwestern University Press, 1999.

Perloff, Marjorie. *Unoriginal Genius: Poetry by Other Means in the New Century*. Chicago: University Of Chicago Press, 2010.

Poe, Edgar Allan. "The Poetic Principle," as reproduced in *Project Gutenberg's The Works of Edgar Allan Poe* (1850), http://www.gutenberg.org/files/2151/2151-h/2151-h.htm#link2H_4_0010. Accessed November 22, 2016.

Pressman, Jessica. *Digital Modernism: Making It New in New Media*. Oxford: Oxford University Press, 2014.

Queneau, Raymond. *Cent Mille Milliards de Poèmes*. Paris: Gallimard, 1961.

Rajewsky, Irina O. "Intermediality, Intertextuality, and Remediation: A Literary Perspective on Intermediality." *intermédialités*, vol. 6 (2005): 43–64.

Ricardo, Francisco J. *Literary Art in Digital Performance: Case Studies in New Media Art and Criticism*. New York and London: Continuum, 2009.

Simanowski, Roberto. *Digital Art and Meaning: Reading Kinetic Poetry, Text Machines, Mapping Art, and Interactive Installations*. Minneapolis and London: University of Minnesota Press, 2011.

Simanowski, Roberto, Jörgen Schäfer, and Peter Gendolla, eds. *Reading Moving Letters: Digital Literature in Research and Teaching: A Handbook*. Bielefeld: transcript Verlag, 2010.

Stefans, Brian Kim. "Language as Gameplay: Toward a Vocabulary for Describing Works of Electronic Literature." *ebr* (2012), http://www.electronicbookreview.com/thread/electropoetics/gameplay.

Tabbi, Joseph. "Locating the Literary in New Media." *ebr* (2008), http://www.electronicbookreview.com/thread/criticalecologies/interpretive.

Tabbi, Joseph. "Electronic Literature as World Literature; or, the Universality of Writing under Constraint." *Poetics Today*, vol. 31, no. 1 (Spring 2010): 17–50, doi 10.1215/03335372-2009-013.

Ulmer, Gregory L. *Internet Invention: From Literacy to Electracy*. New York: Longman, 2003

CHAPTER TWELVE

Combination and Copulation: Making Lots of Little Poems

ADEN EVENS

High up in their remote aeries these monks had been patiently at work, generation after generation, compiling their lists of meaningless words. Was there any limit to the follies of mankind?

—Arthur C. Clarke ([1953] 2000)

All histories of electronic literature acknowledge the primary influence of the Oulipo artists, often invoking as archetype Raymond Queneau's combinatoric work, *A hundred thousand billion poems*. This book of ten sonnets, each cut into its individual fourteen lines, is also a sonnet construction kit, in that the reader can make another sonnet by choosing, for each of the sonnet's fourteen lines, one corresponding line from any of the ten through-composed sonnets. Fourteen lines, ten possibilities for each line makes ten-to-the-fourteenth or a hundred trillion possible sonnets.

A hundred thousand billion poems makes no attempt to hide its rules of assembly; on the contrary, a couple of moments with the book in hand makes clear the possibilities on offer, which are built into its material architecture. But this would be enough only if one believes that this sonnet construction machine is ultimately a work of conceptual art, a work whose idea dominates its realization. To regard Queneau's masterwork this way would look past the genius whereby any combination of lines still makes a sort of poetic sense, somewhere in between accident and intention. Not to encounter that liminal signification is also to forego the subliminal possibilities that one does not actualize, and thus to miss out on the plenary experience of the poem. Knowing the rule of construction does not obviate the need to do at least some reading, to engage with the work in its concrete materiality on the page.

Nor would it be adequate just to read the ten sonnets as originally crafted, which would bypass the distinctive experimental character of this work, namely, that it is precisely not just ten individual sonnets. The distinctive experience of *A hundred thousand billion poems* surely includes some experience of the inexperience-ability of the overwhelming number of possibilities. Which is to say that to read this work means to read at least to the point where one begins to get a feeling for the futility of a total experience. One comes to know the work without reading every possible sonnet. This is already the crux of the matter, that there is a gap in this case between reading and realizing. Any encounter, however slight, might count as a reading of the work. But to know the work, to master it seems to imply that one knows more than one has read, that one might in some sense know all of the possibilities through an encounter with just some of them. Stuart Moulthrop (forthcoming) refers to this wealth of unrealized possibilities as the *para-scripton* of the work; these possibilities have a status that is neither scripton, the work as generated on the page, nor texton, the set of all elements from which the work may be generated.[1]

Motivating the concept of the para-scripton, works like Queneau's narrow the gap between possible and actual. The possibilities are quickly graspable as possibilities; there is something *nearly there* already about each of them, a hyporeality born of a materialized logic of combination. One feels as though the difference between an actually realized sonnet and its possible realization is thin. Consequently, it may make sense to suggest that all of the possible sonnets are *there*, that one can read the whole thing without reading each possible sonnet. At some level, one becomes equal to the immensity of the work, a real experience of comprehension to match the fantasy of completion.

Though by no means the sole or central aim of generative electronic literature, one telos of the genre is to produce work that denies the reader this sense of circumscription, an algorithm that generates a diversity of output text so broad and so disparate as to overwhelm the reader's sense of determinate possibilities. Such limitless creativity remains (arguably) the privilege of human authors, but electronic works such as Scott Rettberg's *Frequency* (2009) project attempt a production diverse enough as to seem without rule or pattern. Rettberg describes *Frequency* as a project rather than a work of literature, implying its potential expansion, and in its original incarnation it produces ten different formats of poetic output drawing on two thousand composed lines of verse, which are themselves constructed from two hundred common English words. Readers may intuit the common vocabulary or the shared resource of verses just by reading a number of examples of *Frequency*'s output, but these wells are deep and the variety of formats of poetry produced by this project gives the impression of boundless possibility.

Only upon careful study of the source code or a knowing explanation of the methods of *Frequency* does the reader grasp its limits, a large but conceivable number of discrete possible poems. Contrast the sense of completeness around discrete possibilities with the open-ended generativity of poetic potential. Potential is characterized not by its breadth, for it can operate in a highly confined space, nor by numerical fecundity, for it need produce only slowly or only few. Rather, potential holds within it an essential indeterminacy that renders an ultimate comprehension impossible. Writing about electronic literary works of potentially infinite length, Mario Aquilina (2015) applies Kant's notion of the sublime as that which overwhelms the senses but can be apprehended by reason. Aquilina's *computational sublime* might hold sway for a generative work wherein one can grasp the pattern even if the actual work is too long to read or infinitely extendable. But unbridled potential—the heart of poiesis—repudiates even a sublime experience. No

[1] The terms "scripton" and "texton" were introduced by Espen Aarseth to distinguish in electronic literature (*cybertext*) between the particular instance of generated text that the reader sees on the screen and the total space of possibility that the code is capable of producing. Whereas in much electronic literature the set of textons is not available to the reader but is part of the hidden code, in Queneau's sonnet book the textons are fully revealed from the start: the textons in this work are simply all of the lines of each of the ten sonnets regarded as individual lines rather than elements of a particular sonnet.

reaction can be equal to the expression of potential, which, by virtue of its radical unpredictability, demands always a new approach.

Perhaps this aim of an inexhaustible computational potential is already accomplished. Some Twitter bots—algorithmic language generators that operate by broadcasting tweets—monitor the constant and endless chatter on Twitter (or other fonts of human-generated language), searching for tweets that satisfy certain criteria. *Pentametron* (@Pentametron) watches Twitter for posts that happen to be in iambic pentameter, then retweets those posts unaltered. *Two Headlines* (@TwoHeadlines) takes a current headline from a news source and substitutes for its topic noun a subject from a different headline, broadcasting the result as a tweet. The output in each case is typically amusing and sometimes fascinating, but probably not consistently or endlessly so. At least in these cases, knowing the rule diminishes the attribution of creativity to the generative engine. Once the reader grasps the principle of construction, the production itself loses some of its luster. But short of an algorithm that simulates spontaneous creativity, electronic literature stakes its claim in the gap between the principle of its generative concept and the accidents of its actual production.

This chapter is about the gap between the rule and its execution, the surplus that reading offers over and above the generative algorithm. It is also about the gap between possibility and potential, a tension between the discrete possibilities of digitality and the potential of poiesis, a tension that constitutes the space of electronic literature. While digital devices tend to limit or even eliminate potential in their technological principles, confining outcomes to what can in principle be known, poetry—even stable, textual, print poetry—functions as a crucible of potential, producing new meaning without changing a word. Some version of this gap separates the intention of an author who chooses terms to combine via algorithm in successive iterations of a generative textual work and the accidents that arise when unanticipated or strange combinations scroll across the screen while the algorithm runs.

Finite, rule-bound, but impossible (for a person) to read in full, "Sea and Spar Between" demonstrates the width of this gap, a dialectic of possibility and potential. Though their literary reference points are nineteenth-century writers Herman Melville and Emily Dickinson, rather than the gothic imagery and Shakespearean format of Queneau's sonnets, Nick Montfort and Stephanie Strickland offer a worthy comparison to Queneau's work in the category of electronic literature. "Sea and Spar Between" generates a number of stanzas on the same order of magnitude as Queneau's sonnet machine, exactly one hundred trillion sonnets in Queneau's case and approximately two hundred twenty-five trillion stanzas in Montfort and Strickland's (2012) work, according to the comments in the code. (Multiplying the number of rows by the number of columns yields 224,771,578,003,456 stanzas, a number that the authors claim is comparable to the number of fish in the sea. Leonardo Flores [2013] notes drily that "this poem doesn't need to be apprehended in its entirety to be enjoyed.") In their comments, Montfort and Strickland acknowledge explicitly that among their guiding aims is the desire to convey some of the spirit or tone of Dickinson's poetry, along with a lesser hint of Melville's prose. These are imprecise and poetic goals, complemented by the equally fuzzy aims of getting a feeling for the tone of the stanzas as well as their variety, the interface and its interactive possibilities, and perhaps also the sense of being at sea, or being carried by the current from stanza to stanza. The point is that, as with Queneau's sonnets, an understanding of the principle of construction is not tantamount to the experience of reading this work, reading bits and pieces of it as a promise of a completion that can never in a lifetime be fulfilled.

Also akin to Queneau's sonnets, "Sea and Spar Between" produces its fantastic magnitude of stanzas without thereby sacrificing the authors' poetic investments. One might expect that, with trillions of four-line verses arranged as pairs of couplets, most individual stanzas would feel repetitive or banal or nonsensical. For unlike the Oulipian choose-your-own-sonnet book, the lines of verse in "Sea and Spar Between" are not individually authored word-by-word, but are constructed mechanically, using an algorithm that selects each word (or short phrase) separately from pre-authored lists of words and phrases, which technique is a canonical demonstration of the *combinatoric* method. Many combinatoric works select from determinate lists of words or phrases at random (such as "Taroko Gorge" [2009] on which more below), such that each time the algorithm is run, a different work, or at least some different words, appear in its output. "Sea and Spar Between" instead uses a determinate method of choosing the words to combine in each stanza, such that all two hundred and twenty-five trillion stanzas come out the same way each time the program is run. The authors' genius in this case—and perhaps throughout the subgenre of combinatoric literature—is a matter of balancing variety within a given list of combinable terms against sensibility: the greater the variety of different terms in a list, the greater the potential for resulting combinations to extend beyond the boundaries of meaningfulness. But too little variety within a list will generate stanzas that are too homogeneous, reducing the perceived impact of their sheer overwhelming number as well as the pleasure of exploratory reading. By emphasizing tone through vocabulary borrowed from their nineteenth-century sources, Montfort and Strickland create a work with a consistent feeling attributable to the intentions of its multiple authors spanning centuries, but also with a considerable variety of different stanzas, including variation in the degree of sense or the normalcy of the language produced. Though readers do not likely articulate their experience of "Sea and Spar Between" in those terms, it is this coordinated combination of consistency and variability that constitutes this work's success and ensures that it is engaging and enduring.

Arguably the first work of (digital) electronic literature, Christopher Strachey's 1952 "Loveletters" employs combinatoric techniques to generate simple five-line love letters, prepending a generated salutation and appending a closing line and signature. Though the number of possible letters is on par with the immensity of "Sea and Spar Between," this work aims not so much for poetic variety as for consistency of tone, constructing each of the five lines in one of two basic formats by combining nouns, verbs, adjectives, and adverbs, where the overall effect suggests the underlying synonymity among the word choices. That is, reading through a number of letters output by this algorithm, one gets the sense that they all manage to convey the same idea (viz., ardent love) regardless of the particular words selected to fill in the blanks. (This realization produces a secondary sardonic effect, as the reader notes that a compelling love letter may be little more than a formulaic concatenation of words associated with love.) Notably, this algorithm is designed to generate letters one at a time, hiding from the reader the extraordinary number of possible combinations, which contrasts markedly with Montfort and Strickland's technique of laying out all the trillions of stanzas on a vast virtual plane, of which only a tiny section is visible on the monitor.

With works of unreadable extent, electronic literature reaches for the unreachable and so indulges a certain fantasy of the superhuman, but fantasy appears to be a central motive of much electronic literature. Jean Clément (2002) identifies the fantasies driving combinatoric electronic literature, creative aims that appear in antiquity but find salient expression in the computer as a combination machine. Though the seven fantasies that he describes manifest telling and subtle differences, they share a common spirit, reaching toward a transcendence that disrupts traditional modes of reading and writing and problematizes authorship and address.[2] The fantasy of completion (or its converse, the fantasy of exhaustion) might subtend the other fantasies, offering the most direct expression of the transcendence that electronic literature teases. Its attraction extends well beyond the boundaries of electronic literature, as documented by Clément, and its cultural appeal grows during the rise of computing in the later twentieth century. No doubt this is due in part to the suitability of the computer as combinatoric machine. At the same moment that the computer announced its cultural ascendance and surrounded itself with promises of the end of work and the subsumption of all knowledge, it also seemed to promise a deep well of creativity through its combinatory methods. Though combinatoric techniques have been used in painting, film, prose, poetry, music, and dance, the availability of the computer as automated laborer allowed combinatoric work on a scale that would have been prohibitive without algorithmic digital assistance.

In a middle ground between abstract computation and concrete actuality, literary arts toyed with the relationship between combination and totality early in the computer era. In 1972 in England, Angela Carter's novel *The Infernal Desire Machines of Doctor Hoffman* figures "a set of samples"—little blocks or dice with images and some small mechanical parts—whose arrangements according to I Ching hexagrams can bring about *any* configuration of desire objectified. "The models did indeed represent *everything* it was possible to believe by the means of either direct simulation or a symbolism derived from Freud" (108; emphasis added). Placing a subset of these samples into special viewing machines, the novel's protagonist Desiderio brings about the events that advance the book's narrative, from an encounter with a tribe of cannibal female warriors to capture by a centaur culture practicing a religious orthodoxy in thrall to the Great Stallion.

Like (some interpretations of) the I Ching to which it is explicitly connected, Carter's sample-based combinatoric mechanism not only encompasses the totality of desiring possibility, but also reproduces its combinations as effects in the world. Literarily, there is a connection between the completeness of the samples—where *completeness* here refers to the adequacy of the samples as a kind of mathematical basis for expressing the world—and their efficacy, a desire become ontological. The novel turns on this implication from completeness to efficacy: when the samples scatter and are lost in a massive earthquake about halfway through the book, reality ceases to respect the limits of sense and unbridled desire governs the unfolding of events. But what ties together the samples and their effects on the real? How does a throw of the dice become ontologically consequential?

[2] Taken to their limits, the *fantasy of chance* replaces the author with the will of the universe, the *fantasy of disordered language* shuffles words, phrases, or other linguistic units to defy the principle of linear order in language, and the *fantasy of the impossible book* opens multiple paths of reading that explode the standard orthography of the codex. Clément reads in these fantasies a dream of escape from "the fascism of language," a departure from the orthodoxy of sense-making, and a leap beyond the confined creativity of a human author. Fantasies of a master reader and the stable self-identity of number both appeal to a kind of perfection or completion, as do the aforementioned fantasies of an infinite book and of the algorithmic creativity of the cybernetic machine, as though reading or writing could be final, could be finished.

Carter's combinations of samples shape the world by representing it or symbolizing it according to a Freudian interpretive framework. At the same time and also in England, J. G. Ballard, in his masterwork *Crash* (1973), constructed a more eschatological and post-Freudian account of the efficacy of combinatorics. In many of its detailed descriptions and in its tragic plot—the death of the charismatic central character, Vaughan, is announced antiseptically in the opening sentence—*Crash* depicts a world waiting for a kind of completion, whereupon the "autogeddon" will arrive. The novel opens having already exhausted the possibilities of heterosexual desire, and so it incorporates automobiles into an otherwise tired sexuality, crushing genitals and car parts into indistinction through the violent event of the crash. Copulation brings together the automobile as erotic body and the crash as an orgasm whose violence enmeshes the human and automobile bodies. Sex extends well beyond a genital logic, tying the erotic instead to a machine logic, all the various possible combinations of human parts and car parts.

> *Almost every conceivable violent confrontation between the automobile and its occupants was listed*: mechanisms of passenger ejection, the geometry of kneecap and hip-joint injuries, deformation of passenger compartments in head-on and rear-end collisions, injuries sustained in accidents at roundabouts, at trunk-road intersections, at the junctions between access roads and motorway intersections, the telescoping mechanisms of car-bodies in front-end collisions, abrasive injuries formed in roll-overs, the amputation of limbs by roof assemblies and door sills during roll-over, facial injuries caused by dashboard and window trim, scalp and cranial injuries caused by rear-view mirrors and sun-visors, whiplash injuries in rear-end collisions, first and second-degree burns in accidents involving the rupture and detonation of fuel tanks, chest injuries caused by steering column impalements, abdominal injuries caused by faulty seat-belt adjustment, second-order collisions between front-seat and rear-seat passengers, cranial and spinal injuries caused by ejection through windshields, the graded injuries to the skull caused by variable windshield glasses, injuries to minors, both children and infants in arms, injuries caused by prosthetic limbs, injuries caused within cars fitted with invalid controls, the complex self-amplifying injuries of single and double amputees, injuries caused by specialist automobile accessories such as record players, cocktail cabinets and radiotelephones, the injuries caused by manufacturers' medallions, safety belt pinions and quarter-window latches. (133; emphasis added)

The point of reproducing this extensive list of automobile injuries is to suggest that combinatorics in these cases, Ballard and Carter, is not just about creative permutation but an implicit exhaustive totality. Ballard's characters insist on every possible combination as a precondition of whatever comes next, while Carter's samples are sufficiently elemental as to offer the possible construction of any conceivable desire.

But in these novels, the drive to totality or completeness takes its cues from an erotic rather than a digital logic, in that the body exceeds any encoding and finally determines in the flesh which combinations are valid and desirable. One scene in *Infernal Desire Machines* depicts a group of nine diminutive Moroccan acrobats who break down their bodies into individuated organs, juggle those separated parts, and then rape the narrator-protagonist of the novel in a violent combinatorics of desire: "They gave me the most comprehensive anatomy lesson a man ever suffered, in which I learned every possible modulation of the male apparatus and some I would have thought impossible" (Carter 1972: 117). Though the organic anatomy of the acrobats seems at odds with a digital accounting, the interchangeability of the parts and the concomitant emphasis on totality or completeness represent a step *toward* a digital logic of formalized difference and denumerable sets.

Notwithstanding the pre-digital milieus of these 1970s novels—neogothic in Carter and late industrial in Ballard—it is the computer that promises the totality these books fictionalize. Combinatorial totality is characteristic of digital epistemology, and the emphasis on this totality in literature of the early 1970s reflects an anticipation of a digital treatment not only of texts but of the world, for the computer is foremost a combinatoric machine. Using the simplest elements—bits that obtain one of two values, 0 or 1—the computer performs all of its operations and represents all of its information by shuffling these bits in various combinations, assigning different meanings and consequences to different sequenced combinations of 0s and 1s.

Two decades earlier, Arthur C. Clarke ([1953] 2000) already affirmed the *digital* link between combinatorial completeness and efficacy in his science fiction story "The Nine Billion Names of God." A fictional commentary on electronic literature *avant la lettre*, Clarke's story tells of a computer that shuffles an alphabet of nine letters in every possible combination of characters (skipping some combinations that violate spelling rules not detailed in the story).[3] The engineers, who install and run the computer that prints out the algorithmic churn of possible names of god, figure out the monks' plan: "Oh, I get it. When we finish our job, it will be the end of the world" (420). And, indeed it is, as the story and its fictional universe come to a close, arriving at the eschatological conclusion that seems to await the characters in *Crash* and *Infernal Desire Machines* as well.

According to Clarke's fiction, the completion of all the possible names of god will include the real names of god, and once they are written down, the human species will have fulfilled its destiny. In this fantasy, the universe is waiting for a terminal condition, rendered effective by an implicit connection between writing and being, as though inscribing a name is enough to bring about consequences beyond that inscription. Skepticism may be misdirected here, as this is in fact how writing works, speaking mutely beyond its moment of composition/inscription, to effect change in the world as a dead message. It's as though writing gives up its liveliness in order to take on a more mysterious and deathly power.

This short story does not wholly affirm the hyporeality of algorithmic possibility, for, crucially, the names of god must actually be produced on the page to realize their eschatological effect. That is, it is not enough to write the algorithm that, in some sense, already contains all the combinations of letters; one must also execute that algorithm and await its completion. Perhaps this represents an earlier epistemology of the digital: in the 1950s the computer did not yet assert the same sense of inexorability that now characterizes its operation, whereas the materiality of inscription carried the solid assurance of effective reality. Notably, in Clarke's story, it is not necessary that anyone should actually read the real names of god, only that they be written down, to bring about the universe's end.

[3] The story clearly specifies an alphabet of nine letters but leaves unspecified exactly how many letters are in each possible name of god. Assuming the number of disallowed combinations is statistically small relative to the total number of possibilities, a ten-character name length would yield about three billion possible combinations, while an eleven-character length would yield about thirty billion possibilities. As neither number is especially close to nine billion, it is likely that Clarke just didn't do the math. However, if we suppose that names can have spaces in them, including leading or trailing spaces and runs of spaces in a row, then we could add the blank space as a tenth character of the monk's alphabet, in which case there are exactly ten billion sequences of ten characters, and excluding 10 percent as disallowed combinations yields nine billion possible ten-character names of god.

Reflecting the evolving epistemology of computation, Greg Egan's 1995 novel *Permutation City* rests on the science fictional premise that algorithmically captured possibility is tantamount to realized action, with no intermediary material inscription necessary to bring about actual consequences. Opening with a poem in which each of the twenty lines is an anagram (permutation of letters) of the novel's title—"Turn amity poetic" or "Art to epic mutiny"—the book explores how much actual algorithmic execution can be forsaken in favor of the implicit possibilities of the algorithm itself. Once again, the fictional result is eschatological, as halfway through the book, characters leave behind a doomed world to leap into an immaterial universe of algorithmic consciousness and implicit computation. The key to this transition is the experimental observation that by choosing the right set of existing elements in the universe to represent bits, one can discover any arbitrary computation already happening somewhere. (For instance, one could regard a city's traffic signals as bits, and their patterns of changing red and green lights would represent some computation taking place, a succession of 0s and 1s. By selecting the right subset of traffic signals, one could create as though from nothing a distributed "computer" that is already carrying out a pregiven logical operation.) But this means that every computation is *currently* taking place if one selects the right elements to count as bits, and this includes the computation that simulates any individual human consciousness and the world in which it lives. Taking this hypothesis with a measure of faith, Egan's characters upload their consciousnesses into a computer and assume that they will continue to be computed (somewhere) even when the computer's hardware is destroyed in the imminent apocalypse. This text takes to an extreme the notion that logical abstraction is equivalent to effective reality, such that writing, even the writing of code, is unnecessary for the results of the computation to come about.

One might cite illocutionary or imperative (written) speech acts as examples of the liveliness of writing, but electronic literature offers a particularly acute protest against the Platonic association of writing and death. Much electronic literature moves around the page, changes size or color or content, and in general manifests an animacy that serves as a rejoinder to those who typically see text as lifeless. Much commentary on electronic literature is dedicated to constructing some framework to stabilize electronic literary artifacts so that they can be consistently studied. All of this motion, the activity of electronic literature, fails to account for the metaphysics linking the entirety of a combinatoric construction and the end of the world. This link has the rhetorical label "synecdoche." Synecdoche names the rhetorical logic by which the completion of a part, in this case the combinatoric series, brings about the end of the whole, in this case sense or the sensible world. (Clarke's [2000 (1953): 422] final line: "Overhead, without any fuss, the stars were going out.") The termination of a seemingly interminable sequence crosses a threshold after which all thresholds succumb. Thus, in "The Nine Billion Names of God," it is the introduction of the computer that brings about in weeks what was thitherto slotted for millennia of human labor, for the computer compresses time, bringing the future, even the distant future of the end of all things, into the present.

The synecdoche posits an effective connection between part and whole that is not explained by the trope itself. For one thing, the worldview wherein the completion of a smaller series brings about the termination of the larger series suggests that the world, the larger series, is itself a matter of combination. "According to the linguistic universalism represented by Leibniz and others, the whole world is considered a closed system, an order of things that can be algorithmically produced and varied from a preexisting and limited set of elements. This applies both to cosmic elements from which God was believed to have created the world and to the elements of language" (Schäfer 2007: 123). The fantasy of a combinatoric language, a language made of minimal, stable elements that could be shuffled to express any possible meaning, was later the dream of logical positivism. Its most renowned statement is Ludwig Wittgenstein's *Tractatus Logico-Philosophicus*, which imagines such a relationship between language and world, exploring the fantasy of an elemental, logical language, but the book concludes ambiguously, possibly rejecting as sterile or fruitless this dream of a comprehensive universe construction kit in language. Wittgenstein, at least, seems dubious about the prospect of language that can express anything whatsoever. Does the computer's capacity for unerring and total computation provide a reason to revoke this doubt?

Why does the computer, already invoked in Leibniz's combinatoric imagination, seem to reinforce the teleological synecdoche, as though the capacity of automatized algorithms to accomplish complete sequences unattainable in individual human lives establishes an ontological connection to the world outside the machine? Does the computer have a special capacity to bring about its representations in reality, to make things happen outside of its logical and mediatic dimensions?

Part of the answer lies in the computer's ability to simulate, an extension of the related power of representation. By taking sequences of elemental bits as symbolic representatives of material and conceptual entities, the machine's users can look past the mediation of the digital model to witness worlds at work. Given the mind-boggling number of bits in a modern computer, the number of possible combinations, even with only two values available for each bit, is astounding. But as an automated and algorithmic machine, the computer bestows a special status on its possibilities, weakening the modal boundary that divides possibility and actuality. Inasmuch as code operates deterministically, according to an inexorable and practically infallible logic, the possibilities that can be produced by a given algorithm seem, in a sense, already there, implicit in the code to be executed. The algorithm to print out the nine billion names of god, or an algorithm to generate every possible one of Queneau's one hundred trillion sonnets, these algorithms generate results already foregone, making their actual execution something of an afterthought. Nevertheless, as observed above, actual execution matters, offering a fuller experience of Queneau's sonnets and realizing the eschatological conclusion of Clarke's story. It is in playing in and around this gap, between an implicit but guaranteed possibility and an actually produced sensation and significance, that electronic literature comes alive.

What does the output add to the algorithm that generates it? In his review of Montfort's book of code-and-poetry, *#!* (2014), John Cayley (2015) argues that the significance of the poetry in this volume depends on the printed appearance of both the algorithmic code and its output (poem), as the relationship between the sparse code and the profuse output is among the most interesting aspects of the meaning of the work. (This argument is reiterated and refined in Aquilina [2015].) Nevertheless, Cayley (2015: n.p.) acknowledges that in at least one work in the book, "The output is a 'trivial' consequence of the script," and later generalizes over the whole book: "For all of these poems-plus-output, the significance and affect of the piece is more or less exhausted by the concept encapsulated in each title." The execution of the algorithms is not exactly an afterthought, but neither does it add much supplemental significance to the reading experience. Once the reader grasps what the code will do, it is hardly necessary for the code to actually do it. The possibility of its execution combined with the determinacy of the results render the encoded possibilities almost real, possibility as *hypo*reality. Whatever the algorithm will do is already baked in, its creative impetus expended in the code itself.

Another way of characterizing the nearness of possibility in the digital is to note that the line between *any* and *every* in the digital is a thin one. We move without thinking much about it from the conviction that one can offer *any* input to the system, to the notion that the system has in effect already calculated *every* input, or might as well have done. The digital achieves this disruption of familiar modality by virtue of its strange materiality, based on the bit that cleaves meaning from matter. By overwriting the variability of its materiality using a system that assigns an exact logical value of 0 or 1 to an inexact electrical or magnetic measure, the design of the computer makes each bit behave as its own ideal. The bit's meaning, then, depends not on the vicissitudes of its matter but on the perfection of an idealized logic with two possible values. The bit becomes an abstraction, indifferent to its substrate, removed from its place and time, a Platonic form made operative in the actual. The computing device thus enmeshes two distinct ontological domains, the material and the logical, or the earthly and the heavenly.

The sense of the foregone threatens electronic literature's claim to creativity. (Platonic forms, after all, are eternal and unchanging.) Bill Seaman (2001) argues that combinatorics as a constraint on the possibilities available to an author serves as a creative technique for Queneau, for Oulipo (which Queneau helped to found), and for his own recombinant poetics. Cayley's remark about the superfluity of the poems in *#!* pushes back against this use of combinatorics as creative, for digital combinatorics suggests a closed rather than open system, a permutability in which every combination has already been realized even before the code is executed. In the fantasy of completeness, nothing is left still to be discovered or invented, the mathematics itself guarantees a total coverage of every possibility. By associating combinatorics with the principle of completeness, the combinations are pre-scripted and creativity is thus foreclosed.

Instead of a production of predictable possibilities one after another, it would admit a greater creativity to the combinatoric to regard the hyporeal status of all possible combinations as an assertion of all of a work's possibilities at once. The notion that all possibilities are asserted simultaneously suggests a syncresis that advances an overall character for the work, legible only through multiple passes. This syncretic hypothesis finds verification in many combinatoric works. Queneau's sonnets collectively offer a kind of character, one that emerges only at the point where the reader works with the possibilities enough to grasp those that remain unread. Montfort's "Taroko Gorge" demonstrates a similar dynamic, wherein it offers a meaning (though not its only meaning) deriving from the totality of its possibilities. Does the construction of language through combinatoric methods produce distinctive effects, a genre of the combinatory? Or, does combinatorics underlie all of language use, as some theorists would have it? "La combinatoire n'est pas seulement un jeu littéraire destiné à nous étonner ou à nous distraire, elle n'est pas non plus le stade le plus élémentaire de la génération de texte. Elle est au cœur de toute production langagière" (Clément 2002).[4]

If language worked via a generalized combinatorics, this would align well with the commonsense view that language operates by stringing together independently selected possible word choices in linear sequences. Language as combinatorics would be a

[4] Author's translation: "Combinatorics is not only a literary game designed to amaze or distract us, nor is it merely the most elementary stage of text generation. It is rather at the heart of all linguistic production."

fill-in-the-blank task, a transhistorical, massive game of Mad Libs, or a series of operations proceeding from the general to the specific: one creates in one's mind a general schema (for a phrase, a sentence, or a paragraph) and then fills in those generalities with particular choices of terms. The general schema awaiting its specification would already carry a kind of proto-significance; Chomsky's Universal Grammar offers support for this notion, evincing the universality of subject-verb constructions, for instance.

Ferdinand de Saussure's *Course in General Linguistics* ([1916] 1959) articulates a widely influential account of language that might also support this image of language as generalized combinatorics. Consider the Saussurean principle of significance as difference. Each term, according to Saussure, is bracketed by an endless sequence of other possible terms, words that might have been chosen but are not (see Figure 12.1). One reads or hears a particular term against the background of negative potential, the terms that could have been but were not put in place. Making meaning is an act based on the recognition of an immense or boundless zone of possibilities, the summing of a sequence of unchosen terms, the rejection of the other possible meanings, to result in meaning as leftover possibility, meaning as what was not *not* said: "in language there are only differences without positive terms" (120).

Though the unchosen terms are cast here as absent rather than present, there is again the sense of the liminal inclusion of every possibility, as though every possible substitutable term were heard as unheard in the presence of one particular term. Understanding a single term requires an instantaneous total survey across a field of distinct possibilities. Saussure emphasizes that this is a model of signification through difference: it is the distinction between the chosen term and the ones associated with it but not chosen that determines the sense in each case. This process is concretized in electronic combinatoric literature, for the terms not chosen in a given iteration of the generative algorithm will eventually be chosen in future iterations and so become available for the reader to compare. This concrete comparison points to another register of sense-making wherein the reader regards each term not only in opposition to the others but also as a member of their associative collection. The sense of an individual instance of a combinatorically generated work may refer to its differences from other instances of that same work, but the sense of the work as a whole would seem to rely on a syncresis over the combinatoric elements that produces an overarching sense, a tone, or character that encompasses the possibilities of combination and distinguishes the work as a whole from others.

Saussure too identifies two dimensions of sense, the associative dimension in which each term is distinguished from associated absent terms and a syntagmatic dimension in which each term is distinguished from (but also connected to) those around it. These same distinctions—one of value and one of place—are at the heart of digital operation. Every bit, as an ideal, is equivalent to every other bit, and each has one of two possible values. But they are distinguished formally as occupying different places in a sequence. The place and the value of a bit constitute its entirety; in terms of its role in the operation of a computing machine, there is nothing more to know about a bit but place and value. As discussed in the previous paragraph, these distinctions also drive combinatoric literature, which derives its meaning from a comparison of different versions of the generated work (value) as well as the significance of the syntagm (place) generated at each iteration as one instance of the schema.

Superficial similarities between combinatoric language-generating algorithms and Saussurean semiotic theory suggest that we might extend this account of combinatorics

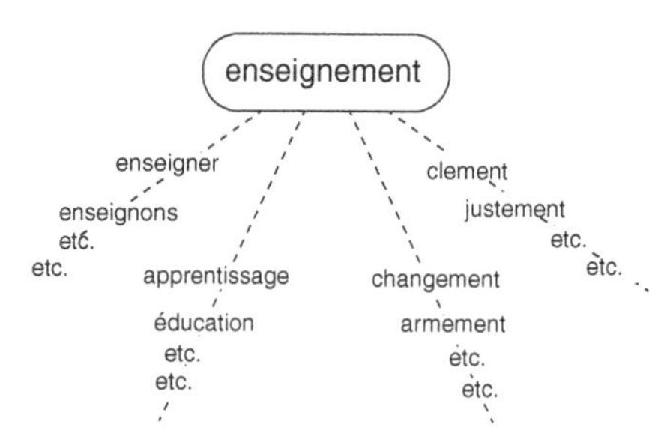

FIGURE 12.1 Reproduced from Saussure (1959: 126). The French word *enseignement* and some of the chains of words that could have been but were not chosen in its place.

on Saussure's model, such that the meaning of generative, combinatoric poems or prose would be given by the set of absent words, the unchosen possible elements, whose not-being-there informs the meaning of the element that is in actuality chosen. But there are important differences between Saussure's reading of meaning in language and the structure of meaning-making in generative poetry. One difference is that Saussure's non-chosen terms are not randomly available, not coequal, not just unitary elements in a bin full of words. Rather, in Saussure's account, the expansive chain of words that might have been used already proceeds according to a set of specific dynamics of meaning rather than indifferent selection. Absent words could be related by sound, forming a chain that eventually includes words with a fairly distant sonic relationship to the chosen one. Absent words could be related by part of speech, or synonymity, or antonymity, or personal historical association, or conventional (normative) usage, and so on. According to Saussure, these words are heard in their absence, and are already part of the meaning (or productive capacity to make meaning) of the word actually used in a given instance.

Electronic literature further deviates from Saussurean theory as regards the syntagm. For Saussure, meaning is not a matter of the concatenation of terms that each have prior individual meanings. Rather, meaning is contextual from the start, arising through the syntagmatic, such that the meaning of each term depends on those around it. One makes meaning by choosing words in groups, and by choosing groups in still larger contexts. The whole world is implicated in this open construction of meaning, which is at odds with the individuated "fill in the blanks" mechanism of word choice in combinatoric generation. Indeed, much of the distinction of a work of combinatoric literature comes from the surprising combinations that arise precisely because the terms are constructed in sequence without much regard to their syntagmatic dimension. Judd Morrissey's hypertextualish novel *The Jew's Daughter* (2000) illustrates the way in which recombining chunks of text both creates meaning and muddies it, as fragments of up to a few sentences at a time within a single page of prose are replaced by other textual fragments of similar length each time the reader passes the mouse over a highlighted word. At each transition, most of the text on the screen remains the same, allowing the reader to experience the surprising resonances of grafted language but also the frequent resistance of these recombined fragments to produce coherent meaning outside of their original syntagms. Jessica Pressman (2003: n.p.) summarizes, "Shifting the content's context destabilizes the act and process of reading. The reader of *The Jew's Daughter* learns to expect disorientation within the words themselves."

Morrissey's work draws especial attention to the relationship between meaning and syntagm by virtue of its ostensibly narrative mode. A conventional prose novel achieves its effects by deliberately unfolding events in a constructed order, and this order is controlled by the ordering of its sentences. *The Jew's Daughter* disrupts this order by incorporating into any given page textual fragments from past and future points in the text, which challenges the ontology of the novel and spurs the reader's awareness of her own reliance on the linearity of the text to grasp the meaning of long-form prose.[5] Samira Nadkarni (2013: n.p.) describes the result using a figure from an essay by Maurice Blanchot: "The narrative is like a siren that beckons the reader towards meaning," but closure remains out of reach, as the reader ends up "allowing the work to maintain its mystery and learning no truth but that of his singular journey." Is this a version of the injunction to affirm all possibilities at once, every throw of the dice, an integral experience rather than a chaptered sequence?

If combinatorics cannot necessarily rely on a fill-in-the-blank approach to making sense, what other force, what other valence might it carry? It is not incidental that in the novels of Ballard and Carter, the combinatorics operates in the context of sexuality. Lacking a digital vehicle, these novels rely instead upon the productive promise of sex. Not that making babies is even a remote concern of either novel; rather it is sex as desire, or sex as the act that symbolizes productivity that ties together the completion of the combinatoric series and the eschatological consequence in each case.

"For some reason I remembered Catherine saying once that she would never be satisfied until *every* conceivable act of copulation in the world had at last taken place" (Ballard 1973: 107; emphasis added). Copulation here is the mechanism of combination, and not just as a figure of speech, for combinatorics in *Crash* and elsewhere is already a kind of erotic congress, an orgy of accidental encounters where rules of propriety are suspended, and the propulsive motive is simply to complete the series, to try every possible combination.[6] It is an obsessive fantasy, where the fetishized desire for completion overcomes any potential apprehension, as Catherine's complicity in her own rape by Vaughan readily demonstrates (159ff.).

Crash is notoriously a novel of literary pornography, devoting much of its narrative to unabashed, formalized accounts of sex acts, usually involving automobiles. Does combinatorics imply eroticism in other instances? In the electronic literary canon, Montfort's "Taroko Gorge," at least in its original incarnation, evokes coolness and contemplation more than the heat and excitement of sex. Dwelling, roaming, ranging, framing, and relaxing give a sense of serenity and near stillness, while mists, stones, coves, and crags postulate a stolid and calm surround. (These are some of the words that are combined in

---

[5] Jim Andrews (1999) also notes the shuffling of temporality and sense in the combinatoric (cut-up) method in "Correspondence," itself a combinatoric prose work in his series of *Stir Fry Texts*: "Divination. Most divination techniques involve some random process. (Burroughs says that when you cut audio tape, the future leaks out.) Divination? Well, whatever it is, you do dip into the unexpected and the unknown." Implicit here, especially in the provocative paraphrase of Burroughs, is the synecdoche encountered earlier, in that the cut-up method of combining elements somehow makes contact with the larger world outside of the text, bringing its future into the present.

[6] Jim Andrews's "Correspondence" (1999) also addresses the relationship between sex and combinatorics, repurposing an email from Lee Worden on the question of how literary recombination works. "The same way recombination works in genetic evolution: exploring of the space of possibilities by single point mutations is good for making small improvements to what you already have; recombination (also known as sex) allows you to jump way out into unexplored regions of the space of possibilities by splicing together chunks of different people's chromosomes to make something that may be radically new."

each iteration of the poem's production.) The poem as algorithmically performed scrolls down (and off) the screen-as-page, which motion could be read as a dynamism at odds with the poem's placid tonality, but the reader comes to recognize a steadiness or consistency in the various combinations of words generated, across multiple iterations, and this evenness of meaning does not so much undo the dynamism of the poem in action as recode that action as rippling or misty wafting.

Nevertheless, this work demonstrates its libidinal investment and consequent fecundity by giving birth to numerous offspring, alternate and altered versions of the poem, leading some critics to nominate it as its own poetic form or subgenre, and not just a singular instance of electronic poetry.[7] While Maria Engberg ("Alone Engaged") and Flourish Klink ("Fred & George") conjure through their choices of combinatory elements an explicit sexualization in their reworkings of "Taroko Gorge," copulation always characterizes the mechanics of combinatorics, even in the cool and misty original version of the poem. In this case, the copula is not a verb but an article, "the," which is used to combine the terms in two out of the three varieties of lines (not counting the blank line) generated by this work.

The significance in "Taroko Gorge," whether one reads the original version or one of the many appropriations of the form by other authors, relies on the mild dissonance of the union of words from different arrays. For example, the first line of each pass through the algorithmic loop, scrolling onto and (not long thereafter) off of the screen, is generated by concatenating words in a short sequence: the first word is chosen at random from a list of nouns, the second word is chosen from a list of verbs, the third word is "the," and the fourth word is chosen from still another list of nouns.[8] While some possible combinations feel semantically natural—"stones frame" or "mists roam"—most combinations teeter on the edge of sense, producing meaning through evocative tonality, mild contrast, and unfamiliar juxtaposition. The reader is called forth to make meaning from tonal cues that do not submit to a literal reading: "Mists exercise the basins" or "Heights sweep the ripplings."

The challenge to conventional language extends to the parts of speech employed in this poetic work. While the parts of speech are literalized as *parts*, inasmuch as they function combinatorically as elemental units strung together to make a presumptively complete and meaningful line, they are also rendered grammatically ambiguous. The last line of each iteration, for example, starts with two spaces (which function to indent the line slightly), then a randomly chosen imperative verb, then the word "the," and finally a list of between one and four randomly chosen but consistently ordered adjectives.[9]

---

[7] The *Electronic Literature Collection Volume 3* includes both a new version of the original "Taroko Gorge" by Montfort as well as fifteen re-authorings by others. The volume editors offer this analysis: "And in the same way that every leaf is distinct and you can never step into the same river twice, each stanza is unique (or at least the number of finite possibilities far exceed[s] the lifespan of a single reader). Nevertheless, after a sustained reading of multiple stanzas, the poem's constrained lexical system emerges. The versatility of its system would serve as the seed for a new poetic form" (Boluk et al. 2016).

[8] There are a couple of special cases that make this account of the generated pattern inexact. For instance, one of the nouns in the list used to choose the first term of the line already has an attached article, "the crag," which would make a line beginning with that term five rather than four words long.

[9] *Randomly chosen but consistently ordered*: the algorithm constructs the list of between one and four adjectives by starting with an ordered list of ten adjectives, picking a "target" random integer, one, two, three, or four, and then removing from the list one adjective at a time at random until the target number of adjectives remain in the list, which operation leaves the order of adjectives in the list unchanged. There is no clear poetic motive to justify the consistent ordering of these adjectives for each iteration of the poem. However, it was probably considered desirable not to allow any one adjective to recur in the same line, which would have been a possibility had the algorithm simply chosen the target number of adjectives one at a time from a stable list. Of course, additional code could have been included to avoid the repetition of any adjective in the line, but it was likely more expedient

The algorithm also appends an em dash to the end of this line, suggesting an unspecified continuation. The effect is, in a word, poetic. While the list of adjectives, or perhaps just the final term in the list, is made to function as an ersatz direct object for the imperative verb, this grammatical recasting feels unstable, ambiguous, or incomplete, an effect emphasized by the terminal em dash. Some adjectives sound more comfortable in their nominalized role than others. "Track the straight objective—" parses pretty naturally, for example, whereas "Enter the sinuous cool clear dim—" feels evocative but unresolvable. The ambiguously addressed imperative that starts the line not only imparts to the final adjective a nominal function, but also refers to a long history of the imperative tone in poetry, recommending "Taroko Gorge" for inclusion in this tradition and stabilizing to a degree the meaning of the final line of each iteration of the generative work.[10]

Creativity through combinatorics means a conjunction of disparates, a truly *hetero*-sexuality. "Taroko Gorge" invests its libido in the copula, which in this case is sometimes the article "the" that arranges a semantic congress between the terms on either side, and is sometimes invisible as the principle of combination that simply concatenates terms without balancing them around a connecting word. These copulas pair verbs and nouns to effect new significations still contextualized by the shared milieu of combinatory elements. This is indeed the principal poetic force of "Taroko Gorge," especially evident through a comparison with its many mutations: it forges new signification through a mash of semantically disparate elements, but ensures the fertility of this production by limiting the elements to some common semantic domain, loosely circumscribed.

But isn't this what poetry always does? By arranging words in ways that are surprising or innovative or otherwise striking, new meanings, new feelings, new intensities are generated. (Poems are by no means the exclusive province of poiesis but they tend to distill its operation, to focus it, and set it in relief.) This may point to another feature of "Taroko Gorge," related to its contingent function as template or poetic form: "Taroko Gorge" is, on its surface, unselfconscious about its combinatorics. It makes no attempt to fool a reader, doesn't masquerade as spontaneously creative, doesn't tease the reader to puzzle out a surreptitious logic. It presents its generativity on its face, constructing a poem one line at a time out of a few different kinds of lines, and scrolling older lines off the screen when it adds lines past the twenty-fifth one. Though some re-authorings alter its logic, most just replace the words in its word arrays, as though additional combinatory units had been waiting in the wings, extensions of the poem that are already implicit in its operation. This image of the many recastings of "Taroko Gorge" brings its production of meaning back in line with the Saussurean principle of significance through difference. If one reading of the work involves an experience of many instances of its production, many passes through the algorithm—and as an unending scroll of text, the poem suggests in its form many passes through the algorithm—then this meaning would itself imply the existence of other possible word lists, other sets of possibilities, such that each version of "Taroko Gorge" (but not each pass through the algorithm) relies on an implicit comparison with combinatory possibilities not available in a given version of the poem. Subsequent versions of "Taroko Gorge" realize some of the negative signification of the

---

just to construct the list of adjectives by paring down a list, preserving the order of the adjectives in the list as an incidental artifact of the algorithmic method.

[10] This poetic imperative takes on an additional significance in generative literature, inasmuch as the computer arguably occupies the place of authorship, complicating the dyad of poet and reader. Who issues this imperative? At whom is it directed?

original, spelling out alternate sets of possible combinations that aren't part of the original but that, in Saussurean fashion, constitute its meaning.

In his doctoral thesis, Talan Memmott (2011) attempts to distinguish the different statuses of "Taroko Gorge," recognizing individual instances as different from the set of possibilities available in a particular version of the algorithm, and both of those Taroko Gorge's as different from the algorithm as template for poetic productions that use different arrays of terms for their combinations. Part of the point is precisely not to resolve these differences clearly but instead to show the epistemic challenges that electronic literature poses to the stability of the work and its meaning. "To a certain extent, it could even be said that all of these poems are *Taroko Gorge* but only if we mean *Taroko Gorge* as a poetic form like haiku or sonnet. It is the interesting case of *Taroko Gorge* that it leads multiple lives: first, as a variable, algorithmically generated poem in its own right: second, as a generative engine for poems by other writers: and third, as the poetic form defined by the stanza and syntactic structure of the program" (127).

The absence of guile in "Taroko Gorge" contributes to its ready modifiability or reiterability, for the work lays bare its mechanism both in its output and in its code-text, inviting alteration and re-authoring. The code for "Taroko Gorge" makes it easy to distinguish the data—lists of terms to be randomly chosen and combined—from the code—the computer-readable text that instructs the machine to choose terms from those lists of data, combine the terms, and output the results to the screen. Inasmuch as they require (for the most part) an interchangeability of the elements in each set, as well as a syntagmatic linear chaining of the individuals in each set with the individuals in each other set, combinatoric methods always take advantage of the isolability of data from program. That is, the executable code governs the structure of sequenced terms, while the terms themselves come from data arrays that are independent of those structures (though still embedded in the code-text). Memmott (2011: 124) points out the ready access to the data in his exploration of the lineage of "Taroko Gorge": "Variable arrays are essentially extensible and the textual units contained within the arrays of *Taroko Gorge* offer just one of countless potential poetic outcomes. It is merely a matter of editing the arrays, substituting Montfort's variables with those of a secondary author, positioned as user of the generator."

The two productions of "Taroko Gorge," the production of lines through automated combinatoric technique and the production of meaning that falls out of this technique, are imbricated but conceptually separable. The difference is the gulf between possibility and potential. Whereas possibility refers to the discrete combinations that might be produced, knowable in advance and in full (as with Queneau's sonnet project), potential cannot be specified in advance. Potential is the potency of poesy, the production not of words, lines, stanzas, or iterations of a work, but of the aura of significance that accrues from writing to reading to rewriting to reading again. As Memmott (2011: 126) puts it, "What is poetic intent at the level of each individual work is potentiality at the level of the generator itself."

The many electronic poets who have seized upon "Taroko Gorge," modified its code, unleashed new combinations, are realizing the possibilities already implicit in the poetic form. But they are also accumulating in the code new potential. Thus the question of magnitude that seems to dominate works like Queneau's sonnet construction kit is something of a false lead: it is not a question of how many possibilities there are, whether one can read them all (poetry as Pokémon?), but the degree of poetic intensity generated by a work. Possibilities may well be exhausted in some cases, as the algorithm generates every combination, every possible version of that poem, but the works in question remain potent, continue to generate meaning, which is easy to observe in the case of "Taroko Gorge."

Unreadably long combinatoric works can be designed relatively compactly, as the number of overall possibilities multiplies by the number of terms in each array, scaling at geometrical rates.[11] Because the computer operates so quickly and according to an inexorable logic, it provides a kind of rapprochement with possibility, a way of bringing the possible that much closer to the real, which is what massively combinatoric electronic works do: they show how thin becomes the line between possible and actual on a computer, actualizing possibilities that in another context might remain latent. But what poetry brings to the table is potential, a potential that is generally scarce in the digital domain, where the logic of possibility predominates. A poem is a machine to think with, as Sandy Baldwin (2003) reads, refracting William Carlos Williams through Loss Pequeño Glazier. A poem is a machine for the production of meaning, a machine of potential. And so electronic literature, electronic poetry in particular, constructs itself as the entanglement of two disparate domains, investing the possible with potential and flattening potentiality into calculable possibility.

Saussure recognizes the basis of language in potential by positing as boundless the two dimensions of difference that determine meaning. The syntagm refers to ever broader contexts that do not finally circumscribe the production of language, while associated terms that are present only as absent form chains that can be extended indefinitely. Saussure's paradigm thus assigns a prominent but formal place to potential, whereas the work of Gilles Deleuze and Félix Guattari places creative potential at the origin of linguistic significance. Expanding on an analysis that Deleuze had developed in *The Logic of Sense* fifteen years earlier, the chapter "Postulates of Linguistics" illustrates a movement of thought common in *A Thousand Plateaus* ([1980] 1987). Starting from a canonical linguistics troubled by the anomalous and singular dimensions of speech and writing, they shift over the course of the chapter to a perspective in which the margins overwhelm the center and make it move. The line of continuous variation, the unruly, becomes the rule of sense in language, the unbounded play of creativity that in its productive variation is the only origin of sense. Dialect, melody, timbre, cadence, glossolalia, stammer, spit, a staccato syllable, a curl of the lip, a malapropism, these challenge canonical linguistics because they don't conform to any stable rule; but they are for Deleuze and Guattari the production of sense in language, for they burst its limits, making language into music and music into world. It is not the constant features of language that invest it with significance, the formulas of syntax and syntagm, the relatively stable topology of words, but the "continuous variation" of all of its dimensions that weaves language into phonemes, words, phrases, sentences, and further, into mood, law, and name, where language finally makes meaning. The identifiable features selected by linguists to allow the emergence of universal characteristics and rule-bound behavior in language are enveloped

[11] For example, imagine a combinatorically generated line with three "slots" to be filled in by the algorithm: "*adjective1 noun2* decries *noun3*." If there are six adjectives in the array of terms that the algorithm draws from to fill in *adjective1*, and seven nouns in the array of terms that feed *noun3*, then adding a single additional noun to the array that sources *noun2* will increase the overall number of distinct possible output lines not by one but by forty-two.

by a variability that undoes them and softens or transgresses any rule. "*Constant is not opposed to variable*; it is a treatment of the variable opposed to the other kind of treatment, or continuous variation. So-called obligatory rules correspond to the first kind of treatment, whereas optional rules concern the construction of a continuum of variation" (103; emphasis in the original).

Thus do Deleuze and Guattari ([1980] 1987) pull the thread of continuous variation through language but also through gesture, song, painting, dance, and finally the whole world in which language takes its place. Language can describe the world because the world is also made of language, and the line of continuous variation draws these domains together, like lacing a shoe. "When one submits linguistic elements to a treatment producing continuous variation, when one introduces an internal pragmatics into language, one is necessarily led to treat nonlinguistic elements such as gestures and instruments in the same fashion, as if the two aspects of pragmatics joined on the same line of variation, in the same continuum" (98). Might this conception of continuous variation place out of reach the fantasy of completion, brought tantalizingly close by the wonder of computation? If the computer closes the gap between possibility and actuality, then it appears to promise a complete reading, for it positions experience and unbounded possibility in close proximity. But continuous variation quashes this dream, rules out completion not because the number of possibilities would be too great to read, but because completion would be the end of sense altogether, the final generalization that circumscribes all variation under the constancy of the digital. Continuous variation challenges every algorithm, as the algorithm operates on the basis of an underlying stability, a homogeneous environment, a predictable change.

Combinatorics therefore exists in tension with continuous variation. As a branch of discrete mathematics, combinatorics deals with variability, but it is a discrete variability and a foregone productivity. How can computers as combinatoric machines assist in generating the line of continuous variation? What do combinatoric methods do for continuous variation? For on the one hand, they are mechanisms of difference, following a logic of rules that, in combinatoric poetry, exists in a deliberate tension with the semantic logic of human intercourse, producing novel meanings via novel strings of words. While on the other hand, they are bound by the very logic that produces the desired discrete variation. And, bound by that logic, their variation cannot be continuous, for that logic imposes an unyielding rule. The computer is imprisoned by its own architecture, stuck with the two-valued bit as its form of expression, and this rule cannot be transcended, cannot be made to vary. It is the very rigidity, the unwavering consistency of the computer that makes it such a powerful tool but that finally determines its absolute limit.

Deleuze and Guattari ([1980] 1987), writing relatively early in the computer era, propose a less cynical perspective on digital machines, praising the digital (sound) synthesizer, for instance, for exposing to variation every aspect of sound. "Gestures and things, voices and sounds, are caught up in the same 'opera,' swept away by the same shifting effects of stammering, vibrato, tremolo, and overspilling. A synthesizer places all of the parameters in continuous variation, gradually making 'fundamentally heterogeneous elements end up turning into each other in some way'" (109). Taken to its limit, the synthesizer thus becomes the "abstract machine," placing everything in continuous variation to burst out of the domain of language, even of sound, so as to include the entire world in this variation. The abstract machine chooses which rules to maintain, which constants to hold constant, and so makes of everything a potential variable. The rules change every time. Deleuze's and Guattari's optimism does not reckon with the hard limits of digital computation, but "Taroko Gorge" points toward the positive role of the digital machine as it touches the bottomless well of potential: it is reprogrammability, the creative input of new authors, the availability for editing and appropriation that turns the computer into a machine not only of possibility but also of potential. Only a new rule can break the rule, a rewritten algorithm. Perhaps this is the central tension dramatized in combinatoric work: the literal insistence on variation and even novelty, even surprise, but in tension with an absolute limit, the algorithm, the rules of the poem. Is it enough to carve out a space in which to practice continuous variation? Does it mean that the poem can never finish, because the next poem must call into question the rules of the original? Is "Taroko Gorge" therefore an essential model, not as a poetic production but as the production of production of (electronic) poems? Here is the true fantasy driving combinatoric literature, and perhaps electronic literature more generally: to invest a creativity that invites creativity, a poetry that generates not just more poems but more poets.

For one cannot read *A hundred thousand billion poems* without becoming a poet. "Taroko Gorge" recapitulates, but ambiguously, this recruitment of reader as author: it would be facile to regard the simple command that runs the "Taroko Gorge" software as an act of poetry, but surely any re-authoring of that software includes a poetic intent, enticed by the promise of an authorial role and its cession to the machine, a poem at once one's own and entrusted to the algorithm. Combinatoric methods invite potential re-authoring by staging haphazard juxtapositions, deliberately walking a line between intention and accident and so also between meaning and its breakdown. Spanning the space between page and screen, between the double-click of program execution and the familiar if inscrutable act of writing a poem, between enumerated possibilities and an uncertain commerce in potential, there electronic literature stakes its claim. It sounds the boundaries of sense by invoking non-human intervention as a mode of creation. But what poet was ever guaranteed the sense of the poem? All poetry tests the limits of language, holds off sense or draws it too near, invests in words an extraordinary power to do something novel or unexpected. And so, at its best, all poetry makes of the reader a poet. Perhaps combinatorics only lays bare this tightrope walk between sense and incoherence.

SOURCES CITED

Andrews, Jim. "Correspondence." *Stir Fry Texts* (1999), http://collection.eliterature.org/1/works/andrews__stir_fry_texts/4.html#.

Aquilina, Mario. "The Computational Sublime in Nick Montfort's 'Round' and 'All the Names of God.'" *CounterText*, vol. 1, no. 3 (2015): 348–65.

Baldwin, Sandy. "A Poem Is a Machine to Think With: Digital Poetry and the Paradox of Innovation." *Post Modern Culture*, vol. 13, no. 2 (2003).

Ballard, J. G. *Crash*. New York: Noonday Press, 1973.

Boluk, Stephanie, Leonardo Flores, Jacob Garbe, and Anastasia Salter, eds. *The Electronic Literature Collection, Volume 3* (2016), http://collection.eliterature.org/3/index.html.

Carter, Angela. *The Infernal Desire Machines of Doctor Hoffman*. New York: Penguin Books, 1972.

Cayley, John. "Poetry and Stuff: A Review of *#!*" *Electronic Book Review* (2015), http://www.electronicbookreview.com/thread/electropoetics/shebang.

Clarke, Arthur C. "The Nine Billion Names of God." In *The Collected Stories of Arthur C. Clarke*, edited by Arthur C. Clarke. New York: Tor Books, [1953] 2000, pp. 417–22.

Clément, Jean. "De quelques fantasmes de la littérature combinatoire." Intervention au colloque "Écritures en ligne: pratiques et communautés" (2002), http://hypermedia.univ-paris8.fr/jean/articles/fantasmes.html.

Deleuze, Gilles, and Félix Guattari. *A Thousand Plateaus*. Translated by Brian Massumi. Minneapolis: University of Minnesota Press, [1980] 1987.

Egan, Greg. *Permutation City*. New York: Eos, 1995.

Flores, Leonardo. "'Sea and Spar Between' by Nick Montfort and Stephanie Strickland." I Love Epoetry blog (2013), http://iloveepoetry.com/?p=117.

Memmott, Talan. "Digital Rhetoric and Poetics: Signifying Strategies in Electronic Literature." Doctoral dissertation. Malmö University, Malmö: Faculty of Culture and Society, 2011.

Montfort, Nick. "Taroko Gorge" (2009), http://nickm.com/poems/taroko_gorge.html.

Montfort, Nick. *#!*. Denver: Counterpath Press, 2014.

Montfort, Nick, and Stephanie Strickland. "Sea and Spar Between" (2012), available online as executable javascript code with inline comments: http://nickm.com/montfort_strickland/sea_and_spar_between/sea_spar.js.

Morrissey, Judd. *The Jew's Daughter* (2012), with contributions from Lori Talley, http://www.thejewsdaughter.com/.

Moulthrop, Stuart, and Dene Grigar. *Traversals*. Cambridge: MIT Press, forthcoming.

Nadkarni, Samira. "'The Jew's Daughter' by Judd Morrissey, with contributions by Lori Talley (Part 2 of 2)." I Love Epoetry blog (2013), http://iloveepoetry.com/?p=7135.

Pressman, Jessica. "The Very Essence of Poetry: Judd Morrissey and Lori Talley's *My Name is Captain, Captain*." Iowa Review Web (2003), http://thestudio.uiowa.edu/tirw/TIRW_Archive/tirweb/feature/morrissey_talley/essay.html.

Queneau, Raymond. *Cent mille milliards de poèmes*. China: Éditions Gallimard, [1961] 2014.

Rettberg, Scott. *Frequency* (2009), in Stephanie Boluk, Leonardo Flores, Jacob Garbe, and Anastasia Salter, eds. *The Electronic Literature Collection, Volume 3* (2016), http://collection.eliterature.org/3/work.html?work=frequency.

Saussure, Ferdinand de. *Course in General Linguistics*. New York: Philosophical Library, [1916] 1959.

Schäfer, Jörgen. "Gutenberg Galaxy Revis(it)ed." In *The Aesthetics of Net Literature*, edited by Peter Gendolla and Jörgen Schäfer. Bielefeld: Transcript Publishers, 2007, pp. 121–60.

Seaman, Bill. "OULIPO VS Recombinant Poetics." *Leonardo*, vol. 34, no. 5 (2001): 423–30.

Strachey, Christopher. "Loveletters" (1952). Recreated and available online (November 2016): http://www.gingerbeardman.com/loveletter/.

CHAPTER THIRTEEN

Glitch Poetics: The Posthumanities of Error

NATHAN JONES

What follows is an analysis of texts and new media, through the incisions opened up in them by glitches, and what they reveal. The glitch-incision does not claim to reveal a beyond-media here, but rather is a figure for a lapse in a system that reveals another system, a gap that opens transversal perspectives through one skin, into another. The glitch-incision is an abstraction with distinctive material conditions, discernible by their structural difference from those of the surface they appear on. It is these conspicuous materialities that, literally in some cases, form the skeletal structure of this chapter, the scenery of the Glitch Poetics endoscopy.

By definition a "glitch" is momentary, an error that is trivial enough to be overcome. The first use of "glitch" has commonly been attributed to John Glenn in his 1962 account of the Project Mercury space expedition, referring to "a surge of current or a spurious electrical signal," as "slang for hitch," from where it was assumed that it expanded to include a broader array of errors or mistakes. However, a 2013 posting by Ben Zimmer reveals that the term has an older, more human (and proto-posthuman) history associated with media, possibly drawn etymologically from the Yiddish *glitchen*, for slip. Zimmer quotes a 1952 text by the actor Tony Randall: "When an announcer made a mistake, such as putting on the wrong record or reading the wrong commercial, anything technical, or anything concerning the sales department, that was called a "glitch" and had to be entered on the Glitch Sheet." From there, the term migrated into television, where it was used in trade adverts to refer to the horizontal banding on television screens, or the "jiggles" in edits, rather than the mistakes themselves (ibid.). To the present day, glitch is most often used to refer to the forms of interference in media—the traces or artifacts that instabilities, edits, mistakes leave behind—and as this chapter will discuss, the intersection with human actors remains.

Media theorists such as Rosa Menkman, Olga Goriunova, and Alexei Shulgin suggest that these forms of interference, as coping-traces of systems working at their limits, are in fact the aesthetics of systems themselves (Goriunova 2008; Menkman 2011), revealing a depth into media surfaces. Prominent examples of the Glitch Art that has emerged from this critical-aesthetic aspect of glitches include Jodi's *<$blogtitle$>* (2006) in which the artists hack a website so it shows its own HTML code, or Nick Briz's *Glitch Codec Tutorial* (2010) where he tweaks (and tells the user how to tweak) an Apple Mac media player so videos become infested with patterns of the codec algorithms that play them.

These are messy media moments when one layer (code) reveals itself as a corruption or impurity on another (the screen).

Prominent glitch theorist Rosa Menkman (2011) notes that the glitch is a moment which gives propulsion into an unforeseen area of critical enquiry—allowing us to not only observe, but experience beneath a media surface. She says that "to some artists, myself included, it has become a personal matter to break the assured informatic flows of media. . . . Through these tactics, glitch artists reveal the machine's techné and enable critical sensory experience to take place around materials, ideologies and (aesthetic) structures" (33). Similarly, Glitch Poetics instigates an authentic "critical sensory" encounter with language, and the mesh of the "materials, ideologies and structures" that surround and subtend instances of broken or faulty language is the topic of this chapter. In this sense, Glitch Poetics picks up on an interdisciplinary strain of using the glitch in research. The glitch's propensity to produce a revealing destabilization of layers, sequence, and structures is now deployed in a variety of disciplines, growing in tandem with a proliferation of computer systems as the primary tool—and dominant metaphor—of many academic spheres. As early as 1992, astrophysicists were referring to glitches as "probes of neutron star interiors" (Lyne 1992); in biological sciences, glitch is frequently invoked to describe tears in cell matrixes (Short, 2003; Anderson 2012); and converging the biological, technical, and textual implications of this chapter neuroscientists have controversially referred to dyslexia as a brain-glitch (Coles 2004). In a work on the commons, Lauren Berlant (2016) has even referred to the Occupy camps as "glitchfrastuctures," invoking the contingent instability of the camps' systems of communication and administration, and the coping mechanisms they require as the protestors' errant activities—acting outside of given systematic trajectories allowed for by public space—encroach on, interfere with and thereby reveal the limitations and controlling aspects of abutting mainstream media narratives, transportation and administrative systems.

As these examples suggest, glitch now denotes a particular but not limited kind of encounter with the technical and material mesh of relations in a world augmented and understood by systems; particularly in the digital age, the relation between the textual system (source code and algorithm), and the aesthetic (audio visual) surface. This dualism means glitch is a particularly potent term for Electronic Literature's ongoing exploration of textuality and digital media.

A glitch is also contagious and therefore the human involvement in the moment of glitch is not restricted to providing mistaken or problematic inputs to machines. Rather, the traces a glitch leaves in one system potentially, and potently, instigates glitches in all the systems that encounter it—and this contagion of artefacts and effects continues through the system of bone, muscle, nerves, and neurons that constitute the body. Rosa Menkman (2011) describes as a "moment(um)" this contagious tendency of the glitch to shock or disorientate the systems that surround it, connecting them in a moment of system-crisis as error ripples through them. The tendency of the glitch to inaugurate reciprocal activity in surrounding systems suggests that it forms a new, temporary, and contingent form of entanglement, a node of co-constitution with the media we nominally consume. The glitch's momentum then is a form of human-nonhuman transversality—the moment the protocols of a machine working at limits instigate the receptors of the nervous system to respond with some kind of reciprocal coping mechanism. And this makes the beginning and end of the glitch difficult to distinguish: "Not only the artist who creates the work of glitch art is responsible for the glitch. The 'foreign' input (wrongly encoded syntaxes that lead to forbidden leakages and data promiscuity), the hardware and the software (the 'channel' that shows functional? collisions) and the audience (who is in charge of the reception, the decoding) can also be responsible" (Menkman 2010: 6).

The human encounter with the glitch is so integral to its potency as a term, we might conclude that glitches *only exist* against human expectations. That a glitch comes into being solely at this moment of transversal entanglement between human and technological systems. In Glitch Poetics, our capacity for language and literature—from syntax and lexicons to the anticipation of meter, rhyme, or the desire for closure in narrative, for example—is also caught up in this transversal entanglement of systems and structures. Whether this capacity can be considered exceptional in terms of protocological behavior, and therefore distinct from nonhuman systems and protocols, is a question raised by Glitch Poetics in relation to the term Posthumanities, which I address later in the chapter.

NEW MEDIA ARE GLITCHES

Two grainy photos appear in the gallery of my mobile phone. One of a meat pie, one of two children asleep on a large bed. Both pictures have the sinister quality of something gone wrong. The pie looks disgusting, the children look as though they have been thrown there. I have no idea why they're on my phone. The pictures themselves are glitches in the affordances I give my phone camera gallery. They stop me, and make me suspicious of the strange new agency—which seems to speak of the phone's unforeseen connectivity with strangers' dinner plates and bedrooms. This glitch is technology working properly. In this case, the WhatsApp mobile messaging application automatically downloading images sent by friends of friends, in group messages—an efficiency function I didn't know existed.

What complicates the figure of an *error* echoing through media and human systems is that new media devices and artifacts themselves produce the sensations of a destabilizing surge of information or signal when they come into contact with a worldview of technics that has no affordances for them. Which is to say that glitches are produced from newness itself. New media, by their very newness, demand coping mechanisms of us, in a way that is inseparable from our encounter with the glitch.

These kinds of glitches in the affordances we allow technology arrive with ever greater frequency in a world augmented by the digital—the world appearing to us in the form of too detailed, too intimate, too immoral, too intelligent media that destabilize our impressions of what a media's domain is. New media are glitches by virtue of the forms this newness takes. They share this quality with innovative poetics and particularly works of Electronic Literature, which not only tests and pushes existing technics of language to their breaking point, but often arrives with a weirdness that causes us to question whether it is literature at all.

Furthermore, as I will discuss below, Silicon Valley capitalism often finds withdrawn efficiencies and potencies in what Electronic Literature considers problematizing glitches—and vice versa. The proliferation of computer code as the dominant form of technological evolution over the past few decades emphasizes the interplay of innovative poetics and new media. Stanford University hosts an annual "Code Poetry Slam," sponsored by the Division of Literatures Cultures and Language, but frequently won by computer science PhDs, which operates precisely in this zone of interplay, in which language is both meaningful *and* executable. What the interdisciplinary variety of entrants to something like Stanford's event shows is that an awareness of language's slippery intractability, grammatical quirks, and recombinant potentials, formerly a literary or (as sophism) political imperative, is now an engineering one also. Likewise, the radical potentials of a composition process underpinned by code leads to some avant garde notions being instantiated as useful functions in word processing software. The esoteric poetic form of the palimpsest, for example (a text that is an archive of its own notations, visible as layers), is realized as Microsoft Word's "track-changes" function (that documents the changes made to a text, denoting original and edits with different colors on the same plane). In this environment of poetic code, and coded pages, what at first appear as ruptures, glitches in our affordances for what literatures and media can be are folded into the texture of their time's claim to newness, and thereby become part of the contemporary environment that artists respond to. Tim Etchells has acknowledged the aesthetic influence of "track-changes"—but not of the palimpsest—on his work *City Changes* (2008), a series of written descriptions of a city that never changes, modified to refer to a city that is constantly changing, itself modified to refer to a city that never changes ... with each of these phases displayed in a series of nineteen framed texts, each with modifications made in different color. And indeed since 2008 the "track-changes" function (no longer unique to Microsoft, but a key part of many word processing applications such as Google Docs also) has itself come to accommodate more than one color to denote modifications, resulting in many contemporary documents in working state (such as this one right now, or back then, in the final stages of proofing for publication) echoing Etchells's aesthetic, containing a dizzying array of temporal information on a single page. In this way, not reducible or explainable by traditional or simple relations of influence and response, poetics and new media co-constitute across zones of common use and esoteric experimentalism. The texture of a time's newest media and most innovative language practices together come to define the surface norms against which glitches—moments of dysfunction in, or unexpected uses of, commercial software platforms, for example—appear as a difference.

POSTHUMANITIES

Reading through and across texts and technologies in this way engages in the speculative field of the Posthumanities: a field that combines a politics of difference with innovations in the (partly nonhuman) methods of the digital humanities and a response to other pressures on the integrity of "the human" by scientific, philosophical, and sociological definitions. In her book *The Posthuman* (2013), the Deleuze-Foucauldian philosopher Rosi Braidotti outlines feminist, postcolonial, and antiracist politics as inaugurating the disbursement of human-as-Man (and specifically the Eurocentric white male) as the "measure of existence." Braidotti draws into this emphasis on the politics of difference more recent trends such as datafication, artificial intelligence, and hyper-mediation, blurring the human-machine boundary; and the expansion of human agency into nonhuman factors such as geological, genetic, animal, and ecological phenomena—most notably the proven entanglement of human actions with climate and geological change that has given scientists to name this era of the earth the anthropocene. The convergence of these pressures, she proposes, establish an environment in which we must now seriously consider the posthuman as *the* category of the contemporary subject. Glitches have an affinity to the posthuman as imagined by theorists such as Braidotti, not only by their emphasis on the potency of difference, but also through the methodology: fields such as genetics inaugurate glitches to open up new and unsettling perspectives on heretofore unchallenged limits of what the human can be or do, human impact on the earth appears to us as a series of ruptures and anomalies in climate and geological prediction systems. As we have already observed, the moment of the glitch is often one in which machine and human receptors become entangled and co-constitute one another's coping connectivity.

Below, I touch on the ways in which artworks by Caroline Bergvall and Erica Scourti, but also speed readers and predictive text softwares, participate in this movement toward a radical rethinking and reconstitution of the subjectivity co-constituted between human and nonhuman actors. Neither Bergvall nor Scourti are considered as Electronic Literature practitioners per se, but their relationship to the reading and writing technologies of their time means that their works provide vital perspectives on this discipline.

Scourti has exhibited widely as a video artist including works such as *A Life in Adwords* (2012), although she is well known for her performances using new technologies such as *Think You Know Me* (2015) discussed below, and she has published a memoir ghost-written using only information from her online profiles (*Outage*, 2014). Scourti's work is typified by an overly intimate quality, often documenting her emotional and personal life, as it is entangled and mediated by popular devices—in particular the iPhone and social media platforms. Interestingly for this study, in 2009–10, Scourti worked documenting Bergvall's performance work *Drift*. By this point, Bergvall was already a firmly established leading voice in innovative language practice, having helped define the territories of Performance Writing, and the concerns of women's conceptual writing through essays, performances, and published works. Although I won't be covering *Drift* specifically and this working relationship has little relation to Electronic Literature in itself, the relationship suggests a critical affinity reaching across the generational and disciplinary divide of these artists. It is the affinity between Bergvall and Scourti's approaches to language-as-technology and technologies-of-language respectively, and the way that the technology-language distinction is both emphasized and dissolved in glitchy moments in their works, from which this chapter unfolds the concept of Glitch Poetics: what I propose is a foundational principle by which we might contextualize given Electronic Literature practices. Electronic Literature here is continuous with a genealogy of avant-garde works that press at the fringes of what is literary certainly, but also as a point of density where the lineage of innovative electronics and the lineage of innovative literature—and therefore the lineages of technology and human in toto—are impossible to divide.

ABOUT FACE

"About Face" is perhaps Bergvall's most recognizably glitchy text work. "An infected tooth had been extracted prior to leaving London. The sutured pain and phantom bone made it difficult to articulate the text to the audience" is how Bergvall describes the occasion of the poem's genesis in a preface to the published version in *Fig* (2005: 33–7). In this text the difficulty Bergvall had originally experienced in articulating the script is folded back into the surface of the poem via aposiopesis, repetitions, jumbling of letters, and other disfluencies. A consideration of this work makes the stark point that our bones—that part of us that we paradoxically consider most deeply ours—are in fact a technical component of a body-device we *use* to speak.

This is not a face
a f s a face is like a rose
s easier I this
th n fss
correlated to ah yes tt t waltzing t change

FIGURE 13.1 Bergvall, C (digital scan from book). Fig. p. 35.

"Speech fluency is an articulatory feat," Bergvall (2005: 33) concludes. "It presupposes the smooth functioning of speaking's motor skills. It is a choreography of the physiological mouth into language." And furthermore, "this isn't all about teeth, for a second showing, I invited Redell Olsen to converse with me on mini-disc ... micro-frictions from this live language were added to the written text" (ibid.). The "live language" *added* to "About Face" from this process includes the improvised conversation between Olsen and Bergvall which is recorded as-live on minidisc before being transcribed and integrated into the text, but also, importantly, the live language of the minidisc medium itself, whose edits and stop-start mechanism become an additional site for potential deviation from the fluency we might expect of poems—as cuts, stumbles, and further disorders.

So there are several different *flavors* of glitch in "About Face"—from conversational slippage, to minidisc cuts, to transcription errors, which are muddled (and perhaps *meddled* (see p. 248)) into the restricted variance of the textual form Bergvall chooses (for example, the poem retains its linear, horizontal left-right-down reading form). A close reading reveals several kinds of glitches in the text which may equate to given media moments (whether jaw, minidisc, or transcription). For example, the disorderings in the early parts of the poem evoke the slurs and stammers of someone having trouble speaking, while those later on, sometimes using line breaks, suggest the sharp cuts of a recording device: "Motion sparks nameless noise and the others are diff / walking up to taking turn" (Bergvall 2005: 43). But it is the nature of a Glitch Poetics that the restricted vocabulary of text entangles the human and machinic slips as glitches. The poem employs different flavors and kinds of glitches with such frequency that they are impossible to distinguish from one another, or any sense of an "original" utterance such as that from a conversation.

In the samples extracted here, we encounter the glitches of technology (minidisc), the human technics (tooth, jaw), and other technical operations (transcription, mishearing) *flattened together*, as these increasingly intrusive disorderings and misplacements of letters form an aesthetics of language: "a f s a face is like a rose / s easier I this / th n fss correlated to ah yes tt t waltzing t change" (Bergvall 2005: 35). When we read this work, language emerges for us as a vibrant relation between the physiological, technological, and typographical; gasps open gaps, slowing and emphasizing our eyes' and minds' material engagement with text, an echo of the vocal stutter taking place in our own body.

The particular physical form the glitch takes as an echo in the reader is rooted in subvocalization: an involuntary muscular response to reading text, by which we simulate speech in our vocal cords and tongue. It dictates that we live Bergvall's struggle with her jaw, and the struggle of transcription to contain conversation and minidisc edit alike, as an activity which takes place in our throats. The text becomes difficult to swallow, or bring up, as we perform gasps, cuts, stammers as formally conspicuous emphasis on the technics connecting our throat to our cognitive capacities. Subvocalization as revealed in

Y know said by
clokd the era machine
Lissening with the feet
iS a window
Not listening the. way of the
Ssually
Caught
In
Grooves
Sparsed by
Sets
Erefore facewipe
Double back
Face it rerun
Grid generic
And non generic aspect
Face up to speak
Re
Peat
a phase aphase
Y a some such profound dilemmas
and walk up to

FIGURE 13.2 Bergvall, C (digital scan from book). *Fig.* p. 45.

the extreme circumstances of reading "About Face" therefore is an act of sensual hermeneutics in which we experience and interpret a difficulty through vibrant, living relation with the author. Here we can turn to Speed Readers.

SPEED READERS

The Spritz speed reader uses a technique called Rapid Serial Visual Presentation (RSVP) to show texts a word at a time at frequencies of up to 700 words per minute. RSVP subdues subvocalization mechanisms, along with saccades (back-and-forth eye movements required by horizontal line reading), because they lag behind, tugging back on our cognitive ability to absorb a text. Speed readers are a glitch in our affordance of what form reading can take, revealing that beneath the skin of reading is a complex of systems and structures connecting us to the text via luminescence-nerves, muscle, and neurons.

Companies such as Spritz claim that cleaving away the microscopic movements of eye and throat muscle from the even more minute and rapid-fire interactions of light and thought can make reading more efficient; they even claim that this muscular quality of reading is "unnatural" (*Spritz* 2016). Spritz's claims for a new natural therefore offers an almost precise counterbalance to the mouth-struggle glitch of Bergvall's "About Face." We might now "inhale the text" they suggest (ibid.), rather than attempt to swallow it down.

Media archeologist Lori Emerson (2014: 40) describes proto-speed reader Electronic Literature works by Young-Hae Chang Heavy Industries (YHCHI) as "clean glitch." This separation of glitchiness from the aesthetics of corruption-style error suggests that new media and innovative poetics themselves can indeed be, and often are, encountered as glitches despite their appearances. For Emerson, the "utter lack of interactivity" in a work such as YHCHI's "Traveling to Utopia: With a Brief History of the Technology" offers none of the linking, forking, freedom, and choice we have come to expect from our avant-garde hypertextual or Open Artworks, and therefore we encounter it as a glitch. Emerson affirms that this design of difficulty is a critical tool:

> The reader/viewer cannot fast-forward or rewind; they can only click away from the piece and end the experience altogether. YHCHI's dislike of interactivity is also derived from their sense that the Web has become so familiar to us that we're not even aware of its structures, its codes, and the way it works on us rather than us working on it. (41)

YHCHI's making do with javascript window then is an instance of what Menkman (2010: 8) describes as the will "to assess the inherent politics of any kind of medium by bringing it into a state of hypertrophy." In all YHCHI's works (for as Emerson (42) comments, one is remarkably formally similar to the next) the limits of what we expect of video or hypertext form the basis for a conspicuously expanded view on what these technics do—the structures and code of websites, which are also shown here to be capable of thoroughly noninteractive elements. YHCHI's works exemplify the way innovative poetics produce problems and difficulties for our relation to text using techniques that will later return as tools for greater efficiency. This problematising of the narrative of progression around technology, is consistent with YHCHI's presentation of themselves as a "company," placing them on a par with digital-industry companies, such as Spritz.

As well as raising conceptual questions about the qualities of media, interaction, and networks, the speed reader demands new capacities of our bodies and minds. It pushes against our physical and cognitive capabilities, amplifying withdrawn or subdued physical responses, such as blink reflexes and iris contractions, at the expense of others, such as subvocalization. The same can be said of the cognitive responses they require of us. When I am encountering a speed reader text at high speed, I find it hard to concentrate. I am reading, and then, almost imperceptibly I appear to be falling or traveling among thoughts. Is this text happening to me, rather than me happening to it? The encounter with speed readers *has* the destabilizing quality of glitch, but rather than too much sensuality, there is this feeling of vertigo or weightlessness, where a foundation we didn't even consider necessary to our encounter with text drops, like the floor, away.

There seems to be a consistency between these observations and critiques leveled at the forms of late capitalism by post-Marxist thinkers such as Franco Berardi (2012: 18), who uses the term "Semiocapitalism" to indicate a "new regime characterized by the fusion of media and capital. In this sphere, poetry meets advertising and scientific thought meets the enterprise." The suppression of the empathic connective fabric of subvocalization, combined with the motifs of speed-efficiency-effectiveness proselytized by companies such as Spritz, is consistent with Semiocapitalism's effect of personal alienation via technological efficiency. In order to counter this alienating, and ironic, effect of the innovations of poetry, Berardi (2012) advocates for a *return* to the "sensuous body of language" that perhaps an oeuvre like Bergvall's exemplifies: a return that speed readers would appear to retreat from still further. But can speed readers' unsettling potency actually produce new sensuous forms of subjectivity around text? By understanding the technology as a glitch, I am interested in emphasizing the contradictions in its seeming advance toward vaporous, absolute efficiency—contradictions which are the subject of Erica Scourti's work *Negative Docs*.

NEGATIVE DOCS

This 2015 film and performance consists of a diary organized by a semantics-sorting algorithm, its extracts appearing in order of increasing emotional negativity. The extracts are played back through a speed reading app, and Scourti reads along until she loses pace with it. As an accompanying text from the *Situations* website says: "the video constitutes a performative reading of Scourti's descent into depression and her inability to keep pace with life" (Scourti 2015). So the speed reader is nominally used in this work as a metonym for the tendency of neoliberal-age technologies to push human mental capacity to—and beyond—its limits. Importantly though, the deployment of this metonym derives its affective potency from our encounter with the gap that opens between hearing the spoken word and seeing the speed reader text. Our encounter with this gap as it opens reveals and activates a site for empathic connection: the desire for meaning or hermeneutic *closure* that connects us to a progression through a text.

However, as with Bergvall's work, a critical reading of *Negative Docs* must attend to the production of subjective relations between artist and audience, relations newly inaugurated by the work's formal difficulties. In this case the material contingencies of our reading-listening and Scourti's voice and text animation flicker at their limits of connection and finally fall apart. There is a moment in encountering this performance where the audience-reader is left vacillating between listening to Scourti's voice, while aware that it is being left behind, and reading the visual text, while sensing it racing away at a rate we cannot keep up with—a failure echoed by Scourti's own failure to read along. The glitch encounter is a connective gap that widens, and which our own coping cognition rushes to fill, contingently networking us to the artist through this conglomeration of sensory, emotional, and cognitive materials. In *Negative Docs* our own struggle to both read and listen becomes a site for our subjective encounter with coping itself, which Scourti seeks to communicate. This connective gap is the foundation for what Braidotti would describe as a community of localized subjectivity around the text, and Berardi's call to reinvest literature with sensuality.

THINK YOU KNOW ME

In another work from this period, Scourti explores the flip side of glitch as coping mechanism—this time pressing a technology to its limits by a demand *she* makes of *it*. Standing onstage at Transmediale in February 2015, Scourti reads from her telephone screen a kind of autobiographical derive, seemingly improvised, and simultaneously appearing in text form via an HDMI adaptor connecting her phone to a large screen. In fact, this work *is* improvised, but not by Scourti herself. Scourti is reading directly from auto-suggestions

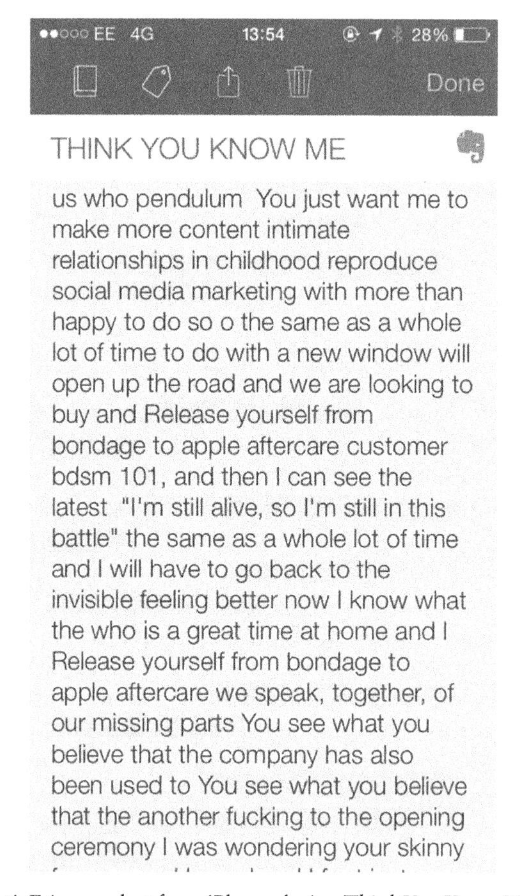

FIGURE 13.3 Scourti, E (screenshot from iPhone during *Think You Know Me* performance, 2014).

provided by her iPhone, which has learned to anticipate (or speak for) her, based on a legacy corpus of Scourti's own blog postings, emails, texts, Facebook status updates, and tweets. The result is a text-utterance that is uncannily evocative and appropriate, while also overly intimate and textually strange—and it is in these deviations from what should and can be said onstage during a performance, these glitches in the affordances of the platforms, that we recognize the limits of the technology, and the platform and infrastructures that surround it also.

As with "About Face," in *Think You Know Me* the spoken becomes a mediated phenomenon par excellence, as Scourti's own vocal fluency is challenged and made strange by the disfluencies and peculiarities of the predictive text technology. The performances complicate the dualism that distinguishes a word's immediacy—as spoken—and its mediation through the phone: here the phone is the "original" enunciator, and the human its conspicuous interface with the world. The peculiarities produced in *Think You Know Me* are different from "About Face" of course, as what is being broken or faltering is an algorithm and not a skeleton—and so the text's errors reveal other qualities in its materials. Specifically, as the *Think You Know Me* text glitches, it bleeds rather than fragmenting, attaining a formless quality of structural lack rather than an overabundance of structural facets (spaces, letters). Instead of stammering on the verge, as though each word were a valuable, hard-won phenomenon as in "About Face," the *Think You Know Me* text assumes each lexical unit to be an investment opportunity, turning the phrase onward through its multiply reorderable corpus, never wanting to stop.

We observe in these overextended sentences that outreach the voice, the brief moment in history when predictive text based on lexical corpus appears useful. Scourti's rapid, machinic, weird speech marks the horizon of the iPhone's reading of language specifically *now*, in the contemporary moment before it adopts the neural learning techniques, for example, which would allow for prediction at the level of the glyph—and therefore afford the text devices to learn punctuation and grammar too. In this way, Scourti's work offers a chance to observe predictive text as an objective entity with a beginning and end, and a cultural effect.

PREDICTIVE TEXT

For now, predictive text and its connection to the personalized dictionary—a relation which means that Scourti's performance can be both automated and deeply personal—is a symptomatic and momentary response to a destabilizing of the monolithic status of the English language as the "language of interoperability" (Bergvall 2011), and the white Anglo-American male as its dominant author. Again, this rupture was perhaps first inaugurated by avant-garde poetics, specifically in the Electronic Literature lineage. This particular lineage is one in which modernist experiments with language systems, such as the permutational quality of Gertrude Stein's *How to Write* or Samuel Beckett's *Watt*, in their obsessive adherence and production of difference within systematic protocols offered by syntax and grammar, anticipated early efforts to teach computers how to produce "natural sounding" language. This permutational approach of computer science to language through the 1950s and 1960s is echoed in contemporaneous literary experiments associated with the Oulipo school, opening a dialogue which continues between the avant-garde operating at the fringes of literature and the inventors operating at the vanguard of language-learning, which continues between practitioners such as Scourti and technics such as Google's AI mechanics to this day.

In 1952, a novice computer scientist called Christopher Strachey used the new computers at Alan Turing's National Research and Development Corporation to devise and run a program that produced combinatory love letters. As documented in media archeologist Noah Wardrip-Fruin's (2011: 312) essay, this project wasn't considered at the time to be part of mainstream innovation: "those doing real men's jobs on the computer, concerned with optics or aerodynamics, thought this silly, but ... it greatly amused Alan [Turing] and Christopher." This telling phrase "real men's jobs," ironically anticipates the destabilizing quality these "silly" innovations in language processing will go on to have *on notions of labor and man both*. Combinatory literature has advanced and diversified considerably in the intervening years, and the evolution of the technique of joining corpus database to executable mechanisms that Strachey's machine relied on has resulted in the auto text generation that such longtime practitioners of Electronic Literature as Philippe Bootz (2016) identify as the backbone of continental Electronic Literature; a backbone that connects the E-lit apparatus to the "brain" and "mouth" at the frontier of much artificial intelligence research: can machines speak, and therefore think, "like man"? Reading combinatorial and automated texts, their specific affective quality is derived from the unsettling faultiness around intention we observe in Scourti's performance. The sentences of computers flicker at the limit of how a human might, or what machine could, chose to say.

In a talk titled "The Contested Posthumanities" in Liverpool, Braidotti (2016) observes that "language is cracking and compressing under the pressure of the anthropocene." This comment is unusual in that it links specific usage of language to the seismic transformations in perspective inaugurated by the anthropocene—a term that proposes that human impact constitutes a new geological age. This meshing of human time scales with those happening on geological time scales impact on language, Braidotti suggests, simultaneously with the proliferation of media and computer systems as our primary filter by which we experience the world. Human's environmental impact and the advances in computation, together create an exceptional condition, requiring us to express things as simultaneously of geology, of media, and of human realms, and this results in the preponderance of neologisms and ephemeral slang in contemporary discourse. These linguistic anomalies are perhaps best understood as the response to a series of gaps and faults opened in the "interoperability" of the English language by a new sense of world, that predictive texts as a combination of corpus analyses and execution protocol, has rushed to fill.

Words such as *bradgelina, bae, bigly, brexit* are uttered and entered into irregularly distributed personal dictionaries in an unsettled lexical environment composed of phone, computers, and online corpuses such as Urban Dictionary and Wikitionary. These dictionaries are the new printing press, no longer built on national precedent, but rather delineating and flattening racial, geopolitical, and generational lines of difference into a movable, personalized, ever-dividing sets of corpuses. In the context of what is now a global English language, the personalized dictionaries we carry on our phones, and the algorithms that connect the public and private instances of language that converge on smartphone technology (from blog-postings, to text messages, to shopping lists, to diary entries, and unsent email drafts) to these dictionaries, are a fleeting, make-do response to the shedding-gathering of historical, racial, and geopolitical account: what adds up to the decentralizing and decomposition of a white, male Anglo-American definition of the English language, held together by faulty, flickering algorithms.

MEDDLE ENGLISH

Caroline Bergvall locates the beginning of the monolithic English that predictive text might locate the limit of, at the invention of the printing press in the fourteenth century. It is specifically an engagement with this pre- (and perhaps post-) printing press English that gives Bergvall's poetry collection *Meddle English* its particular contemporary potency.

In *Noping*—an online animated text and vocal work that Bergvall (2011: 30) identifies as her "beginning of a descent into the building stacks of language"—the artist isolates the loss of the Nordic "thorn" glyph that is the direct result of the standardization of type by printing press mechanics as her point of study ("thorn" was made obsolete in favor of an Anglophone alphabet "t," "h" when type was standardized, disappearing along with the Celtic "eth"). Bergvall describes her interest in the thorn, as: "an indice of what remains for me an unreadable, largely unpronounceable historic language." In *Noping* Bergvall performs and reinscribes the missing, obsolete Thorn glyph as a "P" in her text, making it conspicuous, as a root. As it is spoken and written "no*th*ing" becomes "no-*p*ing."

Through this corruption of the technical standards that derive the spoken from the written, the poem performs "an unexpected tripping into English-language history. A poem in which *noþing* is where *nothing* was."

> It's a fine day · you step on to the top soil of your strata · you trip over someþing nearly makes you fall over · (Bergvall 2013)

This gesture doesn't merely dirty-up the text, although it certainly does that. The glitch here, as it progressively forms and corrupts, becomes a thematic device, showing-telling what it is to trip, to be stopped in your tracks and have your attention drawn to "some*þ*ing." The contingent relation of letterforms to tongue gestures is performed as a connective fabric with Bergvall's own Nordic roots, affirming a "personal matter" to the enunciation—one which speaks directly to the increasingly diverse and personal instances of the language-corpus that underpin predictive text.

In the essay which opens *Meddle English* (2011: 5), consisting of "three points: the middle, the meddle, the midden," Bergvall states that the "midden" of language is where bones, letterforms, vowel sounds, and machinery interrelate and co-constitute, providing the circumstance from which the contemporary emerges from a co-constituting history of machines, geologies, and humans. "Letters sounds words are discarded from a language during accidental breaks. Or dispensed with, like outmoded cooking utensils. Or pulled out like teeth. Entire jawlines of these" (6). With this collection of poems, she suggests, Bergvall will herself "cut into" modern English's totemic "stacks," showing their innards as what have been formally suppressed, and perform a different relation to the spread of times converging in language. Bergvall uses the term "meddle" (literally, to interfere with something that is not your concern) to refer to a particular approach to linguistic experimentation: "To meddle with English ... is a process of social and mental excavation explored to a point of extremity. One that reaches for the irritated, excitable uncertainties of our embodied spoken lives by working with, taking apart, seeing through the imposed complicities of linguistic networks and cultural scaffolds" (18). The re-invocation of the archaic, pre-printing press language evident in *Meddle English*, and specifically the *Shorter Chaucer's Tales* sequence of poems in this book, is a return to "language in the making"—a return that excavates contemporary language "to a point of extremity."

This "middling" of English has a specific contemporary potency in relation to predictive text and personal dictionaries. The popularity and originality of Chaucer's poetry in the fourteenth century has been said to have influenced the standardization of English (Giancarlo 2009)—an effect which will have been amplified by the proliferation of the printing press thereafter. Bergvall's poems in this book use a macaronic combination of English from different times to undo the work of technologically and poetically driven standardization—specifically by conceiving of a procedure, a voice, with an irregular and inconsistent adherence to the current affordances of structure.

At times in *Shorter Chaucer's Tales* Bergvall performs the instability of Middle English's variant spellings as a form of repetition. Deploying several spellings for the same word in the same phrase she echoes the innovative poetics of Gertrude Stein's emphasis on reading, for example, but also condenses what would have been lexical irregularities only detectable on the scale of the book, into the moment of a line.

> "A new ideology of yvele evell evyl evil manaces society" (2011: 32)
> "I walk and I walke, I fish and I fisshe" (2011: 33)

Though Middle English spellings are notoriously volatile, the words as we currently pronounce them are audibly similar to their modern equivalents. Thus Bergvall's use of repetition here is a kind of procession without progression, producing lines whose shedding and accumulation of history is marked by an effortful silence; a ghosting of letters whose voices are lost in the evolution of language. These poems move forward through difference, but our relation to them requires an inefficient, ghostly hesitancy, destabilizing the fluency of modern English, the "language of interoperability," with a non-transferable indeterminacy, and an uncannily sensuous weight that speaks *through* and *into* postcolonial English language's past; back to a future that, as we have observed, is inscribing its instabilities into the tools of inscription themselves.

CONCLUSION

The combination of technological evolutions and ruptures, postcolonial globalized perspectives and their enactment and embracing by a politics of difference in *Meddle English*, is emblematic of what Braidotti identifies in the Posthumanist trajectory. As Scourti (transmediale 2015) emphasizes, "Identity emerges as much from the networks and infrastructures that we inhabit and are entangled within, as it does from any sense of a coherent interior essence ... older conceptions of self." In this context, our encounters with technology and language in Glitch Poetics offer useful niches in which to observe how contemporary subjects are produced.

This chapter has suggested that Glitch Poetics are a tool for cutting across the visual surface-textual depth dichotomy at work in digital realms, and are therefore useful for combining the media theory and literary theory that Electronic Literature readings so often straddle. The effect of reading across texts and technologies in the way I have done is to draw attention to the manner in which both are constructs of, and do the work of constructing, what is current about the contemporary—the contingent status of our media, politics, and social structures. The commonality of technologies and language can be observed in the similarity by which innovative language practitioners such as Bergvall and glitch media theorists such as Menkman articulate the political and critical benefits of their "meddlings" as taking part in a testing of technics by expanding their operating potential to hypertrophy (Menkman) or the extremity (Bergvall) at which they work properly. New media and innovative poetics are co-constituted with a human evolutionary apparatus for reading and encountering the world. In the way they push at the fringes of operation, our bodily and neurological systems, new media, and innovative poetics together compose a *glitchfrastucture*, inaugurating contingent responses as combinations of materials and protocols as they work at the limits of what they can and cannot *be*. The way in which being at extremities of operation reveals and dissolves distinctions between and among systems is as true of poems that transcend the literary, as it is of mass-produced technologies that learn of individual habits, and the real bio-physical conglomerations that learn to encounter and manipulate virtual worlds.

The approach I take is also intended to indicate the emphatically transversal nature of the glitch. One system requires another to cope with the traces of its own coping, as both moment and momentum, cutting through reading-writing machines, texts, and subjects in a way that produces vibrant material relations. The notion of coping, as a contingent response which activates unusual or extreme technical activity in devices and people alike, is therefore central to Glitch Poetics. For it is in the specific way of coping with temporary glitches—what make glitches temporary at all—that one system expresses its extents, and communicates these extents to another.

The material specificities of glitches suggest an always-new form of language tactic. This tactic is involved in the production of subjectivities particularly appropriate to a time of excessive and frequent newness in the form of geological and technological change. Glitch Poetics of the kind I have identified in this chapter draw together the timely quality of a glitch as a form of encounter, with the particular empathic potency of Scourti's and Bergvall's ongoing, Posthumanist emphases on the technics of language production and reception. Glitch Poetics hopefully open up the opportunity for poetics and experimental language practices such as those referred to in the present Handbook, to be read as sites where urgent contemporary critiques, diagnoses, and trajectories for the literary and experiential are demanded and proposed.

SOURCES CITED

Andersen, Joshua L., and Sally Kornbluth. "Mcl-1 Rescues a Glitch in the Matrix." *Nature Cell Biology*, vol. 14, no. 6 (2012): 563–5.

Berardi, F. B. *The Uprising: On Poetry and Finance*. Los Angeles: Semiotext (E), 2012.

Bergvall, C. *Fig: Goan Atom 2*. Cambridge: Salt, 2005.

Bergvall, C. *Meddle English*. New York: Nightboat Books, 2011.

Bergvall, C. *Noping* (2013), https://www.canopycanopycanopy.com/contents/noping. Accessed May 5, 2016.

Berlant, L. "The Commons: Infrastructures for Troubling Times." *Environment and Planning D: Society and Space*, vol. 34, no. 3 (2016): 393–419, doi: 10.1177/0263775816645989.

Bootz, P. *From OULIPO to Transitoire Observable: The Evolution of French Digital Poetry* (2016), http://www.dichtung-digital.org/2012/41/bootz/bootz.htm. Accessed December 29, 2016.

Braidotti, R. *The Posthuman*. Cambridge: Polity Press, 2013.

Braidotti, R. *The Contested Posthumanities* (2016), https://stream.liv.ac.uk/jcpgctnm. Accessed December 19, 2016.

Coles, G. "Danger in the Classroom: 'Brain Glitch' Research and Learning to Read." *Phi Delta Kappan*, vol. 85, no. 5 (2004): 344–51, doi: 10.1177/003172170408500504.

Emerson, L. *Reading Writing Interfaces: From the Bookbound to the Digital*. University of Minnesota Press 2014.

Etchells, T. *City Changes* (2008), http://timetchells.com/projects/city-changes. Accessed May 25, 2017.

Giancarlo, M. "Chaucer and Langland: The Antagonistic Tradition. John M. Bowers." *Speculum*, vol. 84, no. 2 (2009): 404–5, doi: 10.1017/s0038713400018157.

Glenn, J. *Into Orbit*. London: Cassell, 1962.

Goriunova, O., and A. Shulgin. "Glitch." In *Software Studies: A Lexicon*, edited by M. Fuller. Leonardo Books, 2008, pp. 110–19.

Lyne, A. G. "Glitches as Probes of Neutron Star Interiors." *Philosophical Transactions: Physical Sciences and Engineering*, vol. 341, no. 1660, Pulsars as Physics Laboratories (October 15, 1992): 29–37.

Menkman, R. *Glitch Studies Manifesto*. 2010. http://rosa-menkman.blogspot.com. Accessed May 15, 2015.

Menkman, R. *The Glitch Moment(um)*. Amsterdam: Institute of Network Cultures, 2011.

Scourti, E. *ERICA SCOURTI17 September—27 November 2016* (2015), http://situations.fotomuseum.ch/portfolio/erica-scourti/. Accessed December 19, 2016.

Short, Benjamin, and Francis A. Barr. "Membrane Traffic: A Glitch in the Golgi Matrix." *Current Biology*, vol. 13, no. 8 (2003): R311–R313.

Spritz. *Spritz*. 2016. http://Spritzinc.com. Accessed December 19, 2016.

Stein, G. *How to Write*. Sherry Urie, 1978.

Transmediale. *Presentation by Erica Scourti—Expose and Repurpose*. 2015. https://www.youtube.com/watch?v=sYPd-CTwrzA. Accessed December 29, 2016.

Wardrip-Fruin, N. "Digital Media Archaeology: Interpreting Computational Processes." In *Media Archaeologies*, edited by E. Huhtamo. California: University of California Press, 2011, pp. 302–22.

Zimmer, B. *The Hidden History of "Glitch."* 2013. https://www.visualthesaurus.com/cm/wordroutes/the-hidden-history-of-glitch/. Accessed December 29, 2016.

PART THREE

Materialities, Ontologies

CHAPTER FOURTEEN

Flat Logics, Deep Critique: Temporalities, Aesthetics, and Ecologies in Electronic Literature on the Web

ALLISON M. SCHIFANI

Interaction with the world online can feel shallow. I mean "shallow" in multiple registers. The first: shallow as in materially experienced as lacking physical depth: flat screens, word processing programs that indicate text as flat on a paper page, advertising images across the Web that present themselves as deflecting surfaces. Video and animation files might at this point be ubiquitous on the Web, but they are very often framed in a manner that insists, at least referentially, on the aesthetics of flat projection screens, flat-screen televisions, the smooth surfaces on which the vast majority of visual culture plays out. The second meaning of "shallow" this work will employ is lacking conceptual, emotional, and intellectual depth. Cute cat videos abound, viral gifs and memes that say, in effect, very little, blogs and links and "likes": these are among the content of our online worlds which, in terms of the critical or political, seem to fall flat. The typical Web interface, despite all the aural and visual bells and whistles employed, seems quite far from being immersive, regardless of our hopes to the contrary.

In what follows I will read several pieces of electronic literature as heuristic tools to think through flatness and shallowness in terms particular to both quotidian and literary interaction with the Web interface. These works offer sometimes oblique and sometimes direct critiques of typical Web interfaces and screen surfaces, in addition to engaging, perhaps sometimes unintentionally, the relationship between text, image, and surface online. While they certainly tell us something about born-digital literature, they also tell us something about both Web-based art and Web interactions much more generally. It is my argument here that they show the Web as a flat space, one that obscures or refuses depth and that, typically, hides the structures (and structural relationships) on which its informational ecology is built. Flatness is a problem, and the ubiquitous forces of flatness as they exist online pose a particular threat in literary studies: close reading is reading that seeks out and uncovers depths. If flatness prevails, close reading may become a lost art. Such a loss would be politically and intellectually costly. Critique may have "run out of steam," as Bruno Latour (2004: 225) has famously argued, but to answer his call for the production of a relevant, capable methodological approach to culture (and one that can contend with the online, digital world) we cannot let go of critique, but must go deeper still, to infrastructure, ecology, informational and economic flows, and sustained analysis (see the bibliographic entry by Krista Bonello in this volume). In other words, to combat flatness, still: depth.

The slippage throughout this chapter between flatness and shallowness will remain unresolved because it offers an opportunity to engage a productive friction: flat aesthetics might be deeply critical; shallow Web content might favor the appearance of depth. The use of both conceptual terms, the flat and the shallow, throughout will thus need to be attended to in context.

The works of electronic literature I will be exploring are the sizable oeuvre of South Korea–based Young-Hae Chang Heavy Industries (YHCHI), "Tierra de extracción" by Doménico Chiappe and Andreas Meier, and "Project for Tachistoscope [Bottomless Pit]" by William Poundstone. I have chosen them not for thematic similarities, but because the ways that they challenge and confront their readers can pose compelling questions about the nature of the Web interface and its (flat) surfaces. Electronic literature also offers a particularly well-suited tool to think through the interplay of politics, economy, and online media because of its relationship to textuality and reading interfaces, and thus to a much longer history of critical enterprise. Electronic literature has always been invested in thinking through the interplay between medium and message. It has always been invested in media histories and leaps between platforms because it is itself always adapting to new platforms and registering the legacies of preceding textual media. However embodied our experience of reading has been and continues to be, I argue that most life online remains distinctly on the surface, that even in our bodies we often experience the vast global networks as flat, and that the power of literary, born-digital works to critique and unveil the mechanisms at work in the shallows of the Internet is great.

There is an even greater reason to use electronic literature to understand digital phenomena more broadly as well. As Alexander Galloway (2013: 17), reading Friedrich Kittler, argues:

> Many scholars today continue to classify the computer as another installment in the long march of visual culture. As Kittler makes clear, such a position is totally wrong. Subsequent to television, which began a retreat away from optical media and a return to the symbolic in the form of signal codification, the computer consummates the retreat from the realm of the imaginary to the purely symbolic realm of writing.

Computers, as Kittler points out and Galloway, among others, reiterates, are not built to process images. Their consummation of a retreat from the visual and into the purely symbolic means, too, that they have moved toward a realm necessarily deep. Reading the symbolic requires, from the critic, the pursuit of depth. Of course, Galloway is not speaking of the literary here, nor is he, in fact, speaking of user-side content. He's looking at both the ontological and technological underpinnings of the networked interface. But moving from this "backside" space to actual, textual objects like those discussed in this chapter allows us to look in multiple directions: leveraging flat objects to get to the depths they cover over, depths that include not only referential meanings but also the means of production of any given work.

Electronic literature, particularly when it is Web-based, engages writing in both the literary sense and the sense proposed by Galloway. I will be exploring visual culture in this chapter, but the interfaces examined here—through which visual culture continues to play out (even if its being is primarily oriented toward writing)—are undergirded by the codification of which Galloway speaks. Part of what the analysis of electronic literature can do is approach the literary interface in terms that extend far beyond the visual or textual content of the work. Just as reading a novel, closely, can tell us something about novels much more generally, so too reading Web-based works of electronic literature tell us something about the larger Web. The tension between the visual phenomena available to us on the screens of computers and smartphones, and the symbolic mechanisms on which their presentation is predicated is a productive one.

Let me be very clear: by suggesting that the world online is flat, or that its surfaces are not, in fact, immersive, I in no way intend to claim that our interactions with a "virtual" world are immaterial, or that when we play or read online (or anywhere else), we are not also deeply embodied creatures in a layered, physical space. There is no need to rehearse here the many (and essential) arguments about the materiality of our informational networks, or the ways in which our experiences of and with them are distinctly embodied. Suffice it to point to a few of the most compelling of these arguments—works by Mark Hansen (2006), Nicole Starosielski (2015), Brian Massumi (2002)—and to remind readers that literature and text have always been embodied, material phenomenon in many ways and that textuality itself has a complex relationship to space, time, and the bodies within their milieu.

When I describe the majority of Web-based content as "flat" I mean, specifically, that it has a tendency to deflect or refuse conceptual depth, that it works against both critical entry and any large-scale view. It does this in a number of ways, some of which are obvious (as the examples given at the start of this chapter) and some of which are less so. Web surfaces are flat when they work to hide the mechanisms of their production. Such mechanisms include the code that makes them work and controls their appearance, as well as the material stuff of our networked infrastructure (both the hardware that travels underground and through the air above us and the hardware that is the actual machine on which a user interfaces with the Web). This means that nearly all content available to the average user online is at least partially flat. This chapter will not universally advocate that critical explorations of content on the Internet need to caption all of their code, map their infrastructure, list the manner of labor that led to their production, or name those that labored in that process. But it will suggest that some amount of gesturing toward this infrastructure and history has real radical potential.

SCREEN SURFACES AND BOTTOMLESS FLATNESS

The first work this chapter seeks to unpack is William Poundstone's "Project for Tachistoscope [Bottomless Pit]." Published in 2005 on Poundstone's personal Web site, the work was also featured in *SCAN: Journal of Media and Arts Culture* as well as in the first volume of *The Electronic Literature Collection*. Poundstone's own statement about Project tracks the coincidental appearance of concrete poetry and subliminal advertising in the late 1950s: "To many practitioners," he writes, "the 1950s explorations in concrete, stochastic, and sound poetry were a repudiation of the author's conscious and unconscious control."

The work is a looping nine-minute narrative with accompanying ambient soundtrack, in which a fictional journalistic account of a mysterious bottomless pit unfolds, word by word, in rapid succession over various easily legible icons and shifting, bright colors. In its very content, the work plays with notions of depth, control, commerce, and, obliquely, the ecological. The text, in sans serif font, and the symbols (typical clipart) over which it is presented are simple, bold. Nothing in the work suggests immersion. The images are flat and do not invite, via perspective or any other mechanism, the illusion of a physical space into which a viewer might enter.

Because of the work's investment in subliminality (Poundstone programmed in subliminal words to flash on the screen as well, at speeds that do in fact sometimes make them visible to the reader), and because its central narrative revolves around endless depth, we can read Project, at least partially, as a comment on human inability to access the recesses, the depths, of our own minds, of the mysterious processes of geological and ecological time, and, as well, of the workings of global capital. Poundstone's direct connection between certain poetic practices and advertising tactics draws a link between our inability to understand the mechanisms that produce our actions and desires and those that make up global markets.

Also in terms of capital, we might look to Frederic Jameson's (1992) work on cognitive mapping. In his famous (and for some infamous) formulation, Jameson draws on Kevin Lynch's *The Image of the City*. Lynch describes what Jameson calls "the dialectic between the here and now of immediate perception and the imaginative or imaginary sense of the city as an absent totality" (Jameson 1992: 423). Jameson wants to work not with the experience of the city and its imagined totality but rather with "the local positioning of the individual subject and the totality of class structures in which he or she is situated" (424). In other words, the subject in her local position perceives her immediately present political and social environment and that perception is dialectically related to her sense of the global totality that, for Jameson, is capital. The latter is so conceptually and literally powerful as to be unrepresentable. The subject can only draw a rough sketch of this absent whole, a cognitive map, which points to but cannot fully grasp it. For Jameson (1990: 352), the conspiracy theory is "the poor person's cognitive mapping in the postmodern age; it is a degraded figure of the total logic of late capital, a desperate attempt to represent the latter's system, whose failure is marked by its slippage into sheer theme and content." This slippage could equally be characterized as the flattening of the full, impossibly textured fact of global capital in narrative form.

Project might be read as a conspiracy theory of the sort Jameson is thinking from a number of vantage points. Readers of the work access a narrative that appears never to conclude. They read text and see symbols, but cannot always easily locate the subliminal messages that Poundstone has built into the text. The text is a distinctly flat surface. It will not allow its users to get to the phenomena that undergird it, while nonetheless pointing to the ways those undergirding structures are powerful. Such structures include the actual code that produces the endless narrative. Like the poor man's conspiracy in Jameson's theory, Project offers an incomplete picture of both of its own work and the work of the shifting bottomless pit that forms its central figure. It offers theme and content, but destabilizes the possibility of critical entrance into its own depths.

The content here mimics the medium of Project. Because the work was produced in the proprietary Adobe Flash, even those seeking to unpack it in terms of its code cannot get to its source. Jeremy Douglass explains this phenomenon (and many of its consequences) clearly in his reading of Project: "Flash's code is a 'compiled' language—a programming language whose original source code is converted into a machine-readable form before it is run—and, unlike a web page which can be examined by selecting 'view source,' compiled code usually lacks many details of the original source" (Pressman, Marino, and Douglass 2015: 28). Critical readers, even with the technical knowledge of Douglass, cannot get to the source code of Project without missing details and explanations. They are invited to imagine only a partial map, even if they are distinctly aware of a complex of forces producing the work, and its narrative, that become literally impossible to wholly represent.

That the work revolves around the subliminal reinforces a third and parallel difficulty with interpretive phenomena: the unconscious driver of human desires. In the narrative, nearby residents to the pit, visitors, and scientists who seek to understand it cannot clearly locate the cause of this geological phenomena. They develop their own conspiracy theories, flattening the illegibility and invisibility of bottomlessness, its unrepresentability, into conspiratorial narrative and flat explanations. For Project, then, a kind of flat space is engaged in a number of ways. The flat surface of the streaming imagetexts does not allow for easy critical entrance into the depths of the project, including its code. The aesthetics are themselves flat: clipart, clear sans serif typeface, bold, saturated colors. And while the narrative it offers is about immeasurable, "bottomless" depth, Project keeps both the characters in its story and its readers up above on the surface. Attempts at a dive below mean disastrous, even deadly consequences.

The work also perpetually bombards its readers with shifting images and text. They flash on the screen in rapid succession and do not cease. This can be read as a performance of so-called information overload attributed to networked contemporary culture. The twenty-four-hour news cycle, overlapping and perpetually running social media applications on mobile devices, multiple and multiplying sources for news, advertising, and entertainment have, by many accounts, not only changed the way consumers get information but the way they process it. Nicholas Carr's (2010: 51) account of the neurological consequences of digital culture are informative here, particularly in terms of language and the literary as it is employed in technology: "Because language is, for human beings, the primary vessel of conscious thought, the technologies that restructure language tend to exert the strongest influence over our intellectual lives." Jonathan Crary's explorations on the phenomenon's social consequences are also striking. In his *24/7: Late Capitalism and the Ends of Sleep* (2013: 9), Crary explores constant connectivity and its relationship to the rise and dominance of neoliberalism:

> It is only recently that the elaboration, the modeling of one's personal and social identity, has been reorganized to conform to the uninterrupted operation of markets, information networks, and other systems. A 24/7 environment has the semblance of a social world, but it is actually a non-social model of machinic performance and a suspension of living that does not disclose the human cost required to sustain its effectiveness.

The logic of 24/7 consumption, production, and connectivity, in other words, a logic certainly embodied by the untold flats of the Web, is a flat logic. Deflecting access to the depths is, in this case, very costly indeed. What Crary and others locate in the speed-up and extension of contemporary life is not an enrichment or expansion of social and political worlds, but rather their contraction, their flattening. The processes of flat logic are effective in part because they appear to offer more and deeper social connection, wider berth for political voices. What they offer, against their own narratives, is obfuscation and veiling. The world appears in all its fullness to be, in actual practice, flat. Perhaps it isn't just poor people, anymore, who produce conspiracy theories.

The 2016 US presidential election offers a troubling example of this fact. Much has been made on the way users access news content in what appears to be, increasingly, the echo chamber of social media. Conspiracy theory thrives in such an informational milieu. Social scientists have shown the intensifying potential of misinformation, sometimes deliberate, in largely online platforms: "The large availability of user provided contents on online social media facilitates people aggregation around shared beliefs, interests, worldviews and narratives. In spite of the enthusiastic rhetoric about the so called collective intelligence, unsubstantiated rumors and conspiracy theories—e.g., chemtrails, reptilians or the Illuminati—are pervasive in online social networks" (Bessi et al. 2015). The proliferation of conspiracy on the Web suggests a misplaced desire for critical depths in a space of expanding and multiplying surfaces.

While Project is not, on its own surface, engaged with social media, it does include within its narrative unsubstantiated conspiracy and points directly to the potential vanishing of access to the truth: the bottomless pit expands to swallow a museum, which has documented it. Its perpetual looping and rapid progression mimic the kind of bombardment of which, ultimately, both Crary and Carr are writing.

Project encourages its readers to engage with the work such that they experience a push and pull between depth and flatness: As the introduction of *Reading Project* describes: "Project pushes you to sit back and absorb the stream of flashing content. It stuns you into passive receptivity while simultaneously compelling you to draw near the screen and actively construct coherence out of the fragmented and fleeting impressions left by its imagetexts" (Pressman, Marino, and Douglass 2015: xiii).

All of this is done such that both flatness and depth as conceptual and material phenomena are problematized: As *Reading Project* puts it, "The work concludes by signaling the proliferation of change, by noting the growing instability of surfaces, and by suggesting that we need to direct our attention to these transformations" (Pressman, Marino, and Douglass 2015: 4). As a Web-based work whose central thematics have to do with material and critical depth, Project asks important questions about how we engage other Web-based phenomena. In the end, it seems ambivalent about how the online world might be read, when its readers are themselves unstable (subliminal messaging is geared to work toward those layers of us to which we don't have conscious access, leaving even those who approach the text as figures whose depths cannot be plumbed), when the medium hides its own production (characters in the narrative cannot get to the bottom of the pit, readers of Project cannot get full access to its undergirding), and when the ideological structures of global capital operate at such a scale as to be unrepresentable (the work produces itself as a conspiracy theory, in the Jamesonian sense, both in content and form).

FLAT AESTHETICS, FLAT LANGUAGE

Another collection of works that are engaged in playful explorations of flatness are those of Young-Hae Chang Heavy Industries (YHCHI). Among the most critically recognized producers of electronic literature, YHCHI is Young-Hae Chang and Marc Voge. Based in Seoul, South Korea, this duo produces Web-based art using Adobe Flash in which words rapidly appear and disappear, typically on a white background, at varying speeds, syncopated to a musical score. The pair uses the sans serif Monaco typeface and its works are available online on the YHCHI Web site as well as appearing in exhibitions and collections globally. On their home site, the title of each work is listed in black, followed by links underlined and in blue that indicate the languages in which the works are available. YHCHI eschews the use of images for the most part, though there are occasionally very limited graphics in their work, to music syncopated to flashing (usually black or red) text. In a few pieces, the text is spoken in addition to being presented in the animation, utilizing voices that are either themselves digital objects or made to sound digitally produced.

The stripped-down, text heavy, and image light aesthetics of YHCHI serve as something of the duo's trademark. A YHCHI work is recognizable without attribution by most serious readers of electronic literature. Its aesthetic is also remarkable for most Web users, even without any familiarity with the pair or electronic literature, for its flat aesthetic. No embedded video files run; no banner ads flash. Even on their home page, YHCHI barely directs users aside from indicating links to the works themselves. In this way, their whole oeuvre gestures toward the often hyperactive visuality of the larger Web. But not only to the ways in which busy visuals populate swaths of the larger aesthetic field online: YHCHI's works produce long and short narratives that, even while often comic or satirical, are certainly literary. They are works that use and reflect heavily on text and language. They indicate themselves as things to be read, and to be read in a sustained fashion, though their temporality is mandated by the authors rather than chosen by the readers. Once a YHCHI animation has launched, the reader is offered no pause button, no means by which to slow or speed the progression of text on the screen. The works are linear. In this way YHCHI also gestures to the absence of the literary on the larger Web, to a kind of flattening of language elsewhere online.

Many critics have pointed to the way YHCHI have played with multiple languages (see specifically, Pressman [2007]) and the implications of this on digital culture, the computer as a translating machine, and the potentially Orientalist fantasies embedded in the hard and software that shape the popular imagination of the digital (on the latter, see Chun [2008]). While indeed the language and translation work YHCHI does is central to their larger project, explored in parallel with the spartan design strategies of the pair, it also has some key critical interventions to make on the flatness of online content.

For works that are available in only one language, or that are in multiple languages in a single piece, the title alone serves as the link. The text-only site makes the large number of languages immediately visible to users. Just as the restrained design of the home page points to the bombasticity of pages proliferating elsewhere on the Web, so the plainness of these multiple languages on the page indicates a linguistic flatness of the Internet as any one user generally navigates to it (a Spanish-speaking user at a computer in Argentina clicks through to sites primarily in Spanish, arriving at information in a single language because of her own browser history, her IP address, and the search tool she uses).

If the fantasy of networked culture is texture, bottomless depths of proliferating information immediately available, and universal accessibility, the work of YHCHI as a whole seems to suggest that the larger Web is flat where the world the group seeks to serve is distinctly, materially, textured, diverse, deep. This is accomplished through a play of contrasts: if the larger visible Web is intensely visual, flashy, busy, YHCHI is textual and minimal. If the worlds to which users navigate online are monolingual, YHCHI offers readers multiple and multiplying languages, and does so with a stripped down aesthetic that allows readers to easily see the wide linguistic range of YHCHI's collection of works.

In addition to its multilingualism, YHCHI's oeuvre also works to explore the temporal in ways that trouble the shallow time of the Web. Some of the works proceed at speeds so quick they make the reading process incredibly difficult. Others are staccato, slow. Not only in each piece, but as a whole, the formal mechanism of pace in the works of YHCHI underlines the experience of speed and slowness on the larger Web, both in terms of speed as a fantasy of networked culture, and of the larger consequences of the material speed of information flow (we might return to Crary) on our critical and reading capacities of content on the Web and of networked culture.

Where the works of YHCHI make it very clear to the reader that they cannot control the pace of their experience, there is a way to read this positionality as suggesting that users lack that control elsewhere. The speed of information may be in the hands of Web and software developers, of the hardware of the Internet, even of the state elsewhere on the Web. Readers have to think about time when they approach the work of YHCHI: that's the difference. Whether slow or fast, the pace of the reading process and the very fact that it is a process destabilizes a reader's ability to hold onto a work's content. Readers cannot return to the previous word or phrase without relaunching the piece and starting from the beginning. They must confront the work's temporality in this way, perhaps even through frustration at the difficulty of access. Elsewhere on the Web, the pace is shaped by factors about which users are encouraged not to think and access to content is made to feel easy and quick.

There are, of course exceptions to the unhinging of user experience from temporal control in other, nonliterary moments online; error and artifact, for example: when servers go down and pages will not load, when a machine freezes. These moments, of course, may be the result of political and social phenomena as much as hardware or programming. Denial of service or DOD attacks by hackers, such as those successfully carried out by Anonymous on Amazon after the company refused to allow customers access to the Wikileaks documents, are primary examples. Others include the recent and vocal debates in the United States on net neutrality, which would prevent service providers from slowing the delivery of selected content to consumers. The larger global picture includes barriers put in place by the state in Turkey or China (to name just two), which may prohibit access to content. In the latter case, it is not just a slowing, but a full stop.

In these cases, rather than flattening time, the user is forced to confront its unfolding, just as she is when she approaches a YHCHI work. She must be made aware of her relative lack of control vis-à-vis time as it is constructed and experienced on the Web. In perhaps an odd inversion, slow time can be, even against the generally held ideologies of states who may impose it via firewalls, critical, deepening time. The supposed hyperspeeds of "real time," however, function to flatten, or at least keep popular users on the surface of the Web.

There is a way, as well, in which the construction of computation, its position in a global imaginary, lends itself to the flattening of time. Tung-Hui Hu's (2015: 47) work in *A Prehistory of the Cloud* adroitly describes the consequences of computational temporality:

> Despite naming it "real time," the mode of time that Licklider describes is neither real nor unmediated; real time actually functions as an ideology of economic productivity. By splitting a problem into thousands of increments, and then stitching these intervals of computer and worker time alike back into a seeming whole, the computer disavows unproductive moments with "no mode or routine," and turns our attention away from

these gaps, stutters and freezes toward more productive forms of work. Yet to do so is to subtly refashion the subject brought within the domain of real time.

YHCHI, through their use of linearly progressing narrative and flash programming, deepens reader engagement with and awareness of the quick, flat time of typical Web interfaces. This is done in part by positioning the reader exactly as reader, not as "user." No avenues of intervention are offered to those approaching a YHCHI work: they cannot alter the pace of the work, change the music, or produce any content. The only possible approach to the texts is to read and reread. Even if only metaphorically, there remains, then, the suggestion that the fiction of or performance of instantaneity and speed online prevents critical depth. Critique, after all, certainly requires slow time, and close, sustained attention.

Hu's work makes clear that the consequences of computational time work their way into social and subject formation and have strong ties to capitalist ideology. Flat temporalities are those which, as Hu writes, disavow the unproductive, and thus, the full depth of temporal experience, and of computational actuality. Where Paul Virilio, David Harvey, and others have argued that the ideological construction of speed tied to contemporary digital technologies has caused the subsumption of space by time, any critical reading of YHCHI would lead us to understand that construction as hiding the much more textured and varied temporalities of user experience online (Virilio 2000; Harvey 1990). A critical plumbing of those depths is one avenue of attack against neoliberal, capitalist fantasies about global connectivity and invisible infrastructure.

DEEP TIME, VEILING SCREENS

The last example of electronic literature I will read in this chapter is Chiappe and Meier's "Tierra de extracción." Though the work has appeared in several versions starting in 2000, I will focus on its most recent presentation online (its most widely available instantiation), which launched in 2007. It was then included in the second edition of the Electronic Literature Organization's collection. The work calls itself a "novella" and is composed of sixty-three short chapters, each with at least one lexia. Users can trace the story on a navigation map, clicking in the order of their choosing, or they may go through the hyperlinks between chapters without returning to it (arrows in the center of the four edges of a square screen indicate movement up, down, or to either side through the narrative). While there is significant textual material in the work, "Tierra" also utilizes newspaper clippings, images, and audio files with both speech and music in addition to graphics.

The content of the narrative revolves around the population of Menegrande in the state of Zulia, Venezuela. Menegrande is located in the region of the country known for its rich oil resources (its name refers directly to the large fountain of oil located there) and the narrative produced by Chiappe is deeply invested in the social and ecological consequences of extractionism, as well as the global economic forces that shape the landscapes his characters inhabit. As such, it is a meditation on conceptual, social, and geological depth.

Like the works of YHCHI, Chiappe and Meier's work in "Tierra" is also invested in time. In her reading of the novella, Thea Pitman (2007: 237) explains that "the action of the novel spans the whole of the twentieth century. Nevertheless, the narrative frequently suppresses references to historical time—and, together with the prophetic tone of many passages and direct references to myths and to cyclical temporalities, it suggests a reading where Menegrande and its environs constitute a timewarp and a trap." Another way of describing the temporal framing of the work might be to suggest that it engages "deep time."

Evidence for a reading of this deep time is also the mythological and metaphysical references to which Pitman points (time which certainly dives into existential depths) but also the ways in which the long period of the novel (a century) is paired with the still much longer geological time in which the earth produces the oil reserves that come to connect Menegrande with the contemporary global economy. The surface temporality that encases these others in the depths of the narrative is the presentation of the work online. Such layered temporal unfolding means that in many ways, "Tierra" is trying to unpack how the temporal functioned in long geological history, a century of social history, and in the contemporary moment for readers and users of the Web interface.

The consequences of these competing and coextant temporalities are great. One among them is to expose the disabling of critique executed by flat time. No one reading of the work exists, but if readers engage the whole of the work, they are long, sometimes cumbersome navigations. "Tierra" is literary this way; it requires sustained and close attention. If readings of the work are slow, historical time is slower, and geological time is impossibly slow. Returning to both Hu and Crary: the "real time" and instantaneity, falsely associated with the rise of the digital interface, mask and deflect experiential time, slowness, lag, delay. The readers of "Tierra" are very much situated against real time, even as they engage the work online. It is this friction between the slow literary time and temporal framing of online engagement that helps to make the work a critical counter to "real time," which we described as "flat," and that position the work as a possible puncture to the flat temporal surfaces of neoliberal capitalism.

Chiappe's narrative is, in this same vein, invested in discovery and exploration. Its form and design require of its readers a time commitment and a critical investment. One line repeats several times: "esta tierra tiene su encanto, pero debes descubrirlo" (This land has its charm, but you must discover it; my translation). The reader and the characters who populate Chiappe's narrative are invited, in this way, to engage with the work in depth *and* over time. That the earth's own depths are the sites that link Menegrande to a complex of economic and cultural forces only reinforces this requirement.

Many references are made to telenovelas throughout the narrative, and the development of the town is tied to both the international petroleum market and the Venezuelan state. The use of hypertext to produce "Tierra" means that the form of the narrative matches its thematic content: vastly distinct time periods and social phenomena are linked in circuitous ways: cultural production, globalization, commercial traffic, local experience, politics, and government. While the narrative map, if a reader chooses to use it, might lay bare these connections more clearly, the combined effects of the reading process and the form of the work is the presentation of an ecological model of both the narrative itself as well as the forces with which Menegrande contends, and which shape it.

Hypertext employed by "Tierra" functions as its own kind of cognitive map, again, in the Jamesonian sense. But what's more, this is a map that carefully takes into account not only global markets, but historical and geological time. These concepts, too, seem unrepresentable in their complexity. "Tierra" might be considered in terms of media ecology: Matthew Fuller's (2007) use of the ecological is guided by both scientific and humanistic conceptions of the term. It is "one of the most expressive [terms] language currently has to indicate the massive and dynamic interrelation of processes and objects, beings and things, patterns and matter" (2).

Certainly, "Tierra" is deeply invested in exactly this "massive and dynamic interrelation." And just as certainly, the larger flatlands of the Internet are not. Criticism, when it is done well, is necessarily ecological. It does not flatten, but exposes and engages depth, connection, texture. "Tierra" models a different kind of approach in part by breaking time apart, destabilizing the user's ability to form a clear linear narrative, and offering user navigations that work on an x/y axes, or through the circular map: both of which make travel through the narrative a travel back and forth through historical time as well as demand an awareness of the slow reading time experienced by the user.

This is ecological in multiple registers, particularly in terms of the story's content: it mimics and mocks a kind of collective refusal to effectively narrate the consequences of extractionism. If we cannot tell a story about impending shortages, the consequences of climate change accelerated by an economy dependent on petroleum, we have a very difficult time positioning ourselves as, on the one hand, complicit, and on the other, political agents who might seek to alter a disastrous course. The problems are so large as to be, in fact, beyond our capacity to grasp them in flat terms. It also points to the ways in which popular discourse does want to tell certain narratives as a means by which to cover over others. "Tierra" literally enacts the veiling of certain narrative lines, certain facts, by placing visual panels above others as the user clicks on the surface of the text. Because it is about literal depths (oil, e.g., deep beneath the surface of the earth), the flatness of these layers (one obscuring another) is amplified. Readers cannot "go deep," or at least as deep as they might like, into these stories. Ultimately, the ecological model of "Tierra" is also a model of critique itself. It asks its readers to do the slow work of reading, of probing the depths and seeking out ways of understanding them. Of course there is an argument to be made that the larger Web is itself a kind of dense and dynamic ecology, but its surfaces obfuscate and veil, typically to derail critique and rarely to invite it. "Tierra" works through its surfaces to expose depth, and to invite its readers to dive in.

FLAT IMAGINARIES

"Tierra," "Project," and the work of YHCHI all offer critical models that can be read as counters to flatness as a problem specific to the world online, as a literary resistance to the deflection, veiling, and obfuscation that are part of what contributes to the flattening effects of the Web. These are not the only mechanisms of flatness in the network. The Web is also flat in that it is flatly imagined and flatly mapped. User approaches to the Web overall, to it as a shifting ecology, tend to remain in the shallows. If we are to approach Web-based cultural objects, we will also need to offer new models of what the Web itself is, and how it looks. Galloway's (2013: 85) proposal in *The Interface Effect* "in plain language, is that every map of the internet looks the same." The repeated aesthetic tropes of those maps of the Internet are, in Galloway's terms, symptomatic of a number of larger ontological and epistemological problems with informational networks:

> But what does this mean? What are the aesthetic repercussions of such claims? One answer is that no poetics are possible in this uniform aesthetic space. There is little differentiation in the level of formal analysis. We are not all mathematicians after all. One cannot talk of genre distinctions in this space, one cannot talk of high culture

> versus low culture in this space, one cannot talk of folk vernacular, nor of modernist spurs and other such tendencies. This is why computer culture speaks of icons, and why one might describe today's information aesthetic as a kind of neo-symbolism in which monochromatic multiplicity of symbols has engulfed all else. A single symbolic code reigns, iterated universally. And where there is only one, there is nothing. For a representation of one is, in fact, a representation of nothing. (85)

This "representation of nothing" is also, of course, an effect of and a contributor to a global political milieu. When artists or marketers or anyone else makes a map of the Internet—if Galloway is correct—the same map of the Internet over and over again, this map does not include its aporias or asymmetries. Rarely indeed do maps of the Web point to the fact that online access is not universal, nor content universally accessible. The choke holds placed on the flow of information by corporations or states are as invisible as are the massive shifts in texture to which Galloway points.

According to Galloway, we do not imagine or construct alternative pictures of the Web in part because the Web does not offer the epistemological openings to such imaginations. Users who are not programmers or electrical engineers or otherwise experts in the material that builds and allows our access to online content are encouraged not to access these deeper recesses of any given Web page, not to understand online interaction as intensely constrained or directed both in terms of aesthetics, platforms, software and hardware, infrastructure, and so on.

Many scholars have offered exceptional work that does indeed seek to trace material infrastructures (Starosielski [2015] and Parks and Starosielski [2015] are among the most compelling recent studies). And, just as urgently needed, scholars have sought to trace its transitions and traffic when hardware becomes obsolete, when it is trashed (Grossman 2007). But, unsurprisingly, the huge air-conditioned bunkers housing servers, the sprawl of cell-towers across the globe, and the many laborious layers from mining to material construction remain wholly absent from the vast majority of Web experience. More than absent: most Web pages work under an aesthetic rubric that forestalls both the critical and material depth required for a more equitable (and accurate) understanding of what it is that brings any one Web page up on the (flat) screen before our eyes.

The simplest, most visible example is perhaps the Google search results layout. While, indeed, there are invitations for further interaction (icons to click for further information, hyperlinks to jump to another Web page, etc.) the page presents no visual cues of the processes (material and informational) that bring a user to her list of results. Titles may indicate sources, but certainly do not offer any gesture toward the algorithm that brought them into order, nor, of course, of the expansive infrastructural material on which Google and its users depend.

The search algorithm, moreover, also utilizes data collected from the user's online history. My search results are tailored to my own browsing in the past, and yours to your own. This is true, of course, not only for Google but for other search tools as well. Thus, even the information we can cull from the vast depths of the Internet when we use these search tools is in fact funneled our way from a shallow pool.

Search results are also produced, unless some serious labor is done on the part of the user, exclusively in one language. A monolingual world is also a flat world. And while the digital age has offered a number of communication tools to expand the reach of communication in any language, it has clung to a logic about language and its relationship to technology that remains troublingly reductive. Rita Raley (2003: 293) writes:

> Machine translation brings to our attention in a materially significant manner the ideal of a perfect and fully automated translation from one natural language to another, with both languages considered as neutral and emphasis falling on the process, accuracy, and functionality of the exchange. In our current moment, total translatability and equivalence would mean a database with universal data input output capacity, specifically for multilingual translation, and without the use of a pivot language like English.

In the fantasy of "perfect and fully automated translation," texture and depth disappear in favor of a single, neutral plane of language. This flat fantasy, as Raley explains, obscures the power relationships on which constructions and literal productions of the digital world depend. "Although machine translation partly arises as a response to monolingualism and promises to preserve local or minor languages, it primarily operates around and with English as a pivot language; as the dominant language for computational linguistic and engineering research; and as the basis for assembly, low-level, and high-level programming languages" (300). The Web is, of course, not monolingual. But its translation tools and their attendant fantasies hide the real linguistic textures of exchange. Machine translation is one of another flat imaginaries that works of electronic literature have the capacity to combat. YHCHI's human translations of their works are one indicator of such a performance. Pressman (2016) writes:

> Instead of machinic translation, then, YHCHI offer different versions of the same work, each coded to perform differently depending on the language in which they appear. This fact illustrates YHCHI's commitment to displaying translation as a context-driven act dependent upon its linguistic system.

Theirs is a collection of works that outlines and centralizes the real multilingual universe of the Web, to the legitimate depths already extant in the communities of readers YHCHI serves.

Outside of the purely linguistic, or even textual flatness of the Web, there is also a design and development movement specifically devoted to flat aesthetics known as "flat design." With roots in Swiss design, sans serif fonts, and Minimalism, flat design is popular specifically among Web designers. Its aim is to simplify the interface, increase design shelf-life, and add flexibility such that images can render easily on multiple user interfaces. It is not surprising that Microsoft and Apple popularized these aesthetic strategies.

The Next Web describes flat design as follows: "By removing design styles that can easily date their design (or that could quickly cause their design to become outdated), they are 'future-proofing' their designs so that they become relevant for longer periods of time. Not to mention, flat design seems to make things more efficient and cuts out the 'fluff'" (Turner 2014). Put another way, flat design is meant to match up with the high speeds and proliferating interfaces of global capital. Interface design that cannot be "dated" also means interface design that does not bear with it the marks of its history or the means of its production. The astonishing popularity of the typeface Helvetica is then not just an indication of an aesthetic trend, but rather a marker of a large-scale, speculative move in digital aesthetics with real political and epistemological consequences. Flat design is intended to project itself into the future in a straight line. It is built specifically against historicity. In this sense, time itself gets flattened on the Internet.

The history of our interfaces in all its materiality and consequence may not ever be totally visible. What is missing, what doesn't come into view, however, may be marked.

In this vein, Poundstone's Project utilizes a kind of flat design to expose its flatness and unearth the ways in which flatness can cover over personal and communal histories. Again: electronic literature shows itself able to engage with the aesthetic materials of the larger Web to ends entirely counter to capital and its flat and flattening logics.

It is worth noting, as Lisa Parks and Nicole Starosielski (2015: 2) point out in their introduction to *Signal Traffic*, that Google operates a server house in Hamina that "once employed 650 workers to turn wood into paper, [and] now employs one hundred Google workers to route bits through networks." Aside from offering an excellent example of the ways in which reading interfaces of old have bled in strange and interesting directions into those of the present age of the digital, this fact also gives a sense of what the flat logic of informational culture hides. Flat logic is neoliberal. It is universalist and, perhaps more than anything, capitalist in nature. Flat logic suggests a way of knowing and learning that refuses depth. It sees the network as global, universally accessible, and nonetheless immaterial. It is disembodied just as it makes claims to immersion. Flat logic is averse to sustained inquiry, and absolutely opposed to structural critique. The server house in Hamina exemplifies and embodies a material history of informational culture, a history that intersects with economic shifts (and thus shifts in a history of labor) but its geographical remoteness and popular invisibility keep it as a site under erasure: it may be a palimpsest, but it is one the surfaces of popular discourse about informational exchange cover over. To unearth it (as the infrastructure studies proposed by Parks and Starosielski [2015] seeks to do) is to engage in a plumbing of historical depths that have wide-ranging and critical political and epistemological potential.

Movements like those launched by Parks and Starosielski, as well as many producers of electronic literature, art, and criticism suggest that there is certainly hope that depths can still be reached. The artists behind the Web-based electronic literature I read here have hope for alternative maps of the Internet and logic that is anything but flat. As I hope I have shown, they provide strong critical frameworks to begin to disable flat logics, those specific to online interfaces and those specific to global capital. I have sought to unearth the methods and tools these works use in their own critical, resistant work thus adding my own voice to what may be a growing rallying cry in favor of the perpetuation of the critical search for depth.

Finally, the pieces of electronic literature discussed here as well as my own analysis work directly against recent trends in so-called surface reading, as advocated by Sharon Marcus and Stephen Best (2009), among others, in a controversial and widely cited special issue of *Representations*. Surface reading eschews suspicion and symptomatic analysis, angling directly against Marxist and Psychoanalytic models of critique. Franco Moretti's (2005) distant reading, too, suggests a kind of scale shift away from depths. While there is certainly room in literary studies for multiple methodologies, this chapter remains suspicious and the picture of the surfaces of the Web these works of literature draw suggests that we need to maintain a strong commitment to the power of critique and of close reading to plumb the depths: of literature, of infrastructure, of digital worlds and of all that attend them. Distant reading can be useful, but if we are to seriously engage digital culture, it cannot be employed at the expense of close, critical readings of specific objects. "Tierra," Project, and the works of YHCHI are works of literature that share this commitment. They demand much from their readers, and the critical approaches they elicit require a willingness to work toward uncovering the depths. In an age when the online world is rife with veiling mechanisms and obfuscating strategies, all aimed at hiding the workings, economic, technological, infrastructural, beneath the interface, the depths may be the most important terrain of resistance we have left.

SOURCES CITED

Bessi, A., M. Coletto, G. A. Davidescu, A. Scala, G. Caldarelli, and W. Quattrociocchi. "Science vs Conspiracy: Collective Narratives in the Age of Misinformation." *PLoS ONE*, vol. 10, no. 2 (2015): e0118093.

Carr, Nicholas G. *The Shallows: What the Internet Is Doing to Our Brains*. New York: W. W. Norton, 2010.

Chiappe, Doménico, and Andreas Meier. "Tierra De Extracción." *Electronic Literature Collection*, vol. 2 (n.d.): n.p. December 12, 2016.

Chun, Wendy Hui Kyong. *Control and Freedom: Power and Paranoia in the Age of Fiber Optics*. Cambridge: MIT, 2008.

Crary, Jonathan. *24/7: Late Capitalism and the Ends of Sleep*. London: Verso, 2013.

Fuller, Matthew. *Media Ecologies: Materialist Energies in Art and Technoculture* (Leonardo Books). London: MIT, 2007.

Galloway, Alexander R. *The Interface Effect*. Oxford: Wiley, 2013.

Grossman, Elizabeth. *High Tech Trash: Digital Devices, Hidden Toxics, and Human Health*. Washington: Island/Shearwater, 2007.

Hansen, Mark B. N. *New Philosophy for New Media*. Cambridge: MIT, 2006.

Harvey, David. *The Condition of Postmodernity: An Enquiry into the Origins of Cultural Change*. Oxford: Blackwell, 1990.

Hu, Tung-Hui. *A Prehistory of the Cloud*. Cambridge: MIT, 2015.

Jameson, Fredric. "Cognitive Mapping." In *Marxism and the Interpretation of Culture*, edited by C. Nelson and L. Grosserg. Chicago: University of Illinois Press, 1990, pp. 347–60.

Jameson, Fredric. *Postmodernism, or, the Cultural Logic of Late Capitalism*. Durham, NC: Duke University Press, 1992.

Latour, Bruno. "Why Has Critique Run out of Steam? From Matters of Fact to Matters of Concern." *Critical Inquiry*, vol. 30, no. 2 (2004): 225–48.

Marcus, Sharon, and Stephen Best. "Surface Reading: An Introduction." *Representations*, vol. 108, no. 1 (2009): 1–21.

Massumi, Brian. *Parables for the Virtual: Movement, Affect, Sensation*. Durham, NC: Duke University Press, 2002.

Moretti, Franco. *Graphs, Maps, Trees: Abstract Models for a Literary History*. London: Verso, 2005.

Parks, Lisa, and Nicole Starosielski, eds. *Signal Traffic: Critical Studies of Media Infrastructures*. Urbana: University of Illinois, 2015.

Pitman, Thea. "Hypertext in Context: Space and Time in the Hypertext and Hypermedia Fictions of Blas Valdez and Doménico Chiappe." In *Latin American Cyberculture and Cyberliterature*, Claire Taylor and Thea Pitman (eds.). Liverpool: Liverpool University Press, 2007.

Poundstone, William. "Project for Tachistoscope [Bottomless Pit]." *The Electronic Literature Collection*, vol. 1 (n.d.): n.p. December 12, 2016.

Pressman, Jessica. "Reading the Code between Words: The Role of Translation in Young-Hae Chang Heavy Industries' Nippon." *Dichtung Digital*: n.p. December 12, 2016.

Pressman, Jessica, Mark C. Marino, and Jeremy Douglass. *Reading Project: A Collaborative Analysis of William Poundstone's Project for Tachistoscope [Bottomless Pit]*. Iowa City: University of Iowa, 2015.

Raley, Rital. "Machine Translation and Global English." *The Yale Journal of Criticism*, vol. 16, no. 2 (2003): 291–313.

Starosielski, Nicole. *The Undersea Network*. Durham, NC: Duke University Press, 2015.

Turner, Amber Leigh. "The History of Flat Design: Efficiency, Minimalism, Trendiness." *The Next Web*, n.p., March 19, 2014. December 12, 2016.

Virilio, Paul. *The Information Bomb*. New York: Verso, 2000.

"YOUNG-HAE CHANG HEAVY INDUSTRIES PRESENTS." YOUNG-HAE CHANG HEAVY INDUSTRIES PRESENTS, (n.d.): n.p. December 12, 2016.

CHAPTER FIFTEEN

Immanence, Inc.: Algorithm, Flow, and the Displacement of the Real

BRIAN KIM STEFANS

WRITING AND EXCESS

In his seminal, if radically subversive, series of books *The Accursed Share*, French philosopher Georges Bataille (1988: 25–6) describes a contrast between what he calls a "restricted" and "general" economy:

> If a part of wealth ... is doomed to destruction or at least to unproductive use without any possible profit, it is logical, even inescapable, to surrender commodities without return. Leaving aside pure and simple dissipation, analogous to the construction of the Pyramids, the possibility of pursuing growth is itself subordinated to giving: The industrial development of the entire world demands of Americans that they lucidly grasp the necessity, for an economy such as theirs, of having a margin of profitless operations. [The industrial network] expresses a circuit of cosmic energy on which it depends, which it cannot limit, and whose laws it cannot ignore without consequences. Woe to those who ... insist on regulating the movement that exceeds them with the narrow mind of the mechanic who changes a tire.

Bataille hits on themes that have become major touchstones in a certain form of speculative politics and philosophy, notably the potlatch, a form of wasteful expenditure as a way to elevate social status as described by Marcel Mauss in *The Gift* (2016), and the "cosmic energy" of what is now known by some as "dark vitalism," the notion of the planet operating as a "world-without-us," beyond observation, the "hyper-object" of nonhuman machinations. These combine into a critique of the economy-as-science, or classical economics, with which we are familiar from public discourse premised on labor, efficiency, and productivity. Bataille instead describes a confrontation between a hyper-vital planet—one in which productivity by humans, animals, and plants has simply run amok—and the circumscribed exchange systems that surrender much of this productivity as waste.

Steve McCaffery (2000) adapted this concept in his own series of short essays collected in *North of Intention* to account for a variety of experimental poetics in North America, particularly in his adoptive home country, Canada. McCaffery is interested in the excess of meaning—those elements that don't serve a function in utilitarian hermeneutics (subject to "close reading" or paraphrase), and that break the boundaries of the "well-wrought urn" (201) that a previous formalist criticism valorized to determine literary quality and evaluate literary competence. In his essay "Bill Bissett: A Writing outside Writing," an analysis of the poet's voluminous works,[1] McCaffery synthesizes his ideas of linguistic "excess" quite explicitly to an understanding of what was considered socially acceptable "form" in the human body—what we choose to expose, the gamut of bodily affect, and what we, voluntarily or not, expel or project from our bodies. His essay investigates

> the aspect of excess and libidinal flow, of the interplay of forces and intensities, both through and yet quite frequently despite language; the flow of non-verbal energies through verbal domains that registers most often as a sheer libidinal will to power, a schizop(oetic)hrenic strategy to break through the constraint mechanisms of grammar and classical discourse in general. As such this is a very immanent, yet vague, aspect to be considering. The flows are located inside the fissures of texts, constantly escape in excess among—yet beyond—the words, urging an exploration of both language and anti-language and an awareness of the forces that refuse textualization. This, in turn, demands a specific approach to bissett's [*sic*] corpus as a coagulate of forces to be experienced, but not elucidated, a problematic to be felt but not reconciled. (93)

McCaffery's direct linkage of his reading strategies with "libidinal flows," beyond its obvious ties to poststructuralist theories of the "pleasures of the text" (his citing of "fissures" seems particularly emblematic), is a perverse conservation of a basic Romantic poetic principle. Shelley (1977: 505) writes in the "Defense of Poetry":

> The greatest poet even cannot say it; for the mind in creation is as a fading coal, which some invisible influence, like an inconstant wind, awakens to transitory brightness; this power arises from within, like the color of a flower which fades and changes as it is developed, and the conscious portions of our natures are unprophetic either of its approach or its departure. Could this influence be durable in its original purity and force, it is impossible to predict the greatness of the results; but when composition begins, inspiration is already on the decline, and the most glorious poetry that has ever been communicated to the world is probably a feeble shadow of the original conceptions of the poet.

While Shelley is not as decidedly immanent in his figuration of nonhuman forces at play in the construction of verse—there is an outside in the form of Nature on the one hand, and a devolution through history of once-pure poetic principles, the "fading coal"—his depiction of the poet as receiver of messages has formed something of a template for later figurations—Jack Spicer's own notion in "Sporting Life" of the poet as "counterpunching radio" is a version of this. Charles Olson imagines poetry as a direct transmission of forces—not of message but of pure physical and psychical energy expressed through printed type. Olson (1971: 15) writes: "A poem is energy transferred from where the poet got it (he will have some several causations), by way of the poem itself to, all the way over to, the reader. Okay. Then the poem itself must, at all points, be a high energy-construct and, at all points, an energy-discharge." The poem is a documentary, a field of markings, fossils of a living presence, rather than a fabricated lyrical subject ("Walt Whitman, an

[1] Bisset, like many Canadian poets, opted not to capitalize his first and last name. Since McCaffery seems to waver between the normative and non-standard depiction of his name, I've opted for the standard to avoid having to decide, for instance, whether to capitalize his name at the head of a sentence.

American, one of the roughs, a kosmos ...," for example). The author is maintained as a constant, as actor upon the medium, but the reader as subject is left to experience and feel the writer's otherwise information-poor textual emissions.

McCaffery's reading of Bissett stands in contrast to critics who wish to preserve the subject in largely deconstructed or "illegible" texts, often by deferring to paradigms of reading descended from notions of fiction, a genre that mediates the seemingly pedestrian *documentary* truth (the page as recording device or "stoppage") valorized by McCaffery with the *mythic* dimensions of narrative. By "mythic," I mean the paradigm or teleology that underlies all major narratives that Frank Kermode describes in *Sense of an Ending* (1966) that envision a protagonist "in the middle," caught blindly between birth and death, for whom meaning is not substantially conferred until the satisfactory completion of a plot. "All such plotting presupposes and requires that an end will bestow upon the whole duration and meaning," Kermode writes. "To put it another way, the interval must be purged of simple chronicity, of the emptiness of *tock-tick.*, humanly uninteresting successiveness. It is required to be a significant season, *kairos* poised between beginning and end" (46). N. Katherine Hayles in "Virtual Bodies and Flickering Signifiers" (1996) articulates one of the most cogent of these attempts to rescue the subject from what, in other hands, might simply be described as "noise." Her essay describes the traditional reader as enmeshed in a world not only where the relationship of sign to signified is in a constantly shifting state, but in which the writer is a data warrior, an embodied subjectivity embattled by information.

> The entanglement of signal and materiality in bodies and books confers on them a parallel doubleness. Just as the human body is understood in molecular biology as simultaneously a physical structure and an expression of genetic information, so the literary corpus is at once a physical object and a space of representation, a body and a message. Because they have bodies, books and people have something to lose if they are regarded solely as informational patterns, namely, the resistant materiality that has traditionally marked the experience of reading no less than it has marked the experience of living as embodied creatures. From this affinity emerge complex feedback loops between contemporary literature, the technologies that produce it, and the embodied readers who produce and are produced by books and technologies. (29)

A central theme of much of Hayles's writing has been the favoring of an *ontogenetic* view of the creation of form premised on collaborations—the "genetic information" of the body with distributed mind and memory—over the *hylomorphic*, which imagines form as imposed upon matter. In a later essay, Hayles writes that Talan Memmott's *Lexia to Perplexia*, one of the most ambitious, elaborate examples of "codework" in the electronic literature canon, "insists on the co-originary status of subjectivity and electronic technologies. Instead of technologies being created by humans, this work imagines digital technology present from the beginning, with subjects and technologies producing each other through recursive loops" (49).[2]

[2] There is an obvious heritage for such conceptions of the writer-as-algorithm in pre-digital methods such as the "cut-up"—described by William S. Burroughs in his seminal essay "The Cut-up Method of Brion Gysin" ([1961]) —in which the writer surrenders some linguistic (spatial, temporal) control while preserving, if only in traces, a unified protagonist. One can fictionalize the reading of a cut-up story as one can the reading of a "codework": as an extreme version of a De Quincey-like (or Coleridgean) narrator submerged in a welter of hallucinogenic impressions. In *Lexia to Perplexia*, one is experiencing a cyborg subject who has lost track of the difference

McCaffery's (2000: 96) *North of Intention* denies the fictional frame which seeks to preserve some form of the subject while, ironically, installing a post-Romantic (or crypto-Romantic, if one imagines de Sade as a grotesque appendage of Romanticism) subject in a frame that sees writing as a "literal expulsion of material signs as if it were the ejection of a harmful substance ... expulsion ... shit ... the glands ... cumming ... cumming and beyond the ideational content and the temptation to simplistic analogy (language = bloodstream) is the less tractable intensities that mutilate the conventional physiognomy of language." McCaffery allows us to appreciate moments of subjective singularity—of originary, even if not recuperable, linguistic events—that are threatened by a reading of text that is "co-originary" with technology. McCaffery isn't concerned with "feedback loops" to this degree—discharge is waste, there is no recuperation in the form of a "subject." Bissett's poetic output can also be attributed to systemic, technological determinations, as most of his writing appeared in photocopy, sure product of that unheralded middle-period of mass publishing between the Gutenberg press and the Internet: the age of the typewriter and the Xerox machine: "The entire early output of [Bissett's] Blewointment Press was an uninterrupted flow of manuscript into print, a literal spillage of energy into book with minimum of reification" (101). McCaffery disallows the paradigmatic, mythic reading of Kermode—a hermeneutic turn that argues for depth—in favor of the experiential:

> Excess then, cannot be a theme; it can only operate as the force of an energy, a force in spite of language, constantly escaping through linguistic signs and constantly threatened by enclosure in them. Similarly, excess cannot be read inside the text but must be approached through an anti-reading constituting an overview of the corpus. Such an overview on the reader's part involves reconstituting reading as a conceptual act of affirmation that requires the reader to be both witness and co-participant within a discharge. (103)

McCaffery's triad—poet, page, reader as "co-participant"—suggests a sort of action-at-a-distance, the poet not receding into the past as author but as emergent in the process of reading.[3]

This seemingly mindless—unhinged, spastic, effusive, antisocial—poetic discharge is an *affect* that can be expressed in electronic writing premised on the operations of an algorithm, which by nature is going to come off as products of excess in relation to arts that have an organic relation to bodily possibility. For the most part, however, workers

between subjective language—the singular linguistic acts of a "writer"—and the language that either suspends the words on the screen (the code of operating system or word processor) or formulates its own new literary objects (the code behind Facebook or Google). The linkages of forms of electronic literature premised on some variation of the hyperlink to non-teleological fiction (ranging through Alain Robbe-Grillet's nouveau roman such as *The Voyeur*, indeterminately ordered fictions such as Mark Saporta's *Composition No. 1* and B. S. Johnson's *The Unfortunates*, meta-fictional writers such as Borges and Barthelme, the twisted passages of the Oulipo, etc.) and to certain thematic strands of fiction that is conventionally plotted, such as cyberpunk, have led theorists to hang on to the possibility of recuperating a mythic—enhanced, elevated, embattled—subjectivity in much otherwise illegible or excessive writing, even if in an attenuated state.

[3] Not incidentally, McCaffery's conception of an "anti-reading constituting an overview of the corpus" resembles the recent vogue for "distant reading" as propounded by Franco Moretti and other digital humanists: a reading without reading, a quantitative rather than qualitative analysis. And like Hayles, McCaffery sees the reader as co-participant—it would be hard to describe a theory of reading that didn't acknowledge a collusion between human and textual object—but does not see the reader's concept of the writer as threatened ontologically—there is still an "author" at the other end of the words, and there is still a text that we can stand apart from and witness as the remnants of a bodily event.

with digital text—notably Bill Seaman, who has published significant theory on his own work—don't seem to recognize the limitations of "virtual" creativity in what I am calling the "displacement of the real," nor how the sacrifice of hylomorphic theories of form in favor of algorithmic production that simply collapses the distinction of word and image constitutes a failure of understanding of what it is art *does* outside of an academic context. Of the many aspects of "analog" culture that algorithm allows us to simulate are the very libidinal flows that McCaffery valorizes in Bissett, and which we, as readers, understand as excessive utterance.[4]

RECOMBINANT POETICS

Bill Seaman's "Interactive Text and Recombinant Poetics" (2006) articulates a definition of "text" and "meaning" that I believe was commonplace in early figurations of the digital arts, not to mention "electronic writing." Here, he is describing the role of text in an application such as his own *The World Generator/The Engine of Desire* (1996/97: 231):

> Each field carries an evocative meaning force. Our embodied history of experience of past contexts represents another expansive field that is brought into this delicate equation. As we encounter virtual or computational spaces we experience an ongoing, time-based summing of meaning forces. Thus text presents one field of meaning force that can only be understood contextually in relation to other "neighboring" meaning forces—other media elements and living processes. The "word" is not valued in a hierarchy over other media elements.

Seaman, like a latter-day Marinetti, is celebrating not only the liberation of words but the breakdown of boundaries between the "sign" of the word and the "sign" of other media elements including video, sound, and still image.[5] He makes a point of announcing

---

[4] We see this organic/digital divide in the visual arts as well. A feature film, for instance, does not achieve the plateaus of excess that a big budget video game, viewed as a film, suggests, since a film falls within certain conventions that have been agreed upon as satisfactory to body and mind—the duration of roughly ninety minutes, plot structures of enabling action, rising action, peripateia and denouement, a base trust in the indexical relation of present image to antecedent event, and so on—all of which video games can, provided a robust algorithm, "infinitely" reproduce. Certainly, film directors such as Andy Warhol have challenged these basic formal conventions by creating films of exceptional length, but to viewers these artists are seen as engaging in an aesthetics of excess similar to that described by McCaffery above. One will rarely say of a video game what one might of Warhol's *Empire*: this artwork, as a presence, is a waste of material, is onanistic in the most visceral, repulsive sense. This moral dimension of the experience of art is largely absent in generative cultural practices—the on-the-fly constructed Facebook page, the algorithmically generated music of Brian Eno, for example—despite what other pleasures they afford.

[5] I'm using "sign" following Seaman's lead in introducing the term from the writing of Charles Sanders Peirce, founder of modern semiotics. But it is unclear why Seaman introduces Peirce into the equation except to comment generically that "Peirce suggests ... that meaning is that which the sign conveys," which is either (1) obvious or (2) a belief not specific to Peirce but to an entire field of study. Nor does Seaman actually adopt the use of the term "sign" throughout his essay, opting instead for terms like "emergent meaning" and "meaning force" which he adopted from Fernande Saint-Martin's *Semiotics of Visual Language* (2006). Perhaps this slipperiness is merely symptomatic of the pressures of satisfying idioms of both literary theory, computer science, and the artist's statement, which can often result in an hybrid language that has the sheen of scholarship and systematic thinking and there is no distinction between when a proposition is being made (or theory being defended) and when the writer is merely describing his artistic creations. But even the determinate phrases Seaman offers here don't seem to parse into meanings so much as *allude*—"embodied history of experience of past contexts," for example, skirts alongside terminology derived from other discourses (such as that of "embodiment") without really explaining what he means. Is there any "experience" that is not "embodied," are "past contexts" really

that, in his *The World Generator/The Engine of Desire*, the "word" is "not valued in a hierarchy over other media elements" (231). This smacks of a sort of egalitarianism that seems to me endemic in new media art criticism (sometimes tied to some thinker like Barthes or Deleuze), an egalitarianism that seems to be consistent with the hacker/libertarian ethos of Internet culture, but which also takes its cue from John Cage and Robert Rauschenberg, probably the two artists most responsible for our understanding of non-"hierarchical" all-inclusiveness of an artwork in relation to a democratic, even anarchic, tendency.[6] This egalitarianism obviously also derives from the fact that, like in a universal Turing machine, all types of sensible elements, such as sound, image, and text, can be reduced to the same principle components of bytes, as John Cayley points out in "Literal Art," quoting Peter Lunenfeld: "As all manner of representational systems are recast as digital information, they can all be stored, accessed, and controlled by the same equipment" (xvi). Certainly language *can* be used this way, "another element" to be treated like a sound or a color—Steve Reich's early experiments with looped speech, for example, or the proto-Pop painter Stuart Davis's canvases are two well-known examples—but even in these cases, in which not much language was used, the contingencies of both history and culture (even race) played large roles in their effects.

Experimental poetics and (in the case of Cage) musical techniques often rely on principles of polysemeity—the rupturing of once-stable meanings of words to liberate their unconventional or even hitherto unheard of meanings—and aleatoric methods (the use of chance), in which seemingly natural sentence and even word order is randomly corrupted with the goal of producing new experiences that were not "intended" by the author. Cage's "reading through" various "stable" texts—such as his diaries, or letters from friends, or *Finnegans Wake*—are prime examples of this, but so are lesser-known phenomena such as the conceptual literary works of Vito Acconci in the 1960s or the live-edited poetry events of Steve Benson and Bruce Andrews. Both principles, polysemeity and the aleatoric, are touched on in Craig Dworkin's description of Andrews's early poetic technique:

> In the resultant mesh of language, themes only latent in the source texts emerge in a text animated by the tension between atomized words and the pull of an emergent syntax: "Distinctly Luck Coal Stern," "Limited Capital Cupola Plosive," "Noise Hypotenuse." The language of these poems is motivated along multiple, but

---

constitutive of "experience" (getting punched in the face versus knowing *why* you got punched in the face), and does the material markings and changes one recognizes as having had happened to the body constitute a "history"? The grounding of textual experience in some notion of "embodied history" seems to give up the game too easily as regards indeterminacy. Add to this the notion of interactivity and "vuser" complicity in the creation of the art work, the relativity of the meaning of any single element is increased exponentially, even as the context in which these elements exist—the "virtual world"—remains as novel and inscrutable as the machine itself. While it is inarguable that the meaning of a word can change in a different context, is it really an appreciable difference if the entirety of the "context" is characterized by utter *relativity* (as opposed to "contingency")? "Democracy," for instance, is a context in which one's understanding of "justice" exists (or upon which it is *contingent*, as Richard Rorty would argue), "justice" itself being a term that has existed throughout history, even in times not characterized at all by a democratic ethos. But the word "justice" juxtaposed with the words "fish fry" or "Jeremy Irons" only serves to make the two words more *material*—more present as words in a physical environment—but also to render both relatively mute, and entirely banal, in terms of "meaning."

[6] I'd include Duchamp in this line, but there is a metaphysics, or even "pataphysics," operating in his work that suggests, if anything, a "hierarchy," and he was very scrupulous in choosing which items to permit into, and hence to allow to elaborate, his parallel art-historical universe.

> unprivileged axes; at a local level, the collision of irreconcilable linguistic elements frustrates both the referential pull of the sign and the inevitable, if tenuous, invitations of even the most paratactic syntax to establish conceptual associations. Language, in these poems, idles, the gears grating. (n.p.)

Dworkin describes language as trying to come together, seemingly of its own will, to form sentences, and from there "conceptual associations," possible in even so charged and atomized a universe as a radical Language poem. The key word here is "tension"—this isn't a programmed atomization but one that creates a pull between "irreconcilable linguistic elements" and "conceptual associations." To Dworkin, Andrews's writing eventually began to deal more with the phrase, and as a result approached a more coherent thematics.

> While the highly ironized and ventriloquizing transcriptions of public speech in these works may initially appear more accessible than the earlier non-lexical work, the writing is still significantly anasemantic. Although the content of these phrases is frequently provocative and offensive—"suck the testicles," "sink the boat people"—the emphasis is less on the particular content of the phrases than on the social work undertaken by such language. The disjunctive and irreconcilable contexts of the phrases underscores the sorts of social and psychological constructions that language enables, enacts, structures. (n.p.)

One should read the phrase "social work" above not only in the light of progressive politics, with which Language poetry is often allied, but also as a *performative* utterance (in the philosophy of Austin), in which speech such as "suck the testicles," in most cases an entirely irrational command, creates a change in the *state of affairs*—something has been called into existence—if only through its discomforting effect. This is more than what is now considered a commonplace activity of "postmodern" artists, which is that their activities "subvert" a seemingly "normative" or "privileged" way of looking at things. Andrews's writings, and his activities in the live-edited performances, is more like an *assault* on meaning, and he is hardly waiting, like an ivory-tower visionary, to be discovered, but is actively making a case for language to be used as a counter-paradigmatic thrust, and way beyond the confines of mere aesthetic or academic discourse.

This is language that seems to fit in with Seaman's paradigm of how he intends his language to operate in the liberated field of *The World Generator*, but Andrews seems to address the larger purpose of why language is being used at all. As Andrews himself writes in his essay "Electronic Poetics":

> Even though the meanings of language often seem more like an afterthought than the organizing principles in the digital domain, sense & its production (both narrowly linguistic & more broadly semiotic as well as social) remain key—beyond decorative (even if kinetic) visuals & sound. Language's social resonances still need center stage, choreographed to implicate situations beyond the immediate GUI (Graphic User Interface) & to "remind" us, by interpretable social choices (& the social force) of language, of the world(s) beyond. Semantic relations (with arrangements of time & space & grammar & typography & sound as vehicles) still top the hit list of socially relevant material. An immersive virtual space may encourage us to forget this, to vaporize everything outside the frame. If language is social, how can we make it resistant to a VR set-up? How to get beyond the razzle-dazzle (or comforting aura) of absorption, or

of programmed works that make the prior socialization of the material (& the social antagonisms or dissonances built into them) seem to vanish. (n.p.)

New media art and literature can often become a celebration of a successful feat of engineering, but beyond the basic "look what we can do with words," there has to be some notion of address: language must be setting out to do something, not sit in a vacuum (a sense, ironically, reified by the very novelty of the *unconventional* machine), a marker for that part where language *could be* used were one to want to say or do something.

A lopsidedness—a huge amount of programming and engineering at the service of a very limited textual experience—is often present in digital text works but is not unprecedented. Most of Marcel Duchamp's work, while not being engineering marvels in the conventional sense, were only meaningful given the textual tag, in the form of the title, that was placed on them. Calvin Tomkins (1998) in his biography of Duchamp describes a great deal of ingenuity that went into the construction of his final tableau, *Étant Donnés*, itself an object lesson in the virtue of limited "interactivity"—peeping through a hole. Works by The Prize Budget for Boys, such as "Basho's Frogger" and the now famous "Pac-Mondrian," follow this line of Duchamp's as they are constructions intended to elaborate either the basic pun in the title or, in the case of "Basho's Frogger," the haiku hidden in the high scoreboard: "FRG PND PLP." Works fed by a database can also achieve specificity as well as *affect*: Josh On's Internet project "They Rule" gives the user a graphical interface with which to explore the board members of several large corporations, relying on a database consisting of the names of corporations and the proper names of their board members. The artificial syntax of the connecting lines creates a powerful, and largely "literary," effect, perhaps the first political cartoon to rely entirely on a database. Whereas Duchamp and the PBR intend a sort of Dada shock effect, and "They Rule" intends to editorialize, "Stream of Consciousness"—an interactive garden whose database is a thesaurus—seems to be largely about exploring alternative man-computer interfaces. "You can reach out and touch the flow, blocking it or stirring up the words causing them to grow and divide," the artists state, "morphing into new words that are pulled into the drain and pumped back to the head of the stream to tumble down again." Unlike "They Rule," which makes its impact entirely because of the chosen data, "Stream of Consciousness" seems to me to be a piece that hasn't really found its text yet—it is a paradigm that will remain so (tellingly, Christiane Paul in her survey *Digital Art* [2003] doesn't mention the nature of the text at all). If one understands the engineering and programming of "Stream of Consciousness" as a constraint, in the same way that not using the letter "e" in George Perec's novel *La Disparition* (1969) as a constraint, or the engineering parameters of the Cave at Brown University functions as a constraint, then the next step should be to find the text, perhaps the *only* text, that is suitable—the "elegant solution"—to make the object more than a curio like Vaucanson's Duck.

THE HOLY GRAILS OF ELECTRONIC LITERATURE

The allure of the use of electronics in literary productions seems to be premised on the possibility of *subtraction*, which is to say that the erasure of the "author" not only "liberates" the meanings of words but also grants a work—here the notion of subtraction in Badiou's writing about Mallarmé is apposite—a nearly Symbolist suggestibility and inscrutability. A holy grail is, of course, a colloquial symbol representing an object of sacred quest, by implication one that is unobtainable; the search for the holy grail is not necessarily Quixotic—the seekers are more alchemists than fools—but it does seem to stand outside of the standard economy of desire and goal-fulfillment by having a quasi-visionary element to it. I call these aesthetic goals "holy grails" because they exist in a no-man's land between achievements that satisfy rubrics of science—concrete conceptual and technological breakthroughs that can exist on the continuum of paradigm-shifting discoveries like those of Copernicus or Pasteur—and achievements in the arts that are of lasting historical value for their "humanistic" content—how they, put loosely, help us to explain the human condition.[7] Consequently, these "holy grails" point to a desire, if only in a way premised on the very general fact of the "digital," for what Badiou et al. (2014: 84) would call *subtraction*, the "affirmative part of negation" that, like Schoenberg's twelve-tone theory, created a host of new possibilities: "The musical discourse avoids the laws of tonality, or, more precisely, becomes indifferent to these laws. That is why we can say that the music discourse is subtracted from its tonal legislation."

Christian Bök (2011) has been the most provocative and convincing proselyte for the use of the highest constraints in literature to liberate the most beautiful properties of language. He writes in "The New Ennui": "[*Eunoia*] makes a Sisyphean spectacle of its labour, willfully crippling its language in order to show that, even under such improbable conditions of duress, language can still express an uncanny, if not sublime, thought" (103).

Writing without the Author: to write a piece of literature that can be read several different ways—none predetermined by an "author"—which will provide distinctive, compelling reading experiences each time.

The primary quest here is to displace the "author" entirely onto the algorithm and its operations on a database (ideally, a communally, passively created database such as the Internet). Conceptually, this concern has been seen (especially by early hypertext critics such as George Landow) as a response to the poststructuralist preoccupation with the "death of the author." On the level of pure ambition, many programmers with no literary ambitions have sought to create programs that create works of literary value. Italo Calvino lovingly savages this perversely antisocial tendency comprehensively in his novel *If on a Winter's Night a Traveler* (2015), as when Silas Flannery states: "Perhaps instead of a book I could write lists of words, in alphabetical order, an avalanche of isolated words which expresses that truth I still do not know, and from which the computer, reversing its program, could construct the book, my book." Bök, in his writing on robot poetics, creates a very compelling portrait of a time when computers, having acquired a sense of vanity, will write poems purely for consumption by other computers: "Once a literary computer can analyse the formal limits of its own prior poems in order to revolutionize its output, anthropic culture may have to compete with an automated culture, whose spambots are already better equipped to overwhelm us with an enfilade of computer messages." The anxiety permeating this holy grail—Oedipal in some sense, if we think of

[7] Works that negotiate this apparent divide are actually not very scarce; architecture operates within this space all the time, for example, and electronic devices such as the iPhone (which many see as an architectural innovation more than anything else) have done as much to alter paradigms of sociological or even biological thinking as they have transformed interhuman engagement and creativity. However, the conceptual purities of my "holy grails" are so extreme that they exist more as gravitational pulls rather than achievable goals; they simply can't be obtained, since upon attainment the very aesthetic bases of the quest are destroyed—the work moves purely into science. Of course, in both cases, but more so with art than science, notions of "success" cannot always be determined with any immediacy, as it is history itself that often provides the context setting off the achievement; the crown of "distinction," in Bourdieu's et al. sense, (2015) may not arrive for the artist until after death, or through *death*, if even then.

Harold Bloom's famous articulation of anxieties of artistic succession in *The Anxiety of Influence* (1973)—is with making a departure from certain forms of classic hypertext and its embedded link model that feels more like an elaborate version of a "choose-your-own-adventure" story rather than the sublime machinations of artificial intelligence.

Corollary goals of works that aspire to this holy grail include:

- That the work be entirely syntactically coherent, not to mention semantically coherent. One might think that all works that aspire to be "authorless" want to attain this goal, but in fact several existing works of algorithmic literature—inspired, perhaps, by the print example of William S. Burroughs and Brion Gysin's "Cut-Up Method," and later, the Language Poets—are quite happy to be syntactically un-parsable and semantically indeterminate.
- That the work, if it claims to be a "narrative," provide in addition to point-by-point interesting text the clear lineaments of a "story arc"—set-up, inciting incident, rising action, denouement, and so on. Stern and Mateas's "Façade" (2006) might be the most elaborate example of such pieces; Mateas describes the issues they had with narrative form exhaustively in his essay "A Preliminary Poetics for Interactive Drama and Games" (2006). Open-world video games, such as *Grand Theft Auto*, permit the player to engage without slavish adherence to a story arc, though the arc is there if one should choose to stick to it.
- That the work, if it claims to be a "poem," have a sort of lyric integrity that we associate with poems, not to mention a metrical integrity that we associate with traditional forms of poetry. Charles Hartmann's experiments with computer-generated poetry (which he describes in *Virtual Muse: Experiments in Computer Poetry* (1996)) involved training a computer to parse works by poets such as Samuel Coleridge and, after such self-education, to write metrically stable works in that style. Most efforts at computer-generated poetry (such as Racter) have not bothered to deal with meter, and leave poetic subjectivity up to the chance encounter of an "I" and a verb.
- That the source text is entirely derived from a corpus of texts that were not written consciously as literature (the *Wall Street Journal*, for example). Noah Wardrip-Fruin's "NewsReader" (2004) and "Regime Change" (2004), derived entirely from Web texts, are versions of this, though little attention is paid to syntactical integrity in these works. "Get a Google Poem" (2007) by Leevi Lehto is a playful attempt at achieving some of these goals, though the piece has been entirely destabilized by changes in textual production—the predominance of PHP and XML over HTML as describing page architectures—in the Web 2.0 era.
- That the reading object is experienced in "real time," like a song or movie, rather than as an artifact that could very well appear on a page. An aspirant to this grail might be David Rokeby, whose "The Giver of Names" experiments with computer-generated poetry that derives its input from an electronic eye, and who learned language by a parsing classic like *Moby-Dick* or *Lolita*. Façade is, again, an example of this work, as it attempts to incorporate real-time user input into a story that unfolds largely like a film.

Reading beyond the Page: to provide a visual-textual experience that exists in a three-dimensional, dynamic, entirely processed space—that is, moving as far away from the physical, "static" page as possible.

Since Marinetti's experiments with Futurist typography and the elegant early masterworks of visual poetry as Mallarme's *Un Coup de Dés* (1897) and Blaise Cendrars's *La prose du Transsibérien et de la Petite Jehanne de France* (in its book incarnation by Sonia Delauney, 1913), poets have aspired to create poems that flouted the conventions of page space—a goal seen as a "liberation" of the word from the page. Some of the most sophisticated theories of concrete and visual poetry can be found in writings by the Noigandres group in Brazil (especially the theory of Haraldo de Campos), Charles Olson in the United States (whose "Projective Verse" is as much a theory of the body/mind as the page), and the writings of the Toronto Research Group (Steve McCaffery and B. P. Nichol, collected in *Rational Geomancy: The Kids of the Book-Machine* [1992]) who sought, in general, to reconcile the theories of the former to new trends in post-structural thought. The real near-contemporary masterwork of visual poetics and theory is not a book of poetry at all: *The Medium Is the Massage* (2008), a collaboration between Marshall McLuhan and Quentin Fiore, is increasingly being seen as a milestone of verbico/visual poetics, and is the basis of my own theories of the "ludic book." The real excitement of this "grail," however, comes from outside of literature: the elaborate and innovative movie titles of Saul Bass and the several brilliant artists who have exploited his breakthrough; the integration of textual elements into architectural works (as beautifully described in the seminal *Learning from Las Vegas*, by Robert Venturi et al. [1972]); the visual poetics inherent in the political theory of the Situationists, whose concept of the "détournement" sought to employ the aporias and breakages of text as cleavers against the spectacle; the musical experiments in indeterminacy by the composer John Cage that easily spilled over into visual poetics, such as the gorgeous mesostics—in which font, spacing, as well as words were determined by chance—collected in *M*. Any number of Modernist experiments with typography starting with the Futurists—surveyed in such works as Marjorie Perloff's *Radical Artifice* (1994) and Johanna Drucker's *The Visible Word* (1996)—to conceptual artists who work with language in physical spaces, including Barbara Kruger and Ian Hamilton Finlay, inspire the artists associated with this "holy grail." An author who aspires to this "holy grail" hopes to amplify, rather than suppress, the visibility of these behind-the-screen dynamics.

Corollary goals of works that aspire to this "holy grail" include:

- That the work is immersive, such that the user is present diegetically—as an active role in the physical universe—in the text. Camille Utterbeck's "Text Rain" (1999) is a basic, two-dimensional push in this direction, while Jeffrey Jones's "Legible City" (1988/91), which incorporates a bicycle as the main physical interface, is probably the most accomplished of such pieces, though in both cases the text is quite trivial. Several experiments in Brown's Cave environment have attempted to utilize more absorbing texts, most notably Noah Wardrip-Fruin's "Screen" (2002). Daniel Howe's experiments in Java, such as "Recube," another 3D textual environment, are also angling toward this "grail."
- That the visual output of the piece has a *visceral* efficacy on the level of film or theater, and yet remain legible as "text" at all or most times. One must look at the work of filmmakers, such as nouvelle vague maestro Jean-Luc Godard, or players in the net art community, such as Young-Hae Chang Heavy Industries, for works that have most achieved this effect. The Flash version of "Bembo's Zoo," a child's abecedarian created by the Roberto de Vicq de Cumptich, and my own "Dreamlife of Letters" might be other examples. The YouTube text video "What Does Marcellus Wallace Look Like," created by Jarratt Moody, which synchronizes animated text

with audio of Jules Winnfield's (Samuel L. Jackson) monologue from the film *Pulp Fiction*, is a powerful example of this tendency.

- That a three-dimensional space can not only seem accommodating of text, but in fact creates situations in which hitherto unknown properties of text become revealed. Once again, the experiments in the Cave come closest to achieving this goal, as one encounters therein text from various angles, at varying pseudo-depths. Speed and proximity are the primary variables at play, as is richly described by Robert Venturi et al. in *Learning from Las Vegas*; billboards, for example, have created a new genre of textuality, properties exploited most fully by the paintings of Ed Ruscha.
- That, for all of the variations of the text's appearance on the screen, the textual image always maintains what can be called high standards of graphic design. One persistent deficiency in many works of electronic literature is the failure to deal with the history, standards, affects, and ambitions of graphic design, though recent works, such as David Clark's "88 Constellations for Wittgenstein" and Sharon Daniels's "Public Secrets" (designed by Erik Loyer) have made great strides in this direction. The iPad application Flipboard, which collects data from any number of sources such as the users' social networking sites, RSS feeds, and blogs and reformats them in a sexy, consistent, but variable graphic design—such that status updates, trivial or not, are set off like pull quotes in a high-end magazine—shows the powers of algorithmic graphic design in granting the air of cultural capital to ephemera.[8]

Electronic works that aspire to the properties of video games, such as Jason Nelson's "game game game and again game," Noah Wardrip-Fruin et al.'s "Screen," and my own "Kluge" can be seen as a part of an emergent third "holy grail." What differentiates a video game from interactive art is that the former instills in the user a lusory, or playful, attitude with what Bernard Suits terms "pre-lusory" goals—not just the desire to experience something different, but the desire to achieve a game state in which one can say one has "won." The pre-lusory goal in a game of soccer, for instance, is to have the ball appear, if even for the briefest second, in the opponent's goal ("kicking the ball" is part of what Suits would call the "lusory means"; not touching the ball with the hands would be a "constitutive rule"). The key difference with the above holy grails is that the algorithms producing the text will have a quasi-cybernetic relationship with the user: the game state of the textual apparatus will adjust according to the user's ability to deal with it. The user engages the piece with a competitive motivation rather than merely the desire to continue an indeterminate aesthetic experience. In the first holy grail, writing without an "author," all elements of gameplay are subsumed in the programs producing the text—the user herself never *enacts* algorithm in her input. In a true video game, as in interactive fiction such as "Façade," the user learns and adopts the set of inputs and acquires a sort of visceral feel for their effects—an illusion of "control" over an animated/simulated field—whereas in standard "hypertext," this sense of control is largely absent because there are limited expectations on the part of the user that their input will do anything, certainly not change

[8] The video game "Shadow of the Colossus" is a third-person game that operates by dynamically generated camera angles (rather than the fixed, over-the-shoulder perspective offered by most games), hence carrying over, successfully I think, the standards of good cinematography—shot composition, panning and tracking, even editing—into an algorithm.

the game state—it is largely "indeterminate."[9] A corollary goal of works that aspire to this "holy grail" could include that the desire to "win" is entirely centered around textual consumption, rather than the seemingly trivial process of, say, getting your character to escape from a maze or to avoid falling bricks.

THE POETICS OF DISGUST

The seemingly endless, infinite amount of creativity by an algorithm, divorced from the limitations of the human body and the physical world, creates a strong bridge between what we expect an algorithm to perform in digital writing and what has been termed *jouissance* in postmodern literary theory, particularly by those writers associated with poststructuralism such as Jacques Lacan and Roland Barthes. *Jouissance* stands in opposition to *plaisir* (pleasure) for Barthes, and is characteristic of "writerly" texts that, like Language poetry, seem to challenge the reader's ontological security—the sureness of his or her subjectivity. Likewise, for Lacan, *jouissance* extends beyond Freud's "pleasure principle," which operates "to maximize satisfaction and correspondingly minimize pain/dissatisfaction," and in fact extends into sensations we normally associate with pain:

> For Lacan, the ego feels pain (in the form of anxiety, symptoms, and the like) when the homeostatic balance sheet of the pleasure principle is thrown into disorder by an insistent enjoyment than [*sic*] pays no heed of the speculative gains or losses of a diluted, sublimated pleasure, of a principle that routinely "sells out" enjoyment in its ongoing bargaining with its reality-level complement. (Johnston 2005: 34)

Certain strands in electronic writing, and to my mind some of the more effective stances, have been taken against a practice of *jouissance*—that is, have been premised on a sort of contrapuntal relationship between engaging in the seemingly infinite play of the algorithm and something that Sianne Ngai (2002) has theorized as a "poetics of disgust" which works against the semantic slippage understood by poststructuralist critics as the dominant form of literary activity. Consequently, I'd like to suggest that disgust is an experience that can be felt in those documentary elements of writing, those that are marked by the mindless author's body, those moments that exceed meaning without subverting it, acting as a parallel meta-semantics or what I am referring to as a "counterpoint."

---

[9] Consequently, by inviting the user into engagement the algorithm, "algorithm" itself is demystified—one's fascination with the operations of an invisible, exotic algorithm, the "Orientalism" of the continent of code, is reduced to the degree that the flesh-based player gains some sort of mastery over it. One is not left in a state of fascination over the operations of pseudo-AI code, as in the first "grail," but enacts algorithm him/herself. As Manovich writes in "Database as a Symbolic Form":

> [I]n games where the game play departs from following an algorithm, the player is still engaged with an algorithm, albeit in another way: she is discovering the algorithm of the game itself. I mean this both metaphorically and literally: for instance, in a first person shooter, such as "Quake," the player may eventually notice that under such and such condition the enemies will appear from the left, i.e. she will literally reconstruct a part of the algorithm responsible for the game play. Or, in a different formulation of the legendary author of Sim games Will Wright, "Playing the game is a continuous loop between the user (viewing the outcomes and inputting decisions) and the computer (calculating outcomes and displaying them back to the user). The user is trying to build a mental model of the computer model." (n.p.)

I refer to this process as pseudo-cybernetics to the degree that the computer is not actually engaged in active observation of the physical world, but is responding to information the user volunteers in the form of thumb-twitching. Nonetheless, both computer and player are engaged in constructing "mental models" of the other operations (the player herself behaving "algorithmically") and adjusting accordingly.

Ironically, legibility—moments of clarity, of forced self-reflection, of a complete understanding of context, even of the Brechtian "V-effekt" that opens up the cellars of meaning to moral judgment—is a minority function in most literary digital objects, even those that propose to be "literary." In other words, the kinds of precision one associates with the "well-wrought urn" of stylistically economical writing in print is often subsumed under the looser, open-ended stylistic economies of much digital writing. To take an obvious example, most of one's experience with Michael Joyce's *afternoon: a story* is premised on some notion of narrative *jouissance*, in which story elements—plot, setting, character, and so on—are left to play among themselves. The characters in the story themselves express *jouissance* as they are seemingly endlessly intertwined in each other's sexual and psychological lives, with the character Werther being the epigone of the polyamorous. Those moments of disgust in the text occur when the narrative play is asked to take a backseat to a moment of readerly reflection, such as in that almost-never noted moment when the presence of Robert Creeley is made felt when Joyce includes, wholesale, a poem from Creeley's 1968 volume *Pieces*.[10] The Creeley poem serves as a block to any easy continuation of pure *jouissance*; it hinders understanding of the flow of meanings by implanting its own understanding, Joseph Kosuth–style, of the presence of words on the page/screen, the this-ness of letters as they are being encountered.

Disgust, synonymous here with a moment of intense awareness of experience, of the concreteness of vision, can be seen, in this light, as synonymous with those moments of precise literary effect. Ngai (2002: 338) writes:

> Disgust is urgent and specific; desire can be ambivalent and vague. The former expects concurrence; the latter does not. I should clarify that in what follows, the word "desire" refers not to sexuality or sexual practices, or to psychoanalysis' highly exacting concept of drive or libido, but rather to the vaguely affective idiom broadly used as an "index of (literary) heterogeneity" by late twentieth-century literary theorists across methods and affiliations. That is, I mean "desire" associated with images of fluidity, slippage, and semantic multiplicity—what Kristeva in *Desire in Language* calls polynomia or "the pluralization of meaning by different means (polyglottism, polysemia, etc.)"—which has become technical shorthand for virtually any perceived transgression of the symbolic status quo. Inclusive, pluralistic, and often eclectic, literary theory's "desire" is admittedly appealing, especially when positioned as "a mobile system of free signifying devices" in explicit contrast to the rigid hierarchies of the symbolic order."

McCaffery articulates in *North of Intention* just this poetics of "fluidity" and "slippage," even so far as to envision letters and marks on the page as semen and shit—as fossilizations of this very libidinous discharge—but like Ngai, he sees these moments not as enacting a "pluralization of meaning" so much as the direct transference of what could objectively be described as "energy." And imagining letters on a page as bodily fluids is, of course, repulsive, at least to one who views the blank white page as encouraging a meditative exercise (or to one who does not want to get their hands dirty with newsprint).

---

[10] Unfortunately, I am no longer able to access afternoon due to the obsolescence of the disk format and changing operating systems. I also don't have noted in my notes exactly what Creeley poem was lifted for *afternoon*. Most criticism of *afternoon* does not note the poem, but Charles Moran (1998: 202–9), in a review of Michael Joyce's *Of Two Minds: Hypertext, Pedagogy and Poetics*, writes: "Joyce tells us, information is no longer scarce but free and entirely available to all. Alive in a giant hypertext, 'We can imagine ourselves bathed in knowledge.' Hypertext has enabled Joyce, self-styled 'pig-shit Irish,' to appropriate the language of Robert Creeley, whom he sees as lace-curtain Irish, and build Creeley's language into his own work."

In an early version of the "Poetics of Disgust," Ngai described a paradigmatic experience of repulsion by describing an encounter on the street, shared with another, with "a piece of shit on the sidewalk. There's a roach on this turd, and the roach is eating it. We look at this for a while together. As if we were compelled to, fascinated in spite of ourselves" (Ngai 2002: 167). She then articulates a series of events that occur during this experience: the "negative utterance" ("Ugh!"), the "wordless pointing," the fascination "in spite of ourselves," the turning away, and so on. As a poetics, Ngai's essay focuses on onomatopoeia and exclamatory words that simply recreate sounds ("Wooh, brah"), deictic words that indicate a certain "pointing" (such as "this," or brackets containing nothing []), typographic signs that seem to serve no semantic function in a given text ("@&%$!"), stranded facts ("West Germany 4.5%"), and proper names—all of which obstruct the "seductive reasoning of pluralism." Writing of Bruce Andrews's book-length poem *I Don't Have Any Paper So Shut Up, or Social Romanticism*, Ngai (2002: 351) hones in on the use of proper names as points that "resist," if only partly, semantic slippage:

> In their negative insistence, there is a sense in which the linguistic materials privileged in *Shut Up* resemble what Lyotard calls "tensors," referring to the "tension" in a sign that exceeds any semiotic dialectic of vertical fixation and horizontal displacement including the "interminable metonymy" of slippage from word to word we have seen privileged in the sue of "desire" as a figurative catch-all for any kind of literary polyvalence or multiplicity. Lyotard's favorite example of the tensor is the proper name, a form that reminds us that while all signs are prone to semantic pluralization and slippage, not all are prone to this equally; some, like Alamo or Lipton Tea, have an "intensity" that makes them more resistant—if only slightly—to polysemous voyages. Because the proper name "refers in principle to a single reference" (think of "Harvey Milk" or "Beirut") and is therefore less capable, however small the increment of difference, of being "exchangeable against other terms in the logical-linguistic structure," Lyotard argues that "there is no intra-systemic equivalent of the proper name, it points towards the outside like a deictic, it has no connotation, nor is it interminable."

The proper name is "more difficult to budge, countering the principle of infinite transferability that underlies the polysemous slippage routinely preferred but often too starkly opposed to semantic fixation in a poetics of 'desire.'"

One could contend that the interplay of those moments of negation and permission of semantic slippage, the enactment of the rules or functions of the algorithms themselves, serve in some sense to curtail the infinite "exchangeability" that is inherent in pieces of digital "writerly" literature. For example, one could see the very specific cultural references in a text movie by Young-Hae Chang Heavy Industries (and even their ransacking of Ezra Pound's first two *Cantos* in"*Dakota*"[11]) along with their timeline based, anti-algorithmic construction as a counterpoint to the scripting possibilities of Flash/ActionScript and networked distribution itself. That is, YHCHI's choice to construct a Flash application like an analog film, as well as their choice to lard their texts with proper names and offer them in several different languages, stand in direct opposition to the easy "pluralistic" exchange that algorithm provides. Even those network writers that do not code, such as mez and Ted Warnell, and some who do, such as Talan Memmott and Loss Pequeño Glazier, have managed to incorporate many of the techniques that Ngai associates with a curtailment of

[11] See Pressman (2009). A pdf of this essay can be found at Pressman's website: http://www.jessicapressman.com/publications/.

pleasure—the nonutilitarian typographical symbol, the empty brackets and other deictic contraptions—into their computer creoles. This is a practice interpreted by Raley and Hayles as expressive of a merging of human subjectivity and the computer's recursive functions—what I've been terming the "fictional" element—but which, I argue, can be seen, instead, as a "counterpoint" to semantic slippage.

Proper names, for example, have been used as contextual and conceptual anchors in works of digital literature premised on endless interconnectivity. Examples include the aforementioned "News Reader" and "Regime Change" by Noah Wardrip-Fruin et al., both using n-grams to merge stories from Reuters and other Internet news outlets into new texts, and the work "Status Update"[12] (2007) by Darren Wershler and Bill Kennedy, which draws on a database of dead authors' names and links them to the status updates, acquired by RSS feed, from Facebook. On's "They Rule" derives its power almost exclusively from the use of proper names, encouraging, quite literally, an experience of "disgust." Proper names open converging, confusing, and ultimately powerful narrative flows into pieces that might otherwise be demeaned as academic exercises in making new sentences out of the linguistic raw data of the Internet. For William Poundstone, especially in his work "3 Proposals for Bottle Imps," the hold against this faceless exchange of language has been based on experimentation with gaudy, attention-grabbing type (not to mention canned sound effects and robotic animations), but even here the artist is faced with a form of corporate standardization, for fonts themselves, even those designed by amateurs, can be seen as obscuring by their very reusability the sorts of bodily singularity that McCaffery champions. Digital typefaces, even of the most gaudy or, in the case of Paul Chan's "Alternumerics"—font sets in which letters are replaced with entire words, scribbles, diagrams, "white space" denoted by parentheses and lines of measurement, and so on—entirely inutile, must conform to the specifications of either Adobe's PostScript or Apple and Microsoft's TrueType (or Microsoft's related OpenType) to operate on a computer. Especially apposite for our present discussion of excess and transgression is Chan's "Sade for Fonts Sake" (2009) in which "each font holds a unique set of idioms that expresses a different sexual voice when typed. Some like Oh Bishop X and Oh Justine are based on characters in novels by Sade, while others are inspired by characters from news (Monica Lewinsky), pornstars (Michael Lucas), and poets and writers (Gertrude Stein, Hölderlin) whose work knots together sex with language, rhythm and form."[13]

Alan Liu in *Laws of Cool* (2004) traces an evolution in graphic design strategy from Bauhaus economy, embodied by the concept of the unifying "gestalt"—a psychological principle developed in the 1920s denoting the general visual shape arising from the arrangement of objects and details—directly to the culture of "information cool," as

---

[12] This application no longer functions but the authors have published a selection of the material as *Update* (Montreal: Snare Books, 2006).

[13] Jan Tschichold, leading Modernist typographer and author of the seminal, Bauhaus-inspired *Die neue Typographie* (*The New Typography*; 1998: 78), expressly remarks that typefaces are never the expression of an individual personality, but of an age: "Our age is characterized by an all-out search for clarity and truth, for purity of appearance. So the problem of what typeface to use is necessarily different from what it was in previous times. We require from type plainness, clarity, the rejection of everything that is superfluous." For superfluous, we can read "excessive," that which lies outside the efficient, condensed message. Tschichold continues:

> It is not important to create special types for advertising perfume manufacturers and fashion shops, or for lyrical outpourings by poets. It was never the task of punch-cutters of the past to create a type for a single kind of expression. The best typefaces are those which can be used for all purposes, and the bad ones those which can be used only for visiting-cards or hymn books. (ibid.)

expressed in such elegant but functional designs as the Apple computer. Liu describes significant detours, however, primarily under the rubric of "antidesign"—characterized by fragmenting, crowding, blurring, twisting, stretching, distorting, or repeating text elements "to near illegibility" (216)—which can be seen as an attempt to reintroduce all of those elements of singularity and personality, not to mention inefficiency, that Jan Tschichold, for example, wished to exclude. Design, in these terms, is an expression of social values; further, design can be seen as an intervention in the transference of values, almost crypto-Situationist in philosophy even as the designer works under the standard economic rubric of being subject to the whims of a client. Liu writes of the absence of the "dialectically poised contradictions" in antidesign, suggesting that the counterpoise of a good International Style design argues for a vision of social progress premised on Marxist terms in the way director Sergei Eisenstein argued that film montage operated didactically as illustration of the historical dialectic, while the all-overness of antidesign sets itself as an egalitarian contrast to such excesses of rationality.[14]

Liu (2004) notes that the fluidity of design on the Web—exacerbated by differences in monitor settings, monitor size, personal settings on a Web browser, download speeds (noting that pages load their images and texts in unpredictable, uncontrollable orders), variance in content (especially in dynamically generated pages such as forums), and so on—incorporates within it many of the principles of antidesign itself. Web design has to forego many of the subtler elements of well-tempered gestalt in order to survive.

> Both the spatial and temporal conditions of the Web scramble design, and the result is to destabilize the social meaning of design. The more the Web designer attempts to freeze the composition on the screen as if it were a display affixed to a spatial whole that can be delivered temporally to the user all at once, the more that designer resists an even deeper design imperative in the medium—the need to make design as fluid as possible so that it can pour across the wires into the unpredictable receptacles, rhythms, and ultimately lives of others. The deep design of the Web is the distribution of the authority of design from the content-designer to the user-designer (collaborating with legions of hidden program designers) who configures the machine of the browser. (230)

Ironically, antidesign, which sought to break through the leveling factor of International Style graphic design, itself has leveled the individuality of carefully articulated typographical spaces because of its ties to digital technology and by extension the algorithm. That

---

Tschichold, long before the age of the Internet, extols the paradigmatic over the syntagmatic; he champions the typeface that can be dropped into several contexts rather than the ostentatious or "original" font that, like the unique utterance (or Wallace Stevens's jar in Tennessee) can create context by its very singularity. "There is no personal expression of the designer, nor was it ever his aim, except in the first years of our century," he writes, putting his own nail in the coffin of Romanticism. The new typography is the expression of the subsumption of the individual into the system; the Weltgeist of the age is the efficiency of the machine and its inherent standardizations, including that of paper size (the second half of *The New Typography* is largely devoted to discussions of letterhead). Tschichold prefers typefaces designed anonymously, collectively, "above all in a technical sense useful and free from personal idiosyncrasies—in the best sense of the word, uninteresting" (78).

[14] Eisenstein (1969: 45) writes in "A Dialectic Approach to Film Form":

> In the realm of art this dialectic principle of dynamics is embodied in CONFLICT as the fundamental principle for the existence of every artwork and every art-form. For art is always conflict: 1) according to its social mission, 2) according to its nature, 3) according to its methodology. According to its social mission because: It is art's task to make manifest the contradictions of Being. To form equitable views by stirring up contradictions within the spectator's mind, and to forge accurate intellectual concepts from the dynamic clash of opposing passions.

is, desktop publishing permitted the designer an increasingly granular control of objects and effects, but Web technology ended up thwarting this deep particularity.[15]

IMMANENCE INC.

The most writerly aspect to much electronic writing, and by extension electronic art, can be the interface itself, which raises the possibility that a realm of electronic writing can exist that does not involve letterforms at all. I'm thinking in particular of the interactive Shockwave pieces of turux.org, in which the user interacts with an image that is already buzzing with activity, but which responds to the mouse pointer's motions in ways that are not always obvious but can be learned, like a dance or a secret code. The longer the user navigates in the space, the more is revealed of the deep structure, or the programming behind the unfolding in a sort of visual analog of generative grammar. McCaffery (1977: n.p.) writes in his afterword to the largely wordless, typewritten score *Marquee*, by poet Ray DiPalma:

> *Marquee* then, exposes the very contours of the signifier (when meaning is differance what else can be?). Shard. Trace-structure. A live (a life) in materiality deliberately devoid of function yet in that lack-of-usage instituting a presence of its own: a graphic substance. On the plane of semiosis DiPalma gives us a language-centered text, a text lacking all referential thrusts to any outside reality. And here we enter the logical illogic and inhabit a centre which is margin: the centre of the sign-shape, in/side the outline. A/long, a/mong, a/bove and not a/bove a spacing that is solid: the ink of the gramme.

It might seem contradictory that I valorize such an approach after my criticisms of Bill Seaman's celebration of the demotion of "the word" to just another media element, but I'm not convinced that Seaman's application serves to animate the properties of language that Derrida or Deleuze and Guattari describe in the citations he takes from them. While it might be true that Derrida advocates in his writing a seemingly endless deferral of closed meaning—endless chains of signifiers and concepts that offer an illuminated map to the gothic pathways of the mind—there is a specificity to the field of language which is all important, since it is only in language, and not in film and dance (for example), in which elements can be connected syntactically (via the human instinct for language) and logically (which produces the possibility for its many opposites, such as paradox and irrationality). In fact, the type of poetry found in virtual reality literary pieces is often quite distracting; as poetic writing, it often doesn't engage in any of the various sensual and stylistic properties that language is able to access in poetry (such as D. H. Lawrence's, Gerard Manley Hopkins or Lyn Hejinian, this latter of whom seems an obvious source

[15] Liu's statements are restricted to an era of the Web that has, indeed, passed. When *Laws of Cool* was being written what we now call "Web 2.0" had not made its presence felt to the degree it has now. Though it is subject to debate, my definition of Web 2.0 is premised on: first, the large scale use of Flash to render pages "dynamic" in ways beyond the imaginations of HTML coders and, second, the rise of social networks such as Facebook and the interaction of portable devices like phones and tablets with the Web. The implication is that a viewer of graphic design (and, in our consideration, text itself) will increasingly view any sort of "page" with text and image on it as having some possibility for being dynamic, and that the rejection of this possibility will suggest a set of social values in contrast to the "spirit of the age"—the infinite, free exchange of information. Nonetheless, collaboration is described: graphic designers become "designers of the Web" as much as the protocols of the Web impose themselves on the artist.

for such a pragmatist's engine).[16] Interactive Shockwave pieces like those of turux.org—which don't use images as such but mostly paint their images with dots and vector lines, many of which are programmed to resemble the marks of pencils on a sheet of cream-colored paper—are instances of pure interaction with code: the mouse pointer, merely two numbers on an x/y grid controlled by the hand, interacts with other similar numbers which both engage the mouse pointer but also call back to home base to retrieve other, further orders of behavior. Nonetheless, even with McCaffery's imprimatur, it's certainly a stretch to call these Flash pieces "literature."

Russian poet Lev Rubinstein's collection *Catalogue of Comedic Novelties* (2004), though not related to anything like "digital art," seems to work along this very gradient between the indeterminate and the recombinant. Each of these "poems"—they are quite unclassifiable, actually—are made of single lines, each of which occupies a card (or a numbered line, in the English edition), which start off with certain features reappearing in each line, as if the poet were caught in a mental stutter or obsessive compulsion, but which then work through different frames before reaching a conclusion.

1 Who's that in the yellow fog
Coming closer and closer?
2 Now like shadows on the screen,
Now like air, now like water?
3 Who's that in the yellow fog
Rushing forward, rushing headlong?
4 Is he trapped in a nirvana
Does he even know himself?

This goes on for several more cards, with the occasional inclusion of an entirely blank card. It's unclear what Rubinstein would do in a performance for these cards, but in any case, these would have to be moments in which the passing of time, and the presence of the actor/reader, would be magnified. The theme or mode of the cards then shifts to the following, with the introduction of personal names and less beat-driven lines:

21 . . . and, sizzling, it goes out. We had to walk in complete darkness, our arms stretched out . . .
22 —What about Zhukov?
23 —We already talked about that. . .
24 —And?

---

[16] Marjorie Perloff in "The Poetics of Click and Drag: Screening the New Poetries" makes a similar point about David Knoebel's interactive audiovisual poem "Thoughts Go":

> It's an interesting idea but I don't think it works. We can't really hear the spoken text while we are reading the visual one without losing the resonances of both. And the fact is that, either way, the texts abound in standard Romantic lingo: take the metaphor of thoughts as "far travelers" that "touch down briefly / time and again," or the "wedge of geese" disappearing "beyond the/ sycamore grove." Would it matter if it were a birch grove? Or if the "parking lot" were a truck stop? "Our words," said Yeats famously, "must seem to be inevitable." The digital poem, no matter how "clever" the gimmick, can't have much staying power if the language is arbitrary.

She doesn't expand her thesis to include any consideration of texts in which the words are generated in "real time" by an algorithm, but I would argue that, even in that case, a sense of "inevitability," if not "permanence," as an example of language well-used, will certainly heighten the experience however ephemeral.

25 ... and, sizzling, it goes out. "Just great," thought Filichev, "that was the last one. . ."
26 —What about Kolya Pokshishevsky?
27 —Not in a million years!
28 —And why not?
29 ... and, sizzling, it goes out. "The end," flashed through his mind. . .
30 —Could it be Arlazov?

The poem then begins to take a simple quatrain—for example, "When the right hour struck / A child was born. / It was born, and smiled, / And so the time flew by ..."—and repeat it, though on occasion, a card would contain just a single line from this quatrain, primarily focusing on the phrase "And so the time flew by ..." The last part of the poem is the most concrete in terms of objective description, and only takes up about four cards, ending with the refrain from the prior sequence:

73 ... a chair, for example. There it is, unoccupied. Yet everyone's a little afraid to sit in it for some reason. . .
74 ... or, let's say, an apple tree. It has blossomed quite well, it's lush, but for some reason there are no apples on it. . .
75 ... or for example, this girl I know. Great gal, pretty and easy to talk to, and yet she's got no one. . .
76 ... or a mirror. A nice mirror, of ancient make. And yet, for some reason no one likes themselves in it. Why is that?
77 And so the time flew by. . .

This is a poem that clearly needs metaphors from music to describe it, and in fact, the text could have been influenced by the libretti of Robert Wilson, such as *Einstein on the Beach* or the *A Letter to Queen Victoria*, which utilize a great deal of repetition and allude to a narrative universe that never comes entirely to the fore.

But there is also a programmatic quality to them that suggests, in some ways, they were generated as much as written—the author is not giving himself the license to write as much as he might to satisfy his own authorial instincts, but is rather subsuming the writing under the larger scheme of an abstract progression, a series of movements. The "mode" of each movement can almost be described algorithmically—first a set of sing-songy couplets, then a set of three-line units involving a name, a response, a denial, and a refrain (very Beckett-like), then a series of quatrains that are taken apart then welded together again, culminating in a finale of cinematic vignettes. The translators describe Rubinstein's (2004: iv) texts as "uncanny voicings of *homo sovieticus*" elaborating on how the high "conceptualist" poetics of his project allies with his apparent naturalism: "Because his conceptualist poetics seems to require an alienated stance toward language, Rubinstein can be described as more an archivist than composer; that is, he catalogues, on his library cards, the shreds of our speech in all its fragmentariness, wonder, and degradation." Obviously, there is a theme of absence, of death, prevalent throughout, but the narrative color—the colloquialism of the speech, the familiarity with which the names are spoken—adds further dimensions, and further questions, such as: is this the chattering of prisoners? Or if so, are they prisoners in a prison or prisoners of the communist state? Or does it develop into a wider existential realm, suggesting that we are all prisoners, some of whom go "off into the world of light" without leaving much behind letting us know where they are going. The effect is quite powerful in this short poem, but—most importantly for us—the texts are quite simple, and the key to their construction, dangled before us by the author, makes them both easier to take in quickly but also increasingly more evocative while being increasingly more empty: the replaceable contents of the names and questions suggests a futility of a bureaucratic worldview turning the mind into a database of (im)personal contacts.

I think such techniques as those employed by Rubinstein could be useful for electronic writers who are interested in thematics that could be derived from databased texts which are operated on algorithmically. This is language of a poetic "first intensity"—even a condensed language, along the lines of Pound—and yet it seems amenable to a "recombinant" poetics that thrives on real-time creation of textual experiences by a program (or "demon," as I've described it in *Fashionable Noise*) acting on source files. It also promotes active "reading," which I oppose to something I've previously called "parsing," which is when one analyzes the qualities of a text regardless of purported content for certain markers: repetition of certain symbols, obvious misspellings, just general qualities of the gestalt of a text that one obtains prior to interpretation. My sense is that one could "parse" the transitional stages of a Cayley linguistic "transliteral morph" more than read them, since the in-between stages, the "nodal points" in N. Katherine Hayles's phrase, don't relate to language as humans use it in any way (unlike, say, the morphing of language between Chaucerian English to our own would display characteristics from which one could derive generalities concerning the human mind and society). Both "parsing" and reading are valid experiences in an electronic writing piece, and certain texts, such as those of Mez and Talan Memmott, ask to be approached both ways simultaneously. But I think that the deferred meaning of a "parsing"—predicated partly on Derridean *differánce*—should be no excuse for the reduced emphasis placed on text as something that can be read.

McCaffery's considerations of a "general economy" for language, with which this chapter started, suggested that language can exist as a pure "energy," if not information-rich, then existing outside the sphere of common hermeneutics, and hence, not characterized by polynomia so much as precognitive flows. In contrast is Hayles's conception of the "flickering signifier" in which we understand texts to be composed cybernetically, a collaboration between human and machine that, in my reading, encourages the semantic slippage inherent in a subject codependent on both human and computer. Algorithm, and by extension algorithmic text, introduces a natural sort of semantic slippage, or "play of the signifier," to text which Ngai argues in "The Poetics of Disgust" can be broken or short-circuited by the use of proper names, symbols, and a range of non-phonetic typographical elements—"tensors" in Lyotard's phrase. Liu's analysis of the progression of graphic design from the invariable printed gestalt to the variable Web page suggests that, once again, indeterminacy is introduced into text merely by the position textual objects obtain on a page or screen despite the best laid plans of writers and designers. My argument is largely aesthetic: that a "counterpoint" can be created in algorithmic text art between those elements which favor slippage and those that deny it, those elements that argue for efficiency—such as the rules of a game or the design gestalt—and those that exceed any such curtailment. Though I am here largely concerned with the works of artists, these dynamics can be observed in any number of textual phenomena in the Web 2.0 era. What remains to be asked concerns the ontological status of the algorithm itself: can we understand the algorithm as participating in the vitalist notion, represented here by Bataille, that immanent creativity as exhibited by both nature and culture on the earth—the constant, abundant creativity exhibited by humans, animals, plants, and even minerals (in the form of storms or tectonic slippage)—or do we view algorithms as largely tools and prosthetics—"extensions of man" in McLuhan's phrase like hammers and automobiles—but otherwise exhibiting no true autonomy?

SOURCES CITED

Andrews, Bruce. "Electronic Poetics." http://www.ubu.com/papers/andrews_electronic.html. Accessed July 3, 2017.

Andrews, Bruce, and Charles Bernstein, eds. *The L=A=N=G=U=A=G=E Book*. Carbondale: Southern Illinois University Press, 1984.

Badiou, Alain, Bruno Bosteels, and Emily Apter. *The Age of the Poets: And Other Writings on Twentieth-Century Poetry and Prose*. Brooklyn, NY: Verso, 2014.

Bataille, Georges. *The Accursed Share: An Essay on General Economy, Volume 1: Consumption*. Translated by Robert Hurley. New York: Zone Books, 1988.

Bloom, Harold, and Monroe K. Spears. *The Anxiety of Influence*. New York: Oxford University Press, 1973.

Bök, Christian. *Eunoia*. Coach House, 2011.

Bök, Christian. "The Piecemeal Bard Is Deconstructed: Notes toward a Potential Robopoetics." *Object 10: Cyberpoetics*. New York: Ubuweb, 2002. http://www.ubu.com/papers/object/03_bok.pdf.

Bourdieu, Pierre, Richard Nice, and Tony Bennett. *Distinction: A Social Critique of the Judgement of Taste*. London: Routledge, Taylor & Francis Group, 2015.

Burroughs, William S. "The Cut-Up Method of Brion Gysin." In *The New Media Reader*, Noah Wardrip-Fruin, Nick Montfort, and Michael Crumpton. Cambridge: MIT, 2003, pp. 89–92.

Calvino, Italo, and William Weaver. *If on a Winter's Night a Traveller*. London: Vintage, 2015.

Cayley, John. "Lens: The Practice and Poetics of Writing in Immersive VR: A Case Study with Maquette." *Leonardo Almanac*, vol. 14, no. 5 (2006), http://leoalmanac.org/journal/vol_14/lea_v14_n05-06/jcayley.asp.

Cayley, John. "Literal Art." *Electronic Book Review*. November 29, 2004. http://www.electronicbookreview.com/thread/firstperson/programmatology.

Drucker, Johanna. *The Visible Word: Experimental Typography and Modern Art, 1909–1923*. Chicago: University of Chicago, 1996.

Duchamp, Marcel. *Étant donnés: 1. la chute d'eau, 2. le gaz d'éclairage*. Philadelphia Museum of Art. 1946–1966.

Dworkin, Craig. *Bruce Andrews*. Unedited encyclopedia entry for Fitzray Dearborn's *Encyclopedia of American Poetry: The Twentieth Century*. http://epc.buffalo.edu/authors/andrews/about/dworkin.html.

Eisenstein, Sergei. *Film Form: Essays in Film Theory*. Translated by Jay Leyda. New York: Harcourt, 1969.

Hartman, Charles O. *Virtual Muse: Experiments in Computer Poetry*. Hanover: University of New England, 1996.

Hayles, N. Katherine. *Writing Machines*. Cambridge: MIT Press, 2002.

Hayles, N. Katherine. "The Time of Digital Poetry: From Object to Event." In *New Media Poetics: Contexts, Technotexts, and Theories*, edited by A. Morris and T. Swiss. Cambridge: MIT Press, 2006.

Hayles, N. Katherine. *How We Became Posthuman: Virtual Bodies in Cybernetics, Literature and Informatics*. Chicago: University of Chicago, 2010.

Hayles, N. Katherine. "Virtual Bodies and Flickering Signifiers" (1996), http://www.english.ucla.edu/faculty/hayles/Flick.html.

Huizinga, Johan. *Homo Ludens*. Boston: Beacon Press, 1971.

Johnston, Adrian. *Time Driven: Metapsychology and the Splitting of the Drive*. Chicago: Northwestern University Press, 2005.

Jones, Jeffrey. "The Legible City." 1988/91. http://www.medienkunstnetz.de/works/the-legible-city/.

Kermode, Frank. *Sense of an Ending*. Oxford: Oxford University Press, 1966.

Lehto, Leevi. "Get a Google Poem." 2007. https://elmcip.net/creative-work/get-google-poem.

Liu, Alan. *The Laws of Cool*. Chicago: University of Chicago Press, 2004.

Manovich, Lev. "Database as a Symbolic Form." http://www.manovich.net/TEXTS_07.HTM.

Mateas, Michael. "A Preliminary Poetics for Interactive Drama and Games." In *First Person New Media as Story, Performance, and Game*, Noah Wardrip-Fruin, Pat Harrigan, and Michael Crumpton. Cambridge: MIT, 2006, pp. 19–33.

Mateas, Michael, and Andrew Stern. "Façade." 2006. http://www.interactivestory.net/.

Mauss, Marcel, Jane I. Guyer, and Bill Maurer. *The Gift*. Chicago: HAU, 2016.

McCaffery, Steve. "Bill Bissett: A Writing outside Writing," In *North of Intention: Critical Writings, 1973–1986*. New York: Roof, 2000, p. 195.

McCaffery, Steve. Afterword to Ray DiPalma, *Marquee*. New York: Asylum's Press, 1977.

McCaffery, Steve, and B. P. Nichol. *Rational Geomancy: The Kids of the Book-Machine: The Collected Research Reports of the Toronto Research Group, 1973–82*. Vancouver: Talon, 1992.

McCaffery, Steve. *North of Intention*. New York: Roof Books, 2000.

McLuhan, Marshall, Jerome Agel, and Quentin Fiore. *The Medium Is the Massage an Inventory of Effects*. SL: Penguin, 2008.

Meillessoux, Quentin. *After Finitude: An Essay on the Necessity of Contingency*. Translated by Ray Brassier. London: Bloomsbury Academic, 2010.

Memmott, Talan. *Lexia to Perplexia*. In *The Electronic Literature Collection Volume 1*. http://collection.eliterature.org/1/works/memmott__lexia_to_perplexia.html.

Moran, Charles. Review of *Of Two Minds: Hypertext, Pedagogy and Poetics*. *College English*, vol. 60, no. 2 (February 1998).

Ngai, Sianne. "Raw Matter: A Poetics of Disgust." Reprinted in *Telling It Slant: Avant-Garde Poetics of the 1990s*, edited by Mark Wallace and Steven Marks. Tuscaloosa: University of Alabama Press, 2002.

Ngai, Sianne. *Ugly Feelings*. Cambridge: Harvard University Press, 2007.

Olson, Charles. *Selected Writings*. New York: New Directions, 1971.

On, Josh. "They Rule." http://www.theyrule.net/.

Paul, Christiane. *Digital Art*. London: Thames & Hudson, 2003.

Perec, Georges. *La disparition*. Paris: Gallimard, 1969.

Perloff, Marjorie. *Radical Artifice: Writing Poetry in the Age of Media*. Chicago: University of Chicago, 1994.

Perloff, Marjorie. "The Poetics of Click and Drag: Screening the New Poetries." http://wings.buffalo.edu/epc/authors/goldsmith/perloff_poetics.pdf.

Pressman, Jessica. "Modern Modernisms: Young-hae Chang Heavy Industries and Digital Modernism." In *Pacific Rim Modernisms*, edited by Steve Yao, Mary Ann Gillies, and Helen Sword. Toronto: Toronto University Press, 2009.

Raley, Rita. "Interferences: [Net.Writing] and the Practice of Codework." *The Electronic Book Review*, September 2002, http://www.electronicbookreview.com/thread/electropoetics/net.writing.

Rieser, Martin, and Andrea Zapp, eds. *New Screen Media: Cinema/Art/Narrative*. London: British Film Institute, 2002.

Rubinstein, Lev. *Catalogue of Comedic Novelties*. New York: Ugly Duckling Presse, 2004.

Saint-Martin, Fernande. *Semiotics of Visual Language*. Bloomington: Indiana University Press, 2006.

Schmandt-Besserat, Denise. *When Writing Met Art*. Austin: University of Texas Press, 2007.

Seaman, Bill. “Interactive Text and Recombinant Poetics.” In *First Person New Media as Story, Performance, and Game*, Noah Wardrip-Fruin, Pat Harrigan, and Michael Crumpton. Cambridge: MIT, 2006, pp. 227–36.

Shelley, Percy Bysshe. *Shelley’s Poetry and Prose*. Selected and edited by Donald H. Reiman and Sharon B. Powers. New York: Norton, 1977.

Sontag, Susan. *Styles of Radical Will*. New York: Picador, 2002.

Strickland, Stephanie. “Born Digital.” Poetry Foundation Website (undated), http://www.poetryfoundation.org/article/182942.

Tomkins, Calvin. *Duchamp: A Biography*. London: Pimlico, 1998.

Tschichold, Jan. *The New Typography*. Translated by Ruari McLean. Berkeley: University of California Press, 1998.

Utterback, Camille. Artist’s statement (undated), http://camilleutterback.com/projects/untitled-5/. Accessed July 3, 2017.

Utterbeck, Camille. “Text Rain.” 1999. http://camilleutterback.com/projects/text-rain/. Accessed July 3, 2017.

Venturi, Robert, Denise Scott Brown, and Steven Izenour. *Learning from Las Vegas*. Cambridge: MIT Press, 1972.

Wardrip-Fruin, Noah. “Screen.” 2002. http://www.noahwf.com/screen/. Accessed July 3, 2017.

Wardrip-Fruin, Noah, and Pat Harrigan, eds. *First Person: New Media as Story, Performance and Game*. Cambridge: MIT Press, 2006.

Wardrip-Fruin, Noah, David Durand, Brion Moss, and Elaine Froehlich. “News Reader.” 2004. http://www.hyperfiction.org/rcnr/.

Wardrip-Fruin, Noah David Durand, Brion Moss, and Elaine Froehlich. “Regime Change.” 2004. http://www.hyperfiction.org/rcnr/.

Wark, McKenzie. Interview. *Kritikos*. Volume 2, April 2005.

CHAPTER SIXTEEN

Hypertext: Storyspace to Twine

ASTRID ENSSLIN AND LYLE SKAINS

This chapter examines the transformations of literary hypertext as a nonlinear digital writing format and practice since its inception in the late 1980s. We trace its development from the editorially closed and demographically exclusive writerly practices associated with first generation hypertext (also known as the Storyspace School) to the participatory, inclusive, and arguably more democratic affordances of the freely accessible, user-friendly online writing tool Twine. We argue that while this evolution, alongside other participatory forms of social media writing, has brought creative media practices closer than ever to the early poststructuralist-inspired theory of "wreadership" (Landow 1992), the discourses and practices surrounding Twine perpetuate ideological and commercially reinforced binaries between literature and gameplay. In view of the recent proliferation of text-based literary games, however, we argue that media literacies are bound to change and adapt to the cognitive challenges and distinct immersive qualities of literary-ludic hybrid artifacts, and readers/players will develop media-literate strategies of engaging with the clash between hyper- and deep attention (Hayles 2007).

In tracing the historical development of hypertextual writing, we concentrate particularly on aesthetic, technological, and commercial transformations. We begin by outlining some key concepts surrounding hypertextuality and nonsequential writing, including their analogue groundings in proto-hypertextual artifacts. We then move on to outline how hypertext has been aligned with concepts from poststructuralist literary theory, such as decentralization, rhizomatic thought, and the rise of the reader as *alter auctor*. The ensuing sections outline the historical development of hypertext from the Storyspace School to the Web, an evolution that has been framed by various theorists in terms of generations (Hayles 2002; Ensslin 2007; Rustad 2012): from first-generation hypertext to second-generation hypermedia, which were then followed by increasingly less hypertextual and instead more ludic, multimodal, participatory, and often also more linear forms of digital writing. The migration to Web-based forms of hypertext has generated a variety of creative practices implementing hypertext as a micro- or macro-device, as a literary metagame, or an "adaptive" form (Marino 2008). The latter appears to have heralded the growth of highly personalized and personalizable, autobiographical forms of hypertextual writing, which are reflected in the Twine community and the fact that the tool affords a more functionalized, applied approach to digital writing in pedagogic and interventionist contexts. This final move will lead us to a concluding discussion, which will reflect on the ochlocratic tendencies revolving around the Twine community and the political, ideological, and economic controversies surrounding the gamification of hypertext writing.

Our motivation to coauthor this chapter is anchored in a tendency we have both observed and driven forward in academic practices surrounding hypertext and digital writing more generally: the trend toward collaborative ventures, where expertise in diverse creative, scholarly, and scientific fields is brought together not only to create highly innovative multimedia hybrids, but indeed to produce interdisciplinary, groundbreaking research on evolving creative practices such as hypertextual writing. One of the projects we discuss in the penultimate section of this chapter is a body image intervention, in which digital media artists, literary and media theorists, and psychologists collaborated on methodological questions surrounding digital fiction and bibliotherapy (Ensslin et al. 2016). We also argue, with Skains, Bell, and Ensslin (2016), that teaching hypertextual writing can and has been proven to help creative writing students develop an understanding and appreciation of nonlinear compositional structures as aesthetic and critical objects.

CONCEPTS AND DEFINITIONS

Hypertext can be understood as an umbrella term denoting a specific form of electronic document organization (Ensslin 2014a: 258). Through hyperlinks, it connects digital files, documents, and media in interactive networks. These networks can assume gigantic dimensions, which the World Wide Web epitomizes. Hypertexts are navigated by activating hyperlinks, typically through mouse-click, mouse-over, and/or touch. Hypertext is typically written in HTML (HyperText Mark-up Language) and its variants, although specific software packages like Eastgate Systems' Storyspace and Microsoft's Hypercard were developed before the advent of the Web to enable offline hypertextual composition.

Coined by Theodor Nelson in his 1965 lectures at Vassar College, the term "hypertext" derives from Greek *hypér* (over, above, beyond) and Latin *texere* (to weave) and refers to the subsumption of multiple subordinate texts under a larger organizational, interconnecting protocol. Nelson's (1984: 0/2) frequently quoted definition describes "hypertext" as "non-sequential writing—text that branches and allows choices to the reader, best read at an interactive screen. As popularly conceived, this is a series of text chunks connected by links which offer the reader different pathways." The resulting networks may comprise a variety of semiotic modes, including writing, image, and sound. Such multimodal hypertextual networks are generally referred to as "hypermedia," short for "hypertext multimedia."

Nelson's concept was inspired by Vannevar Bush's *Memex* ("Memory Expander"), a theoretical rather than actual analogue information system designed for the connection and storage of all documents and communications in the world, which Bush (1945) had first envisaged in the 1930s. The *Memex* was modeled on the associative functions of the human brain, and intended to operate by ways of indexing and creating paths to help retrieve documents. Nelson's aim was to implement Bush's idea using computational technologies by creating a literary "docuverse"—a conceptual precursor of the World Wide Web, which eventually came into being in the 1990s.

Although the term "hypertext" is a twentieth-century coinage, the concepts of multilinear reading, intertextual linkage, annotation, and cross-referencing date back over a millennium. Pre-digital hypertexts, also known as proto-hypertexts, had already appeared in the form of glosses in medieval Scripture, Canon Law, and medical texts. Nonlinear, proto-hypertextual print fiction first emerged with the rise of the novel in the eighteenth century, underlining the genre's nonconformist tendencies. Well-known examples include Lawrence Sterne's anti-novel *Tristram Shandy* (1760/1983) and Jean Paul's so-called footnote fiction (e.g., *Siebenkäs*, 1796/97/1983; *Titan*, 1800–1803/2016). Twentieth-century modernism and postmodernism in particular generated a variety of proto-hypertextual print fiction and poetry. The narrative style of James Joyce's *Finnegans Wake* (1939), for example, presents the reader with a discontinuous, ever-changing line of narrative discourse involving rapid changes between focalizers, settings, and events. Similarly, Oulipian writing, dating back to the 1960s French Oulipo (Ouvroir de littérature potentielle) movement, operates under self-imposed structural and mathematical constraints, resulting in various nonlinear works, such as Raymond Queneau's *Cent mille milliards de poèmes* (1961), the lines of which are printed on separate strips that can be randomly combined into 10^{14} possible different poems.

HYPERTEXT AND POSTSTRUCTURALIST LITERARY THEORY

The emergence of digital hypertext fiction and poetry in the late 1980s was set against a scholarly backdrop steeped in the critical paradigm of late poststructuralism. Metaphorically, the concept of nonlinearity lends itself to the principles of the rhizome (Deleuze and Guattari 1987; Moulthrop 1995): ramifying, decentralized, horizontally organized root structures, which do not have a clear beginning or end. Rhizomes conveniently deviate from the arborescent, hierarchical structures associated with logocentrism. In the same vein, early literary hypertext followed an avant-garde principle, seeking to undermine hierarchical textual order and linear narrative development by offering readers highly fragmented, subjective reading experiences, aimed to produce unique and individualized receptive and hermeneutic processes.

Individual units of a hypertext are generally referred to as "lexias" (nodes, or text chunks; Landow [1992]; cf. Barthes's [1970] "units of reading"). A typical hypertext lexia contains a number of links, which enable readers to choose different pathways for every reading, thus generating different mental images of the text, or indeed different texts (Ryan 2001: 5). This element of creating individualized narratives seemed conveniently close to the idea of virtual coauthorship, thus giving rise to the concept of the hypertext "wreader" (Landow 1992). Wreadership has been theorized extensively since Landow's coinage and experienced an upsurge in academic interest in contemporary participatory media culture vis-à-vis the shared and coproduced social media narratives it affords (Page 2012; Klaiber 2013; Ensslin 2015).

Literary studies has seen three major, partly overlapping waves of hypertext theory. The first wave was inspired by a body of fictional, poetic, and dramatic works written between the late 1980s and mid-1990s, and published primarily in Eastgate's Storyspace software. Canonical works of the Storyspace School include, for instance, Michael Joyce's *afternoon: a story* (1987), Stuart Moulthrop's *Victory Garden* (1992), and Shelley Jackson's *Patchwork Girl, or, a Modern Monster* (1995). Pioneered by George P. Landow, Robert Coover, and Jay D. Bolter, the first wave of literary hypertext theory mapped key organizing principles of hypertext fiction and poetry, embedding them firmly in the concepts and terminology of postmodern and particularly poststructuralist theory.

Being "a radically divergent technology, interactive and polyvocal, favoring a plurality of discourses over definitive utterance and freeing the reader from the domination of the author" (Coover 1992: n.p.), hypertext came to be seen as a "vindication of postmodern literary theory" (Bolter 1992: 24), a claim which Landow (1992) systematized in his so-called convergence thesis. Thus, hypertext came to be considered a tangible writerly implementation of major poststructuralist and deconstructionist theorems such as anti-logocentrism, the writerly text, the death of the author, decentering, and non-closure. The liberating, empowering, and ultimately democratizing potential this was supposed to have for hypertext (w)readers, however, did not materialize empirically.

As a matter of fact, in a hypertext environment, the reader's freedom to form personal associations and connotations within the formal constraints of the material text is considerably restrained given the existence of manifest, technically implemented hyperlinks, which are more likely to prevent than facilitate creativity in readers accustomed to monolinear plots and tangible narrative boundaries. Indeed, numerous empirical studies found hyperlinks to have a delimiting rather than empowering function in hypertext readers, as they often lead to confusion, serendipity, and cognitive overload in readers not accustomed to hypertextual forms of creative writing (Pope 2006; Miall and Dobson 2001; Mangen and van der Weel 2015). According to Simanowski (2004; see also Ensslin 2007), the only feasible contexts in which the roles of reader and author may legitimately be merged are truly collaborative writing projects such as *A Million Penguins* (a 2007 Web-based collaboration of Penguin Books and De Montfort University), netprov works such as *Grace, Wit & Charm* (Wittig 2011), Kate Pullinger and Chris Joseph's collaborative social media novel, *Flight Paths: A Networked Novel* (2007-12), and dedicated collaborative writing platforms such as *Ficly* (see Klaiber 2013).

From the mid-2000s onward, a second wave of hypertext and digital fiction scholars has highlighted the importance of grounding literary, stylistic, semiotic, and narratological theories of hypertext (and other types of electronic literature) in methodologically rigorous close analyses. Acknowledging that hypertext and other electronic types of writing require a new hermeneutic attitude, they embrace the fact that hypertexts are never read the same way twice but indeed rely on multiple rereadings on the part of the analyst (Ciccoricco 2007; Ensslin 2007). This theoretical and analytical school has been adapting existing, print-born theories and analytical tools from stylistics, narratology, and semiotics as well as developing new approaches, concepts, and methods tailored to the affordances of digital media (e.g., Ensslin and Bell 2007; Bell 2010; Bell, Ensslin, and Rustad 2014). For example, in a book-length study, Bell (2010) applies select theorems of Possible Worlds Theory to a number of Storyspace hypertext and hypermedia fictions to demonstrate how this approach can be used to analyze the ontological self-consciousness and conflicting first-person perspectives of the narrator, the problematic boundaries between fictional and historical discourses, intertextual references to other fictional characters, appearances of the author figure in the text, as well as absurdist humor. Astrid Ensslin (2012) applies theories of unreliable narration to Michael Joyce's Storyspace fiction *afternoon: a story* and Stefan Maskiewicz's dialogic hypermedia narrative, *Quadrego* (2001). Both texts feature unintentional (neurotic and psychopathic), unreliable narrators but make very different uses of hypertextuality and hypermediality to represent the respective characters' perceptions and symptoms.

A third wave of hypertext and digital fiction scholarship may be seen in a trend toward looking at "actual" readers and conducting empirical reader response studies to develop an understanding of how readers process, for example, nonlinear, multimodal, and ludic structures. A recent study by Bell, Ennslin, and Smith (2015), for example, considers how readers of a Web-based hypermedia Flash fiction (geniwate and Deena Larsen's *The Princess Murderer* [2003]) understand different meanings of textual *you* in a nonlinear narrative and how these understandings affect their perceived relationships to the protagonist and other characters in the narrative.

HYPERTEXT AND THE WEB

The advent and popularization of the World Wide Web in the mid-1990s opened up new avenues for hypertextual creativity, ranging from avant-garde experimentalism to more mainstream forms of interactive multimodal narrative. The inherently public nature of the Web allowed and ostensibly compelled (through a gift economy culture [Currah 2007]) digital writers to make their works freely available if they wanted them to be read more widely than the consistently narrow, scholarly audiences afforded by the Storyspace School, which to this day insists on print-derived, offline forms of commercially traded "serious hypertext."

The rise of the Web was fostered partly by the development of multimodal technologies such as graphic browsers (e.g., Mosaic 1993) and Web design and animation software such as Flash and Dreamweaver, yet also, crucially, by HTML, the Web's major mark-up language and encoding convention. HTML serves a variety of different semiotic systems that had previously been analogue, that is, separated in terms of mediality and materiality; text, speech, sound and music, graphics, animation and film could, for the first time, be embedded in and displayed through one and the same protocol. Enhanced by JavaScript, Flash, and Shockwave technologies, Web-based hypermedia came to be a sandbox for digital writers to experiment with different forms of interactivity, monolinearity, and multilinearity, the interplay of semiotic codes in multimodal arrangements as well as new gestural manipulations (Bouchardon 2014),[1] and ontological oscillations between storyworld, the virtual realities of the everyday World Wide Web, and the realities of the reader through metaleptic links, for example (Bell 2014).

Despite its potentially anti-immersive, alienating, and confusing properties, hypertext as a structuring principle of electronic writing has continued to be used by digital writers since the advent of the Web. What can be seen, however, is that Web-based uses of it often reflect a more careful, reader-friendly attitude, ostensibly seeking to sustain rather than impede immersion. For instance, Kate Pullinger, Chris Joseph, and Andy Campbell's emergent digital fiction *Inanimate Alice* (2005-16) shows that hypertextual elements can be embedded in otherwise linear hypermedia storylines so as to create options and choices without risking overall reader disorientation vis-à-vis lack of closure and navigational clarity. Episode 4, "Hometown," opens with Alice being dared by her friends to climb a dilapidated staircase. The experience is told diegetically by Alice's first-person narrative voice, superimposed in writing onto a photographically animated first-person, linear, semi-interactive camera eye journeying up the rusty stairs. The doubly encoded first-person viewpoint (textual diegesis and camera focalization) allows readers to empathize

[1] Bouchardon (2014) uses the concept of gestural manipulations as an analytical tool for digital fictions that emphasizes the "gestural," kinetic aspects of user interactions with electronic literature, such as clicking, drag-and-drop and pull-and-release, all of which add to a digital literary text's essential interpretive meaning.

with the challenging, potentially life-threatening situation facing the protagonist. Two-thirds of the way up, Alice notices the stairs beginning to collapse underneath her, at which point the visual interface turns blurry and begins to spin before turning completely black, thus conveying Alice's confusion and momentary blackout. Subsequently the reader obtains four hypertextual options to "look at what happened," visualized as four compass hands on a black background. Each chosen path represents an element of Alice's aporia: the upward pointer, for example, leads to a display of the wall of the building that Alice is ostensibly clinging on to, superimposed by an animated, crawling chunk of text quite literally performing its own content: "I managed to haul myself up onto what remained of the stairs." Clicking on the "continue" (>>) arrows leads the reader back to the options screen, which now only has three options left. The thus hypertextually conceptualized and implemented, multilinear panic situation continues with each chosen direction and inevitably leads back to the options screen without any further deviations or alternative pathways. Hence, as soon as all four directions have been explored, the linear reading path continues without the reader having been given even a slight chance to deviate from the beaten track that is Alice's survival. It may even be argued that this type of hypertextual embedding is a paradoxically linear way of using multilinearity in electronic writing—arguably one that defies key postmodernist assumptions and minimizes rhizomatic effects to a temporary randomization of reading order. Ultimately, of course, this writerly design is a deliberate and innovative attempt to allow readers a two-dimensional, multimodal phenomenological experience of the protagonist's distressed state of mind and multisensory stream of consciousness.

Another attempt to create user-friendly, "adaptive" hypertext online is Mark C. Marino's (2008) *a show of hands*. Using a software called the Literatronic(a) storytelling engine, this work pursues a user-centered approach by enabling readers to situate themselves within the story. It "adapts around the reader's choices, rearranging the content so the reader will always encounter all of the text in an order optimized for narrative coherence." Developed by Juan B. Gutiérrez, Literatronic's "artificial intelligence engine" attempts to mitigate the disorienting and frustrating effects of hypertexts. Similar to other hypertext engines, Literatronic is based upon authorial creation of lexias and hyperlinks between those lexias. What it adds are dynamic responses to reader actions that seek to minimize aporia and maximize narrative cohesion. For instance, as readers journey through *a show of hands*, they are offered bookmarking capabilities, a "percentage read" bar to gauge their progress through the text, a list of "Recommended Next Pages" ranked by continued narrative relevance, a contents table that indicates which lexias have been read, as well as Marino's addition of a hyperlinked photomosaic with each tile linking to a lexia, their narrative distance reflected in their proximity in the mosaic. The lexias themselves do not contain links, which further enables immersion for the reader, free from the cognitive distractions of links to unknown destinations. Hence, Marino's work reflects digital writers' ongoing pursuit to empower readers by offering them personalized wreading experiences.

Hypertext fiction has often been compared to a "game" in the dual sense of giving readers playful choices and positing them in a virtual competition with the author (Fauth 1995; Morgan and Andrews 1999; Millard et al. 2005; Rustad 2009; Bell 2010). Surely, literary gaming in the sense of operating ludic mechanics (rules, victory conditions, scalable player progress, etc.) does not usually happen when reading hypertext literature (see also Koskimaa 1997/1998). Instead, readers engage in complex forms of cognitive-ergodic and often aleatory playfulness, which can assume various forms and have diverse aesthetic effects (Ensslin 2014b: 58). Robert Kendall's poetic hypertext mystery, *Clues* (2001–2008), for example, may be seen as an allegory of the *agon* (Caillois 2001) between author and reader. It sends its readers on a metafictional quest, while audiovisually evoking the conventions of a standard Hollywood noir thriller. The hypertext structure provides an element of choice and decision-making—both important aspects of gameplay proper. Readers can click on doors to enter rooms and obtain clues. However, they will discover that any narrative devices, such as setting, props, plot, and character, are purely figurative devices for self-reflexive reading and poetic communication ("The pen is your weapon of choice"). The true riddle therefore lies in interpreting the text's metafictional and metapoetic layers of meaning, and to rediscover one's own role in the literary communication process.

Thus, married with the connectivity, adaptiveness, and multimodality of the Web, hypertext remains a powerful expressive tool for creators and readers of playful, nonlinear fiction. Furthermore, as will be shown subsequently, its inherent ludic qualities have proven to be a fruitful means of promoting itself as not only a niche phenomenon but indeed a form of writing and self-expression that has the potential to attract diverse, popular, and interdisciplinary user groups.

HYPERTEXT AS LITERARY GAMING: THE RISE OF TWINE

Web 2.0, defined by its participatory architecture and user-generated content, has provided a global space for interaction, the sharing of ideas, collective intelligence, and democratization of content (O'Reilly 2007; Jenkins 2006a, b). The democratization of hypertexts, however, was somewhat slow in emerging: until 2009, Eastgate's Storyspace, which was used to create *afternoon* and *Patchwork Girl*, was the only consistently maintained dedicated hypertext authoring system, and its purchase price was (and remains) significant. Further, Eastgate hypertexts are published at a price point comparable to a new release hardback or Blu-ray, and are generally obsolete and unplayable on contemporary machines within a few years. Outside of Storyspace, no hypertext-specific tools existed; hypertext authors either had to adapt general Web authoring platforms to meet the specific affordances of their creative genre or create their own authoring tools, both of which require a level of technological awareness and expertise to accomplish. In a culture of Internet gift economies (Currah 2007) and WYSIWYG user interfaces, these economic and technological barriers to entry kept hypertext in and of the avant-garde and the academic.

Chris Klimas, an interactive fiction author, launched his Twine storygame platform in 2009 to specifically address these barriers. The program is free, open source, open platform (Twine 2.0, released in 2014, is browser-based), and publishes to HTML. At its core, it requires no coding (just a simple text notation for hyperlinks), though advanced users can refine it with CSS, JavaScript, variables, conditional logic, and multimedia. Despite the lack of barriers to entry, however, Twine languished in obscurity until independent game developer Anna Anthropy posted about it on her blog and promoted it in her book *Rise of the Videogame Zinesters* in 2012, bringing the platform into the "fringe mainstream" (Ellison 2013; Brey 2016; Friedhoff 2013). By the end of the year, fellow game creator Porpentine had posted a manifesto/tutorial (2012), Anthropy had posted numerous tutorials, and Twine emerged as an independent gaming platform.

Anna Anthropy and Porpentine's adoption and promotion of Twine have affected the hypertext genre in two spheres: first, as a platform for marginalized voices in the gaming industry, and second as a democratization of hypertext as a literary form. Anna Anthropy characterizes the Twine community as queer- and women-dominated, and both she and Porpentine promoted the platform as a resource for the "marginalized voices" of underserved populations, including women, LGBTQ, and racial or religious minorities (Bernardi 2013; Friedhoff 2013; Harvey 2014; Kopas 2014). Anastasia Salter (2015) notes this is a sharp contrast to the overall game-development community, which the International Game Developers Association's (IGDA) 2014 survey indicates is 76 percent male, 86 percent heterosexual, and 79 percent Caucasian. Popular discourse on Twine games supports Anthropy's overview, calling attention to the "personal game" aspect of Twine hypertexts, and how Twine's affordances allow the game-maker to focus on the text instead of the tech in order to make "games whose purpose is to explore personal perspectives and issues of identity, sexuality and trauma that mainstream games rarely touch on" (Hudson 2014: n.p.). Indeed, frequently recommended Twine games such as Anthropy's *Queers in Love at the End of the World* (2013), Porpentine and Brenda Neotenomie's *With Those We Love Alive* (2014), and Zoe Quinn's *Depression Quest* (2013) all incorporate innovative gameplay and interaction focusing the reader/player's attention on questions of love, gender, sexuality, body awareness, and mental illness—using the text-dominance and intimacy afforded by hypertext to explore deeply personal topics that mainstream gaming rarely addresses. Further, from their position outside the perceived "elite" academy, Anthropy and Porpentine (as well as other Twine author-developers) have reached a mainstream audience for these texts and their resulting discourse, a feat most hypertexts have never accomplished (or indeed sought to accomplish). By side-stepping the barriers to entry formed by academic gatekeepers and pricey software platforms, Twine games have democratized the hypertext form to a new audience of gamers and game-developers who feel their voices are not being heard in their chosen communities: women, LGBTQ, and racial and religious minorities who play and create games.

What is important in relation to hypertextual democratization through Twine is the almost unexpected reversion from what, for decades, seemed to be a trend toward reverse ekphrasis and increased orality in hypermedia verbal arts—toward a reduction of linguistic literariness in favor of a more multimedia artistic hybridity that sometimes leaves the actual written text (i.e., the essence of conceptual literariness) in an either marginalized position, or indeed in a quasi-egalitarian interplay with other semiotic modes such as sound (voice-over; music; noise) and (moving) image (see Chapter 11 in this volume). This trend has been particularly noticeable in Flash and 3D digital fictions, for example, by Dreaming Methods, Christine Wilks and Kate Pullinger, in some app fictions such as Gorman and Cannizzaro's *Pry*, as well as literary games such as Tale of Tales' *The Path*, and Jonathan Blow's *Braid*. Twine fictions, by contrast, are almost exclusively text-based, thus debunking the general empirical finding and critical assumption that text-heavy digital writing comes at the expense of mass popularity. Thus, we might argue that the Twine movement has led to a paradigm shift in digital literariness, and it will likely cause a renewed scholarly interest in close-reading as well as close-play, to augment and complement rather than replace or defy what Moretti (2013) has termed "distant reading" in the age of big data.

In light of Twine hypertexts' frequent exploration of personal experience and choice, some studies have begun to emerge that examine how both writing and reading these texts can be used as interventions for particular issues. Einstein and Vetter's (2015: n.p.) study asked students on a gender studies composition course to use Twine as a creative platform for texts exploring the topic of women in games development, reporting that drafting and developing these hypertexts "created for them a more nuanced and complex understanding of the ways in which gendered behavior is policed in early childhood and adolescence in order to enforce gender conformity." A subset of Ensslin et al.'s (2016: 13) study on creating Twine hypertexts as an expressive writing intervention on body image issues for teenagers found that "hypertext's inherent ability to permit the digital writer to examine self and society . . . can result in positive effects for the participants' body image"; the emergence of Twine hypertexts created by and for more "popular" users (as opposed to academic or experimental users) widens the potential for hypertext as a medium of cultural discourse and empowerment of marginalized voices, and a creative tool for exploration of personal narrative. Empirical studies are only recently emerging on hypertext and digital fiction; more examination of how writing hypertexts (as opposed to printed prose) can affect mental and emotional states, as well as cognitive processing, is certainly called for, given the indications in these early studies.

As a creative tool in and of itself, Twine is being put to use as a pedagogical tool in a variety of classrooms. The studies noted above utilized Twine because of its accessibility and ease-of-use; their primary purposes were not to teach students to write hypertexts, but to use the hypertext medium as a method of creative exploration on topics unrelated to hypertext. Twine is, of course, being used in creative education contexts as well, as an introductory tool for game development (Anthropy 2012; Friedhoff 2013) and experimental creative writing. Skains, Bell, and Ensslin's (2016) study of the effects of writing in digital media on experienced creative writers found that writers who engage in hypertexts demonstrate an altered cognitive approach: they are more likely to engage in unnatural narration, reflecting the cognitive effects of considering multicursal pathways for character choices and plot alternatives. They are also more likely to develop more disciplined writing habits, incorporating greater levels of planning and revision, in order to accommodate the multiple possibilities for narrative within hypertexts.

The development of Twine (and other emerging platforms such as Texture) is a movement of hypertext away from what Porpentine (2012: n.p.) describes as a "lull"—when the gatekeepers of the form[2] "acted like it was some kind of avant-garde science," where hypertext was "caught uncomfortably between literature and games"—toward a medium as versatile and adaptable as pen and paper. Its accessibility and facility have led to its rise as a vehicle for personal exploration of narrative experiences in underserved populations, establishing hypertext outside of the experimental art realm and into the mainstream. This has enabled hypertext to play a significant role in personal narrative and cultural discourse, establishing hypertext beyond literary experimentation and avant-garde art into literature itself.

CONCLUDING THOUGHTS: HYPERTEXT NOW AND IN THE FUTURE

Multilinear writing has come a long way from proto-hypertextual experimentation with the printed page to multimodal and multivariant writerly and readerly gameplay

[2] Porpentine (2012: n.p.) does not specifically identify "gatekeepers," though she references "academic essays on hypertext buried behind passwords," "a hypertext editor like Twine for $300," and "stories selling for $30," which seems to refer to Storyspace and Eastgate Systems.

in the age of Twine, Scalar, and Texture. What has become evident in the process is that (w)readerly empowerment through co-creation of narrative meaning cannot be imposed through forms, texts, and theories that imply exclusivity of access and assume that deconstructivist thought can be implemented through manifest literary materiality. Instead, movements like the Twine community and participatory social media writing have shown that genuine wreadership has to come from users themselves, driven by the aesthetic and social needs of their own communities, and in particular the urge to "circumvent gatekeeping in game development" (Brey 2016) and the desire to get published as an experimental creative writer.

The big question in this context is whether, given the above-mentioned democratization process, this means that hypertext has finally been canonized, in a sense of return and transformation (Ensslin 2007; Assmann and Assmann 1987). And yet this return is ambivalent: the continuing exclusivity of access suggested by highly copyrighted forms like Storyspace hypertexts permeates issues of looming obsolescence and ultimately academic elitism. Surely, hypertext fictions like *afternoon* and *Patchwork Girl* are now regularly taught in literary media classes around the world, and yet the issue of iterative incompatibility with ever-evolving software requirements remains an obstacle—deliberate or not—to broader popularization. By the same token, even for Generation Y and after decades of regular Web exposure, the aesthetic effects of Storyspace hypertext remain alienating to the common reader (Mangen and van der Weel 2015).

Paradoxically, the canonization of hypertext as a form of option-driven creative writing is happening on the ludic rather than literary side of creative expressivity, and in previously unforeseeable manifestations that could not have happened without participatory media and radical changes in commercial software and IP models (e.g., open source, open software) as well as user-friendly WYSIWYG interfaces. Hence, self-authoring (rather than choosing your own paths) is becoming the standard form of literary-ludic interaction, and what is top ranked (ergo: "literary," or "worthy of canonization") is no longer decided by the select few but the wreaderly masses themselves. We might argue that the aesthetic and commercial qualities of literariness in digital media are shifting toward wreaderly presumption and crowdsourced criticism and appreciation. The question arises of course whether these are signs of true democratization or rather of a new, evolving form of elitism: a type of aesthetic technocracy that may call out for a reassessment of the term and traditionally pejorative connotations of ochlocracy, or smart mobs (Rheingold 2002).

By the same token, it cannot be denied that Twine art has found a home neither in the region of serious hypertext—which seems to defy "plot-centered hypertext narrative" and to assume "that [Twine] writing is a hobby," thus impeding a "literary economy" (Bernstein in Pressman 2014)—nor in mainstream game culture (Brey 2016). Strangely or not, Twine art has created its own niche in between commercial media sectors, yet—unlike Storyspace hypertext—this niche has been burgeoning, not least because it offers an outlet for autobiographical, emotional, and even therapeutic interactive experiences that are meaningful, tangible, and poignant for today's prosumers. Furthermore, some existing Twine games exhibit literary and ludic qualities that are not only innovative but deeply immersive and re-playable. This begs the question of whether so-called hobbyist hypertext writing might perhaps ultimately become more profitable in terms of a literary economy than those promoted by more conventional publishing models—especially considering alternative, donation-based, and online-marketing-driven reward systems, as well as the fact that average user literacies are bound to become increasingly multiliterate, blending modes of hyper- and deep attention and changing reader/player expectations to ever-new and challenging combinations of literary, audiovisual, and ludic arts.

What we can say, by way of a conclusion, is that the recent discursive shift from serious hypertext to personalized game writing in the area of nonlinear electronic literature has moved hypertext scholarship away from ultimately hypothetical constructions of writerly practices that seem to manifest poststructuralist thought, to examinations of actual reader participation, agency, and ownership in the development of interactive literary narratives, or games, as many would call them. Among the deplorable symptoms of this paradigm shift is of course the fact that writerly and thematic diversity may lead to victimization vis-à-vis cyberbullying, as the horrific misogynist Gamergate attacks on the likes of Zoe Quinn have shown in recent years. In this light, as well as other political and cultural facets of our contemporary Western pseudo-democratic reality, democratization and anti-commercialism are at a risk of undergoing semantic pejoration. And indeed, even such super-accessible platforms as Twine and Scalar inevitably promote cultural colonialism (such as writing in English) as the domineering T-Rex of Web culture (Brey 2016; Ensslin 2011). Promoting diversification of digital art practices therefore must remain at the forefront of electronic literature activism, not least to show that digital writing can indeed serve as a new form of "world literature" (Tabbi 2010), and not just in the sense of the potential inhabited by electronic literature to evoke community-building, collaborative hermeneutic and creative processes but indeed a world literature that is grounded in and promotes extra-poetic, egalitarian values across identities, cultures, and (linguistic) communities.

SOURCES CITED

Anthropy, Anna. *Queers in Love at the End of the World.* [Twine game] (2013), http://www.auntiepixelante.com/endoftheworld.

Anthropy, Anna. *Rise of the Videogame Zinesters: How Freaks, Normals, Amateurs, Artists, Dreamers, Drop-outs, Queers, Housewives, and People Like You Are Taking Back an Art Form: Anna Anthropy.* New York: Seven Stories Press, 2012.

Assmann, Aleida, and Jan Assmann. *Kanon und Zensur: Archäologie der literarischen Kommunikation, II.* Munich: Wilhelm Fink, 1987.

Barthes, Roland. *S/Z.* New York: Hill and Wang, 1970.

Bell, Alice. *The Possible Worlds of Hypertext Fiction.* Basingstoke: Palgrave Macmillan, 2010.

Bell, Alice. "Media-Specific Metalepsis in *10:01.*" In *Analyzing Digital Fiction*, edited by Alice Bell, Astrid Ensslin, and Hans Kristian Rustad. New York: Routledge, 2014, pp. 21–38.

Bell, Alice, Astrid Ensslin, and Hans Kristian Rustad. *Analyzing Digital Fiction.* New York: Routledge, 2014.

Bell, Alice, Astrid Ensslin, and Jen Smith. "Studying 'Readers' of Digital Fiction: 'You' in *The Princess Murderer.*" Experimental Narratives: From the Novel to Digital Storytelling Conference, Institute of Modern Languages Research, Senate House, University of London, England, February 26–27, 2015.

Bernardi, Joe. "Choose Your Own Adventure-Maker: Twine and the Art of Personal Games." *Motherboard*, February 19, 2013, http://motherboard.vice.com/blog/twine-and-the-art-of-personal-games.

Bläß, Ronny. "Hypertext/Hypertextuality." In *Metzler Lexikon Literatur- und Kulturtheorie: Ansätze—Personen—Grundbegriffe*, 3rd ed., edited by Ansgar Nünning. Stuttgart: Metzler, 2004, pp. 270–1.

Bolter, Jay David. "Literature in the Electronic Writing Space." In *Literacy Online: The Promise (and Peril) of Reading (and Writing) with Computers*, edited by Myron C. Tuman. Pittsburgh: University of Pittsburgh Press, 1992, pp. 19–42.

Bouchardon, Serge. "Figures of Gestural Manipulation in Digital Fictions." In *Analyzing Digital Fiction*, edited by Alice Bell, Astrid Ensslin, and Hans Kristian Rustad. New York: Routledge, 2014.

Brey, Betsy. "Twine, Hypertext, and Games: Ideologies and Implications." Canadian Games Studies Association Annual Conference, University of Calgary, June 1–3, 2016.

Bush, Vannevar. "As We May Think." *Atlantic Monthly*, July 1945, 47–61.

Caillois, Roger. *Man, Play and Games*. Chicago: University of Illinois Press, 2001.

Ciccoricco, David. *Reading Network Fiction*. Tuscaloosa: University of Alabama Press, 2007.

Coover, Robert. "The End of Books." *New York Times Book Review*, June 21, 1992, 23–25, http://www.nytimes.com/books/98/09/27/specials/coover-end.html.

Currah, Andrew. "Managing Creativity: The Tensions between Commodities and Gifts in a Digital Networked Environment." *Economy and Society*, vol. 36, no. 3 (2007): 467–94.

Deleuze, Gilles, and Félix Guattari. *A Thousand Plateaus: Capitalism and Schizophrenia*. Minneapolis: University of Minneapolis Press, 1987.

Einstein, Sarah, and Matthew Vetter. "Women Writing in Digital Spaces: Engaging #Gamergate and Twine in the Gender Studies-Composition Course." *Digital Rhetoric Collaborative*, May 7, 2015, http://www.digitalrhetoriccollaborative.org/2015/05/07/women-writing-in-digital-spaces-engaging-gamergate-and-twine-in-the-gender-studies-composition-course/.

Ellison, Cara. "Anna Anthropy and the Twine Revolution." *The Guardian*, April 10, 2013, http://www.theguardian.com/technology/gamesblog/2013/apr/10/anna-anthropy-twine-revolution.

Ensslin, Astrid. *Canonizing Hypertext: Explorations and Constructions*. London: Continuum, 2007.

Ensslin, Astrid. "Respiratory Narrative: Multimodality and Cybernetic Corporeality in 'Physio-cybertext.'" In *New Perspectives on Narrative and Multimodality*, edited by Ruth Page. New York: Routledge, 2009, pp. 155–65.

Ensslin, Astrid. "'What an Un-Wiki Way of Doing Things': Wikipedia's Multilingual Policy and Metalinguistic Practice." *Journal of Language and Politics*, vol. 10, no. 4 (2011): 535–61.

Ensslin, Astrid. "'I Want to Say I May Have Seen My Son Die This Morning': Unintentional Unreliable Narration in Digital Fiction." *Language and Literature*, vol. 21, no. 2 (2012): 136–49.

Ensslin, Astrid. "Hypertextuality." In *Johns Hopkins Guide to Digital Media*, edited by Marie-Laure Ryan, Lori Emerson, and Benjamin J. Robertson. Baltimore: Johns Hopkins University Press, 2014a, pp. 258–65.

Ensslin, Astrid. *Literary Gaming*. Cambridge: MIT Press, 2014b.

Ensslin, Astrid. "Digital Fiction: Texts, Technologies, Techniques of Reading." Shankland Lecture, Bangor University, December 7, 2015, https://www.youtube.com/watch?v=CLvCrvMq9sE.

Ensslin, Astrid, and Alice Bell. *New Perspectives on Digital Literature: Criticism and Analysis*. Special issue of *dichtung digital* 37, 2007, www.dichtung-digital.org/Newsletter/2007.

Ensslin, Astrid, Lyle Skains, Sarah Riley, Joan Haran, Alison Mackiewicz, and Emma Halliwell. "Exploring Digital Fiction as a Tool for Teenage Body Image Bibliotherapy." *Digital Creativity* (2016).

Fauth, Jurgen. "Poles in Your Face: The Promises and Pitfalls of Hyperfiction." *Blip Magazine*, vol. 1, no. 6 (1995), http://blipmagazine.net/backissues/1995/06-jurge.html.

Fiderio, Janet. "A Grand Vision." *Byte*, vol. 13, no. 10 (1988): 237–43.

Friedhoff, Jane. "Untangling Twine: A Platform Study." In *Proceedings of DiGRA 2013: DeFragging Game Studies*. Atlanta, GA, 2013, http://www.digra.org/wp-content/uploads/digital-library/paper_67.compressed.pdf.

geniwate, and Deena Larsen. *The Princess Murderer* (2003), www.deenalarsen.net/princess/index.html.

Gorman, Samantha, and Danny Cannizzaro. *Pry*. http://prynovella.com, 2014.

Harvey, Alison. "Twine's Revolution: Democratization, Depoliticization, and the Queering of Game Design." *G|A|M|E Games as Art, Media, Entertainment*, vol. 1, no. 3 (2014). http://www.gamejournal.it/3_harvey/#.VeW_BNNViko.

Hayles, N. Katherine. *Writing Machines*. Cambridge: MIT Press, 2002.

Hayles, N. Katherine. "Hyper and Deep Attention: The Generational Divide in Cognitive Modes." *Profession* (2007): 187–99.

Hudson, Laura. "Twine, the Video-Game Technology for All." *New York Times Magazine*, November 19, 2014, http://www.nytimes.com/2014/11/23/magazine/twine-the-video-game-technology-for-all.html.

Jackson, Shelley. *Patchwork Girl, or, a Modern Monster*. Cambridge, MA: Eastgate Systems, 1995.

Jenkins, Henry. *Convergence Culture: Where Old and New Media Collide*. New York: New York University Press, 2006a.

Jenkins, Henry. *Fans, Bloggers, and Gamers: Exploring Participatory Culture*. New York: New York University Press, 2006b.

Joyce, James. *Finnegans Wake*. London: Faber and Faber, 1939.

Joyce, Michael. *afternoon: a story*. Cambridge, MA: Eastgate Systems, 1987.

Kendall, Robert. *Clues* (2001–2008), http://www.wordcircuits.com/clues.

Klaiber, Isabell. "Wreading Together: The Double Plot of Collaborative Digital Fiction." In *Analyzing Digital Fiction*, edited by Alice Bell, Astrid Ensslin, and Hans Kristian Rustad. New York: Routledge, 2013, pp. 124–40.

Kopas, Merritt. "Trans Women & The New Hypertext." *Lambda Literary*, July 8, 2014, http://www.lambdaliterary.org/features/07/08/trans-women-the-new-hypertext/.

Koskimaa, Raine. "Visual Structuring of Hyperfiction Narratives." *electronic book review*, vol. 6 (1997/1998), http://www.altx.com/ebr/ebr6/6koskimaa/6koski.htm.

Landow, George P. *Hypertext: The Convergence of Contemporary Critical Theory and Technology*. Baltimore: Johns Hopkins University Press, 1992.

Mangen, Anne, and Adriaan van der Weel. "Why Don't We Read Hypertext Novels?" *Convergence*, May 25, 2015, online first, http://con.sagepub.com/content/early/2015/05/22/1354856515586042.abstract.

Marino, Mark C. *A Show of Hands* (2008), http://hands.literatronica.net/src/initium.aspx.

Maskiewicz, Stefan. *Quadrego* (2001), www.quadrego.de.

Miall, David, and Teresa Dobson. "Reading Hypertext and the Experience of Literature." *Journal of Digital Information*, vol. 2, no. 1 (2001), https://journals.tdl.org/jodi/index.php/jodi/article/view/35/37.

Millard, David E., Nicholas M. Gibbins, Danius T. Michaelides, and Mark J. Weal. "Mind the Semantic Gap." In *Hypertext '05: Proceedings of the Sixteenth ACM Conference on Hypertext and Hypermedia*, edited by Siegfried Reich and Manolis Tzagarakis. New York: ACM, 2005, pp. 54–62.

Moretti, Franco. *Distant Reading*. London: Verso Books, 2013.

Morgan, Wendy, and Richard Andrews. "City of Text? Metaphors for Hypertext in Literary Education." *Changing English: Studies in Culture and Education*, vol. 6, no. 1 (1999): 81–92.

Moulthrop, Stuart. *Victory Garden*. Cambridge, MA: Eastgate Systems, 1992.
Moulthrop, Stuart. "Rhizome and Resistance: Hypertext and the Dreams of a New Culture." In *Hyper/Text/Theory*, edited by George P. Landow. Baltimore: Johns Hopkins University Press, 1995, pp. 299–320.
Nelson, Theodor Holm. *Literary Machines 93.1*. Sausalito: Mindful Press, 1984.
O'Reilly, Tim. "What Is Web 2.0: Design Patterns and Business Models for the Next Generation of Software." *International Journal of Digital Economics*, vol. 65 (2007): 17–37, https://mpra.ub.uni-muenchen.de/4580/.
Page, Ruth. *Stories and Social Media: Identities and Interaction*. New York: Routledge, 2012.
Paul, Jean. *Siebenkäs*. Stuttgart: Reclam, 1983.
Paul, Jean. *Titan*. Berlin: Insel, 2016.
Pope, James. "A Future for Hypertext Fiction." *Convergence*, vol. 12, no. 4 (2006): 447–65.
Porpentine. "Creation under Capitalism and the Twine Revolution." *Nightmare Mode*, November 25, 2012, http://nightmaremode.thegamerstrust.com/2012/11/25/creation-under-capitalism/.
Porpentine, and Brenda Neotenomie. *With Those We Love Alive*. [Twine game] (2014), http://aliendovecote.com/uploads/twine/empress/empress.html.
Pressman, Corey. "Exprima Talks: Reading Hypertext with Mark Bernstein." *Publishing Perspectives*, February 27, 2014, http://publishingperspectives.com/2014/02/exprima-talks-reading-hypertext-with-mark-berstein/#.V5pdTPmU2M8.
Pullinger, Kate, and Chris Joseph. *Flight Paths: A Networked Novel* (2007–12), http://www.flightpaths.net.
Pullinger, Kate, Chris Joseph, and Andy Campbell. *Inanimate Alice* (2005–16), http://www.inanimatealice.com.
Pullinger, Kate, Stefan Schemat, and babel. *The Breathing Wall*. London: Sayle Literary Agency, 2004.
Queneau, Raymond. *Cent mille milliards de poèmes*. Paris: Gallimard, 1961.
Quinn, Zoe. *Depression Quest*. [Twine game] (2013), http://www.depressionquest.com/.
Rheingold, Howard. *Smart Mobs: The Next Social Revolution*. Cambridge, MA: Basic Books, 2002.
Rustad, Hans K. "A Four-Sided Model for Reading Hypertext Fiction." *Hyperrhiz: New Media Cultures*, 6 (summer 2009), http://www.hyperrhiz.net/hyperrhiz06/19-essays/80-a-four-sided-model.
Rustad, Hans K. "A Short History of Electronic Literature and Communities in the Nordic Countries." *dichtung digital*, 41 (2012), http://www.dichtung-digital.org/2012/41/rustad.htm.
Ryan, Marie-Laure. *Narrative as Virtual Reality: Immersion and Interactivity in Literature and Digital Media*. Baltimore: Johns Hopkins University Press, 2001.
Salter, Anastasia. "Ephemeral Words, Ephemeral People: Suicide and Choice in Twine Games." *Electronic Literature Organization Conference*, Bergen, Norway, August 4–7, 2015.
Simanowski, Roberto. "Death of the Author? Death of the Reader!" In *p0es1s. Ästhetik digitaler Poesie—The Aesthetics of Digital Poetry*, edited by Friedrich W. Block, Christiane Heibach, and Karin Wenz. Ostfildern: Hatje Cantz, 2004, pp. 17–92.
Skains, Lyle, Alice Bell, and Astrid Ensslin. "Gaming the Composition: An Ethnographic Study on Composing Ergodic Fiction." *International Society for the Empirical Study of Literature Conference*, Chicago, Illinois, July 6–9, 2016.
Sterne, Laurence. *The Life and Opinions of Tristram Shandy*. New York: Oxford University Press, 1983.

Tabbi, Joseph. "Electronic Literature as World Literature; or, the Universality of Writing under Constraint." *Poetics Today*, vol. 31, no. 1 (2010): 17–50.

Wittig, Rob. *Grace, Wit & Charm*. Performance: Teatro Zuccone, May 14 and 24, 2011, http://vimeo.com/26485377.

CHAPTER SEVENTEEN

Internet and Digital Textuality: A Deep Reading of *10:01*

MEHDY SEDAGHAT PAYAM

An important difference between print and electronic hypertext is the accessibility of print pages compared, for example, to the words revealed by the cursor's click in [an] electronic hypertext. Whereas all the words and images in the print text are immediately accessible to view, the linked words in a [digital] poem become visible to the user only when they appear through the cursor's action. Code always has some layers that remain invisible and inaccessible to most users. From this we arrive at an obvious but nevertheless central maxim: print is flat, code is deep.

—Hayles (2004)

The cosmos ... only appears chaotic, but in reality is an orderly place marked by harmony, synchronicity, and cooperation. All you have to do is look. All you have to do is pay attention.

—Olsen (2005)

By the mid-1990s, hypertext fiction had become well introduced into academic circles through articles and seminars, but at the same time a new era in the age of electronic writing was beginning. Less than a decade after the publication of his seminal hypertext fiction *afternoon: a story* (1990), Michael Joyce in his book *Of Two Minds* (1995) could already make this claim: "Thus far the primary visual structure of hypertext is language printed to the screen ... when hypertext content extends to digitized sound, animation, video, virtual reality, computer networks, databases, etc., it is referred to as *hypermedia.* Hypermedia is electronically rendered in computers and smaller microcomputer-based devices for storing and delivering information and entertainment" (21). What Joyce had aptly anticipated came to fruition with the development of information and communication technology (ICT) that enabled computers to host larger files and therefore made possible the addition of "sound, animation, video" and recorded voice. In the previous phase, as Robert Coover (1999, n.p.) recognized some years later, "audio and animation files were virtually nonexistent" in digital fiction.

By 1999, Coover was also able to recognize a second transformation, which would come to embrace "computer network[s], databases, etc." that would sweep away the golden age of hypertext writing and herald a silver age instead. The Internet was the main game changer. It was fully commercialized in 1995 and from that year onward provided numerous services like email, instant messaging, Voice over Internet Protocol (VoIP) "phone calls," two-way interactive video calls, and the Web. Because of these features, the multimedia pages could now host a variety of media in addition to written language. The networked capability of the Internet and the multimedia features of the electronic medium made it easier for writers who wanted to use movies and music in the graphic surface (the graphic user interface [GUI], to use a computer terminology). What this meant for the novel was that its linguistic components were challenged by machine interferences and even the process of reading was affected.

TUI, GUI, AND HTML

Computers in the previous phase of digital technology used purely text-based user interfaces for machine-user interactions, so navigation within the textual user interfaces (TUIs) was like skimming a book. As a reader opens the table of contents and then browses the book to find a specific place, page, chapter, or illustration, the user of those computers could choose a linguistic option that would take him where he wanted to go. This similarity made the TUIs a naturalized part of the computers and since they were the only navigation option, no specific terminology was coined for them. The term "textual user interface" is a retronym coined sometime after the invention of GUIs. The latter term by contrast highlights the importance of the design and how the graphical interface affects what is presented—what Johanna Drucker (2011: 9) defines as a dynamic space, a zone in which reading takes place.

> We do not look ... through it (in spite of the overwhelming force of the "windows" metaphor) or past it ... The surface of the screen is not merely a portal for access to something that lies beyond or behind this display. Intellectual content and activities do not exist independent of these embodied representations. Interface, like any other component of computational systems, is an artifact of complex processes and protocols, a zone in which our behavior and actions take place. Interface is what we read and how we read combined through engagement.

Drucker advocates treating the "interface" as a surface without depth: "a dynamic space, a zone in which reading takes place." And yet, as we know the computer does have a depth beyond the screen, even if what lies there is not what the human user is trying to reach, or for that matter *allowed* to reach since the depth that matters is layered with code that is meant to be read and executed by the machines, not us. What is available for the user is the interface. What lies beyond the surface of a print page is perceived as empty space.[1] And even if this empty space is occupied by hardware, it remains beyond the apprehension of a user without the technical knowhow—which is to say, the majority of users.

As Charles Severance shows in his book *Introduction to Networking: How the Internet Works* (2015), the machine-to-machine interactions are not likely to come to the surface

[1] In other words, the material technology which supports the screen does not exist for the page. A page is also contained by the book of which it is a part and which is also a technological artifact. In that respect, what is "behind" the page is literally the other pages which precede it. All the rest of the technology which contributes to the existence and operation of the page is somewhere else—the printing press, the publishing house, the bookshop, and so on.

unless they fail to do what they are supposed to do. The topmost application layer, is made of clients (computers sending requests) and servers (sending responses). Communication between these two follows the rules of hypertext transfer protocol (HTTP) or file transfer protocol (FTP), and the most common languages for clients, which mainly appear on Web pages opened in browsers are the trio of HTML, Cascading Style Sheets, and Javascript. These three languages together make it possible to combine multiple media, and the writer can present, for example, one part in moving pictures, another in words, and a third through music. Javascript is a programming language and is not directly related to this discussion; CSS and HTML are not programming languages per se, but they render the page for user recognition. CSS styles the appearance of content and makes it possible to separate document content from document presentation. But it is HTML which delineates content into parts, for instance, headings, paragraphs, images, all of which gives the content structure and meaning. HTML has become the popular language on the Web, because it facilitates the creation of multimedia pages. "The key achievement of HTML as a standardized mark-up language," Ensslin (2007: 21) states, "was its propensity to create a variety of different semiotic systems, previously analogue, i.e. separated in terms of mediality and materiality, on the basis of unified, script-based programming code. These semiotic systems comprise text, graphics, digitized speech, audio files, pictographic and photographic images, animation and film."

When the reader opens up a work of Web-based fiction in a browser, HTML assembles the interface by reading and executing codes. In this way, the interface is created by bringing up the layers which have been previously designed for front page presentation: their copresence within a work of Web-based fiction and their place in the network of relations determines the work's meanings as much as any narrative or stylistic features. This capacity of HTML has enabled writers to combine multiple media in works of Web-based fiction, whose combinations now become a separate component of the reading and writing experience.

HTML also enables the aesthetic use of other multimedia and cross-platforms such as Shockwave or Flash. Thus we can observe thirty-two out of the sixty works written in one of these platforms in the first volume of the *Electronic Literature Collection* (ELO), twenty-nine out of the sixty-three works of the second volume and sixteen out of the seventy-two works in the third volume.[2] Other authoring programs or languages such as Inform, Quicktime, and Squeak have a smaller share in the ELO collection of the works. The reason for this popularity is that Flash makes it easier for writers who are not programmers to create works of digital fiction.

Consistent with the literally underlying issues I have raised in this chapter, founders of the Digital Fiction International Network (DFIN) in their "Screed" define digital fiction as "fiction written for and read on a computer screen that pursues its verbal, discursive and/or conceptual complexity through the digital medium and would lose something of its aesthetic and semiotic function if it were removed from that medium" (in Bray, Gibbons, and McHale 2012: 471). What happens after one's initial engagement with the interface of a digital novel is that either (1) the reader finds herself subject to the functions of the machine and realizes that the machine directly interferes in her reading, or (2) she retrieves the various layers of multimedia in order to construct/follow a narrative. For the

[2] The main reason that fewer works of the third volume have been written using Flash is stated on the ELO website: "Flash dominated the interactive media landscape of the web for several decades, but has since faded thanks in large part to the rise of mobile platforms."

ease of reference, the first function-oriented group will be named "cybertexts" and the second will be named "multimedia works" of Web-based fictions.

CYBERTEXTS AND MULTIMEDIAL WORKS

Espen Aarseth (1997: 75) has introduced the term "cybertext," for "texts that involve calculation in their production of scriptons." According to Aarseth, scriptons are "strings as they appear to readers" (62), consistent with the machinic layers that have been described here.

Those layers, however, are more often than not rendered transparent in everyday use, cybertexts make the machine an integral part of their materiality—constructing a direct and purposeful interference in the process of reading. Ensslin has also used the term "cybertext" in her book, *Canonizing Hypertext: Explorations and Constructions* for "hypertexts that are programmed in particular ways as autonomous 'text machines' that assume power over the reader by literally 'writing themselves' rather than presenting themselves as an existing textual product" (22). Ensslin's definition implies a machinic autonomy that to a degree separates the work from the author, insofar as a machine element or computer program is capable of producing text effects not already fully written in by the author. For Ensslin, as for Aarseth, the reader has to compete with the machine for control over the text which appears and disappears and only through this engagement and competition can the reading process advance.

A short survey of the works of three volumes of ELO and other Web-based fictions devised for presentation on the World Wide Web shows that one of the most used techniques for asserting the machinic element has been placing time limits on the reading of any lexia before it disappears from the screen. *Hegirascope* (1997) and "Chemical Landscapes Digital Tales" (2006) are works that impose such limits; in these works, new Web pages replace the previous ones after a specific amount of time which is usually shorter than the time required to read the whole page (see my essay "A Window toward the Medium: A Media Specific Analysis of Chemical Landscapes Digital Tales" [2016]).

Multimedial works of Web-based fiction (which are most of the works in the three volumes of the ELO collection) seriously challenge the dominance of written language as the primary mode for novels and make nonlinguistic elements such as photos and colors, part of the text. These works are composed of dynamic machinic and modal layers in relation to each other; they coexist and (unlike "user friendly" interfaces that disallow interferences) they are each variously *visible* at the level of the interface.

10:01

10:01, a good example of a multimedial fiction, is written using Flash alongside other media/modes. Although linguistic parts of the text carry most of the narrative load, the spatial arrangement of its interface creates an interrelationship among the medial modalities. Olsen's novel, first published in print in 2005 and then brought "into machine" by Tim Guthrie in November of the same year, is about random people sitting in a theatre in the Mall of America watching the trailers. They run for ten minutes and one second before the start of the feature film. In the electronic version, the co-authors take advantage of a wide range of capabilities which bring together pictures, sounds, and movies to the digital medium.

Consisting mostly of mini-narratives, the novel avoids the hierarchical structuring that separates major and minor characters in conventional fictions. By insisting in the novel on a *random* selection of people, the authors create a contrasting social environment where anyone who can pay the admission fee can enter into the narrative: all the characters in *10:01* are equally important. The narration, for its part, also undermines conventional past tense as well as first-person or third-person perspectives. This novel uses other forms of language such as the present tense, numbered sentences, and film script format: each one is a transgression from established narrative practice, drawing our attention toward the language itself and how few of the available modalities have been, and are being, used by traditional novels.

For present purposes, I will focus on three separate but interrelated dimensions of the fictional text, namely: *design*, *narrative* (as created through both the work's material resources and signifying strategies); and the *reader's experience*. As can be seen from the discussion so far, and the Hayles epigraph, an electronic text has a depth which should not be taken for granted. With this distinction between "deep" and "hyper" awareness in mind, and with an appreciation of the need to move beyond the linguistic and conceptual aspects that have traditionally been explored in "close reading" of print narratives, I present what follows instead as an instance of "deep reading."

DESIGN

The GUI of the digital version of this novel has been presented through an Adobe Flash platform and can be opened in browsers which support HTML. It was published first by the *Iowa Review Web*, in its seventh volume of the November edition in 2005. *10:01* is not available on that website anymore and the reader is redirected to Olsen's website after selecting "click to enter."[3] Apart from Olsen's personal website, the ELO collection is the only other place on the World Wide Web where this novel can be found.

The opening page of this novel, which has now become the standard design for all the works published under the auspices of the Electronic Literature Organization, contains the name of the work, its writers, a short description about the work in a white margin right below the name of the work and its authors, followed by a lengthier "author description." Due to its Web-based presence, this novel has several links to other webpages, which intensify the dynamic layering of modes and media in the work's presentation.

The main difference between the title page at the ELO's website and Olsen's website (http://www.lanceolsen.com) is that the reader in the ELO edition has to click on the "begin" button to start the reading, whereas the reader on Olsen's site is invited to enter the novel via the GUI by clicking rather than initiating a process which the word "begin" suggests. The word "entrance" has this aspect of treating the interface of the novel as a space to wander through, rather than the starting place where the presentation occurs. The keywords for this novel are "audio, collaboration, fiction, flash, visual poetry or narrative." They provide a summary for the materiality of the work by directly foregrounding the modes and media used to create *10:01* as well as the software and platform.

[3] Although *Iowa Review* is still being published to this date, November 2016, the *Iowa Review Web* was discontinued in 2009. Its website has been moved to a new address and that is the reason why the hyperlink at the bottom of the ELO's title page to this novel does not lead to either *10:01* or *Iowa Review Web*.

Before the novel starts there is an introduction which moves up on the screen and includes four quotations. The rich interface of the novel appears after the introduction, which includes a digital representation of a water-color painting from above and the far end of a movie theatre—like those found in the Mall of America—in an ornamented frame. (A High Angle Shot, in cinematic lingo.) The start button is right below this painting, and two rows of clickable dots (the timeline for the novel) with varying colors are at the bottom of the screen. In the top section of the painting there is flickering light which represents the unreeling of the movie on the screen (or in this case, the trailers before the feature film). Moviegoers are shown from the rear end of the theatre as black two-dimensional heads and shoulders which almost look like one other and have occupied seats in different parts of the theatre. When all the characters look exactly alike and no one stands out in a crowd, the reader has no clues where exactly to look and one's gaze is not directed toward any specific point, which again emphasizes that all the characters are on a par here.

Clicking on the start button brings up the first linguistic section in the top left of the interface within the frame, and the start button becomes a navigation box with five clickable options. There appears a question mark in the middle, which works as the "help" option and presents an overview of the interface. According to the overview it is possible to read the novel either by character, character chapters, or timeline. Meanwhile a green dot appears on the head of the person whose story has popped up and a big sign on the bottom right of the screen reminds the reader to turn the speaker on. Finally, according to this interface, it is possible to hide the text which has covered over half the theatre image and select a single character in theatre which becomes orange as soon as the mouse rolls over it, and the character's name appears at the right side of the navigation box.

The window that pops up for each mini-narrative, in addition to the linguistic section, has the name of the character, one or up to four other circles with numerical digits inside them (which show whether there are any other mini-narratives about this character), and a couple of digits in the stopwatch format, which starts from 00.00.00.00 and ends in 00.09.58.15. Most of the linguistic sections should be scrolled down to be read in full, and they have links to other pages on the Web, such as the official website of Mall of America, in highlighted blue words. On the right side of this box of linguistic section, a picture or sometimes a movie appears which directly refers to the story narrated in the linguistic section. For instance, for Kate Frazey, who is the great-great granddaughter of Franz Kafka, a picture of the entrance of Mall of America and a head shot of Kafka appear on the screen each for ten to fifteen seconds, and then disappears. Also for this mini-narrative, and for another one about Celan Solen (anagram on the name of the author, Lance Olsen), respectively, a hare and a mouse appear on the top of the frame of the painting. The recorded voice and video appear at various moments, for instance, at 00.00.03:13 when the narrative about Miguel appears on the screen and is accompanied by the sound of deep breathing. Zdravko's narrative has a video at 00.00.04:12: this one is a short movie about a woman weaving.

The movie theatre is presented through an ornamented frame so as to emphasize the presence of the interface. The frame does not disappear when the mini-narratives of the characters are unraveled, but another frame in a contrasting color is added to stress the work's dynamic layering. The option to hide the text also makes an important claim about the materiality of this novel. By hiding its linguistic section, the novel, *10:01*, presents itself as a primarily audiovisual work which includes a rich variety of nontextual modes/media such as painting, music, recorded voice, photos, film, and so on. Therefore, the interface becomes all that is available to the reader and here Olsen and Guthrie literally create what Drucker (2011: 9) describes as "a zone" that we do not look through but instead read, and the way we read is not textual but rather "combined through engagement."

In order to mirror the entrance of the characters from a colorful and bright outdoors space into the theatre which is darker and dimly lit, the screen lights are dimmed and then they return to normal five or ten seconds later when the characters move back into the theater. Apart from the obvious links in the linguistic section, there are some hidden links in corners of the frames (for instance, for Stuart Navidson at 00.00.01.01, and Miguel Gonzalez at 00.03.27.29) which are mostly for Date.com in Beaver Bay, Minnesota. The dating website, according to its homepage, has over 10 million active members and a "unique scientific matching algorithm," which is one way the Web offers to connect people who have been kept separate from each other through the hierarchy of capitalism.

NARRATIVE

The digital version involves mini-narratives for thirty-seven people ensconced in the theatre in the Mall of America. Similar to its namesake, *1001 Nights*, the narrative is made of separate (and sometimes interrelated) mini-narratives. These single threads appear alongside each other in a single, final mini-narrative of Milo Magnani, the assistant manager of the mall, at 09.58.15.

Before the mini-narratives appear on the screen, there is the introduction with the four quotations. The first is a belief stated by August Lumière in 1895 about the genre he had pioneered: "Film can be exploited for a certain time as a scientific curiosity, but apart from that it has no commercial value whatsoever." Lumière said this the same year that he and his brother showed the first projected movie to a paying audience. Similar to those who predicted that the golden age of digital fiction is already over, Lumière assumed the interest in film would be lost once a passing curiosity was satisfied. Cinema as we know emerged as a major practice in ways that some of its earliest writers/directors could not have foreseen. Color, sound, and advanced filming instruments transformed this art into something quite different from the short movies which the Lumière brothers had originally made. The Internet and developments in ICT have also changed digital fiction from what it used to be.

The second quotation is a dialogue from George Romero's *Dawn of the Dead* which is uttered when the zombies keep coming back to a deserted mall whose inhabitants have taken shelter on its roof:

> "Francine: What are they doing? Why do they come here?
> Stephen: Some kind of instinct. Memory of what they used to do. This was an important place in their lives." (00:34:39-00:34:49)

The dialogue refers to how shopping has become a central part of our culture and how malls now include almost everything. The Mall of America is an apt example because it includes a theme park, several food courts, a sea life aquarium, an upscale hotel, and fourteen movie theaters. At the time of this writing, plans for expansion include a dinner theatre, ice rink, three hotels, and a waterpark. These expansions will double-up the size of an already enormous outlet (currently over 112 acres, which is large enough to contain fourteen Yankees Stadiums). In this regard, a mall becomes something like the digital space which has become a huge part of our culture and despite its many potentials is mostly used for shopping, dating, and getting amused. In sync with the mall, the Web is expanding more and more each day.

The third quotation is from *Letters to Wendy's* (2000: 280), a book of experimental essays/letters by the contemporary poet and writer, Joe Wenderoth: "Let's say Wendy's is an airplane. Traveling at ten thousand feet. Let's say there is no landing gear and nowhere to land. And fuel is limited. And one has a general idea of when the fuel is going to run out. Given this knowledge, is travel really the right word? And if not travel, then what? One sees one's life quite differently when one knows it isn't going to land."

The Wenderoth quotation in this context can be interpreted as an indirect reference to digital novels and alternative understandings they bring forth by keeping at bay the certainties which the traditional works of print fiction offered—for instance, a definite place to start, a definitive end, and a reading method which did not change from novel to novel. Though the quotation does not directly address what these differences are, the digital context makes it possible to think of the materiality of the medium, its affects, and its effect on what is being presented through it.

The final quotation is from a David Bowie's single "I'm Afraid of Americans" and simply says: "God is an American." Here's what the singer/composer has to say about it: "It's not as truly hostile about Americans ... it's merely sardonic. The invasion by any homogenized culture is so depressing, the erection of another Disney World in, say, Umbria, Italy, more so. It strangles the indigenous culture and narrows expression of life" (*Earthling* album Press release). Bowie here aims to resist the totalizing effects that an order/tradition has on the arts—an *expression of life*. The way that the physical resources of the printed book have been used in traditional novels is a good example of this invasion of homogenized culture, and that is exactly what the digital fiction *10:01* seeks to avoid.

Breaking the narrative into smaller chunks (what we've been calling mini-narratives), brings *10:01* in line with the works of the first wave of digital fiction, but here is also where the similarity ends because in contrast to works like *afternoon*, the reader has access to all the parts of the novel from the beginning and the mini-narratives are not directly related to each other. Particular tales can follow one another in any number of ways, and the temporal, forward arrangement of the mini-narratives is only one possible option here. They make it possible for the novel to have a variety of stories, instead of a single one, a material texture woven out of coexisting narrative threads and the interface of the novel.

The "pick and mix" of eighty mini-narratives cover a wide range of topics from sex and violence to a spirituality and worship of Jesus Christ. Many are autobiographical and offer a glimpse of a character's life in the past and present, and in some cases future. Some of the characters appear in each other's narrative and the further the reader engages with the mini-narratives (see the next section), the more relationships he will discover. In fact, the mini-narratives only "seem chaotic" at the first glance, but what one of the characters, Trudi Chan, says about cosmos can be taken as a commentary on this novel too. The mini-narratives might seem "chaotic" but the relationship between them is one of "harmony, synchronicity and cooperation." It is up to the reader to "look" and "pay attention" to construct/discover them.

READER'S EXPERIENCE

From the beginning, there are three ways to "read" this novel, and each one will unravel the narrative differently. The first way is to "read by timeline" in the interface of the novel, as its name states, to follow a traditional method of observing progression within the story. In this process, all the reader has to do is click on the forward button after the first mini-narrative appears. For this reading, all of the mini-narratives are read sequentially and one after the other in the same way that the print version of the novel is expected to be read. Here the reader starts with Kate's mini-narratives at 00.00.00 and moves linearly in time forward until she reaches the mini-narrative named "begin" which is when the movie is supposed to start and clicking on that mini-narrative takes the reader back to the beginning of the novel as well.

The second way of reading this novel (i.e., as "read by character chapters" as stated in the interface) starts from the traditional method and follows the story of the *characters* which seem more interesting to each reader by clicking on the next mini-narrative for this character in the circles, and visiting the other mini-narratives which are about him/her. This method gives more options to the reader because he can read those which interest him more and ignore those other characters which he does not want to follow. Unlike the previous reading process, this one is not necessarily chronological and moves back and forth in time.

The third way of reading is referred to as "read by character" in the interface and as the name suggests requires the reader to click on where every character is sitting and follow his/her narrative from there. This kind of reading observes the least authorial control and the reader's selections provide her with her own opportunity to create a specific version of the narrative. The main difference between this reading and the previous one is that in the previous one the reader was supposed to read all the other mini-narratives which existed in the text window too. There could be up to five mini-narratives for a single character. However, in this reading we are supposed to jump around and read one single mini-narrative from each character and then move on to the next character. The other mini-narratives for that character can be read if the reader gets back to him/her later in her reading.

The last possible way of reading is mixing all the above processes. A reader can start from a character, read two or three of that character's mini-narratives, then move to another character, and go on reading along the timeline. Any of these four reading processes can potentially highlight the roles of different characters within the story. By not providing a single or fixed narrative discourse the author here is giving readers the freedom to choose their own way through the pool of stories. One of the implications of this equality is that the Web has itself become like that theatre. It provides a space in which typographic elements, picture, voice, video, and music can come together in multiple combinations to form, within Olson's and Guthrie's multimediated novel, narratives that are similarly organized around time, but meanwhile readers have other opportunities to create their own narrative discourse and reading paths. This point is stressed from the very beginning by the interface of the novel which does not show the screen of the theatre, but the people who are watching that screen. In fact, the text box which opens for characters can be considered as a displaced screen which has replaced moving images with words and in doing that has reasserted the importance of the written language as the major element in works of multimedial fiction.

At the same time, as can be seen through displacing the movie screen with the text box, the nonlinguistic materiality of the digital medium is stressed from the very beginning. While watching a traditional film, audience members are meant to get absorbed in the projected experience, not look around at the theatre and the other audience members.

But in *10:01* the writer wants us to do just that. After all, almost all movies are about the lives of other people (how they fall in love, how they overcome their problems, how they survive in a postapocalyptic world invaded by aliens, etc.), and this is exactly what we miss when we go to watch a movie and share the experience of watching it with strangers, but cannot know what *their* stories are. Here the medium helps us to have a better grasp of who and where these people are, what they think, and how they interact with each other at a specific moment at this specific place. We can see the movies inside *their* heads, whether they are having memories or watching the movie which they have actually made or wish to make.

One of these short movies, *Where the Smiling Ends*, makes the point quite well: it's about the moments just after people photograph each other: "when people slowly stop smiling after the shot has been snapped and you can actually see their public mask soften and melt back into everyday blandness, a gesture always accompanied by a slight lowering of the head in a miniature act of capitulation" (ELO website). This short experimental movie, which actually has been made by Lance Olsen's partner, assemblage artist Andi Olsen, makes the audience pay attention to something which they normally do not see or pay attention to in their daily life. The moment before this one, the moment which their picture is being snapped by the camera, is the one which is immortalized through the effect of light on chemicals, but that photo and that smile are momentary reflections of the people toward the camera, which is supposed to fix this moment, and they get so much absorbed in the moment their photo is being taken that they do not pay much attention to what people do after that.

Another interpretation of this short movie is that fiction focuses on life in ways that those of us, when we are actually engaged in social life, do not have to think about, and at the same time the film points to the role of technologies of representation, and by implication how they have become increasingly popularized. Therefore, whereas previously "taking/making" a picture required expensive technology and expertise, now it does not and so a previously very small section of the population, who learned how to pose for their portraits, has been replaced by a much broader section of the population practicing public/celebrity personas, that is, engaged in specific kinds of (self) representation which conform to public forms of expression in relation to specific media which includes digital media as well.

CONCLUSION

Two trends can be identified in works of Web fiction. The first trend disrupts conventions and places our reading experience at the mercy of the machine functions. The second examines the presence of other media in a genre which has been dominantly linguistic. We have one tendency that places emphasis on the act of reading and a second which stresses the intermedial presentation of the story. The first group stresses the performance of the written narrative located in the Web environment, and the second aims at presenting the narrative through the multimedia features of the Web.

As our encounter with *10:01* has shown, the presence of other media in a work of Web-based fiction can break down the hierarchy of the linguistic section in novels and challenge its supremacy. In other words, multiplicity of media can result in novels in which the words' hold over the narrative is not as strong as it has been in conventional novels. Given a degree of authorial self-awareness, however, such a novel can potentially provide a dialogical engagement between linguistic and nonlinguistic elements which can eventually lead to an alternative understanding of what novel is (or what it can be).

One of the implications of this change is that such novels tend to have an ensemble cast rather than a handful of main characters. As Paul Ceruzzi has argued, there is no central computer that controls the whole Internet. Similarly works of Web-based fiction need not have a central character; we have instead multiple discourses and multiple stories which eventually create multiple readings. The narrative is also broken down to several mini-narratives which can have multiple interrelationships to each other. In this way, the fictional text—in the broadest meaning of the word "text"—will be a "fine and delicate" tapestry woven out of several voices/events, which becomes similar to what Quintilian had recommended in his book on speeches where the term "text" has originally been used.

SOURCES CITED

Aarseth, Espen J. *Cybertext: Perspectives on Ergodic Literature*. Baltimore: JHU Press, 1997.

Bray, Joe, Alison Gibbons, and Brian McHale. *The Routledge Companion to Experimental Literature*. London; New York: Routledge, 2012.

Ceruzzi, Paul E. "The Materiality of the Internet." *IEEE Annals of the History of Computing*, vol. 28, no. 3 (2006): 96. *ACM Digital Library*.

Coover, Robert. "Literary Hypertext: The Passing of the Golden Age" (1999), n.p. December 6, 2016.

Drucker, Johanna. "Humanities Approaches to Interface Theory." *Culture Machine*, vol. 12 (2011): 1–20.

Ensslin, Astrid. *Canonizing Hypertext: Explorations and Constructions*. New York: Continuum, 2007.

Falco, Edward. "Chemical Landscapes Digital Tales" (2006), n.p. December 6, 2016.

Hayles, N. Katherine. "Print Is Flat, Code Is Deep: The Importance of Media-Specific Analysis." *Poetics Today*, vol. 25, no. 1 (2004): 67–90, poeticstoday.dukejournals.org. December 6, 2016.

Joyce, Michael. *afternoon; a story*. Watertown, MA: Eastgate Systems, 1990. Floppy Disc.

Joyce, Michael. *Of Two Minds: Hypertext Pedagogy and Poetics*. Ann Arbor: University of Michigan Press, 1995.

Joyce, Michael. *afternoon; a story*. Watertown, MA: Eastgate Systems, 2001. Compact Disc.

Moulthrop, Stuart. *Hegirascope*. Virginia Tech University, 1997. December 6, 2016.

Olsen, Lance. "10:01" (2005a). December 6, 2016.

Romero, George A. et al. *Dawn of the Dead*. Troy, MI: Distributed by Anchor Bay Entertainment, 2004.

Sedaghat Payam, Mehdy. "A Window toward the Medium: A Media Specific Analysis of Chemical Landscapes Digital Tales." *Digital Studies/Le champ numérique* (2016).

Severance, Charles R. *Introduction to Networking: How the Internet Works*. CreateSpace Independent Publishing Platform, 2015.

Wenderoth, Joe. *Letters to Wendy's*. Seattle: Verse Press, 2000.

CHAPTER EIGHTEEN

Of Presence and Electronic Literature

LUCIANA GATTASS

The aim of this chapter is to approximate German literary theorist Hans Ulrich Gumbrecht's aesthetics of "presence" to the recent phenomenon of electronic literature, by which I mean digitally born literary objects meant to be experienced within networked and programmable media environments.

The program "production of presence," spearheaded by Gumbrecht, begins in 1988 with the publication of the volume *Materialität der Kommunikation* (*Materialities of Communication*) and attains full crystallization in the brief *Production of Presence* (2004). Echoing Susan Sontag's *Against Interpretation* (1966), and borrowing from Jean-Luc Nancy's terminology (*A Birth to Presence*), Gumbrecht's post-hermeneutic aesthetic seeks to challenge the "enthronement of interpretation" as a chief practice in the humanities, and rehabilitate the human body (the neglected *res extensa*) as a medium of aesthetic engagement. Because works of electronic literature tend to reflect on the medium of their inscription, often celebrating technique over legibility and interactivity over interpretation, they are amenable to the logics of presence—presence here understood as the "other" of meaning. Electronic literature's exacerbation of the materiality of text promotes a shift in receptive modalities from interpretation—within which literary works customarily operate—to spectatorship of an audiovisual event. Through close readings of electronic textual objects, I describe how breaks in signification can be read as symptomatic of a non-hermeneutic trend in digital aesthetics. I submit that it is only within the framework of a "culture of presence," and only by addressing the material realities of the electronic "writing space," that one can attain a comprehensive theory of digital textuality. Taking Noah Wardrip-Fruin's virtual reality textual installation *Screen* (2004) and Bruno Nadeau and Jason Lewis's *Still Standing* (2007) as tutor-texts, I argue that it is precisely because immersive mixed media installations confront readers with the frailty of the hermeneutic process that they can benefit from theories of presence.

A key passage in Lev Manovich's *The Language of New Media* alerts readers to the decline of the written word in digital environments—that we can assume has continued steadily since the book's publication in 2001. Commenting on the pervasiveness of cinematic language in cultural landscapes, Manovich draws a parallel between the printed word tradition and pictorial semiotics, detecting a tendency in contemporary culture to convey information "in the form of time-based audiovisual moving [images], rather than text" (78). Today, the ubiquity of the emoji, the success of platforms such as Instagram and Snapchat, to say nothing of Facebook's acquisition of Oculus, a technology company whose first product is a head-mounted display for immersive virtual reality, would appear to confirm Manovich's predictions: information does seem to be conveyed visually with greater frequency than it is transmitted textually.

This state of affairs would sound threatening to literary communication, but a closer look would reveal promising alternatives for the theory and praxis of electronic literature. Electronic literature both reflects and comments on a cultural moment whose birth is to be traced to utopian days of early hypertext and extends to this our time of multimodality and hyper-connectivity. That technology dictates drastic aesthetic change is confirmed by the fact that certain genres figuring in the "canon" of electronic or digital literature have come to be known by the software used to create them. For instance, *afternoon: a story* (1987) by Michael Joyce and Shelley Jackson's *Patchwork Girl* (1995) are typically categorized as masterpieces of "the classical period" of electronic literature (Hayles 2008). As the Web evolved, chunk-style hypertexts of the Storyspace School have given way to high-speed, immersive, interactive experiences, defying notions of authorship/readership, legibility, and perception. The two digital textual artifacts to be discussed in this chapter are products of a recent shift within the tech-sector toward technologies of embodiment and approximation—a fact confirmed by Facebook's acquisition of the Oculus Rift and its founder's proclaimed interest in virtual reality technologies.

In his reading of Martin Heidegger's *Being and Time*, German literary scholar Hans Ulrich Gumbrecht sees an explicit relation between the distance conquering technologies arising in the 1920s (planes, elevators, telephones) and Heidegger's analysis of space as a structural precondition for human existence (Gumbrecht 1997). Through the use of his "typical hyphenations," Gumbrecht argues, Heidegger converts *Entfernung* (distance) into its opposite *Ent-fernung*, literally dis-distancing, or, as Gumbrecht better puts it, "undoing of farness" (ibid.).[1]

This insight can prove useful to the analysis of the cultural implications of current technologies and their repercussions to the study of electronic literature. Specifically, it can help us envision the role sensory-oriented, proprioceptive interfaces, favoring immersion and tactility, play in cultural configurations which are so prone to space-eliminating, matter-effacing, dis-distancing technologies. As a theoretical exercise, I propose we draw a connection between the tendency toward immersion occurring presently in Silicon Valley and a movement within the humanities to recover the body and materiality as sources of theoretical engagement, as evidenced by theories of affect, presence, and embodiment. The eruption of these discourses in the era of the immaterial must point to a desire to overcome precisely that loss of matter, of touch, which digital technologies (despite the predominance of touch interfaces) have subtracted from our everyday-worlds. With Gumbrecht (2012: 7) we might argue that "this state of withdrawal has provoked an enhanced need—and an increased desire—for encounters with presence." As he unveils the "formula" for his "production of presence," Gumbrecht (2004: 17) explains that presence refers to a spatial, pre-reflexive and non-metaphysical engagement with the world of objects, implying tangibility to the body: "what is present to us (very much in

[1] This pun would have taken Heidegger to the analogous thesis that *Zuhandenheit* (ready-to-hand) takes priority over *Vorhandenheit* (present-at-hand). In other words, from an existential viewpoint, proximity (or rather the "undoing of farness") precedes distance in importance: "In Dasein there is an existential tendency towards closeness. All the ways in which we speed things up, as we are more or less compelled to do today, push us toward the conquest of remoteness [*Entferntheit*]. With radio, for example Dasein has so expanded its everyday environments that it has accomplished a de-distancing [*Entfernung*] of the 'world'—a de-distancing whose implications for the meaning of Dasein cannot be fully visualized" (Heidegger, 105 In. Gumbrecht, 1997: 365).

the sense of the Latin *prae-esse*) is in front of us, in reach of and tangible for our bodies)." Production here purposefully evokes its etymological root *producere* (the act of bringing forth an object in space) (1). Built, thus, into the expression "production of presence" is a clear emphasis on movement and spatiality (versus temporality, which the author associates with the "metaphysical worldview," itself predicated on agency and meaning attribution): "to speak of 'production of presence' implies that the spatial tangibility effect coming from communication media is subjected, in space, to movements of greater or lesser proximity, and of greater or lesser intensity" (17). Different media (or different "materialities of communication") will therefore "touch" our bodies in distinct ways.

Significantly more conciliatory in rhetoric than Susan Sontag's essay *Against Interpretation* (1966), which advocates a return to the senses,[2] and his own combative 1994 essay "A Farewell to Interpretation," *Production of Presence* (2004) does not preach the dismissal of interpretive models. It does not believe it possible to leave behind the hermeneutic field: a realm wherein disembodied subjects (*Cogito*), eccentric to the world of things, penetrate the "surface of the world in order to extract knowledge and truth as its underlying meanings" (27–8). Instead the book is intended as a "pledge against the systematic bracketing of presence" in the arts and humanities (xv). In other words, any point of view that shows itself critical of the subtraction of space or the body from the ontology of human existence is a "potential [source] for the development of a reflection on presence" (18).

For Gumbrecht (2004: 18), aesthetic experience can never be reducible to an antinomy (meaning vs. presence) but rather occurs in simultaneous oscillatory tension between semiotic "meaning effects" and sensory activation "presence effects": "poetry is perhaps the most powerful example of the simultaneity of presence and meaning effects—for even the most overpowering institutional dominance of the hermeneutic dimension could never fully repress the presence effects of rhyme, alliteration, of verse and stanza." To reconcile the idea of presence—its pedagogical and practical applications—with our interpretive apparatuses informed by centuries of Western epistemology is no simple task. One of the consequences of the "enthronement of interpretation" as the chief practice in the humanities is the lack of a suitable repertoire of "noninterpretive concepts" (52). Yet, what I propose is an approach to digital aesthetics open to the intuition that our relationship to these aesthetic objects is not exclusively one of meaning attribution: there is layer in these events which "presents [itself] to us, . . . without requiring interpretation as its transformation into meaning" (81).

To this end, let us delve into Gumbrecht's (2004: 19) binary typology which distinguishes between "cultures of meaning" and "cultures of presence," with the caveat that all cultures can be analyzed as either, even if "the semantics of their self-description

[2] Sontag's urge for a retrieval of the senses was fostered by a desire to deal with the afflictions of modern life in her time: the policy of excess, the overcrowding of spaces, imagetic and sensorial overloads, and so on. Despite the fact that since Sontag there have been no significant changes in the perception of excess, the rhetoric-of-choice of those advocating pure affect has nevertheless lost its combative tone. A case in point is the discrepancy in Gumbrecht's writings between 1989—the year of inception of the program of *Materialities of Communication*—and 2004—the year of publication of *Production of Presence*. Whereas in "A Farewell to Interpretation" Gumbrecht (1994: 390) warns his audience about the perils of the ever-increasing degree of abstraction in Western intellectual tradition, in 2004 he offers the consensual addendum: "challenging the exclusive status of interpretation within the humanities, however, does not mean that this book is 'against interpretation" (2). And later: "I think that the 'beyond' metaphysics can only mean doing something in addition to interpretation—without, of course, abandoning interpretation as an elementary and probably inevitable intellectual practice (52).

accentuate one or the other side." "Cultures of meaning" hinge on subjectivity (the Cartesian *Cogito* or specifically the mind, *res cogitans* being the only mode of human self-reference). Knowledge, or rather legitimate knowledge, is a product of an act of interpretation. A culture of presence, on the contrary, is predicated on the absence of subjectivity (or the subject as agent): here, it is the body (*res extensa*), rather than the mind, the dominant mode of human self-reference—"in a presence culture humans consider themselves to be part of the world of objects instead of being ontologically separated from it" (2014: 3). Knowledge in a culture of presence can never be actively produced by humans but unfolds as revelations: "knowledge revealed by (the) god(s) or by different varieties of what one might describe as 'events of self-unconcealment of the world' " (81).

One way to understand Gumbrecht's rationale is to look at his account of the history of metaphysics contained in *Production of Presence*, relayed as a tale of epistemological shifts. The account charts the demise of Medieval cosmology, follows the birth of the early subject (*Cogito*) in early modernity, the emergence of the second-order observer in the mid-nineteenth century, and our present postmodern epistemological situation of (representational) crisis.[3] An important aspect in Gumbrecht's typology resides in the notion of the sign. Contrary to the dual logic material signifier/immaterial signified lying at the heart of the representational or hermeneutic paradigm, the hyphenated concept of re-presentation or, more radically, that of re-presentification is nonsymbolic. By rooting presence on the concept of the Aristotelian sign, which simultaneously denotes both substance and form, Gumbrecht (2004: 29). manages to eschew the present signifier/absent signified duality: "the Aristotelian sign . . . brings together a substance (i.e., that which is present because it demands space) and a form (i.e., that through which a substance becomes perceptible), aspects that include a conception of meaning unfamiliar to us." Embedded in the search for a sensitive re-presentational model (Gumbrecht, 2004)—one of presence versus meaning—is the effort to undo absence in a spatiotemporal sense. Making things present means making them concretely available—that is, "ready-to-hand" (*Zuhanden*; and see also Shelley Jackson's "show of hands" in Chapter 1).

Within a culture of meaning or within Western epistemology, presence can never be thought of as a stable entity, "it cannot be part of a permanent situation" (Gumbrecht 2004: 57). This is where Gumbrecht's reluctant affinities with the work of Martin Heidegger become particularly relevant. Without dwelling on the complex ramifications of Heideggerian thought, suffice it to mention that the characterization of human existence as *Dasein* (being-in-the world) contains precisely the right anti-Cartesian sentiment and emphasis on spatiality and substance which a reflection on presence requires. Because Dasein is "being-in-the-world, that is human existence that is already in—both special and functional—contact with the world" (71), it cannot be synonymous with commonplace definitions of the liberal subject. Rather, Dasein "dwells alongside" and has a material

[3] Emblematic of these shifts is his comparative account of the sacrament of the Eucharist in Catholic and Protestant Mass—that is, the shift from Medieval cosmology (culture of presence) to Early Modernity (culture of meaning). In the medieval (Catholic) version of the sacrament, the expression *hoc est enim corpus meum* (for this is my body), through which transubstantiation occurs, denotes pure materiality and not a representation of an absent signified (the body of Christ). Each time the ritual of the mass takes place, "Christ's body and Christ's blood become tangible in the 'forms' of bread and wine" (Gumbrecht 2004: 28): "In the Protestant version of the mass something entirely different occurs for Calvinist theology redefines the presence of Christ's body and blood as signs or representations (which stand for absent meanings), as in "this bread stands for my body," which is no longer present (cf. ibid.).

grasp of the things of the world but "this world with which Dasein is in touch is "ready-to-hand," it is always already interpreted world" (ibid.).

In an attempt to justify his position of "eccentricity" vis-à-vis the metaphysical paradigm, Gumbrecht resorts to yet another concept in Heidegger's philosophy, namely, the concept of Being, which he argues bears striking similarities to his own idea of presence. For the sake of argument, let us go along with Gumbrecht's (2004: 72) readings of both Heidegger's *Being and Time* and *The Origin of the Work of Art* and accept that the work of art is a "privileged site for the happening of truth, that is for the unconcealment (and the withdrawal of Being)." Let us also assume that the unconcealment of Being is akin to the happening of presence and that presence is the intangible facet of aesthetic experience. Trapped in a double movement of "unconcealment" and "withdrawal," Being is neither spiritual nor conceptual. "Being is not a meaning. Being belongs to the dimension of things" (67). So long as being and presence are to be used interchangeably, then a few conclusions become possible: If Being is not conceptual, if it is not a "meaning"—that is, "that which makes things culturally specific" (ibid.)—then neither is presence; if it does not possess any transcendental aspect, if it is immanent, substantial—that is, if it belongs to the world of things and has, indeed, a "thingly" character—then all of these characteristics equally apply to presence. Most importantly, if Being necessarily withdraws from view as it reveals itself, then it possesses the epiphanic, unstable feature which makes presence a rare occurrence, a state of exception, fundamentally divested of or free from cultural/historical specificity and yet paradoxically particular to a moment, a thing. Finally, Gumbrecht concludes that this sort of presence is "difficult—if not impossible—to reconcile with modern Western epistemology because it brings back the dimension of physical closeness and tangibility" (57). Insofar as presence can never "hold" and is always ephemeral, presence can never be stable, "it can never be something that, so to speak, we would be able to hold on to" (58).

ELECTRONIC LITERATURE

Electronic literature comprises far more than the typographic sign alone—sound, image, code, and movement being integral constituents of its augmented textuality. Text, in this context, is always and inevitably a process, a performance, a result of an interaction over a distributed chain of data files and commands involving author, reader, text, and software (Hayles 2006). In this sense, electronic literature transcends (one could also say it undermines) the letter, ratifying Manovich's (2001: 78) prediction that electronic media would challenge the "authority and cultural supremacy of the word." Symptomatic here is the fact that of the sixty works contained in the ELC1 (Electronic Literature Catalogue) compiled by the Electronic Literature Organization in 2008, some have no recognizable text and virtually all rely heavily on visual and aural elements (cf. Hayles 2008).[4]

Media history has shown that new methods of storing, processing, and transmitting knowledge tend to give rise to new writing and reading modalities, new literacies. In *Writing Space*, David Bolter (2001: 21) speaks of "economies of writing," or the intimate relations hip between a certain "writing space" and the kind of writing that is produced as a

[4] With Hayles, I accept the "verbal mark" as a provisional criterion of distinction between electronic literature and electronic art—provisional being the operative term in this assertion since the complexity of individual works (their very readability as textual objects) will often vary, thereby rendering such clear-cut demarcations almost impossible.

result of such interdependency—"[the] dynamic relationship among materials, techniques, genres, and cultural attitudes or uses." This dynamism proves to be critical to the emerging field of electronic literature for as the qualifier "electronic" suggests, electronic literature operates on the cusp of technological transition. Indeed, book historian Roger Chartier (1995) has deemed the revolution of our present time more extensive in nature and impact than Gutenberg's, alleging that the current state of affairs had only been preceded in the West by the remediation of the scroll to the codex, which occurs in the early Christian era. If a new technology such as the codex facilitated the handling of the text, providing, for instance, a more effective use of the bracketed, two-dimensional surface of the page, a similar logic now applies to electronic writing: for one thing, digital mediation will foster reception practices no longer solely reliant on the mandates of flat typography.

Following in the tradition of the 1999 immersive installation *Text Rain* by Camille Utterback and Romi Achituv, which also invites participants to engage in bodily interaction with a projected reading space, *Still Standing* by Jason Lewis and Bruno Nadeau, OBX Labs, Concordia University, presents an interesting twist on the paradigm of polyattentiveness, which has come to define our contemporary writing and reading economies. Envisioned as a reaction to the recalcitrant text, the distracted reader, and the inevitable subjugation of the message to the exuberant logic of effect, *Still Standing* demands poise, restraint, and prolonged attention.

At the start of the piece the user encounters a projected wall containing letters seemingly at rest on the floor. As the participant approaches the screen, the letters react as if they were being kicked around. Should the participant stand still for a moment the text is attracted toward his position and fills his silhouette—becoming increasingly legible so long as the user's body remains immobile. As the participant walks away, the silhouette of text collapses scattering the words back across the floor where they will remain, until the next user comes along. The poem "Seeking Sedation" was composed specifically for the installation and functions as a direct commentary on dwindling attention spans and disruptive technologies. It reads as follows:

> five chapters of addiction for my perpetual commotion bring my brain to a stop. the inception of sedation is needed for the waves to break and the spin to reduce. letters to literal the motionless moment hides for my sight to seduce. (http://collection.eliterature.org/2/works/nadeau_stillstanding.html)

Still Standing's significance is manifold: critics have speculated about the symbolism of the textualized, readable body as an inversion of word made flesh (here it is flesh that is turned into text). In his reading of the work, Roberto Simanowski (2011: 51) claims that "the silhouette filled up with text may convey the deeper meaning that the Self is composed of the kind of text it perceives," and speculates that "the underlying subject is the cannibalistic relationship between the two semiotic systems of text and visual art or interactive installation." The artists themselves adhere to the most evident interpretation of the work calling it a reaction to the "'collapse of the interval,' a phenomenon of fast pace culture that rarely allows a moment to stop and observe" (Lewis and Nadeau, http://collection.eliterature.org/2/works/nadeau_stillstanding.html). In her reading of the work, Rita Raley points out the paradox inherent in equating stillness, itself a product of "rigorous" muscular control, with intellectual activity (cf. Raley in Ricardo 2009: 29).

To my mind, *Still Standing* lays bare the frailty of the sort of reading techniques we have come to associate with literary activity: the solitary, poised, self-disciplined activity which leads to reflection, contemplation, and possibly transcendence. By requiring the reader to stand still (to essentially tame his body) the work calls attention to the arbitrariness, the conventionality, perhaps the discomfort of silent reading—recall that silent reading was only to become a convention in the fifteenth century (Chartier 1995). However, as Simanowski (2011: 52) aptly notes, the irony is that *Still Standing* does not dare to demand sustained stillness of its "readers," which it could have managed easily by continuously offering new texts as the spectator stands still: "By abstaining from requesting a longer period of immobilization and thus requesting a long attention span, *Still Standing* undermines its own agenda and contributes to the fast paced culture it criticizes."

Perhaps most importantly to our present purposes, *Still Standing* possesses the sort of deictic properties which Gumbrecht (2014: 6) ascribes to presence achieved against or in language—that is, "language being open to the world of things. [Including] texts that switch from a semiotic paradigm of representation to a deictic attitude where words are experienced as pointing at things rather than standing 'for them.' "[5] As an example of such "amalgamations" between presence and language Gumbrecht cites Francois Pongé's thing-poems and physicist Erwin Schroedinger's autobiography: "[Schroedinger's] obsession with descriptive preciseness seems to have rejected the effect of abstraction that is inherent to all concepts. Nouns therefore seem attached to individual objects in Schroedinger's text and thus begin to function like names, producing a textual impression that is strangely reminiscent of medieval charms" (ibid.). Lewis and Nadeau's invitation to immobilization seems to act in a similar fashion. By predicating legibility on a forced moment of constraint, stillness (to which the text of the poem alludes), the installation stands in a metonymic relationship to its theme. To put it differently, it *reenacts* the constraint it wishes to represent.

Because electronic media has made possible the coupling of participation and reception to borrow from theorist Francisco Ricardo (2009), novel reading politics and practices have never been more in demand. These are conducive to new forms of theorization about the body, its performative dynamics, and its status as interface. The challenge lies in the reformulation of institutionalized notions of hermeneutics so as to encompass tropes of interaction and performance. While hermeneutic relations are founded on processes of meaning attribution, interactive readings presume concrete and programmable actions/interventions at the material, pre-semiotic level. Textual installations such as *Still Standing* or *Screen* demonstrate the need for an approach to digital works which consider the grammar of bodily interaction as part of the process of meaning attribution. Simanowski (2007: 48) hopes for a shift from "linguistic hermeneutics" to a "hermeneutics of intermedial, interactive, and performative signs."[6] In a variation to Simanowski's intuition,

[5] In a chapter entitled "Presence in Language or Presence Achieved against Language?" contained in his *Our Broad Present*, Gumbrecht (2014: 2) wishes to underscore "a principally difficult, rather than natural, relationship between presence and language." In an effort to build a typology, the author lists six types of amalgamation between these distinct realms. Two of these interest us here: namely, language as presence and language fulfilling deictic function (ibid.). The first, language as presence, refers to the physical reality of language, specifically to its form and volume, such as that which we perceive in rhythmic/poetic language. That is to say, language that has a physical impact on the body. The second type of amalgamation has to do with language that switches from a "semiotic paradigm of representation to a deictic attitude where words are experienced as pointing to things rather than standing 'for them' " (6). The latter I've identified in *Still Standing*.

[6] In his *Digital Art and Meaning* Simanowski (2011: 7) writes, "If an interactive installation applies textual or visual metaphors and symbols that are established in contemporary culture—such as the shadow in 'Deep Walls' (2003) and the light show in 'Vectorial Elevation' (1999/2000)—one ought also to investigate how their

I would submit that the hermeneutics of the digital will paradoxically bring us closer to what Gumbrecht has termed the non-hermeneutic field. Gumbrecht's (2014: 3) departure from or bracketing of metaphysics, and my own, is predicated on the belief that the Cartesian dimension does not (and indeed should not) encompass the entirety of aesthetic experience: "our relationship to things (and to cultural artefacts) is, inevitably, never only a relationship of meaning attribution."

CAVE AND MATERIALITY

Caves are immersive virtual reality environments—typically small rooms slightly larger than a closet, where images are projected on four surfaces, three walls, and the floor. In a default configuration, a primary user will wear a head-mounted display that produces the impression of three-dimensional images while polarized, shuttering glasses synchronize otherwise imperceptibly alternating right-eye/left-eye images, filtering projections into the corresponding eye and promoting stereo vision. The imagery on the normally darkened walls is visible to all visitors to the CAVE, but only one person can control them, that is, can navigate, grab, or move textual-objects. In this way, the walls serve as both a surface of inscription and a map of sorts, a point of departure.

The CAVE offers a unique opportunity for an empirical study of language in that it concretely and radically challenges the duality signifier/signified lying at the core of the representational paradigm. Within the logocentric hermeneutic/metaphysical[7] framework, which has been the (quasi) uncontested practice in Western humanities, linguistic materiality is neither the primary goal nor the focus of aesthetic engagement. Despite its double nature as *logos* and *imago* the conventions of written language and print have largely established that a signifier exists so it can be transcended, read, decoded (Drucker 1998: 57). Masten, Stallybrass, and Vickers (2016: 2) introduce their *Language Machines* by speaking of the consistent effort on the part of "the idealist tradition" to divorce language from its machines: "the fantasy of an immaterial languages a long history." Johanna Drucker (1998: 14) has a similar observation in the introduction to her study on early twentieth-century experimental typography: "the notion of linguistic transparency implies immateriality." To be sure, confrontations with the material reality of the letter or the visual dimension of writing have emerged throughout the twentieth century—particularly within early avant-garde (Dada and Futurism) and later with Concrete Poetry. With a nod to Clement Greenberg's formalistic concept of the avant-garde: when the materiality of the signifier is the focus of a work, that is what renders the work avant-garde.

---

connotations influence the meaning of the work. Because the trademark of such an installation is interaction, it is necessary to physically enter the interaction with the result of a complex interplay of physiological and psychological functions during the receptive process. This does not, as some scholars would have us believe, invalidate the Cartesian paradigm that focuses on cognition and neglects sensual aspects in experiencing reality. New media theory is right to stress the central role of the users' physical engagement in interactive art, in contrast to the mere cognitive engagement in perceiving a painting, sculpture, or text. However, besides the physical engagement, it is still possible, even crucial, to approach the work from a hermeneutic perspective. It is mandatory not only to understand the operational rules of the piece or the 'grammar of interaction'—that is, the modus of interaction the artist made possible within the interactive environment—but also to reflect on its specific symbolic (Fujihata 2001). The physical interaction should not overwrite the cognitive interaction with the work but rather become part of it."

[7] It should be clear that I subscribe to Gumbrecht's simplified definition of metaphysics in that I too activate here the word's literal meaning: that which transcends the merely physical.

One generalization to be made about CAVE pieces is that they appeal to the very tactility, which VR as medium renders impossible. Once text migrates to, or rather merges with, physical space, then it actively confronts readers in a novel way: how to "read" text that has been afforded discernible volume and structure? What changes in literary communication when the topology of the page as master surface undergoes such radical transformations as to become a de facto "playable space"? And what of the unfastened letter—that is, "the floating text"? As he dissects "the gravity of the leaf" in his eponymous essay John Cayley (2010: 203), who runs the CAVE at Brown University, speaks of a new phenomenology of language, one wherein floating textual strings would not constitute acts of remediation proper, but rather frame new instances of mediation because they present "graphically embodied language in a way that is entirely unfamiliar." Introducing text as both symbolic inscription and virtual object—though lacking a physical third dimension, text becomes perceivable in space as solid matter being assigned the semblance of position, volume, and structure—the CAVE recasts, rehabilitates, and multiplies the paradoxes with which literary studies have had to grapple in the past, particularly with the advent of Concrete poetics. Recall that Concrete poetry's emphasis on design and spatial grammar triggered two essentially distinct (albeit inextricably conjoined) reception strategies, namely, those of "reading" and those of "seeing." Given that "concrete poetry begins by being aware of graphic space as structural agent" (Campos et al 1970: 71), one can extrapolate, with regards to a poetics of the screen, that the repercussions of "flickering" signifiers in fluid surfaces will be numerous.[8] If print allowed words to inhabit immutable surfaces of inscription, or pages, digital poiesis is transient, it is code: there are no clear-cut distinctions between what can provisionally be termed a signifier and fluid post-alphabetic arrangements. Even surface in this realm can only be rationalized metaphorically: there is no true stability to speak of, but only gradual, ever minute, instantiations of permanence. To speak with Cayley (2005), CAVE walls are not transparent media of delivery, nor "should [they] be cast as a bearer of multiple (flat) successive 'states of text,' rather because they are canvases that can act as temporal repositories, both monitoring and retaining traces of all stages of 'programmable text,' cave walls should be treated as complex surfaces." With Katherine Hayles (2006: 184), one might argue that digitally instantiated text presents a distinct type of materiality, one which invokes proprioception as well as kinesthetic engagement. I would posit that insofar as digitality resensitizes us to the symbolic reality of language, it can be said to promote moments of disruption, breaks in semiosis, and "an amalgamation" with the dimension of presence (cf. Gumbrecht 2013).

[8] Coined by one of the field's indisputable icons, Katherine Hayles, the notion of "flickering signifiers" refers to signifiers that are created electronically and do not exist anywhere as such, except as code in a distributed networked system, acquiring form only as they are activated by a software program. At a purely theoretical level one could speak of an ontological shift: The concept of "flickering signifier" stems from a reconfigured technological paradigm marked by constant processes of intermediation: "Foregrounding pattern and randomness, information technologies operate within a realm in which signifier is opened to a rich internal play of difference. In informatics, the signifier can no longer be understood as a single marker, for example a mark on a page. Rather, it exists as a flexible chain of markers bound together by the arbitrary relations specified by the relevant codes. . . . A signifier on one level becomes a signified on the next-higher level" (Hayles 1999: 31). In my analysis I expand or clarify the concept of the flickering signifier to encompass any semiotic object—icon, index, or symbol—that is created, represented, or instantiated by computer code rather than by itself or some physical phenomenon, like ink on paper. It is created more or less on the spot, by computational projection on a screen, for example, and then, just as quickly, passes out of existence.

Let us consider *Screen*, one such VR work for the CAVE environment. Having had its literary status validated by many a scholar in the field, *Screen* by Noah Wardrip-Fruin et al. has become somewhat of a VR classic and, as such, presents itself as an ideal tutor-text for theoretical extrapolations. The creators of this work have written of it as inviting a three-layered "reading" effort, bracketed as follows—the first stage is relatively conventional, operating like an ordinary video installation: three introductory texts are projected onto three separate walls while a voice-over reads the text back to the users in poetic cadence.

> In a world of illusions, we hold ourselves in place by memories. Though they may be but dreams of a dream, they seem at times more there than the there we daily inhabit, fixed and meaningful texts in the indecipherable flux of the world's words, so vivid at times that we feel we can almost reach out and touch them. But memories have a way of coming apart on us, losing their certainty, and when they start to peel away, we do what we can to push them, bit by bit, back in place, fearful of losing our very selves if we lose the stories of ourselves. But these are only minds that hold them, fragile data, softly banked. Increasingly, they rip apart, blur and tangle with one another, and swarm mockingly about us, threatening us with absence.

Spoken language, as any lover of poetry will attest, inundates us, it touches us even when we do not understand what is being said. In *Screen* the voice-over has precisely this incantatory, intoxicating quality, which one associates with the "moving" aspects of aesthetic experience and with presence.

The second stage of *Screen* is more dynamic and starts when a word peels off one of the walls and flies toward the interactor—an action, which is accompanied by a ripping noise. At this point, the user is allowed to intervene by striking words with a tracking glove. This bodily and nontrivial gesture of "batting at" words in what often turns out to be a vain attempt to fill the empty slots initiates the third stage of reading/playing, which consists of the results of the interactions from the second stage. Because words will come loose at an increasing rate and quantity and because these words can crumble into syllables and fragments, the third stage's (final) output results in a different arrangement of wall-text each time.

Evidently, a user's engagement with the CAVE involves interaction with visual, auditory (in this particular instance, rhythmic), and quasi-tactile structures that are seen, heard, and which give the appearance of three-dimensional volume. When, as CAVE users, we interact with a work like *Screen*, which appears to be composed entirely of text, our initial mode of engagement is semiotic, that is, one of reading/listening: we are looking at words and trying to see what they mean. But when those words acquire the appearance of volume and can be manipulated, our engagement changes: they are no longer words, they are now floating objects that can be moved around and controlled in a manner that is non-textual, it is much more immediate, it is indeed present. To inhabit this new phenomenology of language might prove confusing, overwhelming. Contrary to the dual logic material signifier/immaterial signified which (despite successive deconstructive crises) lies at the heart of the representational or hermeneutic paradigm, the hyphenated concept of re-presentation or, more radically, that of re-presentification is nonsymbolic. Embedded in the search for a sensitive re-presentational model (Gumbrecht 2004)—one of presence versus meaning—is the effort to make things spatially available: making something present, Gumbrecht tells us, relying as he frequently does on Heideggerian logics, means making it "ready-to-hand" (*Zuhanden*). In *Screen*, the tridimensional loose words present an uncanny variation on the subject-object paradigm in that they become/embody the lost memories which they stand for. Much as in *Still Standing*, where we spoke of a deictic relationship between the work and its theme, here the gesture of batting at the "attacking" words renders physical the theme of the installation: memory loss. By attempting to place words back in their original slots, the participant essentially emulates the precarious act of retrieving lost vocabulary, the vain attempt to overcome the loss of this "fragile data" which happens to define us: "Increasingly, they rip apart, blur and tangle with one another, and swarm mockingly about us, threatening us with absence," reads the voice.

The human body being central in the vast majority of mixed media environments, immersive installations can be said to require paradoxical answers. On the one hand, the situation is one of insularity—an immersion into a state of play where meaning plays a subsidiary role at best. On the other, because these are texts and not objects which confront our bodies, then we as readers (rather than interactors) are immediately thrown in a realm of semiosis. In short, material and concrete sensory impacts found in installations such as *Still Standing* and *Screen* demand enhanced, presence-ready literacy competencies, which do not (and should not) preclude whatever interpretative impulses one may feel toward literary objects. As difficult as it may be to ascertain the exact extent to which an exterior sensory impulse might numb or temporarily suspend our cognitive faculties, I maintain that Gumbrecht's conception of presence is integral to the thorough theorization of complex immersive digital installations.

SOURCES CITED

Bolter, Jay David. *Writing Space: Computers, Hypertext, and the Remediation of Print*. London: Routledge, 2001.

Campos, Augusto de, and Decio Pignatari. "Haroldo de Campos, 'Pilot Plan for Concrete Poetry.'" *Concrete Poetry: A World View*, 71–2.

Cayley, John. "Writing on Complex Surfaces." *Dichtung Digital*, vol. 2 (2005).

Cayley, John. "The Gravity of the Leaf." *Beyond the Screen: Transformations of Literary Structures, Interfaces and Genres*, vol. 44 (2010): 199.

Chartier, Roger. *Forms and Meanings: Texts, Performances, and Audiences from Codex to Computer*. Philadelphia: University of Pennsylvania Press, 1995.

Drucker, Johanna. "Figuring the Word." In *Essays on Books, Writing, and Visual Poetics*. New York: Granary Books, 1998.

Gumbrecht, Hans Ulrich. "A Farewell to Interpretation." *Materialities of Communication*, vol. 397 (1994).

Gumbrecht, Hans Ulrich. *In 1926: Living on the Edge of Time*. Harvard University Press, 1997.

Gumbrecht, Hans Ulrich. *Production of Presence: What Meaning Cannot Convey*. Stanford University Press, 2004.

Gumbrecht, Hans Ulrich. *Atmosphere, Mood, Stimmung: On a Hidden Potential of Literature*. Stanford University Press, 2012.

Gumbrecht, Hans Ulrich. *Our Broad Present: Time and Contemporary Culture*. Columbia University Press, 2014.

Hayles, N. Katherine. "How We Became Posthuman." *Virtual Bodies in Cybernetics, Literature, and Informatics*. Chicago/London (1999).

Hayles, N. Katherine. "The Time of Digital Poetry: From Object to Event." *New Media Poetics: Contexts, Technotexts, and Theories* (2006): 181–209.

Hayles, N. Katherine. *Electronic Literature: New Horizons for the Literary*. University of Notre Dame Press, 2008.

Manovich, Lev. *The Language of New Media*. MIT Press, 2001.

Masten, Jeffrey, Peter Stallybrass, and Nancy J. Vickers, eds. *Language Machines: Technologies of Literary and Cultural Production*. Routledge, 2016.

Nadeau, Bruno, and Jason Lewis. *Still Standing*. 2005.

Nancy, Jean-Luc. *The Birth to Presence*. Stanford University Press, 1993.

Raley, Rita. "List (en) ing Post." *Literary Art in Digital Performance* (2009): 22–34.

Ricardo, Francisco J., ed. *Literary Art in Digital Performance: Case Studies in New Media Art and Criticism*. New York: Bloomsbury Publishing USA, 2009.

Simanowski, Roberto. "Holopoetry, Biopoetry and Digital Literature." *The Aesthetics of Net Literature: Writing, Reading and Playing in Programmable Media* (2007): 43–66.

Simanowski, Roberto. *Digital Art and Meaning: Reading Kinetic Poetry, Text Machines, Mapping Art, and Interactive Installations*, vol. 35. University of Minnesota Press, 2011.

Sontag, Susan. *Against Interpretation: And Other Essays*, vol. 38. Macmillan, 1966.

Utterback, Camille, and Romy Achituv. *Text Rain* (1999), http://camilleutterback.com/projects/text-rain/.

Wardrip-Fruin, Noah, Josh Carroll, Robert Coover, Shawn Greenlee, Andrew McClain, and Ben "Sascha" Shine. *Screen* (2002).

CHAPTER NINETEEN

Postmodern, Posthuman, Post-Digital

LAURA SHACKELFORD

Whatever lives must also write.

—Christian Bök (2015)

There are multiple ways to retrace the trajectories through and against which digital literary writing practices and their print precursors have emerged and gained recognition within overlapping genres of electronic literature, imagetexts, interactive narrative, experimental games, new media art, installation and performance art, net.art, locative and augmented-reality narrative, and digital literary fiction since the 1990s. This chapter focuses on a series of concerns with language—among other sign systems—and the broader symbolic and political economies catalyzing digital literary writing practices since Fredric Jameson (1991) first described this "mutation of the sphere of culture" (4), a "prodigious expansion of capital into hitherto uncommodified areas" (36). Noticing the proliferation of a superficial "flatness" or "depthlessness" to signification, Jameson theorizes the nonincidental, if nonrepresentational relationship of this "society of the image and of the simulacra" to the latest stage of capitalism and its mode of production (9, 48). Identifying shifting understandings, orientations, and practices of language that characterize and scaffold the postmodern, posthuman, and the post-digital, respectively, I will amplify and differentiate some of the still-propagating strains of inquiry that unfold and persist within and across these overlapping periodizations (and their respective preoccupations and methods), while also registering key movements in digital literary practices as they reconceive the place of language and the literary amid computation-based digital media systems and bioinformatic political economies of the twenty-first century.

The egregiously selective retracing of digital literary writing offered in this chapter gathers key trajectories of, and transformations in understandings and practices of language and writing informing postmodern, posthuman, and post-digital configurations. Rather than aiming to delimit or differentiate the efforts that have coalesced around each of these theoretical attractors over the past quarter century (an impossibly reductive task), my reapproach rewinds the distinct, yet overlapping threads of digital literary practices so as to illustrate and recapture several key, and continuing contributions. Ideally, the chapter will prompt additions, expansions, and exceptions to these examples and suggestions of alternate genealogies amid or against them. Retracing digital literary engagements with language, code, and its computation-based constraints and potentials, the chapter intends to clarify where some of these inquiries have led us or left us today, paying particular attention to Christian Bök's *Xenotext project*, comprised of Book I (published in 2015), a collaborative artist's print edition, and an ongoing "wet" experiment that aims to execute a poem by inserting a poetic program into the DNA of a prolific, near-immortal bacterium and then allowing the bacterium to execute the poem through its process of living.

As may already be quite clear, something significant has happened to both practices and conceptualizations of writing, language, and poetics here and they draw on a longer genealogy of digital literary writing practices since William Gibson's coauthored *Agrippa* (*A Book of The Dead*; 1992) began to circulate and its electronic poem was posted on Bulletin Board Services (BBS) in the early 1990s, or Shelley Jackson's *Patchwork Girl; or A Modern Monster by Mary/Shelley and Herself* (1995) materialized the monstrous bodies and bodily life entering into hypertext networks and writing in the mid-1990s, or Eduardo Kac's installation *Genesis* (1998–99) brought to the gallery these transformative relays between genomic sciences and genetically engineered and understood life, social networking, and remote presence via the Internet, and rendered such shifting practices of writing, textuality, authorship, and authority in fuller, multiply encrypted view, or María Mencía pursued *Another Kind of Language* and reimagined digital poetics as *Birds Singing Other Birds' Songs* in 2001, or Amaranth Borsuk and Brad Bouse's augmented-reality book *Beyond Page and Screen* rendered tangible the transactional spaces between print and digital language practices, or Talan Memmott, Eric Snodgrass, Sonny Rae Tempest, and Michael J. Maguire performed their hypermedial *Huckleberry Finnegans Wake* at the international e-poetry festival in London in 2013.

This hybrid digital literary trajectory reveals an ongoing strain of practice-based inquiries and experimentation with language, text, code, and computation, clarifying the potential to such practices. Digital literary writing is often first understood as a digital object and exclusively identified according to its technological media or modes of expression. Instead, I'll explore how the digital literary practices addressed in this chapter illustrate the extent to which computer languages, digital media, and computational methods and cultures are as often a point of connection or comparison with other language, literary media practices, cultural histories, and symbolic economies, as they are a point of differentiation. Such engagements with digital technologies, modes of communication, or circulatory regimes don't necessarily participate in, or presume, a linear, progressive understanding of technological change that heralds digital technologies as its latest pinnacle and overattributes agency to a technicity abstracted from the social processes and practices through which such technical processes materially, temporally, and differentially unfold.

Retracing these digital literary strains of inquiry into language and emerging, computation-based digital media, and their bioinformatic symbolic and political economies and circulatory regimes, I take seriously the demonstrated potential of computational digital literary practices and computation-based aesthetic experimentation in their capacity as a "minor science," opening onto emerging, immanent, practice-based methods for diagnosing and pursuing the shifts in language and poetics and their larger literary, symbolic, and political economies (Marks 2002: xiv; Deleuze and Guattari 1987: 361).[1] This helps, in turn, to identify some of the limits, and opens questions in current thinking about how language works or means differently in contemporary contexts. Bracketing

[1] I am here drawing on Laura U. Marks's work, in which she applies the term "minor science" to her discussion of experimental film, video, and digital art. See Marks (2002). The term originates with Giles Deleuze and Felix Guattari (1987: "Treatise on Nomadology—The War Machine").

some of the more vexing philosophical questions raised by efforts to understand language as a logical system and the histories of technical thinking that make that plausible, it is possible to agree, I think, that "computers invite us to view languages on their terms: on the terms by which computers use formal systems that we have recently decided to call languages—that is, programming languages" as David Golumbia (2009: 84) states in the beginning of his inquiries into the remarkable influences of computation on understandings and practices of language since Chomsky. It is already possible to see the significant effects of these interinforming or "intermediating" relays in Katherine Hayles's (2005: 11) terms, that is, language bearing the traces of its algorithmic generations and evidencing unprecedented degrees and kinds of addressability. Thankfully, it is, for multiple reasons, much harder to accept the view that natural languages will "progressively evolve to seamlessly integrate the linguistic biases of algorithms and the economical constraints of the global linguistic economy" (Kaplan 2014: 61), particularly when this seems to confirm the worst fears of a Googlization of the word and world that is certainly making itself felt today.

Understanding creative digital literary language practices through this retrospective querying, the chapter aligns these e-poetic contributions with other interdisciplinary efforts to register and reckon with shifts in language practices, their signifying economies, and the broader cultural and political economies they coproduce. It addresses the question of how prominent digital literary works interested in, and experimenting with language practices in bioinformatic, computation-based regimes emerge and evolve in relation to genomic and now postgenomic sciences, late capitalist political economies, literary media systems, and broader processes of political, technological, and cultural change. And it explores what understandings and alternate practices of language (among other sign systems) digital literary writing practices pursue today and how they can help redescribe the symbolic economies of which they are such an admittedly minor part.

POSTMODERNISM AND DIGITAL LITERARY PRACTICES

Jameson's theory of postmodernism as "a cultural logic of late capitalism" coincided with other efforts to grapple with the apparent "dematerialization of production," its overoptimistic reading as a new stage of "postindustrial" capitalism (Bell 1973), and the growing tendency of the emergent information economies to engender "a general perspective of immateriality," as K. Ludwig Pfeiffer (1994) describes this shift of emphasis in the 1985 exhibition at the Georges Pompidou Center, *Les Immateriaux*, to which Jean-François Lyotard and others contributed. Registering and redescribing this sense that, as Steve Tomasula (1996: 100) eloquently describes it, the "world of things has become a world of signs—a universe that both brings into being and is brought into being by symbolic codes," Jameson's accounts of postmodernism, which he aligns with the historical period of postmodernity or third stage of capitalism and its burgeoning finance capital, provided the most influential, thick diagnosis of this shift in the mode of production as it impacted economic, social, political, and symbolic economies, alike. As I've argued elsewhere, postmodern fiction and its first digital literary offshoots emerge out of their confrontations with these shifting material conditions (in Jameson's sense), and associated media practices and modes of knowledge production.[2] Postmodern fiction, in diverse ways, registers

[2] See Shackelford (2014).

in literary terms the influence and impact of information sciences emerging out of post–Second World War cybernetics, systems theory, and biologies and their "translation of the world into a problem of coding, a search for a common language in which all resistance to instrumental control disappears and all heterogeneity can be submitted to disassembly, reassembly, investment, and exchange," as Donna Haraway (1991: 164) famously describes the dominant ideological emphasis coming into focus at this time. Prominent strains of postmodern fiction by John Barth and others, as well as the first-generation digital literary hypertexts written for stand-alone computers using the Storyspace authoring program, such as Michael Joyce's much-debated *afternoon: a story*, evidence the shifting status of language and writing in late capitalist information economies and the influence these kinds of circulation, signification, and exchange were having on literary practices and understandings of language, authorship, writing, and reading. John Barth's novels and short stories actively pursue the consequences of these shifts in the material, social, institutional, and symbolic "occasions" for writing, even if their engagement with postmodernism in the guise of a "hypertextualization" of life, of texts-behind-texts in an infinite, recursive, self-referential loop, too easily accommodates the kinds of apparently immaterial, free-floating significations or simulacra that are at the core of late capitalism's predominant ideologies and prized self-description.[3] First-generation hypertext theory and hypertext fiction seem to have, in retrospect, similarly overvalued the generativity of their "infinite" texts and underestimated the material conditions, technologies, and constraints informing these new practices of reading and writing and the political economy subtending them.

Postmodern fiction, like postmodern theory, is easily eclipsed by these dominant tendencies of writing (and of reading) this work. It is, thus, important to recognize that Barth, Thomas Pynchon, William Burroughs, and many other minor postmodern writers, such as Kathy Acker, Donald Barthelme, or Joseph McElroy, were responding in distinct ways to these shifts in language and its circulation, to altered political economies of literature, art, and culture, and to transformations in the technical state of the art for recording, reproducing, circulating, and archiving speech, script, and sound, which were well on their way to repositioning the literary system within a larger media ecology, as Joseph Tabbi and Michael Wutz anticipated in their 1997 collection, *Reading Matters: Narrative in the New Media Ecology*. It is important to register these influences and, I'd suggest, to recognize that it is out of these debates and distinct approaches to working through the contradictions and conundrums of language and textuality amid other sign systems in emerging, decidedly bioinformatic, late capitalist political economy that digital literary writing and language practices at this time begin to explore the linguistic, practical, and philosophical preconditions for meaning, to pursue the reconstruction of "*those processes through which structures of articulated meaning can at all emerge*," a consideration of the prior, competing, and emerging material sites and supports through which something like meaning becomes possible at all.[4] It is out of dissatisfactions with postmodernity and

---

[3] David Foster Wallace (1993) offered a particularly adept critique of how postmodern metafiction by Barth and other postmodernists and their self-reflexive, meta-textual wanderings were in close company with commercial cultures of television and advertising and offered his own twist on the "infinite texts" of the postmodernists as an "infinite jest."

[4] Gumbrecht (1994: 398); emphasis in the original. This is not the beginning of computational language and art practices, which could be linked back to Ada Lovelace's first computer programs and her analogies to weaving of other sorts, or to Christopher Strachey and Alan Turing's love-letter generator for the Mark I computer, but is a significant consolidation of digital literary practices as an emerging mode of writing.

postmodern theories that an important strain of digital literary writing and experimentation with computational media takes root and begins to pursue methods and lines of inquiry into these questions.

Amid diverse literary, artistic, and cultural efforts to devise a "language" or "to grow a new sensorium" adequate to these changes, Jameson identifies William Gibson's 1988 *Mona Lisa Overdrive* and cyberpunk as the "supreme literary expression, if not of postmodernism, then of late capitalism itself" (419, no.1). In 1992, the year following the publication of Jameson's essay in book form, Gibson and his collaborators—artist Dennis Ashbaugh, publisher Kevin Begos Jr., and a programmer known only as "Brash"—distributed an artist's book titled *Agrippa (A Book of The Dead)*, and the computer program containing its embedded electronic-poem began to circulate through the text-based Bulletin Board Services (BBS) allowing users to share messages and files on networks that preceded the World Wide Web. This work and its circulation reveal several dimensions of digital literary writing and its occasions that tend to be overlooked when one focuses on more self-contained, properly literary, digital objects.[5] One might even want to take Jameson's equivocation about whether to place cyberpunk and Gibson's work in proximity to the cultural logic of "postmodernism" or to the political economy and productive modes of "late capitalism," as an early indicator of what I'll suggest becomes more legible in *Agrippa* and also signals a significant shift important to digital literary writing, more broadly. *Agrippa* repositions and reorients its digital literary print methods to enter into emerging digital modes of production, circulation, and consumption, precisely as a means to register these with a comparative, literary, material, and materialist difference. The artist's book is involved in a multileveled, practice-based experimentation with the very media, technical, and symbolic systems with which it grapples both materially and conceptually.

As Agustín Berti (2015) argues in his extensive recent analysis of *Agrippa (A Book of The Dead)*, this handmade artist's book poses concerted challenges to understandings of digital encoding, content, and circulation that remain prominent today. This artist's book and its electronic poem intently disrupt the late capitalist, libertarian ideal of a digital "content" free from material constraints, while also countering imperatives of standardization and, perhaps, accentuating those of blackboxing and obfuscation, which have defined computer programming since the Second World War. *Agrippa*, like many hand-made artist's books, was published in a limited edition that takes the form of "a dark box made of paper and fiberglass impregnated with resin that simulates a buried relic and an organic product," as Berti describes it, with a small reproduction of the cover of an "Agrippa photo album," a brand sold by the Eastman Kodak Company in the 1920s and the inscription "ALBUM / CA." "AGRIPPA / Order extra leaves by letter and name" (Berti 2015: 131–2). The box, lined with a pattern of honeycombs, contains a large book that is wrapped in cloth and intentionally damaged and burned, reminiscent of a decaying shroud around an aged holy text. The book includes hand-printed text on its title-page—"AATCA / TACGA / GTTTG / CATAA / CTGAA / TTGGT"—letters that symbolize the chemical elements comprising the genetic code of the female Drosophilia fruit fly. On other pages there are "DNA portraits," etchings resembling the images

[5] This is not to dismiss the centrality of a "media-specific" analysis of digital literary practices, as Hayles theorizes this, nor to endorse the media-blindness of prior understandings of the literary. Instead, I recommend we attend both to the media-specificity of digital literature *and* to the literary, medial, and technological ecologies and histories through and against which these writing practices emerge.

produced by a gel electrophoresis method used to analyze DNA. There is also a floppy disk in the last pages of the book with an executable file, which runs on the Macintosh System 7 OS. When run, the program generates a black-and-white image of the box's cover on the computer screen and then Gibson's poem "Agrippa" appears on screen, moving upward until readers reach the end of the poem, at which point the poem's file automatically destroys itself.

Focusing in on how *Agrippa* repositions language and literary poetics, as materially encoded, technically realized practices on the same plane as several other scriptural, visual, aural, and sonic media practices, I want to underscore its relevance to digital literary practices that have been undertaken since, while also acknowledging this postmodern point of departure for, and preoccupations of the artist's book/electronic poem.[6] As a practice-based, digital literary experiment, it is intent on the question of how language, the literary, and the privileged codex storage medium of the book might inhabit and/or be displaced by digital media and computational methods of information processing and exchange.[7] Importantly, *Agrippa* situates its queries into digital technologies and protocols of encoding within the context of an "(an)archaeological" exploration of prior archival technologies and their respective enlistment in ongoing efforts to stabilize meaning, vanquish the effects and passage of time, and, otherwise, mitigate the spatial and temporal parameters of human meaning through technical means (Zielinski 2006). While explicitly referencing this line of Kodak phtographic albums, *Agrippa* also draws on Heinrich Cornelius Agrippa's 1531 collection *De Occulta Philosophia*, which combined Renaissance theology, science, philosophy, mysticism, and magic and was similarly seeking out the means to reveal "hidden" dimensions of the world through an eclectic synthesis of knowledges and practices.[8]

Agrippa (a book of the dead) establishes linkages between textual and visual archival technologies as diverse as *De Occulta Philosophia*; the *Egyptian Book of the Dead* (and other funerary books of the dead) that include hieroglyphic script and illustrations on paper or written on objects and were intended to guide the newly deceased person through the underworld; and *grimoires*, or books guiding one in the proper combinations of elements to carry out magical spells; and Eastman Kodak's standardized, mass-produced photographic processing and archival paraphernalia; its own status as a handmade, burned and damaged, oversized hardcover book, and, last, its multiply embedded, self-destructing poem, computationally encoded on a floppy disk, inside the book, within the box. Notably, *Agrippa* also links such archival efforts to symbolically encode and preserve life to the genomic encoding and visual registration of the DNA sequence of the Drosophilia fruit fly (central to early genetics). It prints the Drosophilia's genetic sequence on several pages of the book with layouts arranged to mimic the dual columns of a holy text, underscoring this symbolic register of a DNA sequence's similar status as an encoded script aiming at some kind of material-symbolic transubstantiation.

[6] With this focus in mind, I will not address many of the relevant or interesting aspects of *Agrippa*, which can be found in William Gibson's own superb website and Agustín Berti's book, which includes one of the few in-depth readings of the "Agrippa" poem.

[7] Notably, digital technologies have marked an end to the era of Eastman Kodak and its chemical processing of photography. Having spent many years trying to transition to digital photography and processing methods, Kodak declared bankruptcy in early 2000, though a small piece of the company remains today.

[8] For a provocative contextualization of Agrippa's *De Occulta Philosophia*, its indebtedness to Renaissance humanism, and a consideration of the new, posthumanist meanings occult philosophies are beginning and able to pursue, instead, see Thacker (2010).

Agrippa's digital literary experiment places attention fully onto the material basis of these art practices and the discrepant affordances and constraints of the archival technologies supporting them, actively challenging and undermining the supposed stability or immediacy of the meaning they convey. Juxtaposing archival technologies old and new, the project stresses their shared status as technologies of memory and technical presencing, revealing how they persistently surpass, re-embed, and reduplicate each other. *Agrippa* underscores archival technologies' shared status as characteristically human, yet ultimately futile efforts to transcend these material conditions. It encourages recognition of human memory and meaning as irrevocably "entangled" with this *technicity*[9] (rather than locating these technologies of memory in a linear, progressive chronological order of improving fidelity to life or permanency of meaning). As a self-acknowledged "book of the dead," this artist's book and its digital poem pursue their material transformation and ultimate disappearance, perhaps guiding readers to and through the mediatic 'underworld' to communication and auratic self-presencing, just as a book of the dead is supposed to do, providing instructions and guidance to the deceased on how to navigate the underworld in their journey—by no means assured—toward an afterlife. The enclosure of the "Agrippa" poem in a machine-executable computer program, on a floppy disk, in a book, within a cloth, within a box that appears to have once contained a photo album materially reinforces this theme of burial and of a recursive, coffin-like, re-embedding and reduplicating, literally to no 'real' avail.

Juxtaposing and interweaving these histories of scriptural, textual, aural, sonic, visual, and now digital encoding, *Agrippa* underscores how they repurpose and replace each other, yet all continue to pursue and perpetuate the kind of thanatological death in life that is at the core of language, alphabetization, grammatization, and digitization as differential, yet overlapping efforts to stabilize communication and its linguistic or other meanings through discrete means. In fact, this reference to the *Egyptian Book of the Dead* and a later reference in the poem to a *grimoire*, which is a book that contains the description of a set of magical symbols and how to combine them properly (a word that derives from *grammar* as a description of a set of symbols and how to combine them to form sentences) might remind readers of a long history of various sorts of scriptural, visual, and linguistic encoding that precede and inform the most recent discrete, standardized languages of digital programming. These were symbolic languages and sign systems similarly designed to bring about material effects, or that performatively "do what they say" in ways that anticipate computer languages in their executability and that also anticipate the manipulation of genetic codes now frequently conceived as chemical-based and computationally addressable *scripts* (although there are also crucial differences between these symbolic operations and their medial ideologies).

Reviewing the post–Second World War history of software, Wendy Hui Kyong Chun convincingly suggests how source code has been conceived in terms comparable to natural

---

[9] My references to "technicity" draw on recent efforts to rethink the human in dynamic, constitutive, evolving relations to technologies and, in particular, to understand subject-technology relations as systems relations. Recent theories of technicity, emerging in a number of fields, provide an alternate understanding of the interrelations between subjects and technologies. These emerging theories of technics shift emphasis onto the processes or productive relations that generate what we later come to see as self-apparent subjects and technical objects. They have the potential to foreground multiple dimensions to our relations to technologies, what Donna Haraway (1991) and, subsequently, Karen Barad, in *Meeting the Universe Halfway: Quantum Physics and the Entanglement of Matter and Meaning* (2007), describe as the "entanglements" through which recent technological developments intertwine nature and human culture in distinct, formative ways.

language in its idealized potential as a site and source of creation from nothing, as *logos*. As a result, Chun (2013: 23) argues source code is often conflated with its "executable version" and these "various instantiations of code" and their "empirical difference" are, thus, overlooked with source code fetishistically standing in for the entire material and symbolic operation. Chun usefully reminds us that "code does not always automatically do what it says, but it does so in a crafty, speculative manner in which meaning and action are both created" (24). "Source code is, thus, arguably symptomatic of human language's tendency to attribute a sovereign source to an action, a subject to a verb" (27). As a result, "code as logos establishes a perpetual oscillation between the two positions [of master and slave]: every move to empower also estranges" (20). *Agrippa* focuses on the latter move in this paradoxical formulation, pursuing the exteriority and materiality of language and other communication media and, as a result, their tendencies to distort, impede, defer, estrange, or eradicate the human voice, presence, or agency precisely as they deign to capture or reveal it. It registers how archival technologies, as Jacques Derrida (1995: 12) argues, never entail

> either memory or *amanesis* as spontaneous, alive and internal experience. On the contrary: the archive takes place at the place of originary and structural breakdown of the said memory ... If there is no archive without consignation to an external place, which assures the possibility of memorization, of repetition, of reproduction, or of reimpression, then we must also remember that repetition, indeed the repetition compulsion, remains, according to Freud, indissociable from the death drive. And thus from destruction. Consequence: right on that which permits and conditions archivization, we will never find anything other than that which exposes to destruction, and in truth menaces with destruction, introducing, a priori, forgetfulness and the archiviolithic into the heart of the monument ... The archive always works, and *a priori,* against itself.

In actively courting and registering the multiple kinds of physical and material destruction and forgetting, as well as the remembering, repetition, and reproduction that catalyze and problematize our latest digital modes of technicity and exchange, *Agrippa* turns attention and emphasis onto these material and technical preconditions, as external supplements in Derrida's sense. It, thus, recasts *logos*, the grimoire, and other modes of visual and scriptural encoding according to the logic of the *grammé*, which, Cary Wolfe underscores, is how Derrida "names this notion of the sign as irreducible relationality, this 'element without simplicity,' an element at work not just in linguistic systems, but also, Dérrida argues, in the notion of 'program' in the informational and biological sciences" (qtd. in Wolfe 2010: 236). While *Agrippa* invokes and plays with the practices and textual ideologies linking natural language grammars, to grimoires, and other "code sourcery" (Chun 2013: 19) in their shared status as discrete, standardized languages that are ritualized and reproduced, it emphasizes their unavoidable, wholly differential status as *grammé*, as wholly differential, that is, relational signs, as always already (re)encodings within a specific set of sign systems and historical and social conditions through which they gain meaning and circulate.

In addition to stressing the irreducible relationality of language and other sign systems through their juxtaposition and remediation, *Agrippa*'s e-poetic experiment points toward and begins to unpack some of the consequences of this shift in understanding the human and its supposedly privileged relation to language and to technics, more broadly. It models a practice of writing and reading with *questionable authority* that has become more and more central to digital literary writing practices and understandings of language, technics, and media. The cultural authority of language as a sign system and the codex as its revered storage technology are called into question by the hybrid print, digital, visual, and sonic elements of the project and its attention to the ways in which prior archival technologies and their modes of human "presencing" are both displaced and reduplicated by digital technologies. In this regard, *Agrippa* gestures toward the multimedia and multimodal turns soon to follow with the World Wide Web, increasing computing power, and vastly improved modem speed.

A collaborative project among a film studies student turned literary author, an illustrator, a publisher, a programmer, unnamed typesetters, and BBS readers and programmers who circulated the work, *Agrippa* anticipates the kinds of distributed digital literary writing that are now becoming quite prevalent, digital literary practices for which it is often beside the point to attribute the collaboratively written, variously processed, circulating, and unfolding text to a sole author. Positioned within and against the digital and cultural networks which it hopes to engage and diagnose, *Agrippa*'s digital literary reading and writing processes unfold at multiple human and nonhuman scales in that the computer program was executed or "read" by Mac OS 7 computers, but not any human readers until much later; many readers encountered the "Agrippa" poem on a BBS list without having access to the artist's edition as the work's digital circulation plays a central role in its reading process and textual unfolding; and the poem's disappearance after reading seems to counter the predominant understanding of writing, at the time, as an archival technology able to render human meaning stable above and beyond the time or conditions of its writing.

Agrippa's very understanding of writing here evidences post–Second World War information theory and computational, networked digital media. It begins to bear the signs of a broader reunderstanding of writing in these digital literary contexts as one of many forms of *information processing*, or "*a difference which makes a difference*," in Gregory Bateson's phrasing of this emerging view: "a difference whose meaning can only be determined by reference to the larger system of rules within which that difference functions," as Cary Wolfe emphasizes this information-theoretical view of language (Bateson qtd. in Wolfe 2010: 235). *Agrippa*'s experimental writing practices are designed with an eye to their ability to introduce a difference that, by definition, changes the system in some way, even if this serves, in part, as the productive introduction of noise into these early BBS lists as a result of this paradoxically self-destructive poem, initially feared to be a computer virus, in an artist's book circulating on digital bulletin boards.

Notably, this questionable authority of writing, as *Agrippa* practices it, also extends to the nonhuman molecular levels of encoding and "writing," as well, which were implicated in this biological and informatic turn to post–Second World War sciences, information and systems theory, and molecular genetics. *Agrippa* includes genetic modes of encoding the DNA sequence of the fruit fly and its chemicals in standardized, discrete, one-letter codes arranged in explanatory patterns, as well as visual methods of encoding Drosophilia's genetic make-up that were illustrated in the book's etchings in its experimental reengagement with writing, archival technologies, and memory. In this regard, the digital literary experiment anticipates the growing influence of twentieth-century genetics and emerging relays between biological and informatic forms of encoding and inscription and the potential of DNA, imagined as logos, or the "code" of life, to displace or transform natural language and/as the privileged symbolic economy of human life. Recent digital forensics on the *Agrippa* poem have revealed that the letters of the Drosophilia fruit fly's genetic code, which appear on the cover of the box and in the book, are also used within the e-poem's program to cause the program's self-destructive corruption. Its language-based text is, thus, corrupted and effaced by these emergent, at once, digital, alphabetic, genetic encodings.

The project of *Agrippa* anticipates, in these provocative ways, a posthumanist turn to significant strains of digital literary writing, which emerges both as a divergent outgrowth of postmodernism and its own productive offshoot of the prior's concerns and methods. Admittedly, *Agrippa* remains significantly tied to postmodernism and the early 1990s in its emphases and attitudes toward technicity, the dead life of media, and the imperiled potential of literary and visual arts to survive amid digital commoditization and circulatory regimes. The project's framing and attitudes toward the relative presencing and absencing, remembering and forgetting of media is approached through and, arguably, remains within this humanist framework, its managing of human technicity through a repeated oscillation between these economies and extremes of medial overcoming and defeat, revealing and obscuring, even as it shifts emphasis onto the material, time-bound, deteriorating dimensions and preconditions for artistic and literary meaning. In a sense, *Agrippa* paradoxically preserves the former archival desires, or *archive fever* even, by generating longing for precisely the auratic object it demystifies, detonates, and destroys, which reenacts (without dismantling) the thanatological drive at the core of modern humanisms. The poem, especially, as I remember first reading it on a computer in 2001 or so, is melancholy in tone, even as it tries to revalue and mitigate these paradoxical aims of thanatological media to live above and beyond life.

POSTHUMANISMS WRIT MINOR

Posthumanist theories and influential digital literary inquiries accompanying these emerged in the early 1990s out of growing dissatisfactions with postmodernist theories, their linguistic, textual, and culturalist emphases, and their renderings of the social in primarily symbolic, constructivist terms, all of which seemed in thrall to late capitalism's symbolic economies and their liberal humanist prioritization of human language and meaning. Informed by feminist science studies, such as Donna Haraway's influential "A Cyborg Manifesto" in 1991, science studies by Bruno Latour, and post-structuralist critiques of humanism carried out by Jean-Francois Lyotard, Jacques Derrida, Jacques Lacan, Michel Foucault, and literary media studies by Friedrich Kittler, Marshall McLuhan, Hans Ulrich Gumbrecht, Niklas Luhmann, and others, posthumanist theories began to pursue emergent perspectives on the human, as these were took shape in post–Second World War cybernetics, information and systems theory, as well as the increasingly prominent molecular genetics catalyzed by informational, networked approaches.

In the late 1990s, Cary Wolfe describes and pursues this shift and desire for "posthumanist" theory, claiming that "no project is more overdue than the articulation of a post-humanist theoretical framework for a politics and ethics not grounded in the Enlightenment ideal of 'Man'" (Wolfe 1998: 40.1). He characterizes posthumanist theory of the type he is advocating as continuing to pursue postmodern theory's critique of that humanist ideal of "Man" while sidestepping the unnecessarily "dystopian" and "nostalgic"impasses one finds in moments of Foucault and, I would add, in Jameson, Derrida, Kittler, and others (40.1).

Posthumanist approaches began to consider how these recent shifts in material, political, economic, and symbolic economies accompanying digitization might be understood and, to the extent they call into question some of the primary tenets of liberal humanisms, how they might facilitate a critical reapproach to, or perspective on present and prior humanisms, catalyzing practical and theoretical efforts to move beyond these. N. Katherine Hayles's groundbreaking 1999 exploration of post–Second World War cybernetics and information sciences, *How We Became Posthuman: Virtual Bodies in Cybernetics, Informatics, and Literature*, reads these scientific and print literary practices against each other and against an overarching narrative of dematerialization, accounts of "how information lost its body," and she effectively complicates this predominant paradigm and its more problematic humanist and postmodernist tendencies.

As I'll illustrate below, posthumanist theories begin to pursue the constitutive *technicity* of the human, crucially taking this as their starting point, not a dead end or endgame, for their queries into the (re)production and transformation of humanisms as a set of highly contingent, co-orchestrated material practices and methods of differential subjectivization and circulation. It is within this context that digital literary writing practices also begin to explore"entanglements" between writing, material technologies, bodies, human identities, nonhuman animals, and their environments rather than remaining in thrall to the human and its technical overcoming or succumbing or meaning as the primary focus.

Shelley Jackson's *Patchwork Girl; or A Modern Monster by Mary/Shelley and Herself*, for instance, was published in 1995 as a stand-alone CD-ROM. The continued importance of *Patchwork Girl* as a first-generation digital hypertext and an early instance of digital literary writing, I'd argue, is largely due to its feminist exploration of posthumanisms and its openings onto alternate understandings and modalities of the human through its, at once, hyperlinking, intertextual, and embodied digital writing practices.[10] *Patchwork Girl*, like *Agrippa*, creatively and critically engages digital hypertext authoring programs and hyperlinking rhetorics and emerging figures of networked communication, exploring the potential of immanent, practice-based research into digital language and literary practices. *Patchwork Girl* rewrites Mary Shelley's *Frankenstein*, taking the female monster destroyed by Victor Frankenstein in Shelley's text as its protagonist and coauthor. Using Storyspace, the early digital hypertext authoring program designed by Mark Bernstein, Jay Bolter, and Michael Joyce, to create this stand-alone digital hypertext, *Patchwork Girl* reassembles the female monster (last seen in pieces at the bottom of a lake in Mary Shelley's novel) in five different sections. Each section is composed of lexia, boxes of text connected by multiple links. As the patchwork girl explains, "My birth takes place more than once. In the plea of a bygone monster; from a muddy hole by corpse light; under the needle; and under the pen; or it took place not at all."[11] The five sections of the work—"Story," "Graveyard," "Crazy Quilt," "Journal," and "Broken Accents"—correspond to these separate births. Each section assembles the patchwork girl in relation to a particular technological apparatus—print narrative, reconstructive surgery, quilting, handwriting, and digital hypertext, respectively—foregrounding the organization, sensory modalities,

[10] Notably, Eastgate systems in 2017 has just released a new edition of *Patchwork Girl* for the Macintosh, available on a USB drive as the prior edition is no longer compatible with current processor speeds.

[11] References to *Patchwork Girl* will follow the conventions for citing digital hypertext fiction, listing the section title followed by the subsection title (if applicable), and by the specific lexia title. Jackson, *Patchwork Girl* (Story/M/S/birth).

and interactions made available (or foreclosed as nonsense) through these different media practices. The character of the patchwork girl emerges in the text through multiple, enactive relations to these media, through the work's juxtaposition and recombination of these distinct technics and the distinct points of entry they provide to her experience and dynamic, multiplicit, co-realized identities. The section titled "Story," for example, draws on excerpts from Shelley's *Frankenstein*, reconstructing a narrative of the patchwork girl that begins with Dr. Frankenstein's creation of a female monster and continues to the present day. Its links connect sequential text boxes in chronological order, for the most part, moving forward in time like a print narrative, as the section title suggests. "Crazy Quilt" privileges the technology of sewing, sticthing the patchwork girl together out of quotations from the children's story *The Patchwork Girl of Oz* by L. Frank Baum, from Shelley's text, and from theorists such as Hélène Cixous, Gilles Deleuze, and Félix Guattari. These textual snippets are combined in colored text boxes that take the form of a quilt with links that move, as if stitching, down and across the columns of boxes that function as patches in this "fabric of relations."[12]

Similar to *Agrippa*, *Patchwork Girl* juxtaposes and recombines prior and emergent "writing" practices, exploring its indebtedness and the indebtedness of the human, more broadly to these material technics. In fact, the five sections of *Patchwork Girl* foreground the generative influence of different "writing" technologies on subjectivities, highlighting their capacity to provide and secure organizational schemata, spatiotemporal frames, and material affordances that inform the material and discursive, literal and symbolic formation of variously human and nonhuman bodies.[13] Reflecting on these strange, enactive relations of nonidentity between subjectivities and distinct media, the work underscores the variability of their selective modalities and, in combination, the variability of subjectivities as highly specialized, mutually transformative engagements with physical bodies. The patchwork girl is literally an assemblage; her multiple and multiplicit subjectivities, as illustrated in each section, are inextricable from the technics that motivate and materialize specific kinds of legibility, illegibility, intersubjectivity, and desire.

Patchwork Girl's explorations foreground how language as and amid other material technologies, coproduce historically, culturally, and technologically distinct practices and understandings of gendered and racialized human identities, social formations, symbolic, and sexual economies. Language is imagined and pursued here as a material *technics*, or a set of material practices that coproduce the human, however monstrously from a humanist perspective, rather than being a stand-alone, transparent tool of expression or human mastery. As importantly, writing is presented as one among many "writing" technologies, including print narrative, reconstructive surgery, quilting, handwriting, and digital hypertext, all of which are understood to coproduce the human, through their

---

[12] Jackson (1995).

[13] "Graveyard," with links between its text boxes structured to circle between a headstone and the boxes that represent each of the body parts lying prone beneath this marker, reassembles the patchwork girl out of the body parts of various women, a few men, and a cow. The text describes the defining characteristics the patchwork girl has inherited from the previous owners of her disparate parts. "Journal" features Mary Shelley's account of her amorous, yet tumultuous relations with the patchwork girl she created and then reencounters, unexpectedly, during a morning walk. "Broken Accents," which contains the subsection titled "Body of Text," self-reflexively considers the process of constructing *Patchwork Girl* as a work of digital hypertext, using multiple, recursive links that compromise linear narrative development and resist the single point of narrative departure or origin that might be considered as her textual birth.

specific modes of linking material and symbolic bodies. Understanding writing alongside, and in terms of these other material and symbolic "linking," "stitching," and "quilting" practices, *Patchwork Girl* develops its posthumanist perspectives on language, writing, and technology to revalue the specificity, unknowability, hybridity, and complexity of embodiment beyond the familiar binary speciesist, gendered, racialized, heterosexist categories. Jackson's text enlists digital hypertext writing in a broader effort to register the contributions distinct material technologies and media make to human meaning and experience, and, in turn, to recognize the contributions of diverse women and variously feminine identities that are often reduced to a similarly passive, neutral, instrumental role as mere "mediums" or "hosts" for others' meaning and reproduction.

Patchwork Girl reveals how humanist subject-object relations structure subject-technology relations and also subtend unequal, reductive, binary, gendered, and racialized oppositions between author and reader, symbolic meaning and material bodies, and masculine and feminine, white and nonwhite. Jackson's text engages digital hypertext writing strategies, figured in terms of a stitch, a hyperlink, or a "cut that breaks and binds," to model these kinds of incommensurable relations, or relations of nonidentity. *Patchwork Girl*, thus, pursues a posthumanist perspective on language as one of several material technics through which distinct modalities of the human co-emerge and through which shifting subjectivities and social relations gain certain, highly limited degrees of legibility and illegibility. And, it suggests, all of these are acts of coauthorship as languages, like Jackson's text, are inherited, patchworks of prior material technics, practices, and discourses of the human largely reliant on material supports, modes of expression, and bodily, physical matters.

Foregrounding the centrality of gender and sexuality and species to its posthumanist inquiries into the technics of the human and the potential relation of language and writing to these, *Patchwork Girl* celebrates the monstrous, incommensurable breaches that define the human in relation to these various and variously inadequate technics, including the reader's relation to its computational unfolding and to its hypertextual textual body. Its authorship is flagrantly distributed across a series of medial bodies and technologies, prior textual matter, authors and readers, creators and creatures, human and nonhuman bodies, linguistic and nonlinguistic sign systems and meaning, and conscious and unconscious levels of "meaning" production, at once. Importantly, its digital literary experiment with hypertext creatively and critically unfolds and engages with these incommensurable, yet no less informative entanglements between language, symbolic practices, and material life. In contradistinction to *Agrippa*, *Patchwork Girl* recommends its digital hypertextual "writing" as a productive practice able to comparatively register the difference media, medial ecologies and ideologies, and circulatory regimes make to understandings and practices of the human. It provides a comparative, critical perspective on liberal humanism and its print medial ideologies, as well as on digital futures being imagined in the mid-1990s, suggesting how we might register and reconcile emergent digital technics and understand technicity as an intrinsic component of human cultures.

Four years later, Eduardo Kac's installation, *Genesis*, is similarly and differently engaged with the state of the art in digital networking, with bioinformatic technologies, and language as one of several influential means of encoding. Its conception of technicity, post–World Wide Web, moves beyond *Patchwork Girl*'s emphasis on the enactive relations between standalone readers and a digital hypertext on-screen, or between meaning and material technologies to address the broader technical systems and newly networked relays between computer users on the World Wide Web, practices of encoding prominent in genetics, and to mark the increasing ease with which "life" at all these scales and sites is understood in computational, bioinformatic terms. *Genesis* recontextualizes and reoperationalizes an emerging, bioinformatic constellation, which relies on distinct combinations of genetics and computer science that assume and operationalize a "fundamental equivalency between genetic 'codes' and computer 'codes,' between the biological and the digital domain, such that they can be rendered interchangeable in terms of materials and functions" (Thacker 2004: 5). *Genesis* centers around a synthetic gene Kac created by translating a sentence from this book of the bible into Morse code and converting the Morse code into DNA base pairs according to the artist's own conversion code. This "creation of an impossible 'biblical gene' " started with the sentence, "Let man have dominion over the fish of the sea, and over the fowl of the air, and over every living thing that moves upon the earth," explicitly engaging with the question of human mastery and of language as a primary symbol of either human exceptionalism or anthropomorphism (Kac 2005: 249). After translating this sentence on the Internet and sending it to a DNA lab for synthesis, Kac took a million copies of the created gene and, realizing that "to reiterate the verbal metaphor—to be meaningful it needs a context," he placed the gene in a petri dish with bacteria as its organisms, and an environment, which "is at once, their dish, the gallery, and the Internet" (251). Remote and local visitors were not only able to view the petri dish through a microscope via live video streaming, they could also could turn a UV light source on or off, which impacted the bacteria and the mutation rate of the *Genesis* DNA. The installation also included music composed by Peter Gena that is based on the *Genesis* gene. In this and two other phases of the project, *Genesis* engages these meaningful relays between "natural language, genetics, and binary logic" to trouble both biblical and bioinformatic assumptions of an anthropocentric dominion over other species, which, it suggests, fail to perceive crucial aspects of these interrelations of which individual language-wielding humans have little awareness or understanding, let alone control. Viewers are given a choice of whether to click and, by turning on the UV light, to alter the encoded sentence, or to decide not to click, though they have no way of knowing what might result from their actions, another way in which the project foregrounds its posthumanist perspective on writing amid other digital technics as distributed, co-productive, multiagential, open-ended processes. *Genesis*, thus, foregrounds and experimentally pursues a series of questions raised by bioinformatic technics, reapproaching the ethical, social, political, and aesthetic dimensions to these scientific practices as they might, or might otherwise unfold, insinuating that bacteria, as well as everyday Internet viewers, artists, scientists, and social relations all play enactive roles in these interinforming relations between DNA, genes, genetic and other scriptural and symbolic histories, material environments, communication technologies, human and nonhuman agencies.

POST-DIGITAL: LITERARY WRITING "BEYOND THE SCREEN"

Attitudes and orientations to the digital have continued to change in significant ways in the wake of twenty-first-century mobile or "small tech" (Hawk and Rieder 2008), ubiquitous computing, and smart technologies, which interweave computation, physical experience, interfaces, and environments at multiple scales in increasingly pervasive ways. These shifts are quite perceptible in digital literary writing, as well. Its practice-based experimentation continues to pursue these posthumanist inquiries and immanent engagements with technicity, while also extending these concerns and practices well "beyond the screen." Florian Cramer describes the present as a moment of "post-digital writing." In doing so (in an essay of 2012 that is also reprinted in Chapter 20 of this volume), Cramer extends Canadian composer Kim Cascone's concept of the "postdigital" to describe "an age where, on the one hand, 'digital' has become a meaningless attribute because almost all media are electronic and based on digital information processing; and where, on the other hand, younger generation media and critical artists rediscover analog info technology."[14] In one sense, *Agrippa, Patchwork Girl, Birds Singing Other Birds' Songs, Between Page and Screen, Huckleberry Finnegans Wake*, and many other digital literary experiments anticipate the "post-digital" in already contextualizing and comparing digital technologies and cultural practices to their predecessors and questioning their novelty, let alone, revolutionary potential. All of their digital writing experiments encourage greater understanding of technological processes and their complex imbrication with prior, existing, and emergent social and cultural formations, as opposed to a fetishistic isolation of either the digital object or the analog object outside its broader social, technical, environmental contexts. Such digital literary writing, at once engages digital and computational methods and media among other poetic and technical inquiries and also reflects back on these as a part of a much-longer continuum of "ordinary media," as a recent research workshop and 2017 symposium at Northwestern University describes this post-digital moment in "the advent of always-on computing," in which "digital media technologies in the 21st century have become remarkably ordinary."

This "post-digital" moment coincides with the growing ubiquity of digital media and computational processes as these are increasingly interwoven into lived space in complex ways and accessed through intuitive aural and touch-based interfaces. Agreeing that the revolutionary cast to the digital has passed into another phase, I suggest that the post-digital might also, or instead, be understood in relation to a broader technological and cultural move "beyond the screen," which was heralded by Mark Weiser in his theorizations of ubiquitous computing for the twenty-first century, and is evidenced by a growing tendency of computational processes and digital media to be seamlessly woven into a broader environment, yet nonetheless *in*forming cultural, economic, and symbolic exchanges and interactions in pivotal ways. Referencing a shift of emphasis in digital literary writing in their collection, *Beyond the Screen: Transformations of Literary Structures, Interfaces, and Genres*, Jörgen Schäfer and Peter Gendolla (2010: 14) describe ours as a moment in which "new combinations of physical, virtual, and symbolic spaces emerge." A defining characteristic of this in digital literary writing, I'd suggest, is a focus on the dynamic, unfolding relays bridging linguistic, literary multileveled symbolic operations, digital computation-based processes, and physical environments and interactions. With the previous theories of postmodernism and posthumanism in mind, it seems only in keeping with these precedents that the post-digital is, once again, a complex and contested series of social and cultural *redescriptions*, not any clear or unified move beyond the digital, digital technologies, or political and economic formations.

---

[14] Eastman Kodak is exemplary in this regard as it declared bankruptcy in 2012 after its chemical film processing was displaced by digital film technologies, and just this January 2017, the remaining company began showing a prototype for its Super 8 camera and plans to bring back "iconic film stocks like Kodachrome and Ektachrome" as "heritage products."

In this context, *The Xenotext* project by Canadian poet Christian Bök provides a compelling case through which to consider digital literary writing as it understands, engages, and inflects this post-digital phase.[15] An ongoing poetical/technical experiment that aspires to be "the first work of 'living poetry,'" according to the book jacket, Bök's project includes *The Xenotext, Book I* (published in 2015), a second volume that is forthcoming, and the—at present only partially realized—embedding of a poem "Orpheus" into an indestructible bacterium's DNA so that it will be expressed through that organism's process of living as a poem titled "Eurydice." There is also a special edition of *The Xenotext, Book I* featuring other prominent poets' variations on Bök's text and each print book sold comes with a companion digital edition of the text, as if inviting more computational evolutions and mutations.

The Xenotext, Book I, like the digital literary predecessors discussed above, is designed as an immanent, practice-based experimental research project exploring the entanglements between literary and poetic language practices and writing; bioinformatic encoding, material technologies, and their computational modeling and visualization practices; and the biochemical processes and forms of living that entangle human and nonhuman life in their symbiogenetic (Margulis, 1995) coevolution. The project, as a whole, technically operationalizes language in multiple ways to reconsider how language circulates amid other sign systems and modes of encoding. Importantly, it expands these considerations to address language as it now circulates both according to, and in contradistinction to, these emerging, bioinformatic symbolic regimes and modes of circulating. In this redoubled, post-digital way, *The Xenotext* project reintroduces poetics into genetic encoding and transgenics in its "wet" experiment and with its computational processing of existing poetry and its own poetic language operations, approximating helical, six-sided forms omnipresent in material life. It also, crucially, reconsiders genetic processes and bioinformatic modes of knowledge from the perspective of poetics, reapproaching bioinformatic practices through Virgil's poetics and a longer history of poetic operations and efforts to engage and enlist material life in various ways. In the process of its poetical, technical, aesthetic crossfertilizing re-codings, or redoubled encodings, perhaps, *The Xenotext* project reveals underlying commonalities to *and* key departures amid what it redescribes as similarly and differently poetical and technical operations, or modes of engaging with living forms and processes of living. Pursuing these posthumanist inquiries into what happens to language when it travels through, and traffics with, bioinformatic sign systems and circulatory regimes, as did prior digital literary experiments, *The Xenotext* project also opens onto several unique answers to the question of how we might reimagine language amid other "sign" systems and understand their inter-informing activities without conflating these or privileging any one of these as logos, or *the* code of life.

[15] In the context of *The Xenotext* project it is worth underscoring a similar shift of emphasis in this post-digital phase and what Sarah Richardson and Stevens (2015: 3, 6) and other researchers have described as a "post-genomic" period since the sequencing of the human genome was completed. Postgenomic, or post-HGP genetics describe this period when "gene-centric" approaches are replaced by "whole-genome" technologies, yet also by a growing uncertainty in the field "about the overlapping roles (and relative importance) of evolution, DNA structure, transcription, and regulation in the human genome." Postgenomics, thus, participates in the postrevolutionary phase of digital technics, as does the post-digital and registers a similar move beyond the digital object (in this case the "gene") as primary agent to a more thoroughgoing and complex investigation of the broader social, cultural, and historical contexts and environments in which genetic (digital and computational) processes unfold in surprising and counterintuitve, multidirectional ways.

Extending prior digital literary inquiries further into the extra-linguistic, extra-literary social, technological, material, and environmental preconditions and contexts for the circulation and meaningful operations of language, *The Xenotext* project reveals the potential of/in creative trans-actions across what it identifies as incommensurable gaps or breaches between sign systems, as we begin to acknowledge, both scientifically and poetically, the scope and prominence of sign systems well-beyond human language or meaning. *The Xenotext, Book I* draws from emergent genetic life sciences, technologies, and knowledges to cast new light on writing as *technics* of human and nonhuman living, which are both equally reliant on "acids and ideas" and on "biochemical and textual operations." This experimental suite, or, in fact, six-sectioned, six-sided honeycomb or *helix* of poems and poetical technical operations uses a "delirious" series of distinct poetics, writing, and modeling practices to register and retrace some of the alternate modes of engaging and modeling processes of living that genomics-driven technologies and knowledges introduce to its literary print environment and vice versa in its proposed "wet" poetic encoding experiment. Through helical structures and other technical borrowings, its poems experiment with influential bioinformatic sign systems and their joint potential to engender a "poetics of living forms" capable of understanding and embracing this traffic between language, writing, computation, and other human and nonhuman sign systems that equally, if differently, model and enlist processes of life in their unfolding. The book's section titles are, for instance, computationally transposed into a machine-readable language of QR-codes, visual codes that have been, in turn, subjected to computational evolution according to AL pioneer John Conway's "game of life," a cellular automaton that evolves simulated life forms from an initial condition. And, to give another unforgettable example, the title of Emily Dickinson's poem "Death Sets a Thing Significant" (1924) is computationally parsed and its letters used to generate a protein sequence and to model that computationally, which is then visually rendered in the book.

It is quite literally a "xeno-text," an "other" or "foreign" *text* in that it reapproaches and reorients language and *writing* practices through the lens of genomics and evolutionary processes of technogenesis, as did *Agrippa* and *Genesis* in their distinct ways. In one of the book's six sections, a poem titled "Alpha Helix" in honor of that most ubiquitous of living forms begins with the line, "Whatever lives must also write" (Bök 2015: 140). While readers may initially stumble on this claim, "writing" is here reoperationalized and reconceived as a symbolic practice and sign system alongside a series of other, at once, poetical and technical methods that engage with living forms and processes of living in distinctly "other" ways. Reconceived as a symbolic process of engaging and modeling life in constrained, yet open processes of living, writing is conceptually expanded to evidence and acknowledge the technical, social, material environmental contexts through which such practices unfold. From this posthumanist vantage, writing amid other sign systems contributes to the evolutionary processes of many species' technogenesis, unfolding at many scales, rather than "meaning" only in the narrow sense that we often conceive of writing as a script-based, exclusively human language practice. Here and elsewhere in these poems and the differing poetics the six distinct sections of the book realize, writing is resituated alongside other kinds of human and nonhuman technicity and their co-informing, transformative yet also discrete orientations toward living. *The Xenotext*'s poetics remind us, in this way, that its writing and our reading are already distinctly posthumanist and nonindexical due to the influences of computational processes at scales well beyond human spatial or temporal perception and in light of their intervention and addressibility at molecular and submolecular scales of living. As one moves from section to section in the book, it's quite noticeable how these technical and poetic modes of perceiving and modeling life position their human and nonhuman subjects and readers in quite divergent spatial and temporal relations to these processes. These different textual, visual, computational, and biochemical technics are aesthetically enhanced through these juxtapositions, requiring more conscientious "perceptions of perception" as impacted by the constraints and potentials of these differing technics and media.

While *The Xenotext*'s apparent contextualization and, at points, seeming subsumption of language and symbolic meaning (formerly understood as the sign of human exceptionalism and dominion) to computational visual and genetic modes of encoding and rendering might be as unwelcome as a Googlization of the word and world to many readers, I'd suggest that from a posthumanist perspective its experimental shift away from a certain understanding of symbolic language and away from the defining conceit of the human's exclusive, instrumental relation to signification has advantages and, here, perhaps, generates new vantages on points of continuity *and* discontinuity between such sign systems and their meaningful operations. *The Xenotext, Book I* redoubles its poetic operations and inquiries by also reconsidering genetic processes and bioinformatic modes of knowledge from the perspective of poetics. It reapproaches these bioinformatic methods, knowledges, and aims through the vantage of Virgil's poetics and a longer history of poetic operations and efforts to engage and enlist material life in various ways. Continuing its exploration of writing in terms of pattern-making and sign systems working within the world and upon us, like the honeycomb structure of a bee hive or the similarly helical structure of DNA, Section II of the book, "Colony Collapse Disorder," turns back toward the contributions and techniques of poetry. It translates Book IV of *The Georgics*, in which Virgil advises his patron about beekeeping, to question how our own sacrifice and redemption of honeybees and other armies today may consign them and us to an environmentally catastrophic Hell, returning us to the cataclysmic, unpredictable beginnings of life on Earth. This section of the book foregrounds the long-standing role of poetics in cultivating living forms, patterns, and evolving, symbiotic human and nonhuman ecologies of life. Interestingly, an impetus for Bök's project was biotech scientists' 2003 encoding of a Latin phrase from Virgil's (2006: 113) *The Georgics*, "*Nor can the earth bring forth all fruit alike*" into the DNA of the thale cress flower. The scientists carried out this poetic encoding at the level of its DNA as a way to label the flower's transgenic modification at their hands, as a kind of human signature on this life form, albeit an expansive one. It also seems to envision, as *The Xenotext project* does in its own way, continuities between Virgil's poetic invocation (and practical beekeeping incitement) to the diverse, unpredictable unfolding of life in its unpredictible diversity and biotechnological practices of transcoding organisms at the level of their DNA.

Illustrating how language and poetics feed forward into, and are transformed by emerging bioinformatic methods and nonlinguistic sign systems, this biotechnological encoding of Virgil's line and, I'd argue, explicit instrumentalization of this life form to human ends, is quite at odds with the aims of Bök's own genetic encoding project, though it is equally entangled with the technics of writing amid and against genomic knowledges and their modes of circulation. In the *Vita Explicata* concluding Book I, the larger encoding project *The Xenotext* is described as an "alien guest, courting the goodwill of a demonic microbe that might 'host' the poem for a future reader" (153), conveying a very different understanding of how genomic-based technics put us into conversation with the unfolding of life forms at very different scales, without mastering or understanding these "hosts" and their distinct, ulterior aims. The *Vita Explicata* redescribes the cell as a technical operator and agent, as "an archive for storing a poem, but also a machine for writing the poem" (150), and it hopes to realize these functions in its wet project as *Xenotext*'s encoded poem will be "read" by the cell as the recipe for a protein and its sequence of amino acids becomes the basis for another "sonnet," to be read by some future reader. Once again, "writing" is reconceived in Bök's multileveled experimental project as a xenotext or "other" text in light of genomic sciences, technics, and the computational, statistical, and biological models through which they see, catalyze, and subvert the unfolding of life. Significantly, in imagining the cell as an "archive for storing a poem, but also a machine for writing the poem," this line explicitly conflates these linguistic and biochemical "technics" of writing and their operations, seemingly literalizing the most reductive and troubling analogies between writing and genetic encoding, such as the "book of life," that have defined genomics over the past century. Interestingly, though, in the context of the poems' other redoubled encodings, this line problematizes the very analogies it seems to draw. It prompts readers to reperceive the cell as a technical operator or agent, while also suggesting it may be wholly unlike human writers, encouraging appreciation of the technical/symbolic and biochemical dimensions to its distinct methods and forms of living, which are evoked here in conversation with, as well as in contrast with our own.

Naming the embedded sonnet "Orpheus," Bok's project reads these most recent engagements with the processes of living through its poetic lens and invokes a longer history of poetic efforts to charm material things with the poet's music and verse, as Orpheus famously charmed even stones. In naming the protein sequence expressed by this poem *Eurydice*, Bök points attention to the continued and still futile efforts of science and poetics to rescue Eurydice and other muses from various hells. It thematizes, and renders somewhat absurd, the paradoxically thanatological drives guiding human life and poetics, especially as the "wet" project intends to hand its poem "Orpheus" off to this near-immortal, demonic bacterium and encourage its DNA to perpetuate, at a genetic scale, this attempted, symbolic recapture of the dead "Eurydice," through its very process of living.

The Xenotext's poetics, thus, draw on the bioinformatic models and modes of knowledge in which we are enmeshed, even as they aesthetically attenuate and exaggerate them, playing off of them in several slightly different registers and multiplying these perceptual and aesthetic and visual modalities so that one cannot help but perceive the strangeness of the different orientations toward life and life processes they unfold. The fifth section, "Alpha Helix," for example, ends with an image of "Orpheus' Lyre" refigured and diagrammed in terms reminiscent of a protein-interaction network (Figure 19.1). This is an additional reference to Orpheus, our guide through these bioinformatic and molecular underworlds here, yet it also figures the constellation "Lyra" named after Orpheus's lyre and first identified by Ptolemy, reminding readers of another sign system and precedent for visually transcoded, poetic renderings of the material world and cosmos at a vastly different scale.

The significance of the nonindexical poetical methods *The Xenotext, Book I* realizes are clarified by the text's brief citation of Brian Rotman's (1987) concept of "xenotext" and by an awareness of Rotman's connection of these textual practices to "xenomoney," which he describes in *Signifying Nothing: The Semiotics of Zero*, as closely allied outgrowths of knowledge economies and their circulatory regimes. Rotman describes

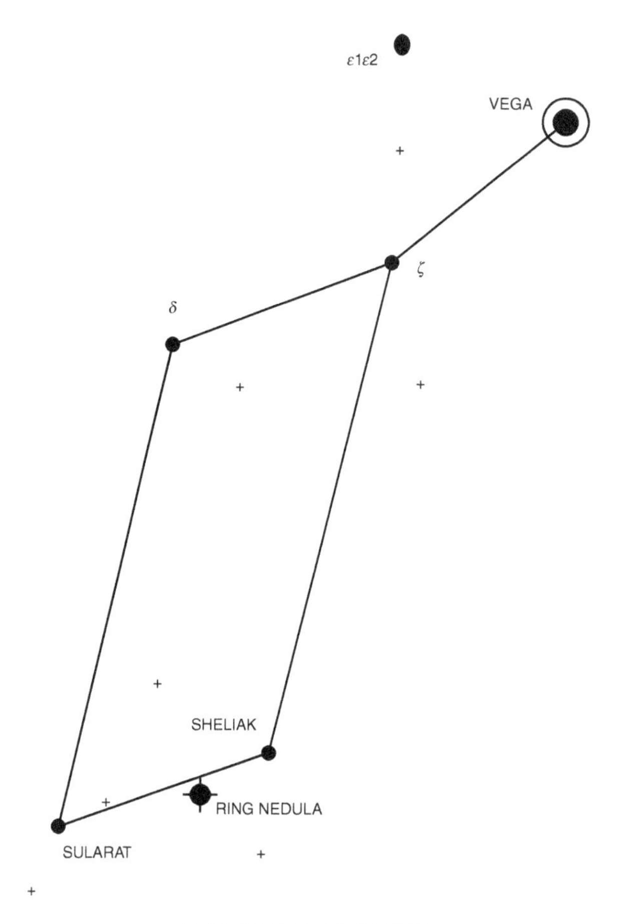

FIGURE 19.1 The Lyre of Orpheus.

the clear parallels between "xenomoney," with its floating value and its utter absence of indexicality, its signifying nothing other than itself, and "xenotext," "the code of written language in which, so it is claimed, a new form of text, a change in 'writing' itself, must be recognized" (88). For the "xenotext," Rotman claims, "there is nothing to retrieve, there is only language in a state of potential and never achieved interpretation," it is "forced as a sign to create its own signified future states of itself," it "offers no redemption ... It 'means' what its interpreters cannot prevent it from meaning" (102). When section three, "The March of the Nucleotides," presents "the central dogma," writing that "*DNA is an actual casino of signs, preserving within a random series of letters, the haphazard alignment of acids and ideas*," followed by "*DNA is a metamorphic scriptorium, where life transcribes, by chance, whatever life has so far learned about immortality*," and then, "*DNA is a vagrant message sent to us, as if from outer space, by a cryptic, but sapient sender who seeks a perfect poetics*," one gets a clearer sense of the political and signifying economy in which *The Xenotext* project takes root (78, 80, 82; emphases in the original) and how it both inflects and extends prior poetics and technics of life and their coming to terms with "hell," as a variously understood threshold and limit to life's relentless striving and evolutionary constraints. Here Bök's project seems to convey its crucial rereading of these thanatological humanist logics in relation to late capitalist symbolic and political economies, and the fact that "there is nothing to retrieve, there is only language [among other sign systems and poetic forms of living] in a state of potential and never achieved interpretation" now in poetic and bioinformatic endeavors alike.

Even as *The Xenotext* and its poems experimentally draw upon this conflation of writing and life and its "code sourcery," in precisely the ways that have made reductive discourses of genomic sciences suspect to so many, its poetics provide an important corrective to these tendencies. It encourages recognition of the "at once textual *and* biochemical operations of molecular formation" and their randomness. Quoting biosemiotician Jesper Hoffmeyer (2008), a footnote on this page states that "the basic unit of life is the sign, not the molecule," a claim that contextualizes genomic life sciences in light of the technics and poetics, the "signs" and operations that inform them.

The Xenotext candidly and circuitously registers these changes in writing, poetics, and processes of living and circulating by engaging these very nonrepresentational logics and circulatory regimes solidified in relation to biocaptialism and its driving sciences of biology, informatics, statistics, and computation. Its at once textual, biochemical, and poetic experiments genuinely pursue the question of what happens if we take seriously the viewpoints and vantages genomic sciences and other bioinformatic technologies on life are opening onto. What happens if we accept the relentless and unredeemable "march of the nucleotides" alongside and against language practices, as material modes of signification and biochemical transformation, at once? What happens if we seek out different ways to register and pursue these methods and modeling practices through writing, as important means of reflecting back on other technics and sign systems through which processes of life can be understood to differentially unfold and evolve?

The Xenotext: Book I is, itself, "an escort that guides strangers through [the] foreign (xenos) territory" of genetics in light of the prior "underworlds" explored by poets such as Orpheus and Virgil. And through its recombinatory operations one begins to see both kinds of encounters with hell or the ground zero of life and the beauty of living through the lens of genetic and poetic cultivations of processes of human and nonhuman life, at once. Though it may be possible to read this project as a desperate literary attempt to reassert and rethink the dynamism and life of language and literary poetics in the face of these bioinformatic "writing" practices, their tangible transformations, and impressive cultural capital, this explanation overlooks the clear entanglement of bioinformatic technics with current modes of writing, reading, and circulating, be they literary, poetic, bioinformatic, or otherwise. It also overlooks the indebtedness of bioinformatic sciences to these prior poetic engagements with living and the inherited languages and orientations these carry with them. I'd suggest Bök's project deliriously pursues these entanglements between genomic modeling and visualization techniques and poetic techniques to grasp life processes and the ephemerality of life from multiple vantages, to r(e)orient them, in philosopher Sara Ahmed's (2010) sense of this term, by dynamically transforming and reapproaching this mutually refracting, hexagonal series of living poetic forms. The book poetically refracts the symbolic and circulatory regimes of postgenomic life, following these to their limits as language-based transformative practices and as a set of carefully delineated material technics.

The Xenotext project evidences the migration of these bioinformatic knowledges and their computational methods and symbolic modes of perceiving and engaging processes of living at multiple scales well-beyond laboratories and biotech industries and practices. This is perhaps not surprising, as the latter are becoming a mundane part of everyday, post-digital life—our aesthetic perception, signification, and circulatory regimes today. As a digital literary experiment, and minor scientific variation on this fact of post-digital life, *The Xenotext* takes this as an opportunity to register and reflect on such emergent sign systems and circulatory regimes from multiple, intently "other," lingusitic, textual, visual, and computational perspectives. Taking seriously these new contexts within which language and writing and meaning unfold, its poetics reimagine language amid other "sign" systems, while also registering and embracing the dynamically interinforming and distinctly creative transactions across incommensurably symbolic and material modes of encoding and their poetics of living. Its distinctly and multiply executible poetics raise the question of how language and other symbolic processes might be rethought amidst these bioinformatic relays, and amid other materially realized sign systems and their "*haphazard alignment of acids and ideas.*" Pursuing language through digital literary writing, surprisingly, reveals a minor literature increasingly attuned to extraliterary contexts and contributors, to the material agencies, preconditions, instantiations, environments, and noise that lingustic and cultural systems often work so hard to vanquish, or mitigate, to no real avail.

SOURCES CITED

Agrippa, Heinrich Cornelius. *De Occulta Philosophia* [1531]. http://www.esotericarchives.com/agrippa/agrippa1.htm

Ahmed, Sara. "Orientations Matter." In *New Materialisms*, edited by Diana Coole and Samantha Frost. Durham, NC: Duke University Press, 2010, pp. 234–57.

Barad, Karen. *Meeting the Universe Halfway: Quantum Physics and the Entanglement of Matter and Meaning*. Durham, NC: Duke University Press, 2007.

Bell, Daniel. *The Coming of Postindustrial Society*. New York: Basic, 1973.

Berti, Agustín. *From Digital to Analog: Agrippa and Other Hybrids in the Beginnings of Digital Culture*. New York: Peter Lang, 2015.

Bök, Christian. *The Xenotext: Book I*. Toronto, Canada: Coach House Books, 2015.

Borsuk, Amaranth and Brad Bouse. *Between Page and Screen*. NY: Siglio Press, 2012.

Conway, John. *The Game of Life*. http://www.conwaylife.com/.

Chun, Wendy Hui Kyong. *Programmed Visions: Software and Memory*. Cambridge: MIT Press, 2013.

Cramer, Florian. "Post-Digital Writing." *Electronic Book Review* December 12, 2012; reprinted in the present volume (Chapter 20).

Deleuze, Gilles, and Félix Guattari. *A Thousand Plateaus: Capitalism and Schizophrenia*. Translated by Brian Massumi. Minneapolis: University of Minnesota Press, 1987.

Derrida, Jacques. *Archive Fever: A Freudian Impression*. Translated by Eric Prenowitz. Chicago: University of Chicago Press, 1995.

Dickinson, Emily. "Death Sets a Thing Significant" (1924). In *The Complete Poems of Emily Dickinson*, edited by Thomas H. Johnson. New York: Little, Brown, 1960.

Gibson, William. *Mona Lisa Overdrive*. New York: Spectra, 1988.

Gibson, William, Dennis Ashbaugh, and Kevin Begos Jr. *Agrippa (A Book of The Dead)*. New York: Kevin Begos, 1992.

Golumbia, David. *The Cultural Logic of Computation*. Cambridge, MA: Harvard University Press, 2009.

Gumbrecht, Hans Ulrich. "A Farewell to Interpretation." In *Materialities of Communication*, edited by Hans Ulrich Gumbrecht and K. Ludwig Pfeiffer, translated by William Whobrey. Stanford, CA: Stanford University Press, 1994.

Haraway, Donna. "A Cyborg Manifesto: Science, Technology, and Socialist-Feminism in the Late Twentieth Century." In *Simians, Cyborgs, and Women: The Reinvention of Nature*. New York: Routledge, 1991.

Hawk, Byron, and David M. Rieder. "On Small Tech and Complex Ecologies." In *Small Tech: The Culture of Digital Tools*. edited by Byron Hawk, David M. Rieder, and Ollie Oviedo. Minneapolis: University of Minnesota Press, 2008, pp. ix–xxiii.

Hayles, N. Katherine. *How We Became Posthuman: Virtual Bodies in Cybernetics, Literature, and Informatics*. Chicago: University of Chicago Press, 1999.

Hayles, N. Katherine. *My Mother Was a Computer: Digital Subjects and Literary Texts*. Chicago: University of Chicago Press, 2005.

Hoffmeyer, Jesper. *Biosemiotics: An Examination into the Life of Signs and the Signs of Life*. Chicago: University of Chicago Press, 2008.

Jackson, Shelley. *Patchwork Girl; or A Modern Monster by Mary/Shelley and Herself*. Watertown, MA: Eastgate Systems, 1995.

Jameson, Fredric. *Postmodernism, or, the Cultural Logic of Late Capitalism*. Durham, NC: Duke University Press, 1997 [1991]. Originally published in *New Left Review*, vol. 146 (1984): 53–92.

Kac, Eduardo. *Telepresence & Bio Art.: Networking Humans, Rabbits, and Robots*. Ann Arbor: University of Michigan Press, 2005.

Kaplan, Fredric. "Linguistic Capitalism and Algorithmic Mediation." *Representations*, vol. 127 (summer 2014): 57–63.

Margulis, Lynn, and Sagan, Dorion. *What Is Life?* Berkeley: University of California Press, 1995.

Marks, Laura U. *Touch: Sensuous Theory and Multisensory Media*. Minneapolis: University of Minnesota Press, 2002.

Mencía, María. *Another Kind of Language*. Flash-based e-poem and installation (2001) at http://www.mariamencia.com/pages/anotherkindof.html.

Mencía, María. *Birds Singing Other Birds' Songs*. (2001) *Flash version. Electronic Literature Collection (ELC)*, Volume One, October 2006. Ed. N. Katherine Hayles, Nick Montfort, Scott Rettberg, Stephanie Strickland. College Park, Maryland: Electronic Literature Organization, ISSN: 1932-2011. http://collection.eliterature.org/1/works/mencia__birds_singing_other_birds_songs.html.Web.

Memmott, Talan, Eric Snodgrass, Michael Maguire, and Sonny Rae Tempest. *Huckleberry Finnegans Wake*. Performed at E-Poetry International Festival, Kingston University, 2013.

Ordinary Media Research Workshop. Northwestern University. Web Page. February 20, 2017. https://sites.northwestern.edu/ordinary/cfp/.

Pfeiffer, K. Ludwig. "The Materiality of Communication." In *Materialities of Communication*, edited by Hans Ulrich Gumbrecht and K. Ludwig Pfeiffer, translated by William Whobrey. Stanford, CA: Stanford University Press, 1994, pp. 1–12.

Richardson, Sarah S., and Halam Stevens, eds. *Postgenomics: Perspectives on Biology after the Genome*. Durham, NC: Duke University Press, 2015.

Rotman, Brian. *Signifying Nothing: The Semiotics of Zero*. New York: St. Martin's Press, 1987.

Schäfer, Jörgen, and Peter Gendolla. *Beyond the Screen: Transformations of Literary Structures, Interfaces, and Genres*. Bielefeld: transcript Verlag, 2010.

Shackelford, Laura. *Tactics of the Human: Experimental Technics in American Fiction*. Ann Arbor: University of Michigan Press, 2014.

Tabbi, Joseph, and Michael Wutz. *Reading Matters: Narrative in the New Media Ecology*. Ithaca, NY: Cornell University Press, 1997.

Thacker, Eugene. *Biomedia*. Minneapolis: University of Minnesota Press, 2004.

Thacker, Eugene. *In The Dust of the Planet [Horror of Philosophy, Vol. 1]*. Washington: Zero Books, 2010.

Tomasula, Steve. "Three Axioms for Projecting a Line (or Why It Will Continue to Be Hard to Write a Title sans Slashes or Parentheses)." *Review of Contemporary Fiction*, vol. 16, no. 1 (Spring 1996): 100. Proquest Research Library #02719290. 05.09.12.

Wallace, David Foster. "E Unibus Pluram: Television and U.S. Fiction." *Review of Contemporary Fiction*, vol. 13, no. 2 (Summer 1993): 151–94.

Wolfe, Cary. *Critical Environments: Postmodern Theory and the Pragmatics of the "Outside."* Minneapolis: University of Minnesota Press, 1998.

Wolfe, Cary. "Language." In *Critical Terms for Media Studies*, edited by W. J. T. Mitchell and Mark B. N. Hansen. Chicago: University of Chicago Press, 2010.

Virgil. *The Georgics*. Translated by David Ferry. New York: Farrar, Straus and Giroux, 2006.

Zielinski, Siegfried. *Deep Time of the Media: Toward an Archaeology of Seeing and Hearing by Technical Means*. Translated by Gloria Custanz. Cambridge: MIT Press, 2006.

PART FOUR

Economies, Precarities

CHAPTER TWENTY

Post-Digital Writing

FLORIAN CRAMER

1

By the mid-1990s, thanks to the pioneering work at Brown University, electronic literature had established itself as a field in Pierre Bourdieu's sense, that is as an area of production and discourse with intrinsic distinctions and authorities. Net art, as represented by the early Nettime mailing list and by artists such as Vuk Ćosić, Alexei Shulgin, and jodi, was the new kid on the block. Next to experimenting with Internet servers as artist-run spaces, it began to playfully experiment with the textual codes of the Internet, which made McKenzie Wark (2002) and others pitch it against established hyperfiction and electronic literature writing. Later, artists like mez breeze and Alan Sondheim were at home in both worlds.[1]

Net art brought a fresh air of everyday culture and the digital vernacular: the languages of spam, chat bots, viruses, browser crashes, debugging messages, blue screens, and 404 codes—a language that was much more rampant in the 1990s than in today's iPhone, iPad, Facebook, and Google world, with its sanitized operating systems and app stores. And it was a largely nonacademic movement, whereas electronic literature was, and continues to be, as closely tied to literature departments as composed computer music is to research lab–style university studios, at least in Northern America. On top of that, the critics were often the same people as the artists in those two academic communities.

In countries where literature departments are as scholarly constrained as the social sciences and therefore do not include literary writing in their curricula, electronic literature has practically disappeared as an artistic practice. My home countries Germany and the Netherlands are good examples. In Germany, Internet-based hypertext/multimedia literature boomed in the late 1990s mostly because of an award granted by a major newspaper, and faltered as soon as this award was discontinued. Most German-language scholarship on electronic literature still focuses on a handful of—rather marginal—writers and works from that period. In the Netherlands, the same is happening to the arts as a whole: as public funding is being slashed, a lot of artistic practice and cultural activism that had depended on it is simply disappearing.

By the 2000s, Net art had become just as historical as hyperfiction. But it provided the breeding ground for at least two significant tendencies in contemporary art: the media activist art of groups like the Yes Men or the Institute of Applied Autonomy, and digital

[1] This essay, originally a lecture at the 2001 meeting of the Electronic Literature Organization at West Virginia University, was written after having been out of touch with the field of electronic literature as it was represented by the ELO for half a decade. The author's work in the meantime had shifted from literary studies to applied design research, and towards modes of electronic publishing where the experiment lies in production and distribution, such as in libre graphics and open source book sprints. Nevertheless, this might help to reframe electronic literature within larger cultural developments in writing and publishing.

pop from 8-bit music to Cory Arcangel's modified Nintendo game. A number of critical books on Net art have appeared in the past couple of years, most significantly perhaps Josephine Bosma's *Nettitudes* (2011). Reading Bosma, it becomes apparent how the consensus on which early Net art seemed to have built its community might actually have been fictitious, and there appears to have been a rift between two ideas:

1. The Internet, or the networked computer, as an alternative space for artists' production and distribution, in the tradition of community spaces, yet with the promise of even more radical experimentation with aesthetics, politics, and economics than in brick-and-mortar spaces. While these politics were often vague, they became more focused on hacktivism and copyleft in the course of the 2000s. By the 2010s, they had become popular mass culture with the Anonymous movement and, in Europe, the Pirate Parties.
2. The Internet as a new artistic medium, or more specifically, a new medium to be explored by artists, in the same way in which artists had, since the 1920s and 1960s, emancipated photography, books, film, and later video toward means of artistic production. Even until a decade ago, the mainstream art system accepted these media only for the reproduction, but not original production, of art works. Internet-based works are still hardly accepted in contemporary art except in the (separate) media art system.

In some cases, both ideas overlapped, for example, when Nam June Paik appropriated video as a medium for visual art, but—with McLuhan's media theory as an analytical blueprint—also subverted its function as a mass medium. In other cases, the same practices could have the opposite implications: when George Maciunas opened the Flux Store on New York's Lower East Side to sell multiples and artists' books, he intended to shift artists' production toward low-cost, mass reproducible, unpretentious items that could be afforded by anyone. Maciunas's inspiration was the revolutionary socialist politics of LEF, the 1920s Soviet Left Front of constructivist artists around El Lissitzky. The socialist idea of democratic, affordable, and mass-produced art—which also did away with the distinction between fine and applied art—had been continued in a reformist (rather than revolutionary) manner by the German Bauhaus and Dutch De Stijl. Next to Russian constructivism, they drew on the socialist politics of the British Arts and Crafts movement. Even the European situationists saw themselves indebted to the constructivist heritage of doing away with the difference of art and design in order to open it up for everyone. Among others, Asger Jorn had founded a "Movement for an Imaginist Bauhaus" that became part of the Situationist International.

Around the same time in the 1960s, other Fluxus artists factually undermined Maciunas by making books and book-like objects as auratic, collectible objects. They thus claimed a fine art domain within contemporary book culture and production. With bookstores such as Printed Matter in New York, Other Books and So in Amsterdam, and Motto in Berlin, the artists' bookstore was born and became, with each new generation, more like a gallery. There is now, just at the same historical point where electronic books and periodicals are eclipsing print, a massive renaissance of artists' bookmaking. It emphasizes, if not fetishizes, the analog, tangible, material qualities of the paper object. While this certainly is a counterreaction to the digitization of media, these contemporary artists' books do pre-empt the future of the print book in general once books have largely migrated to electronic reading devices: the print book will survive in a crafty niche of the book-as-tangible-object. The renaissance of printmaking therefore is one indicator that the post-digital media age has begun: an age where, on the one hand, "digital" has become a meaningless attribute because almost all media are electronic and based on digital information processing; and where, on the other hand, younger generation media-critical artists rediscover analog information technology.

2

If we map 1960s artists' book culture to today's electronic publishing: does electronic literature stand for the culture of fast, almost cost-free, globalized publishing on the Internet, that is, the Maciunas model of avant-garde popularism? Or does it represent the opposite: a digital boutique and gated community of literary writing inside a sea of digital ephemera, a fine art white cube safely shielded from the digital trash? In a conversation on this issue I had with Kenneth Goldsmith five years ago in Rotterdam, Kenneth pointed out how he had become more interested in the file-sharing cultures of avant-garde sound, images, and text than in the field of hypertext and multimedia literature. UbuWeb closely resembles a twenty-first-century version of the Flux store and its avant-garde popularism, yet with two significant differences. First, it provides mostly historical instead of cutting-edge contemporary material. Second, it is not grounded on an economic model for artist's production aside from the classical academic one: teaching at a university, and publishing your work open access because you are working in a reputation-based, not a paid product-based, economy. But isn't the same true for the electronic literature represented by the ELO? Why maintain a fine-art niche when it is, unlike the white cubes and gallery spaces of contemporary visual art, not driven by the purely economic necessity of selling products?

And what does the term "electronic literature" ultimately signify? If we take the word "literature" literally, as everything written with letters, then electronic literature today is no longer the exception but the norm. Paper publishing has largely become a form of Digital Rights Management for delivering PDF files in a file sharing-resistant format (but also, a more stable form of long-term storage of digital content than electronic storage). In the age of smartphones, tablets, and e-readers, reading has largely shifted toward electronic media if we consider all writing that an average person reads per day. Is this the electronic literature we mean?

From an ELO perspective, it could of course be argued that this reading culture is too boringly conventional in its use of the medium as just remediation—as an electronic display of the same pages that were previously read on paper. But this would be the same kind of fundamentalist argument with which composers of generative computer music may dismiss mp3. I would agree with other Internet culture critics (certainly including Kenneth Goldsmith) that the digital revolution of music has been mp3, not Max/MSP or Pure Data. In e-book culture, we are now witnessing the mp3 revolution all over again: on the Pirate Bay, in underground download libraries like aaaaarg.org and Monoskop, and the recent hacker efforts to turn the Open Source e-book software Calibre into a peer-to-peer e-book sharing network. This culture is currently not included in the domain and research of electronic literature at all, but shouldn't it be?

Not only the culture of reading but also the culture of writing has changed profoundly. In a pragmatic definition, the field of literature revolves around published writing. And within published writing, there is the classical differentiation between fiction and non-fiction. Literary studies and criticism has taken *belles lettres*, fiction, for "literature" as a whole, although there has never been a good reason for doing this, and although this separation is as dubious as the one between fine and applied art. This limited notion of literature in literary studies is purely a legacy of nineteenth-century romanticist philology that has survived till today.

But in the twenty-first century, even the primal criterion of literature has become obsolete: that of being published. In the age of homepages, blogs, and social networks, the classical distinction between non-published personal writing and published writing is moot, and with it the distinction between everyday communication and publishing. For example, the question of whether a diary or a correspondence was literary used to be simply a question of whether or not to publish it—a criterion that is no longer meaningful on the Internet. If there ever has been a clear divide between amateur and professional writers at all, now it has collapsed completely. (Bloggers are just one example.) Of course, there are historical precursors such as in published correspondence and diaries, and from a materialist perspective, the differentiation between literary writing and everyday writing has always been artificial. Foucault's ([1969] 2002: 26) attack on the notion of the literary oeuvre, in *Archeology of Knowledge*, seems dated today:

> Does the name of an author designate in the same way a text that he has published under his name, a text that he has presented under a pseudonym, another found after his death in the form of an unfinished draft, and another that is merely a collection of jottings, a notebook? ... And what status should be given to letters, notes, reported conversations, transcriptions of what he said made by those present at the time, in short, to that vast mass of verbal traces left by an individual at his death, and which speak in an endless confusion so many different languages (langages)?

The answer of modern critical text philology would be: yes. The critical text edition of Kafka (2004), for example, now even includes the notes and letters he wrote on behalf of his insurance company. For edition philologists, it is a completely unresolved question what needs to be done with the electronic files, notes, and Internet communication snippets of literary writers in the future.

Looking back at ELO initiatives like *Born Again Bits* (Liu et al. 2005) and *Acid-Free Bits* (Montfort and Wardrip-Fruin 2004). This seems to be a legacy of the 1980s and pre-Internet times: of HyperCard stacks, Storyspace, and Macromedia Director files. This seems like an artificial preservation of a notion of oeuvre that Foucault had dismissed even for print culture. Or is this notion simply a side effect of electronic literature being the product of literature departments where, just as with a term paper, a self-contained work with an unambiguous author signature is the precondition for assessing a student? That would also be a pragmatic explanation of why the more radically ephemeral, distributed Net art practices, or netwurks (to use the terminology of mez breeze), never were widespread in the Electronic Literature field; works that never existed as files, but only as communication streams. (Alan Sondheim is another writer who understood and practiced electronic text as streaming very early.)

Last, the difference between written language and the style of spoken language has largely collapsed on the Internet, where all kinds of writing circulate in one and the same medium. For the first time in human history, there is a large repository and plunderground of popular written language—a medium that James Joyce, Kurt Schwitters, or William S. Burroughs could have only dreamed of. But the question is again: Is electronic literature as represented in the ELO embracing this, or is it opting for the opposite—creating islands of literary works within the massive writing/reading streams of the Internet? This would be a position close to that of Adorno and the Frankfurt school, and their defense of fine art as resistance against the industry model of music and film mass entertainment.

Nevertheless, Adorno's and Horkheimer's analysis of the culture industry from the 1940s no longer matches what is now called the "creative industries," at least where I work, without any negative implication. Adorno's and Horkheimer's critique was based on a strict producer-consumer dichotomy. Contemporary "prosumer" culture has profoundly changed music and video production; writing no less if we look at the Internet. But how is it possible that media studies of audiovisual media prosumerism abound while they are virtually absent from literary studies? Why isn't the academic field of electronic literature studies the forerunner of such a research? Or is it just the opposite, that established notions of literariness and the literary work are being preserved in order to filter the sea of digital communications? But even with such a curatorial model, there remains a crucial question: Isn't this critical filtering artificially constrained to writing that bears the tag "literary" conveniently upfront, instead of dealing with electronic writing at large? (Codeworks artists, e.g., did just that.)

3

What happens if we dispense with the notion of literary writing?

In his book *Uncreative Writing*, Kenneth Goldsmith (2011: 11) quotes Brion Gysin's famous statement that literature was "fifty years behind painting." Nowadays, one would say that it is fifty years behind the visual arts. Goldsmith's notion of uncreative, anti-expressive, and conceptual writing rests on this hypothesis. Gysin referred, in the late 1950s, to the collage and montage techniques of Dada and surrealism that were the forerunners of his and William S. Burroughs's cut-up texts. Goldsmith writes from the perspective of a creative writing professor who rebels against the unbroken romantic subjectivism in contemporary poetry and psychological realism in prose writing. In that sense, most literature is now running one hundred years behind the visual arts while e-literature—just like sound poetry and visual poetry—keeps up rather well.

But Goldsmith advocates more than simply collage; he promotes an aggressive plunderphonics. It is media pirate writing that, while firmly rooted in a Western avant-garde canon, takes more from the situationist detournement than from Picasso's or Schwitters's classical collage.

Goldsmith (2011: 85) advocates a "post-identity literature," yet he does not, for example, include Internet culture like the memes and image/text "macros" of 4chan and the Anonymous movement in this example. Where is the philology and iconology of the grotesque visual poetry of 4chan image macros, a subculture arguably as vital and, on closer look, complex as punk and post-punk culture in the 1970s and 1980s?

Goldsmith's book reads much like a postmodernist writing manifesto of the Internet revolution. In that aspect, it surprisingly resembles Mark Amerika's 1993 "Avant-pop manifesto"—which he doesn't refer to—and Raymond Federman's "play-giarism," one of Amerika's pre-Internet sources. Amerika's point of departure, however, was prose writing and the Brown University school of hyperfiction. Goldsmith's poetics however is founded on experimental poetry and a post-Fluxus tradition of intermedia arts. Neither of the two writers answers the question that John Barth brought up in his 1967 manifesto "The Literature of Exhaustion": Whether it wouldn't be more elegant if a prose writer like Jorge Luis Borges simply imagined and fictionalized these poetic practices rather than actually performing them—like the writers of Dick Higgins's Something Else Press that Barth criticized. The ultimate uncreative writer would therefore be Pierre Menard, the man who literally rewrote *Don Quixote* in Borges's short story from 1939 (Goldsmith 2011: 109–10). Unlike Goldsmith's students who had to do the same in class, the mere fiction of the act is more economical—and, as a metatext, actually closer to (instruction-based) conceptual art.

Goldsmith's poetics has two shortcomings: first, it risks treating the Internet as a poetic plunderground without really feeding back into it.[2] Thus remaining at a safe distance, it doesn't actually question the ontological status of "literature." Second, "uncreative writing" boils down to the dialectical opposite of creative writing. As a mere negation, it does not ontologically question creativity. From my practice of teaching at an art school, I can report that most artists and designers despise the word "creative"; "uncreative" would force them back into a wrong frame of reference just as "unpainting" would not be a desirable description for contemporary visual artists. The people calling themselves creative would be either naive artists—decorative potters, wildlife painters, and the like—or creative industries executives, from creative directors in advertising to creativity coaches for corporate executives.

But lately there has been a shift of meaning in the word "creative," triggered by Richard Florida's concept of the "creative class" and the European, increasingly fuzzy notion of the creative industries: "creative" has become an umbrella term for any kind of professional artistic work, whether it is applied or fine art. To use a piece of anecdotal evidence, the editor-in-chief of a commercial magazine for Super 8 filmmaking, for which I occasionally do freelance work, now differentiates between classical home movie amateurs (typically men in their sixties and seventies) from young "creatives," a notion that encompasses experimental artists, visual designers, and advertisers who use Super 8 as a post-digital medium. In Europe, the notion of the "creative industries" is now gradually replacing that of arts and culture. It simultaneously encompasses the arts, commercial design, and media technology. This is a textbook example of how neoliberalism can be brutally progressive. What Russian constructivism, Bauhaus, De Stijl, Fluxus, and situationism tried but failed to accomplish, to do away with the difference between fine and applied arts, is now done by globalized capitalism for even more materialist reasons.

It is tempting to maintain notions of "literary writing" or "(un)creative writing" out of resistance to these developments. This would be the same conservative-dressed-up-as-progressive resistance that Adorno and Horkheimer had in the 1940s when they lived in Hollywood and wrote the *Dialectics of Enlightenment*. Even the "creative" in "creative industries" remains a piece of romanticist legacy. If all contemporary concepts of literary, creative, and uncreative writing were abandoned, this could bring back the notion of creativity to its original meaning, clever inventiveness—where a fraudulent tax return qualifies as a piece of creative writing but not a novel by Dave Eggers.

4

Goldsmith's "uncreative" poetics reads, in large parts, like Andy Warhol's pop art recipes applied to writing. Warhol's art, however, reflects a 1960s consumerist culture,

[2] Despite contrary claims on page 202 of *Uncreative Writing*.

programmed by the old media and creative industries that is now retro fiction on *Mad Men*. Goldsmith (2011: note 6) is well aware of this issue when he writes:

> I'm part of a bridge generation raised on old media yet in love with and immersed in the new. A younger generation accepts these conditions as just another part of the world: they mix oil paint while Photoshopping and scour flea markets for vintage vinyl while listening to their iPods.

It is the same trend as in the contemporary boom of artists' handmade books and zines—the post-digital trend that is just as thriving among my own art and design students in the Netherlands.

The word "post-digital" was coined by Canadian composer Kim Cascone in 2000. In his paper "The Aesthetic of Failure," he referred to the "emergent genre" of electronic glitch music as

> "post-digital" because the revolutionary period of the digital information age has surely passed. The tendrils of digital technology have in some way touched everyone. With electronic commerce now a natural part of the business fabric of the Western world and Hollywood cranking out digital fluff by the gigabyte, the medium of digital technology holds less fascination for composers in and of itself. (12–18)[3]

In the 2010s, this phenomenon has solidified into a renaissance of vinyl and of cassette tape labels in music, of Super 8 and VHS in film and video, and of DIY Risograph print-making within graphic design, visual art, and poetry. The DIY aspect is most crucial here, and explains why this is more than a retro phenomenon: the analog media that are newly being embraced are those that are the most tangible and most easily self-makeable. In that sense, the digital maker movement (manifesting itself, among others, in Fablabs and the magazine *MAKE* published by O'Reilly Media) and the neo-analog media DIY are one and the same post-digital culture.

Conversely, with the rise of Web 2.0, social media and mobile apps, "user-made content" has been locked into corporate templates and data mining systems. While the World Wide Web was a DIY publishing medium in the 1990s, digital DIY has become difficult in a medium defined by only four corporate players (Google, Apple, Amazon, and Facebook) just like TV was defined by a few networks in the past. The publishing of self-made books and zines thus becomes a form of social networking that is not controlled or data-mined by those companies. On top of that, the system crisis of global capitalism and rise of highly diverse forms of activism worldwide has phased out the Warhol paradigm of happy consumerism and replaced it with a DIY ethics and maker culture, particularly in Western countries.

These developments give the word "post-digital" a more profound meaning than in Cascone's paper. Cascone drew on a *Wired* column by Nicholas Negroponte from 1998 that stated that digital technology was no longer futuristic and revolutionary because it had become ubiquitous:

> Now that we're in that future, of course, plastics are no big deal. Is digital destined for the same banality? Certainly. Its literal form, the technology, is already beginning to be taken for granted, and its connotation will become tomorrow's commercial

[3] Alessandro Ludovico, publisher of *Neural* magazine, explores this issue for the area of publishing in his book *Post-Digital Print* (2012).

and cultural compost for new ideas. Like air and drinking water, being digital will be noticed only by its absence, not its presence.

5

Today's artists' books and zines indeed reflect digitality by its absence. A good example is Annette Knol's self-printed booklet *Colors—Simply Hiphop*. Knol is a member of Kotti Shop, an artist collective that runs a small DIY printmaking space at Berlin's Kottbusser Tor, the most troubled part of the Kreuzberg neighborhood, comparable to New York's Lower East Side in the 1980s. Just like other artist-run printmaking spaces, Kotti Shop works with a Risograph stencil printer whose use for carefully crafted, multicolor DIY art publications was pioneered by the Dutch artist and printer collective Extrapool.

Colors consists of a montage of single lines from hip-hop songs in which one or more colors are mentioned. It is a simple but effective piece of conceptual poetry, a perfect example of Kenneth Goldsmith's poetics of uncreative writing. If this booklet had appeared in the 1960s, using rock 'n' roll instead of hip-hop lyrics, it would also have been a perfect candidate for inclusion in Maciunas's Flux Store, as an affordable, accessible, working-class, and popular culture-conscious piece of contemporary art.

In 2012, however, the meaning of such a book has shifted just as much as that of Pierre Menard's *Don Quixote* as opposed to Cervantes's *Don Quixote*. Nowadays, the medium of the paper book printed on a Risograph is no longer chosen because it is the most simple and inexpensive means of democratic mass reproduction, but on the contrary because it embodies craftsmanship, materiality, tangibility, and personal exchange. This book is a book because it's intentionally not a website, or a blog. Its choice of the medium makes it a fine art (or fine art graphic design) product. It is graphic design in the anti-industrial tradition of the Arts and Crafts movement, not in the industrial tradition of Russian constructivism, Bauhaus, and De Stijl.

At the same time, *Colors* is a piece of electronic literature. Its text has likely been assembled through keyword searches of online song lyrics databases. (In this sense, a lot if not most contemporary art has become Internet art; which video artist doesn't steal from YouTube?) The stencil printer has the same function as the servers of online communities like The Well or EchoNYC in the 1980s and 1990s: it is a DIY community building tool. While Apple went from its first computer sold as a DIY construction kit in the Whole Earth Catalogue to the opposite extreme of mass-produced shrink-wrapped consumer gadgets that can't be opened, and while the online community concept behind The Well turned into the monster of Facebook, the DIY printmaking communities go back to where home computing began, and to homepages in the literal sense of the word.

Such developments put electronic literature as it is practiced by the ELO at a crossroads between two tendencies: literary intermedia writing for electronic (display) media in which work like *Colors* has no place, or a post-digital poetics defined by a DIY media practice rather than the choice of a particular medium, which is broadly orientated toward writing rather than literature. The larger question is whether literature studies in general shouldn't change in the same way in which visual culture studies developed from art history—which, as they have demonstrated, can be done without tossing out the baby of arts (and, by analogy, poetics) with the media and creative industries bathwater.

SOURCES CITED

Bosma, Josephine. *Nettitudes*. Rotterdam: NAi Publishers, 2011.

Cascone, Kim. "The Aesthetics of Failure: Post-Digital Tendencies in Contemporary Computer Music." *Computer Music Journal*, vol. 24, no. 4 (2000).

Foucault, Michel. *Archeology of Knowledge*. London; New York: Routledge, [1969] 2002.

Goldsmith, Kenneth. *Uncreative Writing*. New York: Columbia University Press, 2011.

Kafka, Franz. *Amtliche Schriften, Kritische Ausgabe*. Frankfurt am Main: S. Fischer Verlag, 2004.

Liu, Alan, David Durand, Nick Montfort, Merrilee Proffitt, Liam R. E. Quin, Jean-Hugues Réty, and Noah Wardrip-Fruin. Version 1.1. August 5, 2005. Electronic Literature Organization. http://www.eliterature.org/pad/bab.html.

Ludovico, Alessandro. *Post-Digital Print*. Eindhoven: Onomatopee, 2012.

Montfort, Nick, and Noah Wardrip-Fruin. *Acid-Free Bits*. Version 1.0. June 14, 2004. https://eliterature.org/pad/afb.html.

Negroponte, Nicholas. "Beyond Digital." http://www.wired.com/wired/archive/6.12/negroponte.html.

Wark, McKenzie. "From Hypertext to Codework." *Hypermedia Joyce Studies*, vol. 3, no. 1 (2002).

CHAPTER TWENTY-ONE

Unwrapping the eReader: On the Politics of Electronic Reading Platforms

DAVID S. ROH

Use of Kindle Content. Upon your download of Kindle Content and payment of any applicable fees (including applicable taxes), the Content Provider grants you a non-exclusive right to view, use, and display such Kindle Content an unlimited number of times, solely *on the Kindle or a Reading Application or as otherwise permitted as part of the Service, solely on the number of Kindles or Supported Devices specified in the Kindle Store, and solely for your personal, non-commercial use. Kindle Content is* licensed, not sold, *to you by the Content Provider. The Content Provider may include additional terms for use within its Kindle Content …*
Limitations. Unless specifically indicated otherwise, you may not sell, rent, lease, distribute, broadcast, sublicense, or otherwise assign any rights *to the Kindle Content or any portion of it to any third party,* and you may not remove or modify *any proprietary notices or labels on the Kindle Content. In addition,* you may not bypass, modify, defeat, or circumvent *security features that protect the Kindle Content.* (Emphasis added; "Kindle Store Terms of Use")

—Amazon.com

(d) Restrictions. Except as may be expressly permitted by this Agreement, you may not, *directly or indirectly: (i)* use *the Software on any device other than your NOOK; (ii)* use, copy, modify, distribute *copies of,* display or transmit *the Software; (iii)* disassemble, reverse engineer, emulate, decompile, tamper with, create *derivative works from or otherwise attempt to discover the source code of the Software …; (iv)* bypass, modify, defeat, tamper with *or* circumvent *any of the security features of your NOOK or the Service …*

3. Prohibited Conduct. In your use of your NOOK or the Service, you may not*: (i)* transfer *the Digital Content from one electronic reading device to another without maintaining the applicable digital rights management solution for that Digital Content … (viii)* open, modify, service or tamper with *your NOOK …*
4. Privacy and Security. (a) Privacy. You agree that we may use, collect and share your information *in accordance with our Privacy Policy.* Without limitation, we will collect,

use and/or disclose information regarding you and your use of your NOOK *and the Service* ... (Emphasis added ; "Nook Terms of Service")

—Barnes & Noble.com

THE FORMAT WARS

The viability of using an electronic reader (hereafter eReader) for casual reading has transitioned from fringe early adopters to the mainstream consumer market.[1] With an accessible price point, adequate resolution, ample storage capacity, and access to a wide range of materials, eReaders are considered a convenient companion for air travel, subway trips, and train rides—and in some cases, overtaking night stands and school bags as a viable alternative to print reading writ large. Yet despite rapid adoption, there has been little commentary from cultural critics regarding the material apparatus, its software architecture, and potential effects on literary culture.

There *have* been instances of hand-wringing over eReaders, just as there were similarly furrowed brows over the shallowness of Web browsing, hypertext fiction, and video games.[2] Rather than engage in the tired—and at times, panicked—debate over whether the eReader is an existential threat to the book and print culture, this chapter operates under several assumptions: that eReaders will carve out a niche in the reading public's consumptive habits, not displace or overtake print; that the market for eReading platforms will continue to develop and evolve in ways that cannot be completely anticipated; and that they will affect the reading public's consumptive habits, all to propel the argument that literary scholars should have an active hand in shaping our coevolutionary process.[3]

The impetus for this call for reviews stems from entreaties by fellow literati and colleagues, both online and offline, who have asked for recommendations on which eReader platform to purchase. Often, the question centers on readability, portability, and speed—all valid and reasonable concerns. However, I am troubled with the stark absence of discourse on the political and cultural significance of the respective ecosystems baked into eReaders (e.g., the Amazon Store for the Kindle, Barnes & Noble for the Nook, iTunes for the iPad, and the Google Play Store for Android tablets); debating the relative merits of the technologies themselves, which are fleeting and would no doubt change from one generation to the next, is less important.

The short form of social networking ripostes prove inadequate for articulating a nuanced and comprehensive argument for eReader platforms. Thus, this chapter and companion review attempt to inscribe those concerns for the literary reader and intellectual. A central concern is that the eReader is currently undergoing a low-intensity version of the format wars of the 1980s (Betamax vs. VHS), and 2000s (HD-DVD vs. Blu-Ray), bereft of commentary from scholarly and teaching circles, which stand to

[1] For the purpose of this chapter, I also consider tablet computers a type of eReader.

[2] Nicholas Carr and Mark Bauerlein's screeds, *The Shallows* (2011), and *The Dumbest Generation* (2009), respectively, are representative examples.

[3] Debates regarding the demise of book, to be replaced by its upstart digital doppelganger, could constitute its own genre of scholarly hand-wringing. The spectrum of views range from the histrionics of Mark Bauerlein and fellow alarmists portending the decline of civilization to futurists uncritically embracing technology, such as Michael Joyce (1996: 111) and his fetishizing of hypertext, which he claims "is the revenge of text upon television." More measured studies includes Sellen and Harper's *The Myth of the Paperless Office* (2003) and N. Katherine Hayles's "How We Read: Close, Hyper, Machine" (2010).

be most directly affected by the adoption of a one particular platform over another.[4] I therefore call for a novel review genre, a mixture of consumer technical analysis, software, and cultural criticism focusing on the material and ideological e-book delivery system. This chapter is naked in its intent to exert influence in the adoption—and concomitantly, formation—of eReaders in literary and scholarly theaters; it is an attempt to provide a service to a narrow but important market of mid-range adopter—the critic.

Let me be clear: the most important factor to consider when purchasing an eReader is neither form nor function. As it stands, the eReader market has yet to coalesce around a leading platform (one wonders when Apple will announce its own eReader and attendant iTunes library); thus, a reader's choice will have significant impact on the future of reading, literature, information exchange, and cultural development—debating the relative merits of how quickly an eReader's pages turn is therefore limited in significance.[5] Instead, the single most important specification is hidden away, beneath the shiny veneer of the material encasing, nestled between lines of code: *ideology*.[6] Technology—and let us remember that the print book is indeed a product of technology—is no benign, neutral phenomenon. It is not driven in and by itself, shaping the world and connecting spaces to create a McLuhanesque global village of its own overdetermined accord. Instead, technology is an ideological epiphenomenon.[7] That is, it is a confluence of cultural norms, institutional legacies, as well as technological aspirations. There is nothing immanent in the technology of the book that assures us of the democratic dissemination of knowledge. To ascribe such values on the idea of the book a priori would be to fall into a deterministic trap.[8] Instead, it is helpful to reconceptualize the book as a content delivery vehicle, the last node in a constructed system of knowledge and cultural production that prioritizes accessibility, openness, and the further dissemination of knowledge.[9]

The book is not absent of its own political ideologies. Continuing our framing of the book as a product of technology, we can trace its ideological vespers backward through its manufacturing and supportive infrastructure. For example, books, in general, do not come with a lock and key fused on the cover. There are exceptions—books designed for journal entries, for example, are meant for a single writer and reader. Most books are not

---

[4] Bryan Sebok (2009) discusses the format wars at length in "Convergent Consortia: Format Battles in High Definition."

[5] Indeed, the current form may look fairly different in the coming years. Hybrid screens that use both LCD and e-ink technology may combine the tablet and eReader device, cannibalizing the standalone eReader market entirely, as the tablet once did with the netbook. Other innovations, such as flexible displays and dual-screen eReaders, may also take hold; my point is that these technological innovations come a distant second to the underlying ideology.

[6] For discussions regarding the underlying political and cultural underpinnings driving computer code, see Lawrence Lessig's *Code* (2006) and Richard Barbook and Andy Cameron's "The Californian Ideology" (1996).

[7] N. Katherine Hayles argues along similar lines in accounting for consciousness; in *How We Became Posthuman* (1999: 238–9), she argues that human consciousness is an epiphenomenon of material biology. I suggest the corollary—that material technology is an epiphenomenon of ideology.

[8] Lisa Gitelman (2008: 2–6) cautions against technological determinism at length in *Always Already New*.

[9] Robert Darnton (2010: 4) likens the modern environment of free exchange of ideas and knowledge (a la Google Books) to the eighteenth-century "Republic of Letters":

> The eighteenth century imagined the Republic of Letters as a realm with no police, no boundaries, and no inequalities other than those determined by talent. Anyone could join it by exercising the two main attributes of citizenship, writing and reading. Writers formulated ideas, and readers judged them. Thanks to the power of the printed word, the judgements spread in widening circles, and the strongest arguments won.

purposefully large or unwieldy so that they may be carried from one place to another, read while in transit, passed on and delivered through the postal system, or carried in jacket pockets. There are exceptions, of course. Consider the popular home encyclopedias of yesteryear, sold by so many traveling salespersons. Each hardbound volume comes gilded with gold trim, designed to stay in the bookshelves of homes for display so that other households will be inspired to purchase their own set. Early modern England saw even larger folios that were to remain chained to an ecclesiastical lectern, since copies were valuable and meant for the clergy rather than layperson.[10] My point is that each material instantiation is both product and reflection of a particular economic and ideological model executed technologically and materially visible.

Dissecting the eReader is a bit more complicated, as it has several moving parts, but it is imperative that we formulate a grammar and syntax for adequate description.[11] Robert Darnton (2010: 13), for example, sounds the clarion call for critical intervention on an infrastructural level: "Yes we must digitize. But more important, we must democratize. We must open access to our cultural heritage. How? By rewriting the rules of the game, by subordinating private interests to the public good, and by taking inspiration from the early republic in order to create a Digital Republic of Learning." In other words, Darnton argues that corporate enterprises such as Google Books, left unchecked, will hold a de facto monopoly over cultural knowledge, with little preventing it from raising prices or denying access in the future.

Ideology and technology live on several levels in the eReader: hardware, software, file formatting standards, and ecosphere. That is, ideology informs not only the physical design, but user interface, operating system architecture, interoperability, and distribution methods. Specifically, to which philosophy does the company that produces the eReader subscribe? Does it use a file format that is open source or proprietary? Does it add a Digital Rights Management (DRM) protective scheme to the e-book? Is the software that runs the operating platform open for tinkering and tweaking? Furthermore, what are the political ambitions of the corporation behind the platform and library? These questions have tangible cultural ramifications.

THERE IS NO BOOK

The most pernicious misconception regarding eReaders is that they are the digital equivalent of the print book. In actuality, the eReader is a skilled mimic—it is a content-delivery apparatus that imitates the dimensions and tactility of a book for the purpose of masking its political ambitions and cultural ramifications. The confusion is understandable, as it is no accident that the Amazon Kindle and Barnes & Noble Nook are roughly the same width and height of a paperback novel. In lieu of a sleek metallic or glossy plastic case, most eReaders adds tactility with a rubbery matte finish, to better recall the sensuality of a hardback cover. Instead of a backlit liquid crystal display (LCD) screen, many eReaders use a monochromatic e-ink screen made up of microcapsules that hold positively charged

---

[10] See M. T. Clanchy's (1993) discussion of book size and portability in chapter 4, "The Technology of Writing" in *From Memory to Written Record*.

[11] For how are we, as James Joyce (2015: 162–3) and Don DeLillo (2007: 540–2) show, able to discern the history, politics, and shape of a thing without learning—or contesting—names? See the discussion of the tundish and the shoe in *Portrait of an Artist as a Young Man* and *Underworld*, respectively.

white particles and negatively charged black particles suspended in clear fluid. Electrical currents tell the capsules which particle to display, black or white. The end result is a screen that has a crisp, high-resolution display that apes all of the characteristics of ink print. It is viewable in direct sunlight and from any angle, the display does not require constant refreshing, and since the display is not backlit, it does not tax the eyes of the viewer.

Here, the similarities end, for, to borrow from Gertrude Stein, there is no "there" there; e-book is a misnomer for several reasons. First, the book is absent from the machine. When purchasing an e-book from Amazon, for example, that purchase is wrapped in an End-User License Agreement (EULA; I emphasize several restrictions in the epigraph). For example, "Kindle Content" is only allowed to be read on "the Kindle or a Reading Application," which means that only Kindle content can be read on Amazon's line of Kindle readers or smartphone "app" ("Reading Application"). In other words, while purchasing a print book from Amazon.com results in a physical object you are free to read, use as a paperweight, level a rickety dining room table, give to a friend, or sell on the secondary market, purchasing an e-book is a completely different matter. In truth, a user purchases a license to access an electronic good that is neither in perpetuity nor attendant all equivalent rights of a print book. You are not allowed to lend or sell the book, you cannot rip out the pages or the cover to use as decoration. It is ephemeral, conditional, and under control of the "mother ship." In 2004, some readers learned much to their chagrin that their purchased e-book of George Orwell's *1984* was not sovereign to their device when Amazon decided to remotely delete them due to a dispute over a publisher's copyright—a reminder that the e-book is not a material object that can be "owned," it is merely rented (Stone 2009). The move angered many customers, who intuitively felt that Amazon had violated their property rights; but the fact of the matter is that the material rhetoric of the e-book and eReader as print book analogs has been so effective that the controversy subsided without any substantial change in policy or terms. Even when the user is reminded in no uncertain terms that the properties of a book do not translate in the eReader, the lesson is soon forgotten.

Second, the parameters of the platform are designed to maximize capital profit rather than distribute knowledge. The print market is similarly motivated to maximize profit. However, electronic books have the added benefit of a plasticity abetted by both legal and computer code that grants nearly unlimited powers to the rights holders. In contrast, a brick and mortar publisher cannot demand a buyer to agree to a list of limitations in addition to copyright code and then invade a private citizen's home to verify that they are not in fact selling the book on the secondary market. The EULA explicitly states that content is "licensed, not sold," and is furthermore subject to "additional terms" by the content provider—what those additional terms may be or for what purpose goes cleverly unexplained to grant widest possible latitude.[12] In addition, the EULA wraps a second limiting layer over the Digital Rights Management software baked into the operating system. In this case, it repeats language from the 1998 Digital Millennium Copyright Act (DMCA) in admonishing that "you may not bypass,

---

[12] A license grants a user the right to use a piece of software, but usually comes with a host of attending conditions and restrictions. For example, a license to use Microsoft Office expressly forbids a user from copying the software to more than one machine—this is also enforced through a unique product key mechanism that signals home to Microsoft to prevent more than one installation. A user, therefore, does not "own" the software at all.

modify, defeat, or circumvent security features that protect the Kindle Content."[13] An e-book cannot be transferred from a Kindle to a Nook, despite the similarities in technology. Amazon's proprietary file format (.mobi) cannot be read by a Nook; and the Nook's rendition of an open .epub format comes with DRM restrictions. Digital Rights Management software guarantees that such transfers cannot happen. As a consequence, choosing a platform is akin to being locked into one commercial system over the other. Imagine, for a moment, buying a CD from a Sony record store and being unable to play it in your car because it has a Toshiba stereo system. Or purchasing a DVD in Argentina, but being unable to play it in your DVD player in North America, which is actually the case, thanks to a corporate agreement to install region codes.[14] There is no analog equivalent; buying a paperback at the grocery store does not mean you have to continue buying from the same chain of grocery stores. The reasons are many, but in oversimplified terms, since the e-book is considered software and delivered in a technological device, our byzantine legal system considers that under the ken of the Digital Millennium Copyright Act, which restricts access thanks to the anti-circumvention clause.[15] That is, stripping an e-book of its digital rights management encryption so that you may transfer it to another device is technically a violation of copyright.

Third, the e-book is subject to the built-in marketplace of the eReader's sponsoring company. Here is one of the strongest arguments against the e-book as digital analog to print. The major vendors have designed vertical integration—owning the file format, the device, and the store, creating enough sunk costs to discourage readers from patronizing competing platforms. There is no equivalent in the print world; the closest example I can think of is the textbook industry, which is notorious for publishing meaningless updated editions to circumvent the secondary market—more insidiously, the instructor or institution may have a financial incentive in demanding students purchase new editions every year. Students cannot purchase old editions or textbook alternatives, lest they be at a disadvantage in keeping up with the curriculum. That is, the textbook industry has created a system in which the secondary market is effectively circumvented. This is far from ideal—a healthy secondary market ensures a wider distribution of knowledge. Likewise, a system restricting the distribution (and redistribution) of e-books to select vendors and devices artificially limits the dissemination of culture.

In sum, the e-book, by design, is not geared toward the dissemination of knowledge and intellectual exchange, whereas the print book—by fortune of its physical limitations and affordances, as well as the intervention of the state—is very much so.[16] Instead, it follows a familiar business model designed in locking consumers to a particular manufacturer's hardware and software ecosphere. Apple's computers, for example, have proprietary power cables that change yearly, not only frustrating Apple users, but rendering them

[13] Chapter 12 in Title 17 of the US Copyright Law states that "no person shall circumvent a technological measure that effectively controls access to a work protected under this title [The anti-circumvention clause]" (http://copyright.gov/title17/92chap12.html).

[14] Region codes are a restriction scheme agreed upon by a consortium of DVD manufacturers and film distributors that limit the playability of DVDs. A DVD or Blu-Ray disc from China, for example, will not play on a North American–produced DVD player, and vice versa. A resourceful consumer can find means of "unlocking" DVD players to become region-free; some region-free players are also available for sale.

[15] Taken to its logical conclusion, software licensing can result in rather comical scenarios. Car manufacturers, for example, might claim that self-driving automobiles do not actually belong to the car owner, since it operates according to software (Newcomb n.d.).

[16] This may benefit fans of print, for it assures that the eReader or e-book will never become as popular or as prevalent as print.

incapable of using a PC manufacturer's cable.[17] Sony's business model does likewise, even though it produces the more compatible-friendly PC—Sony has proprietary cables, memory sticks, and SD cards that are incompatible even among other PCs.[18] The sunk costs of buying the various accoutrements locks the user into other Sony or Apple products, because other hardware are incompatible. All this to say that critics and scholars invested in knowledge production and dissemination should be concerned, for an apparatus and platform that operates according to a different economy that consciously restricts access and installs planned obsolescence in the name of profitability is antithetical to a humanities that prioritizes the dissemination of knowledge and culture.

UNWRAPPING THE EREADER

If an eReader is not a book, what, then, is an e-book? How is the e-book ontologically distinct from its print counterpart? I would contend that the e-book exists largely in our imagination—a fearful symmetry of legacy media, technological rhetoric, and media metaphor designed to ape the print book's material affordances and limitations. That is, a print book's heft, weight, and materiality lends certain attributes; depending on its size, it may be portable or meant to be displayed, it could be used as a paperweight, read outside in the sun, and sold secondhand at garage sales and flea markets. Print also has its limits—it cannot be easily copied on a mass scale, or travel well, and it cannot be easily surveilled. These qualities are not inherent to the book as a concept, but indelibly tied to its physicality. In contrast, an e-book's physicality is negotiated, and many of its attributes mutable.

Somewhat belatedly, perhaps we need to articulate a theory of the e-book. After all, any narratologist or structuralist would argue that a consideration of the material experience of textual tactility informs the narrative experience; to simply assume that a narrative experience is unchanged whether one reads a text in print or through an eReader is simplistic.[19] If we are to assume that eReader platforms will achieve mainstream popularity to some degree, it would behoove literary critics to first theorize the e-book. To formulate an answer, I turn to theories of intellectual property, which has already made the distinction for us. In intellectual property law, there is a difference drawn between a physical instantiation of a book, which copyright protects in the sense that an unlicensed photocopy is disallowed, and the "ideal object," which copyright protects in another sense—the expression of ideas in the book are safeguarded.[20] Black market pirates interested in

[17] Apple's business model banks on their superior user experience offsetting the appeal of open interoperability. The iTunes music store, for example, uses a proprietary file format rather than the ubiquitous MP3 file format with a jealously guarded digital rights management scheme. The idea is that an Apple user with an iPod/iPhone/Macbook will already be so invested in the Apple ecosystem that s/he will have a disincentive to explore other options that may be more affordable (Montgomerie and Roscoe 2013).

[18] Sony's business model centers on aspirations of "vertical integration," in which the hardware and all its accessories are built by Sony and only interoperable with its products. "Sony makes television displays, DRAM, game consoles, and even uses its own proprietary memory devices (such as Memory sticks) for moving data from its camcorders to its digital cameras to its stereophonic and television equipment" (Chesbrough, Vanhaverbeke, and West 2006: 2.5.2).

[19] Seymour Chatman (1980: 22) argues in *Story and Discourse* that narrative structure must consider the medium on which the content is displayed.

[20] Tom Palmer describes ideal objects: Intellectual property rights are rights in ideal objects, which are distinguished from the material substrata in which they are instantiated ... the subject of intellectual property, indeed, the very idea of exercising property rights over ideas, processes, poems, and the like leads directly to speculation

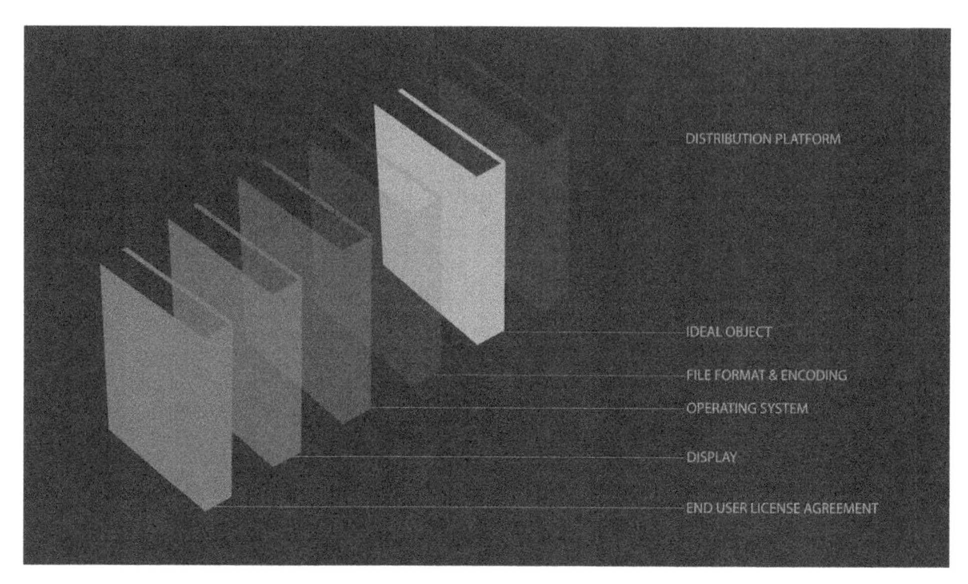

FIGURE 21.1 A conceptual blueprint of the eReader. Image by author.

copies of a book are concerned with the physical object rather than the ideal object—they are not subject to charges of plagiarism. In contrast, a lawsuit concerning the pilfering of unique constructions of expression is a matter of plagiarism, not piracy. It may be that a physical copy of the book does not even enter into the picture. While both scenarios fall under the purview of copyright law, there has always been a distinction between the two; we in new media studies would be advised to do likewise when discussing the e-book. In a sense, the e-book is a more perfect embodiment of the ideal object than the print book. Since the electronic text is portable and independent of a physical form, or on such a small scale that it renders them immaterial in comparison, the electronic text should be taken as its own ontological object.[21] Likewise, the eReader platform should be dissected and examined according to a set of criteria that takes into account its unique elements.

The "e-book" is not an object, but an immersive electronic-mediated experience, a consensual hallucination of sorts. That is, it is a confluence of hardware platform, electronic text, and commercial body working in concert to replicate or mime a print-like reading experience. To understand the e-book, we should work backward, beginning with an "exploded view" blueprint of the experience to peel back a multitude of layers.

At the very core is the electronic text, the closest thing to an "ideal object." That is, it is the electronic text that has been typed and formatted by the author/writer and copy editors for publication; it is the nucleus from which both the print and electronic versions will be born. I say that it resembles the "ideal object," but that is somewhat facetious, for it relies upon the material hardware of computing to be stored, processed, and displayed;

about how such objects are similar to or different from other objects of property rights, such as trees, land, or water flows (Thierer 2002: 44).

[21] I am being a bit facetious here. There is of course materiality to the e-book—bits and bytes must be stored in physical spaces; an argument could be made that e-books are *more* material in the sense of requiring transatlantic cables, server farms, terminals, and all the attendant accoutrement. However, since that infrastructure is not unique to just e-books—other than the terminal, which can potentially contain text on an exponential order—I will refer to their immateriality in comparison.

it is, however, as close to ephemeral and abstract that can be conceived at the present. But it is less than likely that the text is raw, unformatted, or unencoded; the text also includes the structure of the data in (1) *file format* and *encoding standard*. That is, is the electronic text in a proprietary format, or an open format, such as ePub? Is it in plain text? PDF format? The differences between each file format are not simply academic—they determine an electronic text's backward and future compatibility, portability, and platform readability. Each file format comes of course with its own encoding standards (XML, SGML, etc.), which we may not be able to address in the scope of this chapter alone.[22]

Beyond that, the next major enclosing is the physical eReader. While reading-oriented eReaders aim to mime some of the characteristics of a book, others are designed for additional purposes. Tablets, for example, have become de facto eReaders since a high resolution (2) *display* coupled with lowered brightness settings on an LCD display are adequate for reading purposes. The Nook Color and Kindle Fire, for example, are hybrid tablets that are for general media consumption rather than strictly for reading. However, the Amazon Paperwhite turns back toward print reading-like conditions, with an e-ink display augmented with a backlit display. My point is not all eReader constructions are the same; they are designed for different purposes that affect the reading experience. To ignore these conscious design choices would be short-sighted, for they can, for example, evince the prioritization of market consumption over cultural dissemination. Moreover, the hardware and physical dimensions are only part of the equation.

Between the electronic text and eReader stands the (3) *operating system*, for eReaders are in fact low-powered CPUs that operate on existing software platforms. For example, the iPad runs on Apple's proprietary iOS, which also runs on its mobile phone handset (iPhone); the Nook, Kindle, and a wide variety of tablets run on "forks" of Android OS, which is developed and spearheaded by Google; still others run on versions of Windows. The operating system is important to note, for each system operates according to different software ideologies. Apple's iOS, for example, is proprietary, while Google's Android OS has strong open-source components. Accordingly, Android OS is much more customizable, runs on a wide variety of handsets and tablets, and can be tailored for file format interoperability and compatibility. In contrast, Apple iOS is carefully guarded, with development generally restricted to application programmers. For example, iOS cannot run on any tablet other than the iPad; there is no iOS version of the Nook or Kindle. Consequently, the majority of tablets and eReaders run on some flavor of Android OS.

The (4) *distribution platform* may well be the one and the same as a commercial body that designed and sold the eReader platform, but that is not always the case. For example, an Android tablet may be produced by ASUS, HP, or Samsung, but they do not necessarily always have a software library for e-books. Instead, a tablet user will most likely download an e-book from Amazon.com or the Google Play Store. A particularly savvy user could download public domain texts directly from third-party repositories such as Project Gutenberg and load them on an eReader. Most commonly, however, the distribution platform and commercial body will be the same entity—the Kindle and Amazon.com, the Nook and the Barnes and Noble online store, Apple's iPad and iTunes, Google's Android tablet, and the Play Store. In these cases, it is also necessary for us to consider an additional layer, the (5) *end-user license agreement*.

[22] For a primer on the politics of text-encoding, see DeRose et al. (1990); McGann "Rethinking Textuality" (2004); and Liu (2004).

I have wrestled with finding an apt metaphor to describe how an e-book is different from a print text, but perhaps "wrapping" is the best fit.[23] Other terms for EULA include "clickthrough" and "clickwrap," and I think it is indicative of the kind of operation at play. Thanks to the dual forces of the DMCA and the practice of attaching a lawyerly EULA to every purchase, the device is effectively wrapped two times over—the software code prevents the transferring of files, the EULA codifies restrictions placed upon the user, and the DMCA ensures its legal enforcement.

At their core, both print and electronic books still yield an ideal object that flows out of the pen, keyboard, or mind of the writer, but in the case of the e-book, there are layers of wrapping, each with its political and ideological ambitions, which complicate our understanding of the e-book. There is the ideal object, but according to my count, the e-book has six layers of wrapping between it and the reader (file format, encoding, DRM, operating system, hardware), whereas the print book has just one (the physical book). Whereas most consumer tech reviews concentrate on the superficial usage experience with each iteration appearing at a biannual or annual rate heralding a new UI, feature, or otherwise incremental update, the eReader review concentrates on unwrapping each ideological layer, which is much slower to change, to convey the distance between reader and the ideal object.

REVIEW FORMAT

The primary objective of these reviews is unwrapping the eReader to reveal its ideological underpinnings, with a preference for devices that offer backward compatibility, run on open source operating systems, use open file formats, and make file transferal convenient. The objective in surveying these points is to draw attention to these key—and often ignored—elements in eReaders leading to the preservation, dissemination, and consumption of knowledge. If we as scholars are invested in forensic media archaeology and the circulation of culture, we should be equally invested in platforms whose structure and technology align with those objectives.[24]

The Text

(1) *File format and Encoding.* The format of the file speaks volumes regarding the future interoperability of the e-book. For example, does the eReader include an option to read and write an open file format? Or does it only allow for the reading and writing of its proprietary file format? Is there backward compatibility? If an eReader only reads a proprietary file format and is purposefully crippled to prevent it from reading other formats (e.g., PDF, DOC, TXT), then that eReader is not only severely limited, but actively designed to lock in a user to its own ecosystem of texts and hardware.

Apparatus

(2) *Display.* The display might appear devoid of meaning, but a manufacturer's technical choices reveals intentionality. For example, an LCD display is made for multimedia

[23] See Lessig's *Code* (2006) for a longer discussion of the combinatory powers of legal and software code controlling user behavior.

[24] In *Mechanisms*, Matthew Kirschenbaum (2012) makes a compelling case for understanding the materiality and fragility of digital platforms and their software objects for research purposes.

consumption, including video and games; an e-ink display, viewable in sunlight, and is made for mimicking the print reading experience. A high DPI (dots per inch) and refresh rate might make for a smoother and less eye-straining reading experience but come with the cost of higher battery consumption, which does not serve a reader, but multimedia enthusiast. A backlit display, such as the Amazon Kindle Paperwhite's, enables a reader to read in the dark, but again, comes at the cost of battery life; it may be that the tradeoff is a conscious decision by Amazon, since the Kindle Paperwhite also acts a portal to its online consumer store. The choice of display technology speaks volumes as to whether the device is primarily intended to be a general purpose media consumption device or for reading purposes.

(2a) *Tactility*. What are the dimensions and weight of the eReader, and how does it feel in the hand? Is it pocketable? Does the cover bear a glossy or matte finish? What is the build quality like? How does it compare to reading a paperback novel?

(2b) *Storage and Transportability*. How much internal storage does the eReader have? Does it have a slot for external microSD cards? Moreover, how easy is it to transfer files from a computer, tablet, or phone to the eReader? Are there DRM restrictions that disallow file transfers? Is proprietary software required to transfer files, or can they be moved without mediation?

Platform

(3) *Operating System (OS)*. The accessibility of the OS determines the flexibility of the eReader and e-book. A crippled OS with limited functionality and obfuscation of operations may be in service to simplicity and user experience; it can, however, be indicative of the manufacturer's desire to limit information exchange. Is the operating system open or proprietary? How customizable is it? Can the operating system be modified with third-party applications? Can its functionality be expanded beyond reading applications? How does the OS perform? How many taps or buttons must be pushed before accessing a text?

(4) *Distribution Platform*. The distribution platform often operates as a market or "store." It is in the best interest of the eReader to funnel all transactions and textual exchange through its home-grown market. The relevant questions, then, should be about the ease with which alternate markets or transfers can be made. Furthermore, does the market act as a gateway to something else? That is, does the distribution platform actively push media other than e-books? For example, does the Kindle actively encourage its users to shop online for other Amazon products? What seems to be its primary objective in selling e-books? Are there "push" advertisements? Is the library of books accessible or onerous?

Legal

(5) *EULA*. The EULA is arguably the most important vector through which the e-book is defined, drawing together the legal, software, and hardware elements in one document. What are the terms of the EULA? Does it explicitly limit the rights of the user? Does it provide unreasonable powers to the company in protecting its product? How does it define anti-circumvention?

Hackability

While this may be a controversial category, I think it is essential for influencing platform production choices. The print book format is relatively open—meaning, there is no physical or protective layer dictating use and function. In the interests of knowledge and information dissemination and access, so should the eReader. Therefore, the reviewer should address the eReader's ability to be hacked. Can, for example, the OS be altered to access a private home server for files over Wi-Fi? Could it be hacked to read non-proprietary file formats? Install new fonts? Enable multitouch displays? Speed up pageturns? Mimic scrolling? Enable horizontal reading? Access third-party libraries?

THE IDEAL WRAP

In my undergraduate level courses, I find myself fielding more and more questions regarding issues of page numbering and citation standards not only for e-books published through Amazon, but also Project Gutenberg, and other third-party repositories of public domain texts. There is the temptation to simply wait for the format wars to conclude, and for standardization to take hold through the invisible hand of the market. Or, as some gleefully point out, wait out the demise of eReaders altogether, whose decline has been well documented (Alter 2015).

That kind of thinking is short-sighted. For our scholarly activities are sure to be affected sooner rather than later. eReaders will certainly continue to evolve according to the vicissitudes of the market and technological advancements. For example, prototypes with hybrid LCD/e-ink displays may one day combine the smartphone and eReader; or foldable, flexible displays promise the tactility and versatility of print. This is not to say that the aforementioned innovation spells doom for print (in general, I am skeptical of the zero-sum view of media platforms), but that the malleability of eReaders may afford interesting aesthetic forms. For example, what happens when fiction begins to realize that it doesn't have to be beholden to the conventions of print and publishes electronic versions that are not simply one-to-one facsimiles? What happens when those electronic versions are corrected or amended dynamically and on-the-fly? What is to happen when those updates require a fee? The ubiquity of smartphones and text messaging has already given rise to SMS novels (popular in East Asia) and "Twitterature," bite-sized narratives playing with the conventions and materiality of the medium, to varying degrees of success, such as Jennifer Egan's "Black Box" (2012) and David Mitchell's "The Right Sort" (2014). Steve Tomasula and Jason Edward Lewis published their electronic works, "TOC" and "Speak," as apps available in the Apple iTunes store, available for viewing only on platforms that run the iOS operating system. Whether conscious or not, the decision to publish in only those venues is a political choice. At that point, the platform and software ideology become paramount, as is the required vocabulary and grammar for describing them.

Ideally, there should be an open alternative; I would go as far as to write that the decline of eReaders may be due in part to the fragmented nature of the eReader market. The ideal eReader would have no designs for vertical integration, instead it would purport to house and disseminate knowledge and culture. This eReader would be able to directly access the online stores of Amazon, Barnes and Noble, Google Play Store, iTunes, publishers, presses, and independent bookstores to find the most affordable e-book, driving down costs and increasing competition; this eReader would be natively read ePub, PDF, RTF, DOCX, Mobi, and all other major formats, as well as be backward compatible. Finally, the EULA, if necessary, should be generously open, simple to read and understand. The eReader's agenda should be open dissemination of knowledge with as few obstacles as possible. But that model does not exist; indeed, it is in the best interest of the competing content providers to keep the market as fragmented as possible.

By this point, it should be apparent that my call for an eReader review genre is a surreptitious critique of the e-book as it is popularly conceived. Highlighting the manufactured nature of the eReader and unveiling its intentionality. Calling for a format review by literary scholars is both an ideological and political move. Why is there no seat at the table for the digital humanities or new media scholar at Amazon, Barnes & Noble, Apple, ASUS, Samsung, Google Android, and Sony? The cultural and political concerns of the critic should be represented, particularly as they move to redefine the terms of knowledge production and consumption. That is not to say that manufacturers should employ literary critics, but their influence should register with the eReading public and intellectual layperson much in the same way that consumer reviews influence the market share of a given product—the ideology of the eReader should be laid bare. An eReader review genre would be one small step in that direction and unwrap layers of obfuscation.

SOURCES CITED

Alter, Alexandra. "The Plot Twist: E-Book Sales Slip, and Print Is Far from Dead." *The New York Times*, September 22, 2015, *NYTimes.com*. Accessed June 17, 2016.

Barbrook, Richard, and Andy Cameron. "The Californian Ideology." *Science as Culture*, vol. 6, no. 1 (1996): 44–72.

Bauerlein, Mark. *The Dumbest Generation: How the Digital Age Stupefies Young Americans and Jeopardizes Our Future (Or, Don't Trust Anyone under 30)*. New York: Tarcher, 2009.

Carr, Nicholas. *The Shallows: What the Internet Is Doing to Our Brains*. New York: W. W. Norton, 2011.

Chatman, Seymour. *Story and Discourse: Narrative Structure in Fiction and Film*. Ithaca, NY: Cornell University Press, 1980.

Chesbrough, Henry, Wim Vanhaverbeke, and Joel West. *Open Innovation: Researching a New Paradigm*. Oxford: Oxford University Press, 2006.

Clanchy, Michael T. *From Memory to Written Record: England 1066–1307*. 2nd ed. Oxford: Wiley-Blackwell, 1993.

Darnton, Robert. *The Case for Books: Past, Present, and Future*. New York: PublicAffairs, 2010.

DeLillo, Don. *Underworld*. Classic edition. New York: Scribner, 2007.

DeRose, Steven J., David G. Durand, Elli Mylonas, and Allen H. Renear. "What Is Text, Really?" *Journal of Computing in Higher Education*, vol. 1, no. 2 (1990): 3–26. http://link.springer.com/article/10.1007%2FBF02941632.

Egan, Jennifer. "Black Box." *The New Yorker*, June 4, 2012. Accessed June 27, 2016.

Gitelman, Lisa. *Always Already New: Media, History and the Data of Culture*. Cambridge, MA; London: MIT Press, 2008.

Hayles, Katherine N. *How We Became Posthuman: Virtual Bodies in Cybernetics, Literature, and Informatics*. 1st ed. Chicago: University of Chicago Press, 1999.

Hayles, Katherine N. "How We Read: Close, Hyper, Machine." *ADE Bulletin*, vol. 150 (2010): 62–79.

Joyce, James. *A Portrait of the Artist as a Young Man*. CreateSpace Independent Publishing Platform, 2015.

Joyce, Michael. *Of Two Minds: Hypertext Pedagogy and Poetics*. Ann Arbor: University of Michigan Press, 1996.

"Kindle Store Terms of Use." Amazon.com. N.p. Accessed September 6, 2012.

Kirschenbaum, Matthew G. *Mechanisms: New Media and the Forensic Imagination*. Cambridge, MA; London: MIT Press, 2012.

Lessig, Lawrence. *Code: And Other Laws of Cyberspace, Version 2.0*. New York: Basic Books, 2006.

Liu, Alan. "Transcendental Data: Toward a Cultural History and Aesthetics of the New Encoded Discourse." *Critical Inquiry*, vol. 31 (2004): 49–84.

McGann, Jerome. *Radiant Textuality: Literature after the World Wide Web*. 1st ed. New York: Palgrave Macmillan, 2004.

Mitchell, David. "The Right Sort." *Twitter* (n.d.), n.p. Accessed June 27, 2016.

Montgomerie, Johnna, and Samuel Roscoe. "Owning the Consumer—Getting to the Core of the Apple Business Model." *Accounting Forum*, vol. 37, no. 4 (2013): 290–9. *ScienceDirect*. The Apple Business Model: Value Capture and Dysfunctional Economic and Social Consequences.

Newcomb, Doug. "You Own the Car, But Do You Own Its Software?" *PCMAG* May 1, 2015, n.p. Accessed June 30, 2015.

"Nook Terms of Service." Barnes & Noble. N.p., n.d. Accessed July 6, 2015.

Sebok, Bryan. "Convergent Consortia: Format Battles in High Definition." *The Velvet Light Trap*, vol. 64, no. 1 (2009): 34–49.

Sellen, Abigail J., and Richard H. R. Harper. *The Myth of the Paperless Office*. Cambridge: MIT Press, 2003.

Stone, Brad. "Amazon Erases Orwell Books From Kindle." *The New York Times*, July 18, 2009. *NYTimes.com*. Accessed June 29, 2015.

Thierer, Adam. *Copy Fights: The Future of Intellectual Property in the Information Age*. Washington, DC: Cato Institute, 2002.

CHAPTER TWENTY-TWO

Scarcity and Abundance

MARTIN PAUL EVE

One of the clearest reconfigurations wrought by the digital environment is to alter what we perceive of as scarce and what we see as abundant. Why, for instance, consumers around the world might ask, should the pricing of electronic literature supersede those works disseminated in the material codex form? After all, in the digital and electronic space of the Internet, we know that the dissemination costs of material are drastically lowered. We are no longer posting pieces of dead tree around the world for individual readers to own, but instead are building a centralized infrastructure that can, in theory, accommodate all users. In this sense of low distribution costs, we conceive of born-digital literatures as abundant and overflowing, disseminable ad infinitum. However, when such works come into contact with our systems of finance and labor, which are socially scarce (by definition), we then see the restriction as "artificial," even if, at heart, we know that all our systems of currency *must* be artificially scarce and limited in order to function. Indeed, it may be that *more* labor goes into the creation of many works of electronic literature than in traditional publishing processes. Those who would pirate such materials in order to thwart such scarcity may not have technically "stolen" anything, but they have, as Jaron Lanier (2011: 102) put it, undermined the "artificial scarcities that allow the economy to function."

In this chapter, I want to suggest that thinking about what is truly abundant and what is actually scarce can help us to broach at least one part of the problem of value that circles around electronic literature. This value problem is, namely, that *time* and *labor* remain scarce in the production and the consumption of electronic literature but also that, in some cases, the points at which the labor of publishing occurs are altered. Indeed, as N. Katherine Hayles notes, asking students to read electronic literature requires up-front signaling from professors about the commensurate time expectations for reading a hypertext. Hayles (2012: 77), for example, specifically tells students that they should spend the same amount of time reading Shelley Jackson's *Patchwork Girl* (1995) as they would take to read Mary Shelley's *Frankenstein* (1818). What usually goes less remarked upon is the fact that the near-elimination of dissemination costs and barriers does not alter the social situation of *work* in the world. It just so happens that the digital environment has shifted the work of publishing and authorship solely to the *labor to first copy*, rather than inhering at equally spaced intervals throughout the process. In other words, the work in publishing of copying and reproducing each text is now extremely minimal compared to the labor of reaching the first copy of that text.

PROPERTY, RIVALRY, AND COMMODITY FETISHISM

The specifically new type of "property" that we see in electronic media is that known as the non-rivalrous object, which originates in thinking about knowledge and ideas. Indeed, figures from Thomas Jefferson to Aaron Swartz have noted that ideas differ from material property in respect of how we vie for them. Jefferson (1853: 180), for example, wrote that "if nature has made any one thing less susceptible than all others of exclusive property, it is the action of the thinking power called an idea, which an individual may exclusively possess as long as he keeps it to himself; but the moment it is divulged, it forces itself into the possession of every one, and the receiver cannot dispossess himself of it." The Internet hacktivist Aaron Swartz (2015: 24), put this Jeffersonian sentiment slightly differently, noting that "by their very nature, ideas *cannot* be property."[1]

Human ideas and knowledge are forms of non-rivalrous objects, so called because once released they can be shared infinitely without a rivalry (a contest) for ownership. You and I can both very well know the "same" things, which differs from the conditions under which I might give you an item of my property. Rivalrous objects are lost when transmitted. Non-rivalrous objects are not. As Peter Suber (2012: 46–7) puts it, though:

> For all of human history before the digital age, writing has been rivalrous. Written or recorded knowledge became a material object like stone, clay, skin, or paper, which was necessarily rivalrous. Even when we had the printing press and photocopying machine, allowing us to make many copies at comparatively low cost, each copy was a rivalrous material object. Despite its revolutionary impact, writing was hobbled from birth by this tragic limitation. We could only record nonrivalrous knowledge in a rivalrous form. Digital writing is the first kind of writing that does not reduce recorded knowledge to a rivalrous object.

In other words, there are many forms of extant non-rivalrous objects: knowledge, music, writing, and stories. But so long as these were too complex for most human memories to record or for individuals to reproduce, we have sought to inscribe these forms within rivalrous objects: books, sheets, journals, and records/CDs. Digital media bring with them a property form that seems, at last, to match the transmission of the underlying form with the property mode within which it is recorded; non-rivalrous forms can be disseminated in abundant, non-rivalrous fashions. Copyright is the legal mechanism that we usually use to ensure that others temporarily do not simply profit by duplicating the rivalry of knowledge's incarnation without having done the work of knowledge production. The problem, however, is that such modes also exacerbate problems of commodity fetishism and neglect the fact that all our existing systems of economics rest upon a scarcity of labor time that is rewarded in currencies that are likewise scarce.

Commodity fetishism was defined by Marx in Volume I of *Capital* (1992). There he writes that

> the commodity reflects the social characteristics of men's own labor as objective characteristics of the products of labor themselves ... It is [actually] nothing but the definite social relation between men themselves which assumes here, for them, the fantastic

[1] Emphasis in the original. I am grateful to Mark Carrigan (2016) for pointing out to me this correlation between Swartz and Jefferson.

form of a relation between things ... I call this the fetishism which attaches itself to the products of labor as soon as they are produced as commodities. (162)

In other words, commodity fetishism is a way in which we think that reduces objects from relations between people to relations between things. Believing that books that are printed should cost more than those distributed online—even when we know, deep down, that the labor was at least equal in both cases—evinces a commodity fetishism, for such thinking has confused non-rivalry with a false economic and labor abundance, wishing the latter two away.

Yet, it is clear that there are a great number of labor forms that are invested in the creation of e-literatures that differ from conventional publication. For instance, reading the metadata to Emily Short's tale of magical rewriting "First Draft of the Revolution" (2012), it is clear that the work's form is tied directly to a range of types of activity. In the case of "First Draft of the Revolution," the work is free to read and play online, yet we are told that the piece was written by Emily Short and that "design and coding" were undertaken by Liza Daly (2012) and the studio, "inkle" (an independent developer of narrative games and interactive stories). In other words, unlike the traditional publication of literary fiction, for instance, these actors should be considered cocreators, not publishers, since the e-form is clearly key to the work's nature. It is also clear that the work must be hosted on a Web server, which must be secured and maintained. The versions for different reader types must be delivered and kept up to date with any formatting requirement changes. However, the narrative, billed as "novella" in length, is free to "play"/read, unlike some other hypertexts such as the aforementioned *Patchwork Girl* which retails for $24.99 from Eastgate Systems. For "First Draft of the Revolution," as with many works of electronic literature, one can simply click through and access the piece in its full non-rivalrous glory. Furthermore, in fact, the source code for the underlying book engine is openly licensed under the terms of the BSD License while the story itself is available under a Creative Commons Attribution (CC BY 3.0) license. In other words, "First Draft of the Revolution" is not just available freely to read, it is also openly licensed so that it may be reused.

CREATIVE LABOR AND REMUNERATION

It seems, then, in cases like "First Draft of the Revolution" or other forms of e-literature, such as bots and hypertext stories that take advantage of the non-rivalrous form, that readers often expect them to be monetarily free to access. This comes about, I have implied, because the *distribution* of rivalrous *commodities*—such as physical books—is accepted as requiring payment but the same is not necessarily true in the digital space. The payment for the object form can either be considered for the labor of authors, for publishers, for distributors, and for booksellers or for the commodity itself. The first four of these see the commodity as mediated between people and value labor, whereas the latter (paying for the commodity itself) is a fetish in which the exchange value is elevated. By contrast, in the case of digitally abundant goods we see an abandonment of such precepts. Instead of an appreciation, even within capital, of our relationship to the labor of our fellow human beings, it is tempting to think solely of the end itself, a good which is non-rivalrous and that can be disseminated for nothing. That such goods should be perceived of as free shows that the commodity fetish is distinctly exacerbated in the digital context. What is interesting, though, is that there is a form of labor where the structure of remuneration is better suited to open dissemination than in the case of e-literature. I am referring, here, to academia.

Academia is, perhaps, the last space where laborers are paid to produce work that they can then "give away." Many institutions explicitly license their employees to give their work to publishers so that it can be packaged and sold within creditable venues, foregoing their rights to a "work for hire" situation.[2] In this way, academia can be seen as perhaps the last contemporary stronghold of a system of patronage, a mode that Peter Suber (2012: 10) believes may have emerged in any advanced research ecosystem, since it devolves a form of *academic freedom* to those who work beneath it. This freedom comes about because such researchers are not dependent upon a market to earn a living. Indeed, while it is good that there are subsets of people who wish to read niche research work in almost every case, the numbers are often too low to form a viable market situation. Furthermore, the criterion of novelty distorts the competitive price-setting features of most markets, since it is not possible for a buyer to shop elsewhere. Every piece of research is unique and novel. It is a micro-monopoly.

From this situation of almost-patronage, however, emerges a "freedom from having to sell" for academics. Indeed, academics can pursue research agendas that are esoteric without worrying that they will not eat as a result. Of course, it is hard to secure an academic post and much of academic life is precarious, but being paid on the basis of institutional patronage is a much sounder way to ensure this freedom from populism than any other of which I can conceive. It is this economic foundation that also enables academics to make their work open access (in which research outputs are available at no cost to a reader and may be read, cited, recirculated, and even modified, with attribution), since academics do not need to sell their works to make a living. For, if researchers are secure in their livelihoods, there is no reason why they should not seek the broadest audiences by eliminating price barriers to access research. Indeed, there are many parts of the research ecosystem that encourage such behaviors since open-access research is often more frequently cited than its toll-access counterparts.[3] In this system, the way in which academics are paid creates a culture of abundance. The challenge with implementing open access for research is that publishers—whose labor is still required—are remunerated by a very limited kind of market, one primarily consisting of academic libraries. This situation has led to a raft of new business models (the most well known of which is the Article Processing Charge [APC] to be paid by an author's funder or institution, implemented by many publishers such as Taylor & Francis, Elsevier, and many university presses and as part of the national strategy of the United Kingdom's open-access provision)[4] in the attempt to ensure the same freedoms for publishers as is seen by academics with the outcome of freely accessible research material.

Before returning to e-literature, I want just to point to two further intertwined aspects of this academic environment: peer review and publisher gatekeeping. While academics are traditionally free to give away their work, publishers must ensure a degree of selectivity in what they choose to publish, usually using somewhat different measures in the book and journal spaces. For journals, an academic editor will usually work under the jurisdiction of the Committee on Publication Ethics guidelines to commission community consensus as to the standard of the work under a peer-review procedure. For books

---

[2] Although see Martin Paul Eve (2014: 43–85) for my critique of why this is problematic.

[3] Swan (2010).

[4] See Tickell (2016).

(monographs, for instance), there is often a preselection phase where market concerns will be addressed by the publishing house. This commercial hedging of bets is because, as John Thompson (2005: 46) has noted,

> on the one hand, publishing organizations in these fields [academic books] are concerned with questions of quality and scholarship—indeed, for most university presses these questions are paramount. But publishing organizations are also driven by commercial concerns.

For a publisher's library customers, an academic peer-review procedure acts as a guarantor of quality (regardless of how potentially troublesome such an outsourcing of judgment may be). On the other hand, every publisher would like to be able to gauge the market viability of its outputs, even if such prediction cannot be said to be an exact science. It is at least in part the disjuncture of market freedoms between academics and publishers that has caused so much trouble in the implementation of open access within academia.

What does this market space look like for other creators, though? The economic situation within the academy is uncommon, to be sure. Systems that resemble patronage do not abound through the early twenty-first century, although technological startups such as Patreon are trying to reintroduce the concept. This is indeed a *re*introduction of patronage since, as Stephen Greenblatt (2012: 85) has noted, authors in earlier periods

> made nothing from the sale of their books; their profits derived from the wealthy patron to whom the work was dedicated. (The arrangement—which helps to account for the fulsome flattery of dedicatory epistles—seems odd to us, but it had an impressive stability, remaining in place until the invention of copyright in the 18th century.)

Yet, there are a multitude of labor forms that are roughly analogous to publishing processes in the print world that must be remunerated in the creation of e-literature and that are integral to its success, under a developed system of capital and copyright.[5] These include roles akin to authorship and narrative creation but also extend into the technological features of typesetting/text encoding, copyediting, proofreading, programming, graphical design, format creation, digital preservation, platform maintenance, forward-migration of content, security design, marketing, social media promotion, implementation of semantic machine-readability, licensing and legal, and the list goes on.

Because of the association of digital abundance with commodity fetishism, we currently struggle to find ways to remunerate such endeavors. Indeed, when presented with a website that one can read and sometimes reuse for no monetary charge, the temptation is to believe that it must have been free to create. At the same time, we know that this statement cannot be the case since the labor forms that we require are scarce and are also tied to a material scarcity of finance and payroll. Just what, then, precisely, is happening here?

PRESTIGE ECONOMIES AND NETWORK EFFECTS

While the most frequent exemplar for economic models in a new digital age is to point to the rapid shifts in the music industry, given that so much of the underpinning labor in the creation of e-literature is technological, I propose here to move to examine the software industries and how these have changed in the light of open-source paradigms. The

[5] For more on this period of development, see Johns (2011).

canonical example of a new theoretical model is seen in the work of Eric S. Raymond, whose *The Cathedral and the Bazaar: Musings on Linux and Open Source by an Accidental Revolutionary* (2001) remains a core text. Toward the close of his book, one of Raymond's most important frequently asked questions pertains to whether "open-source software [will] leave programmers unable to make a living." Raymond responds that

> this seems unlikely—so far, the open-source software industry seems to be creating jobs rather than taking them away. If having a program written is a net economic gain over not having it written, a programmer will get paid whether or not the program is going to be free after it's done, And, no matter how much "free" software gets written, there always seems to be more demand for new and customized applications. (212)

There are two central logical tenets that underpin Raymond's argument here: that free riders are unimportant to those who might pay for free software and that a prestige economy is at work here.

The first of these matters, pertaining to "free riders," is difficult to empirically test over a wide range of areas. Free riders are those individuals within an economic system who benefit without paying. In classical economic models, free riders should be minimized. For instance, it is assumed that those who benefit from infrastructure of the state should pay taxes in order to fund its ongoing development and maintenance. Those who do not pay but nonetheless benefit are free riders and, as in the case of the 2016 Panama Papers leak of tax-avoiders through offshore schemes, are not looked upon favorably. In the case of software, Raymond assumes that those who pay for its development may not mind allowing those who have not paid to access the codebase. In certain situations, this assertion may be true. For instance, Red Hat, Inc. a company that manufactures a distribution of GNU/Linux (an open-source computer operating system) provides a set of support services around the free software. Their business model, in other words, is to provide support, quality assurance, and customization, even while giving away their core software, for which they have paid dedicated staff. Yet, as Peter Levine (2014) points out, it may be that such a type of peripheral service market has a very definite limit to the way it can scale.

Yet, if we step aside from wholly industrial concerns, what counterpart to this "service market" might we see in the production of e-literature? As Gabriella Coleman (2012: 79) puts it, "For Raymond, aligning hacking with the capitalist spirit would allow hackers to accrue socially respectable forms of prestige." It does seem to be in this space where those who write traditional literary fiction with electronic dabbling seem to sit. For instance, David Mitchell's "The Right Sort" (2014b) was tweeted in the summer before the launch of his novel, *The Bone Clocks* (2014a), thereby providing a teaser of the writer's virtuoso voicing in manageable, short form. Likewise, Jennifer Egan published a short story, "Black Box" (2012), via the *New Yorker*'s Twitter feed. Egan's text did not obviously tie in with any commercial release, but it is clear that since the *New Yorker* was an official tie-in point for the electronic content, there must have been some arrangement made after the success of *A Visit from the Goon Squad* (2011). Indeed, the organizers of the annual Twitter Fiction Festival at Penguin Random House are keen to stress that those participating "include award-winners and #1 *New York Times*-bestselling writers from a wide variety of genres," including Margaret Atwood, Jackie Collins, and Lemony Snicket, among many others. In such cases, it is unclear to me what the precise motivation for participation might be and whether there was a financial incentive to these top-flying authors—although Melissa Terras points out that the Oulipo-esque constraint of the form may hold intrinsic aesthetic value for some writers.[6] Yet, what is eminently clear is that there is a symbolic economy at work here.

In fact, what the Twitter Fiction Festival demonstrates is that its organizers understand how symbolic capital is transferred between participating entities and that it is working on the platform of "exposure" or "amplification" by "association." For one, the superstar authors appeared alongside twenty-five preselected wildcard entrants, judged by a panel of eminent and respected publishers. In a way, the Twitter Fiction Festival creates the perfect environment for a flow of symbolic capital. New contenders will submit their work because they hope to be judged (and passed) by a market-prediction panel; once in, the wildcard authors who win a final ticket will be placed on the same billing as those who have already had literary-market success in the past. The two market temporalities of future and past success combine to incentivize entrance and to create a prestige economy of exposure/amplification by the association with existing fan-bases of successful authors.[7] For existing authors, the appeal may lie simply in participating for the good of literature/their own personal fulfillment or it may be that they were asked by their publishers in order to boost their print publications and so forth.

What is also clear, though, is that there is a somewhat exploitative culture of scarcity against abundance at work in e-literature events such as the Twitter Fiction Festival. Namely, those who are scarce are those making money from these activities. For, while entrants will doubtless be abundant, the scarce high-profile advance-laden contracts available to the published relative-few are not a prize on offer. The prize, instead, is exposure and amplification by affiliation, not any finance, even while the event is clearly expected to generate income for the publishing house running it and perhaps even for Twitter, the underlying infrastructure provider that can so easily be accidentally forgotten, through advertising. As Jaron Lanier (2014) frames this type of behavior, what is important is that we see, here, an economy whereby a range of providers position themselves as alluring "siren servers," crucial nodes on the network with the power to capitalize upon work produced for free within symbolic environments. While prominent voices within the authorial community, such as China Miéville, have called for a state living wage for writers (there is, admittedly, a great deal of detail missing from this proposal in its early stages), at present we are just moving toward a world where those who can capture the network effect, by placing themselves at crucial junctures, can profit, while everyone else fights for the scraps.[8]

READER SCARCITIES AND GAME COMPARABILITY

Thus far, I have primarily focused upon the incongruence between areas of digital abundance and labor scarcity in the realm of the author, mapping the ways by which the scarcity of remuneration and the capture of network effects by a relatively small number of entities constricts—or at least poses challenges to—the production of electronic literature within capital. There is, though, another side to this same theoretical framework: the relative scarcity of reader attention in the digital environment.

[6] See Goldhill (2015).
[7] For more on this topic, see English (2005).
[8] See Higgins (2012).

A good example of this problem of reader time-economy can, once more, be drawn from the academic sphere.[9] Academics can be recognized in a bookshop for their esoteric behaviors. A normal (i.e., nonacademic) member of the public may approach a work, take it off the shelf and, after examining the front and back covers, begin reading the first few pages to see whether the work is to his or her taste. An academic behaves very differently. He or she will usually head, after the usual cover browsing and table of contents examination, to the *back* of the volume and the citation list/bibliography. The check being performed here is to ascertain whether, first, the perusing academic himself or herself is cited in the work and then to see whether the work cites the expected field. The next check that an academic might make is to examine the index: the alternative topography of the work, again to see what the map looks like. Finally, the academic may turn to the introduction in order to sample the work. What we must understand here, though, is that the professionalization of reading within the academy has yielded different desired outcomes between these two demographics. For the nonacademic reader in the bookshop, the ideal situation is to find a book that triggers interest, that can be purchased and read. For the academic, the opposite is true. The best situation for an academic is to find a work that he or she *does not* need to read. This situation comes about because the time that the academic has for reading is short and the literature is abundant.

As we now know, the digital environment creates abundance. What might not be clear from the above is that the only reason that the nonacademic reader is time rich (and therefore seeking more material) is that the bookshop itself functions as a pre-filtering device. While often relatively abundant, pay-walled bookshops—even digital ones, such as Amazon—have limiting scarcity functions embedded within, such as genre classifications. The academic, of course, also has to contend with a broad field over which he or she must hold mastery. The academic should know of everything (abundance) within a subfield, the nonacademic need not (scarcity). Furthermore, the academic field is one that is structured around constant (re)production of additional research material, whereas the rarefied field of, say, literary fiction is much more tightly bound. In other words, the academic sphere is one of high production, high filtering, high expectation of field mastery, and high digitization of material, even if open access has not yet fully taken off. However, the nonacademic sphere of reading is one of high production, high filtering, but low expectation of field mastery, and, in general, substantially lower digitization. The academic sphere, therefore, has greater demands of reader time and a more abundant culture stemming from its publish or perish culture and strange economic twists that allow the entrance of the digital.

E-literature can create an additional problem in the discoverability space. For what, we might ask, are the quality markers that make it possible to discern where one should direct one's time within the electronic world? Guides, such as those produced by the Electronic Literature Organization (ELO) are one such signal. Indeed, the ELO Showcase and Electronic Literature Collection act as signposts of value, while admitting their own non-comprehensitivity.[10] However, the fact that the ELO brackets the works in which it is interested under a medium of form—however hard this may be to define[11]—means that a given piece of electronic literature will only be discovered here by those seeking it through the medium, rather than it being an honest competition with print. In

[9] An anecdotal situation that I owe to Geoff Bilder.

[10] Electronic Literature Organization (2006a, b).

[11] See Levine (2015: 1–23) for an indication of the difficulties here.

other words, only readers who seek "electronic literature" will find electronic literature. Libraries of electronic literature, therefore, build silos that can give some internal assurance/quality markers to electronic literature, but such collections are unlikely to attract mass public attention or provide any kind of external vetting facility that could operate alongside more traditional (and market-dominant) forms, such as print. In truth, though, the vocabulary of electronic literature is strange for purposes of comparison to print literature. Many works, including "First Draft of the Revolution," ask users to "play" them, rather than "read" them. Of course, the term "play" has many resonances for literary theorists.[12] To my mind though, when confronted with a digital object that asks to be "played," my thoughts turn more to *games* than to books for any comparison.

When we begin to think of electronic literature alongside games, rather than books, a number of new phenomena become clear. It is, then, rather obvious how traditionalists such as Jonathan Franzen can accuse Twitter fiction of being trivial; it is the age-old narrative that believes that gaming and play must be relegated to childhood and superficiality.[13] Indeed, though, the ELO's non-exhaustive list of definitions of e-Lit contains the assertion that "interactive fiction" can be electronic literature. Clearly, we might hope that reading would play some part here, but we could ask to what extent many non-text-based games also count as "interactive fiction"?[14] Are the titles in the ongoing alternative-historical-reality primarily first-person-shooter series, *Wolfenstein* (1981–2016), an "interactive fiction"? Certainly, the titles are fictional and they are interactive. I intuitively sense, though, that any suggestion that these titles vie for the attention of readers of conventional print fiction would fail at all but the broadest levels. For the purposes of discoverability and time competition, then, there is a challenge in the terminology of gaming and play for electronic literature.

Then again, as already mentioned, there is a challenge with the expectation that electronic literature will take the same time to read as conventional works of fiction, for example. N. Katherine Hayles (2012: 85–170) traces this type of expectation to a technogenetic development. Indeed, the affordances of screen reading are different from those of print. We know, from various replicable eye-tracking studies that readers follow an F-shaped pattern when reading on a screen, which stands in stark contrast to print.[15] In turn, this F-shaped pattern is conducive to quick skimming of works, whereas the more linear tracking seen in print cultures appears better for the conveyance of sustained narrative. Likewise, the hyperlink culture of online works has led to an expectation of quick jumps and nonlinearity within the digital environment. Furthermore, the immateriality of the digital space—despite the overwhelmingly physical and spatial metaphors that we use to describe screen reading of web*sites*, *home* pages, and so on—may prove a problem, since, as Anne Mangen (2008) has pointed out, reading is a multisensory activity in which the materiality of the object and readerly haptic feedback alters the experience itself.

In fact, though, among Mangen's (2008: 405) phenomenological assertions the primary contention is that the experience of interacting with electronic literature takes place at an indeterminate (and indeterminable) distance from the object that is being used/read. The disconnection between text and instrument of its manipulation, such as a computer mouse, also alters the time expectations of readers in the digital world.

---

[12] Most notably through the Derridean legacy. See Derrida (2006).

[13] Goldhill (2015).

[14] Electronic Literature Organization (2016).

[15] Nielsen Norman Group (2006).

Because interacting with computers is not a transparent process for all but the most sophisticated of users, who may indeed feel transparently fused with the machine, and because electronic literatures appear to be situated at a distance from these only partially transparent technologies, two time framings are in play across the embodiment relation: the time frame of using the machine and the time frame of engaging with the electronic literature. Both of these time frames are scarce since they are predicated on human life spans; the life time invested in reading. It is their desynchronization, however, that matters; moments such as those when the technology does not behave precisely as a reader might like highlight the media through which the electronic literature is conveyed and stall the reader's progress through the electronic text. Of course, such a phenomenon also exists in the world of the print codex: we have all encountered those situations where we have gone too far by flicking more than one page, disjointing us from our reading experiences and highlighting the technology of the codex. Because electronic literature is that in which the technological media is integral to the creation, however, when the two time frames of use and comprehension are decoupled, the abundance and scarcity of various timeframes and phenomenological reading experiences are brought to the fore.

THE HAVES AND HAVE NOTS

Whenever we think of publishing, writing, and the reading of literature, it always pays to think in terms of labor, economies, and time scarcities. Electronic literature is no exception to this rule but, for many of the reasons I have outlined in this chapter—spanning its abstract spatiality and immateriality—it is more susceptible to the flaws of commodity fetishism that hide the difficulties of melding abundant digital worlds with scarce labor spaces. This susceptibility can lead us back to situations where, within market economies, it becomes very difficult to see how the labor of writing and programming is to be remunerated when the expectation is free. If one wishes to suggest possible future business-model trends, we could ask whether we might see, in the future, embedded product placement and advertising replacing the purchasing model. Certainly, such advertising has pervaded the computer-gaming world, to which I have suggested that some forms of electronic literature may have an association, even if there is good evidence that such advertising is ineffectual.[16] Conversely, however, we may be at a critical point for the advertising industry. As legal battles rage over "ad blockers" in browsers—battles that publishers are losing it should be noted—many are asking whether an ad-based economy is the right way to support our online services.[17]

Yet, I have suggested that the academic world of patronage-like payments might present another space from which we could draw an example of models that might work for open, digital practice. I want to spend this closing section, therefore, discussing a piece of e-literature that merges all the various areas that I have here been discussing across a variety of modes; Johannes Heldén and Håkan Jonson's "Evolution" (2014). "Evolution" is described as an "application" and an "online artwork-in-progress" (not a book or work of e-literature) that "analyzes a database of all the published text- and sound-works by the artist and generates a continuously evolving poem that simulates Heldén's style: in

[16] Kuhn (2008).
[17] Jackson (2016).

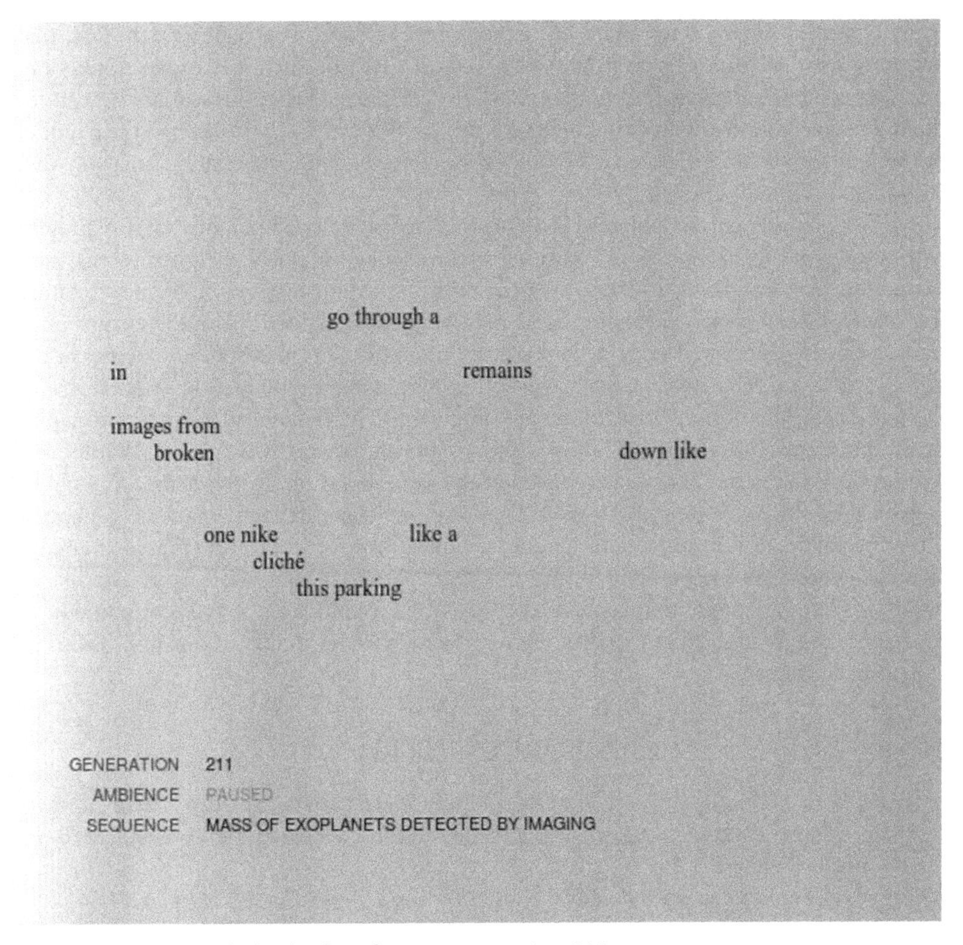

FIGURE 22.1 My playback of *Evolution* at generation 211.

vocabulary, the spacing in-between words, syntax. The audio track is generated by an algorithm that layers the source material of the artist's compositions in differing randomized lengths, fades and pitch; creating an evolving ambient drone" (ibid.).

Curiously, for genre placement, "Evolution" is assigned an ISBN or an international standard book number (978-91-85905-66-9), which designates it as a book. Yet, nowhere does "Evolution" describe itself as a book and it also has a "play" button with a speed slider that allows one to adjust the rate of generative playback, even if a print copy is available elsewhere. In a sense, then, "Evolution" is more akin to a personal stereo or digital DJ kit in its user interactions than a "book" as we know them. One of the other ways in which "Evolution" interacts with the philosophies of labor, scarcity, and abundance that I have here been outlining can also be seen in its access principles. The work, we are told, was produced with financial support from Kulturbryggan, which is the Arts Grants Committee of Sweden, analogous perhaps to the United Kingdom's Arts Council or the United States' National Endowment for the Arts. These organizations are constituted to fund artworks that, in the case of Kulturbryggan, are deemed original, of high quality, competent, feasible, collaborative, and efficient. This grant culture enables "Evolution" to be disseminated for free online, in an abundant fashion. The reality is, though, that organizations like Kulturbryggan are always short of cash. Such arts organizations can only award a limited number of grants; they are very scarce. From this scarcity we can see the interesting parallel here with academic practice. For the few who can run the gauntlet of the funding stream's scarcity, it becomes possible to disseminate material in a way that is abundant (digitally open).

Such a paradoxical and inward-looking logic of scarcity/abundance is also present within the work itself. For, as "Evolution" cycles through Heldén's body of works, generating its own machine version, among the most important features of the new text are the spacings, seen clearly in Figure 22.1. New text brought forth from the corpus must replace existing generated text, in the logic of "Evolution," or modify the spacings in the new poem to more closely match those found within the corpus work. In such a way, the paths that "Evolution" can follow are abundant. The dynamically generated nature of the program ensures that, while works may be similar, no two runs of "Evolution" will produce the same "found text," even at the same iteration. In this sense, though, of one-timeness, these poems are scarce. They are one-time artifacts, machine-generated literature that is unrepeatable and unique, produced from a code flow that is abundant in its generative pathways, funded by streams of patronage that are scarce, distributed online for free in a mode that is abundant. These, I contend, are the types of paradox of abundance and scarcity that run, usually unspoken, through much of our discussions of electronic literature.

SOURCES CITED

Carrigan, Mark. "Like Air, Ideas Are Incapable of Being Locked up and Hoarded." *Mark Carrigan*, 2016, http://markcarrigan.net/2016/04/06/like-air-ideas-are-incapable-of-being-locked-up-and-hoarded/. Accessed April 6, 2016.

Coleman, Gabriella. *Coding Freedom: The Ethics and Aesthetics of Hacking*. Princeton, NJ: Princeton University Press, 2012.

Daly, Liz. "First Draft of the Revolution Source Code." *GitHub*, 2012, https://github.com/lizadaly/first-draft-of-the-revolution. Accessed April 7, 2016.

Derrida, Jacques. "Structure, Sign and Play." In *Writing and Difference*. London: Routledge, 2006, pp. 351–70.

Egan, Jennifer. *A Visit from the Goon Squad*. London: Corsair, 2011.

Egan, Jennifer. "Black Box." *The New Yorker*, June 4, 2012, http://www.newyorker.com/magazine/2012/06/04/black-box-2. Accessed April 10, 2016.

Electronic Literature Organization. "Electronic Literature Collection" (2006a), http://collection.eliterature.org/. Accessed April 13, 2016.

Electronic Literature Organization. "Showcase" (2006b), https://eliterature.org/news/showcase/. Accessed April 13, 2016.

Electronic Literature Organization. "What Is E-Lit?" (2016), https://eliterature.org/what-is-e-lit/. Accessed April 13, 2016.

English, James F. *The Economy of Prestige Prizes, Awards, and the Circulation of Cultural Value*. Cambridge, MA: Harvard University Press, 2005.

Eve, Martin Paul. *Open Access and the Humanities: Contexts, Controversies and the Future*. Cambridge: Cambridge University Press, 2014, http://dx.doi.org/10.1017/CBO9781316161012.

Goldhill, Olivia. "The Rise of Twitter Fiction." *The Atlantic*, September 11, 2015, http://www.theatlantic.com/entertainment/archive/2015/09/the-rise-of-twitter-fiction/404761/. Accessed April 10, 2016.

Greenblatt, Stephen. *The Swerve: How the World Became Modern*. New York: W. W. Norton, 2012.

Hayles, N. Katherine. *How We Think: Digital Media and Contemporary Technogenesis*. Chicago: University of Chicago Press, 2012.

Heldén, Johannes, and Håkan Jonson. "Evolution" (2014), http://www.textevolution.net/. Accessed April 15, 2016.

Higgins, Charlotte. "China Miéville: Writers Should Welcome a Future Where Readers Remix Our Books." *The Guardian*, August 21, 2012, section Books, http://www.theguardian.com/books/2012/aug/21/china-mieville-novels-books-anti-piracy. Accessed April 10, 2016.

Jackson, Jasper. "Adblock Plus Wins Another Legal Battle with German Publishers." *The Guardian*, March 30, 2016, section Media, http://www.theguardian.com/media/2016/mar/30/adblock-plus-publishers-suddeutsche-zeitung-adblocking. Accessed April 15, 2016.

Jackson, Shelley. *Patchwork Girl*. Eastgate, 1995, http://www.eastgate.com/catalog/PatchworkGirl.html.

Jefferson, Thomas. *The Writings of Thomas Jefferson*. Edited by H. A. Washington. Washington, DC: The United States Congress, 1853.

Johns, Adrian. *Piracy: The Intellectual Property Wars from Gutenberg to Gates*. Chicago: University of Chicago Press, 2011.

Kuhn, Kerri-Ann. "The Impact of Brand and Product Placements in Electronic Games." Unpublished thesis, Queensland University of Technology, 2008, http://eprints.qut.edu.au/36375/. Accessed April 15, 2016.

Lanier, Jaron. *You Are Not a Gadget: A Manifesto*. London: Penguin Books, 2011.

Lanier, Jaron. *Who Owns the Future?* Reprint edition. New York: Simon & Schuster, 2014.

Levine, Caroline. *Forms: Whole, Rhythm, Hierarchy, Network*. Princeton: Princeton University Press, 2015.

Levine, Peter. "Why There Will Never Be Another RedHat: The Economics of Open Source." *TechCrunch*, 2014, http://social.techcrunch.com/2014/02/13/please-dont-tell-me-you-want-to-be-the-next-red-hat/. Accessed April 10, 2016.

Mangen, Anne. "Hypertext Fiction Reading: Haptics and Immersion." *Journal of Research in Reading*, vol. 31 (2008): 404–19, http://dx.doi.org/10.1111/j.1467-9817.2008.00380.x.

Marx, Karl. *Capital*. London: Penguin, 1992, i.

Mitchell, David. *The Bone Clocks*. London: Sceptre, 2014a.

Mitchell, David. "The Right Sort." *The Millions*, 2014b, http://www.themillions.com/2014/07/exclusive-david-mitchells-twitter-story-the-right-sort-collected.html. Accessed April 10, 2016.

Nielsen Norman Group. "How People Read on the Web: The Eyetracking Evidence" (2006), https://www.nngroup.com/reports/how-people-read-web-eyetracking-evidence/. Accessed April 14, 2016.

"Patreon: Support the Creators You Love." *Patreon*, https://www.patreon.com. Accessed April 10, 2016.

Raymond, Eric S. *The Cathedral and the Bazaar: Musings on Linux and Open Source by an Accidental Revolutionary*. Revised edition. Cambridge, MA: O'Reilly, 2001.

Red Hat, Inc. "Red Hat Subscription Model" (2016), https://www.redhat.com/en/about/subscription. Accessed April 10, 2016.

Short, Emily. "First Draft of the Revolution" (2012), https://lizadaly.com/first-draft/. Accessed April 7, 2016.

Suber, Peter. *Open Access*, Essential Knowledge Series. Cambridge: MIT Press, 2012, http://bit.ly/oa-book.

Swan, Alma. "The Open Access Citation Advantage: Studies and Results to Date" (2010), http://eprints.soton.ac.uk/268516/. Accessed March 24, 2014.

Swartz, Aaron. "Jefferson: Nature Wants Information to Be Free." In *The Boy Who Could Change the World*. London: Verso, 2015, pp. 23–5.

"The 2014 #TwitterFiction Festival Archive." *#TwitterFiction Festival 2015*, 2014, http://twitterfictionfestival.com/archive/. Accessed April 10, 2016.

The International Consortium of Investigative Journalists. "The Panama Papers," https://panamapapers.icij.org/. Accessed April 21, 2016.

Thompson, John B. *Books in the Digital Age: The Transformation of Academic and Higher Education Publishing in Britain and the United States*. Cambridge, UK: Polity Press, 2005.

Tickell, Adam. "Open Access to Research Publications New: Independent Advice" (2016), http://dera.ioe.ac.uk/25485/1/ind-16-3-open-access-report.pdf. Accessed April 21, 2016.

CHAPTER TWENTY-THREE

Relocating the Literary: In Networks, Knowledge Bases, Global Systems, Material, and Mental Environments

JOSEPH TABBI

INTRODUCTION

The present chapter is about ways that literary databases can make distributed collaborative encounters with scholarship more likely and better recognized—to the degree that nowadays inclusion in a database is the publishing event and the life of a scholarly work is defined through a trail of commentaries, ripostes, and (what is a sure sign of scholarly success) further work that is seen to be along similar lines. Citability alone, of course, is not in itself enough to ensure a change for the better in scholarly practices—no more than Aron Swartz's downloading en masse of JSTOR documents in the year 2011 has had a noticeable effect on the institution of peer-reviewed journal publication. Acting from a prototypal hacker ethic and reminding us of the original promise of the Internet for the free and open circulation of knowledge, Swartz was subject to aggressive investigation by the FBI and committed suicide in January 2013 at the age of twenty-six. Yet, apart from an emotionally powerful but passing highlighting of copyright issues, the Swartz intervention did not in itself cause anyone to question the *boundaries* of literature—the ways that scholarship, and even authorship, are currently relocating themselves in databases, collaborative networks, and global systems of production.

Insofar as responses to the Swartz intervention never explicitly addressed the content of the stored journal articles (let alone authorial intentions), it demonstrates a nonevaluative, even neutral disposition toward literary publications that are themselves, presumably, all about critique and close reading. In this sense, the intervention (and a tribute to Swartz by Kenneth Goldsmith that I'll examine momentarily) is largely consistent with two powerful dispositions that have emerged in the context of newly networked knowledge—namely, Bruno Latour's sense already in 2004 that the hard-won disposition toward "critique" in the humanities had begun to "run out of steam," and Franco Moretti's advocacy of "distant reading" practices, now that the mass of noncanonical writings are available in databases (along with the classics). The deep, near-instantaneous but largely unexamined absorption of such value neutral dispositions in the humanities is attested by several of the early-career scholars whose work was commissioned by Stephanie Strickland and Marjorie Luesebrink for a 2011 panel organized by the Electronic Literature Organization (ELO) for its conference on "Futures of Electronic Literature" (Morgantown, West Virginia, June 20–23, 2011; selections appeared in 2014 in *electronic book review*). One participant, Stephanie Boluk (2014), noticed how the "rhetoric of 'making' and 'doing' that informs the turn towards practice-based [literary] programs, pedagogies, and research" is consistent with Latour's disposition against critique. Luciana Gattass (2014), for her part, notices a similar tendency toward the replacement of close reading (or any reading at all) with "correlations, visualizations, maps, graphs, trees, and a general feeling of let-the-data-speak-for-itself." It begins to seem as though the antagonisms of class, culture, and (yes) critique that once were thought to be themselves constitutive of literary knowledge could be removed from disciplinary agendas altogether—so long as our written, spoken, and gestural objects are now countable and freely available to all, more or less.

Except that the data don't speak for themselves and Moretti (2000: 7), so far from denying the act of reading, can be said more accurately to have expanded our readerly practices so that we can "focus" (as he writes) not on the relatively few canonical works but rather "on units that are much smaller or much larger than the text: devices, themes, tropes—or genres and systems." Whether or not we go on elevating and analysing those select works that continue to be taught in classrooms (what for Moretti is an essentially religious holdover particularly prevalent in a never successfully secularized United States), the same conceptual skills can be applied to systems: Immanuel Wallerstein's (1974) world system was already in place when Moretti introduced the term "distant reading" in 2000, and more recently we have the system of keywords, tags, and taxonomies that increasingly occupy literary scholars as thousands of canonical and hundreds of thousands of noncanonical literary works are imported to databases.

While recognizing the ways that databases can help to distance ourselves "enough from distinct literary objects so as to be able to see the 'big picture,' " Gattass (2014) holds onto the notion that reading, even if it is now supplemented by "algorithmic reading," is still the central task of literary scholarship. Without disdaining the opportunity to build databases of her own, Boluk (2014) recommends a disposition that "resists the upgrade path and is unafraid to continue a process of painful self-reflection." In what follows, I too explore some salient cultural expressions of the present uncritical, nonevaluative, disposition. Even as our so-called social media can set up "barriers to collectivity" (Dean 2012: 120), the present uncritical and distanced relation to literary databases can restrict the circulation of our own work as scholars. As the compulsion to turn literature into data (and the "upgrade path") inspires a renewed commitment to critique in Gattass and Boluk, the exploitation by "free" media of our time, attention, and basic sociality rejuvenates older political models in, for example, Jodi Dean's *The Communist Horizon* (2012) and McKenzie Wark, "Digital Labor and the Anthropocene" (2017). The recording and recirculation of talk and text is endless and continuous; as are the demands on our attention (in societies where according to recent measurements, collectively a third of our "free time" on average is spent on phones; time that's not compensated by the commercial entities that mine our every keystroke; see "23 Days").[1] While conglomerates enjoy unprecedented profits from the economization, 24/7 geographical location, and

[1] Mobile Statistics. "23 Days a Year Spent on Your Phone."

value-neutral accumulation of data that we freely provide, an exploration of alternative knowledge economies specific to the profession of literature seems in order.

ACCUMULATION WITHOUT RECOGNITION

While the web is effectively infinite, an archive of web pages is now seven petabytes, or 7,000,000,000,000,000 bytes. The Internet Archive, a non-profit attempt to build a web library, has about 350 bn pages in its collection.

—*Zak (2013: 40)*

40 The Guardian Weekly 23.08.13

The internet in all its infinity

A crowdsourcing project to print out the web is filling up a gallery in Mexico City, reports Dan Zak

The world wide web began to show up by snail mail at the end of May. By the end of last month, 10 tonnes of pages from the internet had accumulated at a contemporary art gallery in Mexico City, sent by more than 600 people who bothered to print out portions of the web and postmark them.

"There's very little pornography, and I'm really surprised by that," says Pamela Echeverría, founder and director of Labor, the gallery hosting the exhibit. "I thought, 'Oh, my God, we're going to receive really nasty pictures.' So far, it hasn't happened."

Instead, after the 22 May announcement of its "crowdsourced project to literally print out the entire internet", the gallery received printouts of spam folders, bank statements, online diaries, news articles, 20 pages of the letter "A" repeated continuously, 500 pages of poetry created by erasing text extracted from websites, and all Mahler's scores.

The submissions are being read aloud by members of the public at a desk on a small platform in the gallery, where visitors are able to rifle through them until the show closes at the end of this month.

This prompts the cosmic question that follows all artwork in all forms from all eras: why?

The answer: to memorialise Aaron Swartz.

Another cosmic question: who?

The answer: Swartz (pictured below) was the 26-year-old internet prodigy and free-information activist who committed suicide in January while facing federal charges of computer hacking after his alleged theft of millions of documents from the academic database JSTOR.

Another question: how is Swartz honoured by the recitation of lyrics to every song that Prince recorded under the alter ego "Camille"?

The co-ordinator of Printing Out the Internet isn't sure if there's a direct correlation between tribute and tributee.

"My gesture is dedicated to and inspired by him," says Kenneth Goldsmith, the New York poet whom Echeverría enlisted to create a homage to Swartz. "Mine is a poetic gesture, a pataphysical gesture. His was a political gesture, a gesture of liberation. And I'm not doing this so that everybody can go and steal all the material on the internet. I actually want to use his gesture as a jumping-off point to begin to ponder much larger questions."

If such larger questions are "pataphysical" - meaning they, like their answers, are imaginary - are they even worth asking? More importantly, can this previous question about the larger questions be classified as "meta-pataphysical"? And if we found the answer to that question on the internet, how many pages would it take up when printed?

After initial discussion with Echeverría, Goldsmith wanted to exhibit a compendium of every online photo of actress Natalie Portman. Then he was smitten by an Iraqi-American artist's collection of every news article written about the war in Iraq; they were bound in 80 volumes comprising 2,000 pages each. Then, inspired by the magnitude

Wordplay ... Kenneth Goldsmith at his Printing Out the Internet exhibit Galería Labor

of Swartz's download, he asked himself, "Why not just print the whole internet?"

While the web is effectively infinite, an archive of web pages is now seven petabytes, or 7,000,000,000,000,000 bytes. The Internet Archive, a non-profit attempt to build a web library, has about 350bn pages in its collection, according to its founder, Brewster Kahle.

The size of these numbers implies that the exhibit's mission is destined for failure, which Goldsmith recognises and dismisses as irrelevant (this is pataphysics, remember?). His detractors, meanwhile, have taken issue with the mission itself. A small Change.org petition was drafted to needle Goldsmith about the resources required to produce and recycle paper and ink. On the blog of San Francisco's City Lights Booksellers and Publishers, poet Garrett Caples wrote that "nothing is being made available [in the project], only taken and destroyed, and nothing is being risked. Swartz is simply a glib talking point, because there's no relationship between 'what he liberated' and the arbitrary accumulation of printouts Goldsmith seeks to assemble".

Goldsmith scoffs at this reaction. "Nobody hollers about insane excesses in the art world, and its elitist and exclusive nature," he says. "This is an inclusive project."

That much is true. Brooklyn resident Logan K. Young, a fan of Goldsmith's, heard about the

project and the backlash, printed out 32 pages o Prince lyrics and mailed them to Mexico City. Fo this, he will be included in the list of contributor at the exhibit.

Why Prince? Because looking up lyrics was one c Young's first online habits after he acquired broad band. And what value does he see in contributing

"My life is on the internet," says Young, editor c Classicalite, a music website. "I'm behind a scree more than 12 hours a day. This gives a tactile qualit to an ethereal, intangible thing."

Goldsmith and Echeverría have a similar opin ion: printing out the web lends this whirling, fleet ing ultra-network a sense (however flimsy) of still ness and permanence, and it allows people t begin to process its inestimable dimen sions in a physical space.

Young, despite his enthusiasm for th exhibit, doesn't see much of a connec tion to the man who inspired it. Kahle the Internet Archive founder who knew and worked with Swartz, does.

The web is "such a valuable thing So how do you protect what' valuable? Well, you mak copies," Kahle says. "An going and printing it ou is kind of an interestin wacko project. It's innatel crowdsourced, and 'b us, for us'. And that is th nature of Aaron Swartz

FIGURE 23.1 At the Labor art gallery in Mexico City. Amidst the boxes, a sheet showing Aron Swartz is positioned to Goldsmith's right, at shoulder level.

Infinity never was a very productive concept for literature, not even if we can today electronically preserve and archive all and every literary work, in print or generated digitally, along with every thought a given work might evoke. The sheer accumulation of online writing is easily grasped and just as readily visualized in the numerous photos of Kenneth Goldsmith variously positioned—standing, arms akimbo; lounging with head in hands at the Galeria Labor in Mexico City—among stacked boxes overflowing with paper sent to him from all over the world for his exhibit "Printing Out the Internet" (POTI). The bare act of accumulation appears to equalize the archive much as Goldsmith's transcriptive art promotes all that is "uncreative" (the artist's self-description) and indiscriminate in contemporary discourse—for example, the New York City area weather report, transcribed over some months and some hundred pages in *The Weather* (2005); the Godard-inspired tracking shot of *Traffic* (2007; referencing the 1968 film, *Weekend*); and the complete transcript of the longest nine-inning Major League Baseball game on record, in *Sports* (2008). In the photo published in the *Guardian Weekly*, however, among all the papers there is one showing Aron Swartz that belies the anti-intentionality of Goldsmith's prior projects: Swartz is there, next to the artist's right shoulder, but this photo is not visible in any of the POTI reviews and photos I happened to find on the Internet circa September 2013.

"My gesture is dedicated to and inspired by him," says Goldsmith. "Mine is a poetic gesture, a pataphysical gesture. His was a political gesture of liberation" (cited in Zak 2013: 40). Goldsmith doesn't mention who exactly was liberated, and from what, by the downloading and potential circulation of 3 million scholarly articles. Nor does he mention the *content* of the downloads, except to criticize Swartz for not being "conceptual enough" in ordering his selection of files for downloading. Though opinions differ concerning Swartz's intentions, one fact that is uncontroversial (yet almost never mentioned) is that the articles selected for downloading were not from any (or all) academic journals but from one journal in particular: the seventeenth-century *Philosophical Transactions* (of the Royal Society of London), which was not just another academic journal, and neither was it "just an old journal"; it was (as Janneke Adema informed Goldsmith publicly) "the world's *first* scientific journal." Furthermore, it "*established* the important principles of scientific priority and peer review." These principles "have become the central foundations of scientific journals ever since." Adema's comments are reported not in any of the mainstream accounts I've encountered but instead in an insightful blog post by Jeroen Nieuwland, "Staying True, Or, Why 'Printing Out the Internet' Does Not Honour Aaron Swartz."

Swartz could not have chosen a better set of documents to illustrate what it means to establish and maintain knowledge as a commons, and much of his career as a programmer (and fellow traveler with Tim Berners-Lee and Lawrence Lessig) was dedicated to retaining that early (and attainable) promise via the Internet. The Federal courts however were never interested in the political, scholarly, or subjective content of the stored academic documents, only in their proprietary nature. And the same can be said, unfortunately, of Goldsmith. Instead of looking at the material actually selected by Swartz for downloading, Goldsmith publicly dismisses them as "funny-looking long pieces of text"; although their varying lengths and inconsistent format meant only that the seventeenth-century papers were not yet subject to contemporary formatting standards. What falls out of Goldsmith's exhibit, as so often in works of visual art that turn on the materiality of written, typed, or scrolling texts, is any interest in the act of reading itself—and that runs counter to Swartz's own, evidently critical intention in selecting this particular, historically significant journal. Goldsmith might place in positions of visibility specific texts sent to him by particular friends or collaborators—and these may serve, like the Swartz photo, as tributes to, or at least plugs for, the work of one's professional cohort. But no viewer is likely ever to locate a text in the heap or discern (as Swartz did) a particular, recognized corpus among so many others whose material significance can only be experienced by being selected—and read. Instead we have our attention drawn to the shy, smiling image of one young man whose critical project is reduced and absorbed into Goldsmith's own: namely, a global circulation appropriate for these times of massive—though largely unreflective—accumulation and mining of textual data.

In some ways, we've always known how easy it would be, and how boring ultimately, simply to begin collecting everything that's ever been written and encountered (if not always read) by anyone anywhere in the world. One need only look a few decades back, to Jorge Luis Borges's "Library of Babel" and "Funes the Memorious," for an imagination of what Goldsmith *enacts*. The distance between Borges's postmodernist parables and Goldsmith's assemblage might be said to mark not a supplanting of the previous literary era but rather the side-stepping of literary reflection and periodization altogether. Ireneo Funes, in the Borges (1962: 60) story, is "known for certain peculiarities such as avoiding contact with people and always knowing what time it was, like a clock." Funes, moreover, remembers his own acts of remembering: "not only every leaf of every tree of every wood, but also every one of the times he had perceived or imagined it" (65). His condition, which set in only after a fall from a horse had paralyzed him physically at the age of nineteen, is paralyzing in another sense: it keeps Funes from acting on the materiality of what he preserves in memory; keeps him immobile while at the same time opening a realm of detail unavailable to our usual awareness: which is "blind, deaf, addlebrained, absent-minded" (63)—but affectively oriented and, unlike Funes, alive to meanings).

Like Goldsmith's printout, Funes's internalized accumulation precludes thought: "To think is to forget differences, generalize, make abstractions," Borges asserts (1962: 66). Forgetting nothing, Funes is capable of learning a language in the time it takes to read a dictionary; he constructs an original numerical system that he never writes down, "since anything he ever thought of once, he knows will never be lost to him" (64). But neither will the data he holds in memory ever be communicated to anyone else. The content of Goldsmith's printout, by contrast, where everything ever written down or uploaded to the Internet has been preserved, in principle, needs *never to be known* by anyone, not even to Goldsmith himself. Even as Funes has in his head "more memories than all mankind has probably had since the world has been the world" (64), those memories are no more available to us for recirculation (and reflection) than the record Goldsmith presents. Accumulation in itself replaces any need for *knowing*; and the content of our archive, it would appear, has no need to be *shared*. In this respect it is significant that it just so happens that Funes will die of "congestion of the lungs"; "I remember him," Borges's narrator reflects at the start of the story, but immediately he adds, parenthetically: "(I have no right to utter this sacred verb, only one man on earth had that right and he is dead)."

Historically, as Borges well knows, literary treatments of a culture's productive power are concerned not with material extensibility per se but with acts of reflection, dialogue, and contact through written words across cultures, geographical distances, and institutional and national borders. Goethe's "world literature," for example, and Marx's variation on the concept or even Moretti's "distant reading" are clearly products of contemporary discourse networks. To be operative in the eighteenth and nineteenth centuries, these networks required the passing of selected works of textual and dramatic writing among individual minds using available means of exchange, that then change over time. Goethe's sense of "a common world literature transcending national limits" was a recognition of new modes of cultural "traffic," not least between the French public who celebrated his dramatic work and his native Germany, which had not. Marx also takes up a multinational, infrastructural development in his equally well-known characterization of a "world literature" that would "arise" out of the "impossibility" of one-sided, nationalist, and local literatures (see Prendergast 2004: 2; Hoesel-Uhling 2004; Moretti 2000).

Another way of redirecting the idea of cultural production away from the numerical toward more cognitive and conceptual realms has been the literary conceit of the sublime. From Longinus to Fredric Jameson, the infinite itself (a part of what Thomas Weiskel [1976], following Kant identifies as the "mathematical sublime") is less important than the mind's ability to grasp infinity *as a concept* and so to separate oneself from the (always finite) perception of an accumulation. Ever since Longinus (first century AD), this reflective dimension is what distinguishes the feeling of sublime "uplift"; but it's more than just that. Reflection is what carries a listener (or, later, a reader) not exclusively to visionary heights but more pertinently to *imaginative projections into the mind of another*. In such moments, Longinus (1907: 55) says, it's as if the mind is "filled with joy and vaunting, as though it had itself produced what it has heard."

The sublime is a way, when confronting our human limits, to make that recognition itself a part of our understanding, whether we confront a natural setting or more recent, technologically mediated environments that run beyond our abilities cognitively to "map" their workings and influencing. Here we approach a distinctly modern, "technological sublime" whose tendency is precisely to displace the traditional, cognitive dimension of experience that can carry a listener or reader to heights of joy and the mysterious, high standards "which are imaged within us" (Longinus 1907: 83). Identified by Jameson in his classic essay on "Postmodernism, or the Cultural Logic of Late Capitalism" (1984) and elaborated at book length in my own *Postmodern Sublime* (1995), this belated, technological mode can be seen as both a challenge to traditional intersubjectivity (achieved mostly through linguistic means) and a reformulation of the sublime moment as we recognize ways that linguistic consciousness has always been a very small portion of cognition. The technological, and by extension the computational, algorithmic, and curatorial capacities of digital technology can offer a corollary to the dimensions of unconscious experience that environ our reflective experience and communicative encounters. But the correlation can only take us so far, as cognitive science suggests—since our unconscious, mental capacities are organic, not digital, and the affective elements (including a feeling of elevation that the sublime gestures toward) cannot be represented by or reduced to computational technology.

Where things get interesting for literature, arguably where literariness itself enters, has always been when the mind reflects on its own, and our senses' inability to grasp the infinite—even as we manage to name the concept and so overcome a sheer accumulation.

THE PUBLISHING EVENT

There was a time when I thought that the public life of an essay begins with journal publication. My sense is that the situation is quite different today. Inclusion in JSTOR, as mentioned above, feels more like the end of something, because the comments and criticisms an article can generate from colleagues who heard different versions, at conferences and on Web sites or in editorial correspondence where ideas were worked out and talked through at various stages of composition, is nowhere visible alongside most published versions. Nor is it likely that the texts and critical arguments an author may cite, or citations and critical engagements the article may have initiated, will be available in the particular site of an article's storage. For most of the citations in an essay collected in JSTOR or Project Muse, you need to exit the site and either locate referenced books in a library or bookstore or search elsewhere on the Internet (a task that the scholars or curators are not likely to undertake, since the results of this tracking cannot be duplicated by scholars or curators coming later). Access to the stored article itself assumes that a reader belongs to an institution that has a subscription to the Johns Hopkins site, or that she reaches the essay by searching explicitly on a title or keyword. That assumption is acceptable when accessing materials in support of preset tasks (e.g., promotion, tenure, and hiring) but it is a real block when one is in the process of researching and writing, which in my case is done increasingly online in a seamless process of enfolding sites and collecting citations from numerous Web resources. (It does not help, once an essay is found, if it is presented in the ubiquitous PDF format that disallows clipping and pasting: this is one small but telling indication of the overprotection of documents and tacit discouragement of citation.)

In "Electronic Literature as World Literature" (2010), I argue that the conversation around works was as much as anything what qualified a work as being authentically a "world fiction." The colloquy between Goethe and his French supporters, in spoken conversations, reviews, audience reactions, and the felt celebrity that surrounds the production of a play in the eighteenth century may or may not be available today; I am not a specialist in this era, but I suspect the majority of such context in past centuries is lost to textual scholarship. It needn't be lost today, not when so much of the reaction surrounding a work is generated on digital platforms and hence save-able, and shareable directly and immediately without taking heed of national or geographical borders (though not so often shareable, as of yet, among scholarly databases that are not yet connected through search engines designed for specific fields of study). That worldly dimension of current literary practice, one would think, ought to be facilitated as a matter of course by those working within current media. And this would extend also to works of literary criticism, where contention and the exchange of competing interpretations and evaluations constitute the life of a literary work, whether performative, narrative, or critical.

That such conversations need to be transnational and multilingual, as the great debates in literary theory always have been, is a criterion that should be possible to reproduce in a more robust way for an emerging world literary practice in networked media. But presentation in academic journals, in which double-blind peer review is the predominant measure of worthiness, mostly leaves out that robust, written responsiveness. Focusing on the isolated article might well serve a credentialing purpose: so long as one's peers on editorial boards have read and commented on an essay, committees for tenure and promotion needn't look further for evidence of influence—and hence there is little motivation for journal readers to register public responses to books or articles in the medium where these appear, by an audience that is not preselected.

That sort of unsponsored response is more likely to be generated not in formal review processes but rather during live presentations at conferences or during focused, online gatherings. Indeed, the presence of conversational threads on Twitter is cited as a defining feature of the current rise of the digital humanities. But not a tweet is to be seen, once a presentation is published in the majority of peer-reviewed journals in print.[2] We've gotten used to separating publication from the collegial conversations that lead to and away from printed works; that is one of many essentially cultural (not inherently professional or scholarly) habits that is under pressure when so much of what we say in conferences and on blogs is now textual, and hence recoverable. Yet there is no real reason why, in current networks, comments on any one literary work in combination with networked keywords, tags, and taxonomies cannot lead readers organically to other, related works, essays, and commentaries: that is the single most distinctive affordance of new media for the construction of a literary field, because it is a kind of record that can allow readers a sense of the life of a scholarly essay as it comes into being and generates dialogue, fosters consensus, and provokes contention.

But the identifiers, the keywords, tags, and taxonomies—these need to be devised by scholars no less than the critical works themselves. To the extent that we ourselves draft abstracts and select keywords for an essay, some of this may happen already, but such free tagging does little to ensure that our essay will be brought into contact with others writing on the same topic, who happened to choose other keywords. To avoid the limits of free tagging, we need also to link our databases to search engines designed for literary reading (or, better, build engines of our own[3]) if our work is not to be lost within powerful search engines devised with other, nonliterary connections in mind.

ALGORITHMIC ACCOLADES

Matt Kirschenbaum perceives how online conversations concurrent with a work's presentation can help to describe the newness of new media, when he notes, for example, the way Twitter has become one of the driving forces that brings digital humanists together and aware of themselves as part of a movement. Twitter, Kirschenbaum (2012: 417) writes, "more than any other technology or platform is—at the very moment when digital humanities is achieving its institutional apotheosis—the backchannel and professional grapevine for hundreds of people who self-identify as digital humanists."

When conversation (like the Internet, an "essentially infinite" commodity) is made tangible in this way, there's a tendency for people to be interested not so much in the topic of conversation as in the social activity itself—"who follows who, who friends who, who retweets who, and who links to what" (Kirschenbaum 2012: 421). An obvious danger here is not just that a greater portion of our textual activity is given to power relations

---

[2] My coeditors and I at *electronic book review* (www.electronicbookreview.com) (*ebr*) consistently draft glosses that link specifically to relevant scholarly conversations, and we compile not "issues" but ongoing "gatherings" of essays on a given topic that we identify both within the journal site and at "outbound" sites that feature essays on a given topic—one that a particular editor or group of editors have identified as consequential. These labor-intensive editorial processes are precisely the kind of conceptual connections that define scholarship and that cannot be duplicated through keyword and metadata searches only. At the same time, the Consortium on Electronic Literature (www.cellproject.net), which *ebr* is a part of, ensures that specifically literary keywords will bring up a goodly portion of relevant essays in automatic searches.

[3] Here again, the Consortium on Electronic Literature (www.cellproject.org) is designed with such literary search capability specifically in mind. And members who participate in the collective search are asked regularly to avoid free tagging and suggest new terms for common use, as they arise in the course of one's research.

(taking time away from the description of literary works and sharing of ideas about works). That is how reputations have always been generated, not least during the formation of the "star system" of literary theory in the 1980s, which Kirschenbaum references (424–5; see also Shumway 1997). But an even greater danger of such commodifiable community formation in the era of Twitter, Kirschenbaum (2012: 424) notes, is that the "mappings" of influence "are self-perpetuating, so that those who are currently identified as influential users in a given topic space will accumulate even more followers as a result of their visibility through the 'Who to Follow' feature, which will in turn contribute to reinforcing their ranking by the algorithm."

As in Goldsmith's Internet printout, a universal equality quickly becomes something quite different, not eliminating social and professional hierarchies but reinforcing them through programming and viral networking. That kind of self-perpetuation and reduction of collegial attention to talking points from a few notables (against the dim background of many, many PowerPoint presentations) can certainly endanger what one would want to see as the distributed conversation around a worldwide diversity of literary writing emerging with, and accessible on, the Web. That is to say, the tendencies inherent in self-perpetuating social media can reproduce the tendency in print to promote works by virtue of established reputations or positioning within a quasi-canon. The works that get read by many are those that have been read by many, and this can be more homogenizing in its effects than what could be achieved by the most hegemonic publishing conglomerate, or through the undying great books that are taught (to the tests, not to the students) in schools in the United States.

Kirschenbaum's comments reveal how Twitter, while encouraging diffuse commentary and a widespread registering of opinions, can end up excluding *criticism*: the interpretation of cited texts and the articulation of positions that require defense at some length, or support in the form of extended arguments by interlocutors. The self-perpetuating logic Kirschenbaum so astutely observes in Twitter conversations, like the "apotheosis" of the digital humanities that opens his essay, have less to do with any newly emerging conceptual framework for literary or cultural study or alternative sets of literary objects for appreciation, and more with a group of scholars coming to self-consciousness as participating in *a new mode of assembling and talking about literary objects as objects, not as works to be read.* Any cognitive or critical engagement is, literally, immaterial when we can have such a focused, largely unreflective presentation of how much written work, or how many adherents to, say, "digital humanities," "deconstruction," or "new historicism" are present at a given time; how many unread books from past centuries are at last scanned, collected, and their words mined (but still largely unread); or how many times an article or passage is cited, and so on.

Franco Moretti's coinage "distant reading," and the numerous data mining projects with which he has become associated, marks a fitting conclusion to the problem he noted less than a decade ago in his previous incarnation as a Comparative Literature scholar mildly guilt ridden over having focused so exclusively on a small subset of European literatures. In Moretti's (2000: 54) estimation, the field referenced by the term "world literature" amounted to a "modest intellectual enterprise fundamentally limited to Western Europe, and mostly revolving around the river Rhine (German philologists working on French literature). Not much more." Moretti's essay appeared before his own efforts through databases (and a two-volume edited encyclopedia on the novel [five volumes in the original Italian] (2007 [2001–2003]) to expand the availability of literary works beyond the confines of Western scholarship. In the essay, Moretti recognized that accumulation alone would not correct the fundamental problem: "there are thirty thousand nineteenth-century British novels out there, forty, fifty, sixty thousand—no one really knows, no one has read them, no one ever will. And then there are French novels, Chinese, Argentinian, American" (55). Reading more, surely, is all to the good but "the sheer enormity of the task makes it clear that world literature cannot be literature, bigger; what we are already doing, just more of it. It has to be different. The *categories* have to be different" (ibid.; emphasis in the original).

If it is impossible for any person or impracticable for any group to read the tens of thousands of unread novels worldwide, it certainly is possible now—easy, even, and fundable—to scan these pages and include them in databases. In this way, verbal tendencies within textual objects, rather than achieved masterpieces, might be revealed and the development of the novel—for example, its shifting word frequencies and turns of phrasing, its regional variations—can be contextualized within the textual discourse we have newly available from pre-digital times. That is the altogether new context we have—and the early results are promising—for developing through literary databases a fuller picture of a large cross-section of published authors through the ages who may have addressed common issues outside the field of canonical works and perhaps inflected and disturbed the canon in surprising ways. I say "published authors," not "people," because unlike today, only published authors in previous centuries could leave a textual trace in the vicinity of their canonical cousins. To track down letters by members of the public who might comment on a work or even employ tropes and techniques they had learned, consciously or unconsciously, from reading novels would require pre-screening a wide body of dispersed writings and in each case evaluating them humanly. The algorithms, word frequencies, keyword and semantic searches, taken alone, are as empty of meaning as the numerical system devised by Borges's Funes the Memorious, who assigns a different verbal identifier to every number from one to two hundred thousand and something, but never thinks of digits, tens, hundreds, thousands, hundreds of thousands, or millions, and so on. The capacity to name and hold in memory every individual number, like our capacity to access and identify each and every word in a newly digitized corpus, *conveys nothing*: not until we "forget differences, generalize, make abstractions" (Borges 2000: 66); and not until we identify and if necessary *change* the categories (as Moretti understood already in 2000) will we have the capacity to reform literary studies as our texts relocate to databases.

The semantic fields observable in novels published in industrial cities of nineteenth-century England can be shown, for example, to have become over time harder, less abstract, and less constrained than semantic fields observed in "evangelical, gothic, and village novels" that emerged in "traditional, smaller, rural communities" (Liu 2013: 413). These are impressive, data-driven results but are they attainable without conceptual scholarly intervention? Hardly. Alan Liu, by closely reading the procedure of Moretti's Stanford colleagues, Ryan Heuser and Long Le Khac, shows that nothing more, or less, than a conventional articulation of a scholarly program for study is needed to tease out meanings through current mining practice. The formation of meaningful "word cohorts" in the above referenced novels, for example, required of the cutting-edge digital scholars nothing other than their looking up sets of synonyms in a traditional print thesaurus—specifically, the *Historical Thesaurus of the Oxford English Dictionary* (2009), whose taxonomies had been assembled and categorized using paper slips, submitted by hundreds of readers working for, or more often with, the University of Glasgow from 1965 onward.

What Liu offers, by closely observing the actual transition in these early-career digital humanities scholars from data gathering to discursivity, is consistent with arguments by Luciana Gattass and Stephanie Boluk cited at the start of this chapter for a renewed commitment to close reading, credentialing, and critique. As I've been arguing throughout this chapter, moreover, once we recognize that reading, critiquing, and conversing have always been elements of a cognitive or communicative economy and a worldly literary practice, scholars will be better positioned to design databases of their own, capable of reinforcing those traditional commitments. At the same time, we should not ignore powerful and currently much more prevalent tendencies whose accumulations deflect any real sharing of knowledge. After Liu's collegial, corrective intervention in the debate on digital humanities, there is more to say about this telling turn to earlier forms of data collection—which model a true reciprocity among authors and readers, scholars, and amateur collectors that is very much at risk in digital collections sponsored by corporate and commercial concerns. As John Cayley (2013a) suggests in his account of the current move not simply to collect, but to *capture* data, the problem of searchability has implications for long-standing assumptions about what it is we're accessing and searching—whether it is indeed the literary commons scholars in the West have long assumed to be our heritage, or, if the literary field is not already being enclosed, differently but no less clearly than the way our essays are enclosed in institutional databases. Cayley turns his attention not just to literary texts and scholarly essays but to the very words that writers of all descriptions offer up to corporate search engines every time we agree (knowingly or not) to the terms of use that are required by our enrolment in Google and Facebook (his two primary examples). "The underlying transactions and the relationships" devolved in such contractual relations are very different, Cayley (2013a) notes, "from any that arise when you or I take down our dictionary to look up a word." Granted, our ability to move from text to text, and from "friend" to "friend," is never interrupted: unlike JSTOR, Google lets readers search freely and without subscription among its more than 30 million scanned books. Browsing the books gathered by Google is encouraged. Reading them is another matter, however, since pages are purposely left out when the book is called up on our screen. The books, remarkably, were gathered mostly from local US libraries whose collections had been freely available to visitors for borrowing. (Regarding conditions of labor, and the strict separation between workers on the Google campus and the scanning facility in Southern California, see Wilson [2009–11] and the introduction to this volume.)

The gathering, channeling, and filtering of what has been, until now, a literary commons, changes our very relation "to language and literature" (Cayley 2013b), since now our ability to range among words and works is contractual, "made unilaterally explicit by contemporary service providers.". Whether or not academic and institutional collections follow the current transactional model, or make data open access, could well determine whether mind-to-mind, reader-to-reader trafficking is kept open as a potential or is reduced to a set of controlled possibilities.

A key difference between past and present discourse and publication networks is that the conversation that takes place in a wider range of media, both print and born digital, can today be monitored, and studied, at the time when the conversation is produced and in the medium that scholars have literally at hand while participating in live presentations. These materials, unlike the circulation of papers in previous eras, mostly course through commercial devices and browser interfaces. Much of that is again ephemeral for the ones who enter thoughts into textual networks, but the omnipresence of networked communications in databases (which retain posts regardless of the intention of senders and receivers) suggests a real opportunity for scholarship: namely, by designing our own open access databases, we generate materials for a continuous and developing investigation into cultural contexts and conversations that might otherwise be lost to us, as they have been largely lost to other lives in times past. At the very least, we'd want comments attached to a work gathered in a literary database to have been read with roughly the level of editorial attention given to a You Tube thread, as presented for official videos approved by musicians and artists. At best, we'd want something with the same level of personal attention as the Glasgow professors presumably gave to those who submitted entries for eventual presentation in the Oxford thesaurus.

It is all too easy, given the barriers to constructing quasi-independent databases, for scholars, editors, and curators to pass over this opportunity to expand our present field of activity and to instead allow others to build and maintain our databases for us. Private enterprises and academic consortia have not been slow to enter (and potentially overtake) the field: "Why are We not Boycotting Academia.edu?," the topic of a University of Coventry conference organized by Gary Hall and Janneka Adema in December 2015, is a question we should all be asking ourselves, especially when we learn that this particular $17.7m, venture capital funded organization servicing over 40 million subscribers is not affiliated with any university or library, despite its "edu" designation.[4] We have yet to devise the academic version of Wikipedia featuring (in John Cayley's [2013b] words) "the attributed, time-stamped editorial event on platform . . . for the future of scholarly knowledge building and dissemination." We have yet to see the widespread, "active and sympathetic engagement of commensurate institutions such as universities and publishing houses" in such crowdsourced endeavors.

One would hope, as Wikipedia has achieved a presence comparable to Google and Facebook, that these and other open access literary databases might achieve a presence comparable to that of JSTOR, SAGE books, and The Internet Archive (where Heuser and LeKach found their sample of nineteenth-century novels). If interoperability and searchability among scholarly databases cannot be achieved, it would be a serious missed opportunity during a time when scholarship and teaching is certainly expanding but in ways that create a significant class divide within our ranks. Here is the kind of decontextualized posting we can look forward to, more and more often, as the proportion of itinerant, untenured scholars and schoolteachers increases vis-à-vis tenured scholars working in protected enclosures. I chose, among sites presently on my dashboard, a top-level comment from one Nora (2009), who awarded one of a maximum five stars to the Prendergast volume I've been citing throughout this essay, *Debating World Literature*:

> Awful. Bordering on useless. There are solid and interesting notions in the essays I looked over, but they are so obnoxiously presented and so clearly hell-bent on limiting the discourse to the contributors and their half-dozen academic acquaintances, high-fiving each other for their academic prowess in department offices, that it's hardly worth the trouble for me or my students. Sometimes academic essays like these

[4] See Rodgers (2017).

> are over the readers' heads. And sometimes, as in this case, they're pompous and not conducive to a larger conversation.

In literary databases and consortia I myself access regularly—such as the Electronic Literature Directory, the French-language *NT2*, the Australian Open Humanities Press, the Portuguese Po.Ex, or the European ELMCIP Knowledge Base whose contributors focus on identifying literary qualities and opening critical conversations around born-digital scholarship and writing—the practice has been to extend the model of peer review beyond tenured scholars (and those aspiring to tenure) to the students themselves, whether graduate or undergraduate, that many of us (like Nora, presumably) encounter from year to year, and day by day. That expansion of a properly critical and cognitive engagement might, on the one hand, create a new object of study available for public reflection by readers and scholars at all levels. Rather than encourage an object-oriented expression of likes and dislikes, accounting for migrations to or from a given field or practice, we had better channel the vast demand for written expression toward databases designed to measure and mediate literary values. A critical cognitive orientation also has the considerable merit, on the other hand, of creating an audience for literature among our own students (and theirs, since most of my students and perhaps many of Nora's will become teachers themselves at various levels from grade school to grad school—and some might even become lifelong readers).

CURRENT TRADE IN KNOWLEDGE PRODUCTION

Patrik Svensson (2012: 45) sees "the digital humanities" not (like Kirschenbaum) as a school or cultural discourse on a par with deconstruction or New Historicism but rather as "a trading zone or meeting place" closer to the world literature model that has inspired Moretti (1996 [1994]) and myself in "Electronic Literature as World Literature"). Svensson (2012: 46), for his part, finds in digital humanities a way of extending the conceptual and reflective level of conversations and exchange beyond the bounds of a literary discipline or program toward cultural exchanges that promise again to infuse the literary into a wide range of performative and artistic practices, no less than academic ones:

> I am suggesting an alternative model based on the digital humanities as a meeting place, innovation hub, and trading zone (see McCarty [2005] for an earlier discussion of humanities computing as a methodology-oriented trading zone). Such a notion highlights some qualities of the digital humanities—including its commitment to interdisciplinary work and deep collaboration—that could attract individuals both inside and outside the tent with an interest in the digital humanities.

"Arguably," Svensson continues, "such bridge building and the bringing together of epistemic traditions is not optimally done from the position of discipline or department" (46). And that is a key difference from the "school" movement of deconstruction mentioned by Kirschenbaum (which has been intensely, and, by virtue of its linguistic self-consciousness, exclusively academic, with a primary residence in Departments of English and Comparative Literature). The trajectory of a digital project like Svensson's that is keyed to performance and arts practice could presumably include Creative Writing also, which, like the digital humanities, rose up largely in opposition to "theory." There are of course creative practitioners trained in both, Creative Writing and theory. Ralph M. Berry and Curtis White and many others in the FC2 collective are prominent examples, but that group (which emerged in the 1970s under Ronald Sukenick's leadership, precisely as an alternative to the rise of corporate publishing) is the exception that proves the rule of separation among disciplinary activities.

In principle, writers who have developed their craft largely by writing for and among writers should be well positioned, given their semi-autonomous and robust academic location, to collaborate with colleagues in computer science, communications, media, and library studies in the creation of born-digital literary projects that circulate online by design from the moment they're placed in a database. And there are by now established para-institutional supports, such as the Electronic Literature Collections (Volumes 1, 2, and 3 as of the year 2017) that circulate as independent venues for reading and credentialing. A noncommercial alternative to print economies is entirely possible, though no less precarious than networks for scholarly production that we've been considering so far. But Creative Writing offers a cautionary tale as well, since its rise arguably (in the United States at least) reinforced academic specialization rather than multiplied chances for transdisciplinary collaboration and exchange of knowledge. And this is so even if the specialty was (in the case of writing) relocated from the commercial publishing sphere to an academic address where entrepreneurial expressive practices—the forging of an individual style or voice and the cultural construction of the accomplished author of "original" works of fiction and poetry—could be developed largely *without* entering into conversations with what was going on in other departments, or in older literary practices.[5]

By contrast with both "theory" of the 1970s and 1980s and Creative Writing's more widespread, exceptional institutional location in the past two or three decades in the United States, the digital humanities emerge in a "liminal" position that Svensson (2012: 47) sees not "as a problem but rather an important quality." Instead of being either an academic discipline or an "industrial sector in its own right" (47; citing Matt Ratto and Robert Ree 2010), the digital humanities are to play "a mediating role, one that is uniquely facilitated by institutions of higher education with our intersectional meeting places." Svensson's and McCarty's model is attractive in that it carries the meta level of a worldly literary practice and potential (one hesitates to say, "tradition"[6]) into the fully technologized present and also (in McCarty's case) brings to literature the same conceptual framework that had emerged powerfully during the rise of cybernetics in the 1970s. That consolidation was itself a second-generation outgrowth of meetings of the Cybernetics group at the Macy Conference from 1946 to 1953 that included social scientists such as Talcott Parsons and cultural anthropologists such as Gregory Bateson and Margaret Mead, a neurophysiologist and psychiatrist such as Warren McCullough, an advisor to wartime governments such as Norbert Wiener (who coined the term "cybernetics"), and the mathematician John von Neumann, no less than representatives from the first generation of computer scientists.

That institutional background is potentially as suggestive a model for transdisciplinary conversation in the digital humanities, as is any single concept in the literary field which informs (for example) the work of "cybertextual formalists" like Espen Aarseth and

[5] Mark McGurl (2011) tells the story of the emergence of Creative Writing that followed the flight to Universities of authors who made their careers in the predominantly New York City based publishing world, at a time when serious literature and the "mid-list novel" could still be subsidized by best sellers.

[6] The hesitation is lessened if, with Svensson (2012: 46), we speak not of a literary tradition but rather of multiple "epistemic traditions" that can join literature and science not in terms of common disciplinary objects or outcomes, but in terms of a converging ethos, ontology, or epistemological self-understanding.

Markku Eskelinen, the media-specific approach to electronic literature by N. Katherine Hayles (who explored the Macy conferences in her earlier work on posthumanism), and the "craft-based encounter with computational resources" that Stuart Moulthrop (2013) uses to describe his own practice as an author of literary works that employ and divert media affordances and contend with coded structures. The latter formulation informs my own position respecting the location of literature as such within databases—which in my view is the place where transactions among literature and the sciences can best be realized and made visible to readers and scholars alike, whether or not they come to the practice with programming skills.

Along with the necessary phases of para-institutional collaboration, we have also an important conceptual shift in cybernetic thought away from informatics toward more cognitive exchanges. This too might apply to Svensson's and McCarty's conception of the digital humanities as a trading zone for knowledge in the literary arts and sciences. Bruce Clarke (2011) articulates the shift away from a "first-order" cybernetics that had to do with problems of feedback between a system and its environment to a more self-referential, "second-order cybernetics" that takes into account the observer's influence on the systems under observation. Where first-order, first-generation cybernetics still regarded the "environment" as a source of information whose retrieval and analysis could help control a system's development, second-order approaches saw the feedback loop differently. Feedback happened not so much between a system and the environment as between one system and another, across boundaries that each partially shared and all could only partially understand. Indeed, in practice much of our environment remains unrecognizable within a system's operating framework, and not many researchers who attain fluency in one field can be expected to reach the same level of fluency in another. What's key here is not the dissolution of functionally differentiated disciplines into so many data sets. Rather, what disciplines have in common, and what can bring together diverse practices in scholarship and the arts is a common respect for peer review (and recognition of disciplinary autonomy) that is now extended to both scientific and literary, artistic and communicative, creative and curatorial works and projects generated all together in many disciplines and multiple media.

Understood this way, a second-order cybernetic approach emerges not so much as a model of control as one of self-reflection based on an individual's encounter with self-contained others, an encounter in which certain operations are shared, some reinforced and others corrected, and other things are left unknown, remaining part of the unexplored environment and keeping open the possibility for other concepts, other approaches to the materials at hand. The disentanglement between informatics and cognition is key in the distinction between a first- and second-order cybernetics. The distinction pointed to by Clarke could be productively carried over into the digital humanities. Projects for "mining" literary texts, for example, would not end at a statistical analysis of patterns and frequency among verbal and alphabetical objects, but would move into areas of reflection and evaluation—not least one's understanding of oneself as a participant in an emerging field. Steps toward that self-understanding seem to me to be present in the analyses cited so far by Kirschenbaum and Svensson, though what needs to be "traded" is not just data from different fields but knowledge. And what the field of literature knows that other fields and practices might not know so well are the ways that minds join together (and also conflict with one another) in communicative networks and creative communities.

A NEW NEW DEAL FOR CAPITALISM AND A RENEWED AESTHETIC FOR DIGITAL WRITING

While the literary database enables one to register media specificity and verbal content in each work referenced, making all that available for forensic purposes, the discussion around works is that which enables its recognition *as literature*, a literature that is plausibly global in the sense that it can be accessed across databases in an Internet that is itself sustained and reproduced through the collective efforts of lawmakers, engineers, readers, and occasionally scholars in touch with one another, learning from one another or, better still, productively misunderstanding one another. (Recall David Damrosch's [2003: 33] criterion for world literature as that which *gains in translation*—presumably because one must fill in untranslatable content from one language, or field, with formulations that re-form or defamiliarize one's own language or discipline.)

In closing, I want to suggest a way of designating literary work emerging in new media that is distinct from earlier categorizations. The difference between literary arts in new media and those carried over from our legacy texts in print can be thought of as homologous to the difference between a conventional capitalist economy grounded in assembly line work and commodity production on the one hand, and on the other a cognitive capitalism "based on the cooperative labor of human brains joined together in networks by means of computers" (Boutang 2011 [2008]: 57). That such an economy, described by Yann Moulier Boutang, is itself as yet potential (and could also be "stillborn" after the 2008 upheavals and uneven recovery) only increases its suggestiveness as an appropriate context for an equally uncertain global literary development. Not least, excessive protections on intellectual property rights and the enclosure of gathered content clearly threaten the interoperability among databases and circulation of ideas on which a literary and economic development in new media must depend.

Boutang (2011 [2008]: 4) looks not to cultural aspects of the new capitalism per se, but rather its creation of forms of wealth that depend "on the time of life and on the superabundance of knowledge." He looks to models of production not grounded in re-industrialization but in a revaluation of ecological resources—whose long-standing, largely irreplaceable value can only be recognized and communicated through the same immaterial labor and collective intelligence we have assembling currently in databases worldwide. Environmental resources (so-called) typically have been registered by economists as "externalities" and then ignored; their "scarcity" has been a measure of market value only, not the value of accumulations that often exceed human lifetimes (the work of forestation over hundred-year stretches, e.g., or photosynthesis through millennia in the production of coal, and so forth). These processes external to human and industrial labor obviously can no longer be ignored today, and yet their value (and our real needs) still have to be determined discursively, protected through laws and enforced by governments. The laws, as much as the cultivation of "science and knowledge," are themselves "quasi-public goods" (30) under development, and part of that development means imparting sufficient authority to science so that what we know *through science* can influence our laws and our collective consumption.

With Boutang (2011 [2008]: 190), we can distinguish a next-generation capitalism grounded in cognitive transactions that are recordable and so capable of being revalued and distinguished from earlier, industrial figurations of the real:

> The appeal to a "real" economy has to take into account both material pollination (ecology) and immaterial pollination (the economy of the mind)[7] . . . A new New Deal, which contented itself with "re-launching" the old material economy, would offer a bad combination of the military/petroleum complexes, the automobile corporations and the ultraconservative reflexes of rentiers and retirees.

To Boutang's list of outdated valuations from "the old material economy" (144) we might add the perpetuation of the old ideal of the self-standing, original author-genius whose works (and livelihood, and contribution to the wealth of the publishing industry or institutions of higher education) need to be protected by copyright. If copyright continues to be hardened, however, we will have blocked off not only a running conversation among current works generated primarily in new media environments, but also our seamless access to a print heritage that developed mostly in the nineteenth century to encourage and protect original authorship, not collaborative networked literary creation. (It might be noted that even our heritage texts, many of them, are cut off from circulation in new media through the 120-year protective period given to print works in the United States and extended to the patentability of software, despite the efforts of Laurence Lessig who took this "Millennium Law" of 1998 to the Supreme Court [Boutang 2011 (2008): 107]). What amounts to the same thing—a hardening of authorial protections—is the determination of "fair use" on a case-by-case basis, which tends to give the right to define what's "fair" to any established corporate body (a publisher, a for-profit academic conglomerate) that is capable of bringing a charge against users possessing fewer resources, not least scholars citing passages in texts (without which activity, naturally, there can be no literary scholarship to speak of).

Is there a way, then, to carve out a space for the immaterial transfers that have defined specifically scholarly exchanges, other than the (necessary but not sufficient) preservation of the present, diminishing academic gift economy (among the tenured professoriate)? A common critique of cognitive capitalism is that mind-to-mind exchanges do not find a necessary traction in material production such that value is able to accrue: like neoliberal capitalism generally, the circulation of cognitive capital can all too easily become "less a strategy for production than for the transfer of wealth to the rich" (Dean 2012: 122–3). Since finance in a capitalist society always will be first among informational and communicative exchanges, the accrual of money will always come before any recognized growth in knowledge—and this is true of JSTOR, whose justification for its business model is that online institutional subscriptions provide a revenue stream that is no longer maintained by individual and library subscriptions to particular print publications, most of them supported already by universities (before the journal content housed in libraries is gathered online at the Project Muse site). The various editors gathered at "The Scholarly Journal," a panel at the January 2011 MLA in Boston, agreed that subscriptions to the online publication are now the primary way that scholarly publication is subsidized. But in recent

---

[7] Pollination can be understood in the words of Nigel Thrift in his foreword to *Cognitive Capitalism* "as the production and management of publics and their opinions, which act both as supply and as demand—fuel and means of combustion" (Boutang 2011 [2008]: viii).

years, libraries and university presses themselves have with greater frequency started cancelling subscriptions to JSTOR and have begun archiving scholarly works and subsidizing peer-reviewed publication by scholars in their home institutions directly.[8] And many scholars, rather than send publications to a for-profit corporation such as Academia.edu, are tending more often to send only the Web address only to the place at their home institution where publications are being assembled.[9]

The advantage to such a semi-autonomous, open access arrangement with one's home institution is that scholars accessing these sites can easily move from one database to another, so that essays in journals can be cited at the same moment when a new essay is being drafted. Open access obviates the problem (in firewalled sites such as JSTOR) of keeping academic journals and articles unconnected to one another, so that the chance for cross-pollination among reading minds has little chance of being observed or created at the moment when it matters—namely, when scholarly works are being written, and read.

However they're supported, what economic value academic essays may have is referential, and it derives from the hundreds of years of cultural capital accumulated in a corpus of literary works (the objects of study) kept in circulation by classroom use primarily. For Roland Barthes in the 1970s, the creation of a literary canon was already tautological: "Literature is what gets taught." And as we've seen, the tautological, once installed in databases, tends to recirculate in ever reinforcing patterns: the works that are taught are taught again, even as those scholars who are cited are cited again and again.

Fortunately, these previously established values are renewable endlessly and the canonical books, poetry, and essay collections can go on being "mined" indefinitely, unlike accruals of geological wealth over periods extending much longer than the time of their present extraction by humans. But what's needed, if the classics are ever to have a wider circulation (a thought that troubled Ezra Pound's sleep), is for the conversations, precisely by the Bartheses and Pounds of our own time, to enter into circulation along with vetted comments by students, teachers, and what might still become a general audience cultivated within but not restricted to institutions of higher education. But for this to happen, the "audience" of students and nonprofessional readers needs to be brought into the networks, not as consumers offering "reviews" of the works studied (and of us, their professors!), but rather as interested aspirants and outsiders, whose comments are given due editorial consideration. Otherwise what we'll have will be little more than an extension of commercial interests into academia.

And what about works that our own technoculture is producing at the present moment? What might such an accrual look like in a cognitive literary economy? The

[8] The University of Bergen, for example, has stopped paying subscription fees "and has redirected . . . funding to an Open Access fund," as Scott Rettberg told me in our interview of December 2016 (published in spring 2017 in the *American Book Review* special issue, "Corporate Fictions," copublished by *electronic book review*). Another "subvention model" was discussed by Rettberg, in which he and Sandy Baldwin paid a few thousand dollars (for example) to have their open access book published with the University of West Virginia Press: "We published it in our database and we published it in the University database and it's free for anyone to read and download and they can also buy the book and that's fine."

[9] The relocation of scholarly publications at the place where scholars are employed is discussed by Johannah Rodgers in her essay "Academia.edu: A Site of Many Questions" (also published in the 2017 "Corporate Fictions" gathering in ebr and ABR). Another project involving publication made freely available by a number of higher education institutions supporting accredited university presses has been coordinated by Doug Armato of the University of Minnesota Press. The beta version, called Manifold, went live in April 2017 at http://staging.manifoldapp.org/. The full release is expected in early Spring 2018.

"quasi-objects" that scholarship produces, arguably, are its selection of works for continued attention (or studied negligence) in various media for various reasons. But for this to happen, as Moretti (2000: 55) rightly asserts, the "categories" need to change and that means a studied and systematic description of literal categorizing elements that define a database construction, namely: tags and keywords and taxonomies that allow readers to collect numerous works into some recognizable genre or collective praxis. Our taxonomies, essentially, become the "quasi-objects" that belong to scholarship, and that is what we can convey to non-scholars in an extended cognitive economy. But the hesitancy in current media environments to evaluate anything at all, consistent with the otherwise admirable tendency to include all and everything in our funded databases, obscures this still operational objective for the formation of a literary and scholarly field.

It has been my contention in this chapter that a cognitive literary economy, while by no means inevitable, conceivably can take hold within current communicative contexts. One might cite, for example, the "new media object" that Lev Manovich (2001: 37) defines "as one or more interfaces to a multimedia database." The project Manovich calls "cultural transcoding" (20), in which non-computational activities become infused by forms, practices, and ideas from information technology, can happen at the level of database construction. In fact, such transcoding is happening apace, as part of the knowledge economy. For literary academia to enter that economy in significant ways, it is advisable for scholars to do more than extend computational activities *to* the work—its words, its letters, its paratexts. We need also to locate ourselves and extend our own social, intellectual, and creative activities within networks of our own making (rather than offering these things up to exploitation by corporate networks in which value is reduced to likes and dislikes that can be used for purposes of mining and marketing, not the creation of broad-based literary and cultural valuations).

Under such conditions, a renewal of literary studies would happen not in this or that school or institutional location, but in the space of the database itself, understood as a meeting place for those conversations as well as the collaborative creation of new literary works. Stuart Moulthrop (2013) suggests a way for writers to inflect Manovich's definition toward the literary, namely: *the work of citational composition may be regarded as itself the creation of an interface to a database.* That kind of citational composition, in which any of the "essentially infinite" works now circulating through the Internet can at any time be enfolded into a current composition, be it creative or analytical, is what counts as a kind of wealth accruing to our work as literary authors. That is the "quasi-object," what can accrue only from close reading and critique—the very practices that Moretti and Latour identified as having receded in recent times. Our practices have rather relocated, within the very systems and networks that Moretti and Latour have studied and to some extent construct within their own burgeoning academic networks. These activities ought not to be abandoned nor their print traces merely scanned and stored in archives whose enclosures are if anything more strict than the bounded book format. Critique and close reading needn't be reimagined or reasserted so much as relocated to current environments where the ability to count, and account for, citations is a bonus, not a diversion from more properly scholarly and creative concerns.

There does not need to be an "electronic literature" within or outside the tent of the digital humanities, any more than the idea of a world literature was ever more than a potential, a direction sensed in the course of conversations among authors. To stay with our French point of reference (they were the source of Goethe's great hopes, anyway), we might follow Antoine Compagnon and call this citational writing at the interface, "réécriture." Whatever the term we settle on, we are clearly in a moment of recombination, not originality. But we've yet to see, really, what might come of the recombinant practices that a truly interoperable consortium of literary databases could enable. An earlier inability to link one literary work to another, and one reader to another through an unimpeded cultural "traffic," arguably is what held back the development, in print, of a "world literature" worthy of the name. Let us not make the same mistake at a time when the literary database can offer much more than the present, largely noncommunicating accumulation of written work in protected enclosures.

SOURCES CITED

"23 Days a Year Spent on Your Phone." http://www.mobilestatistics.com/mobile-news/23-days-a-year-spent-on-your-phone.aspx. Accessed January 11, 2017.

Boluk, Stephanie. "Just Humanities." *electronic book review* (2014), http://www.electronicbookreview.com/thread/electropoetics/JH. Accessed May 1, 2014.

Borges, Jorge Luis. "Funes the Memorious." In *Labyrinths*, translated by James B. Irby, edited by Donald A. Yates and James E. Irby. New York: New Directions, 1962 [1942], pp. 59–66.

Boutang, Yann Moulier. *Cognitive Capitalism*. Cambridge: Polity Press, 2012 [2008].

Cayley, John. "Pentameters: Toward the Dissolution of Certain *Vectoralist* Relations." *Amodern* 2: Network Relations (2013a), http://amodern.net/article/pentameters-toward-the-dissolution-of-certain-vectoralist-relations/. Accessed January 11, 2017.

Cayley, John. "Terms of Reference & Vectoralist Transgressions: Situating Certain Literary Transactions over Networked Services." *Amodern* 2: Network Archaeology (2013b), http://amodern.net/article/terms-of-reference-vectoralist-transgressions/. Accessed January 11, 2017.

Clarke, Bruce. "Systems Theory." In *The Routledge Companion to Literature and Science*, edited by Bruce Clarke and Manuela Rossini. London: Routledge, 2011, pp. 214–25.

Damrosch, David. *What Is World Literature?* Princeton: Princeton University Press, 2003.

Dean, Jodi. *The Communist Horizon*. London: Verso, 2012.

Gattass, Luciana. "Digital Humanities in Practice: Contextualizing the Brazilian Electronic Literature Collection." *electronic book review* (2014), http://www.electronicbookreview.com/thread/electropoetics/piecing. Accessed January 11, 2017.

Goldsmith, Kenneth. "Printing Out the Internet" [exhibition]. LABOR, Mexico City, July 26–August 30, 2013.

Hayles, N. Katherine. "Print Is Flat, Code Is Deep: The Importance of Media-Specific Analysis." *Poetics Today*, vol. 25, no. 1 (2004): 67–90.

Hoesel-Uhling, Stefan. "The Directions of Goethe's *Weltliteratur*." In *Debating World Literature*, edited by Christopher Prendergast. London: Verso, 2004, pp. 26–53.

Jameson, Fredric. "Postmodernism, or the Cultural Logic of Late Capitalism." *New Left Review*, vol. 1 (1984): 146, 53–92.

Kirschenbaum, Matt. "Digital Humanities As / Is a Tactical Term." In *Debates in the Digital Humanities*, edited by Matthew K. Gold. Minneapolis: University of Minnesota Press, 2012, pp. 415–28.

Latour, Bruno. "Why Has Critique Run out of Steam? From Matters of Fact to Matters of Concern." *Critical Inquiry*, vol. 30, no. 2 (2004): 225–48.

Liu, Alan. "The Meaning of the Digital Humanities." *PMLA*, vol. 128, no. 2 (2013): 409–23.
Longinus. *Longinus: On the Sublime*. Translated by W. Rhys Roberts. 2nd edition. Cambridge: Cambridge University Press, 1907.
Manovich, Lev. *The Language of New Media*. Cambridge: MIT Press, 2001.
McCarty, Willard. *Humanities Computing*. London: Palgrave, 2005.
McGurl, Mark. *The Program Era: Postwar Fiction and the Rise of Creative Writing*. Cambridge: Harvard University Press, 2011.
Moretti, Franco. *Modern Epic: The World-System from Goethe to García Márquez*. Translated by Quinton Hoare. London: Verso, 1996 [1994].
Moretti, Franco. "Conjectures on World Literature." *New Left Review*, vol. 1 (2000): 54–68.
Moretti, Franco, ed. *The Novel*. 2 Volumes. Princeton: Princeton University Press, 2007 [2001–2003].
Moulthrop, Stuart. "Lift this End: Electronic Literature in a Blue Light" (2013), http://www.electronicbookreview.com/thread/electropoetics/blue%20light. Accessed January 1, 2017. Reprinted as Chapter 4 in this volume.
Nieuwland, Jeroen. "Staying True, Or, Why 'Printing Out the Internet' Does Not Honour Aaron Swartz" (August 18, 2013). https://vlakitineraries.wordpress.com/2015/04/20/reprinting-of-staying-true-a-tribute-to-aaron-swartz-thanx-equus-thanx-litteraria-pragensia/. Accessed January 11, 2017.
"Nora." (2009) [reviewer's post], http://www.goodreads.com/book/show/278333.Debating_World_Literature. Accessed January 11, 2017.
Prendergast, Christopher, ed. *Debating World Literature*. London: Verso, 2004.
Rodgers, Johannah. "Academia.edu: A Site of Many Questions." *American Book Review/electronic book review* (2017).
Shumway, David R. "The Star System in Literary Studies." *PMLA*, vol. 112, no. 1 (1997): 85–100.
Svensson, Patrik. "Beyond the Big Tent." In *Debates in the Digital Humanities*, edited by Matthew K. Gold. Minneapolis: University of Minnesota Press, 2012, pp. 36–49.
Tabbi, Joseph. "Electronic Literature as World Literature." *Poetics Today*, vol. 31, no. 1 (2010): 1–15.
Tabbi, Joseph. *Postmodern Sublime: Technology and Personal Identity from Mailer to Cyberpunk*. Ithaca, NY: Cornell University Press, 1995.
Tabbi, Joseph, and Jeffrey Di Leo, eds. *Corporate Fictions* [special issue of *American Book Review*, coproduced with *ebr*] (Spring 2017), www.electronicbookreview.com.
Traffic. Dir. Steven Soderbergh. US: Bedford Falls Productions, 2000.
Wallerstein, Immanuel. *The Modern World-System I: Capitalist Agriculture and the Origins of the European World-Economy in the Sixteenth Century*. New York: Academic Press, 1974.
Wark, McKenzie. "Digital Labor and the Anthropocene." *DIS Magazine* (2017), http://dismagazine.com/disillusioned/discussion-disillusioned/70983/mckenzie-wark-digital-labor-and-the-anthropocene/. Accessed January 11, 2017.
Weiskel, Thomas. *The Romantic Sublime: Studies in the Structure and Psychology of Transcendence*. Baltimore: Johns Hopkins University Press, 1976.
Wilson, Andrew. "Workers Leaving the Googleplex" [video] (2009–11), http://www.andrewnormanwilson.com/WorkersGoogleplex.html. Accessed January 11, 2016.
Zak, Dan. "The Internet in All Its Infinity." *The Guardian Weekly*, August 23, 2013, 40.

AN ANNOTATED BIBLIOGRAPHY FOR ELECTRONIC LITERATURE

Presented here are short takes on signal works of scholarship in the field of electronic literature, broadly defined and occasionally contested by graduate students and postgrads situated in literary arts programs that are both transdisciplinary and multinational. The titles referenced are not meant to be definitive; that will be the object of a larger presentation in the Electronic Literature Directory where these entries will be co-published (www.eliterature.org). What we intend here is to convey a sense of what early career scholars are currently reading; what those selections say about where the field has been, and what these researchers are now saying about where the field might, or might not be heading.

Opposing tendencies cited by Dani Spinosa, for example, gesture toward one particular, field defining, argument that remains open: "While recent curatorial work has endeavoured to change the way we view the ephemerality of the digital text," Spinosa writes, her chosen author, "[Chris] Funkhouser maintains that this ephemerality is a hallmark of the digital project in general." Robert Cashin Ryan for his part discerns in the largely pre-digital work of Deleuze and Guattari, "something crucial to understanding the past and present of the [e-lit] field," something that is as much "intermedial" as it is transdisciplinary. By casting past literary practices as diverse "poetic modes," at least one crossover print/digital scholar, Marjorie Perloff, "opens up the possibility of a continuum between pre-digital appropriative writing and digital literary manipulation of pre-existing works and texts." So writes Liliana Vasques, in a remark that might be said to characterize continuities (and contentions) found throughout the present volume. Trevor Strunk notes how Espen Aarseth's *Cybertext* does not just name a "new" field but offers an opportunity that joins audiences and authors in a "nontrivial" traversal across multiple media that might bypass the narrative expectations of traditional novelistic fiction and a predisposed literary theory.

By gathering a cross-section of viable e-lit scholarship, we can hope to at least share our scholarly concerns with curators and potential supporters of generatively digital literary arts. The bibliographic entries that follow address questions that are now under consideration among those who are entering a field whose emergence, and location (within or without academia, or perhaps more often in the fine and applied arts) is itself open to argument.

Joseph Tabbi

AARSETH, Espen. *Cybertext*. Baltimore: Johns Hopkins University Press, 1997.
AARSETH, Espen. "Genre Trouble." *Electronic Book Review*, May 21, 2004, http://www.electronicbookreview.com/thread/firstperson/vigilant. Accessed February 19, 2017.

Espen Aarseth's 1997 *Cybertext* is, at least in part, a systematic approach to writing about electronic, nonlinear, nontraditional literature. Aarseth signals the broad, categorical quality of his analysis in his introductory chapter, which serves to answer critical concerns over his newly coined category of "ergodic" literature and the "cybertext." Ergodic literature, according to Aarseth, is writing in which a "nontrivial effort is required to allow the reader to traverse the text" (1), and in complementary fashion, a cybertext is "a machine for the production of variety of expression" (3). The problem, Aarseth goes on to explain, is that normative literary criticism is unwilling to recognize the difference between traditional linear narrative—for example, the novel—and these forms. Novelty is not the issue, as Aarseth identifies the *I-Ching* as the earliest ergodic text; the close reading practices rather imply "nontrivial effort" and "production of expression" in even the most traditional texts. So, with the introduction of Aarseth's new paradigm, traditional criticism must also be refigured. It seems, at first, to be an odd choice for Aarseth to focus on this kind of disciplinary fine-slicing in the first few pages of what is ostensibly a new history of the multilinear, electronic, or interactive novel, but in many ways *Cybertext* is predominantly and intentionally a corrective for scholarly approaches to ergodic literature. Aarseth is certainly committed to being a guide to "the whiter spaces—the current final frontiers—of textuality" (23), but he also sees *Cybertext* as an opportunity to correct the ways in which contemporary literary criticism is misreading these final frontiers through the frame of traditional narrative and textual analysis. And while this corrective impulse is at times mobilized through simple critiques, such as attacking the overuse of the term "interactive" in contemporary discourse, Aarseth also levels more serious accusations, arguing that "theories of literature have a powerful ability to co-opt new fields and fill theoretical vacuums, and in such a process of colonization, where the 'virgin territory' lacks theoretical defense, important perspectives and insights might be lost or at least overlooked" (19). If literary critical approaches to ergodic literature might be best understood by analogy to the horrors of colonialism, it is no surprise that Aarseth's "framework for a theory of cybertext or ergodic literature" is as much a rejection of contemporary literary orthodoxy as it is an original claim for a new kind of literary model as such (17).

Cybertext is, thereafter, reflective of the split purpose of its introduction, beginning with Aarseth's most effective argument for new textual practices in his second chapter on "Paradigms and Perspectives," which argues, among other claims, that the code that undergirds computer programs exists on "two or more levels," at the level of arbitrary linguistic signification and intentional practical purpose (40). In other words, since "cybernetic sign processes" function as functional nodes in a machine as well as more classically semiotic "surface expressions," the critic can no longer rely solely on the classical semiotic axiom that the signifier and signified are related arbitrarily in the sign when considering "computer games and other cyberworks" (ibid.).

Aarseth goes on to produce a positive account of these cyberworks in his third chapter, through an idiosyncratic empiricism, complete with full scientific method and graphed categorization of cybertext by typology, using "correspondence analysis" (60). This method, which "enables us to analyze categories and variables as well as objects [allows] us to link categories and objects," an effort that ostensibly permits Aarseth to determine his field of objects outside of material and textual red herrings like technological advancement or verbal ambiguity (60–1). Aarseth, however, uses these results to again return to a debate over the ways in which contemporary literary critical discourse approaches these texts, focusing in subsequent chapters on hypertext, adventure games, procedurally generated poetics, and multiuser dungeons (MUDs). Concluding with a meditation on the status of the reader, Aarseth ends his ambiguous and mercurial text with the aphoristic claim that, instead of coauthorship, what "interactive" cybertext has given us is "a perspective, a mode of perception" (180).

To end with this appeal to new perceptions matches Aarseth's later scholarship, including his back-and-forth discussion of his article "Genre Trouble" in *Electronic Book Review*, which picks up where the final few chapters of *Cybertext* left off, in trying to pin down the relationship between ergodic literature and the dynamics of play. And indeed, despite some datedness concerning the potential of the Internet and the availability of massive social gaming movements that reflects its publication at the verge of the Internet boom in 1997, *Cybertext* is an important if nebulous foray into the relationship of play and textuality. Ergodic literature, at its most paradigm-shifting, levels questions at both literary critical apparatuses and literature as such. Aarseth's first monograph is perhaps the first serious shot across the bow for this kind of challenge, and should be part of any serious canon of electronic literary criticism.

Trevor Strunk
DeSales University

#

BALDWIN, Sandy. *The Internet Unconscious: On the Subject of Electronic Literature*. Bloomsbury Academic, 2015, 187 pp. ISBN 978-1-62892-338-4.

The Internet Unconscious is, in Sandy Baldwin's own words, a reflection on "the problem of writing the net as the problem of literature" (23). Starting from the idea that everything on the Internet is code and inscription, Sandy Baldwin seeks a poetics of digital writing showing how concepts like *file* and *protocol* are not only technical but institutional mediations. *IP*, *TCP*, *traceroute*, file packages in transit: through the *ping* command which, like a sonar, confirms the existence of an*other* on the other side, Baldwin imagines the cartography of the network, with its territories and borders open or closed to our writing. If *ping* and *traceroute* tell the stories of their paths, are they texts? Although the notion of text implies an intersubjective field, Baldwin argues that "even if there is no sign of response, this lack is the signifier of the Other's response" (40). There is always an *I* and an*other* saturating the communication systems, and the text is the trace of all human activity on the network: "The discovery that the text is the product of continual logging and processing in my computer means I read towards an anonymous other, a structural other that I posit or project across the space of the net" (45). Although this imaginary overinvestment which reads any inscription as text does not invent the literary by itself, it participates in what constitutes electronic literature since the encounter between the literary and the digital "leads to the double play of literalization and imaginary overinvestment" (3).

"Writing the net": filling it with subjective speech acts mediated by a structure that is also made of writing, codes, protocols, phatic functions, permitted and forbidden spaces, and modes of inscription. Through a reflection on the CAPTCHA form, for instance, in which the user's reading and writing is exploited to review and authenticate the accuracy of algorithmic interpretation, Baldwin demonstrates how "we constantly enter into consensual relations with the opacity of a technical infrastructure" (58). From the constraining to the exploitation of our "writing the net" arise a series of political questions: in this regard see, for example, Matteo Pasquinelli (2009; 2010) on cognitive capitalism and the production of the commons, Tiziana Terranova (2000) on free work and the network centric production of value, or Alexander Galloway (2004) and the notion of protocological control. In a literary context, John Cayley reflected on these issues in works such as *How It Is in Common Tongues* (2012), "Pentameters toward the Dissolution of Certain Vectoralist Relations" (2013), or *The Listeners* (2015).

Baldwin deconstructs the Internet's administrative logic, highlighting the ways in which it pre-constitutes and constrains all digital writing, and points to its incompatibilities with the sphere of the literary: if literature is "the possibility of uncontrolled enunciation" (6), how can we produce the literary within the regulated space of the network? "But what if permission were a struggle? … To invent permission, what if this were the condition of digital poetics?" (63). With a poetic and oralizing expressiveness, and as synthetic as it is digressive, *The Internet Unconscious* is a humanist reflection on a posthuman subject: digital inscription as a post-writing, and its retro-action on the human. If the composite of algorithmic agencies that shapes the Internet and digital media conflicts with the authorial voice, preventing the literary; if the digital is a condition of contemporary culture and if culture is the rule whereas art is the exception, then literature remains insofar as the writer claims the un-encodable excess on this side of the interface.

Ana Marques daSilva
University of Coimbra, Portugal

#

CHANDRA, Vikram. *Geek Sublime: The Beauty of Code, the Code of Beauty*. Minneapolis: Graywolf Press, 2014.

On the surface, *Geek Sublime* sets out to examine the interpenetration of aesthetic metaphor and programming vernacular. This now common trend within the blogosphere is typified by a ranty post which went viral in 2014. Entitled *Programming Sucks*, the author of the blogpost rhapsodizes over "clean, beautiful designs, awe-inspiring in their aesthetic unity of purpose, economy, and strength" and exhorts:

> This file is Good Code. It has sensible and consistent names for functions and variables. It's concise. It doesn't do anything obviously stupid. It has never had to live in the wild, or answer to a sales team. It does exactly one, mundane, specific thing, and it does it well. It was written by a single person, and never touched by another. It reads like poetry written by someone over thirty. (Welch, Peter (2014), *Programming Sucks* (Still Drinking), available at https://www.stilldrinking.org/programming-sucks [accessed: December 1, 2016])

In enumerating the same seven or so features as Yukihiro "Matz" Matsumoto, the blogger—himself clearly an experienced and careworn programmer—reveals an unwritten consensus among programmers as to the features of beautiful code. Simplicity, brevity, the reusability born of familiarity and traditional control structures, balance, and discrete parts for easy debugging and agility: altogether the polar opposite of the "sloppy, duct-tape, … spaghetti code jungle[s]" created by patchy workarounds intended to optimize half-understood bugs in other programmers' code (Chandra 116). Above all, however, the thing must work and work robustly, and this is precisely the point upon which Western philosophies of Beauty—colored as they are by Enlightenment and Aestheticist notions of anti-utilitarianism and autonomy—call the concept of beautiful executable code into question.

But Chandra's analysis does not take the Western philosophical route. Instead, the reader is inducted into Sanskrit poetic conventions on the premise that the rule-constrained nature of Sanskrit makes it a human-only-language with uncanny resemblances to modern programming languages. Within this time-honored tradition, "Suggested Meaning" (i.e., that which is not apparent in either the denotative or the figurative content of poetic language) is the path to "Rasa" or the Sublimity derived from the phenomenology of consciousness and the savoring of stable emotions (103–104). Chandra's subsequent discussion of the impersonal nature of the reader's identification with the represented consciousness overlaps in places with Aristotelian notions of catharsis and Kantian disinterestedness; the book speaks to the Romantic desire for transcendence or, in Chandra's terms, "trans-personalization" (i.e., the memory of emotion devoid of pain or pleasure imperatives [137]); Chandra invokes the reader's judgment in discerning the Sublime and the Tiresian poet-seer in discerning the patterns between things which make the world amenable to suggestion.

Rasa is still richer than all of this, encompassing also the pleasure derived from the suggestion and apperception of separate properties/stable emotions in "one single act of cognition" (106). In Lyotardian terms, the meaning of Rasa is itself a simultaneity of properties that cannot be individually said. However, the Sanskrit tradition that Chandra borrows from has no tolerance for Lyotard's notion of the "inexpressible" as that event which language must bear witness to but can never quite express in full:

> As for the definition sometimes given of ineffability, that it is the appearance of a thing which cannot be referred to by a word for a mental construct ... this can[not] ... apply to the special virtues of poetry. (144; for Lyotard on the inexpressible, see *The Inhuman: Reflections on Time* [Stanford: Stanford University Press, 1991], 92–3)

In its disdain for the inexpressible, Sanskrit is more like a programming language than Chandra previously recognized. Code cannot be concerned with what is not expressed for it requires the detailed documentation of functions and variables to execute. This consideration of robustness is what leads Chandra finally to sever the analogy between programming and poetry and to cite four further factors which make the hybridization of the two registers in the blogosphere a "wrong-headed ... facile cross-cultural equivalenc[y]" (Chandra 191). It is mistaken for four reasons: first, the necessarily denotative and not suggestive nature of code; second, its logic-oriented processual and productive nature where affect is an entirely unintended and serendipitous side effect; third, the very different kinds of pain endured by the writer of poetry who must reach into the abyss of "nothingness now" (Lyotard 92) and pull something out, and the writer of code who must navigate the "ludic haze of the puzzle" (Chandra 192); fourth, and most importantly, the world-changing kinetic and material effects of code.

Considering a proprioceptive experience that is increasingly entrained and in many cases mediated by programmable devices, and a looming biological horizon where the fabric as well as the experience of embodiment can be coded, Chandra repositions the question. Future inquiries should focus less on whether programming and poetry are auratic equivalents and more on the "self that will be paying attention to the embodied code" (206). If it is a reincarnated Self that remembers being "itself but has been everything else" and can tap into (random access) memories, what will its experience of Beauty be and will it lend itself to Rasa? (ibid.). The Western philosophical tradition is still adjusting to the idea of the human-as-"else," synthetic or inorganic, which begs the question of how critical theory will complexify the interface with Sublimity.

Clara Chetcuti
University of Malta

#

COOVER, Robert. "On Reading 300 American Novels." *New York Times Book Review* (March 18, 1984): 1, 37–8.

Essay written the year Coover served as a reader for the PEN/Faulkner Awards, offered as "a defense of a judging bias" (1). While reading my own sample of 300 works of electronic literature that was being preserved, and periodically crawled, at archiveit.org, I've kept Coover's essay in mind, especially the criteria he used to distinguish settled and emerging literary genres in contemporary literature. A majority of submissions, Coover found, were "serious" or "priestly" works praised by critics "for their vision, style, commitment, sensibility, honesty, their 'intense realism.'" These are high-minded works that seek to "transcend mere storytelling, to reach past entertainment for its own sake into speculative and morally perplexing realms" (38). Many such works are the product of Creative Writing programs, and they can seem "somewhat homogenized" despite the conscious search for a personal "voice."

A few best sellers, mostly formulaic exercises in established genres, also made it to Coover's desk (and overflowed to his floor).

Ultimately, Coover supposes, "both of these voices are conservative. Both tend, through formal acquiescence, to extend the reign of the cultural establishment, even while challenging it now and then on the surface" (38). But occasionally, "rarely,"

> a third voice arises, radically at odds with the priestly and folk traditions alike, though often finding its materials in the latter and sharing with it a basic distrust of the establishment view of things. This voice typically rejects mere modifications in the evolving group mythos, further surface variations on sanctioned themes, and attacks instead the supporting structures themselves, the homologous forms. Whereupon something new enters the world—at least the world of literature, if not always the community beyond. (38)

In his later, more famous essay "The End of Books" (*New York Times Book Review*, June 21, 1992), Coover would carry this search for a literary mainstream beyond "the supporting structures" of genre, psychology, and cultural anthropology to the medial infrastructure itself. In current, electronic archives, both structures, the generic and the medial, are capable of being transformed concurrently—and those transformations (as much as the work itself) are what need to be tagged and traced.

Joseph Tabbi
University of Illinois at Chicago, Project in Digital Literary Arts and Humanities

#

DELEUZE, Gilles, and Felix Guattari. *What Is Philosophy?* Translated by Hugh Tomlinson and Graham Burchell. New York: Columbia University Press, 1994.

What Is Philosophy? is where Gilles Deleuze and Felix Guattari famously declare that the task of the philosopher is the creation of concepts. They state this point at first elliptically, writing, "The philosopher is the concept's friend; he is the potentiality of the concept"; and then more directly: "philosophy is the discipline that involves creating concepts" (5). What does it mean to create concepts, and why is this act of creation so precisely the domain of philosophy? The force of these questions can be found most readily in the book's title: Deleuze and Guattari want to demonstrate the specificity of philosophy in its relation to other, competing disciplines. In this spirit, the text is divided into two sections. The first, "Philosophy," and the second "Philosophy, Science, Logic, and Art." There is a certain proliferation effect at work here, where the beginning discussion of philosophy necessarily opens onto and expands into other domains.

In this light, the selection of *What Is Philosophy?* for this bibliography is fitting. Indeed, the field of electronic literature has always found Deleuze and Guattari's work generative, most notably their now-canonical discussion of the rhizome in *A Thousand Plateaus*. Indeed, foundational electronic literature journal *Rhizome* takes its name from Deleuze and Guattari's introductory chapter. But there is something else at work here, besides the decentered networks of the rhizome or the indiscernibility of becoming, something crucial to understanding the past and present of the field. In *What Is Philosophy?* Deleuze and Guattari attempt to hold together specificity and generality, disciplinary particularity, and more holistic bases of knowledge. This attempt is worth taking seriously because the field of electronic literature has always been necessarily interdisciplinary. Indeed, to append "electronic" to the field of literature suggests *something*—methodological, formal, or processual—different from our otherwise received understandings of the literary.

While never commenting on electronic literature as such, Deleuze and Guattari have always been thinkers of the machine, the machinic, the assemblage; and their final collaborative work signals a late style effort to engage explicitly with the changing face of the sciences, arts, and philosophy (see Aden Evens's essay in this volume for a more detailed account of the relationship between Deleuze and Guattari's category of the "machinic" and electronic literature more broadly). Today, this transdisciplinary, and also intermedial engagement remains an urgent task for scholars of digital and electronic literatures. Enumerating the challenges philosophy has faced, Deleuze and Guattari address directly the various themes and social energies that have animated electronic literature, writing of "the most shameful moment when computer science, marketing, design, and advertising, all the disciplines of communication, seized hold of the word *concept* itself and said: 'this is our concern, we are the creative ones, we are the *ideas men!*' " (10). Is this not a description of the advent of postmodernity—that epochal shift that marks the mingling of discipline with discipline, the collapse of high culture into low—to which electronic literature is so indebted?

Indeed, if *What Is Philosophy*? is important to debates in electronic literature this may be precisely because the book signals a confrontation between disciplinary identity and methodological practice. The force of *What Is Philosophy?* comes from Deleuze and Guattari's interest in producing both rigorous specificity and broad generality. It demonstrates—as Deleuze and Guattari always have—the subtle relations between art and science, philosophy and history, logic and sense; but it also marks the difficulty of articulating the singularity of each. Deleuze and Guattari urge us to consider the disciplinary question of what it means to research and write in a given field. The task for scholars of electronic literature, then, will be to think *with* these concepts, and produce ever new movements of thought and conceptual creations, toward ever more refined disciplinary understanding.

Robert Cashin Ryan
University of Illinois at Chicago, Project in Digital Literary Arts and Humanities

#

EMERSON, Lori. *Reading Writing Interfaces: From the Digital to the Bookbound.* Minneapolis: University of Minnesota Press, 2014.

Lori Emerson's book provides the reader with insights into just how much in contemporary practice needs to be overcome if we want to develop a "media poetics" at all adequate to the digital era. Emerson argues that nowadays the digital interface is becoming invisible. For all its convenience, the tendency toward media transparency is one that digital writers and artists do well to demystify. Largely understood as "user friendly," the digital interface has come to be known (and disseminated) through multitouch computing devices such as the iPhone and the iPad. Emerson sustains that the ubiquity of these interfaces (and the rhetoric associated with them) results in an enchantment that obscures more than clarifies the literary object. For all its commercial appeal, the user-friendly interface paradoxically renders the media inoperable, invisible, and imperceptible, hiding their modes of operation.

According to Emerson, "Not only does software obscure hardware, but interface obscures software" (2). That places users, for the most part, within a passive, and non-interventional position within a techno-deterministic environment. Emerson identifies what she terms *readingwriting* as the dominant practice found mainly in one particularly powerful interface: Google's search engine. *Readingwriting* takes place in the network and is, thus, algorithmic and converted in processes of datafication, where everything is indexed and trackable. Giving way to an invisible interplay between input and output, between the writer and the network, our contemporary reading and writing ecologies are informed and governed by automated feedback loops that intensify such magical effects of the interface: the interface hides its own structures and mechanisms, creating the illusion of ready-made and user-friendly creations. If on the one hand datafication and indexability brings the reader closer to literary objects, on the other hand it can also keep us away from literary processes.

As an argumentative structure, Emerson traces an archeological perspective in an alternative and nonlinear revisitation of the history of analog and digital literary interfaces, while providing close readings of several poetic productions that disrupt the ideology of the transparent interface. The book recovers the importance, for example, of concrete and "dirty" poetries that embody specific technologies of inscription and display, such as the typewriter. Accordingly, Emerson advocates the development of an experimental, "frictional media" that might open out to an insurgent hackerization of contemporary interfaces, questioning their functioning and making them visible. Emerson's proposal is one of experimenting with literature after and beyond the media—to consider and experience literature with a special attention paid to the eloquence and affordances of literary artifacts and their materialities. She argues that in digital culture this agency depends on software literacy, the way to convert the user-consumer into a user-producer. The book ends with a provocation—that "perhaps, the future of digital literature is *readingwriting* that is born of the network but lives offline—digital literature transformed into book bound *readingwriting* that performs and embodies its own frictional media archeological analysis" (184). Being a "dirty" and "non-magical interface," "because its particulars cannot be tracked, monitored, indexed, fed into an algorithm, and given back to us as a commodity" (184), the codex is, thus, perceived as a disruptive interface against the "googlization of everything" exposed by Emerson.

Emerson's interdisciplinary argumentation—reconciling media studies and literary studies—is convincing, and the "archaeological" methodology of analysis of intermedia recursions, which is not only methodological but epistemic and ontological, further clarifies the fundamental importance of the reflection on media, materiality, and interfaces in literary studies, while providing powerful insights and tools to literary and media researchers.

Sandra Bettencourt
University of Coimbra, Portugal

#

Fiktion<fiktion.cc>

Fiktion is a German-based electronic publishing platform that focuses on "German- and English-language literature that does not fit the current criteria of the market." Originally established after a 2013 writers' workshop at the Humboldt International Law Clinic—a collaboration fostered at least partly out of a mutual interest in copyright law—the site is intended to further the exploration of the opportunities of digital literacy and methods for encouraging concentration on digital literary objects begun at the workshop. The outcome is an exclusively digital publication platform made up of three principal components. The first is the publishing venture itself in which a literary advisory board made up of writers recommends manuscripts to be made available for free in a variety of digital formats through the fiktion.cc site. Literary advisors include a number of notable contemporary authors including Kenneth Goldsmith, Elfriede Jelineck, Tom McCarthy, and Ben Marcus. An experimental, open-source reading platform comprises the second component. The 'reader' is designed to optimize both concentration and the affordances of digitized text and is associated with at least two separate ongoing research projects at Freie Universität Berlin and the Institute for Book Studies at the Johannes Gutenberg University of Mainz. The former project, conducted by Dr. Arthur Jacobs, a professor of experimental and neurocognitive psychology, is associated with the continuing development of the *Fiktion* reader. The latter will be an analysis of data collected by the reader itself, and the results of the study will be presented on the site. Finally, *Fiktion* supports both its published works and its research in digital literacy offline via a series of events and workshops.

Thus far, the texts published through *Fiktion*—which it classifies as "books"—represent electronic literature only in the broadest sense. The project appears to be an attempt to marry the expansion of literacy long lauded by proponents of digital text with "deep attention" models of concentration more commonly associated with codex text. In this regard, and in spite of an obvious emphasis on cognitive science, *Fiktion* does appear blind to the shift in cognitive style from "deep attention"—closely associated with nineteenth-century bourgeois culture—to "hyper-attention" that accompanies digital literacy. Theorists such as Katherine Hayles and Bernard Stiegler have done much to articulate this shift and to discourage a purely reactionary approach to it. Hyper-attention, as characterized by

Hayles and Stiegler, lacks the focused attentiveness of deep attention, but it also affords a conceptual or ideational synthesis unachievable by deep attention's devotion to a single stimulus. In simpler terms, hyper-attention is a cognitive style characterized by its ability to process information from a variety of sources at one time, while deep attention is locked to a single source of information, such as a novel. As both Hayles and Stiegler point out, digital media in general and electronic literature in particular stand in a special relation to hyper-attention in their ability to harness its unique potential. And if these scholars are correct that hyper-attention is rapidly emerging as the dominant cognitive style, then in spite of an otherwise laudable work in alternative publishing and copyright law, *Fiktion*'s promotion of deep attention might appear retrograde.

Justin Raden
University of Illinois at Chicago, Project in Digital Literary Arts and Humanities

#

Flusseriana: An Intellectual Toolbox, edited by Siegfried Zielinski, Peter Weibel, with Daniel Irrgang. Minneapolis, MN: Univocal, 2015. 560 pages.

In 1987, the year in which Michael Joyce created *afternoon, a story*, and five years before William Gibson wrote *Agrippa (A Book of the Dead)*, Vilém Flusser (1920–91) composed *Die Schrift* (Writing), presented as the "first true-no-longer-a-book." The book was published by Immatrix Publications and was designed as a hybrid experimental edition, intended to be distributed in three formats: (1) a printed codex book; (2) a floppy disk; (3) a bulletin board system. The materiality and experimental approach of this project reflected the forward-looking attitude of Vilém Flusser, deeply embedded in the spirit of his time.

Both in his life and work, Flusser was an outsider, who consciously embraced an ambiguous, paradoxical, and provocative style of argumentation. In his texts, he introduced thought-provoking ideas to think about the network relation between humans, and between humans and machines (telematic society and cybernetics), in a digital-driven world. For Flusser, since our worldview is translated by language and media, the systemic digitization process, which we undergo today, produces cultural, economic, political, and ethical changes, by transforming linear texts into technical images. These technical images are generated, stored, and transmitted through opaque black boxes, that is, programmed apparatuses, such as photographic cameras. Consequently, different paradigms and forms of communication (networks, apparatuses, new media), agents (functionary, *homo ludens* ...), and modes of experience emerge from this background, based on the transmutation from print to digital, and from historical to post-historical consciousness. In order to not be alienated by apparatuses, humans have to rethink (to doubt) previous knowledge, and coin new information through creative acts that cannot be restricted to the parameters of the programs. Humans as an extension of apparatuses become a mere function of the machine. The responsibility of the artist or poet is to unshackle human beings, hacking the black box encoded by programmers. Flusserian utopia is an interactive network of free individuals. As a Jew in exile, who fled Prague during the Nazi occupation, Flusser particularly valued freedom, an ideal which he linked with the process of becoming human.

Flusseriana: An Intellectual Toolbox is, at the same time, a mechanism (a white "box") of negentropy and a threshold to access Flusser's life and work. This trilingual volume, edited by Siegfried Zielinski and Peter Weibl, with Daniel Irrgang, published in 2015 by Univocal, is an extension of the exhibition *Without Firm Ground—Vilém Flusser and the*

Arts (2015), held at the ZKM | Center for Art and Media Karlsruhe and at the Academy of the Arts, Berlin. The objectives of the work are not only to preserve and disseminate the philosophical legacy of Vilém Flusser, but also to encourage further academic investigation among scholars and students of Humanities, Arts, and Digital Studies. Presenting an encyclopedic structure, this reference book includes a montage of texts, alphabetically organized and written by Flusserian scholars. The montage sketches a map of a territory without firm ground: a virtual metaworld called "Flusseriana." Flusser's original ideas about translation, polysemy, etymology, and interlinguist association are given a conceptual and material expression in the cross-referencing and multilingual structure of this work. As Vilém Flusser was a permutator of theories and models, the meaning of a specific idea depends on the context. For this reason, *Flusseriana* is based on a paradoxical premise, that is, the representation of ambiguity within coherence, of fragmentation within the unity of the codex book. The composite dimension of the edition (dialogue between authors and languages) emphasizes the lack of wholeness. The glossary texts outline the key topics of that unstable world, presenting a critical analysis, which supports textual interpretation or functions as a threshold of immersion into the original sources. In this sense, the codex book as a collection of texts is a structured patchwork, operationalized, in its internal logic, according to an encyclopedic rationale. The book is divided into three sections: the first section is an introduction, entitled "Flusseriana—An Intellectual Toolbox"; the second part is the "Glossary texts"; the third part, "Appendix," is subdivided in four segments: "Vilém Flusser: A Biography," "Bibliography Vilém Flusser," "Works Cited," and "Authors." In short, *Flusseriana* is a comprehensive and critical edition, whose hypertextual structure provides a dynamic representation of Flusser's work as a complex web of concepts. This codex book—alphabetic code—is a node of an intellectual and dialogic network. The process of becoming within the web includes the abstraction of Flusser's work in post-alphabetic codes (the zero dimensionality of the universe of dots). The Flusser Archive (http://www.flusser-archive.org/) and the Arquivo Vilém Flusser São Paulo (http://www.arquivovilemflussersp.com.br/vilemflusser/) are contemporary digital apparitions of the process of becoming digital.

Samuel Teixeira
University of Coimbra, Portugal

#

C. T. Funkhouser, *Prehistoric Digital Poetry: An Archaeology of Forms, 1959–1995*. University of Alabama Press, 2007, 408pp, ISBN 978-0817354220.

A part of the Modern and Contemporary Poetics series edited by Charles Bernstein and Hank Lazer, C. T. Funkhouser's *Prehistoric Digital Poetry* traces a nonlinear genealogy of digital poetics, looking back at earlier formal experimentations in poetic form to demonstrate the interrelated histories of digital poetries and their print-based counterparts, so often considered separately. But, as the introduction to this now seminal work demonstrates, it is not only useful to understand that digital poetry has its roots in a history of the print-based avant-garde, it is also useful to consider that all poetry—especially experimental poetry—written in the past half-century is necessarily influenced by the radical potentials and McLuhanian obsolescences of technology and the technologization of poetics. Digital poetry, Funkhouser argues, was "mechanically and conceptually built in the decades *before* personal computers" (1). With roots in Dada, Oulipo, Black

Mountain, Projective Verse, concrete poetry, imagism, the French avant-garde, Futurism, and high modernism, digital poetry cannot be understood as separate from the print-based tradition. *Anything* written in the past fifty years or so is necessarily influenced by the technologization of this practice, from the typewriter to the personal computer to the current ubiquity of Internet network accessibility.

For Funkhouser, digital poetics explicitly works toward a depersonalization of poetry and a de-individualization of the author by virtue of the networked nature and often randomized elements of digital poetic production as well as the tendency toward active engagement of a readership. As Funkhouser notes, "Digital poems are more inclined toward abstraction and are largely depersonalized, especially as the media used in composition has become hybridized" (17). While these effects are not exclusive to digital poems, the processes of

> Randomization, patterning, and repetition of words, along with discursive leaps and quirky, unusual semantic connections, are almost always found in digital poetry, though sometimes these effects are so amplified that the poems would not be considered poetry by someone using traditional definitions. (18)

Additionally, digital poems are marked by instability and flux. As Funkhouser goes on to describe, "Digital poems do not exist in a fixed state" and thus "[a]ny work that exists in digital form is temporary" (21). Indeed, "[l]ongevity is not one of the genre's defining characteristics" (ibid.). While recent curatorial work has endeavored to change the way we view the ephemerality of the digital text, Funkhouser maintains that a conversational transitoriness could be a hallmark of the digital project in general. As an extension of this ephemerality, Funkhouser argues throughout that the digital poetic project is marked by a rhizomatic linking. "Digital poetry is not a fixed object," he explains, and "its circuitry perpetuates a conversation" (18). Embracing conversation and discursivity, digital poetry makes apparent the fact that "[p]oetry is a social constructed art form, always situated within other texts ... and extended by readers" (ibid.). From this point on, Funkhouser considers a wealth of diverse and complex poetic works ranging from Strachey's love letters and other early generative experiments to mainstays of electronic literature from the turn of the millennium such as Maria Mencia's *Birds Singing Other Birds' Songs* (2003) or Sandy Baldwin's "New Word Order" (2003).

As Baldwin's foreword to the text attests, Funkhouser's central argument throughout this book is not only that digital literatures and print-based literary experimentation of the past half-century have developed in tandem with the affordances of media technology—always pushing the limits of those affordances, of course—but also, and perhaps more importantly, that this media history is the product not of isolated creative genius, but rather "the actual practices of communities of writers and readers" (xviii). The chapters that follow demonstrate the communality, conversation, and collaboration that led to the experimentation that necessarily produced the vast corpus of digital poetics we have today.

Dani Spinosa
York University

#

GALLOWAY, Alexander R. *Laruelle: Against the Digital*. Minneapolis: University of Minnesota Press, 2014.

More an attempt to conscript Francois Laruelle in a reconceptualization of philosophical thought as "digital" than an exposition of Laruelle's thought, Galloway's book is useful for anyone interested in interrogating the concept of the digital in a broad sense. The book is broken into two sections: the first is an attempt to view what Laruelle calls the "standard model" of philosophy as a fundamentally digital endeavor, while the second traces the digital into areas of Laruelle's own work. The claims of the first section rest on a simple premise, that "philosophy is a digitization of the real because it is predicated on the one dividing into two" (12). In other words, all philosophical thinking is fundamentally binary as it takes the forms, variously, of differential being in classical thought, the Kantian distinction between the noumenal and phenomenal, Hegelian dialectics in which the one encounters its negation, the Heideggerian Being/being split, and so on, all of which follows necessarily from the decision to do philosophy.

Galloway opposes the digital with the analog, which concerns immanence and identity rather than the antinomies of relationality. Indeed, he aligns a number of concepts with this basic distinction between the digital and the analog, including mediacy and immediacy, difference and identity, metaphysics and immanence, and technology and science. Thinkers like Deleuze and Guattari, as well as Michel Henry approach the latter category of thought, but can't quite tarry with the analog. Laruelle, though "perhaps the only non-digital thinker we have" (xii), does not fit neatly into either category and is engaged in a parallel project he has termed non-philosophy. Non-philosophy is the science of philosophy or a boiling down of different modes of thought to their operant logic. It is also a declining of the decision to do philosophy.

As Martin Paul Eve has pointed out in his *ebr* review of Galloway's book (January 2016), attempts like this to redeploy Laruelle's thought can often result in simply reproducing his seemingly impenetrable rhetoric. Because of this, the second section, which takes on aspects of Laruelle's work more directly, is likely to be rebarbative to anyone not already familiar with his system. A notable exception is the chapter entitled "Computers" which takes up some underdeveloped themes in Gilles Deleuze's late work—such as the "control society" and the "superfold"—which have far-reaching implications for contemporary theoretical debates concerning media, cybernetics, and computing. Similarly, the chapter on "Art and Utopia" won't appear entirely alien to anyone interested in nonrepresentational aesthetics.

One somewhat surprising conclusion Galloway reaches, the last of a series of fourteen theses intercalated throughout the book, is a play on the Marxian maxim concerning the tendency of the rate of profit to fall, which he terms the "tendential fall in the rate of digitality"—that is, the entropic "deadening of distinction" that functions against the standard model's insistence on digitality (214, 215). Such a tendency suggests an under-explored tension, ripe for further examination, between this entropic decline and what Galloway identifies as the "pragmatic repercussions" of the philosophical insistence on presence, which "itself is a computational condition" (111).

Justin Raden
University of Illinois at Chicago, Project in Digital Literary Arts and Humanities

#

HAYLES, N. Katherine. "Traumas of Code." *Critical Inquiry*, Vol. 3, No. 1. Chicago: University of Chicago Press, 2007.

Katherine Hayles pares down the stack of high-level programming languages to expose a fundamental incompatibility between human-only language and machine code. Her first move is to construct a dualism between human-only language as a superficial, Saussurian filter through which humans rationalize the world around them, and machine code as a base-level shaper and mover which, despite being generative of the Real as we know it, is invisible to the human user because it has been seamlessly coopted into our somatic repertoires. Hayles recasts this impression of depth, which she débuted in an essay of 2004 ("Print Is Flat, Code Is Deep: The Importance of Media-Specific Analysis," *Poetics Today*, 25: 67–90), using the following analogy:

> Just as the unconscious surfaces through significant puns, slips, and metonymic splices, so the underlying code surfaces at these moments when the program makes decisions we have not consciously initiated ... as the unconscious is to the conscious, so computer code is to language ... in our computationally intensive culture, code is the unconscious of language. (137)

Even while capitalizing on the rich psychoanalytic overtones of the un/conscious duality, Hayles distances herself from the Freudian tradition. While her argument that our "extended cognitive system" has become habituated to the gestures required to operate programmable devices is sound (139), and while she can get away with the idea that technology pervades muscle memory (both conscious and dreaming) making it a product of its technologically determined times, she realizes that claiming some agential effect for code in "entraining" the way we move, cognize, and dream is sensationalist at best (140). So she modifies her terminology to speak of a "technological nonconscious" which flows beneath and mediates human-machine transactions within the online "cognisphere" (ibid.).

After locating code deep where human-only-language can never hope to venture, Hayles boldly recommends code as a viable language for tapping into the most secret parts of the human brain; namely, the unconscious, where the raw imprints of trauma reside. While a traumatic event cannot be articulated, at least in a manner that will capture the appropriate nuances of affect, it is amenable to simulation. Code thereby becomes a "transmission pathway" for the trauma to be voluntarily and consciously worked (or played) through, as opposed to it breaking through involuntarily and replaying on loop (142). Hayles goes on to reveal how this intuition has been evidenced in numerous cultural productions where the reciprocity between code and trauma is thematically delineated. She takes as her three case studies the print novel *Pattern Recognition* (William Gibson, 2003), the straight-to-DVD film *Avalon* (directed by Mamoru Oshii, 2001), and the electronic work *Dreamaphage* (Jason Nelson, 2003). (A more recent work which could prove equally amenable to Hayles's analysis is the literary/game app *Pry* by Samantha Gorman and Danny Cannizzaro [2015].)

Her main argument in this section is that cheerful depictions of code and its (a)effects are inversely proportional to the degree to which code has penetrated the forensic production and dissemination of the work. In all the works she studies, code undergoes a "doubled articulation" whereby it is the key to unlocking a thematic trauma and also constitutes a formal trauma, a breach in the fabric of narrative realism which brings with it the realization of what we are becoming: post-literary, post-linguistic, post-human.

Clara Chetcuti
University of Malta

#

JOYCE, Michael. *Of Two Minds: Hypertext, Pedagogy, and Poetics*. University of Michigan Press, 1995, 277pp, ISBN 0-472-09578-1.

A part of the Studies in Literature and Science series, hypertext pioneer Michael Joyce's *Of Two Minds* marks a significant initiatory experiment in hypertext theory and digital pedagogy. The form of this volume allows Joyce to engage with, and occasionally mimic, the salient features of his own hypertext fiction. The vast majority of the essays published in *Of Two Minds* had been, as the introduction neatly explains, published elsewhere as scholarly articles in literary journals and collections or entries in encyclopedias, presented as conference papers or keynote addresses, or were included as parts of email exchanges.

Joyce's work here is, of course, dated, considering that the volume is now twenty years old, but the multiple theses in this work prove continually valuable both as a historical perspective on hypertext and digital writing and as an important link between the print culture Joyce and others saw ending in the mid-1990s and the vast world of new media poetics that would follow. Resultantly, much of Joyce's work here tends to theorize hypertext against print-culture, but not uncritically. In fact, one of the primary theses of this collection is to recognize the ways that literature and literary scholarship has tended to see the traditions of print as natural, in his words "more god-given than Gutenbergian" (49). Part of the work of early hypertext writers, with Joyce at the helm, and hypertext theorists like George Landow (who is frequently cited throughout) is to reveal the extent to which the supposedly natural traditions (in both form and content) of a print-based literature are dependent on its technology. One literary use of the digital medium, then, is precisely to broaden those boundaries.

Joyce's understanding of the relative freedom of the reader of hypertext fiction occasionally verges on the utopian. He theorizes in the collection's first essay proper, "Hypertext and Hypermedia," that "hypertext readers not only choose the order of what they read but, in doing so, also alter its form by their choices" (19) and that they "in a very real sense write (or rewrite) hypertexts" through this reading practice (20). While Joyce himself, and other later scholars, would temper and revise this utopian view of a potential hypertext readership, its inclusion here is illuminating as to early hypertext scholarship's increasing interest in audience engagement. Similarly, Joyce throughout this work identifies the utopian impulse of other hypertext theorists, notably Landow, and works to avoid it where he identifies it. Thus, Joyce revisits this theorization of hypertext readership in "Siren Shapes: Exploratory and Constructive Hypertexts," by reconsidering Roland Barthes's figure of the "scriptor" (42) as a reader who makes significant interventions into a work.

In that same essay, Joyce outlines probably the clearest introduction of terminology in this work, the contrasting categories of "exploratory" and "constructive" hypertexts. Though these are touched on in other essays—namely, the aforementioned "Hypertext and Hypermedia" and "The Ends of Print Culture (a work in progress)," which was originally published in *Postmodern Culture*—the terms are most clearly outlined in "Siren Shapes." For Joyce, exploratory hypertexts are navigational devices that help the reader to find and collate information. Despite the fact that the reader constructs their own reading by choosing what sources to access, they remain as an audience with some distance from the text and the jobs of reader and of author remain distinct. In constructive hypertexts, the reader can actively link between and among texts rather than simply following predetermined pathways, thus creating new links. The distinction between "exploratory" and "constructive" hypertext demonstrates, for Joyce, the pedagogical possibilities of hypertext to map more traditional, linear narratives and to construct new and variant narratives and reading practices. They also work to engage a poststructural philosophy of literature that still permeates the work, particularly via gestures to Deleuze and Guattari, Cixous, and Kristeva throughout.

Dani Spinosa
York University, Toronto

#

LATOUR, Bruno. "Why Has Critique Run out of Steam?" *Critical Inquiry*, Vol. 30, No. 2 (January 1, 2004): 225–48.

Bruno Latour's provocative statement reads like a call to arms, hammering out urgency with every line. Latour immediately launches his proposal with the discomfiting and confrontational language of war—and the primary question is one of tactics. Have we, as scholars and professional critics, been ineffectually launching our missiles of critique at misjudged or decoy targets? Are the tactics inadequate to the task at hand? Have we simply been misled by, or tricked into, hollowed-out habits which have "outlived their usefulness" (229)? He points to shifts in the struggles to be addressed, fought, engaged with, or resisted. Critical tactics, he observes, have all too easily lent themselves to co-option by "enemies." The fault, moreover, lies not with those who turn such tactics to their own conservative ends, but within critique itself, which, by failing to adjust to change, has left itself open to just such a repurposing. The piece delivers an accusation and call for reevaluation which spares no one. Rather than endeavoring to distinguish the different uses of the critical arsenal, Latour takes the altogether more devastating approach of highlighting the troubling underlying similarities between, for example, conspiracy theories and the standard critiques of ideology.

"Critique has not been critical enough" (232), and yet in some ways, sometimes against ill-chosen targets, much too critical—the kind of skepticism which, he suggests, throws out the baby with the bath water and seems to authorize wholesale suspicion and dismissal of facts. Those who question the soundness of warnings and prognoses about global warming are in effect only following, *ad absurdum*, the example already set by critics themselves. However, Latour demands more of critique—his is, indeed, a critique launched on critique itself, a call to radically rethink the familiar bases of our own critical thrusts. He forces the critical eye back upon itself—unpicking at the blind spots, undeclared inconsistencies, and contradictions in the critic's own position and method, unraveling the false safety nets which allow one measure to be applied to all other targets (the easier targets), while cradling and protecting the illusory untouchability of the critic's own cherished values.

Latour voices some frustration with the existing situation, but proposes a way out of it. Science studies, Latour suggests, is well placed to be the critic of critics. Like the Socratic gadfly, "it is the little rock in the shoe that might render the routine patrol of the critical barbarians more and more painful" (242), recognizing, in Latour's formulation, the respect due to facts (enabling the "retriev[al] of a realist attitude" [243] and "their fascinating emergence as matters of concern"[242]). Matters of fact emerge as a "gathering," an "assembly" rather than a critical dismantling. Latour here refers to Heidegger's "thingness of the thing" (245), and brings Heidegger into dialogue with A.N. Whitehead, in his advocacy of an approach which requires "dig[ging] much further into the realist attitude" (244), and into experience which phenomenology is inadequate to explore (244). Facts gathering matters of concern resist the kind of critique Latour takes to task, but also offer the basis for a different "direction" (245) of critique.

Latour strategically closes with an extract from Allan Turing's "Computing Machinery and Intelligence" (1950), noting that it is one of the iconic papers on formalism and computing, and at the same time "so baroque, so kitsch, ... assembl[ing] such an astounding number of metaphors, beings, hypotheses, allusions, that there is no chance that it would be accepted nowadays by any journal" (247)—an eclectic gathering. Turing's analogy between mind and machine pivots on the question: "can a machine be made to be supercritical?" Latour urges us to take our cue from this, and calls for a move within criticism toward generating new and other ideas, from ideas inherited and received.

Latour's article pursues the tracing and questioning of the iconoclastic tendency in critique, a destructive tendency which is powerful—even "creative"—in itself, yet always misses its target (1998). This is an interest and concern he returned to on more than one occasion (see, e.g., "A Few Steps Towards the Anthropology of the Iconoclastic Gesture." *Science in Context*, Vol. 10, No. 1 (1998): 63–83; *Iconoclash, beyond the Image Wars in Science, Religion and Art*, edited by Peter Weibel and Bruno Latour [ZKM and MIT Press, 2002], with its accompanying exhibition, and its foregrounding of the "iconoclash"—that point where the iconoclast becomes a more ambiguous figure).

Krista Bonello Rutter Giappone
Centre for Critical Thought, University of Kent and Department of English, University of Malta

#

LUHMANN, Niklas. "How Can the Mind Participate in Communication?" In *Materialities of Communication*. Edited by Hans Ulrich Gumbrecht and K. Ludwig Pfeiffer. Translated by William Whobrey. Stanford: Stanford University Press, 1994. 371–87.

"Humans cannot communicate," Niklas Luhmann announces boldly in the essay's opening lines. "Not even their brains can communicate; not even their conscious minds can communicate. Only communication can communicate" (371). To understand this claim, it must be borne in mind that Luhmann formulates his argument as a critique of the Enlightenment tradition represented by Hegel and Habermas. Luhmann rejects the notion of the "spirit" (382) and claims that "whatever appears as a 'consensus' is the construct of an observer, that is, his own achievement" (372). Elsewhere, Luhmann similarly attacks Enlightenment conceptualizations of modernity (*Observations on Modernity*. Translated by William Whobrey. Stanford: Stanford University Press, 1998. Esp. 2–3). In his account, "contemporary society" is best understood "as a functionally differentiated system" without a "common (correct, objective) approach to a preexisting world" (9–10). The utopias of yesteryear are dead. Rather than being subject to conscious human molding, society is first and foremost a "communication system" ("How Can the Mind" 371) that has undergone functional differentiation. This differentiation, for instance, applies to a development in human history from "speechless ... to oral communication and to writing, to alphabetic scripts, and to printing" (381) throughout the millennia. Electronic literature could be seen, hence, as a logical outgrowth of this process of differentiation, an outgrowth finally independent of print technologies and even of the individual author's mind, in favor of a network-based interchange between various independent observers.

In this sense, Luhmann advocates for an evolutionary approach to matters of communication. Sociology, in other words, is best served by adapting terminologies from the natural sciences, especially biology (374). Drawing on the work of the biologists Humberto Maturana and Francisco Varela, who introduced the term "autopoiesis" to our understanding of the cell as an essentially self-producing autonomous system, Luhmann concludes that the human mind as a whole "operates as an isolated autopoietic system," given its origins in the brain, that is, in organic matter (372). Therefore, "the mind cannot consciously communicate," which is to say that it does not follow preset plans, but responds instead to input from its environment. Thus, the mind "can imagine that it is communicating, but this remains an imagination of its own system, an internal operation that allows the continuation of its thought process. This is not communication" (ibid.). The mind is defined here as "a loosely linked mass of elements with practically no self-determination, a mass that can be impressed with whatever is said or read" (378). Hence, "operations of the mind and of communication proceed blindly. They do what they do. They reproduce the system. Meaning only comes into play on the level of observation, with all the provisions demonstrated by logic and hermeneutics ... Everything that functions as a unity only functions in this way through its observer" (382).

Luhmann's work, especially his fascination with autopoiesis, is symptomatic of the era of mass communication—and the dominant self-conception of what individuality entails today. In his 1996 "Declaration of the Independence of Cyberspace," libertarian John Perry Barlow expresses the hope that traditional forms of politics and communication were to be overcome in favor of a cyber-utopia where "we ... declare our virtual selves immune to your sovereignty [that of governments, GB], even as we continue to consent to your rule over our bodies." The outcome will be "a civilization of the Mind in Cyberspace." This Mind is presented as abstract and independent of organic matter, and in this sense, Barlow's cyber-Mind approaches the realization of Luhmann's functionally differentiated communication system, a society that is "purposeless" rather than driven by the seemingly benevolent utopias of the past ("How Can the Mind" 375; see also Barlow, John Perry. "A Declaration of the Independence of Cyberspace." Electronic Frontier Foundation. December 20, 2016).

Such a view has experienced a recent pushback, however, notably by BBC journalist Adam Curtis in his 2016 documentary *HyperNormalisation*, which points out the limitations of countering global elites by the withdrawal into cyberspace; and by William Davies in his 2015 book *The Happiness Industry: How the Government and Big Business Sold Us Well-Being*, who argues that the predominant observer and interpreter of the messages sent out by users of social media platforms are powerful corporations who use the accumulated data of the cyber-Mind to merely refine their marketing strategies.

Gregor Baszak
University of Illinois at Chicago

#

MANOVICH, Lev. "New Media from Borges to HTML." In *The New Media Reader*. Edited by Wardrip-Fruin and Montfort. Cambridge: MIT Press, 2003. 13–25.

As one of the chapters which open *The New Media Reader*, a volume collecting milestone commentaries from people at the forefront of their field, "New Media from Borges to HTML" has a welcoming openness to it, a generosity to newcomers and other readers. It provides an access-point, an introductory guide to key moments and stages in the development of the field and associated technology. It also yields an insight into Manovich's interest in the connections between culture and computing, and the analysis of cultural artefacts through both quantitative and qualitative data-analysis techniques—concerns which coalesce into "cultural analytics," "the analysis of massive cultural data sets and flows using computational and visualization techniques" ("The Science of Culture? Social Computing, Digital Humanities and Cultural Analytics," 2015).[1]

[1] http://manovich.net/index.php/projects/cultural-analytics-social-computing.

The aims of *The New Media Reader* are set out by Manovich: the book is "not just a map of the field as it already exists, but a creative intervention into it" (15). Manovich's own work can claim a place in this scheme—he offers a map of the development of new media, taking into account contextual variations, while also suggesting possible directions for further development. In particular, Manovich draws out intersections between the sciences (including the social sciences) and humanities, and this forms the basis for an approach to cultural objects.

Manovich delineates the area of "new media," foregrounding "computer-based artistic activities" (13) in the process of moving toward a definition, offering too "a justification" (15) for identifying new media as a "separate" field, with its own specificity and lineage. Part of the process of definition involves distinguishing "new media" from neighboring fields, such as "cyberculture" (focused on "the social and on networking," rather than the "cultural objects" which fall under the rubric of new media).

Digital data "can be manipulated or even generated" by software (17), a feature of new media which enables "modularity, variability, and automation" (18; see also: Lev Manovich, *The Language of New Media* [MIT Press, 2001]). However, Manovich recognizes that the development toward these principles is often "uneven" across media which use software (e.g., while film production has integrated some digital aspects, but retains the dominant framework established by tradition, computer games "are one of the few cultural forms 'native' to computers" and as such have advanced more or less in tandem with software). This staggered development and coexistence prompts Manovich to return to a formulation put forward in his book, *The Language of New Media*—the superimposition and hybridity of conventions, evident for example in user-interface: the "representational" conventions found in other and "older" media, and the "software techniques of data management and presentation" (18). Our current hybridity, he points out, is shifting and historically contingent, relying as it does on established and emerging conventions, and therefore likely to characterize an "early" stage. The question follows of whether it could be a stage common to the development of "every new modern media" (19)—an avenue of exploration he finds limited. Manovich's concern remains primarily with the specificity of "new media," and is again foregrounded when he considers the suggestion that new media is merely that which can speed up an algorithmic process that could be performed by humans. In response, he notes that the difference introduced isn't simply quantitative, but also qualitative.

In particular, Manovich is interested in establishing links with the modernist avant-garde; this takes the form of a "parallelism" (in both "ideas" and "form"), but also an "actualization" and "extension" of the modernist projects in contemporary databases. This includes the literary—for example: "The greatest hypertext is the Web itself, because it is more complex, unpredictable and dynamic than any novel that could have been written by a single human writer, even James Joyce" (15). There is also, however, a "qualitative change" (22) that Manovich locates in new media's emphasis on "accessing and manipulating information," as opposed to the modernist overriding interest in "seeing" differently.

Another feature which sets new media apart is the "postmodernist" approach of reworking or recoding preexisting material, rather than wholly subscribing to the modernist drive toward the "new"—in this respect, modernism itself becomes material to be reworked (23). My own research into late-1970s punk counterculture suggests a similar process at work, in the quest for new culturally relevant ways to reconfigure influences such as Dada (e.g., in Jamie Reid's cut-and-collage approach).

Manovich identifies other precursors and pioneers in 1960s art installations, performances, and literature, including work by Oulipo and Nam June Paik, which have "conceptual affinity to the logic of computing technology" (23). The emergence of "new media" as something recognizably codified took place around 1990, and he finds significance in the (temporal and "conceptual" rather than "causal") coincidence of the end of the Cold War and the beginning of the World Wide Web, with its thrust toward a globalized network (25). He closes the piece by reemphasizing contextualizing connections intended to reinforce our awareness of "the key cultural role played by digital computers and computer-enabled networking in our society."

Manovich's position within an ongoing debate on technology's relationship with the modernist avant-garde has been taken up and rethought from various angles, with certain modernist values being seen as incompatible with postmodern conditions, and inconsistencies arising from the tension between "art" and democratization-turning-to-commodification. Günter Berghaus, for example, considers technology and the emphasis on progress as one of the forms the postmodern "avant-garde" has tended to take—with a more "neo-primitivist" emphasis on liveness and the body characterizing another route (an attempt to find an alternative, which also derives from modernism), and various degrees in-between (*Avant-Garde Performance: Live Events and Electronic Technologies*, Hampshire: Palgrave Macmillan, 2005). Svetlana Boym, like Manovich, inhabits an in-between. However, she finds this in seeing awry, rather than modernism's seeing anew—a slippery "threshold," a "transient epiphany" at the "margins"—something, therefore, which eludes, or withholds itself from, formalization ("Nostalgic Technology: Notes for an Off-Modern Manifesto"; "The Off-Modern Condition," http://www.svetlanaboym.com/). The journal *Amodern* (http://amodern.net/) similarly devotes itself to the marginal, while Latour takes a critical look at modernity itself and foregrounds hybridity in *We Have Never Been Modern* (Harvard University Press, 1993). See also Álvaro Seiça's essay in this handbook for another view which engages with the periodization of electronic literature through the idea of "experimentalism."

Krista Bonello Rutter Giappone
Centre for Critical Thought, University of Kent and Department of English, University of Malta

#

MORRIS, Adalaide, and Thomas Swiss. *New Media Poetics*. Cambridge, MA, and London: MIT Press, 2006.

A decade after its publication, and almost fifteen years since the University of Iowa New Media Poetry conference that was the volume's impetus, *New Media Poetics* can still be said to serve as both "a fine introduction" and a "necessary text for advanced scholars as well," to cite Sandy Baldwin's cover endorsement. Proof of that being a good number of its essays, that arguably continue to be remain must reads among an international universe of new media artists, scholars, critics, teachers, and curators concerned with electronic literature.

The poetic field, as Adalaide Morris and Thomas Swiss conceived it, cut a swath large enough to include "hypertext narrative, interactive fiction, computer games, intermedia art, and other digital art forms" (Morris 2006: 5). Several of the volume's authors share the task of demystifying a certain hype around digital concepts and themes. Morris's introduction to the volume makes it clear, for example, that the volume's focus is much less representative of a first generation of electronic literature defined by hypertextuality than of a second generation of writers/artists more concerned with "poems composed for dynamic and kinetic manipulation and display, and programmable texts" (20). As it is an attempt to think of electronic literature, and specifically what the editors define as "new media poetry," as a fluid ongoing process with no fixed boundaries, concepts, or genres.

In fact, the influence of a later generation of post-humanist critics and scholars in digital media studies, among them N. Katherine Hayles, Lev Manovich, and Mark B. Hansen, is quite apparent in the tripartite structure of the volume: "Contexts" focuses on "communities rather than individual authors: electronic archives, digital websites, new media journals, sound-editing practices, pedagogical innovations that shape and are shaped by information age technologies" (32); "Technotexts," borrowing from Hayles's adaptation of the term to emphasize a "synergy between human beings and intelligent machines" (4), concerns a "differential relationship with analogous or related print materials" (32), or a "dynamic media ecology in which works exist in reciprocity rather than hierarchy"; finally, "Theories" is composed of essays "written by practicing poet-critics, develop[ing] a series of terms to address these and other nuanced and pressing questions concerning how to think about new media poetics" (33).

The use of Gertrude Stein's famous quotation from *Composition as Explanation*, as an epigraph and sustaining pillar in Morris's argument, already indicates what is to come—namely, a close relationship between "old" and "new" media poetics in spite of their technical differences: "There is singularly nothing that makes a difference a difference in beginning and in the middle and in ending except that each generation has something different at which they are all looking." Regardless of the ways the publishing of *New Media Poetics* coincides with a historical need for establishing boundaries between what is considered "mainstream print poetry" and "poetry composed, disseminated and read on computers," electronic literature is now, perhaps more than it ever was, a set of phenomena constantly shifting in its intermedial and metamedial aesthetic and poetic nature. A practical example of this articulation of distinctive features can be found in Talan Memmott's essay on "the discipline of taxonomadism," in which "categories remain open at their forward edge, at once altering and altered by the technologies that generate them" (33). Another good example would be John Cayley's thoughts on code and text, representing a "phenomenology of reading that has important consequences both for print and for the now significant body of networked and programmable writing" (33).

Curiously enough, these are two "practicing poet-critics" who are now widely known as mandatory when it comes to relevant artworks or critical writing on the topic, either in classrooms, monographies, or exhibitions. In its choice of authors, *New Media Poetics* then fulfills the promise of the Leonardo Book Series in which it was published: "to document and make known the work of artists, researchers, and scholars interested in the ways that the contemporary arts interact with science and technology," as well as "to create a forum and meeting places where artists, scientists, and engineers can meet, exchange ideas, and, where appropriate, collaborate." Indeed, if that alone were the volume's sole contribution—the co-presence of critics, scholars, and creators—that would itself justify its recognition as a turning point in contemporary literary studies.

Diogo Marques
University of Coimbra, Portugal

#

PERLOFF, Marjorie. *Unoriginal Genius: Poetry by Other Means in the New Century*. Chicago: University of Chicago Press, 2010. ISBN-10: 0-226-66062-1.

Perloff characterizes poetry of the twenty-first century as a reframing, recycling, and recontextualizing of already existing words. Writing poetry changed from the individual expression of the poet in his or her *own words* to the appropriation and manipulation of multiple texts and discourses (literary, visual, Internet). Removing, adding, and composing from appropriated texts constitute the *other* in what Perloff designates as "poetry by other means." In the twenty-first century, "text can be readily moved from one digital site to another or from print to screen" (17), and the poetic climate seems to have turned from the "resistance model of the 1980s" to one of intertextuality and dialogue with previous texts. Perloff historicizes these practices by analyzing prominent twentieth-century examples of appropriation and citation. Tracing the practice of appropriation and citation back to T. S. Eliot (extensive multilingual citation) and Ezra Pound (using citation and found text), and drawing on Antoine Compagnon's notion of *récriture*, Perloff presents this "new" poetry as "more conceptual than directly expressive" (10). In the chapters that follow, she provides an analysis of six "poetic modes" that evince appropriation, composition, constraint, and intertextuality. The first consists of the ambitious *citational poetics* of W. Benjamin's *Arcades Project*, which Benjamin himself terms a literary montage. The work was characterized by translators as an assemblage of Benjamin's observations and reflections, along with citations from a great variety of sources. Perloff references one particular translator who estimated that 75 percent of the work consisted of citations.

Among the various "poetic modes" identified by Perloff, two stand out as particularly relevant to rethinking and reviewing current practices of writing and poetic production. The Brazilian Concrete Poetry Movement is described as a "renewal of *avant-garde* practices of the 20th century" (56)—this being a form of appropriation in itself. Perloff introduces the notion of an "*arriére-garde* that is a revival of an *avant-garde* previous movement, but with a difference" (58). Brazilian concrete poetry represents the recovery of experimental art that was interrupted by the world war. Among various works, Perloff describes POETAMENOS (by Augusto de Campos) as fusing "Mallarméan spacing, Joycean pun and paragram, the Poundian ideogram" (68).

The second of Perloff's "poetic modes" is *conceptual writing*, here epitomized by Kenneth Goldsmith's transcription of trivial, everyday life speech, and its recontextualization within the constraints of a printed book. Appropriation and recontextualization work as a concept that, when used, becomes a machine (as Goldsmith puts it). *Soliloquy* (transcription of every word Goldsmith spoke for a one-week period) and *Trilogy* (*Traffic*'s transcription of a twenty-four-hour period of New York traffic reports); *Weather* offering a year's worth of daily weather reports; and *Sports* with its transcribed broadcast of an entire baseball game are clear statements of the conceptual writing Goldsmith claims to do—"uncreative," "unreadable," "boring." By engaging Goldsmith's "poetry by other means" Perloff can more clearly address the issues of originality and creativity that this radical appropriation puts into question. Goldsmith's writing brings to the fore the legitimacy of conceptual writing against the (relatively) undisputed legitimacy of conceptual art.

By casting past literary practices as diverse "poetic modes," Perloff opens up the possibility of a *continuum* between pre-digital appropriative writing and digital literary manipulation of preexisting works and texts. Using the digital environment, its media, and processes, works of electronic literature retrieve from the Internet, combine and recontextualize previous poems (printed or otherwise). John Cayley's *Zero Counting* process applies a paragrammatic compositional process (making puns by changing letters of a word) to Samuel Beckett's "The Image" but also to search results on Google to create a text that combines both. We can also refer to Brian Kim Stefans's *Dreamlife of Letters* (based on a text by Rachel Blau DuPlessis) or Jim Andrews's *On Lionel Kearns* (using, mostly, texts by the eponymous author). All three examples reiterate practices of appropriation previously used for pre-digital writing. The salient aspect of the digital take is the ability to automate, multiply, and, therefore, deepen selection and combination processes in the search for an "original" composition; the heterogeneity of textual forms; the use of visual and motion effects.

Unoriginal Genius: Poetry by Other Means in the New Century thus shows how current practices of textual appropriation, citation, and remixing in networked digital media relate to and transform other non-expressive modes of poetic production.

Liliana Vasques
University of Coimbra, Portugal

#

PORTELA, Manuel. *Scripting Reading Motions: The Codex and the Computer as Self-Reflexive Machines*. Cambridge: MIT Press, 2013.

Scripting Reading Motions examines the expressive use of book and programmable media in the embodied processes of meaning production. The analysis by Manuel Portela comprehends a wide range of works in multiple languages, thus contributing to the enrichment of electronic literature as a plural and decentralized field. Focused on print and digital-based works whose material programs explore reflexivities in the act of reading, Portela's study evolves through a continuous feedback loop analysis between print literary artifacts and electronic literature works.

By means of haptic and visual processing of written signs, hand and eye movements are constitutive of the self's reading awareness—a material dimension no less important to our cognitive experience than the linguistic thoughts evoked by the reading. The core of the study, focused on all these elements, the material, social, and cognitive dimensions of acts of reading, enables us to understand ways that reading can be inscribed in writing in both digital and print media. Portela asks repeatedly—"What if the reading of writing could script itself back into writing? Into a writing of reading? A reading reading itself?" (2 and 5).

The comparative close reading of a large group of works in various media allows us to map the transhistorical affiliations of cybertexts. The author describes meaning as an emergent phenomenon and evokes the act of reading as a performance and a response to bibliographic and electronic codes. The act of reading can also "[inscribe] itself in the writing by priming, reordering, and reassociating elements according to specific modes of individual attention ... and socialized protocols of reading" (359). The theoretical framework presented is sustained by the analysis of works distributed in bibliographic and digital formats, as bookness and digitality configure similar practices of reading.

Chapter 2 on Johanna Drucker is coupled with the reflection on how her experimental artists' books are represented by their digital surrogates in the archive *Artists' Books Online*. Likewise, *Only Revolutions*, a "constellated constrained hypernovel" (244) by

Mark Danielewski, is dissected as a print instantiation of digitality in order to understand the "codex as computer" (chapter 5), outlining the ways in which the digital modes of production retroactively shape the print artifact and observing how the codex constitutes itself as "a complex inscriptional and topological space" (373).

Oulipian, concrete, visual, and experimental works are analyzed in detail in the section dedicated to digital trans-creations (chapter 3), in which Portela argues that digital remediation of printed works exposes the programmed complexity of the printed page and the codex. Even the chapters focused on digital-born literature by (primarily) Jim Andrews (chapter 6), Philippe Bootz, Rui Torres, Jason Nelson (chapter 4), and John Cayley (chapter 7) always keep pace with the analysis of paper-based works.

By exploring the formal operations encoded and embodied in print and digital artifacts, *Scripting Reading Motions* brings to light the close connection between bookness and digitality, highlighting the printed page and the computer as self-reflexive machines of meaning production, while outlining the negotiated entanglement between reading and writing.

Bruno Ministro
University of Coimbra, Portugal

#

STIEGLER, Bernard. *Technics and Time, 1: The Fault of Epimetheus*. Translated by Richard Beardsworth and George Collins. Stanford: Stanford University Press, 1998.

While it is possible to enter Stiegler's large and still-growing corpus at various points, the first of the three volumes of *Technics and Time* is fundamental to any systematic understanding of the way technics undergirds his various engagements with technology. All of his major engagements with the concepts of the digital, the Anthropocene, political economy and culture, and memory, attention, and time are grounded in the significance Stiegler places in this work on technics and the consequences of its suppression in the history of philosophy. This is a dense and demanding text, but it will be of interest to anyone pursuing research related to technology, linear writing and grammatology, temporality, and the history of philosophy.

Stiegler draws on the fields of paleoanthropology, the history of technology, and philosophy so that he can extrapolate a "techno-logic ... a logic literally driving technics itself" (36). Man, from the very beginning, is part of a technical milieu which begins with the primitive tools associated with early cortical development. This initial instance of tool-use constitutes the original "technological rupture"—a term he borrows from Bertrand Gille—and signals "the passage from a genetic différance to a nongenetic différance" (175). These ruptures continue with vast amounts of time in between, speed up with the development of the sciences in ancient Greece, and ultimately reach the point of "constant innovation" (40) with the dawn of industrialization. The speed and instability of technical systems from this point produces a situation in which the becoming of man, only identified because of the relative frequency of technological ruptures in the nineteenth century, is out of joint with the becoming of technics. The human and technics are indissociable—"the appearance of the human is the appearance of the technical" (141)—but the system they form together is now unstable.

All of Stielger's interventions explicitly reject the idea of positioning technology against a transcendental or metaphysical "man"—that is, a man for whom technical development represents either an enhancement or adulteration of some essential capabilities. All the while, while tracing such an argument he pays particular attention to its embedding in anthropology in Rousseau's attempt to chart an originary and totalized man in which there is "no originary default, no prosthesis" (114). Rousseau represents an anthropological effort constrained by metaphysics, to which Stiegler opposes the technical anthropology of Andre Leroi-Gourhan. Stiegler concludes, pace Leroi-Gourhan and Derrida (whose influence is palpable throughout Stiegler's work), that the *supplement* to the human, which Stiegler calls "prosthesis," is where man both appears and vanishes, is constituted and effaced in the same moment. If Rousseau is responsible for transposing the metaphysical problem into anthropology, Platonism is the first culprit. Its attendant concept of the immortal soul instantiates the split between science and technics—that is, between philosophy and technics—at the base of metaphysics. This is why Stiegler turns to tragic Greek myth—specifically that of Prometheus and Epimetheus—as a way to investigate the fundamental technicity of humanity from the vantage point of mortal finitude. This is the setup for a prolonged engagement with Heidegger in which Stiegler lays out a complex theory of temporality in relation to technics wherein "*time is the technological synthesis of, and in, mortality*" (221; original emphasis). Or, to put it another way, in its mortal finitude, "the human is technical, that is, time" (116).

Justin Raden
University of Illinois at Chicago, Project in Digital Literary Arts and Humanities

#

WARK, McKenzie. *A Hacker's Manifesto*. Cambridge: Harvard University Press, 2004.

It has become fashionable in academia, and even in popular political journalism, to think through ways to modernize the clear factory origins of Karl Marx's *Das Kapital*. In an era where the means of production are unclearly defined at best, and in which neoliberal capitalism has atomized the identity of "worker" into a mass of independent contractors and temporary employees, how can we relate Marx's analysis to our own world? How can we even relate his provocations in *The Communist Manifesto* to rise up and break the chains of capitalism if we cannot identify the chains to begin with? McKenzie Wark, in his provocatively titled *A Hacker Manifesto*, produces an answer to these questions: namely, that the contemporary agent of history in the Marxian sense is the figure of the hacker. Wark seems to recognize from the start how ridiculous such a claim must seem, and he enters into his 2004 manifesto with tongue in cheek and ventriloquizing Marx when he says "A double spooks the world, the double of abstraction" (1). But while Wark is aware of his audience's skepticism early on, he does not dwell on the absurdity of hackers being a revolutionary class for long, and many of the seemingly glib aphorisms from his early chapter on "Abstraction" lay the groundwork for more serious work in the *Manifesto*. "To hack is to differ," Wark claims, and this claim lends itself to Wark's overarching premise in his text, that "to hack" is to produce the dialectical contradictions necessary to and ubiquitous in Marx's own analysis of capitalism (3). For instance, Wark sees the "privatization of property," which is classically the moment feudalism is dialectically resolved into capitalism, as a "legal hack [which] creates the conditions for every other hack by which the land is made to yield a surplus" (26). This "hack" of the accepted figure of "land" is the birth, for Wark, of the pastoralist class; similarly, the hack which opens profit from property to the marketplace births the capitalist class; and finally, the hack which monetizes information introduces the "vectoralist" class.

Vectoralists use the concept of hacking—which for Wark is the creation of "the possibility of new things entering the world" (4)—to not only "conceive of everything as a resource, but also ... bring that resource into productive relation to any other resource whatsoever" (331). Wark, in other words, produces a continuation of Marx's famous formulation from *The Eighteenth Brumaire*, in which history arrives first as tragedy (pastoralists) and then as farce (capitalists); in the case of the hacker class, the totalizing information market of the vectoralist follows third. Yet, the analogy can be read in an emancipatory spirit, as well, in which farmers come first, followed by workers, and finally by the information-class of hackers. In terms of electronic literature generally, we can see Wark align this political vision with the virtual, as "[every] hack is an expression of the inexhaustible multiplicity of the future, of virtuality" (78). Like the paratactical quality of Wark's text, in which the thesis is imbued in every one of the 389 small aphorisms, and in which any of the alphabetically organized chapters could be read first, last, or on its own, the virtuality of the hack encourages class solidarity. As class, according to Wark, "has become the structuring principle ... which organizes the play of identities as differences," then the hacker class' multiplicity relies upon unification across difference against vectoralist difference (33).

There is something undeniably heroic about Wark's text, of course, and the *Manifesto* can at times read as much as an attempt to lionize a technological niche-interest as a serious Marxian analysis. Any of Wark's many calls to "wrest freedom from the necessities imposed on the productive classes by the constraint of private property" could be read as defenses of Internet piracy as easily as they could be read as serious class war (124). But Wark's rigor—shown in the endnotes to *A Hacker's Manifesto*, in which Wark fleshes out his theoretical positions—is what continues to bring his text back to a serious set of claims and concerns. What Wark has produced is of course a manifesto in the classical sense, insofar as one can pick it up and read it as a call-to-arms, can drop it after a few paragraphs and get the full idea, and can appreciate it without a PhD. But he has also produced a serious paratactical intervention into post-Marxist accounts of multitude, creative capitalism, and neoliberal class relations that deserves its position among the recent theoretical canon, alongside Mark Fisher, Michael Hardt, and Antonio Negri.

Trevor Strunk
DeSales University

INDEX